CRITICAL SURVEY OF
MYTHOLOGY AND FOLKLORE

Heroes & Heroines

CRITICAL SURVEY OF
MYTHOLOGY AND FOLKLORE

Heroes & Heroines

SALEM PRESS
A Division of EBSCO Information Services
Ipswich, Massachusetts

GREY HOUSE PUBLISHING

Cover: Vintage engraving from *Illustrations by H. C. Selous of "Hereward the Wake"* by Charles Kingsley. Published by Art Union of London, 1870.

Critical Survey of Mythology and Folklore: Heroes & Heroines, 2013, published by Grey House Publishing, Inc., Amenia, NY, under exclusive license from EBSCO Information Services, Inc.

∞ The paper used in these volumes conforms to the American National Standard for Permanence of Paper for Printed Library Materials, Z39.48 1992 (R1997).

Publisher's Cataloging-In-Publication Data
(Prepared by The Donohue Group, Inc.)

Critical survey of mythology and folklore. Heroes and heroines / Grey
   House Publishing. -- 1st ed.

   p. : ill., maps ; cm. -- (Critical survey of mythology and folklore ; [2])

   Includes bibliographical references and index.
   ISBN: 978-1-61925-181-6

   1. Heroes--Folklore. 2. Women heroes--Folklore. I. Grey House Publishing, Inc. II. Title: Heroes and heroines

GR515 .C75 2013
398.27

ebook ISBN: 978-1-61925-186-1

PRINTED IN THE UNITED STATES OF AMERICA

CONTENTS

PUBLISHER'S NOTE

Critical Survey of Mythology and Folklore: Heroes and Heroines, by Salem Press, presents critical essays on mythology and traditional literature from a wide range of periods and cultures of the world. This volume offers an in-depth examination of one of the major subjects in traditional literature—the trial and quest of the hero and heroine, which often involves strange places, monstrous beings, and extraordinary acts of bravery. Designed for college students, the aim of this collection is to advance the study of traditional literature as an important activity in cultural and literary analysis. Toward this end, essays emphasize the major approaches to analyzing mythology and folklore, including such commonly studied topics as gender, cross-cultural meaning, and religion, among other areas of interest.

Readers will appreciate the diversity of literature in this collection, which offers mythology and fairy tales in equal measure, as well as selections from popular legends and rarely studied oral traditions. Major figures in the genre are represented, including Homer, Ovid, Thomas Bulfinch, and Andrew Lang. In addition, tales from American Indian, African, Oceanic, and East Asian traditions, among other world cultures, are included. The editor's goal was to provide an inclusive collection that, while representative of the most studied literature, offers critical essays on cultural subjects rarely covered in collections. The essays will establish for students and their teachers, as well as general readers, the social and cultural significance of reading and studying traditional literature.

ESSAY AND VOLUME FORMAT
The collection includes forty essays, each approximately seven thousand words in length. The top matter of each essay includes reference information on the author (when available), the country or culture of origin, the period in which the myth or tale originates, and the genre. Following a standard format, critical essays provide a condensed version of the story, introducing principle characters and actions, developed from authoritative sources. These condensed myths and tales will prepare readers to go on to read the primary sources in their entirety. An in-depth analysis, of approximately three thousand words, follows, grounded in the leading scholarship in the field. To emphasize the opportunities for comparative

study, particularly in such a diverse collection of literature, the final section of the essay offers a cross-cultural analysis, linking the primary myth or tale with other literature across eras. In addition, each essay includes a sidebar note that introduces either greater contextual background or links to the other arts, including painting, film, and poetry. Each essay offers a bibliography of additional readings for further research.

The volume is organized according to six chapter themes highlighting major subjects in the literature, including tales of miraculous births and the initiation of the young hero, the adventures of trial and quest, and the cunningness of the culture hero. The aim of the thematic organization is to establish the ways in which stories of human desire, cultural origin, and familial relations, to name a few of the subjects, intersect among myths and folklore across a wide range of periods and cultures.

SUPPLEMENTAL FEATURES
- "Maps and Mythological Figures" presents eight maps and charts detailing the cultural or geographic placement of many of the deities, authors, and tales in the volume.
- "Mythology in the Classroom" explains major approaches to studying mythology and fairy tales.
- A sample lesson plan, on the Greek heroine Penelope, accompanies the essay on teaching mythology in the classroom. The aim is to provide one model for comparative analysis.
- A timeline lists major authors, publications, and events related to mythology and traditional literature.
- A chronological index of titles and a culture and country index offer supplemental information on the overall coverage of the volume.

CONTRIBUTORS
Salem Press would like to extend its appreciation to all involved in the development and production of this work. The essays are written and signed by scholars and writers in a variety of disciplines in the humanities. Without these expert contributions, a project of this nature would not be possible. A full list of contributor's names and affiliations appears in the front matter of this volume.

INTRODUCTION

The mythic hero may well represent the most important archetype in mythology. In the many stories of the hero and heroine across cultures, common thematic and narrative elements reappear, so much so as to become cultural shorthand for the exploration of human verities. Courage, sacrifice, and strength may serve as the central conceit around which the tale unwinds, while honor, compassion, and love reveal an inner life in the hero's tale. The adventures of Odysseus in Homer's *Odyssey* are as much about his cunningness in battle as they are about his struggle with his own desires. *Critical Survey of Mythology and Folklore: Heroes and Heroines* illustrates the many forms of adventure crossed with cultural meaning in traditional world literature.

Joseph Campbell defined the hero as "someone who has given his or her life to something bigger than oneself." While the hero's story generally follows the familiar narrative of courage and adventure, the underlying story is deeply rooted in a journey toward self-discovery and transformation. Perhaps it was his talent as a storyteller as much as the power of myth that propelled Campbell, a scholar of comparative religion, into the American popular consciousness in the 1980s. In several interviews with Bill Moyers, aired on PBS, Campbell wove a thoughtful story about the interconnectedness of myth and religion, and his depiction of the hero's call to adventure, the subject of his *Hero of a Thousand Faces* (1949), presents a very old story about what he called the "monomyth": the hero or heroine embarks on a journey that ultimately tests the individual's capacity for spiritual transformation for self and community. The greatest mythic heroes, from Odysseus to Christ, Sir Gawain to Saint George, have answered the *call to adventure*, a decisive moment when the hero must act in an extraordinary fashion. On closer inspection, Campbell identifies stages of the hero's life and journey that, for many readers of mythology and viewers of films, may well be familiar themes. This collection, however, offers readings that uncover the complexity of these themes against a broad backdrop of multiple traditions.

The hero or heroine may be anointed well before the call to adventure, through a miraculous conception or by extraordinary circumstances following a birth. The infant Moses, discovered in the ark of bulrushes, is the story of an incredible delivery toward a course of events that alters the culture. Infants Romulus and Remus are left to die in the river Tiber but, through miraculous events, are saved and later restore their grandfather, the rightful king, to the throne. A common story line that follows a miraculous birth is the initial challenge experienced in childhood, as the young hero may encounter a moment of recognition that he is, somehow, different. He then embarks on the first of many transformative experiences. J. K. Rowling's Harry Potter series illustrates many of the patterns represented in the journey of the young hero-to-be. As an infant, Harry Potter is marked with a scar, a lightning bolt on his forehead, the first strike by the forces of evil aligned against him long before he is aware of his own powers. "That ain't no ordinary cut on your forehead," he is told. "A mark like that only comes from being touched by a curse, and an evil curse at that." Rowling's story illustrates the complex struggle the young Harry must endure in his journey toward recognition and his acceptance of the call. Harry Potter represents only the best-known contemporary story to depict a pattern of birth and initiation in the hero's journey.

Stories of initiation, such as Harry Potter's, illustrate the importance of trial and quest as a path toward self-discovery and transformation. In fact, the quest, whether for an object or a place, is the singular theme around which many of the most important tales develop. Sir Gawain and the search for the Sangreal come to mind, as does Jason's search for the Golden Fleece. In the *Odyssey*, two stories define the nature of trial and quest, those of Odysseus and his wife, Penelope. While Odysseus searches for his way home to Ithaca for ten years, Penelope must draw upon her cunning to deceive the suitors and hold off an unwanted marriage. Courage, endurance, and skill are virtues that often characterize the hero in the quest, and aspects of an emerging psychological or spiritual complexity align with each stage of the journey. For example, Heracles must endure a series of twelve challenges, or labors, to atone for his actions in the killing of his sons. He successfully accomplishes each of the seemingly impossible tasks, each victorious encounter—often against fantastic creatures—illustrating the qualities of cunning, honor, and virtue. Heracles travels far and wide, each task a microcosm of each stage in the transformation of the human character and psyche. The fantastic creatures in many of these stories reveal that the quest often occurs in a strange, altered symbolic order of the universe.

The theme of monstrosity occurs throughout world mythology and folklore. Dragons, giants, and half-human creatures serve multiple roles in the adventure of the hero. If the apogee of the quest is the transformation of the hero's outer and inner worlds, such extraordinary change must take place in a hyper-reality of monstrosity and human otherness. In the various accounts of Theseus and the Minotaur, the city of Athens must sacrifice young men to a creature at regular intervals. In order to end the cycle, Theseus travels to the depths of the labyrinth to battle the Minotaur, a creature with the body of a man and the head of a bull, whereupon he slays the beast. An unnatural and irrational order into which the hero must enter, the labyrinth is inextricably linked to the framework of the quest story. The descent into the underworld, which goes by many names across cultures, is similar to the labyrinth, as the hero is removed from the present order of the world above. This domain is both a physical and psychic disruption in the life of the hero. The monstrous and, consequently, the site of the monstrous, are often designed to alter the language of human understanding.

The cultural meaning of the hero's journey is most often defined by a decidedly masculine narrative that seems to limit the way we can speak of the heroine. The heroine in Western literature, for example, may be the object of the quest, as in the story of Tristan and Iseult. In mythology, primordial deities often represent such gendered roles as the mother goddess of the heavens, earth, and sea; or they may represent aspects of feminine beauty, compassion, and fertility (the Greek pantheon would include Gaia, Persephone, Athena, and Aphrodite). Yet, the quest can be a story of spiritual and psychic transformation, which may be grounded in its differences according to culture but cuts across gender nevertheless. The Trung sisters, the legend goes, fought during the wars for Vietnamese independence from Chinese rule in the first century CE. In Vietnamese arts, they are illustrated as fierce warriors riding elephants into battle. The sisters are among the most important heroines in Vietnamese culture, called upon for multiple purposes, political and cultural, in the Vietnamese wars of independence. The legends of Joan of Arc (France) and Tomoe Gozen (Japan), also grounded in history, likewise share heroics, proof that the hero's quest can be overgeneralized as strictly a male endeavor. Nonetheless, rather than simply defining a common narrative of battlefield heroism, some stories reveal the important ways in which the heroine may differ from male heroes. The Trung sisters suggest, for example, the significance of matriarchy in the formation of a cultural and national identity. The tales selected for this volume will illustrate the imaginative complexity of the heroine figure.

The hero and heroine, as the Trung sisters reveal, represent the imaginative, as well as artistic, formation of a cultural identity. The *culture hero* acts not as an individual but as a member of a community, or at least comes to the realization that he or she embodies something larger than the self. While many of the tales in this collection may capture these ideals, the culture hero more strictly acts with an ethos of community. The tale of Robin Hood (Robyn Hode in the collection), for example, represents the complex role of insider and outsider, an outlaw who steals from the rich and gives to the poor, or so the legend goes. In the several versions of the tale, the outlaw is defined by allegiance to the underclass and in resistance to aristocracy. The blurred line between right and wrong is a common feature of the culture hero across cultures. And, in many cases, the culture hero adopts an animal form in doing his work. The Coyote hero in North American indigenous folklore, for example, is a trickster with powers of great cunning, transformation, and invention who may perform good deeds for the community. That is to say, the culture hero often embodies the greater aspirations of the community.

The diversity of stories analyzed in this volume provides a rich portrait of the hero and heroine in literature around the world, as well as the myriad of reasons that the hero or heroine is called upon by the culture to perform the extraordinary. The supplemental sections on cross-cultural influence in each article, as well as the sidebars that examine the uses of myth and folklore in art and literature, will provide a greater understanding of the significance of these long-told stories.

CONTRIBUTORS

Adam Berger, PhD
New York, New York

Pegge Bochynski, MA
Beverly, Massachusetts

T. Fleischmann, MFA
Dowelltown, Tennessee

Ashleigh Imus, PhD
Ithaca, New York

Judy A. Johnson, MLS, MTS
Clark State Community College

R. C. Lutz, PhD
Bucharest, Romania

Allene Phy-Olsen, PhD
Austin Peay State University

Katherine Sehl, MA
Concordia University

Theresa Stowell, PhD
Morenci, Michigan

MAPS AND MYTHOLOGICAL FIGURES

ANCIENT GREECE

EPIRUS

OLYMPUS

PALLENE   SITHONIA

PINDUS

Peneius

HESTIAEOTIS

THESSALY

AEGEAN SEA

TRICCA

THESPROTIA

MAGNESIA

IOLCUS

Acheron

PHERAE

Enipeus

Acherusian Lake

PHYLACE

PHYTHIA

EPHYRA

MELITAEA

TYMPHRESTUS

PHTHIOTIS

ACARNANIA

Sperchius

TRACHIS

LEUCAS

Achelous

AETOLIA

DORIS

LOCRIS

DIRPHYS

Evenus

PHOCIS

AMPHISSA

PARNASSUS

COPAS

CHALCIS

ITHACA

PLEURON

BOEOTIA

OECHALIA

LOCRIS

DELPHI   HYRIA

THEBES   AULIS

CALYDON

OROPOS

CEPHALONIA

THESPIA

MARATHON

*CORINTHIAN
GULF*

ALCYON ISLANDS

MEGARNIS

ACHAIA

SICYON

ELEUSIS

ATHENS

ERYMANTHUS

CYLLENE

CORINTH

HYMETTUS

ELIS

*Itymphalion
Lake*

CORINTHIA

ATTICA

Peneius

STYMPHALUS

NEMEA

SARONIC GULF

ELIS

Ladon

MYCENAE

ARGOLIS

ARCADIA

ARGOS

TIRYNS

IONIAN SEA

PISA

EPIDAURUS

OLYMPIA

NAUPLION

TROZEN

LYCOSURA

TEGEA

PELOPONNESE

MESSENE

SPARTA

MESSENIA

PYLOS

AMYCLAE

LACONIA

*SEA of
CRETE*

ANCIENT
GREECE

TROY

ASIA
MINOR

*MEDITERRANEAN
SEA*

CRETE

GREEK MYTHOLOGICAL FIGURES

The Major Titans	Cult of the Twelve Olympians	Bestiary of Ancient Greece
Koios (Coeus) Northern cosmic pillar holding heaven and earth apart **Krios (Crius)** Southern cosmic pillar **Kronos (Cronus)** God of time and the ages **Hyperion** Eastern cosmic pillar **Iapetos (Iapetus)** Western cosmic pillar and titan of mortal life **Mnemosyne** Goddess of memory, words, and language **Okeanos (Oceanus)** A primeval deity of the earth-encircling river **Phoibe (Phoebe)** Goddess of intellect **Rhea** Goddess of female fertility **Tethys** Mother of the rivers and springs **Theia** Mother of sun, moon, and dawn **Themis** Goddess of natural order and divine law	**Aphroditê (Aphrodite)** Goddess of beauty, love, procreation **Apollôn (Apollo)** God of prophecy and oracles, music, and healing **Arês (Ares)** God of war, battle, and manly courage **Artemis** Goddess of hunting, wilderness, and animals **Athênê (Athena)** Goddess of wise counsel, war, and heroism **Dêmêtêr (Demeter)** Goddess of agriculture, grain, and bread **Dionysos (Dionysus)** God of wine, vegetation, and pleasure **Hêphaistos (Hephaestus)** God of fire, metalworking, and sculpture **Hêrê (Hera)** Goddess of women and marriage **Hermês (Hermes)** God of animal husbandry, travel, language, and writing **Poseidôn (Poseidon)** God of the sea, rivers, flood, and drought **Zeus** God of sky and weather, justice, and fate	**Khimaira (Chimera)** A fire-breathing monster slain by Bellerophon astride the winged horse Pegasus **Drakôn Kolkhikos (Colchian Dragon)** Guard of the Golden Fleece; slain by Jason **Kêtos Aithiopios (Ethiopian Cetus)** A sea monster slain by Perseus **Grypes (Griffins)** Lions with the head and wings of eagles **Harpyia (Harpies)** Directed by Zeus to steal away people from earth **Hydra Lernaia (Lernaea)** A nine-headed water serpent slain by Hercules **Drakôn Ismenios (Ismenian Dragon)** A giant serpent slain by Cadmus **Drakôn Ladôn (Ladon)** A hundred-headed dragon slain by Heracles **Drakôn Pterôtoi (Winged Dragons)** Two winged serpents used by Medea to escape Corinth **Pythôn (Python)** A giant serpent slain by Apollo **Seirênes (Sirens)** Three sea nymphs who sang to lure sailors to drown

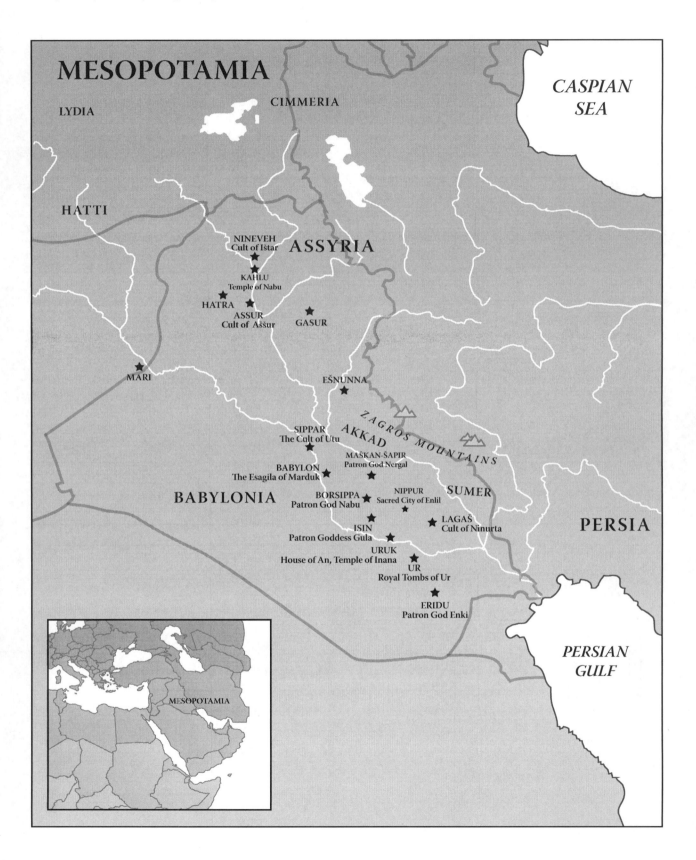

MESOPOTAMIA

LYDIA

CIMMERIA

CASPIAN SEA

HATTI

NINEVEH
Cult of Ištar

ASSYRIA

KAHLU
Temple of Nabu

HATRA

ASSUR
Cult of Aššur

GASUR

MARI

EŠNUNNA

ZAGROS MOUNTAINS

SIPPAR
The Cult of Utu

AKKAD

MAŠKAN-ŠAPIR
Patron God Nergal

BABYLON
The Esagila of Marduk

SUMER

NIPPUR
Sacred City of Enlil

BABYLONIA

BORSIPPA
Patron God Nabu

LAGAŠ
Cult of Ninurta

PERSIA

ISIN
Patron Goddess Gula

URUK
House of An, Temple of Inana

UR
Royal Tombs of Ur

ERIDU
Patron God Enki

PERSIAN GULF

MESOPOTAMIA

MESOPOTAMIAN MYTHOLOGICAL FIGURES

Sumerian ca. 3500 BCE–2000 BCE The settlement of temple towns in honor of the gods and goddesses; the height of Sumerian civilization	**Babylonian and Assyrian** Babylonian (ca. 2000 BCE–500 BCE) and Assyrian (ca. 2400 BCE–600 BCE) periods	**Demigods, Heroes, and Kings**
An Sun and heaven god	**Adad** God of storms	**Alulim** First king of Eridu
Ašnan (Ashnan) Goddess of grain fields	**Anšar (Anshar) and Kišar (Kishar)** Primordial gods	**Apkallu** Seven sages
Dumuzid Food and vegetation god	**Anu** God of the sky	**Ašur (Ashur)** God of all Assyria
Enki Water, creation, and fertility god	**Apsû** God of the underworld	**Atra-hasīs** Boat builder of Great Flood myth
Enlil Rain, wind, and air god	**Aruru** Mother goddess	**Bel** Sage of the gods
Ereškigala (Ereshkigal) Goddess of the underworld	**Dagan** God of grain and fertility	**Dumuzid** Shepherd king; fertility god
Inana Goddess of sexuality, fertility, and warfare	**Ea** God of wisdom, waters, crafts, and magic	**Enkidu** Natural man, lord of the forests and wildlife
Ki Earth goddess; consort of An	**Ellil** God of earth and wind	**Ĝeštinana (Geshtinanna)** Goddess of wine; sister of Dumuzid
Lahar Goddess of cattle	**Ereškigala (Ereshkigal) and Nergal** Goddess and god of the underworld	**Gilgameš (Gilgamesh)** Demigod; King of Uruk
Namma Primeval sea; birth to An and Ki	**Gula** Goddess of healing	**Gudgalanna (Gugalanna)** The bull of heaven
Nanna or Nanna-Suen God of the moon	**Ištar (Ishtar)** Goddess of love, procreation, and war	**Huwawa** God of the cedar forest
Ninĝišzida (Ningishzida) God of vegetation, underworld, and innkeepers	**Mammu** God of mist and craft	**Lamaštu (Lamashtu)** Demoness; slayer of infants and children
Ninhursaĝa (Ninhursag) Mother goddess	**Marduk** God of magic	**Lugalbanda** Father of Gilgameš; warrior king
Ninlil Healing and mother goddess; consort of Enlil	**Nabû** God of wisdom and writing	**Namtar** God of death
Ninurta God of war and agriculture	**Nintinuga** Goddess of healing	**Ninsun** Goddess and mother to Gilgameš
Sumugan God of the plains	**Nuska** God of light and fire	**Pazuzu** King of the demons of the wind
Utu God of the sun	**Šamaš (Shamash)** Sun god	
	Sîn God of moon; son of Enlil	
	Tammuz Demigod of vegetation	
	Tiāmat Primeval sea	
	Zaltu Goddess of strife	

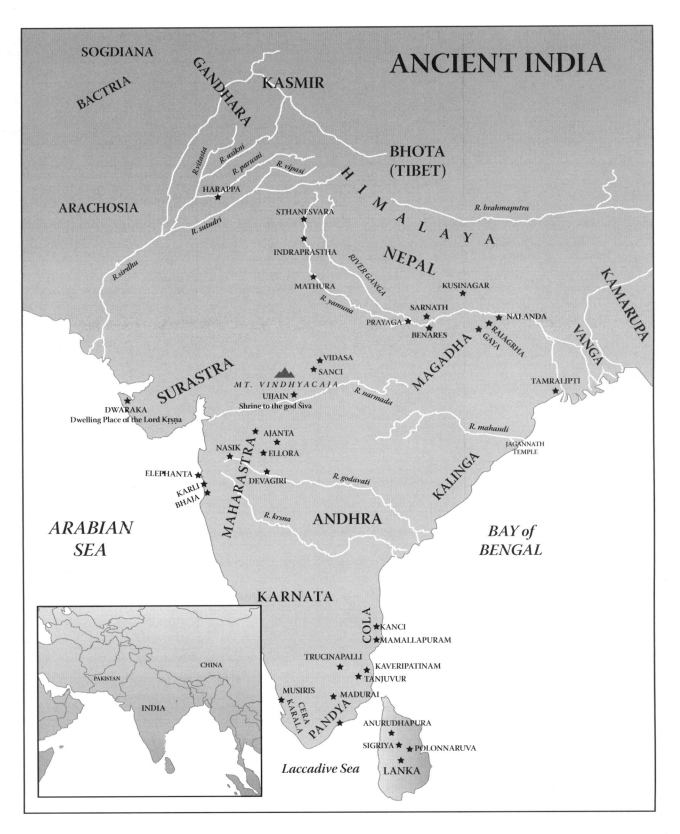

ANCIENT INDIA

SOGDIANA

BACTRIA

GANDHARA

KASMIR

BHOTA
(TIBET)

ARACHOSIA

R. vitasta
R. asikni
R. parusni
R. vipasi
HARAPPA

R. sutudri

R.sirdhu

STHANESVARA

HIMALAYA

R. brahmaputra

INDRAPRASTHA

RIVER GANGA

NEPAL

MATHURA

R. yamuna

KUSINAGAR

SARNATH

KAMARUPA

PRAYAGA

BENARES

NALANDA

VANGA

GAYA
RAIAGRHA

MAGADHA

SURASTRA

VIDASA
SANCI

MT. VINDHYACAIA
UIJAIN
Shrine to the god Śiva

R. narmada

TAMRALIPTI

DWARAKA
Dwelling Place of the Lord Krsna

R. mahandi

JAGANNATH
TEMPLE

AJANTA

NASIK
ELLORA

ELEPHANTA
KARLI
BHAJA

MAHARASTRA

DEVAGIRI

R. godavati

KALINGA

R. krsna

ANDHRA

ARABIAN
SEA

BAY of
BENGAL

KARNATA

COLA
KANCI
MAMALLAPURAM

TRUCINAPALLI

KAVERIPATINAM
TANJUVUR

MUSIRIS

CERA
KARALA

MADURAI

PANDYA

ANURUDHAPURA

SIGRIYA
POLONNARUVA

Laccadive Sea

LANKA

CHINA

PAKISTAN

INDIA

HINDU MYTHOLOGICAL FIGURES

Vedic Deities ca. 1500 BCE–300 BCE The *Rig Veda, Sāma Veda, Yajur Veda,* and *Atharva Veda*	Puranic Deities ca. 300 BCE–1000 CE Brahmā, Viṣṇu, and Śiva texts	Avatars of Viṣṇu (Vishnu) The divine descent of Viṣṇu, in order of incarnation
Aditi Mother of many of the gods	**Brahmā** Supreme being or creator	**Matsya** The great fish
Agni God of earth	**Durgā** Warrior goddess	**Kurma** The tortoise
Brahmā The creator, preserver (Viṣṇu), and destroyer (Śiva)	**Gaṇeśa (Ganesh)** God of prudence and policy; the elephant-headed god	**Varāha** The wild boar
Dyauṣ pitā God of the sky	**Lakṣmī (Lakshmi)** Goddess of love, beauty, and prosperity	**Narasiṃha** The man-lion
Indra God of the air	**Kālī** Goddess of time and change; the black one	**Vāmana** The dwarf
Karṇa God of love and desire	**Kāma or Kāmadeva** God of love and desire	**Paraśurāma (Parashurama)** Rāma with axe
Pṛthvī (Prithivi) Goddess of earth	**Kārttikeya** God of war	**Rāma** Hero of the Rāmāyaṇa
Pūṣaṇ (Pushan) God of meeting	**Hanumān** The monkey god	**Kṛṣṇa (Krishna)** The adorable one
Mitra and Varuṇa Rulers of day and night	**Pārvatī** Consort of Śiva; reincarnation of Satī	**Buddha** The enlightened one
Sarasvatī Goddess of the river	**Sarasvatī** Goddess of wisdom and science; mother of the Vedas	**Kalki** Destroyer of time; avatar yet to come
Skanda or Kārttikeya God of war	**Satī** Consort of Śiva; reincarnated as Pārvatī	
Soma God of intoxicating juice (soma plant); god of the moon	**Śiva (Shiva)** The destroyer	
Sūrya God of the sun	**Tvaṣṭṛ (Tvastar)** God of a thousand arts	
Uṣas (Ushas) Goddess of the dawn	**Varuṇa** God of the ocean	
Vāyu God of the winds	**Viṣṇu (Vishnu)** The preserver of cosmic order	
Viśvakarmā (Vishvakarma) Architect and workman of the gods	**Yama** Judge of men; king of the unseen world	
Yama God of the infernal regions		

WESTERN EUROPE

NORWAY
Peter Christen Asbjørnsen
Jørgen Engebretsen Moe

SWEDEN

DENMARK
Hans Christian Andersen

NORTH SEA

IRELAND
Samuel Lover
Patrick Kennedy

POLAND

ENGLAND
Andrew Lang
Edgar Taylor
Joseph Jacob

NETHERLANDS

GERMANY
Johann Karl August Musaus
Jacob and Wilhelm Grimm
Benedikte Naubert

BELGIUM

English Channel

LUXEMBOURG

CZECH
REPUBLIC

FRANCE
Charles Perrault
Catherine Bernard
Madame Le Prince de Beaumont
Madame d'Aulnoy

AUSTRIA

SWITZERLAND

SLOVENIA

BAY of
BISCAY

ITALY
Giuseppe Pitrè
Laura Gonzenbach
Domenico Comparetti

*Adriatic
Sea*

*Mediterranean
Sea*

The Great Folklorists of Europe

The term *fairy tale,* first coined by Marie-Catherine d'Aulnoy in France in 1697, describes a genre of traditional literature that emerged in various cultures throughout the world. This list presents a selection of major authors and publications of fairy tales in Western Europe that have shaped the cultural imagination of authors and readers for generations.

Charles Perrault (1628–1703; France)
- *Histoires ou contes du temps passé* (*Stories or Tales from Times Past,* 1697)
- First publication of "Le petit chaperon rouge" ("Little Red Riding Hood")

Marie-Catherine d'Aulnoy (1650–1705; France)
- "L'île de la félicité" ("The Isle of Happiness," 1690)
- Introduces the term *conte de fées,* or "fairy tale," in 1697

Catherine Bernard (1662–1712; France)
- *Inès de Cordoue* (*Inez of Cordoue,* 1696)

Gabrielle-Suzanne de Villeneuve (ca. 1695–1755; France)
- First publication of "La belle et la bête" ("Beauty and the Beast," 1740)

Jeanne-Marie Le Prince de Beaumont (1711–1780; France)
- "La belle et la bête" ("Beauty and the Beast," 1756)

Johann Karl August Musäus (1735–1787; Germany)
- *Volksmärchen der Deutschen* (*Fairy Tales of the Germans,* 1782–1786)

Benedikte Naubert (1752–1819; Germany)
- *Neue Volksmärchen der Deutschen* (*New Fairy Tales of the Germans,* 1789)

Karoline Stahl (1776–1837; Germany)
- *Fabeln, Mährchen und Erzählungen für Kinder* (*Fables, Tales and Stories for Children,* 1818)

Jacob Grimm (1785–1863; Germany) and **Wilhelm Grimm** (1786–1859; Germany)
- *Kinder- und Hausmärchen* (*Children's and Household Tales,* 1812)
- *Deutsche Mythologie* (*German Mythology,* 1835)

Edgar Taylor (1793–1839; England)
- *German Popular Tales* (1823), first English translation of Brothers Grimm

Thomas Crofton Croker (1798–1854; England)
- *Fairy Legends and Traditions of the South of Ireland* (1825)

Hans Christian Andersen (1805–1875; Denmark)
- *Eventyr fortalte for børn* (*Fairy Tales Told for Children,* 1835)

Samuel Lover (1797–1868; Ireland)
- *Legends and Stories of Ireland* (1837)

Peter Christen Asbjørnsen (1812–1885; Norway) and **Jørgen Engebretsen Moe** (1813–1882; Norway)
- *Norske folkeeventyr* (*Norwegian Folktales,* 1842)

Svend Hersleb Grundtvig (1824–1883; Denmark)
- *Gamle danske minder i folkmunde* (*Danish Popular Tales,* 1854)

Laura Gonzenbach (1842–1878; Italy)
- *Sicilianische Märchen* (*Sicilian Fairy Tales,* 1870)

Patrick Kennedy (1801–1873; Ireland)
- *Fireside Stories of Ireland* (1870)

Giuseppe Pitrè (1841–1916; Italy)
- *Biblioteca delle tradizioni popolari siciliane* (*Library of Sicilian Popular Traditions,* 1871)
- *Fiabe, novelle e racconti popolari siciliani* (*Sicilian Fairy Tales, Stories, and Folktales,* 1875)

Domenico Comparetti (1835–1927; Italy)
- *Novelline popolari italiene* (*Italian Popular Tales,* 1875)

Charles Deulin (1827–1877; France)
- *Les contes de ma Mère l'Oye avant Perrault* (*The Tales of Mother Goose from Before Perrault,* 1879)

Andrew Lang (1844–1912; Scotland)
- English translation of "Beauty and the Beast" (1889)

George McDonald (1824–1905; Scotland)
- *Dealings with the Fairies* (1867)

Joseph Jacobs (1854–1916; England)
- *English Fairy Tales* (1890)
- Revision of "Beauty and the Beast" (1916)

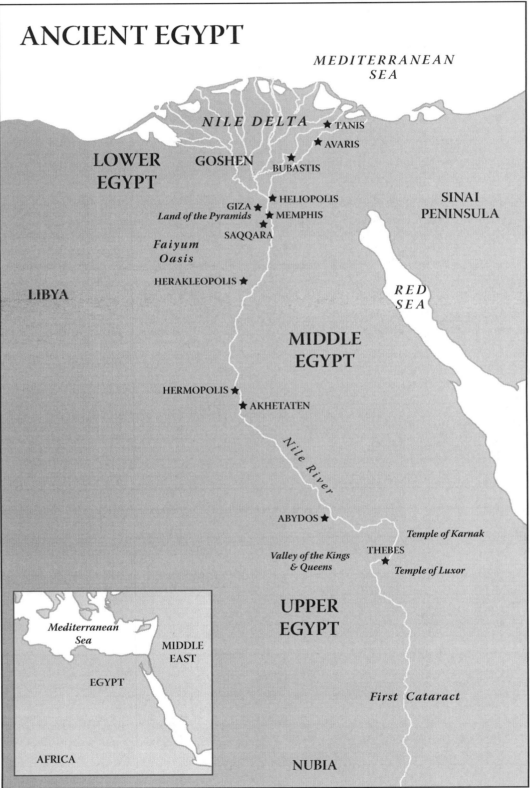

EGYPTIAN MYTHOLOGICAL FIGURES

Aker
God of the earth; protector of the eastern and western horizons

Amen (Amun or Amon)
Supreme god of all gods; primeval deity

Amen-Ra (Amun-Ra or Amon-Ra)
Chief among the gods

Anubis
God of funerals and embalming, depicted with a hound's head; anointer of the dead

Aten (Aton)
Solar creator deity worshipped monotheistically under Amenhotep IV (Akhenaten); represented by a disk

Atum (Tem)
God of the sun and creator of the universe; father of twins Shu and Tefnut

Bastet (Bast)
Goddess of cats, pregnant women, music, dance, and prosperity; depicted as a cat-headed woman

Geb and Nut
God of the earth and goddess of the sky; sibling spouses who bear Isis, Osiris, Nephthys, and Set

Hapi
God of the Nile, flooding, and fertility

Hathor
Goddess of sexual love, dancing and music, and destruction; depicted as a cow; a symbolic mother of the pharaoh

Horus
God of the sky; depicted as a falcon-headed man; son of Osiris and Isis

Isis
Goddess of motherhood and great magic; sister-wife of Osiris; a symbolic mother of the pharaoh

Khonsu
God of the moon; sometimes depicted with head of a hawk

Mut
Goddess of Thebes; wife of Amen; a symbolic mother of the pharaoh

Nephthys
Funerary goddess; sister-wife of Set

Nun
Primeval waters from which Atum emerged

Osiris
God of the dead and ruler of the underworld; brother-husband of Isis; depicted as a mummy with white crown

Ra (Re)
God of the sun and lord of all gods; depicted with the head of a falcon

Set (Seth)
God of chaos and violence; brother-husband of Nephthys

Shu
Primeval god of sunlight and dry air

Sobek
God of pharaonic power; depicted as a crocodile or part-crocodile

Tefnut
Primeval goddess of moisture; sister and consort of Shu

Thoth
God of knowledge and writing, magic, and the moon; provider of mathematics, medicine, and astronomy

EAST ASIAN MYTHOLOGICAL FIGURES

Ba Xian (Pa Hsien): The Eight Immortals of Daoism (Taoism)	Major Shintō Spirits
Cao Guojiu (Ts'ao Kuo-chiu) Associated with a tablet of admission to the court of the Song dynasty	**Amaterasu** Kami of sun; ruler of heaven
Han Xiang (Han Hsiang-tzu) Associated with the peaches of immortality; said to make flowers grow and bloom at will	**Ame no Uzume** Dancing goddess of the dawn and laughter; patron of drama and performance
He Xiangu (Ho Hsien-ku) A beautiful maiden depicted with the magic lotus blossom in hand; patron of unmarried women	**Fūjin** Kami of wind
Lan Caihe (Lan Ts'ai-ho) The wandering singer associated with the flute and cymbals; patron of the poor	**Hachiman** God of war and peace, culture, and divination; protector of children
Li Tieguai (Li T'ieh-kuai) Associated with the crutch and medicine gourd; patron of pharmacies	**Inari/Inara** Kami of rice, prosperity, and fertility; associated with foxes; shown as both male (Inari) and female (Inara)
Lu Dongbin (Lü Tung-pin) Possesses a magic sword; able to fly and walk on clouds; associated with the elixir of life	**Izanagi and Izanami** Primordial sibling spouses who created the earth
Zhang Guolao (Chang Kuo-lao) An old man usually astride a white mule and associated with matrimonial happiness	**Kaze no Kami** Kami of wind
Zhongli Quan (Chung-li Ch'üan) Associated with a fan of feathers or palm fronds; the messenger of heaven	**Ninigi** Kami of rice and plenty
	Raijin Kami of thunder
	Ryūjin (Ryūō) Sea kami or dragon king who lives in Ryugu and controls the tides with tide jewels
	Suijin A water spirit
	Susanoo (Susano-Wo) Kami of storms who captures the eight-headed, eight-tailed dragon Koshi
	Tenjin Kami of learning and calligraphy who aids those learning difficult lessons
	Toyotamabime Daughter of the sea kami Ryūjin (or Wata-tsumi) who becomes a sea monster
	Tsukuyomi (Tsuki-Yomi) Kami of the moon and night

CENTRAL AND SOUTH AMERICA

Gulf of Mexico

CHICHÉN ITZÁ

TENOCHTITLÁN

ATLANTIC OCEAN

2 **1** **3**

5 **4**

CENTRAL AMERICA

Caribbean Sea

6

PACIFIC OCEAN

Amazon River

7

8

MACHU PICCHU

CUZCO

SOUTH AMERICA

9

10

CIVILIZATIONS

1 TOLTEC 900–1200 CE AND AZTEC 1325–1521 CE

2 TEOTIHUACÁN 100 BCE–750 CE

3 OLMEC 1200–100 BCE

4 MAYA 100–1542 CE

5 ZAPOTEC AND MIXTEC 300–1524 CE

6 CHIBCHA 1200–1538 CE

7 MOCHICA 100–1000 CE AND CHIMÚ 1000–1471 CE

8 CHAVÍN 1000–500 BCE

9 TIAHUANACO 600–1000 CE

10 INCA 1200–1535 CE

CENTRAL AND SOUTH AMERICAN MYTHOLOGICAL FIGURES

Aztec Gods	Maya Gods	Inca Gods
Chalchihuitlicue (Chalchiuhtlicue) Goddess of freshwater and storms; protector of infants and women giving birth **Chicomecóatl** Goddess of mature corn **Coatlicue** Goddess of the earth; mother of Huitzilopochtli **Huitzilopochtli (Uitzilopochtli)** God of sun and war; depicted as a bird **Mictlantecuhtli** God of the dead and ruler of the underworld **Quetzalcóatl** God of Venus, the sky, wind, agriculture and fertility, and writing; patron god of priests and rulers; depicted as a feathered serpent **Tezcatlipoca** Supreme god of sun and darkness, north and cold, war and death, fortune and misfortune; sees the future with his smoking mirror; brother of Quetzalcóatl **Tlaloc** God of rain, mountains, and fertility; depicted with huge fangs **Xipe Totec** God of the springtime, vegetation, and regeneration; patron of metalworkers **Xolotl** God of bad luck, illness, lightning, and twins; protector of the night; depicted as a deformed dog	**Ah Puch (or Hun Came and Vucub Came)** Ruler of the lowest underworld realm; depicted as a skeleton or decaying body **Bacabs** Four gods who support the skies at the four points of the compass **Chac (Chaac)** God of rain, thunder, and lightning and of fertility; discoverer and provider of corn **Itzámna** God of the sky and sun; granter of writing, religion, and medicine **Kinich Ahau** God of sun and fire by day; jaguar ruler of Xibalba, the underworld, by night **Pauahtun** Four-part god who holds up the sky at the four points of the compass; god of thunder and lightning	**Apo (Apu)** God of the mountains **Illapa (Ilyap'a)** God of storms, thunder, and lightning **Inti (or Apu-punchau)** God of the sun, vegetation, and growth; face depicted with emanating golden disks and rays **Mama Cocha (Mama Qoca)** Sea mother goddess **Mama Quilla (Mama Kilya)** Goddess of the moon; sister-consort of Inti; face depicted as a silver disk **Pachamama** Earth mother goddess **Viracocha (Huiracocha or Wiraqoca)** Creator of sun, moon, earth, sky, stars, and human beings; father of Inti and Mama Quilla

Norse Mythological Figures

Major Norse Gods and Goddesses	Other Female Figures in Norse Mythology
Balder Beloved of the gods; son of Odin and Frigg	**Norns** Three maidens who decide the fates of all living creatures
Bragi God of poetry and music	**Valkyries** Warrior maidens who gather fallen heroes to Valhalla, the palace of Odin
Frey God of fertility, harvest, peace, and prosperity	
Freya Goddess of fertility	
Frigg Goddess of the earth and of marriage; wife of Odin	
Heimdall Watchman of the domain of the gods	
Idun Goddess of eternal youth; wife of Bragi	
Loki Deceiver and rescuer of the gods	
Njörd Sea god; father of twins Frey and Freya	
Odin Father god; god of the sky, knowledge, poetry, war, and death	
Thor Thunder god; son of Odin and Frigg	
Tyr Bravest of the gods, known for his justness	

CRITICAL SURVEY OF
MYTHOLOGY AND FOLKLORE

Heroes & Heroines

BIRTH AND
PROPHECY

Birth of Athena and the War with the Giants

Author: Hesiod; Pindar; Pseudo-Apollodorus
Time Period: 999 BCE–1 BCE
Country or Culture: Greek
Genre: Myth

OVERVIEW

As one of the great divinities of ancient Greece, the goddess Athena has extensive mythical origins stemming from many traditions that all contribute to the complicated divinity familiar to historians today. As one of the twelve Olympians, Athena is most commonly described as the goddess of wisdom and war, the protector of strongholds and heroes, and the inventor and master of skillful crafts and weaving.

The different traditions do not all agree on the story of Athena's birth. Most of the later traditions describe Athena as the daughter of Zeus, the all-powerful god, and Metis, the most intelligent and crafty of goddesses. In this story, Zeus is compelled to swallow Metis, who is pregnant with Athena, which leads to Zeus giving birth to Athena from his head. Some sources suggest that different deities assist Zeus in opening his head, including Hephaestus, Prometheus, or Hermes. Many sources ascribe the birthplace of Athena to the river Triton. Within this tradition, Athena is usually described as emerging from her father's head dressed fully in the accoutrements of war, heralding her birth with a screeching war cry.

Another tradition regards Athena as the daughter of Pallas, a winged giant, whom Athena is forced to kill when he attempts to violate her chastity. In these and other sources, Athena uses his skin as a defensive aegis and ties his wings to her feet. It is perhaps due to this lineage that Athena is often described with the surname Pallas, as Pallas Athena. A Libyan tradition suggests that Athena is the daughter of Poseidon. In this account, Athena is educated by the river god Triton along with his daughter Pallas, whom Athena eventually kills. According to Herodotus, Athena becomes angry with her father and goes to Zeus, who makes her his own daughter. Some scholars attribute this lineage as providing her with the surname Tritogenia (Tritogenia Athena), which can be loosely taken to mean "Triton birth"; other scholars suggest that Tritogenia has etymological origins in the ancient Boeotian word for "head," associating the surname with Athena's birth from the head of Zeus.

Myths regarding the births of the gods are extremely significant in defining who the gods are and what they will come to represent. Born from Zeus's head and having inherited the cunning intelligence of her mother, Metis, Athena's character is often considered the harmonious blend of power and wisdom. However, her birth from the head of Zeus also serves to align her more closely with a male deity than a female one, and as such, Athena often occupies a space between the male and female genders. Her birth from the head, rather than from male or female genitalia, corresponds with her characterization as a chaste and virginal goddess, hence her epithet Parthenos ("virgin"). Thus, Athena was often perceived by the ancient Greeks as an ethical deity, attributed with presiding over law, authority, and justice, as well as with founding the ancient court, the Areopagus. Born dressed in war armor, Athena is also described as the goddess of war and battles and the protector of heroes and cities under siege.

SUMMARY

The story of Athena's unusual birth is recounted in numerous Greek sources. Although among the following sources the fundamental and crucial aspects of Athena's birth from Zeus's head remain unchanging, the details surrounding this climactic moment are told differently from version to version.

In an account by Hesiod, who makes three references to the birth of Athena in the *Theogony*, Zeus consorts with the goddess Metis, the clever daughter of Oceanus and Tethys. Metis becomes pregnant with the goddess Athena. Fearing that Metis is pregnant with the son who has been prophesized to overthrow him and following the advice of Gaia and Uranus, Zeus takes Metis into his hands and swallows her whole. As Metis is known for her wit and cunning, her offspring are feared by Zeus and his parents as threats to his power. Even though they know that Athena, equal in strength and intelligence to her father, is to be born before Metis conceives a son, Zeus takes no chances and swallows Metis ahead of time.

After swallowing Metis, Zeus gives birth to Athena—fully arrayed in the arms of war—from his head. The birth takes place on the banks of the river Triton; Athena remains hidden there for some time. In his last reference to the birth of Athena, Hesiod reports that along with Athena, Zeus also conceives Deino ("the awful"), Agestratos ("the host-leader"), Atrytone ("the untiring"), and Potnia Egrekydoimos ("the queen who revels in tumults, wars, and battles"). Jealous of Zeus's adultery and of his ability to reproduce without her, Hera conceives the god of fire and craftsmanship, Hephaestus, on her own.

In the *Olympian Ode*, the Greek Theban poet Pindar provides a similar description of Athena's birth, but with some variation. According to Pindar, Athena springs from Zeus's head in Rhodes with the assistance of the god Hephaestus, who wields a bronze axe at Zeus's head in order to open it. As she springs out from her father's head, Athena screams a terrifying war cry that makes Uranus and Gaia shudder. Following her birth, the sun god Hyperionides (also known as Helios) constructs a shining altar and founds the rites of sacrifice—a gift that makes both Zeus and Athena very happy. Following this, Pindar tells of Reverence, the daughter of Forethought, bringing joy and valor to the people of Rhodes, where Athena was born. In the acropolis of Lindus (Lindos), a precinct is founded for the goddess—although it is without a holy fire. Zeus brings a saffron cloud upon the people of Lindus and causes it to rain gold. Athena endows the people with the gift of skill, enabling them to excel in craftsmanship.

In Pseudo-Apollodorus's *Bibliotheca* (*The Library*), even though Metis turns herself into many forms as a way to evade Zeus, he rapes and impregnates her. While pregnant with Athena, Metis tells Zeus that after she

"Zeus slept with Metis, although she turned herself into many forms in order to avoid having sex with him. When she was pregnant, Zeus took the precaution of swallowing her, because she had said that, after giving birth to the daughter presently in her womb, she would bear a son who would gain the lordship of the sky. In fear of this he swallowed her. When it came time for the birth, Prometheus (or Hephaestus, according to some) by the river Triton struck the head of Zeus with an axe, and from his crown Athena sprang up, clad in her armor."

Bibliotheca

gives birth to Athena, she will bear a son who will claim kingship of the sky. Fearing the fulfillment of Metis's prophecy, Zeus swallows her. When Athena is ready to be born, Prometheus (or Hephaestus) assists Zeus by prying his head open with an axe. Athena springs forth, fully clad in battle armor.

Pseudo-Apollodorus then describes Athena's role in the Gigantomachy, the war with the giants, following her birth. The gods receive an oracle that none of them will be able to defeat the giants without the assistance of a mortal. With the help of Athena, Zeus calls upon his part-mortal son Heracles to assist in defeating the giants. With Athena's counsel, Heracles fires an arrow at the giant Alcyoneus (Alkyoneus) and then drags him outside of Pallene, where he dies. As another giant, Enceladus (Enkelados), attempts to flee, Athena throws the island of Sicily at him. While she fights, Athena is protected by the skin of Pallas.

ANALYSIS

Born from Zeus's head, fully dressed in armor, Athena not only enables Zeus to secure his role as the all-mighty authority of the gods, but also temporarily forces Zeus to occupy the typically feminine domain of childbearing.

According to some versions, Hephaestus or Prometheus temporarily acts as midwife while Athena emerges prepared to enter the masculine domain of war. While Athena's femininity is never questioned—it is even revered as being exemplary—her birth and the figure she comes to represent occupy exclusively male realms in a rather abstruse way. Athena affirms the patriarchal order by not threatening Zeus as a potential successor and by being born without the necessity of a mother. Yet although she is renowned throughout classical Greece as the protector of patriarchal dominion, she simultaneously represents a certain level of feminine autonomy that feminists throughout the ages have come to identify with.

Accounts that relate the birth of Athena usually narrate in a way the makes it seem that Athena's birth occurs *ex nihilo*, outside the chronological ordering of the universe. However, her birth puts an end to a recurring myth of succession. As related by Hesiod in the *Theogony*, Gaia, the earth, conceives Uranus, the sky or universe, through parthenogenesis, and together they form the first divine union. Fearing that his children may try to usurp him, Uranus stuffs them back into Gaia until one of their children, Cronus, equipped with a sickle provided by Gaia, cuts off his father's testicles and in so doing succeeds his father. Cronus forms a union with Rhea and begins to have children with her, but fearing the prophecy from his parents that one of his children will try to succeed him, he becomes nervous—like his father—and decides to eat all of his children as soon as they are born. Unhappy with this, Rhea hides one of their children, Zeus, and gives Cronus a rock to swallow instead, leading him to regurgitate all of their children. Zeus eventually overthrows his father and imprisons him in Tartarus.

Much like his predecessors, as supreme authority of the universe, Zeus is faced with the same prophecy that he will be succeeded by one of his offspring. In almost every ancient myth, a prophecy cannot be undone and is always brought to fulfillment. In the most classic example, even when King Oedipus tries to avert the prophecy that he will kill his father and couple with his mother, his attempts to avoid his fate actually lead him to fulfill it. This is certainly true of Zeus's grandfather, Uranus, and of his father, Cronus. However, when Zeus learns that his second child with Metis, a son, will overthrow him, he successfully averts his fate by swallowing Metis while she is pregnant with Athena. In some ways, Zeus's action combines the ideas of his forefathers. Much as Uranus does to Gaia, Zeus attempts to force Metis into a perpetual state of being with child, since she is pregnant with Athena when he swallows her. Perhaps more obviously, much as Cronus does, Zeus decides to solve his problem by consuming it.

For ultimately unknown reasons, Zeus succeeds in averting his fate. Some critics argue that Zeus's success is largely the result of his complete absorption of the female. Although Uranus and Cronus are each undone by one of their sons, their female partners play a decisive role in their demise. Gaia hatches the plan to stop Uranus, making the sickle herself and giving it to her son Cronus, who is only responsible for executing the plan. Similarly, Rhea hatches a plan of her own, hiding her son and tricking Cronus by giving him a rock. These female deities of the earth defeat their partners with cunning and intelligence—features that Metis personifies. Of the three female partners in the succession myth, Metis should be poised as the one most likely to evade her partner and potentially outsmart him. However, despite being known as a shape-shifter and as the epitome of shrewdness and wisdom, Metis is overcome by Zeus. Pseudo-Apollodorus even suggests that Zeus rapes Metis.

Zeus thus averts his fate and secures his role as a universal authority in a way that fundamentally eradicates feminine autonomy and establishes male supremacy and the patriarchal order. Some scholars argue that even though Gaia and Rhea have instrumental roles in defeating Uranus and Cronus, they could not effectively execute them without the assistance of their sons. Without any male to help Metis, her shrewdness and her ability to shape-shift are for naught. As Christopher P. Long notes, "In swallowing Metis, Zeus accomplishes what his father and grandfather could not: He takes full possession of the feminine dimension of the generative process, and in so doing secures his own ultimate autonomy" (69). Yet, even further, Zeus's abolishment of Metis is evidence for the hegemony of male power. As Susan Carter argues, "Metis [is] ultimately unable to avoid Zeus' advances, despite her shape-shifting. . . . if the goddess of wisdom (and cleverness) could be overcome, then surely a mortal woman would not stand a chance in denying a man" (210). By giving birth, Zeus shows that he has not only consumed feminine autonomy, but he has also absorbed it through his ability to reproduce offspring on his own.

Athena's birth is not viewed by Zeus as a potential threat of succession, but instead viewed as a triumph. According to Susan Deacy, "The scheme ends not with the threatened son, but with the daughter who, warrior and warmonger that she is, will not seek to overrun her father" (30). Athena is not a threat to Zeus because she is female, and despite her masculine affinities, her celebrated portrayal as a chaste virgin solidifies her harmlessness toward Zeus and his established order. Yet the question remains as to why Athena is portrayed in such a masculine way, since it is her femininity that defines her lack of a threat to Zeus. Deacy argues that the myth of Athena's birth establishes her close relationship with her father. She notes that as a female warrior, Athena ought to be a subversive and transgressive female figure, further perpetuating the transgressive nature of her birth that forces males to occupy the feminine domain of childbearing. Instead, Athena uses her power in unison with her father's from the very moment of her birth when she assists Zeus and Heracles in defeating the giants. The myth of Athena's birth establishes the patriarchal order, and through the accompanying myth of the Gigantomachy (Battle of the Giants), Athena protects the order that her birth established.

As with other myths that relate the births of gods, the myth of Athena's birth completely defines her character. Many critics compare the differences between Athena's birth and two other well-known Greek stories of divine birth, those of Aphrodite and Dionysus. According to Hesiod's genealogy, Aphrodite, the goddess of sexual love and desire, is Athena's great-aunt, yet Aphrodite could not be more different from her. The only similarity between the births of Athena and Aphrodite are that they are birthed somewhat asexually by their fathers. Yet, whereas Athena's birth establishes the masculine authority of her father, Aphrodite's birth is the product of Uranus's emasculation by his son at the behest of Gaia. When Uranus's castrated testicles fall into the Mediterranean Sea, Aphrodite rises from the foam they produce and the sea carries her to the shores of Paphos, Cyprus. As the asexual product of her father's genitalia, Aphrodite's character becomes completely defined by sexuality. Many of her myths involve her engaging in tragic romances with handsome mortals or being involved with matters of love and sexually charged emotion. Similarly, she is often portrayed nude with full hips, posing seductively. Dionysus's masculine sexuality, on the other hand, is often attributed to his birth from Zeus's thigh, a region close to Zeus's genitals.

Unlike the births of Aphrodite and Dionysus, there is nothing sexual about Athena's birth. It might be logical to assume that Athena is nurtured inside Metis even after

being swallowed up by Zeus and that, before emerging from Zeus's head, she might have actually been birthed through her mother's genitalia; however, all of these details are elided in every extant telling of the myth. More important and defining is that Athena is born from Zeus's head, perhaps the farthest physical location from sexual organs and, metaphorically, the most antagonistic to the heart and sexual body. Much like Dionysus's birth, prior to which he is extricated from his mother's womb and sewn into Zeus's thigh, Athena's birth from a man establishes her affinities to the masculine and her strong relationship with her father. Athena alone is granted exclusive access to Zeus's aegis and to his thunderbolt. Although Athena's intelligence and perspicacity are likely inherited from her mother, who personifies these things, her birth from her father's head usurps that inheritance by acting as a symbolic metaphor: Aphrodite is born from genitals and thus presides over matters of the genitalia; Athena is born from the head and thus presides over matters of the mind.

The prevalence of masculinity surrounding Athena's birth has subsequent implications for her character and how she was understood by the classical Greeks. Carter argues that "the mythical precedent of Athena's birth from Zeus's head is used in early Greek society to argue that father alone can beget a child" (210). Since Athena does not have, and presumably does not require, the nurture and care of a mother, the myth of her birth secures a certain degree of "father right" that had real consequences for the classical Greek judicial system and general societal ordering. In the extant Attic drama from fifth-century BCE Athens, the myth of the birth of Athena is invoked in four different tragedies, and in almost every instance the invocation is used to function "as a counter to some form of matrilineal ideology" (Leitao 167). The most well-known of these references is found in the *Eumenides*, the final play of Greek tragedian Aeschylus's trilogy *Oresteia*.

In the final play of the trilogy, the heroic protagonist, Orestes, is about to go on trial in Athens for murdering his mother, Clytemnestra. In the first play, *Agamemnon*, the titular character, the husband of Clytemnestra and the father of Orestes, returns home to Mycenae after spending ten years leading the Greeks against the Trojans during the famous Trojan War. Prior to leaving, Agamemnon had sacrificed his daughter Iphigenia in order to divine what his prospects would be against the Trojans. While he was away, Clytemnestra, who was angry with him for sacrificing their daughter, began an

HISTORICAL CONTEXT

The Panathenaea was an ancient festival celebrated in Athens to honor Athena, the patron deity and namesake of the prominent Greek city-state. The festival was reportedly founded by Erechtheus (or Erichthonius), a mythical king of Athens, 729 years before the first Olympiad, but was revived in 566 BCE by the Athenian archon Pisistratus. Although the festival was originally exclusively a religious festival, it eventually developed into a larger festival that included a sports competition that came to be known throughout the Greek world as the Panathenaic Games. The Panathenaic Games were held every four years and extended the length of the festivities by three or four days, thus they are referred to as the Greater Panathenaea; the Lesser Panathenaea, which lasted a shorter time and was more exclusively religious, was held every year. Although never superseding the Olympic Games in importance, the Panathenaic Games were considered the most important athletic competition in Athens.

Among the many sporting events that the games hosted were chariot racing, boxing, wrestling, rowing, pancratium (boxing and wrestling), a pentathlon, javelin throwing on horseback, mock infantry battles, the *euandrion* (contest of strength), the *pyrrich* (military dance), the *apobatai* (type of chariot racing), and even a torch race from Piraeus (Athenian seaport) to the Acropolis of Athens. Along with the sporting competitions, the Panathenaic Games also included artistic competitions in which participants could be awarded for the best recitation of Homeric poetry, for the best performance on the *aulos* (reed instrument) and *cithara* (type of lyre), and for the best singing performance.

Most important, however, was the religious ceremonial aspect of the festival, which involved a procession to the Erechtheum, a temple on the acropolis. The procession showcased the peplos, a large robe woven by the *ergastinai* (maidens of Athens) and paraded through the streets until it reached the Erechtheum, where it would be used to dress the statue of Athena Polias. As the procession prepared to enter the acropolis, a sacrifice of one cow was offered to Athena Nike, followed by a hecatomb ("sacrifice of a hundred oxen") to Athena Polias. The meat from this sacrifice would then be used for a huge feast on the last night of the festival.

---

adulterous affair with Aegisthus. Learning of his return, Clytemnestra devises a plan and murders Agamemnon in their home, closing the first play. In the following play, *The Libation Bearers*, Orestes returns home to find that his mother has murdered his long-absent father. After being met by the ghost of his father and conversing with his sister, Orestes conjectures that he must seek his father's revenge in order to purify the polluted and cursed house of Atreus. Assuming a disguise, Orestes enters the house and murders his mother and Aegisthus.

Haunted by the Furies (chthonic deities who avenge patricide and matricide), Orestes flees to Athens. There, he faces the Athenian law courts, presided over by Athenian jurors—but most importantly by Athena. The purpose of the trial in essence is to determine whether Orestes should be considered guilty for the crime of murdering his mother or whether he is innocent because he performed just action to avenge the crime against his father. Following the prosecution, the jurors arrive at a tie

and call upon Athena to cast the deciding vote. In order to explain her reasoning to the audience, Athena invokes the story of her birth: "There is no mother who bore me . . . I am entirely my father's child. As a result, I will not give greater weight to the fate of a woman who kills her husband, the overseer of the home" (qtd. in Leitao 167). Her mother completely forgotten, Athena arrives at her decision to acquit Orestes based entirely on the notion that Zeus is her sole parent. As David Leitao explains, "Athena, who had no mother of her own, does not think much of the Furies' argument about the primacy of the mother-child bond, a retrograde position that provides justification for mothers who kill their husbands in favor of their children" (167). Ultimately, as a motherless goddess, Athena's affiliations are entirely with the father and with the male in general.

In the *Eumenides*, Athena is presented as the enforcer of gender boundaries and distinctions, though she herself manages to transgress the boundaries and distinctions that a female mortal would have faced. While there is no example of a case like Orestes's actually occurring in the Athenian courthouses, the firmness of patriarchal ideology espoused by Athena, their patron goddess, was deeply engrained in the society. Despite the goddess's authority and importance throughout Athenian culture, had she been a human living in the democratic polis (city-state), she would not have even been considered a citizen. While Athena was upheld as the protector of the patriarchal domains of politics and war, the sanctity of her virginity also enabled her to be regarded as the exemplary female: skilled at weaving, pottery, and other crafts. Thus, the goddess is active and exemplary in distinctively feminine and masculine spheres that were divided in fifth-century Athenian culture and, most bafflingly, whose separations were enforced by the very goddess who unified them.

Although it is complicated for contemporary scholars to interpret Athena's role in Greek and Athenian society, it appears to have been no less complicated for the Greeks who worshipped her. In Athens, Athena was revered as the founder of the ancient Athenian law courts and the protector of the city. However, in their society, "while female citizens had important roles in the religious worship of the community, they were completely barred from participation in political, judicial, and military affairs" (Pomeroy et al. 97). Women labored almost exclusively in the manufacture of pottery and woven garments. Their craftsmanship would be showcased during the Panathenaea, an annual religious festival held in honor of the goddess during which a new robe (peplos) made by the women of Athens would be brought to adorn the statue of Athena Polias ("Athena of the city") in the Erechtheum (or Erechtheion), a temple on the acropolis. Women's education was limited to the instruction of their fathers, if their fathers chose to provide it, whereas higher-class men partook in different educational institutions. This included mentorship, necessary political engagement, and even more exclusive involvement in artistic engagements and competitions, symposia, and so forth. The fifth-century BCE in Athens also heralded the intellectual movement of the sophists, "practitioners of wisdom." These intellectuals came from all over the Greek world to Athens to engage in philosophic discourse.

According to Deacy, Athena's ability to transcend gender boundaries and norms made her an appealing figure to use as a means of exploring these supposed boundaries. She explains, "The Greeks were fond of exploring Athena's similarities with other pugnacious females, notably the Amazons, the enemies of patriarchy *par excellence*, whose society represented as a matriarchy, and who, on various occasions in myth, launched invasions of Greece" (31). However, as within the *Eumenides*, comparing Athena with Clytemnestra or the Amazons only made clearer to the Greeks that she represents the exemplary female and that although she occupies male realms, she also upholds them. Yet, even as an exemplary female and upholder of gender boundaries, Athenians such as Aristophanes voiced their discomfort over the apparent oddity of Athena's masculinity. In his comedy, *The Birds*, set in Athens, Aristophanes's characters have the following exchange:

CHORUS: What god, then, shall be our city's protector? For whom shall we weave the peplos?

EUELPIDES: Why not keep Athena as City-Goddess?

PISTHETAIROS: How could a city be well-ordered where a woman-god stands in full armor, and Kleisthenes works the loom? (qtd. in Hurwit 235)

Anxiety toward women in Greece's patriarchal culture was sometimes expressed as anxiety toward the confusing masculine goddess of Athena, who at times crosses into boundaries defined as exclusively male.

The curiously gendered nature of the deity has enabled her followers to use her as a symbol of antagonistic movements. Many different feminist-oriented organizations named for Athena have been founded to further involve women in fields that are acknowledged as being traditionally male, such as science, engineering, and technology. For many, the goddess of supreme wisdom, who in her mythology never seeks union with a male, is a powerful feminist figure and a potential model. A symbol of both female and male power, Athena—and her prominent role in Athenian culture—continues to puzzle scholars and historians.

CROSS-CULTURAL INFLUENCE

With the defeat of Persian king Xerxes I's army at the battle of Salamis in 480 BCE, the Athenians embarked upon a historic golden age as the victorious naval power of the Greek world; however, they also found their city in ruins, the acropolis (high city) having been sacked and destroyed by the Persian army. This, despite their triumph, did much to weaken the morale of the Athenian people, who had been war-stricken for years. In order to boost the morale of his citizens and to secure Athens' position of leadership in the ancient Greek world, Pericles, the Athenian statesman and elected archon famously labeled the First Citizen of Athens by Thucydides, devised a vision for Athens that would involve the beautification of the city and the flourishing of cultural institutions and festivals. On his agenda, Pericles imagined a redesigned acropolis that would include temples to honor the gods—the most important of these temples being the Parthenon, dedicated to the patron goddess and protector of the city, Athena Parthenos. For Pericles and the Athenians, the rebirth of their Athenian polis and the birth of Athenian democracy were inextricably tied to the birth of Athena and what her divine sanctions represented to them.

As the namesake for the ancient Greek city of Athens, the goddess Athena took a central role in Athenian culture and society. In many ways, of all of the twelve Olympians, Athena's figure and character made her the most appropriate deity for a society that prided itself on intellect. In fact, during the Greco-Persian Wars that preceded the building of the Parthenon, the Athenians took a central role in the fight against Persia along with the Spartans; the brilliance and brute strength of the Spartan army was sharply contrasted by the Athenians, who won battles through strategy and cunning. Following the Greco-Persian Wars, which established the Athenians as leaders of the Greek world, Athens, much like its patron goddess, assumed the role of "protector" of the Greek world. Athenians established the Delian League, which included a treasury that was collectively invested in order to fund defense against other potential war threats.

Many other defining characteristics of Athena led to her presiding over crucial and distinctive aspects of Athenian culture. As the ethical goddess of justice, Athena was the natural figure to represent great law courts that the newly democratic society prided itself upon. She was considered the founder of the Areopagus, the ancient court that functioned as the supreme court and tried the most serious cases. In situations when the jury could not make a decision, Athena was said to have made the deciding vote, as in Aeschylus's *Oresteia*. Her authority extended into the artistic and domestic realms as well, particularly when it came to her presiding over women's activities. Her unmatchable skill at weaving is an important aspect of the goddess that was celebrated during one of Athens' largest festivals, the Greater Panathenaea. This religious festival honored the goddess with various ritual ceremonies, athletic games, and artistic competitions.

The Athenians celebrated the history of Athena becoming their patron deity in a popular mythical account of a competition between her and Poseidon. In the myth, both Athena and Poseidon are interested in the patronage, so in order to make a decision the Athenians establish a contest. They ask the gods to present an offering; whoever has the best offering will be chosen. Poseidon makes his offering first by striking a rock powerfully with his trident and producing a stream of water. Athena follows Poseidon, producing a blooming olive tree by striking her spear into the ground and planting an olive branch in it. The mythical king Cecrops of Athens is very impressed with Athena's offering of peace and prosperity and thus selects Athena, naming the city after her.

The mythical contest between the gods and naming of Athens was one of the motifs that decorated the Parthenon. The building of the iconic temple began around 449 BCE when the Athenian archon Pericles proposed its construction to the assembly. It would be built between 447 and 432 BCE. Recruiting the finest architects and artists throughout the ancient Greek world, Pericles sought to construct a building on the acropolis that would leave an indelible impact on its observers and that would convey perfection, prosperity, and power to all visitors and citizens of the city. Blending both Doric and Ionic elements, the building was in many regards the first of its kind and was also the largest building in the world constructed entirely of marble. The rectangular structure had a ratio of eight columns on the width ends and seventeen columns running the length of the rectangle, a ratio that was deemed by the architects and engineers as being aesthetically pleasing (Pomeroy et al. 275). In fact, the architects of the building were so concerned with the aesthetic perfection of the structure that much of how the Parthenon appears to look is actually the product of an optical illusion.

Although the columned building seems to consist exclusively of perfectly straight linear patterns running parallel and perpendicular to each other, in actuality, there is not a single straight line in the structure. In *Ancient Greece: A Political, Social, and Cultural History*, Sarah B. Pomeroy, Stanley M. Burstein, Walter Donlan, and Jennifer Tolbert Roberts explain:

> Athenian architects were well aware that from a distance the eye would perceive perfectly straight columns as thin in the middle and appearing to fall outward, and

a perfectly horizontal foundation would appear to droop toward the center. Consequently, they took pains to create optical illusions by subtle swelling (*entasis*) of the midportion of the columns, by tilting the columns toward the interior lest they seem to be falling outward, and by curving the middle of the floor and steps upward as though a wind were blowing under a rug. (275)

At the center of the building, the mid-portions of the steps are actually four inches taller than they are on the respective ends of the steps. Such meticulous ingenuity and foresight had never yet been matched. From afar the building, poised on the top of the acropolis, appeared to be hovering over the city. The clever attention to such details was a fitting and duteous tribute to the city's patron goddess. With the Parthenon, the Athenians were able to showcase the impressive attributes that they shared with Athena: skillful craftsmanship, cunning strategy, and intimidating ingenuity.

The brilliance of the Parthenon's inherent structure was matched by the friezes and motifs that decorated the building, depicting the honored goddess. Although partially lost, it is generally agreed upon that the eastern pediment depicted the renowned birth of Athena from the head of her father. Fortunately, Jacques Carrey drew images of the Parthenon in 1674 that usefully inform interpretations of the damaged pediment. Yet even in 1674, the central figures of Zeus and Athena were already gone. The motif drawn by Carrey depicts Athena and Zeus at the center, surrounded by various other figures. Most scholars agree that the left side of the pediment in Carrey's artwork depicts Helios, a horse pulling the sun god, Dionysus reclining, Persephone and Demeter seated beside each other, and Artemis turning away from the central figures. From the center out to the right is Hestia seated by Dione, Aphrodite leaning affectionately against Dione (mother of Aphrodite in *The Iliad*), and another horse that is thought to belong Selene or Nyx, personified deities of the moon and night.

Some speculate over the mythical accuracy of this depiction. While there are many varying accounts of Athena's birth, no account includes a divine audience of that size on hand to witness the birth. Some scholars criticize the fact that neither Hephaestus, Hera, nor Prometheus are depicted, since they all are commonly recorded as being involved with or present during the birth. Other scholars have identified these deities in place of some of those described above. Among those who assert that the pediment undoubtedly portrayed the mythical birth of the goddess, there is a debate as to whether the pediment should be treated as an artistic interpretation and hyperbolic glorification of the birth scene or as an additional historical source offering yet another version of Athena's birth. Regardless of these debates, the eastern pediment was a telling parallel to the western pediment, which depicted the contest of Athena and Poseidon and the founding of Athens with its patron deity. The motifs chosen for these two pediments directly aligned the magnificent birth of the goddess with the birth of the great Greek city.

As impressive as the outside of the Parthenon was, the inside of the temple rivaled it with the awe-inspiring statue of Athena Parthenos located at the end of the great hall. Standing at a daunting forty-foot height, the now-lost statue of the goddess prompted awe and wonder from its observers, who would have met the goddess's feet at eye level. Phidias, the sculptor and a friend of Pericles, was renowned throughout the Greek world as the greatest sculptor of divine figures. Among his many impressive creations, he also constructed the statue of Zeus at Olympia, which is considered one of the lost wonders of the ancient world. The statue of Athena Parthenos, covered in gold and ivory, stood with a six-foot figure of Nike (victory) in her left palm. The impressive sculpture was built in parts so that were the city to face the threat of war or thieves, it could be easily taken apart and protected. Behind the statue and locked in a back room were kept the possessions of the goddess, which included the Athenian treasury and eventually also the treasury of the Delian League. Outside the Parthenon was another statue of Athena sculpted by Phidias. Clothed in her military armor and equipped with a spear, the goddess's statue could reportedly be seen by sailors coming into Athenian harbors.

The Parthenon is representative of how important Athena was to the Athenians and is in essence the architectural epitome of what Athena represented to them. By depicting her birth along with their own, the Athenians, who were at the time in the process of regeneration, imagined themselves to be born out of the same power and wisdom as their patron deity. The temple, which has left behind the impressive legacy of being the most copied structure in the world, represents the impressive ingenuity of a people inspired by the great goddess of intelligence and authority. The imitated architecture of the Parthenon—used for government buildings, banks, courts, and museums across the Western world—still symbolically represents what the Athenians coveted of their patron goddess: stability, safety, justice, wisdom, and power.

Katherine Sehl, MA

BIBLIOGRAPHY

Aeschylus. *Eumenides*. Ed. Alan H. Sommerstein. Cambridge: Cambridge UP, 1989. Print.

Apollodorus. *The Library of Greek Mythology*. Trans. Keith Aldrich. Lawrence: Coronado, 1975. Print.

Aristophanes. *The Birds*. Trans. William Arrowsmith. Ann Arbor: U of Michigan P, 1961. Print.

Carter, Susan. "Athena and the Mirror." *She Is Everywhere! An Anthology of Writing in Womanist/Feminist Spirituality*. Ed. Lucia Chiavola Birnbaum. New York: iUniverse, 2005. 209–25. Print.

Deacy, Susan. *Athena*. London: Routledge, 2008. Print.

Hesiod. The Works and Days, Theogony, *and* The Shield of Herakles. Trans. Hugh G. Evelyn-White. Mineola: Dover, 2006. Print.

Hurwit, Jeffrey M. *The Athenian Acropolis: History, Mythology, and Archaeology from the Neolithic Era to the Present*. Cambridge: Cambridge UP, 1999. Print.

Leitao, David D. *The Pregnant Male as Myth and Metaphor in Classical Greek Literature*. New York: Cambridge UP, 2012. Print.

Long, Christopher P. "The Daughters of Metis: Patriarchal Dominion and the Daughters of Between." *Graduate Faculty Philosophy Journal* 28.2 (2007): 67–86. Print.

Pindar. The Odes *and Selected Fragments*. Trans. G. S. Conway and Richard Stoneman. London: Dent, 1997. Print.

Pomeroy, Sarah B., Stanley M. Burstein, Walter Donlan, and Jennifer Tolbert Roberts. *Ancient Greece: A Political, Social and Cultural History*. New York: Oxford UP, 1999. Print.

Cyrus the Great

Author: Herodotus
Time Period: 999 BCE–1 BCE
Country or Culture: Persia
Genre: Legend

OVERVIEW

Many heroes, both historical and mythical, have been granted tales of a miraculous birth or preservation. Cyrus II, who was king of Persia from 550 BCE to about 530 BCE, is one such figure. Fragments of his story appear in several ancient texts. Of these, Herodotus gives the most complete account, a tale of multiple families and generations.

Sometimes known as the first historian, the Greek writer Herodotus lived during the fifth century BCE. His *Historiai Herodotou* (424 BCE; *The History*, 1709) contains information about Cyrus and the Achaemenid Empire over which he ruled. The work is commonly divided into nine books because the ancient copies of the text required nine scrolls. Herodotus's stated aims in that work are to record the stories of both Greeks and non-Greeks and to relate how the two groups faced conflict. In contrast to the bards, such as Homer, who invoked heavenly powers as they began writing, Herodotus aimed to use his own research and observation to write.

Herodotus is the major source of information about his own life. He asserts that he was born in Halicarnassus, now known as Bodrum, Turkey. If his work is factual, he visited several areas of the Greek world. His ability to write indicates that he came from a family of means, one able to afford a teacher. He may have served in the army; he describes battles, though not from the viewpoint of a commander. Scholars conjecture that he died sometime after 429, which is the year of the last incident he recorded. That was also the summer of the great plague in Athens; he may have died the city at that time.

Major characters in Herodotus's work include Astyages, a powerful regent of the Medes, whose rule over

an empire that dominated the Middle East extended from about 584 BCE to 550 BCE. His daughter, Mandane, is married off to a Persian man of lower birth, Cambyses (Kambyses). Their son is Cyrus (Kyros), the hero of the tale. Harpagus (Harpagos) is Astyages's relative and confidante; Harpagus's slave Mithradates is a cattle herder. Mithradates's wife is named Spako, which means "bitch" in the Median language, a name that is significant in the mythology; many myths involve abandoned children being suckled or raised by female animals, such as female canines, properly known as "bitches."

The folkloric and mythic elements of Herodotus's account will be examined through the lens of work done in the early twentieth century by folklorists Antti Aarne and Stith Thompson. Aarne created and Thompson expanded a classification of the motifs used in Western folktales and fairy tales. The numeric system is similar in concept to the Dewey decimal system used in classifying library books. Each category has a letter and number designation, such as AT S42, which represents the "cruel grandfather," applicable to the analysis of Cyrus's story. The archetype of the hero has been most fully explained by the work of the twentieth-century academic and author Joseph Campbell. Although Cyrus was a historical figure, the passage from Herodotus pertaining to him contains mythic elements.

SUMMARY

Like many rulers, Astyages is superstitious and dependent upon his court astrologers and magicians. When he dreams that from his daughter Mandane will come a flood of water so great as to fill not only their city but also all of Asia, he consults his magicians for an interpretation. They relate that her child will rule over this great region. To prevent a loss of his own power, Astyages marries her to Cambyses, a Persian commoner, not his equal in blood or rank. During the first year of the marriage, however, Astyages dreams of a vine that comes from Mandane and covers Asia. The interpreters of dreams suggest that the child Mandane is carrying will usurp Astyages's power.

To prevent this from happening, Astyages sends for Mandane, who is living in Persia, intending to kill the child. He entrusts the task to his servant Harpagus, telling him to kill the boy and dispose of his body. Although Harpagus agrees, he weeps when he arrives home, explaining to his wife that the boy is his relation and the king has no male heirs. Wanting to protect himself when Mandane comes to the throne, he passes on the task to a slave, Mithradates, who herds cattle in the mountains. Harpagus charges him with exposing the child on the mountains, saying that he will return to see it has been done.

On his way home, Mithradates, who assumes the child has been born of a slave, hears the truth of the child's origins. Mithradates's wife is in labor that day, but their child is stillborn. His wife, named Cyno (Kyno) in Greek and Spako in Median, suggests they raise the baby as their own and expose the dead child. This they do and, three days later, summon Harpagus to see the exposed dead body. The cattle herder and his wife bring up the living child, whom they do not call Cyrus.

The truth of the boy's noble birth comes out when he is twelve and playing with other boys. They elect him as their king, and he acts accordingly, assigning them tasks. When one of the boys disobeys, Cyrus beats him. The boy complains to his father, who goes to Astyages. Cyrus is summoned to answer for beating a boy of higher rank, and he defends himself on the grounds of having been elected king. Cyrus willingly submits to Astyages's judgment, which indicates to Astyages that his own grandson stands before him.

Astyages calls for Mithradates, who at first claims the boy as his own blood son. As he is being led off to be tortured, however, he confesses the truth and begs forgiveness. Astyages's wrath is directed at Harpagus, who is summoned and tells the truth at once.

Astyages states that he had regretted the boy's death, particularly after Mandane's laments, and is glad all has worked out so well. He asks Harpagus to send for his own son to greet Cyrus and to be present at a feast he is preparing to honor the gods who have planned all this.

Harpagus's son is about thirteen years old. When he arrives at the palace, Astyages has him butchered, cut into pieces, and then roasted. To the rest of the guests Astyages serves lamb, but he places before Harpagus his own cooked son, with the head, hands, and feet reserved

"Lord, he has only received his due. For the boys in the village, he being among them, were at play, and made me their king, believing me to be the best adapted thereto. And the other boys did as they were told, but he was disobedient, and did not mind me at all. For this he has received his reward. If I have deserved punishment, here I am at your service."

"Cyrus"

in a basket. At the conclusion of the meal, Astyages inquires if Harpagus has enjoyed the meal. When Harpagus answers that he has, the servants reveal the head and other parts of his son. Harpagus does not react in anger or sorrow, but says the king has done well.

Astyages once again calls his magicians and relates the story of Cyrus's survival and the revelation of his identity through playing king, asking what it means. The magicians state that the king has nothing to fear now, because the playacting has fulfilled the prophecy that Cyrus would become king. Astyages therefore calls the boy and sends him to Persia to his overjoyed parents, who had believed him dead.

Cyrus relates to them the story of his being saved from exposure and of Spako caring for him. His parents interpret this to mean that a wild animal suckled Cyrus, a common motif in hero tales.

When Cyrus is grown, Harpagus incites him to attack the Medes. Although victorious, Cyrus does not slay his grandfather, who has been taken prisoner, but instead keeps him near and cares for him. Cyrus then reigns over the Persians and the Medes.

ANALYSIS

The Finnish folklorist Antti Aarne followed in the footsteps of other European romantics who were concerned about the loss of ethnic cultures in the wake of rapid industrialization and urbanization. Attempts to classify motifs in fairy tales and folklore began as early as 1864. In an article published in 1908, Robert Harry Lowie

HISTORICAL CONTEXT

Cyrus II, known as Cyrus the Great, lived from about 585 BCE until about 529 BCE. He was the son of Cambyses I, king of Anshan. He became king of the Medes and the Persians in 558 after overthrowing his grandfather, Astyages. He may be best remembered for his conquest of Babylon, which had been the dominant power of the era.

Following this success, he permitted the Jews, whom the Babylonians had captured, to return Judah (2 Chron. 36). The Jewish prophets Isaiah and Jeremiah had prophesied this release even before the captivity had begun. According to Isaiah, God referred to Cyrus as his "shepherd" (Isa. 44:28).

In addition, Cyrus allowed the returning Jews to rebuild the temple, which the Babylonians had destroyed. He also returned the sacred items from that temple, which the Babylonian king Nebuchadnezzar II had captured as spoils of war. According to Ezra 1, a biblical text attributed to a priest who accompanied the captives back to Jerusalem, this was a considerable treasure, including thousands of silver and gold vessels and knives.

In 1879, a cuneiform text now known as the Cyrus Cylinder was discovered. It indicated the release of captives from east of the Tigris River. This does not include Judah, however, and thus does not confirm the biblical account. Rather, it indicates continuity of the tradition of allowing for repatriation of conquered peoples, along with the rebuilding of temples and care of the local deities.

Cyrus continued the conquest of neighboring lands, establishing the Achaemenid dynasty. His empire extended from the Indus River to the Aegean Sea. It was so vast that a successor, Darius, divided it into districts known as "satrapies," administered by "the eyes of the king." Befitting his heroic status, Cyrus was killed in battle against the tribe of the Massagetai.

dichotomies between the worldviews of his upbringing and those that he studied. Later, while studying abroad, he was influenced by early twentieth-century writers, artists, and thinkers of Europe. In 1934, he began a teaching career at Sarah Lawrence College that lasted for nearly four decades. Academic life enabled him to write and publish a number of theoretical works on mythology. His *Hero with a Thousand Faces* (1949) brought awards and recognition. Between 1959 and 1968, he published the four-volume collection *The Masks of God*. At his death in 1985, Campbell was working on a projected five-volume set, *Historical Atlas of World Mythology*, of which four volumes are complete. Campbell, who had studied the work of psychoanalyst Carl Jung, believed that myths were projections of the self.

Campbell was also familiar with the work of Otto Rank, a colleague of Sigmund Freud. Born in 1884, Rank served as an assistant to Freud for two decades, until disagreement over methods of analysis divided them in the mid-1920s. Before the split, however, in 1914, Rank published *The Myth of the Birth of the Hero*, which in turn had an influence on Campbell. Among the stories Rank considers in this text is Herodotus's account of the birth and upbringing of Cyrus.

Although a historical figure, Cyrus is furnished with a story of birth and upbringing typical of heroes. The hero cycle encompasses three major rites of passage: birth, initiation, and death. Although little information is provided about the hero's childhood, a crisis occurs around the age of puberty that demonstrates his being destined for greatness. Herodotus focuses on Cyrus's birth and crisis point in his narrative. In doing so, he incorporates at least six points in the hero cycle that Lord Raglan identified in *The Hero: A Study in Tradition, Myth, and Drama* (1956). Raglan found that among heroes in myth, history, and legend, twenty-two distinct aspects may be found. These include an attempt to kill the hero, often by his father; the child being taken away from harm; and foster parents in a distant land rearing the child. In addition to these,

highlighted the advantages of a uniform classification scheme for mythology. Two years later, Aarne published the *Verzeichnis der Märchentypen* (Tale type index). The American Stith Thompson translated and expanded the index of motifs, which was published in English as *The Types of the Folktale*, with revisions in 1928 and 1961. Tale types receive the designation AT to honor the work of these two men. This index contains A to Z classifications, with submotifs.

A second figure in comparative mythology and folklore, Joseph Campbell, had a tremendous impact through his decades of teaching, lecturing, and writing. Born in 1904 into a New York Roman Catholic family, he became obsessed with American Indian cultures and the four further points pertain to Cyrus: little is said of his childhood; Cyrus reaches his future kingdom as a young man; he is victorious over a king; and he begins to rule the kingdom himself.

The motif "Culture-hero is hidden in order to escape enemies" (AT511.2.3) clearly applies to the Cyrus legend. According to Herodotus, the king orders Cyrus, his grandson, to be exposed, but the child is saved from certain death through the beneficent scheme of Mithradates and his wife, who raise the child. In this sense, Cyrus is the hero hidden in plain sight. The tale also incorporates AT511.3.1, "Hero raised in seclusion," which refers to being hidden from harm but not in isolation.

Aarne-Thompson motifs S300–S399 concern abandoned or murdered children. Both of these types occur in the Cyrus legend: Cyrus is meant to be abandoned, with his death the intended outcome, and Astyages has Harpagus's unnamed son murdered. Generally, it is the child's father who makes the attempt on his child's life. In these instances, however, Astyages, grandfather of Cyrus and distant relative of Harpagus's son, is the figure planning abandonment and accomplishing murder. S301 is the category for children who have been exposed and left to die but are rescued, as Cyrus is. Harpagus's son is murdered for revenge, which is classified as S302. As an absolute ruler, Astyages considers Harpagus's abrogation of his direct will to be both a personal slight and defiance of his kingship, and he demands revenge.

As Susan M. Bernardo states, "children's fates are often tied to the fates and situations of their mothers, broader needs for political power, and fear of prophecies of the burgeoning power of the child" (408). All three of these factors are in play in Herodotus's narrative of Cyrus. Astyages's primary concern is to consolidate and maintain his power over the Median Empire. To that end, he arranges the marriage of his daughter, Mandane, to a man in another kingdom, one not of noble birth. Astyages acts in such manner because of prophetic dreams that indicate his daughter's offspring will threaten his hegemony. Astyages's dreams—one of a river overflowing Asia and one of a vine encompassing Asia—both not only indicate the extent of the future empire but also suggest wild and rampant growth. According to motif AT M371, one of the motives for abandonment is to circumvent a prophecy's fulfillment, which occurs in Herodotus's narrative.

Abandoning a child in a remote area either to die or to be killed by wild animals falls within the rubric of AT S, "Unnatural Cruelty." Motif S40 is classified as "Cruel Grandparents," a designation applicable to Astyages, who features as Cyrus's most prominent relative in the story. Indeed, aside from being named and begetting his son Cyrus, Cambyses does not factor much in this tale. He is included in the rejoicing at Cyrus's return near the end of the legend but, like Mandane, has no speaking parts.

The wide variety of themes and motifs from the Aarne-Thompson system indicates the way in which even historical figures are prone to have embellished elements in their biographies. In the absence of verifiable details, a story must be created. Although historians conclude that Herodotus was reporting faithfully what he had been told, this does not preclude mythic and folkloric elements from influencing the tale.

Turning to Campbell's insights on myth brings the awareness that myth is "the dream of the world." Further, Campbell writes that "dream and myth are of the same logic" (*Myths* 70). Thus, the presence of dreams in motivating Astyages's actions clearly indicates a mythological aspect to the tale.

Campbell also notes that even in cases in which the hero is a historical figure, the makers of legends will weave adventures that are appropriate to a heroic status. Campbell suggests that these adventures, which are often mythic journeys, could be symbolic of one descending into the psyche. In this regard, he follows Jungian theory. Cyrus being called to answer for himself before the king at twelve years of age aligns with this motif.

It is noteworthy that in his defense before Astyages, Cyrus does not make excuses. He merely explains that the son of Artembares was not obedient and therefore deserved to be whipped by a king. He says, "If I have deserved punishment, here I am at your service" (Rank 28). Through this statement, Astyages realizes the true identity of the young man before him. The true royal nature merely states the truth and accepts consequences. In the same way, in the Bible, when Joseph and Mary locate Jesus in the temple after he has been missing from the family group for three days, he asks, "Do you not know that I must be about my father's interests?" (Luke 2:49). The young men in each story identify with royalty.

In analyzing Rank's *Myth of the Birth of the Hero*, Campbell refers to a four-part pattern, calling it a neurotic daydream of dissociation from true parents. The pattern is of an individual who imagines divine or noble birth, exposure or exile as an infant, adoption by a lowly family, and the hope for restoration. This "daydream" leads in some rulers to an ego that identifies with a god, rather than an ego appropriately extinguished in the presence of a god (*Masks* 74).

A similar result is implied when Astyages's assumes what might be the prerogatives of a god, determining who is permitted to live and who will die. Astyages's charge to Harpagus is delivered almost casually:

> My dear Harpagos, I shall charge thee with an errand which thou must conscientiously perform. But do not deceive me, and let no other man attend to it, for all might not go well with thee. Take this boy, whom Mandane has brought forth, carry him home, and kill him. Afterwards thou canst bury him, how and in whatsoever manner thou desirest. (Rank 25)

Although the command is delivered briefly, all the components are strictly set forth. Harpagus violates every one of them. He deceives Astyages for twelve years; he assigns the task to another, one of the king's cattle herders; and he does not carry the boy to his own home or kill and bury him.

Instead, Harpagus, who emerges in this tale as a man of more honor than the king, entrusts the task to Mithradates. He explains his actions to his wife as being motivated (not unlike the king's actions) by a desire for self-preservation. The boy is a blood relation, a fact that, for Harpagus, argues against committing the murder. More important, Astyages has no male heir; thus, one could infer that upon Astyages's death, Mandane will rule. Harpagus concludes that she is not likely to look favorably on the murderer of her son. Yet for Harpagus's own safety while Astyages lives, the child must be killed. Thus, he passes on the unpleasant task of murder to one further down the social scale. Mithradates also intends to kill the child for reasons of self-preservation, fearing that Harpagus will require his "disgraceful death" if the child lives (Rank 27). It is Spako who supplies the solution of substitution.

In general, the wives in Herodotus's *History* are noteworthy for their quick thinking and tender hearts. As Carolyn Dewald points out, they often remind their male peers of the way society must proceed, and they act to ensure the stability and continuance of the family. Although Mandane seems to have nothing to say concerning either her marriage or the removal of her son, the wife of the herder, Spako, thinks and acts decisively to save the life of the infant prince. Like other women in *The History*, Spako comes up with a creative solution that is not apparent to the men in the narrative.

True to his earlier threat, Astyages, once the truth is revealed, punishes Harpagus by murdering his son, who is roughly the same age as Cyrus. The mythic motif of the death of the substitute is familiar to Western readers through the Christian myth of Jesus Christ, who substitutes and sacrifices himself for all humankind. The motif is also beautifully rendered in novels, such as Charles Dickens's *A Tale of Two Cities* (1859), in which Sydney Carton accepts death for Charles Darnay out of love for Lucy, Darnay's wife. However, in the Cyrus legend, the son of Harpagus does not choose to act as a substitute; on the contrary, he is murdered as casually and brutally as Astyages had intended for his grandson to be. The earlier death of a substitute, the herder's stillborn son, furthers the theme of doubling, which occurs throughout the legend.

Doubling is also present in the use of a basket. When the stillborn child is exposed early in the story, it is placed in a basket. At the feast after the recognition scene, the head, hands, and feet of Harpagus's son are placed in a basket to be revealed only after Harpagus has feasted on his own son's flesh.

All of this multiplication must then be removed so that Cyrus can stand alone and heroic. As Rank points out, "The hero in the various duplications of himself and his parents, ascends the social scale from the herder Mithradates, by way of the noble Artembares, who is high in the king's favor, and of the first administrator, Harpagos, who is personally related to the king—until he has himself become a prince" (86).

Although Harpagus outwardly accepts the judgment of Astyages, saying that what the king has done is just, he apparently does not forgive or forget the murder of his son. According to Herodotus, it is he who later joins with the adult Cyrus in overthrowing Astyages and establishing a new kingdom.

Herodotus gives the reader a charming anecdote, a sort of metamyth, near the end of the account. He states that upon reuniting with his birth parents, Cyrus gives an account of how he has lived. Spako, his foster mother, is often mentioned kindly. Mandane and Cambyses hear her name and associate it with an animal bitch, which, Herodotus tells his readers, explains how the idea that Cyrus was suckled by a she-wolf became popular.

Combining the insights of mythological types, as outlined by Aarne and Thompson, and those of myth theorists, including Rank and Campbell, readers gain appreciation for the richness of Herodotus's version of Cyrus's birth, preservation, and restoration to his rightful princely state. Elements common to Western mythology appear throughout the tale of this Persian prince.

CROSS-CULTURAL INFLUENCE

The theme of children abandoned to the elements at birth appears in many cultures. Two such versions of this mythic motif are the third-century Greek novel *Poimenika ta kata Daphnin kai Chloen* (*Daphnis and Chloe*, 1587), which shares features with the Cyrus story, and the Shakespearean romance *The Winter's Tale* (ca. 1610–11), which has thematic similarities.

In both texts, anagnorisis (the recognition scene) is a key plot device. Aristotle wrote of the device in the *Peri poētikēs* (ca. 334 BCE–23 BCE; *Poetics*, 1705); it literally refers to a sudden insight leading from ignorance to knowledge. Anagnorisis often involves the recovery of abandoned children by their true parents. It is most famously used in Sophocles's *Oedipus Rex* (ca. 429 BCE). Although often associated with tragedy, it also occurs in comedy and epic; in later literary history, it appears in novels. Perhaps one of the first examples of its use in a novel is in *Daphnis and Chloe*.

Daphnis and Chloe was based on ancient legends that Longus shaped into an early novella of four books, written around the second century CE. For this work, Longus uses the method of ekphrasis, writing about a piece of art. His prologue indicates that while hunting, he came upon a cave with paintings that told the story he then relates. Only at the end of the work does the reader realize that the two main characters of the tale are responsible for creating the paintings.

The novel details the events throughout one year, although it begins by telling the backstory of the two main characters. Abandoned as children with tokens indicating a connection to wealth, both Daphnis and Chloe are found by childless herders and subsequently reared as their children. A goatherd, Lamon, and his wife, Myrtale, adopt the boy, Daphnis, who has been suckled by a goat. Two years later, Dryas, a shepherd, discovers an infant girl being cared for by one of his ewes; he takes her home to his wife, Nape. They raise the girl as their own.

Although both fathers ensure that their children receive an education befitting their real (but concealed) estate, both men are later instructed in dreams to make the children herders. Spending a great deal of time together, because they tend their flocks together, the two young people, by then in their teens, fall in love.

Each of the adolescents survives a series of narrow escapes and adventures that test their love, a mysterious feeling for which they have no name. They are under the protection of gods and nymphs, as well as under the tutelage of an old man who instructs them about love and its remedies. Although Daphnis is initiated into sexual activity by an older married woman, Chloe remains virginal, as was expected of a young, unmarried woman of the time.

In the final book of the work, Lamon's master arrives for the harvest festival. When Lamon brings out the tokens that he found with Daphnis, the master recognizes them. He had instructed that Daphnis be killed through exposure because he and his wife already had two sons. Daphnis was the fourth child, and there were not enough resources to provide for him, a common reason for abandoning children. Meanwhile, one of the older sons has died, so the parents rejoice at finding their youngest son again. At a feast, Dryas brings forth Chloe's tokens to indicate she is worthy of Daphnis, even in his new status. A rich man at the gathering, who had once been poor and unable to support children, recognizes the tokens and claims his daughter amid general joy. Daphnis and Chloe marry, but despite their status and wealth, they continue to prefer country life to that of the city.

Both *Daphnis and Chloe* and Herodotus's tale of Cyrus present a common mythic and folkloric theme, one familiar even to modern children who feel mistreated. Secretly highborn, the child has somehow been placed in the care of common folks. At a future point in time, he or she will be rescued and receive both riches and the restoration of proper status. The motif is always that of a child from riches being raised by people of lower status, never the reverse. This is the case in both the tale of Cyrus, a prince who is meant to be killed by exposure but is instead entrusted to the care of a cattle herder, and in the novel *Daphnis and Chloe*.

Another component of the theme is the way that the children surpass the common folks in their beauty, manners, and intelligence. Longus notes that Daphnis and Chloe are better looking than the peasants around them and are thus something of a wonder. Cyrus naturally assumes kingly command and prerogatives when playing a game with his peers. Although *Daphnis and Chloe* was not transcribed until later, both stories originate from a time before the Common Era; it is impossible to know which might have influenced the development of the other. However, the plot seems to have been a familiar one in ancient Greece.

Another major work that shares the common trope of a highborn infant left for dead and then rescued, *The Winter's Tale* was first performed privately in 1611. No clear date of composition has been assigned. In 1611, playwright William Shakespeare was nearing fifty years old, with most of his masterpieces written. *The Winter's Tale* is set in the period of his romances, following closely productions of *Cymbeline* (ca. 1609–10), another romance with a jealous husband and lost children, and *Pericles, Prince of Tyre* (ca. 1607–08). It precedes *The Tempest* (1611), which some scholars regard as Shakespeare's farewell to the theater. The First Folio, published in 1623, is the source for this work.

Because paternity was not an issue that could be resolved fully until modern times, a woman's sexual activity and the products of her fertility were often suspect. For Leontes, the king of Sicilia in *The Winter's Tale*, sudden suspicion leads to the accusation that his best friend, King Polixenes of Bohemia, has committed adultery with his wife, Hermione. She is heavy with child, and Polixenes has been visiting for nine months. When Leontes fails to persuade Polixenes to extend his stay, he then asks his wife to plead the cause. Hermione's success arouses Leontes to jealous rage. He has Hermione imprisoned and sends a trusted servant, Camillo, to murder Polixenes. Instead, Camillo warns the wrongly suspected king, and they both escape to Bohemia. In prison, Hermione delivers a girl, whom her gentlewoman Paulina presents to the king. Despite the physical resemblance, the king refuses to acknowledge the baby as his own. Instead, he first commands that the girl be burned alive. Later, he softens the decree to abandonment, commanding Antigonus, one of his lords:

> We enjoin thee,
> As thou art liege-man to us, that thou carry
> This female bastard hence, and that thou bear it
> To some remote and desert place quite out
> Of our dominions, and that there thou leave it
> Without more mercy, to its own protection,
> And favor of the climate. (2.1.173–79)

The young son of Leontes and Hermione, Mamillius, dies shortly after, in fulfillment of the prophecy given by Apollo's oracle—the king will have no male heir if the lost is not found—that Leontes has disregarded. The reference is to the baby, whom Antigonus, in a dream, has heard Hermione name Perdita, meaning "lost." No sooner has Apollo's judgment been read than Mamillius,

who has been ill, dies. At her trial, Hermione faints at the news; Paulina, the wife of Antigonus, later tells the king that Hermione is dead.

Antigonus takes the baby, who is wearing clothing to which is pinned a paper with the name Perdita written on it, to Bohemia. Money is also placed with the infant. An old shepherd finds and raises her with the help of his son. Sixteen years pass, during which Perdita grows into a beautiful young woman. As act 4 opens, she and the son of Polixenes, Florizel, are preparing for a rustic spring festival. Disguised, Polixenes and Camillo arrive in an attempt to discover where and with whom Florizel has been spending so much time. The two young people, who have pledged their love, disregard Polixenes's displeasure at the idea of his son marrying a shepherdess. At Camillo's direction, they escape and head for Sicilia. The shepherd and his son seek Polixenes to reveal Perdita's true identity.

At the beginning of act 5, Florizel and Perdita arrive at Leontes's court, quickly followed by Camillo and Polixenes. Leontes pledges his support of the young couple, still unaware that the princess is his daughter, though he later admits he thought of Hermione when he saw the girl. In the final scenes, Leontes learns the truth, and Paulina reveals a "statue" of Hermione that comes to life. Hermione tells her daughter that, because the oracle extended hope that the lost might be found, she has remained alive to greet her.

The play depicts what can occur in a male-dominated society, where it can be dangerous to be a wife, mother, or daughter, Shakespeare indicates. One of the ladies at court tells the king's young son, Mamillius, "We shall present our services to a fine new prince" (2.1.16–17). Daughters are a liability and not especially wanted. The custom during Greek and Roman times was to expose unwanted children to the elements, a custom that Leontes follows. When Emilia gives news of the royal birth that has occurred in prison, Paulina, that most staunch supporter of Hermione, first asks, "A boy?" (2.2.24). One wonders if a male child would have received the same fate or if the birth of a prince would have softened Leontes's heart.

As a young woman, Perdita becomes an object of contention between Florizel and his father, Polixenes, as well as a potential danger to her shepherd father and foster brother. Even Polixenes, who is generally a more reasonable and sympathetic character than Leontes, expresses the possibility of male violence against women. In his anger at his son's affection for a mere shepherdess, however lovely, the alienated Polixenes threatens Perdita: "I'll have thy beauty scratch'd with briers and made more homely than thy state" (4.4.425–26).

One might ask why, in the early seventeenth century, Shakespeare created a play concerning a lost royal child whose true identity is masked for years in a rustic life. For theater audiences of the early seventeenth century, royal progeny and succession were important themes. Beginning with the death of Henry VIII in 1547, issues of succession had troubled the English court. Henry's son, Edward, had died young and childless. The rule of Henry's daughter Mary resulted in a strict Catholic monarchy that caused the deaths of many, a reign that earned her the name Bloody Mary. Under Elizabeth I, who began to rule in 1558, a more moderate return to the Anglican faith ensued, but intrigue surrounded her rule, as she died childless and left her heir undetermined. In 1603, James VI of Scotland, a close relative of Elizabeth, began his reign as James I of England. Like Elizabeth, he was a patron of theater, and the King's Men performed for his pleasure and that of his wife, Anne.

Along with most monarchs of his era, James believed in the divine right of kings to rule, and he wrote two treatises on the subject. Like Leontes and Polixenes, he was concerned with the succession—particularly since the lack of an obvious successor to Queen Elizabeth I had created such turmoil and political jockeying before her death. Only three of James's children survived childhood; his son Charles would take the throne in 1625. Thus, the twin issue of lineage and the survival of royal children remained of prime importance to the monarch, Shakespeare's patron, at the time *The Winter's Tale* was written and first performed.

The parallels between Herodotus's tale of Cyrus and Shakespeare's story of Perdita are several. First and most obviously, jealousy plays a major role in motivating action. Leontes is unreasonably jealous of his wife, fearing she has been unfaithful. Astyages is jealous for his own power and security, sending away his grandson for fear of a prophecy. Both men intend death for their offspring, then resort to an ancient custom of exposing children in the elements. In both cases, people of low birth rear the children and their true identities keep from them.

Clearly, mysteries of origin and status make for good plots. Longus and Shakespeare both knew and took advantage of this fact, creating memorable works that have survived for centuries.

Judy A. Johnson, MLS, MTS

BIBLIOGRAPHY

Bernardo, Susan M. "Abandoned or Murdered Children: Motifs S300–S399." Garry and El-Shamy 404–8.

Bieman, Elizabeth. *William Shakespeare: The Romances*. New York: Hall, 1990. 66–89. Print.

Campbell, Joseph. *The Hero with a Thousand Faces*. New York: Pantheon, 1949. Print.

—-. *Masks of God: Occidental Mythology*. New York: Viking, 1964. Print.

—-. *Myths of Light: Eastern Metaphors of the Eternal*. Novato: New World, 2003. Print.

Dewald, Carolyn. "Women and Culture in Herodotus' Histories." *Women's Studies* 8.1–2 (1981): 93–128. Print.

Garry, Jane, and Hasan El-Shamy, eds. *Archetypes and Motifs in Folklore and Literature: A Handbook*. Armonk: Sharpe, 2005. Print.

Morgan, J. R., ed. *Longus: Daphnis and Chloe*. Oxford: Aris, 2004. Print.

New Oxford Annotated Bible. 3rd ed. New York: Oxford UP, 2007. Print. New Revised Standard Version with the Apocrypha.

Rank, Otto. "Cyrus." *The Myth of the Birth of the Hero: A Psychological Exploration of Myth*. Trans. F. Robbins and Smith Ely Jelliffe. New York: Journal of Nervous and Mental Disease, 1914. 24–38. Print.

Shakespeare, William. "A Winter's Tale." *The Riverside Shakespeare*. Vol. 2. Boston: Houghton, 1974. Print.

Underberg, Natalie. "The Hero Cycle, Various Motifs in A." Garry and El-Shamy 10–23.

Hainuwele

Author: Traditional Wemale
Time Period: 2499 BCE–1000 BCE; 1901 CE–1950 CE
Country or Culture: Indonesia
Genre: Myth

OVERVIEW

The Hainuwele story is a traditional myth of the Wemale tribe on the island of Ceram, in eastern Indonesia. Ceram is one of the islands of the Maluku (or Moluccas) archipelago, which runs east of Timor and west of New Guinea. The inhabitants of the Maluku Islands have always depended on trade. Many of the islands of the archipelago have poor soil, making sustainable agriculture impossible, and few can grow enough rice to feed their populations. By trading locally available goods—such as fish, turtles, shells, and exotic birds—the tribal peoples were able to obtain the products they needed to survive and flourish.

The Maluku Islands have long been the source of wealth for outside merchants as well. From the early medieval period on, the Maluku Islands were a main source of spices such as cloves, mace, and nutmeg, valuable trade commodities that went east to China, and west to India, the Middle East, and Europe. As such, the Maluku Islands are better known to the outside world as the Spice Islands. Feathers from birds of paradise were also gathered on the Maluku Islands and were traded abroad as expensive luxury goods.

The constant flow of merchant ships in the medieval period, mainly from other parts of Indonesia, India, and China, to the Spice Islands brought a variety of goods to the people of the Maluku archipelago. Foreign treasures—such as ivory, gold ornaments, musical instruments, forged iron weapons, ceramics, and textiles—are still passed down from generation to generation among the families of the Maluku Islands. These vestiges of a bygone era of trade are evidence of the huge influx of wealth that the spices trade brought to the remote archipelago.

Hainuwele, the protagonist of story that describes the formation of the traditional social order of the tribes of western Ceram, has the unusual gift of excreting valuable goods. This detail surely reflects the fascination foreign treasure held for the people of the island. Despite her supernatural ability to give gifts, the people of the tribe grow jealous and eventually kill the young heroine. Hainuwele's murder by people who do not understand her power, then, points to the potentially disruptive force of foreign trade.

The Western world first learned of the Hainuwele myth when German scholars from the Frobenius Institute (Frobenius-Institut), named for the famous early German ethnologist Leo Frobenius, led an expedition to the Maluku Islands in 1937 and 1938. The ethnographers working on the expedition recorded many of the myths of the tribal people they encountered throughout the archipelago. The Hainuwele myth was first described in Western academic literature by the German anthropologist Adolf E. Jenson.

Based on Jenson's work with it, two prominent mythologists became interested in the Hainuwele myth. These were Mircea Eliade, a Romanian professor at the University of Chicago, and Joseph Campbell, the American who pioneered comparative mythology as a popular subject. It is through two scholars, and particularly Campbell, that the Hainuwele myth is now widely known within the English-speaking anthropological community, where it has become a template for understanding the myths of other peoples.

SUMMARY

The Hainuwele myth begins by stating that the nine families of humans originally come from Mount Nunusaku, where they grew out of a bunch of bananas. They then settle in the western area of Ceram, between Ahiolo and Varoloin. These early families call the place the Nine Dance Grounds. One of the people of the original nine families is a man named Ameta, which means "dark," "black," or "night." Ameta is a hunter and, according to some translations, one who mainly works in darkness. Ameta has no wife or children. On one hunting trip, Ameta's hunting dog scares a wild pig, who escapes by swimming into a pond. The pig becomes exhausted and drowns, and Ameta pulls it out. When he gets the pig to shore, he sees that there is a coconut stuck to its tusk, which is a new sight to humans since coconut trees do not yet exist.

Ameta takes the strange nut home and covers it with a cloth decorated with a snake motif and goes to bed. He dreams that a man has told him to plant the nut in the ground so it could grow, and in the morning, he does so. Three days later, it is a tall coconut palm, and three days after that, it blossoms. Ameta climbs the tree to gather blossoms, but he cuts his finger and bleeds on a leaf, returning home to treat his injury. When he returns three days later, he finds that a human face is growing out of the leaf where his blood had spilled. After three more days, a body of a person is growing, and after three more, he returns to the tree again and finds a little girl.

When he goes to sleep that night, he dreams of a man who tells him to cover the little girl with the cloth with the snake motif and bring her home. The next day, he carefully carries her down from the tree and names her Hainuwele. Three days after being brought to Ameta's home, Hainuwele has grown into a nubile maiden, and Ameta discovers that Hainuwele has an unusual power. When she defecates, she does not produce normal feces, but instead bears valuable gifts, such as Chinese ceramics and gongs. Ameta grows very rich because of his adopted daughter's strange talent.

Not long after Hainuwele comes to live with Ameta, the nine families of people hold a sacred Maro Dance (which traditionally lasted for nine days and involved the women sitting in a circle handing betel nut to a nine-fold spiral of men dancing around them). On the second day of the dance, Hainuwele is invited to sit with the women in the circle, which makes her happy. Instead of handing the men betel nut, however, she gives them coral, which delights everyone. Each night, Hainuwele gives the men more and more valuable gifts. On the third night, she distributes Chinese ceramics; on the fourth, larger Chinese porcelains; on the fifth, large bush knives; on the sixth, copper boxes; on the seventh, golden earrings; and on the eighth, large gongs.

The people grow jealous of Hainuwele's talent and plot to kill her. On the ninth night of the dance, they dig a deep hole in the center of the dance circle, and the

"He [Ameta] descended cautiously, took her home, and named her Hainuwele. She grew quickly and in three days was a nubile maiden. But she was not like an ordinary person; for when she would answer the call of nature her excrement consisted of all sorts of valuable articles."

"Hainuwele"

men dancing in the spiral slowly edge her into it and bury her. Her cries are muffled by the music of the Maro Dance. When his adopted daughter fails to return home, Ameta becomes very worried. He takes palm fronds and sticks them in each of the dance grounds used over the past nine nights. When he sticks the palm branch in the last one, it comes up with blood and hair, so he knows Hainuwele is down there.

Ameta then digs up his dead daughter, cuts her body into many pieces, and reburies it all around the dance ground. He keeps her arms, however, and presents them to the goddess Satene, who had emerged from an unripe banana when people came out of ripe bananas at the beginning of humankind. The pieces of Hainuwele that Ameta buried grow into beneficial plants that have never existed before, especially the tuberous food plants that the people of Ceram come to depend upon for food.

Satene shares Ameta's grief and is very angry at her people for having committed murder. She builds a gate at the dance grounds and tells the people to try to pass through if they want to move to another place with her. The people try, but not all are able to pass it. The ones who do not come through are turned into animals that have not existed before. Those who do pass are smacked with Hainuwele's severed arms. The people who approach Satene on her left have to jump over five sticks of bamboo; the ones who come to her right have to jump over nine.

Satene then tells the people that she is leaving humankind. If they want to see her again, she says, they will have to do so only after they have died and passed through eight mountains. She then goes to live on a mountain in the southwestern part of Ceram. From then

HISTORICAL CONTEXT

The story of Hainuwele is a traditional myth of the tribal people of Ceram, an island in the Maluku chain in eastern Indonesia. The Maluku archipelago, which runs east of Timor and west of New Guinea, is remote and its islands are mostly of poor value for growing subsistence crops. The people of the Maluku chain traditionally harvested locally available products and traded with other islands.

Despite the limited fertility of their soils, the Maluku Islands have long been sources of exotic flavorings, such as cloves, mace, and nutmeg. They are also home to birds of paradise, valued for their exotic plumage. Hence, the Maluku Islands have been visited by enterprising maritime merchants throughout recorded history. By the first century CE, merchant vessels from India and China were routinely passing through Indonesia, bringing spices and other exotic materials to their home markets and for sale to the Middle East and Europe. The first written evidence of the spice trade taking place in the Maluku area comes from the Chinese Han dynasty, which lasted from 206 BCE to 220 CE.

It was this increasingly lucrative trade that allowed the Indianized states of Southeast Asia to develop, and the otherwise unassuming Maluku Islands were at the epicenter of the most important trade route of the medieval period. Hence, the Maluku archipelago became known to the world as the Spice Islands. External wealth flowed into the Maluku chain, especially gold, ivory, weapons, and ceramics. Foreign objects are still valued as heirlooms by the families of the region. However, the massive inflow of foreign material wealth must have been disruptive to traditional society, as is suggested by the myth itself.

The Hainuwele myth was first recorded by ethnographers on an expedition from the German Frobenius Institute in 1937 and 1938. It was written about in German by Adolf E. Jensen, and then repeated by a number of scholars, including the popular comparative mythologist Joseph Campbell. The Hainuwele myth has therefore come to be considered by scholars as representative of a myth category found throughout the Indonesian archipelago and, indeed, the world.

on, the people are divided into the Fivers and the Niners, depending on whether they had approached Satene on the left or the right, and there are also all kinds of animals on the earth after this event, whereas only humans existed before it.

In Jensen's original rendering of the Hainuwele myth, the deceased and dismembered coconut girl is ultimately reborn as the moon. This detail is not included in Campbell's English translation. As Jensen explicitly explains, she remains in the sky as a constant reminder of the cycles of fertility.

ANALYSIS

The structural approach to the analysis of myth, as championed by the French anthropologist Claude Lévi-Strauss, is chiefly interested in symbolic binaries, the relationship between opposite symbols in myth narratives. Derived from the field of linguistics, wherein the most basic element of speech is the phoneme, the structural approach to myth seeks to uncover the basic elements of the narrative, which Lévi-Strauss called "mythemes." It then aims to understand the opposed pairs of mythemes in a narrative and uncover the cultural truth that exists in the tension between them.

The structural approach to myth analysis—with its pretentions to be a systematic and even mathematical way to unpack complicated and confusing narratives—is no longer in favor among most anthropologists. One important reason for this is that the structural approach does not provide much insight into what the people living within the culture from which the myths derives actually think about them, but instead imposes an external, Western logic on culturally specific stories. Even with this known limitation, however, the structural approach does have some strengths. It certainly provides a way to closely read and symbolically interpret myths, even if the conclusions of these symbolic interpretations are acknowledged to be subjective and speculative.

This twofold realization—that structural analysis of myth affords interesting ways to see beneath the surface of traditional narratives but that these insights are ultimately subjective rather than absolute—led to a flourishing of new anthropological theories about mythology. Among the most prominent was a field called interpretive anthropology, most notably championed by the American scholar Clifford Geertz. He famously described culture as "a system of inherited conceptions expressed in symbolic forms by means of which men communicate, perpetuate, and develop their knowledge about and attitudes toward life" (Geertz 89).

Geertz's approach retained structural anthropology's interest in using symbols, and often dualistic symbols, to get beneath the surface meaning of mythical narratives. On the other hand, it did not hold to Lévi-Strauss's pretentions that such analysis could be done in a sterile, mathematical manner. Instead of attempting to break myths down into formulaic calculations, Geertz suggested the use of what he called "thick description," or thoroughly investigating the reasons behind actions in cultural events or narratives, to gain insight into their deeper meanings.

It is fitting to borrow from Geertz's concept of interpretive analysis in making sense of the Hainuwele myth, both because it is a symbolically rich narrative that probably expresses several historical realities cloaked in the tale's mythical language, and because Geertz himself conducted his fieldwork in Indonesia. Just like Lévi-Strauss's structural approach, it will allow for a thorough survey of the myth while paying attention to some of the important mythemes and symbolic dualities it expresses. In the end, however, it will not yield an ideologically neutral breakdown of the Hainuwele tale, but rather a living interpretation of the story from Ceram, which is now known as one of the most important narratives in the field of comparative mythology.

The Hainuwele myth begins by describing the emergence of people from a bunch of bananas on Mount Nunusaku, at a time prior to the narrative of the story of Hainuwele herself. The opening lines introduce one of the most important mythemes of the tale: the contrast between the human and plant kingdoms. Many of the main events of the story involve the transmutation of plants to people, and vice versa.

It also introduces an important contrast in geographical settings that is repeated in the myth—the contrast between the high mountainous terrain of the people's origin and the lowlands where they dwell during the present time of the narrative, in an area they call the Nine Dance Grounds. It is worth paying attention to the fact that there is a correspondence between the original nine families of humankind and the nine dancing grounds of the dwelling place. The repetition of multiples of three becomes important for quantities and time in the myth.

The first protagonist of the story, Ameta, is initially described as an unusual figure. He is a hunter, associated with blackness and darkness, who specializes in hunting in the night. This sets up the important contrast between day and night; the main events that drive the story happen not during the day, the usual time for human activities in a preindustrial society, but at night. Ameta is also introduced as not having a family at all, which would of course have been uncommon for an adult man in a tribal community.

The action of the story begins when Ameta goes hunting with his dog, at night, according to his normal routine. His hunting dog scares up a pig, an animal that the tale later indicates does not exist at this point. Ameta and the dog chase the pig into a pond, and it tries and tries to swim away, but grows exhausted from the effort and drowns. When Ameta retrieves the pig, he finds a coconut on its tusk, which is like nothing he has ever seen before since coconuts also did not exist before this point.

The presence of a pig at this early point in the myth despite a later claim that it did not exist yet would seem to be a mistake in the narrative; it is, however, worth considering that a pig would have been a familiar prey and sacrificial animal to a Wemale audience, and this fits with the theme of useful food products that did exist before making their first appearances in the unfolding of the myth. In dualistic terms, there is an implied contrast between known and unknown valuable objects, with the pig and the coconut representing the new, unknown products entering the world of tribal Ceram for the first time. The contrast between known and unknown things is certainly another very important duality expressed in the Hainuwele myth, and it may even be said to be central to the story's overall message.

Ameta took the strange nut home and covered it with a cloth bearing a snake motif before he went to sleep. This detail is of quite some symbolic importance to understanding Wemale culture. First of all, the tribes of the Maluku Islands associate cloth with coolness, femaleness, and the womb. Woven products are "linked with notions regarding fertility both of the earth and the woman" (De Jonge and Van Dijk 125). The serpent motif on the cloth is also significant, as the Wemale have other myths describing a time before creation when snakes, perhaps representing the generative male power, roamed the world creating things. The coming together of the cloth and the snake, then, represents the dual aspects of male and female fertility, and that presence magically imbues the coconut with the life force that becomes Hainuwele.

In his sleep, Ameta is visited by a man in his dream. He tells the hunter that he must plant the strange nut in order for it to grow, which he does as soon as he wakes up. This facet of the myth further underscores the power of the night, the time of dreams.

The multiples-of-three motif is then repeated with the description of the growth of the coconut tree. Three days after Ameta planted it, it grew into a tall tree; three days later, it blossomed. Ameta climbed the tree in order to gather some blossoms to brew a beverage. Some scholars, including Campbell, see this passage as an indication of Ameta's desire to brew an intoxicating beverage from the blossoms of the mysterious plant and suggest that there may have been an old Wemale ritual that "would correspond nicely" to the "maiden-moon-animal" formula in ancient Mediterranean mythology (Campbell 195).

When Ameta returned to the tree three days after dripping blood onto the leaves, he saw that there was a human face growing on the tree where he had bled. This image is interesting, for among the tribes of the Maluku Islands "vital strength is handed on to following generations via the woman's blood in the womb" (De Jonge and Van Dijk 143). On the other hand, it is the male contribution—which is considered to come from the outside world—that gives a person his or her social identity. Hainuwele, then, is generated entirely without woman's blood, and wholly from man's blood, associating her with the outside world rather than the traditional tribal world.

Hainuwele continues to grow on the tree, with her progress witnessed by Ameta in increments of three days so that after three more days a body grows and then three more days there is a little girl. From the time of his spilling blood on the tree to Hainuwele's generation as a fully-formed child, then, is nine days. After he witnesses her as a child, Ameta is again visited in his dreams by a male figure who tells her to carry her home in the same snake-embroidered cloth, symbolically giving birth to her as a human being. The day after his dream, Ameta climbed up the tree, and then very carefully climbed down, bringing the strange child to his home and adopting her as his daughter.

Ameta soon discovers that Hainuwele is not a regular girl. When she defecates, she produces valuable foreign objects, such as "Chinese dishes and gongs" according to the Campbell translation (180). This fits with her coming from the hitherto unknown coconut and being generated from a man's blood (an outside force) and not a woman's. Ameta soon grows rich due to his daughter's odd gift.

Next, the myth describes how the people hold the sacred Maro Dance, which lasts for nine days and involves the women sitting in the middle of a spiral of men around them and handing the men betel nuts. This dance physically manifests the idea of the woman as the domestic and the man as the foreign, and the handing out of betel nut may be read as the traditional domestic product of the Ceram islanders. In a sense, then, the point of the dance is to domesticate the male sphere. Campbell says it is possible to detect a "labyrinth theme" in the spiral of male dancers (195). It is also worth considering the spiral as an image of a coiled snake, the ancient Wemale image of male generative power.

Hainuwele is very happy to be invited to sit with the women and give out gifts to the men, as this marks her as an accepted member of the tribal group. However, she defies traditional protocol. Instead of giving out betel nut, she gives out progressively more valuable foreign trade goods, including coral, Chinese ceramics, and metal tools. The men are at first happy to receive such valuable products from the outside world but are said to grow suspicious of Hainuwele's unusual power. The tension here is between traditional domestic goods and new foreign goods, and ultimately the men of the tribe decide they cannot allow Hainuwele to live.

This episode marks the turning point of the myth from a story of miraculous riches to a tragedy. Many analysts have suggested that it reflects the coming of the Europeans and the culturally disruptive influence of colonialism. That would put the date of the myth around 1512, when the Portuguese first came to the Spice Islands. However, there is no reason to think that this episode does not reflect a much earlier, and in some ways more dramatic, clash of cultures.

Metal technology first came to the Maluku peoples around 500 BCE, as a result of an emerging trade network linking China with India. This trade network was certainly well established by the time of the Han dynasty (206 BCE–220 CE) and largely replaced the overland Silk Road, which had become dangerous due to political chaos, as the main conduit of goods between western and eastern Asia. The goods transported by the merchant sailors traveling between China and India were exactly the trade goods described in the Hainuwele myth, such as metal knives and boxes, coral from the other islands of the Indonesian archipelago, and Chinese ceramics.

The new metal technology dramatically affected the cultures of the peoples of the Maluku Islands. The new link to the international trade route, and the blade technology it brought, led to an outbreak of intertribal warfare, head-hunting, and the establishment of "a hierarchical society with leaders, freemen, and slaves" (De Jonge and Van Dijk 21). It is therefore entirely possible, and indeed likely, that the Hainuwele myth dates back to this earlier cultural disruption and not merely to the sixteenth-century arrival of the Europeans.

As the myth continues, the men of the tribe then plot to kill Hainuwele, which they do by digging a hole in the middle of the ninth dance ground and edging her into it with their dancing spiral. Once she is in the hole, they stomp the earth firm, as though planting her in her grave. Ameta, worried that his adopted daughter did not come home after the ninth night of dancing, then takes the unusual measure of poking palm fronds into each of the dancing grounds to locate her body. When he pokes a frond into the ninth one, blood and hair sticks to it, and he knows she is buried there. This strange episode in the myth serves to further identify Hainuwele's lifeblood and human body with the coconut from which she came. She is, after all, a being that brings together the dual categories of plant and human.

In his grief, Ameta digs up his daughter's body, cuts it into pieces, and reburies them throughout the dancing grounds. This is clearly symbolic of a new way of farming, as the root vegetable crops introduced to the island are cultivated in exactly this way. The myth explicitly states that the plants that people come to depend upon, especially tubers, came into being through Ameta's replanting of Hainuwele's body.

Ameta presents Hainuwele's severed arms, perhaps representative of palm fronds or the upper, green portion of root crop plants, to the goddess Satene. Satene, who is also identified with plants and with difference since she came from an unripe banana when the ancestors emerged from a bunch of bananas, is troubled by the murder of Hainuwele. She commands the people to pass through a spiral gate, perhaps again representative of the labyrinthine nature of mysterious powers suggested by Campbell, if they want to move away from their current home with her. The ones who are able to

pass the gate become fully human, but the ones that do not become all the animals of Ceram, including useful ones like pigs.

As the newly formed people approach Satene, she hits them with Hainuwele's arms, in this case embodying the power of plants over the human world. The ones who came to her left had to jump over five sticks of bamboo, and the ones who came to her right had to jump nine bamboo sticks. This act divides them into Fivers and Niners, or the first modern division of Wemale social order. There is in this episode a theme of plants and cultivation leading to specialization and social hierarchy, which was probably born out historically with the changing economy of Ceram as the Maluku Islands entered into trade relationships with the wider world.

After dividing animals from humans and splitting society into factions, Satene announces that she will be leaving her people. She says that if they want to see her again, they must die and pass through difficult ordeals. She will be living on a mountain in the southwest of the island, and to get to it, they must pass eight other mountains. Satene, then, will be living on the ninth peak of this mysterious mountain range. This obviously repeats the multiples-of-three motif found throughout the myth, and the division between highlands and lowlands. The highlands are the space of the gods, whereas the lowlands are the home of modern, fully formed people.

The final image from the Hainuwele myth, as rendered by Jensen, is of the moon. Hainuwele is reborn not only as all the plants useful to humankind, but also is identified with the moon. There is an interesting correspondence between the appearance of Hainuwele's original form, the coconut, and the full moon. Its cycles reflect the cycles of fertility. Moon cycles were traditionally used to mark the passage of time and indicate when to plant and harvest the crops that sustained the people of Ceram.

CROSS-CULTURAL INFLUENCE

The Wemale of Ceram, like the other tribal inhabitants of the Maluku Islands and other areas of Indonesia, are descended from Austronesian migrants who came to the region sometime around 2500 BCE. These early pioneers spoke related languages and shared a similar way of life. They probably introduced new forms of agriculture, including the cultivation of root crops, coconuts, and rice to the remote islands that they settled. Although the tribal peoples of the region are extremely diverse, as is to be expected in a landscape made up of small islands, they do share some common cultural traits, especially in their mythologies.

Elements of the Hainuwele myth are reflected throughout Indonesia and New Guinea and offer evidence of a common Austronesian cultural past. Throughout the Austronesian cultural zone, as among the Wemale, women are associated with coolness and moisture, while men are associated with heat and dryness. As such, women are often identified with plants, which grow from the cool, moist earth, while men are considered to be closer to animals.

One source of evidence of this connection comes from a cycle of myths from New Guinea that associate women with sago palms. One tale, which comes from the Bola tribe, describes a village of only men, who have no women to marry. A young hunter, desperate for a wife, sees a beautiful woman living in a sago tree. He camps out beneath the tree until she comes down and woos her by saying that he will do all the work and she can just relax. They marry and have a baby. One day, the man grows tired of doing all the work and orders his wife to clean the baby's diaper in the stream. When she does so, she turns to mush like an overripe sago fruit and drains away.

In the myths of the Austronesian cultural zone, women are usually not just associated with plants in general, but the most important life-sustaining plants—the staple foods that feed the masses of people. An interesting variant of this theme comes from Bali. The tales of Dewi Sri feature an Indianized heroine, but she almost certainly reflects a far older indigenous goddess. In the stories of Dewi Sri, she is described as controlling the cycles of rice germination and ripening. She is also associated with the monsoon, which again reflects the Austronesian connection between women and coolness and moisture.

Another Indonesian myth, from Java, is even more reminiscent of the Hainuwele story. In it, a serpent brings a magical jewel from the underworld that grows into a beautiful girl named Tisnawati. When she grows to maturity, a sky god called Batara Guru wants to marry her, but she refuses and dies. She is buried, and a myriad of useful plants grow from her corpse. Her head grows into a coconut palm, her teeth grow into corn, her hands grow into bananas, and her vagina grows into rice.

A very similar myth from the island of Sunda bears the same close resemblance to the Hainuwele tale. In this one, a serpent named Antaboga gave birth to a girl through crying. The girl, Nyi Pohaci, is pursued

by Batara Guru but is not interested in marrying him. On the advice of the other gods, she eats the fruit of paradise to resist him, but soon she is unable to eat any other food and dies. Her grave yields a bounty of useful plants, such as coconut palms, bamboo, and rice. A lunar nymph named Dwi Nawang Sasih shows the people how to cook rice. Miraculously, one spike of rice was enough to feed a hundred people because it multiplied when cooked. However, this miracle ended when Dwi Nawang Sasih's husband, King Siliwangi touched the kitchen utensils and caused Dwi Nawang Sasih to return to the sky as the moon.

In all of these related tales from the Austronesian cultural zone, a basic foodstuff is "symbolized anthropomorphically" and humanity's discovery of it is "narrated in terms of killing" (Hamerton-Kelley 44). In a good number of them, including one from the Indonesian island of Flores in which the original human ancestors are dismembered and buried, planting pieces of the corpse yields a bounty of new cultigens, just like in the Hainuwele tale. The protagonist in these tales is nearly always a female born through an unusual process. There is frequently a reference to moon in these tales, and often the protagonist herself is reborn not only as useful foodstuffs, but as the moon itself. The discovery of a staple crop through the death of a heroine of a key foodstuff also tends to mark the beginning of human society.

The Hainuwele myth has also had a strong cross-cultural influence that goes far beyond the Austronesian cultural zone. This is due to the history of its scholarly investigation. The Hainuwele myth was first recorded by Western scholars during an expedition from the Frankfurt-based Frobenius Institute in 1937 and 1938, spearheaded by Adolf E. Jensen. The Frobenius Institute, founded by the pioneering German anthropologist Leo Frobenius, began conducting anthropological field research in 1925. Its members went on scores of research expeditions throughout the world, collecting a large amount of mythical data from diverse and often radically different cultures. As such, the analytical outlook of the Frobenius Institute's members tended to be quite cross-cultural in nature.

In one sense, this cross-cultural approach to analysis was in keeping with an older tradition in anthropology. In the late nineteenth century, the field was dominated by cultural evolutionists—scholars interested in understanding a universal history of human culture and establishing an evolutionary model of culture by tracking cultural progress from its most primitive to most advanced forms. This aim, which corresponded to an emerging theory of evolution in the field of biology, ultimately resulted in racist, ethnocentric findings of little lasting value. It did, however, involve a fairly rigorous process of comparing and contrasting ethnographic information from diverse human cultures, which was also of paramount importance to researchers working with the Frobenius Institute. In the early twentieth century, British researchers including Bronislaw Malinowski, E. E. Evans-Pritchard, and A. R. Radcliffe-Brown, who can really be said to be among the first influential modern anthropologists, tended to shy away from the cultural evolutionists' interest in cultural comparison and instead focused on specific, local knowledge in their chosen field research areas.

Meanwhile, anthropology in Germany was heavily influenced not only by anthropology in Britain and America, but also by the works of German psychologists. In particular, the investigations of Carl Gustav Jung affected the analytical approach of the Frobenius Institute's researchers. Jung developed an interest in the human unconscious as a force that transcended cultural difference. He himself traveled to different countries to further his investigations, and he championed a frankly comparative method to better understand what he described as the "collective unconscious," or basic in-built processes of the human mind.

Research into myth and religion played a key role in Jung's attempt to comprehend this collective unconscious. Jung, and those social scientists influenced by his work, compared mythological tales from different cultures to uncover universal themes within them, which were considered to reflect something of the collective human unconscious. Although the approach has been severely criticized by many social scientists for its tendency to take myths out of their specific cultural contexts—and to link unrelated tales together by virtue of superficial similarities—there is no doubt that the approach Jung envisioned has helped to shape the modern field of comparative mythology.

It was in this intellectual climate that the Hainuwele myth came to assert its true cross-cultural influence. When Jensen first brought the myth that he had recorded on his expedition to the Ceram to the attention of German social scientists, he called the character Hainuwele herself a "dema deity," or lower manifestation of the divine than the higher gods. Stories that attribute the discovery of food, especially tubers from the ground, with violence toward and usually the death of a dema

deity became, in his analysis, versions of the Hainuwele mythologem—the term "mythologem" referring to a seemingly related cluster of mythical tales. The Hainuwele myth therefore became a prototype for understanding thematically similar, if culturally unrelated, myths from all around the world. He described parallels from India, other areas of Indonesia, New Guinea, and South America.

Jensen contrasted Hainuwele-style myths with those that told of the origin of food crops through theft from a divine being, which he compared to the Prometheus myth, the well-known Greek tale of the theft of fire from the gods. In his view many of the world's myths relating to the origin of food could be described as belonging either to the Hainuwele mythologem or the Prometheus mythologem. Based on Jensen's work, the Hainuwele tale became a staple story used by comparative mythologists to understand myths from both inside and outside of the Austronesian cultural zone.

Joseph Campbell, who first translated the Hainuwele myth into English, considered the story to have close parallels to the story of Persephone. According to Greek mythology, Persephone was the daughter of the chief god Zeus and the goddess of the harvest, Demeter, and was therefore a "dema deity," to use Jensen's terminology. She was abducted and forcibly married by Hades, the god of the underworld, and eventually became revered as the queen of the underworld. In ancient times, Greek people considered Persephone to be a representation of edible vegetation. They prayed to her in the spring to ensure a healthy harvest.

Campbell, like many of the German anthropologists associated with the Frobenius Institute, took an approach that borrowed heavily from the psychology of Jung. A prolific and accessible writer, he became the single most influential comparative mythologist. His books generated interest not just in academic circles, but gained favor with a wider popular audience. Campbell's use of the Hainuwele story in making sense of world mythology ensured that it would retain an important place in the analysis of myth for generations to come.

Adam Berger, PhD

BIBLIOGRAPHY

Barnard, Alan. *History and Theory in Anthropology.* Cambridge: Cambridge UP, 2000. Print.
Bonnefoy, Yves. *Asian Mythologies.* Chicago: U of Chicago P, 1991. Print.

Campbell, Joseph. "The Ritual Love-Death." *Masks of God: Primitive Mythology*. Vol. 1. London: Secker, 1960. Print.

Chambert-Loir, Henri, and Anthony Reid. *The Potent Dead: Ancestors, Saints, and Heroes in Contemporary Indonesia*. Honolulu: U of Hawaii P, 2002. Print.

De Jonge, Nico, and Toos Van Dijk. *Forgotten Islands of Indonesia*. Hong Kong: Periplus, 1995. Print.

Geertz, Clifford. *Interpretation of Cultures*. New York: Basic, 1973. Print.

Hamerton-Kelley, Robert, ed. *Violent Origins*. Stanford: Stanford UP, 1987. Print.

Jensen, Adolf E. *Myth and Cult among Primitive Peoples*. Chicago: U of Chicago P, 1951. Print.

Leeming, David. *Myth: A Biography of Belief*. Oxford: Oxford UP, 2003. Print.

---. *Mythology: The Voyage of the Hero*. Oxford: Oxford UP, 1998. Print.

Lévi-Strauss, Claude. *The Savage Mind*. Paris: Librairie Plon, 1962. Print.

Li Qingxin. *Maritime Silk Road*. Beijing: China International, 2009. Print.

Slone, Thomas. *One Thousand Papua New Guinean Nights*. Oakland: Masalai, 2001. Print.

Smith, John Z. *Map is Not Territory: Studies in the History of Religions*. Chicago: U of Chicago P, 1978. Print.

Lohengrin, the Knight with the Swan

Author: Jacob Grimm; Wilhelm Grimm
Time Period: 1001 CE–1500 CE
Country or Culture: Germany
Genre: Legend

OVERVIEW

The literature surrounding the legendary British ruler King Arthur is expansive, with the mythologies of the individual warriors and knights of his Round Table and the Council of the Holy Grail all having developed over centuries of storytelling. While rooted firmly in the history of Britain, these stories extended throughout Europe, so that in legend, the holy and just knights travel throughout the world, righting wrongs and championing chivalry.

From the brief narrative of the knight of the swan, the story of Lohengrin became a much more complex one. Lohengrin himself became a figure of purity and holy chivalry, representing the faith of Christianity as exemplified by the Holy Grail and the order of knights set to protect it. The woman he rescues is named Elsa, a troubled and castigated woman in her society who ultimately succumbs to the temptation of others and asks her husband to explain his origin to her. Through these expansions, the legend becomes an exploration of love and faith. Lohengrin is an impossibly idealized hero figure, and while Elsa connects with him both romantically and spiritually, that connection is short lived, brought to an end by Elsa's own doubts and imperfect nature. Lohengrin himself even becomes a Christlike character, saving Elsa as well as the people of Brabant but ultimately needing to depart for a more holy land (the Council of the Grail) when Elsa's imperfect fate becomes evident. This narration of salvation and faith, however, does not rest on familiar moral grounds but instead is inseparable from the romantic and erotic attraction between Elsa and Lohengrin. It is this component of the legend that caught the interest of subsequent generations of writers and allowed the character of Lohengrin to find a second life in the world of modern opera, the romantic and spiritual struggle between faith and doubt proving itself to be the type of timeless narrative that thrives on the stage as much as in myth.

The story of Lohengrin, the knight with the swan, is one example of the Arthurian legends combining with regional folktales and mythologies. In Germany, variations of a legend about the knight of the swan had circulated for centuries, becoming especially popular in medieval times. These legends tell of a knight mysteriously arriving to save a woman in need. The knight falls in love with the woman and marries her but insists she never ask about his true origin. When she inevitably does so, he leaves as mysteriously as he came. While these folk stories rarely explain who the knight actually is, in the thirteenth century, German poet Wolfram von Eschenbach rewrote the knight of the swan narrative, clarifying that the mysterious white knight is actually summoned from King Arthur's holy court. In Eschenbach's poem *Parzival*, a much longer narrative of the quest for the Holy Grail, he expanded the Lohengrin myth enough so that it caught the attention of later writers. From then on, the legend remained relatively popular, eventually being recorded by famous folklorists Jacob and Wilhelm Grimm. The version analyzed here is from mythologist Otto Rank's discussion of the Grimms' tale.

SUMMARY

The Duke of Brabant has no male heirs, only an unmarried daughter, Elsa. Hoping to secure some sort of future for his name, the duke suggests that a warrior in his service, Friedrich, might make a good husband for his daughter. After the duke dies, Friedrich falsely claims that Elsa has been promised to him. Elsa denies this, so Friedrich complains to the emperor, who declares the matter should be settled in battle. Elsa is given the opportunity to select any man to go to battle on her behalf against Friedrich in divine combat. According to the tenets of divine combat, the victor of the battle would be the one whom God has decided is in the right.

Unfortunately, Elsa cannot find any knight to take her position in battle. Despondent, she prays to God, pleading for him to send a noble person to protect her honor. As she prays, a small bell rings in the Council of the Grail. The Council is held a great distance away from Brabant, and it is there that the legendary knights of King Arthur meet to discuss their business and to honor the sanctity of the Holy Grail itself. Hearing the bell, they know that their divine assistance is needed, and Lohengrin agrees to rescue whoever is in need. Lohengrin then gathers his supplies and loads up his horse. However, before he can depart, a swan pulling a skiff comes down the nearby River Scheldt. Lohengrin takes this as a divine sign and instead boards the skiff, not even bringing with him food, as he knows that God will provide on the trip. He then floats down the river for days, the swan occasionally plucking fish out of the water to feed him.

Elsa has gathered her council together to seek advice when, seemingly out of nowhere, Lohengrin arrives on the bank of the river, pulled there by the great white bird. Lohengrin climbs out of the skiff with his armor and sword, and the swan immediately departs. Elsa quickly tells Lohengrin of the wrong that has been done to her by Friedrich, and Lohengrin agrees at once to be her champion in battle, knowing that hers must be the cause that he has come to defend. In little time, Friedrich is summoned so that he and Lohengrin can meet in combat in front of the emperor. Lohengrin, with the skill of a knight of the Holy Grail, quickly defeats Friedrich, who confesses his lie and is therefore executed at the emperor's orders. Elsa is then given over to Lohengrin in marriage, a condition the knight gladly accepts, as they have already fallen in love; he insists only that she never ask about his ancestry or his previous home. If she ever does, he says, he will leave her at once, never to return.

Lohengrin lives happily for some time as a champion of his new emperor and a dutiful husband to Elsa. He goes to battle to defend their land against invaders and treats his people with kindness. This is all interrupted, however, when he one day triumphs over the Duke of Cleve in a friendly jousting competition, upsetting the duke from his horse with a javelin. The Duchess of Cleve, embarrassed by her husband's defeat, begins to disparage Lohengrin in public, saying that he is obviously a good Christian but that his lack of noble ancestry is unfortunate, implying that he might not be a proper fit for the Duchess of Brabant. Elsa, although she knows better, is deeply troubled by the duchess's words.

"The hero of the Grail defeated Friedrich, who confessed having lied to the duchess, and was executed with the axe. Elsa was awarded to Lohengrin, they having long been lovers; but he secretly insisted upon her avoiding all questions as to his ancestry, or whence he had come, saying that otherwise he would have to leave her instantaneously and she would never see him again."

"Lohengrin"

Eventually, unable to contain herself, she asks Lohengrin where he is from while the two lie in bed together. She tells him that she knows in her heart that he must be a noble person, but for the good of her children, she needs to know it for sure. For two nights, Lohengrin ignores her questions; at last, on the third night, he agrees to give her an answer in the morning.

The next day, Lohengrin gathers his people and publicly declares that he had come from the Council of the Grail and that his father was the famous knight Parsifal. He then bends to his knee and kisses his two children, born of Elsa, before declaring that it is time for him to depart. The swan appears again and takes Lohengrin back to the Grail. While Elsa spends the rest of her years in grief over the loss of her husband, her son, also named Lohengrin, is taken in by the empress and raised as one of her own.

ANALYSIS

"Lohengrin, the Knight with the Swan" is the most famous of a subgenre of legends that are generally referred to as the knight of the swan tales. These stories contain many core narrative elements present in the Lohengrin legend, the most characteristic being the presence of a mysterious knight who arrives on the back of a swan to save a damsel in distress. These swan tales were popular throughout medieval Europe and included a related set of legends, those of the swan children, that were continually woven into the fabric of European mythology.

In this tradition, the familiar legend of the knight of the swan was connected in the thirteenth century with the Arthurian legends of the Knights of the Round Table, and the mysterious savior was at last given a name: Lohengrin.

The connection with the Arthurian legends highlights the divine nature of Lohengrin, directly linking the knight with the Christian god. This link is necessary in understanding the somewhat bizarre plot that follows. Although Lohengrin is adamant that his wife should never ask about his origin or his true nature, there is never a reason given for this demand. Instead, the mysterious nature of the knight and his insistence that his past should remain unknown is simply accepted, both by the legend and by Elsa. While this seemingly unfounded demand might come across as preposterous to some modern readers, it does enhance the link between Lohengrin and the Christian tradition he represents. He is a divine hero, and just as the role of the faithful in most forms of Christianity is to accept God for what he is and never doubt one's belief in Christ, so too must Elsa accept Lohengrin for who he claims to be, sans proof. To express doubt or to ask for proof of his noble heritage would be to fail in her faith, a failure so severe that it would end the relationship. "Lohengrin, the Knight with the Swan," then, blends this spiritual devotion with the erotic and romantic love Elsa feels for her husband, creating a savior who is tantalizingly human but ultimately inaccessible.

The beginning of the tale sets up a clear dichotomy between the impure and deceitful motives of Friedrich and the noble, pure motives of Lohengrin in relation to Elsa. Friedrich attempts to gain Elsa as a wife, and thereby gain control over the duke's estate, by lying to the emperor and manipulating the hierarchy of power in the court system, which would have ensured his marriage to Elsa if she had actually been promised to him. Friedrich here is an unambiguous villain, and so when the emperor declares that the matter will be decided by "divine judgment" (Rank 59), it is already obvious that Friedrich will meet his downfall. Morality is always clearly defined in this legend, linked to the noble systems of the court, which are in turn linked to the belief systems of medieval Christianity. By modern standards, the lack of power granted to Elsa is certainly immoral, as her refusal to marry Friedrich should be enough. However, in the context of the medieval German court (Henry I the Fowler being the first king in this era of German history), the needs and desires of a woman were considered essentially unimportant, with all matters being decided by divine will and by the ruling men. In this way, the legend presents Friedrich as a villain not because of his mistreatment of Elsa but because he deceives the systems that decide marriage and property rights, using a political system closely aligned with God in order to advance his own material interests. Instead of validating Elsa's will in order to remedy this wrong, the conflict is moved up the ladder of power to be decided by God, regardless whether that decision ultimately benefits her or not.

In contrast to Friedrich's blatant villainy, Lohengrin is presented as purely noble and well intentioned. He is summoned directly by Elsa's prayers to God, hearing the sound of the bell that indicates her distress while in the Council of the Grail. In the popular literature and legends of the time, Arthur was considered an exemplar of chivalry, knightly traditions, and noble behavior. In addition, by obtaining the Holy Grail, the Council of Arthur drew a direct connection to Christian divinity. The Grail itself was believed, at various points in history, to have been a stone that fell from heaven or the chalice from which Jesus drank at the Last Supper. By obtaining the Grail, the Knights of the Round Table proved their holiness, not only becoming pinnacles of both Christian morals and medieval chivalry but linking the two concepts with one another. Lohengrin, then, comes into the legend from a place of unquestionable virtue, validating the systems of political power that Friedrich attempts to manipulate. As such, he should be understood not simply as a knight, there to protect the virtue of a lady, but rather as a savior summoned by God.

The start of Lohengrin's quest is marked by his extreme faith and virtue, with the knight following the signs presented to him by God. In the same way that Lohengrin will come to make a seemingly arbitrary demand of Elsa to never ask about his origins, he in turn is presented as a figure who accepts the will of God for what it is, unconcerned with his own well-being as long as he knows he is being faithfully submissive to that will. This is made clear when the swan appears, pulling the skiff, for the first time. Lohengrin has already loaded his horse, but he forgoes this mode of travel in favor of the swan, which he immediately assumes to be a divine messenger. He even goes so far as to leave behind his food, undoubting that God will provide him sustenance. Lohengrin here is a figure fully committed to an idealized fate, floating down the river on a boat pulled by a swan and peacefully unconcerned with his destination or his means of sustenance. The image is unworldly and

MYTH INTO ART

Following its premiere in Weimar, Germany, in 1850, Richard Wagner's operatic version of *Lohengrin* became an instant favorite of fans and critics alike. Over the next twenty-five years, productions were staged across the world, with the most famous actors and musicians of the day offering their own interpretations of the characters.

Original productions of *Lohengrin* held themselves to fairly traditional staging and costuming, even as Wagner's musical choices went against some operatic traditions. Within the confines of traditional costuming, however, the story left ample room for decadence and lavish displays. The arrival of the swan, the expansive cast, the many duels, the fantastical wedding scene—all of these components gave directors the opportunity to create a world onstage that was as unreal as the idealized romance Lohengrin and Elsa share. As the stage was often crowded with elaborately dressed noblemen and serfs, the tenth-century atmosphere Wagner summoned was typically romantic, true to the spirit of medieval times yet larger than life in its styling.

As the opera has maintained its popularity into the modern day, the contemporary tendency toward experimentation and unconventional choices in opera has allowed directors to conceptualize the fantastical aspects of the narrative in new ways. A 2010 production, for instance, conceived of the chorus as a group of lab rats, helplessly following the commands of their leaders. Other productions have stripped down the costuming, presenting the characters in plain clothes with little or no set behind them in an attempt to emphasize the emotional core as something that transcends time and context. While it is still common to see the play produced in traditional style, new productions of *Lohengrin* are as likely to depart from Wagner's conception as to hold true to it.

almost magical, just as Lohengrin's faith and chivalry also border on fantastical, achieving a morality that seems to transcend the mundane world. As this is the method through which he enters the life of his future wife, their romance is made inseparable from his divine connection and faith.

The swan itself is also a symbolically loaded figure. Swans are consistently present throughout Western mythology, often as the animal form assumed by a human or a god in a romantic tale. In this tradition, the swan represents a link between the spiritual world and the physical world, even if that link often occurs for less-than-holy purposes, as when the Greek god Zeus famously takes the shape of a swan in order to seduce the mortal Leda. In addition to this symbolic history, the swan that Lohengrin rides is made even more mystical by the simple fact of its unusualness, the bird of course being an inappropriate animal to pull even a small boat. Taking all of this into account, the swan becomes less of a vehicle and more of a herald, announcing that the knight it carries comes from some other realm, a place that does not follow the rules that govern Brabant. Like all other aspects of the legend, this aspect of the story is reminiscent of Christian theology, with the divine hero exiting the spiritual realm and entering the world of humans just as Jesus lives as a god among men. While it would be imprecise to read the legend as a direct metaphor for Christianity or the narrative of Jesus, the heavy influence of Christian mythology is here blended with the mythology of the swan, indicating Lohengrin's separation from Brabant even as he arrives there.

Once he lands on the shore, Lohengrin transitions seamlessly into his role as protector and husband of Elsa. The swan leaves Lohengrin at the riverside next to Elsa and her gathered council, the knight immediately agrees to take up her just cause, and the battle is fought before the eyes of the emperor, all in quick succession. The expediency with which these events follow each other speaks to the predestined nature of the legend; Lohengrin's quest being holy, there is no reason to stall. While the conflict between Lohengrin and Friedrich is in many ways at the core of the narrative, the actual drama of that conflict is treated as being much less important than the subsequent relationship between Elsa and Lohengrin. The lack of details and the swift resolution—"the hero of the Grail defeated Friedrich, who confessed having lied to the duchess, and was executed with the axe" (Rank 60)—only serve to highlight the heavenly nature of the justice. Indeed, as it is declared early in the legend that God would decide who is right and who is wrong in the matter of Elsa's marriage, there is no doubt how this battle would turn out.

In all the swift victories and unambiguous chivalry of the myth, the strange and secret demand made by Lohengrin that Elsa should never ask about his ancestry stands out as an unexpected detail. This command is a product of the combination of romantic and spiritual devotion that defines Elsa's relationship to Lohengrin. Her role and her limited power are made clear through the legend itself, which declares that "Elsa was awarded to Lohengrin" (60), treating her as a piece of property that can be won by others. Just as her romantic relationship is defined by a lack of power, so too is her spiritual relationship one in which she lacks the agency to make her own choices or achieve any sort of complete knowledge of her partner. Elsa here is in a conflicted position. She clearly shares a romantic and erotic love with Lohengrin, the two having already been lovers before their marriage. Yet this romantic love is only one component of her spiritual devotion to the divine knight, and that divinity ultimately trumps any erotic connection. Regardless of the seeming incompatibility of these relationships, however, both the erotic and the spiritual are brought together by the fact of Elsa's subordinate role, the duchess forced to accept each position without question.

The mystery surrounding Lohengrin makes him into an unusual type of lover and husband. In Christianity, the mystical realm of God and the heavens are left intentionally unknowable to humanity. The mystery associated with the divine is not considered a troublesome component of the relationship between humanity and the spiritual realm; instead, the fact that people cannot receive "proof" of God is an integral part of the Christian faith. To have faith despite a lack of concrete proof is to be a true believer, while belief based on concrete evidence is not a true faith at all. By this logic, Lohengrin's demand parallels the implicit demand of Christianity: to ask for proof is to indicate a lack of belief and is therefore considered sinful. As with all aspects of this legend, however, the understanding of Lohengrin's demand must encapsulate the romantic relationship as well as the spiritual. By keeping his history as a Knight of the Round Table secret, he remains in some ways still distant from his wife. He might live with her and raise children with her, but she can never know him as fully as he knows her, and he will always maintain the power of that mystery, having access to a knowledge she can never have. Taken together, these two elements create a sort of dream lover: heavenly and ideal, yet always slightly removed from

the reality of the household and the marriage, never truly there.

The period in which Lohengrin lives with Elsa is likewise a somewhat unreal period, defined by "peace and happiness" (Rank 60) as well as the fair rule of Lohengrin and the safe defense of the city against invaders. This time is idyllic precisely because the roles of the government and of spirituality have been so perfectly melded together through Lohengrin's chivalry. In marrying Elsa and taking on her inheritance, thus becoming a duke, Lohengrin brings a level of holiness to that title. The code of chivalry that the Knights of the Round Table idealized was itself based on a union of the highest morals, combat skills, and faith in God. The reality in most European societies, however, was not one in which the ruling class and knights practiced perfect ethics and effortlessly defended their land against invaders but rather one that strived for a perfect society but thrived on manipulation and extortion (seen earlier through the behavior of Friedrich). By marrying Lohengrin, Elsa does briefly create a space in which something nearing paradise can exist. However, that paradise is as mythical as Lohengrin himself and therefore cannot be sustained in the real world.

When Elsa finally succumbs to temptation and asks about Lohengrin's identity, she does not do so for reasons based on her spiritual or erotic attachment to him. Instead, it is the question of his nobility and his connection to a royal court that eventually drives Elsa to defy his command. The criticism made by the Duchess of Cleve makes this distinction clear, as she complains that "Lohengrin may be brave enough, and he seems to be a good Christian; what a pity that his nobility is not of much account" (Rank 61). As Lohengrin has never given any person cause to doubt his virtue or strength, this criticism has to be cleverly worded so as to attack the one aspect of his character that is vulnerable. While it was certainly possible for a person without noble lineage or a connection to a court to be holy, there was a strong link between royalty and divinity at that time. By implying that Lohengrin does not have a noble connection, the duchess is implicitly criticizing his value as a husband and as a spiritual man, even though those qualities are otherwise beyond reproach. Especially because this accusation puts the nobility and future of Elsa's children at risk, she finds herself tormented by the question, no longer able to suppress her curiosity.

When Elsa breaks Lohengrin's command, she likewise breaks her faith, demonstrating at last that she is incapable of belief without proof. Lohengrin's response to this is not to immediately disappear but rather to reveal his true nature and history before departing. The moment of the reveal roughly parallels the story of Jesus in which the resurrected savior appears once more in the flesh before ascending to heaven, revealing his true nature to all those who doubted him, the apostle Thomas included. Just as Jesus departs after allowing Thomas to confirm his true nature by touching his wounds, so too must Lohengrin depart after he offers proof of his holy origin. There is nothing for Lohengrin to gain by revealing his noble lineage and connection to the Council of the Grail, and he could have lived happily with Elsa while maintaining his secret, his property and noble class secured by his marriage to her. However, he not only makes this declaration but further reveals that "God had sent him from the Grail" (Rank 61). By declaring his divine nature, he puts an end to the doubts of the Duchess of Cleve and of his wife while going one step further: because the revelation shows that he is not simply a noble person but a knight acting on God's behalf, their doubt and Elsa's refusal to follow his command become a sign of their own sinful, unholy natures.

Although Lohengrin has lived among the people of Brabant and even taken a noblewoman as his wife, with the truth of his holiness revealed, he must return to the Council of the Grail, the only place appropriate for a divine hero. While the majority of the legend describes a glorious period in which divinity enters the mundane world, protecting the people there and righting wrongs, by its conclusion, those two realms are proven incompatible after all. A holy knight may be able to briefly enter the kingdom and love may be made fleetingly possible, but ultimately the doubt that defines humanity and unbelievers cannot coexist with the pure spirituality represented by the knights of the Holy Grail. Likewise, we might at times encounter lovers who seem impossibly pure, coming into our lives to save us from our own misfortunes, but such a romance can only exist behind a gauze of mystery. It is for this reason that the swan returns at the conclusion of the myth. White and silent, it takes Lohengrin away once more, leaving behind the devastated Elsa and her two children and confirming again the divide between ourselves and our ideals.

CROSS-CULTURAL INFLUENCE

Despite the long history of legends concerning King Arthur's court and the knights of the swan, the story of Lohengrin ultimately came to thrive not through folklore and written narratives but through the medium of opera.

The first and certainly the most impactful operatic version of the story of Lohengrin was written by the German composer Richard Wagner. Wagner was an innovative and sometimes controversial composer, known for his tendency to favor tonal irregularities and to break away from conventional patterns of sound. He also wrote under the heavy influence of German romanticism; romanticism was a nineteenth-century movement that took inspiration from the medieval period, which many romantics believed featured a near-ideal unity of art and society. Most romantics saw the modern era as suppressing strong emotions, in stark contrast to the medieval era and medieval legends, which were filled with intense emotional highs and lows, alongside melodramatic transformations and deaths. They hoped to reconnect with such emotions through art, nature, and the sublime. In his return to the medieval and the seemingly unmitigated spiritual experiences offered there, Wagner selected the story of the mysterious swan knight as the basis of his opera *Lohengrin*, one of the masterpieces of his oeuvre. The composer spent the summer of 1845 in deep study of several medieval versions of the epic, piecing them together slowly until he had created a sort of patchwork plot, primarily true to the older versions but with his own edits and additions throughout. He then spent the next several years composing the music.

Wagner's *Lohengrin*, while thematically very similar to the original versions of the legend, also includes quite a few departures. Elsa is accused of murdering her brother, the duke, in order to inherit his lands, a fact that heightens the risk she faces in her trial with the emperor while also pointing to the prevalence of corruption in the political system. She also has a vision of Lohengrin arriving on his swan following her prayers to God, allowing her to recognize the knight and making more evident the connection between her mysterious savior and the Christian god. The opera's conclusion is also markedly different; it is revealed that the swan had all along been Elsa's brother, transformed by witchcraft, and the departure of Lohengrin results in Elsa's death. Perhaps the greatest difference, however, is the character of Ortrud, who, in Wagner's version, is the wife of Friedrich. Ortrud is the primary person responsible for planting the seeds of doubt in Elsa's mind and encouraging her to ask Lohengrin the forbidden question. She does not do this out of jealousy or pride, however, as the Duchess of Cleve does in the original legend. Instead, Ortrud is presented as a pagan witch, praying for wickedness and deceit from her gods and attempting to upset Elsa's place in the kingdom so that she might one day claim it for her own people and religion. She and her husband, Friedrich, whose life is spared at the start of the opera, are major characters, conspiring in the woods outside of town and eventually barging into the wedding of Lohengrin and Elsa to accuse the knight of sorcery. There are consistent warnings made throughout the opera against evil and pagan magic, and the sense of witchcraft lingers as an atmospheric danger. With this addition, Wagner amplifies the existing Christian reading of the text, composing an opera that stresses the tension between faith and disbelief, between a thriving Christian tradition and what Wagner saw as misguided, unbelieving traditions of alternative spiritualities. In this version, the eventual failure of Elsa and subsequent departure of Lohengrin comes to represent the removal of all people from pure piety.

While the failure of Elsa and others remains evident at the conclusion of the opera, it is important that the majority of the dramatic action is taken up not by this failure but by Elsa's consistent attempts to maintain her faith in an unjust world. She is not simply coerced into marriage, as is the case in the Arthurian legend. Instead, she is the object of abuse and manipulation by a powerful witch and her wicked husband, her entire family and their assets under assault. Further, the very systems that should protect her—the legal systems of the court—are instead twisted by Ortrud so that they work against her. In addition, Wagner firmly sets the opera within a historical period of warfare. The dramatic action begins with King Heinrich gathering his soldiers to defend against Hungarian invaders, and the threat of these invaders is continually present in the background of the main narrative, with a march against the Hungarians even overlapping with the wedding of Elsa and Lohengrin. In contrast to the original myth, which only mentions war as a brief aside, Wagner keeps the sense of impending danger and uncontrollable political violence present, increasing the helplessness of the characters against the greater threats of the outside world.

For these reasons, Wagner's decision to introduce Ortrud into the plot is integral to understanding his own interpretation of the legend. As the culture of the nineteenth century underwent a crisis of faith, with scientific and philosophical developments shaking the core of Christian belief for many Germans, Wagner and others sought ways to maintain a revised sense of faith in a rapidly changing world. Elsa becomes a character trapped in a similar conflict, her only option seemingly being a turn to God and to prayer while others urge her to doubt her savior. In this turn, she is still left with a fundamental paradox: she relies on God and trusts that he cares for her, yet lives in a world plagued by deceit and corruption. It is this paradox that ultimately seeds Elsa's doubt of Lohengrin.

Elsa also becomes something of a blissfully naive figure in Wagner's interpretation. In contrast to the hand-wringing and frightened Elsa of the original myth, the wronged woman in Wagner's opera seems to be at peace with her position from the start, the vision of the swan knight assuring her that everything will work out for the best. For much of the remainder of the narrative, this is the idealized and nearly pure Elsa that Wagner portrays. She stands on a balcony and sings a quiet and gentle song to the breezes, is praised by everyone in the kingdom, and has a series of duets in which she celebrates her love with Lohengrin and the happiness it brings her. This version of Elsa is so quick to acquiesce to her faith that she borders on becoming a ridiculous figure. However, it is important to remember that this bliss is based on her close proximity to Lohengrin and, by extension, her close pious connection to God. Elsa floats through most of the opera in a state of joy, not in order to present an uncomplicated portrait of Christian belief, but rather to magnify her fall from that faith when she finally doubts Lohengrin, the bliss of uncomplicated belief proving itself too good to be true.

Despite the conflict between Christianity and paganism, however, Wagner's *Lohengrin* should not be taken as a straightforward celebration of Christian faith. Instead, as a romantic writer, Wagner was interested in the cultural and social shifts of his time, particularly the many movements in art and philosophy that valued the individual and subjective experiences. In this context, the failure of Elsa is also in many ways the failure of Lohengrin, a mysterious knight who is unable to win the true faith of his beloved or to live unscathed in a world populated also by pagans and nonbelievers. Lohengrin is quite literally a figure from the past, an otherworldly apparition who defies the laws of man, and as such is fundamentally incompatible with the medieval world (as he would also have been with nineteenth-century Europe). When he exits the stage of the opera and returns to the Council of the Holy Grail, he does still represent pure Christian piety, but it is a piety in retreat from the human world. While the severed connection between Christianity and humanity is a failure, that retreat also opens up a new space, with Elsa and her brother briefly reunited as rulers, able to make their own decisions free of Lohengrin's commands or Ortrud's meddling influence. In Wagner's version, this is a decided shift toward individualistic spirituality, implying that if pure faith is incompatible with human nature, a new, romantic form of Christianity would need to emerge. The need for new systems of belief becomes most evident through Elsa's death. Even as she came to doubt Lohengrin, she remained the pinnacle of faith throughout the opera; without the possibility of that faith, she simply cannot exist in the new world that follows.

Lohengrin has become one of the most widely performed and highly regarded operas of all time, with the "Bridal Chorus" from the wedding of Elsa and Lohengrin becoming popular through the modern day as "Here Comes the Bride." While the general reading of the play as an exploration of the tension between belief and disbelief has been the dominant interpretation, audiences have also found occasion to celebrate the romantic spirit, heightened emotions, and engaging plot. Importantly, the opera has also come to define the relationship between modern audiences and the legend of Lohengrin. Wagner, in his romantic portrayal of medieval times, transported an aging narrative into the modern era. By crafting the story with his innovative music and deft storytelling, he allowed audiences to access that narrative with fresh attention. From this renewed interest, a reinvigorated engagement with the legend began, with Lohengrin himself becoming a popular figure in modern opera. Additional operas based on the Lohengrin legend, including several parodies of Wagner's opera and Salvatore Sciarrino's popular 1982 retelling, have found wide audiences across the Western world. Regardless of context, however, the legend of Lohengrin remains popular because of its core concerns—namely, that universal tension between belief and doubt, between romance and despair. More than any other writer, Wagner has defined the modern understanding of Lohengrin, and it is his knight of the swan who continues to captivate audiences around the world.

T. Fleischmann, MFA

BIBLIOGRAPHY

Cicora, Mary A. *Modern Myths and Wagnerian Deconstructions: Hermeneutic Approaches to Wagner's Music-Dramas.* Westport: Greenwood, 2000. Print.

DiGaetani, John Louis. *Wagner outside the Ring: Essays on the Operas, Their Performances, and Their Connections with Other Arts.* Jefferson: McFarland, 2009. Print.

Gurewitsch, Matthew. "Her Brother's Keeper." *Opera News* 62.13 (1998): 24. Print.

"Lohengrin." *Opera News* 70.10 (2006): 54. Print.

Rank, Otto. "Lohengrin." *The Myth of the Birth of the Hero and Other Writings.* New York: Vintage, 1959. 59–64. Print.

Turzynski, Linda J., and Walter E. Meyers. "Parzival." *Masterplots.* Ed. Laurence W. Mazzeno. 4th ed. Vol. 8. Pasadena: Salem, 2011. 4315–18. Print.

Williamson, George S. *The Longing for Myth in Germany: Religion and Aesthetic Culture from Romanticism to Nietzsche.* Chicago: U of Chicago P, 2004. Print.

Moses in the Ark of Bulrushes

Author: Traditional Jewish
Time Period: 2499 BCE–1000 BCE
Country or Culture: Southern Levant
Genre: Myth

OVERVIEW

Moses—rebel prince, emancipator, lawgiver, and prophet—has haunted the popular imagination as have few other figures of sacred history, myth, legend, or fiction. According to the Bible, his equal did not exist in all Hebrew tradition, because he was the only prophet who knew God "face to face" (Deut. 34:10). Whether as the horned colossus of Michelangelo's sculpture, enthroned in the basilica of St. Peter in Chains in Rome, or as a robed Charlton Heston in Cecil B. DeMille's film *The Ten Commandments*, most people in the Western world have a ready mental image of Moses. But the Bible does not present him first performing his wonders in Pharaoh's court, arguing with God at the burning bush, or even contending with the rebellious Israelites in the Sinai desert. He first appears in Jewish scripture as a threatened infant, with a sentence of death on his head, floating precariously down the Nile in a tiny ark. In the ancient world, little care was usually taken to preserve accounts of the early lives of heroes, so the few details that were transmitted to future generations are, therefore, especially tantalizing, however smothered in myth they may be.

Orthodox Jews, Christians, and Muslims accept Moses is a thoroughly historical figure, vouchsafed by their holy books. While some secular scholars have contended that Moses is purely mythological, most students of history and archeology do believe that he was a real person around whom legends gathered. But attempts to corroborate the events first narrated in the Bible have been largely unsuccessful. Judaism has traditionally credited Moses with the authorship, under divine guidance, of the first five books of scripture, the Pentateuch. Though his death and burial are described therein, this

has not been seen as contradictory because he is credited with prophetic foresight. But whether or not he wrote the Pentateuch, it is still appropriately known as the "five books of Moses," or Torah, because his personality dominates the text.

The prevailing scholarly opinion today—though not shared by all—is that the Pentateuch is a compendium of oral traditions and earlier writings. This documentary hypothesis of authorship was formulated by German scholar Julius Wellhausen (1844–1918). Wellhausen identified the chief sources of the text as "J" (the Jehovist or Yahwist), "E" (the Elohist), "D" (the Deuteronomist), and "P" (the Priestly). They are so designated because of stylistic features, preoccupations, and the names by which they refer to God. The Pentateuch in its present form, according to this theory, emerged near the end of the fifth century BCE. Rabbinical Judaism has traditionally calculated the dates of Moses's life from about 1571 BCE to 1452 BCE. Christian scholars have generally dated him even earlier, while secular scholars who concede his historical reality have suggested a variety of dates.

While Moses's career forms the major epic of the Hebrew Bible—his deliverance of the Israelites from Egyptian slavery, his receiving of the Ten Commandments from God while encamped in the desert, and his leading of the Israelites to the border of the Promised Land—the beginning of his life is especially significant because it provides the necessary backdrop against which his subsequent journey unfolds. The Bible, in typical laconic fashion, sets forth the plight of baby Moses. He comes from the priestly tribe of Levi, and his birthplace is in the Egyptian province of Goshen, where his people have been enslaved. Although a brother, Aaron, appears later in the biblical book of Exodus, mention is initially made only of a sister called Miriam. From birth, Moses is condemned under Pharaoh's edict that all male children of the Israelites are to be killed. To give the baby a chance of survival, his parents set him afloat in the

Nile, with his sister stationed nearby to watch over him. The fifth person in the infancy narrative is an unnamed royal princess, daughter of the murderous pharaoh, who comes to bathe in the Nile and finds the child.

Though Exodus remains the chief source of Moses's nativity narrative, embellishments later appeared, some of them adding desired details to the intriguing, though brief, biblical account. Flavius Josephus, a Jewish historian of the first century CE, is valued for the information he provides surrounding biblical events and personalities, gathered from many oral and written traditions. Though born in Jerusalem to Jewish parents, Josephus served two Roman emperors, Vespasian and Titus. Noting the Roman fascination with things Jewish, Josephus sought to introduce Romans to the history and religion of his people properly in *The Antiquities of the Jews* (ca. 93 CE), placing his subject in the broader context of the Greco-Roman world.

A further source of lore comes from a wealthy, highly sophisticated Hellenistic Jew, Philo of Alexandria (ca. 10 BCE–ca. 45 CE). Though he wrote at length about the Law of Moses and the Pentateuch, his chief concern was in presenting Judaism as a rational, philosophical system, acceptable to learned Greeks. Following a method developed by Greek philosophers in their readings of Homer, Philo heavily allegorized the Bible, particularly when it came to accounts of the miraculous. He sought to prove through his writings that Jewish thought was equal to that of pagan Greece, and his conception of God resembled the transcendent deity of the Greek philosophers more than the involved, suffering, loving, and sometimes angry God who wrestles with Moses in Exodus.

Through the centuries, rabbinical embellishments of the biblical narratives continued. Other tales of Moses, often from the oral tradition, came to be included in the Talmud, an enormous collection of Jewish law and lore, and the Midrash, rabbinical commentaries on biblical texts. When Christianity emerged from first-century Judaism, the Jewish scriptures were adopted as the Old Testament. Christians thought of Jesus as "the New Moses," though they believed him to be greater still. Early compilers and readers of the Christian scriptures, the New Testament, interpreted the sacred Jewish writings as a catalog of symbols and foreshadowings of the coming messiah, whom they recognized in Jesus. They saw in the infancy account of Moses a keen parallel to the birth narrative of Jesus.

Another sacred scripture in which Moses appears prominently is the Qur'an, the holy book of Islam. He is mentioned in 502 verses, more than any other prophet. The Qur'an adds details of Moses's infancy not found in the Hebrew Scriptures. Moses is believed to have foretold the coming of Mohammed, the prophet to whom the Qur'an was revealed. It is even likely that Mohammed identified in some ways with Moses, since both were children reared by foster parents and were called to rescue a people from idolatry.

While many tales have been told of the infancy of Moses, some of them contradictory, questions have arisen almost from the beginning about the child's origin, what his position was in the pharaoh's court, which pharaohs he knew, and how much influence the wisdom of Egypt had on him. Folklorists have noted that the story of his infancy follows the familiar archetypal pattern of great heroes and rulers who were abandoned or threatened at birth, were reared by foster parents, and achieved their destinies through struggle and hardship.

SUMMARY

The Pentateuch provides a clear explanation of the plight of the Israelites in Egypt at the time of the birth of Moses. In a series of lively narratives, the books of Genesis and Exodus relate the wanderings of the patriarchs. Some four hundred years previous to Moses's birth—though biblical chronology is sometimes difficult to follow—Joseph, the favorite son of the patriarch Jacob, is sold into slavery by his jealous brothers. Slave traders eventually take him to Egypt. While there he becomes the servant of Potiphar, an honorable Egyptian official. Through treachery and the lust of Potiphar's wife, he ends up in prison, but he is able to earn his release through his gift of dream interpretation. By forewarning Pharaoh of a coming famine throughout the land, he gains favor in the court and becomes an adviser to the ruler. Eventually the famine drives his entire family to Egypt, where they settle and establish their clans. By the time Moses appears a few centuries later, they have become a prolific people within the great nation.

At Moses's birth, the ruling pharaoh no longer honors the accomplishments of Joseph. To enhance his reign, the pharaoh enslaves the Israelites and puts them to work building cities and other structures to display his might and dominance. Fearing a possible insurrection or, as some versions of the legend assert, warned by astrologers that a male of their number would cause him woe, he decrees that all male Israelite children be thrown into the river. Why a ruler so in need of slave labor would decide on this method of population control is not clear, but whatever the reason, Moses, like other Israelite male infants, is given a death sentence at birth.

When Pharaoh instructs the midwives who attend the Israelite women to kill all male children, they choose not to heed him and instead try to save the children. Hearing of this, Pharaoh questions them. They respond that "the Hebrew women are not as the Egyptian women; for they are lively, and are delivered ere the midwives come unto them" (Exod. 1:19). This vitality and fecundity of the Israelites was later embellished by storytellers who report that the women did not merely have children but gave birth to "litters."

These midwives later became objects of curiosity as the legend grew. One source claimed that they were Egyptian women who had converted to the Israelite way of life. Whatever their loyalties, Pharaoh, it is said, becomes so preoccupied with the slaughter of the innocents that he attempts to beguile the midwives, first with flattery and later with amorous propositions, which they promptly reject. The midwives are rewarded for their valor with fine homes and families.

Either warned by God—according to some accounts—or simply through maternal love, Moses's mother, Jochebed, refuses to allow her "goodly child" to be destroyed (Exod. 2:2). She cares for him in secret, and when it becomes impossible to hide him any longer, she fashions a *teiva* (ark) of bulrushes, sealing it with bitumen and pitch and placing it by the river. The Hebrew word *teiva* translates more properly as "chest," but it is the same word employed for Noah's ark in Genesis. "Bulrushes" probably refers to the familiar papyrus stalks that were abundant around the Nile and figure so prominently in the artwork that would later commemorate the event.

Whether through a fortuitous coincidence, a clever connivance of Jochebed, or divine providence, the daughter of Pharaoh comes with her ladies-in-waiting to bathe in the river. While Moses's sister, Miriam, watches attentively from the banks of the river, Pharaoh's daughter spies the tiny ark floating among the brush and sends her maids to retrieve it. On opening it, she sees the child, who bursts into tears. The kindhearted princess recognized at once that this is an Israelite child. (Exactly how she knows this—whether by the weave of the cloth surrounding him, his appearance, his circumcision, or some other factor—is not made clear, however.) The princess takes pity on the child, and when his sister emerges from her hiding place and

"And when she [the mother] could not longer hide him [Moses], she took for him an ark of bulrushes, and daubed it with slime and with pitch, and put the child therein; and she laid it in the flags by the river's brink. And his sister stood afar off, to wit what would be done to him.

And the daughter of Pharaoh came down to wash herself at the river; and her maidens walked along by the river's side: and when she saw the ark among the flags, she sent her maid to fetch it. And when she had opened it, she saw the child: and, behold, the babe wept, and she had compassion on him. . . . "

Exodus

offers to find a wet nurse for the child, she is pleased to offer wages for the service. Thus, Moses's own mother is secured by Miriam to become his first caregiver. Later, the child is returned to the princess, who adopts him as her own son.

Because Pharaoh's daughter has retrieved the child from the river, she calls him Moses, meaning "drawn out" in Hebrew, the language of the Israelites. Secular scholars have also suggested that the name is derived from the Egyptian *mose* or *messes*, which, added to a proper name, means "born" or even "son of," as in the name of the important pharaoh Rameses.

Other storytellers were quick to fill in details or clarify perplexities only hinted at in Scripture. According to Exodus, when God first calls the adult Moses, speaking to him from a burning bush and giving him the task of liberating the Israelites from slavery, one of the reluctant Moses's first excuses is that he is "slow of speech, and of a slow tongue" (Exod. 4:10). This led to the conjecture that there was some speech impediment traceable to early childhood. In his *Antiquities of the Jews*, Josephus relates an episode not in the Bible but certainly from the Jewish oral tradition. Moses, Josephus alleges, is from the beginning an attractive, intelligent child, much loved by his adoptive mother and even a favorite pet of Pharaoh himself, despite warnings of court soothsayers that the alien child in their midst would bring trouble. One day when Pharaoh holds him, little Moses seizes Pharaoh's crown, throws it on the floor, and tramples on it. While this might have been dismissed as a playful antic of an innocent child, the suspicious court sees sinister intent. Only the actions of his adoptive mother save Moses from her father's anger.

In some later versions of this tale, the action cannot be entirely dismissed, and a test is devised to determine whether the child should be punished. Two cups are placed before the child. One cup contains precious jewels, the other a burning coal. In choosing the jewels, Moses would reveal exorbitant ambition, thus threatening Egyptian power. His life would be forfeit. As his small hand reaches out to take the dazzling jewels, an unseen angel seizes it and brings it down on the coal. Quickly putting his burning hand to his mouth, little Moses burns his tongue and lips, making him forever unclear of speech. Dreams were always important in ancient times, and Josephus additionally relates that Amram, Moses's biological father, is given a revelatory dream before the child's birth. It reveals that his son would deliver his nation from bondage and be revered ever after by all humankind.

Readers of the Bible have longed to know more about the gracious princess who adopts and nourishes Moses. Josephus provides her a name, Thermuthis. He writes that she has no children of her own and, thus, places Moses in line to become ruler of Egypt. She continues to love, educate, and protect him, even against suspicious courtiers. Rabbinical tales further elevate this Gentile woman. According to the rabbis, she eventually converts to monotheism, rejecting the gods of Egypt, and at the end of her life, she is taken directly to paradise.

Some of the ancient rabbis also sought to explain the first encounter between the baby and the pagan princess, adding a few miraculous incidents. God, they say, sends a plague of scorching heat down upon Egypt. To cool off, Pharaoh's daughter seeks the waters of the Nile. When she sees the little ark bobbing in the water, her arm becomes elastic, growing so long that she is able to reach the basket herself. At the touch of the ark, she is cured of fierce boils that had broken out on her skin. Other rabbis contend that the princess flees to the waters

of the Nile in order to purify herself from the idolatry she constantly witnesses in the pagan court of her father. Her attendants, according to this account, do not receive the baby lightly and try to persuade her to abandon him. But God sends the angel Gabriel (who does not appear at this juncture of the biblical scriptures) to bury these evildoers alive. God himself then bestows upon the princess the name of Batya, meaning "daughter of God" (Kirsch 53–54).

The Bible does not give the age or marital status of the princess. Still, the versions of the myth that report that she is childless provide further motivation for her adoption of Moses, in addition to her natural compassion. Philo of Alexandria, attempting to impress his Greco-Roman and Hellenized Jewish readers, is more philosophical in his presentation of Moses's life. For this reason, he minimizes the extravagant details in the infancy narrative in *De vita Mosis* (*The Life of Moses*). According to Philo, from the beginning Moses displays the perfection that would be admired in any Greek or Roman hero. Philo does not mention an ark of reeds, writing only that the child's parents expose him on the banks of the river and depart in tears, leaving him to the care of God. Philo contends that in order to confuse her father, the princess pretends to be pregnant, using "contrivances" to make herself appear thus (qtd. in Kirsch 61). After the proper time, she presents Moses to her father as her biological son.

Not surprisingly, Moses became a central figure in Jewish mystical traditions and later movements among the Jews of the Diaspora. Lubavitch Hasidic lore tells that Moses's mother, Yocheved, is born "between the boundary walls" of Egypt, belonging neither to Egypt nor to the Holy Land. Thus, she possesses a vision in which geographic and cultural limitations are transcended, a universal vision she bestows on her son, making him especially fit for leadership. After Pharaoh's decree, Moses's parents choose to live apart and thus deprive Pharaoh of future victims. But their wise daughter, Miriam, tells them it is their duty to have children, saying, "Your decree is worse than Pharaoh's." While he only wishes to rid the Israelites of males, she tells them, their choice would put an end to the Israelites altogether. Persuaded by her impeccable logic, her parents reunite and beget Moses.

The Hebrew Bible reports no miracles attending the birth of Moses. Yet according to Lubavitcher legends, miraculous signs and portends abound at his birth. The house of his parents is filled with a radiance symbolizing

MYTH INTO ART

A lesser-known but particularly arresting depiction of Moses in infancy is the work of Simeon Solomon (1840–1905), the youngest son of a middle-class British Jewish family. Hovering on the edges of the Pre-Raphaelite brotherhood, Solomon was admired for his draftsmanship and his early work inspired by Shakespearean and biblical subjects. Children were a special favorite. Although the prophet Jeremiah's childhood is not mentioned in the Bible, Solomon envisioned it in an 1862 contribution to the British Royal Academy titled *The Child Jeremiah*.

More significant, however, was an oil painting of two years previous, *The Mother of Moses*, an important achievement for a twenty-year-old artist. Composed in subdued shades of brown and umber, the painting focuses all attention on the mother and sister of Moses, while the face of the infant, held in his mother's arms, is not visible. Solomon had found his models in his own British Jewish community, elegant and stately women whose features were believed at that time to be distinctly Semitic. Leaving out the overly familiar Egyptian motifs employed by other artists and illustrators—palm trees, lotus blossoms, even bulrushes—Solomon clearly intended to celebrate Jewish womanhood and the Jewishness of Moses, which was beginning to be challenged by revisionist scholars who were attempting to identify the laws and traditions of Israel's revered prophet with the higher aspirations of ancient Egyptian civilization. The spiritual radiance of Miriam, Moses's sister, as she gazes on her brother, the future lawgiver, was almost certainly inspired by Solomon's own deeply religious sister Rebecca, a painter concerned with women's issues.

the enlightenment the infant would bring to humankind. Because Egypt is filled with astrologers, soothsayers, and magicians, Moses, growing up in the royal court, is well situated to learn the wonder-working skills he later uses so effectively when he confronts Pharaoh to demand the liberation of the Israelites and when he parts the Red Sea.

The Qur'an, the holy book of Islam, gives high honor to Moses. God, according to the Qur'an, commands the mother of Moses to put her son in the Nile, assuring her that the river will cast him up gently. The Qur'an also tells how Moses is restored to his natural mother through the planning of his sister, after Moses rejects the breasts of the Egyptian wet nurses. At this point, the Qur'an deviates from earlier accounts. Now it is Pharaoh's wife, traditionally called Āsiya, who rescues the child, convinces her husband to allow her to adopt him, and loves him as her own (Q28:1–13). This righteous foster mother further desires to become a true believer, though she lacks the strength to revolt against her own people and their pagan beliefs.

The Qur'an adds an interesting encounter between the adult Moses and Pharaoh, who reminds him that he had been brought as an infant to the court, stayed there for several years, and enjoyed many advantages. Now, his foster father wants to know why he is so ungrateful. Moses replies that although he committed ungrateful deeds in his misguided youth and fled the court in fear, it is now the Lord of the Worlds who gives him wisdom and calls him to rescue the Israelites (Q26:16–24).

ANALYSIS

Every passage, personage, and episode of the Bible has been subjected to endless analysis. The story of Moses in the bulrushes lends itself as well to various interpretations. Sir James George Frazer, a renowned Scottish anthropologist and folklorist, identified familiar patterns in the Moses infancy story. He noted that, as reported in the Bible, it contains features echoed in folktales from throughout the world. Many ancient documents and orally transmitted stories speak of how a mighty hero or future king was exposed at birth and daringly escaped early death. Frazer believed these elements of romance and foreshadowing were probably "picturesque touches added . . . to heighten the effect of a plain tale which [the narrator] deemed below the dignity of the subject" (439).

The ancient Romans had their legend of the founding twins, Remus and Romulus, saved by a woodpecker and nourished by a she-wolf. These inconvenient offspring of a vestal virgin and the god Mars had been given to servants who were ordered to place them in a tiny ark and drown them in the overflow of the Tiber (Frazer 447–48). They were, however, fortuitously rescued and preserved by caring animals. Other kings and heroes of antiquity made much of the myths surrounding their birth. The ancient Greek tragedies of Sophocles explore the legend of King Oedipus, who, because of a dire prophecy before his birth, is sent with a servant to be exposed to the elements. The servant ties his feet to a tree branch—hence his name, meaning "big foot" (446). He is later found and adopted by loving parents who rear him in ignorance of his origin. The Babylonian king Sargon the Elder (ca. 2600 BCE) claims conception by a "lowly woman" and a father he never knew. Born in secret, he is then placed in a basket of rushes closed with pitch and cast into the river. He is rescued by a drawer of water, who rears him as his own son, and is taught to be a gardener. But through the love of the goddess Ištar (Ishtar), he becomes king and rules for many years (450). A similar myth surrounds the birth of Cyrus II of Persia, according to the Greek historian Herodotus (444).

Even in far away India, as celebrated in the national epic, the Mahābhārata, a king's daughter conceives a child by one of the gods. Fearing the disapproval of her parents, she puts the child in a basket and places it in the nearby river. A childless couple find the baby, marvel at his beauty, and raise him as a skilled archer (Frazer 451–52). A legend from high in the Himalayas, where Semitic narratives were probably unknown, states that Trakhan, king of Gilgit, is enclosed as an infant in a wooden box and deposited by his mother in the river, to be found and reared by a peasant family and eventually restored to his royal heritage (453).

A feature of these narratives that aroused the interest of Frazer was the casting of the infant into the water. In numerous cultures throughout history, a child of disputed origin was tested by throwing him in a river. If the child sank, he or she was declared a bastard; if the child surfaced or swam, he or she was proclaimed a legitimate heir (454).

More realistically, political scientists today point out that slave rebellions, revolutions, and important social movements are rarely instigated by the oppressed themselves; rather, they are typically led by privileged members of the disadvantaged community or others who identify with the downtrodden and refuse to tolerate the injustice they see around them. Examples include educated and urbane reformers such as Mahatma Gandhi, a legal scholar, and Martin Luther King Jr., a member

of a professional middle-class African American family. So, it is not unusual that Moses, in appearance and education an Egyptian, would become the liberator of the enslaved Israelites, ultimately recognized as his own people.

The early Christians saw Moses as a clear forerunner of Jesus. "Out of Egypt have I called my son," states Matthew 2:15, quoting the Old Testament book of Hosea; though originally a reference to Moses or the Israelites themselves, this appeared to Christians to be a clear foreshadowing of the Holy Family's flight into Egypt. This journey, according to the gospel of Matthew, is made to protect the life of the Christ child from the wrath of King Herod. This wicked and paranoid ruler, led more by superstition than by piety, believes an unnamed child who would threaten his rule is soon to be born. Consequently, he orders the slaying of male babies, known as the Holy Innocents.

Christians found other similarities between baby Moses and baby Jesus. Moses is placed in the bulrushes; Jesus is laid in a manger. Joseph, the legal father of Jesus, is told in a dream that an extraordinary child is to be born in his family, and Jewish legend reports that the father of Moses experienced a similar dream. Jesus's mother also receives prophetic messages from angels. The sister of Moses is Miriam; the mother of Jesus is called Mary, a name derived from Miriam. Though early Christians did not embellish the story of Moses's birth and childhood, they treasured the infancy story as a parallel to the nativity of Jesus. The midwives who protected the Israelites were also recalled in medieval Christian discussions of what would become known as "situation ethics," when the question arose about the propriety of lying to protect human life.

In the latter part of the twentieth century, the literature of the past was scrutinized by a new school of interpreters, women with a concern for the status and achievements of their gender. Along with secular literature, sacred books proved favored hunting grounds by both feminist literary critics and feminist theologians such as Ilana Pardes and others. They have pronounced the daughter of Pharaoh one of the most admirable figures in sacred history and have observed that in the nativity accounts of Moses, men play few positive roles. Moses survives because a network of compassionate women protects and nourishes him, with sympathies and concerns that transcend religious and tribal boundaries. First are the midwives—whether Egyptian or Israelite—who refuse to kill him and help his mother save his life.

Then his sister patiently watches over the tiny ark in the Nile. The daughter of Pharaoh adopts him as her own son, while his natural mother is allowed to nourish and instruct him. Even as an adult, he is befriended by the daughters of the priest of Midian, who take him to their father, who in turn provides employment and shelter as Moses waits for his divine call. Some feminists have likened these women to the goddesses who protected pagan heroes from the evils that surrounded them at birth.

CROSS-CULTURAL INFLUENCE

Moses intrigued the originator of psychoanalysis, Sigmund Freud, one of the most influential thinkers of the twentieth century. Freud's engagement with Moses was tied to his ambivalent feelings about his own Jewish identity as well as his developing theories of psychoanalysis. Against the pleadings of several of his Jewish friends, he published his controversial work *Moses and Monotheism* in the midst of the Nazi persecution of his people. Although the book was initially published in 1939, after Freud had fled his home in Austria and found refuge in England, it has endured many reprintings and translations and continues to exert influence in popular culture. Historical and biblical scholars have remained highly critical of Freud's interpretation, pointing out his fast-and-loose handling of chronology and his disregard of much historical and archeological scholarship. Recognizing that much of his text could be seen as an exercise of the imagination, Freud at first thought of calling his book "a historical romance" but ultimately concluded that his speculations were likely true.

Freud's thesis was basically as follows: the monotheism that has long been the pride of Judaism was not native to the Israelites but came from the Egyptians. Egyptian history does record a pharaoh, Amenhotep IV, who decreed that his nation would worship the sun god, Aten (Aton), exclusively. This pharaoh even changed his own name, in the custom of ancient rulers, to Ikhnaton (Akhenaten or Akhenaton), in honor of his god. Historians do not agree whether he actually believed in only one god or merely determined that this god alone would be worshiped by his people. Yet Freud appears to have believed that the faith of Aten was truly monotheistic, rejecting anthropomorphic conceptions of deity, any belief in an afterlife (which had become an obsession with other Egyptian rulers), and the sorcery that attended paganism. But in ancient Egypt, the priests of rival cults could not be convinced, and after Ikhnaton's death, polytheism resurfaced among the people. Some

followers of Aten remained undercover, Freud believed. Moses was one of them, not really an Israelite but an Egyptian nobleman, possibly even a priest. He was also, according to this theory, an absolute monotheist. When the religion of Ikhnaton was threatened by extinction, Moses took matters into his own hands. Finding foreigners living among the Egyptians, he decided to teach the Israelites the faith of Aten, introduce among them the Egyptian rite of circumcision, and lead them out of Egypt. Though successful at first, Moses later discovered his task more difficult than he had assumed, as he found himself the leader of a stubborn, muttering people who resumed idol worship as soon as his back was turned.

In their desert wanderings, Freud suggested, the Israelites encountered the tribes of Midian, who worshipped a fiery, volcanic god named Jahve (Yahweh). Among the Israelites, the two gods became fused, thus leading to the seeming contradiction between the jealous anger and the infinite mercy of God. A second Moses, a Midianite priest, came forth. The Israelites subsequently murdered the original Egyptian Moses, leaving only hints in their traditions and scriptures of what had really transpired. In line with his psychoanalytic theories, Freud said the ancient Israelites acted out an oedipal fantasy: the murder of the spiritual father.

In crediting monotheism to ancient Egypt, Freud antagonized his fellow Jews; he seemed intent on depriving Judaism of its greatest contribution to humankind, its recognition of a single supreme deity. He was also defying secular scholarship dominant since the German Enlightenment, which questioned the historical reality of Moses. If Moses had existed at all, many German Higher Critics contended, only a part of his legend would be authentic. They believed that monotheism had developed gradually from polytheism, through henotheism, the worship of only one god among many gods. They preferred to credit developed monotheism to the great writing prophets of Israel, who came long after Moses.

But Freud did find one credentialed scholar who appeared to agree with him, at least in part. This was biblical scholar Ernst Sellin, whose views had been published in Berlin in 1922, to little scholarly acclaim. Sellin had concluded from his studies that Moses was indeed a monotheist and lawgiver. He further believed that Moses might well have been an Egyptian, rather than an Israelite.

Freud's critics have been many. Religious scholars and students of history and archaeology alike have pointed out his factual errors. Even psychologists, many of whom have either rejected or modified Freud's therapeutic theories and methods, have found his venture into biblical history amateurish and questionable. One of the most articulate and entertaining critics of Freud's interpretation is Rabbi Jonathan Sacks. In the essay "Freud's Great Freudian Slip," he calls *Moses and Monotheism* "a strange work if ever there was one," noting first that its author chose an odd time, the Holocaust, to attack a fundamental article of Jewish pride. Acknowledging that Freud made much of the many legends of the hero's precarious infancy, Sacks bases his refutation of Freud precisely on the infancy stories themselves. He argues that Freud failed to see the importance of the major deviations the Moses story has from the archetype. "What Freud failed to realize is that the story of Moses is not a myth but an anti-myth. It takes a myth and turns it upside down," Sacks asserts. Moses is the biological child of humble people, of slaves, rather than a rejected son of the nobility or the gods, as in other such myths. Rather than being adopted by a peasant or an animal, Moses is brought up in a royal palace.

In the antimyth, the rabbi finds a profound message. As elsewhere in the Jewish prophetic tradition, God's favor falls not on those of high estate or wealth but on people of character. As the child of slaves, Moses's career demonstrates that it is not power that matters but the courage to fight against injustice and tyranny.

Sacks clearly recognizes that in his exploration of Moses, Freud was working out his own conflicted feelings about his religion, admiring the cultural heritage but struggling with Judaism. That is why Freud missed what Sacks calls "one of the most powerful moral truths the Bible ever taught": "A child of slaves can be greater than a prince. G-d's standards are not power and privilege.

They are about recognizing G-d's image in the weak, the powerless, the afflicted, the suffering and fighting for their cause." Sacks concludes that Freud missed an opportunity to comfort fellow Jews during their time of peril, during the Holocaust. From the relative safety of England, he failed to realize that the story of baby Moses was one of the most powerful narratives of survival and hope.

Allene Phy-Olsen

BIBLIOGRAPHY

Doré, Gustave. *The Doré Bible Illustrations*. London: Dover, 1974. Print.

Feiler, Bruce. *America's Prophet: Moses and the American Story*. New York: Harper, 2009. Print.

Frazer, James George. "Moses in the Ark of Bulrushes." *Folk-Lore in the Old Testament: Studies in Comparative Religion, Legend, and Law*. Vol. 2. London: Macmillan, 1919. 437–55. Print.

Freud, Sigmund. *Moses and Monotheism*. Trans. Katherine Jones. 1939. New York: Random, 1967. Print.

The Holy Bible. New York: American Bible Soc., 1999. Print. King James Vers.

Kirsch, Jonathan. *Moses, A Life*. New York: Ballantine, 1998. Print.

Maier, Paul L., ed. and trans. *Josephus, The Essential Works*. Grand Rapids: Kregel, 1994. Print.

"Moses: The Birth of a Leader." *Chabad.org*. Chabad-Lubavitch Media Center, 2013. Web. 6 Mar. 2013.

The Qur'an. Trans. M. A. S. Abdel Haleem. Oxford: Oxford UP, 2005. Print.

Sacks, Jonathan. 2012. "Freud's Great Freudian Slip." *Chabad.org*. Chabad-Lubavitch Media Center, 2013. Web. 6 Mar. 2013.

Wright, Melanie. *Moses in America*. New York: Oxford UP, 2003. Print.

Romulus and Remus

Author: Plutarch
Time Period: 1 CE–500 CE
Country or Culture: Roman
Genre: Myth

OVERVIEW

Thanks to the intriguing image of infant twins suckled by a wolf, many people are familiar with the ancient Roman myth of Romulus and Remus. Yet the twins' time in the care of the nursing wolf is just one of many gripping episodes in this story of the founding of Rome, which has fascinated and flummoxed scholars and general readers alike with its compelling drama and peculiar features.

Many versions of the story exist, including that of Plutarch, a Greek historian who lived from 46 to 120 CE and recorded the story of Romulus and Remus in *The Lives of the Noble Grecians and Romans,* also known as *Parallel Lives.* In his account, the Alban king Amulius overthrows his brother Numitor's kingdom and tries to force Numitor's daughter to remain a virgin, but she becomes pregnant with twins. Amulius attempts to have the twins killed, but Romulus and Remus are first nursed by a wolf and protected by a woodpecker and then raised secretly by Faustulus, Amulius's herdsman. As young adults, the twins are brave and virtuous, superior both physically and morally. Although they work as shepherds for Amulius, their true identity is revealed to the king through a series of events resulting from a conflict with Numitor's herdsmen. Before Amulius can take action, Romulus and Remus, aided by forces hostile to the dictatorial king, overthrow him and restore Numitor to power.

The brothers then return to the land where they were raised to found their own city, but Romulus murders Remus after a dispute spirals out of control. Romulus then buries his brother and founds the city on his own, establishing its social structure and providing it protection. However, because the city lacks sufficient women,

he orders his army to abduct the Sabine women, sparking a series of military conflicts. Eventually, the women choose to remain with their Roman husbands, and Romulus begins to conquer additional territories and establish sacred Roman institutions. After he divides land among his soldiers and returns hostages without the senate's consent, he mysteriously disappears. Plutarch states that he has been either murdered by the senators or deified by the gods. Romulus's friend confirms his deification, leading the Romans to worship Romulus as Quirinus.

Plutarch's account is especially interesting because of its inclusion of many alternate versions of his story, which he nonetheless presents as valid history. This presentation constantly reminds readers of the tenuous nature of the details surrounding Rome's origins. Following earlier writers, Plutarch connects the hero Aeneas to Romulus and Remus to reconcile two very different myths of Rome's origin, a problem that has intrigued historians. A comparative analysis underscores the radical differences between the Romulus and Remus story and the Roman poet Virgil's account of Aeneas to explore how the myths served different periods of Rome's development. Although both myths existed long before the height of the Roman Empire, some historians believe that the Romulus and Remus story suggests a popular myth that was appropriate for Rome as a city-state, whereas Virgil is known to have developed the story of Aeneas to represent Rome as an empire.

SUMMARY

Plutarch's account of the origin of Romulus and Remus is long, incorporating numerous alternative accounts and digressions, but a single narrative comprising many of the most important elements of the story can be discerned. After summarizing many different versions of Rome's origin story, Plutarch introduces "the story which is most believed and has the greatest number of vouchers" (16). He states that the kings of

"While the infants lay here, history tells us, a she-wolf nursed them, and a woodpecker constantly fed and watched them; these creatures are esteemed holy to the god Mars, the woodpecker the Latins still especially worship and honor. Which things, as much as any, gave credit to what the mother of the children said, that their father was the god Mars."

The Lives of the Noble Grecians and Romans

Alba descended from Aeneas, the hero who came to Italy after the fall of Troy. When brothers Numitor and Amulius inherit the throne, the latter suggests two equal shares and sets the kingdom as one share and an equivalent sum of money as the other. When Numitor chooses the kingdom, Amulius uses the money to usurp the kingdom from his brother. Next, fearing that Numitor's daughter, Rhea Silvia, might produce an heir, Amulius forces her to become a vestal virgin, a priestess of the goddess Vesta. When Rhea Silvia becomes pregnant soon after, however, Amulius has her sequestered until she gives birth to twin boys "of more than human size and beauty" (16). Amulius orders a servant (possibly Faustulus) to dispose of the children, so the servant places the twins in a trough, intending to throw the trough into a river. When he finds the river swollen with rushing waters, he simply leaves the trough near the bank. The river eventually overflows and gently carries the trough to "a smooth piece of ground" (16).

Soon after, a she-wolf approaches to suckle the infants, and a woodpecker feeds and guards them. Plutarch notes that these animals are sacred to Mars, the Roman god of war, whom some Romans believed to be the boys' father. The servant Faustulus discovers the twins, and he and his wife, Acca Larentia, raise them as their own in secret. As the twins grow, their pleasing physical appearance "intimate[s] their natural superiority" (17), and they both prove to be courageous, becoming famous for hunting, capturing thieves, and protecting the weak. Romulus, however, displays particular wisdom, projecting "the idea of being born rather to rule than to obey" (17). Working with Faustulus as Amulius's herdsmen, the twins, along with their fellow shepherds, have a quarrel with Numitor's shepherds and drive them away. One day when Romulus attends a sacrifice, Numitor's shepherds take advantage of his absence and capture Remus. The herdsmen accuse Remus in the presence of Numitor, who requests justice from Amulius for his servants' misdeeds. Amulius gives Remus back to Numitor to punish as he sees fit, but when the latter is impressed by Remus's physical and mental superiority, he invites the shepherd to reveal his identity. At this point, Remus confesses that he has recently heard that Faustulus and Larentia are not his true parents and that he and Romulus were abandoned as infants and nurtured by beasts. Hearing this and suspecting that the twins are in fact his grandsons, Numitor confirms the story with his daughter.

Meanwhile, Faustulus entreats Romulus to help rescue his brother and reveals the full details of their birth. Faustulus then attempts to take the trough in which the infant twins had been originally placed to Numitor, but on his way he is stopped and questioned by Amulius's guards, one of whom recognizes the trough and seizes Faustulus for questioning. Faustulus is forced to admit that the twins are alive, but he says that they live as shepherds far from Alba and that he had intended to bring the trough to reassure the boys' mother. Alarmed, Amulius sends a messenger to question Numitor about his knowledge of the twins, but the messenger allies himself with Numitor and urges him to act swiftly against Amulius. Having gathered citizens and other forces opposed to Amulius, Romulus attacks the city from the exterior while Remus rouses forces from within. Together they overthrow Amulius, restore Numitor to power, bestow due honor on their mother, and depart from Alba to found a city in the land where they were raised.

The twins disagree, however, about where to found the city, with Romulus choosing Roma Quadrata, or "Square Rome," and Remus favoring the Aventine Mount. They decide to settle the matter via divination, the ancient art of predicting the future through omens. Romulus wins when he sees twelve vultures, whereas Remus observes only six. Believing that Romulus has cheated, Remus ridicules and obstructs his brother's work in building the city walls. When Remus leaps over the walls, Romulus (or perhaps a character named Celer,

Plutarch notes) kills him, and Faustulus is also killed in the conflict. Romulus buries Remus and founds his new city, establishing a sufficiently large population, a military, and a patrician class. The city lacks wives for its new inhabitants, however, partly because of the foreign, humble, and suspicious origin of many of the new citizens, a number of whom are escaped slaves and criminals. Romulus thus has his army abduct the Sabine women during a festival and forces the women to marry the men of his city. This sparks a series of armed conflicts between the Sabines and Romans, but eventually, the women intervene and ask the Sabines to allow them to remain with their new husbands and children.

The rest of Plutarch's account concerns the institutions established by Romulus, his military victories over various territories, and his growing arrogance as king. When Numitor dies, Romulus inherits the throne in Alba, but wanting to "court the people," he gives the people governing power, thus encouraging "the great men of Rome to seek after a free and anti-monarchical state" (27). Romulus then, without the senate's consent, divides the lands acquired by war among his soldiers and returns hostages to the Veientes, a conquered people of Tuscany. Shortly after, he disappears. Some Romans claim that the senators murdered him and cut his body to pieces, while others believe that Romulus was taken up by the gods as the sun darkened. A close friend of Romulus, Proculus, testifies that he encountered the deified Romulus, who told him, "By the exercise of temperance and fortitude, they shall attain the height of human power; we will be to you the propitious god Quirinus" (28). The Romans henceforth worship Quirinus as a god.

ANALYSIS

The myth of Romulus and Remus is a story of Roman origins, but many aspects of the tale remain shrouded in mystery. Ancient writers present the myth as history, leading many scholars to focus on verifying its details. Yet certain features, such as the exposed children and the nursing wolf, have clear parallels in Greek and other myths, inviting symbolic interpretations. Some of the myth's unusual features, however, particularly the function of Remus and his disturbing murder by Romulus, have resisted easy explanation. In fact, the myth's many unflattering elements, such as the possible rape of the twins' mother, the portrayal of Faustulus's wife as a prostitute, and Romulus's fratricide and connections with suspect characters have bedeviled scholars, with some nineteenth-century scholars even proclaiming the

story to be fabricated anti-Roman propaganda. Furthermore, the story is radically different from that of Aeneas, the other Roman hero whose story was eventually coordinated with the Romulus and Remus myth. A comparative analysis of Plutarch's story and Virgil's account of Aeneas reveals the different cultural and political functions of each tale. Although Aeneas was known as a Trojan hero, and the story of Romulus and Remus existed long before Virgil and Plutarch wrote their respective accounts, the stories' differences can be explained in relation to general historical circumstances at the time of their emergence. Although Plutarch wrote at the end of the first century CE, he presents the myth as a biography of Romulus and thus largely reports the story as it developed when Rome was a city-state. In contrast, Virgil was commissioned to create an epic worthy of the Roman Empire, which accounts for his development of Aeneas as a cosmopolitan and complex hero.

One of the most notable features of Plutarch's account is the extent to which he offers alternate details. These alternate details, in fact, make up the bulk of the story. Plutarch highlights the importance of these other possible accounts from the first sentence, stating, "From whom, and for what reason, the city of Rome, a name so great in glory, and famous in the mouths of all men, was so first called, authors do not agree" (15). He proceeds to outline the various alternate claims about the founding of Rome, including the theory that the Pelasgians were the city's founders, the story of a Trojan matron named Roma who incited other women to burn their ships and thus forced the Trojans to stay and found a new city, and other stories. He continues this practice throughout the biography, even in sections of the story he views as valid. For example, he notes that some people call the twins' mother Ilia, others Rhea, and still others Silvia. He offers two accounts of the twins' paternity, mentioning both the god Mars and Amulius himself as possible fathers. Faustulus is said to be the name of the servant who places the infant twins in the trough, the one who raises them, or possibly both. When discussing how the wolf suckles the twins, Plutarch states that *lupa*, the Latin word for "wolf," was also used to refer to prostitutes, leading some chroniclers to suggest that Faustulus's wife, Larentia, known to be a woman of ill repute, is the real nurse who suckled Romulus and Remus. He even introduces doubt about the deaths of Remus and eventually Romulus himself, stating that either Romulus or Celer kills Remus and that Romulus is either chopped to bits by the senators or deified. At every turn, Plutarch reminds his readers of the tenuous nature of key facts of his biography.

At the same time, however, Plutarch presents the story as authoritative. He introduces his account as the one with the most "vouchers" and names the historians Diocles of Peparethus and Fabius Pictor as his sources (16). He provides dates, albeit without years: Romulus founds his city on April 21 and disappears on July 28 in the thirty-seventh year of Rome's existence. Plutarch claims that the abduction of the Sabine women occurred four months after the city's founding and notes that some say only thirty women were taken, while others claim as many as seven hundred. He also clearly favors certain accounts; reporting that certain historians believe that Romulus carried out the abduction simply because he was warlike and because oracles had proclaimed Rome's destiny for war, he writes that "this is not very probable," instead favoring the idea that there were not enough women in the city (21). When he supports suspiciously dramatic details, such as the twins' overthrow of Amulius, he quells the reader's doubt by saying that events such as these "would not wholly be disbelieved, if men would remember what a poet fortune sometimes shows herself" (18). On the other hand, he rejects Romulus's deification as a "fable" (28). Finally, also bolstering the text's historical status is the inclusion of many Roman institutions that actually existed, such as the *patres conscripti*, the Roman senate.

These competing tendencies encourage readers to view Plutarch's narrative as a valid history that is careful to acknowledge all accounts but that also ranks them authoritatively. The narrative prompts modern readers to want to know more about the "actual" role of the various players in the founding of Rome, to ascribe a meaning somehow more "truthful" than mere metaphor or symbolism. Thus, as T. J. Cornell documents in the essay "Aeneas and the Twins: The Development of the Roman Foundation Legend," some scholars have focused their attention on the validity of the story itself, asking crucial questions regarding the age of the story, the meaning of the myth's more unsavory details, and the story's relation to the apparently incompatible story of Aeneas as one of the progenitors of Rome.

The Romulus and Remus story shares many features with other hero myths. As J. N. Bremmer and N. M. Horsfall report in *Roman Myth and Mythography*, myths from around the world frequently include a principal hero who is of illegitimate parentage, with a mother whose father is a native prince. The hero's father is either a god or stranger, and the exposure of the hero's identity follows an omen. The hero is suckled by animals and later raised by a childless shepherd. After serving abroad, the hero returns triumphantly to overthrow an oppressive sovereign, liberate his mother, found a city, and experience an extraordinary death. The murder of a younger brother appears in some of these stories as well. Stories similar to the Romulus and Remus myth include the Greek myth of Perseus, whose mother, Danaë, is confined by her father, Acrisius (Akrisios), after an oracle predicts that his grandson will kill him. Nonetheless, Zeus takes the shape of a shower of gold and impregnates Danaë. When Acrisius discovers this, he casts mother and son out to sea, but they survive, and Perseus is raised by a fisherman. In some accounts, Perseus later fulfills the oracle's prophesy by accidentally killing his grandfather. Another well-known story of a child cast off into the water is the biblical story of Moses, who as an infant is sent in a basket down the Nile after the Egyptian pharaoh orders all male Israelite infants to be killed. Rough parallels to the motif of nursing animals are found in Asian myths, some of which claim that various groups "derive their origin from a wolf as ancestor" (Bremmer and Horsfall 31). The theme of the noble youth raised by shepherds is widespread in Greek myths such as the story of Paris. These parallels reveal that the Romulus and Remus story conforms to a model that to some degree is cross-cultural.

Yet the story's many unpalatable features have made it difficult for some readers to accept Romulus as a heroic figure at all, let alone as the founder of Rome. The rape of Rhea Silvia, the presentation of a predator as a nurse, and the depiction of foster mother Larentia as a prostitute have all troubled readers. Cornell reports that some versions depict Romulus and Remus as cattle bandits and their followers as "an unsavory rabble of vagabonds, murderers and thieves" (8). Romulus possibly cheats in the divination contest intended to resolve the dispute over the future city's location and then promptly kills Remus, whose role and meaning in the story have not been conclusively explained. As founder, Romulus plans and executes the rape of the Sabine women and, at least according to some accounts, is ultimately murdered by the senators. These details combine to present an impressively unsympathetic founding father. Ancient societies were aware of this problem, and as Cornell notes, enemies and other detractors used the story to critique Roman power. Moreover, scholars have noted that the story as a whole seems incompatible with the other foundation myth of Rome, which celebrates Aeneas its hero. For this reason, some historians have argued that the Romulus myth was actually fabricated as anti-Roman propaganda relatively late. However, Cornell, Bremmer, and Horsfall successfully refute this thesis based on the story's appearance in the third century BCE at the latest and the Romans' perpetuation of the myth.

Radically different from the Romulus and Remus myth, Virgil's *Aeneid* invites comparison with the story of the twin brothers. The nearly ten-thousand-line poem presents Aeneas not as the founder of Rome but nonetheless as the chief hero of the city's origin story. The story recounts Aeneas's escape from the city of Troy after its sacking by Greek forces and his arduous wanderings through the Mediterranean, which eventually lead him to Latium, where he fights and wins a brutal war. The poem is often divided into two parts; books 1 through 6 recount the hero's escape from Troy and his wanderings at sea, while books 7 through 12 focus on the battle once Aeneas and his companions arrive in Italy.

The story opens with Aeneas and his followers sailing toward Italy, but the goddess Juno, inimical to the Trojans, convinces the wind god Aeolus to generate a storm to wipe out the Trojan fleet. Neptune, god of the sea, intervenes just in time, and Aeneas's few remaining ships arrive in Carthage, on the coast of Africa. There, Aeneas meets the queen, Dido, and recounts the fall of Troy and the events preceding his arrival in Carthage.

After the Greek warrior Ulysses devises the scheme of filling a giant wooden horse with Greek warriors, thus giving the Greeks the ability to enter Troy undetected, Aeneas wakes to find the city burning and under attack. He initially fights but soon realizes the Trojans are doomed. Rescuing his son and father but not his wife, Creusa, whose ghost delivers a moving farewell speech, Aeneas and his followers escape on a fleet of ships. Book 3 recounts their adventures as they sail the seas and meet Trojan survivors and fantastic creatures such as the Harpies and the Cyclopes. Aeneas completes his narrative, and the story returns to the present in Carthage in book 4. Venus causes Dido to fall in love with

MYTH INTO ART

The bronze sculpture known as the Capitoline Wolf is one of the most famous and controversial Roman sculptures. Housed in Rome in the Capitoline Museums, the large sculpture is 75 centimeters (about 30 inches) in height and 114 centimeters (about 45 inches) in length and is a representation of the mythological she-wolf nursing the twins. The lean wolf stands alert on four legs with her ears raised and head turned to gaze directly at the viewer. Romulus and Remus are depicted as healthy infants feeding from the wolf's full udders. They are sculpted in a very different style from the wolf, with round bodies and hands upraised as they nurse.

The sculpture is well known as a representation of the Romulus and Remus myth, but it is also a perfect symbol of the historical and interpretive puzzles surrounding the myth itself. Rather than shed light on some of the mysteries regarding Rome's most important legend, the sculpture serves as another problematic piece of the puzzle. For centuries, scholars believed that the wolf was an ancient Etruscan piece dating to the fifth century BCE and that the nursing twins had been added by Antonio Pollaiolo in the fifteenth century. In the early twenty-first century, however, new dating methods indicated that the sculpture was actually created in the thirteenth century CE, a suggestion that had also been made by several nineteenth-century scholars but largely ignored.

Aeneas, and the ever-scheming Juno negotiates with Venus to join the queen and the hero in marriage, but Jupiter sends Mercury to remind Aeneas of his duty to lead his people to Latium. When Aeneas departs, Dido tragically commits suicide in one of the most famous episodes in Western literature.

Aeneas and his followers next arrive in Sicily, where they hold games to commemorate the death of Aeneas's father, Anchises. During the games, Juno incites the weary Trojan women to set their ships aflame, but Jupiter quells the blaze with a rainstorm. In book 6, the sibyl, priestess of Apollo, accompanies Aeneas to the underworld, where the spirit of Anchises delivers a lengthy prophecy of his son's destiny in Italy. The remainder of the poem focuses on Aeneas's arrival in Latium and the lengthy war that results from his engagement to Lavinia, the daughter of King Latinus. Turnus, king of the Rutulians, also wishes to marry Lavinia and is thus Aeneas's chief opponent. Juno incites war in various ways, even sending one of the Furies to afflict the people. Aeneas allies himself with King Evander of the Arcadians, and numerous battles between the two forces ensue. The poem ends with a single combat between Aeneas and Turnus, whom Aeneas ruthlessly stabs after he sees his enemy wearing the belt of Pallas, the slain son of King Evander.

It is interesting to consider Virgil's reasons for choosing Aeneas rather than Romulus as his epic's protagonist, given the latter's role as founder of Rome. To explore this question, one must first review the stories' chronology. Most scholars believe that the legend of the twins existed by the early third century BCE, but Bremmer and Horsfall argue for an even earlier date, suggesting that the story originated early in the sixth century BCE. Aeneas appears as a brave warrior in *The Iliad*, the first of two epics attributed to the Greek poet Homer and likely written in the eighth century BCE. Cornell states that by the fifth century BCE, Greek writers had linked Aeneas to Rome, and archaeological evidence from the ancient Etruscan civilization reveals objects that connect Aeneas with Italy. Thus, the Aeneas legend and that of the twins existed in Italy quite early and were eventually stitched together in an attempt to create continuity. Neither story was used to replace the other, in part because Aeneas could not logically be the direct founder of Rome; Troy is believed to have burned in approximately 1200 BCE, but Rome was not founded until 753 BCE. Thus, Plutarch and other writers identify Aeneas as an ancestor of Romulus and Remus. Likewise, Romulus and Remus are mentioned several times in the *Aeneid*. In book 1, Jupiter reassures Venus that Aeneas is destined to reach Italy, where Rhea Silvia (called Ilia in the poem) will become pregnant by Mars and bear twin boys. Jupiter continues,

> Afterward, happy in the tawny pelt
> his nurse, the she-wolf, wears, young Romulus
> will take the leadership, build walls of Mars,
> and call by his own name his people Romans.
> (1.373–76)

In this speech, Jupiter also mentions Romulus and Remus as future lawgivers of Rome. Later, when Aeneas encounters the spirit of his father in the underworld, Anchises points to Romulus as a future soul already marked for greatness, proclaiming that "under his auspices / illustrious Rome will bound her power with earth, / her spirit with Olympus" (6.1047–49). Romulus and Remus are also mentioned in book 8 when the shield that Vulcan forges for Aeneas is described. Here, the twins appear with the wolf on the shield as part of a prophetic narrative outlining Rome's future glory. The twins are thus celebrated as noble leaders in all of these references, which avoid or change the unflattering details of earlier accounts, such as Remus's murder.

Despite this celebration, Virgil chose Aeneas as his hero, likely for several reasons. Virgil was commissioned to write the *Aeneid* by the Roman emperor Augustus and worked on the poem between 29 and 19 BCE, at the height of Rome's imperial power. In commissioning the *Aeneid*, Augustus sought the composition of a poem celebrating Rome as a world empire. To create such a work, Virgil needed a single hero, not twin brothers, and a far more cosmopolitan and virtuous figure than Romulus. In addition to being a world traveler, Aeneas, unlike Romulus, embodies the Roman virtue of *pietas*, or duty. Aeneas is also an appropriate choice because he is rooted in the Greek epic tradition as a warrior who survives the Greeks' sacking of Troy. Virgil needed to match the achievements of Greek epic poetry, which greatly overshadowed Roman efforts. Thus, it made sense for him to choose as a national hero someone who could be viewed as a credible counterpart to the likes of Achilles, Odysseus, and other Greek heroes. Moreover, Aeneas fits the bill because he is the son of Venus, the favorite goddess of both Julius Caesar and Augustus. Bremmer and Horsfall note that Caesar even proclaimed himself a descendant of Venus through his aunt Julia. Yet because the gap in dates prevents Aeneas from being the actual founder of Rome, Virgil elevates his story brilliantly by creating a double perspective that highlights Aeneas's ancient *pietas* through the glorious lens of the current empire. Thus, Virgil's characters repeatedly prophesy that Aeneas will settle in Latium and that his descendants will one day rule the world. In this way, Virgil turns Romulus and Remus into supporting actors for Aeneas, who becomes the chief Roman hero.

Plutarch wrote after Virgil, but as a Greek historian writing a biography of Romulus, he records the legend as it has been passed down, with all its variations. In *Remus: A Roman Myth*, T. P. Wiseman argues that the myth of Romulus and Remus actually developed long before Plutarch and before the Roman Empire, originating when Rome was a city-state. He also argues that readers' discomfort with the unpleasant details of the Romulus and Remus story represent a postimperial interpretation; in other words, many origin myths include rape, murder, and other heinous crimes, but people especially object to such details in this myth because it appears to degrade what eventually became one of the most revered civilizations in history. Wiseman argues that the Romulus and Remus story developed locally and orally and was dramatized at festivals and that its details emerged and shifted based on the changing political and social realities of early Rome. Determining the nature of these historical realities is difficult. Cornell suggests that the twin brothers might have reflected the dual guardian gods of the state, but when the leadership structure emphasized a single ruler, Remus was no longer needed. Bremmer and Horsfall note that Rome's powerful rivals had a similar legend, suggesting that the Romans and their neighbors developed similar versions of the story to reflect contemporary military conflicts. Wiseman theorizes that Remus's death might be a veiled reference to a human sacrifice that occurred at the city's founding. Although it is impossible to know everything that the ancient Romans believed about their city's origins, the myth of Romulus and Remus reveals a great deal.

CROSS-CULTURAL INFLUENCE

Although the myth of Romulus and Remus is typically treated quite seriously in literature and drama, Irish poet T. F. Dillon Croker provides a lighter take on the story in his one-act burlesque *Romulus and Remus; or, Rome Was Not Built in a Day*, published in 1859. A burlesque is a musical stage performance that pokes fun at a serious subject—in this case, the founding of Rome. Quite popular in Victorian England, this type of burlesque does not include the risqué features that became associated with the genre in the twentieth century. Croker's treatment is typical of the English genre, and while his puns are deliberately bad, his absurd treatment is often hilarious. Culturally, his lampooning of one of the major Roman myths may reveal historical significance as a humorous critique of nineteenth-century British imperialism.

The story begins in the palace of King Amulius. As the curtain rises, soldiers and other courtiers sing lightheartedly about the cruelty of the king, a murderous tyrant who makes a practice of killing his subjects every day: "Every day as sure as the clock, / Somebody here had his head on the block" (9; sc. 1). Amulius enters and requests beer but then thinks better of it, declaring, "I beg to state / the state is in a state that's rather queer, / so I must not be found in one of beer" (10; sc. 1). As Amulius begins to address his master of the guard, the chorus bursts in and interrupts him, commanding him to sit. The chorus then sings boisterously as it supplies background information, introducing Numitor as Amulius's brother and Rhea Sylvia as Numitor's daughter.

The chorus punctuates its song with a quick refrain reminiscent of a show tune:

> Killing, thrilling,
> Singing, flinging,
> Drowning, crowning,
> Reigning, gaining,
> Nursing, cursing,
> Flying, spying,—
> In it there is some. . . . (11; sc. 1)

After the chorus falls silent, Amulius converses with his guard to confirm that his orders to kill Numitor's son and to make Rhea Sylvia a vestal virgin have been carried out. The guard confirms these deeds, but Amulius prefers that Rhea Sylvia be locked in a dungeon rather than a convent. When the guard reassures him that she is safely cloistered, Amulius suddenly calls her a martyr and suggests that she be rewarded with food.

The guard departs, and several citizens challenge Amulius to reconsider his cruel actions toward his relatives. He silences them until the guard rushes back to announce that Rhea Sylvia has given birth to twins. Amulius first refuses to believe him, but when the guard insists, Amulius in a rambling response first orders the twins drowned, then considers having them strangled, and finally reconsiders once again. He warns the guard not to be persuaded by Sylvia's objections and commands that she also be drowned. The guard begs Amulius to reconsider and forgive Rhea Sylvia, but he callously refuses: "Oh no, I sha'nt, so shye her in the river. / I never gainsay anything I order" (18; sc. 1). The guard leaves, and Amulius reports his dream that Rhea Sylvia had two sons who ended up fighting over the throne, but he rebukes his citizens when they express surprise. He grows indignant when the chorus questions his certainty that "affairs will go on swimmingly," reminding them that their job is to explain—"I act" (19; sc. 1). Declaring his fatigue, Amulius then departs for a nap.

The chorus reenters to explain Faustulus's discovery of the twins and the wolf nursing them, with much comic reference to the double entendre of *lupa* meaning both "wolf" and "prostitute." The scene shifts to show a wolf singing silly nursery rhymes to the twins. Faustulus enters in search of his sheep, singing "Little Bo Peep." He spies "Mrs. Wolf" nursing the twins and takes them from her as the animal growls (22; sc. 2). He departs with the infants after a brief song. Rhea Sylvia enters with two ruffians who plan to throw her in the river. She tries to dissuade them, even offering money, but they refuse in a series of comic songs, telling her that bribes will not work only to reveal that someone else has paid them more than she. After a further exchange of tunes between the ruffians and Rhea Sylvia, they drag her off, and the chorus appears to condemn the ruffians' lack of conscience. They close by announcing that scene 3 is ready to begin.

The next scene opens with Laurentia wondering why Faustulus has not returned home. He then enters, complaining that she has deliberately left him out in the rain with squalling infants. Grateful for the babies, she begs forgiveness for her pettiness. Faustulus asks for brandy as his wife makes dinner; she serves him beer, and after they eat, he tells her to care for the infants and goes to bed. The scene ends, and the chorus enters to announce that the twin boys have grown up, but their behavior leaves something to be desired, as "they've been trained up in ways they should not go" (35; sc. 3). Scene 4 begins with Romulus and Remus, who are portrayed as dandies, applauding peasants who dance for them. Romulus announces that they have overthrown Amulius with the quip, "As an impediment he did esteem us,— / We had the same esteem for him, eh, Remus?" (36; sc. 4). He declares that there is no place like Rome but then remembers that it does not yet exist. This leads into the brothers' disagreement about where to found the city. Romulus proposes they count vultures, and Remus agrees after annoying Romulus with his sarcasm. Romulus admits candidly in an aside that he intends to cheat, and they depart.

The chorus enters and orders the peasants to dance to prove that dancers in Rome equal those in Spain. The dancers obey until Romulus and Remus return, arguing about who saw more birds. They break into song, with Remus accusing his brother of drinking and Romulus commanding Remus to "march, march, march. / And help [him] to found / Here a city renowned" (40; sc. 4). They argue a bit more, and Romulus begins to lay bricks for the walls of his city, urging Remus to help him. Instead, Remus jumps over the wall and kicks some of the bricks over. Romulus threatens to strike his brother, and they argue again, with much wordplay on the Latin word *as*, which signifies a type of Roman coin but also sounds similar to "ass." Romulus strikes Remus several times as they continue to argue; he finally knocks Remus to the ground and laments his use of excessive force, stating, "What have I done? I only meant to mill him. / Alas, it strikes me that last stroke

may kill him" (43; sc. 4). He quickly gets over his fratricide, however, glibly saying, "No evil thought against you shall I cherish, / But you knock'd down the wall and so must perish" (43; sc. 4).

After Romulus throws the body of Remus into a ditch, Numitor enters, and Romulus announces that he has restored his grandfather to power. Romulus attempts to leave before his murder is discovered, but suddenly the spirit of Remus appears, declaring, "Never say die" (45). The spirit of Rhea Sylvia appears to announce that it is only right for her to appear at the end of a burlesque: "Not rearing you, yet I'll bring up the rear" (46; sc. 5). Romulus then begs any reporters who happen to be present not to write of his fratricide, but the chorus promptly tells him, "It is in history." Romulus retorts, "Then never mind" (46; sc. 5). The chorus and Romulus beg the audience to judge them leniently and not take offense; the performance concludes with Rhea Sylvia, Romulus, and Remus singing comic songs in succession.

Croker effectively creates comedy through diction, rhyming couplets, puns, and music. The colloquial diction creates an absurd incongruity between the ostensibly serious subject matter of the Roman twins and the characters' speech. When Amulius first appears in scene 1, he behaves ridiculously, asking for beer and addressing his people as "noisy rascals" (10). Similarly, when Laurentia delays in opening the door to Faustulus, he stands outside complaining, "Aint' she a long time opening the door!" (30; sc. 3). Rhyming couplets, pairs of lines that rhyme and have the same meter, are a standard feature of English burlesque and are used to great effect in Croker's burlesque. Most of the dialogue is made up of these couplets, such as when the chorus ironically asks, "Well, gentle critics, what is it you say, / Do not you think this is a heavy play?" (20; sc. 1). The couplets create a singsong effect, drawing attention to the characters' speech and underscoring their silly messages. Croker also frequently uses puns, many deliberately bad, such as when Romulus describes Remus: "An innate ass! Had he been less inflated, / He would not have been thus ass-ass-inated" (44; sc. 4). Such puns are another standard feature of the burlesque genre and make the tone not simply light but absurd. Finally, Croker's use of music is meant to be humorous, as characters regularly break into songs that were popular in Croker's day. This technique is somewhat problematic for the modern reader, to whom most of these songs are unknown. A few exceptions, such as the use of the still-familiar song "Little Bo Peep," convey Croker's intended effect.

Although humor is obviously the chief objective of this burlesque, the cultural significance of Croker, who was of Irish descent, lampooning a myth of imperialism is worth considering. Croker wrote when the British Empire was still strong, despite the loss of its American colonies late in the previous century, and controlled numerous colonies around the world. The English established a presence in Ireland in the twelfth century and seized and colonized territories there in the sixteenth, leading to a bitter struggle that lasted through the poet's time and into the twentieth and twenty-first centuries. For these historical reasons, it is possible to read Croker's parody of the Romulus and Remus myth (and thus implicitly the Roman Empire) as a veiled reference to the empire that oppressed Ireland. Supporting this possibility are Croker's direct references to England, such as when Amulius's guard tries to persuade the king to spare Rhea Sylvia. Amulius refuses, ordering the guard to throw her in the Tiber River, and states, "In Rome, to act like Romans is the rule, / And this is Rome, it is not Liverpool" (18; sc. 1). Here, Croker pokes fun at the English city Liverpool in a way that implies the inferiority of the city compared to Rome. Similarly, when the ruffians insist that they must cast Rhea Sylvia into the river, they jokingly reassure her by saying that at least the Tiber does not smell as bad as the Thames, a major river that flows through London: "Unlike the Thames, in one respect, 'tis well, / You'll find the tide is stronger than the smell" (27; sc. 2).

These jokes are intended chiefly as entertainment, but at the very least, they invite the audience to compare the British and Roman empires and suggest a veiled critique of Britain's domination. Given the long, troubled history between the English and the Irish, it is not hard to imagine that some in Croker's audience might have appreciated his burlesque of imperial power both Roman and Victorian.

Ashleigh Imus, PhD

BIBLIOGRAPHY

Bremmer, J. N., and N. M. Horsfall. *Roman Myth and Mythography*. London: Inst. of Classical Studies, 1987. Print.

Carandini, Andrea. *Rome: Day One*. Trans. Stephen Sartarelli. Princeton: Princeton UP, 2011. Print.

Cornell, T. J. "Aeneas and the Twins: The Development of the Roman Foundation Legend." *Proceedings of the Cambridge Philological Society* 21 (1975): 1–32. Print.

Croker, T. F. Dillon. *Romulus and Remus; or, Rome Was Not Built in a Day*. London, 1859. Print.

Plutarch. *The Lives of the Noble Grecians and Romans*. Trans. John Dryden. Chicago: Encyclopedia Britannica, 1952. Print.

Virgil. *The Aeneid*. Trans. Robert Fitzgerald. New York: Vintage, 1984. Print.

Wiseman, T. P. *Remus: A Roman Myth*. Cambridge: Cambridge UP, 1995. Print.

TRIAL AND QUEST

Gilgameš and Huwawa

Author: Traditional Sumerian
Time Period: 2499 BCE–1000 BCE
Country or Culture: Mesopotamia; Iraq
Genre: Myth

OVERVIEW

In 1853, the Assyrian archaeologist Hormuzd Rassam was conducting fieldwork at the site of the ancient city of Nimrud in an area now part of Iraq. It was in this excavation that Rassam found the first copies of *The Epic of Gilgamesh* (ca. 2000 BCE). Although Rassam could not decipher the tablet or place the myth, he immediately understood its potential importance. While twenty more years passed before a translation of the epic was published, scholars around the world soon came to recognize its significance. Although literally unheard of for thousands of years, *The Epic of Gilgamesh* was the oldest piece of surviving literature in the world, coming likewise from the oldest human civilization. Through the twentieth century, further fragments of the myth were discovered, and academics began to understand the development of a myth that was foundational to human culture.

One of the core stories of *The Epic of Gilgamesh* is the story of Gilgameš (Gilgamesh) and Huwawa. In this myth, Gilgameš is the warrior king of the city of Uruk (or Erech), a role he inherits from his father, a king, and his mother, a goddess. Gilgameš works to advance the city, building strong walls to protect it from outside invaders. When the story of Gilgameš and Huwawa begins, the king decides that he will travel into the distant cedar forests where the giant Huwawa lives, taking with him his constant companion and beloved ally, Enkidu, to complete the quest. The journey is inspired by Gilgameš's need to establish a legacy, knowing that his renown will last beyond his mortal death. It is also, however, a quest for the cedar resources of the forest, which were unavailable in the region of Uruk yet were valuable to the development and growth of the city. While

he and Enkidu eventually complete their quest, gathering the cedar and slaughtering Huwawa through a mixture of deception and brute strength, they are ultimately chastised by the god Enlil for not instead welcoming Huwawa into their civilization.

Gilgameš and Huwawa is an important story in both the development of the character of Gilgameš and in the study of Sumerian civilization. Gilgameš is a figure who constantly struggles with the reality of human mortality. While he will try to achieve immortality following the death of his beloved Enkidu later in the myth, at the point of the story of Gilgameš and Huwawa, he has accepted that death is inevitable. In response, the king turns to civilization and to community—to his reliance on Enkidu and to the ongoing culture of Uruk—to form a meaning and a legacy that can transcend death. Gilgameš never truly finds peace in his crisis of mortality, but the myth of Gilgameš and Huwawa affirms that human civilization offers some solace, even when the humans themselves struggle through their own flaws and failings.

SUMMARY

Gilgameš, the king of the Sumerian city of Uruk and a demigod, decides one day that he should head into the distant cedar mountains. The mountains are protected by a monstrous beast named Huwawa, but they also contain valuable lumber, which is difficult to obtain in the Mesopotamian region. Gilgameš knows that even though he cannot live beyond death, he can establish a legacy of fame by entering the cedar forest.

Gilgameš's companion and dear friend, Enkidu, agrees to travel with his master into these mountains, but he reminds Gilgameš that anything having to do with the cedar forest is the business of the sun god, Utu. Because of this, Gilgameš first makes a sacrifice of a young goat to Utu. The god responds, asking why Gilgameš would take on such a task when he is already a noble person. Gilgameš answers that even though he is

---

"Look, Enkidu, two people together will not perish! A grappling-pole does not sink! No one can cut through a three-ply cloth! Water cannot wash someone away from a wall! Fire in a reed house cannot be extinguished! You help me, and I will help you—what can anyone do against us then?"

—"Gilgameš and Huwawa"

---

the king of a city, he constantly sees there the death and disease that are inherent to humanity. He realizes that he too will one day die—that not even a human with a goddess as his mother can overcome death. However, he can travel into the mountains to establish his bravery and legend, and if he reaches a place beyond where his story will be remembered, he can establish there the glory of the gods instead.

Utu is moved by Gilgameš's plea, and in response, he gives Gilgameš seven warriors, all of whom have magical gifts and know the different routes of the earth. With these warriors to guide him, Gilgameš also heads to his city, where he demands that any man without a wife or a mother should join him on the quest. Quickly, fifty men volunteer their services as well. The small army assembled, Gilgameš travels with the guidance of Utu's warriors, passing through the valleys of the mountains. He crosses seven mountain ranges filled with cedar in this way before finally, after the seventh mountain range, coming across the cedar forest he seeks.

Gilgameš and his army begin to cut down the cedar forest, making piles out of the logs. Deep within the forest, hidden in his lair, Huwawa senses the presence of the men, and their actions make him tremble. As Huwawa's terrible aura reaches across the mountain, Gilgameš and his men all grow weary and finally collapse in sleep. As night approaches, Enkidu awakes and tries desperately to rouse anyone else. He sees the sun passing and knows that the protection of Utu will soon fade, and he feels the terrible presence of Huwawa. When at last Gilgameš wakes up, however, he scolds Enkidu for treating him

like a child who would return home frightened rather than complete his quest.

Enkidu and Gilgameš argue, with Enkidu insisting that Huwawa is a beast to be feared and Gilgameš insisting that if the two friends stay loyal in battle, they will succeed. Before they can conclude their argument, however, Huwawa appears before them, his eyes filled with the look of death. Gilgameš is so frightened he can barely move. Huwawa addresses him, declaring that Gilgameš is a noble and glorious person and that he should have nothing to fear. Gilgameš touches the ground at Huwawa's feet and lies, saying that he has come only to find where in the mountains Huwawa lives. He even offers his older sister to be Huwawa's wife. When Huwawa accepts this offer, he gives up a little bit of his terrible aura to Gilgameš, and Gilgameš's men begin to cut down the cedar again.

Gilgameš continues in this way, offering his little sister to be Huwawa's concubine and again receiving some of the monster's aura. He offers him many gifts, including the food of the gods, the mountains, and even precious gems. As Huwawa takes these gifts and slowly gives up his aura, the cedars are likewise cleared away. At last, Gilgameš walks up to Huwawa gently, pretending to offer the monster a kiss out of respect but instead attacking him at the last minute. Huwawa bears his teeth, but Gilgameš manages to conquer him, capturing the monster in a net. Huwawa begs mercy from Gilgameš and from Utu, and for a moment, Gilgameš's heart softens; he orders Enkidu to free Huwawa. Enkidu, however, insists this is a horrible idea, and when Huwawa argues with Enkidu as well, Enkidu quickly cuts the monster's throat, putting the head inside a bag.

Enkidu and Gilgameš take the head of Huwawa to Enlil, the god of the storm. Enlil, however, only scolds them, saying that Huwawa should have been treated with respect and dined with the king and his friends. In retaliation, Enlil uses his power to take the auras of Huwawa away from Gilgameš. He quickly divides those auras, giving them to the rivers, the forests, the lions, and other natural wonders and deities.

ANALYSIS

Ancient Mesopotamia, nestled between the Tigris and Euphrates Rivers, is generally believed to be the birthplace of Western civilization. It was home to some of the first large urban areas in human history (built around 5000 BCE) and seems to have been the first region in which writing and literature emerged. As such, the few pieces of Mesopotamian literature that survive into the modern day offer a unique glance into the history of humanity and the concerns, both philosophical and utilitarian, that drove early culture.

Of those surviving works of literature, *The Epic of Gilgamesh* is the most widely studied today, just as stories of Gilgameš seem to have been some of the most widely enjoyed in the ancient Mesopotamian world. The king of the great city of Uruk and the son of a mortal man and a goddess, Gilgameš was a legendary hero in the culture, with superhuman strength and desires. Despite his status as a demigod, however, Gilgameš was also a figure confronting some of the core questions of humanity, primary among them the meaning of life in the face of mortality. The question of mortality is particularly relevant considering that Mesopotamian culture, in a stark contrast to most cultures that followed, did not include belief in an afterlife or an undying soul. This conflict between inevitable death and the desire to live is brought to the forefront during the myth of Gilgameš and Huwawa. In it, Gilgameš, along with his beloved companion Enkidu, risks his own life by traveling into distant cedar forests to establish fame and renown, their legends theoretically living on even after they have died. While not an attempt to achieve true immortality (Gilgameš will somewhat foolishly take on this quest later in his life), the battle with Huwawa can be understood as an early attempt to sustain civilization and history, crafting meaning that transcends death even if individuals cannot do so.

The myth of Gilgameš and Huwawa begins not with Gilgameš alone deciding to conquer the monster, but rather with Gilgameš and Enkidu together, conspiring in their plan and offering support to each other. Although he is described in the text as Gilgameš's slave, Enkidu is, by this point in the mythology of Gilgameš, the companion, soul mate, and constant ally of the warrior king. At the start of his life, Enkidu is a wild man, born out of the clay of the earth and living an uncivilized life. It is only through Gilgameš that Enkidu is brought into the civilized world, and even then, he often demonstrates shadows of his wilder, uncivilized past. At the same time, Gilgameš is as dependent upon Enkidu as Enkidu is upon him; when the two first meet, Gilgameš is a violent and oppressive ruler, and Enkidu championls the citizens of Uruk, teaching Gilgameš to treat his people with respect and dignity. Although the two meet in physical battle, they almost immediately become inseparable friends, each reliant on the other to keep them

grounded in the civilization and culture of Uruk. While Enkidu is taught by Gilgameš to suppress his wild nature and behave in a respectable way, Gilgameš is taught by Enkidu that he should not rise above his people but live respectfully among them. It is with these histories behind them that the two heroes decide to seek out the cedar forest, hoping to establish their own legacy beyond the walls of Uruk.

The destination of the cedar forest is also an important component of the meaning of their quest. While Gilgameš declares simply that he hopes to "establish my renown there" (line 4), the forest represents more than an unexplored and dangerous landscape in which he can prove his might. The region of Mesopotamia was a fertile land with many opportunities for irrigation and agriculture; however, it had limited lumber resources. The cedar forests nearby, although often at a great distance from early cities such as Uruk, were home to rich lumber resources, valuable to the growth and sustainability of these urban areas. In establishing his renown in the forest, then, Gilgameš is also establishing the continuation and growth of his civilization. This is highlighted by the fact that early in the mythology of Gilgameš, he is celebrated for building a cedar wall around the city, an accomplishment that wins him the respect and support of the population he protects. That this forest is also at a remove from that civilization and guarded by Huwawa only amplifies this meaning, with Gilgameš literally marching into the frightening and unknown wilderness as a champion of human culture.

When Gilgameš seeks the blessing of the sun god, Utu, for his quest, the link between the expansion of civilization and the struggle against mortality is made explicit. When Utu asks Gilgameš why he would ever want to battle Huwawa, Gilgameš describes the constant death seen in the city of Uruk. Gilgameš is aware that he cannot overcome this death and that he too will one day join the corpses floating in the river. However, what he can do is to establish his legend in the mountains, ensuring that people will speak of him and his accomplishments long after he is gone. It is important that Gilgameš is presented as a figure who accepts the inevitability of death but who still struggles with the meaning of that mortality. While there is no perfect solution, civilization and the newly arisen culture of Uruk seem to offer the best compromise for Gilgameš: his mortal body cannot live forever, but his accomplishments and the legends of his strength can continue as long as the Sumerian civilization is able to pass along their stories.

Considering that their quest is in essence a journey to champion their city, it is fitting that Gilgameš and Enkidu do not travel into the mountain alone, but with a small army gathered from Uruk. This army is carefully selected to include only single men or pairs of two men together, while men who have either wives or mothers to support are excused from the quest. This selection process shows both social stratification and the rising importance of the military in the culture of Uruk. In addition to being one of the largest cities in the entire world at the time, Uruk was also a city with a developing military located in a region under near-constant invasion. It was therefore necessary that the job of defending the city be balanced with the other tasks necessary to maintain the thriving Sumerian culture protected within its walls. That Gilgameš selects his army with careful attention to the other needs of the citizens (such as the necessity placed on men to provide for and protect their mothers, wives, and children) shows that he has learned the lesson Enkidu urged upon him in the past. He has it within his power to gather an army bigger than any other on earth, yet he limits it in size based on an obligation to treat his people with dignity and kindness.

With all the resources of the city properly gathered, Gilgameš and Enkidu travel into the wilderness in order to challenge Huwawa and fetch the cedar lumber. The myth clearly defines the extreme nature of the journey, stressing through repetition that the warriors must cross seven mountain ranges in order to reach their destination, a place Gilgameš recognizes by instinct. The extremity of the quest is typical of any heroic epic, a genre that thrives on thrilling adventure and superhuman strength. In the case of Gilgameš and Huwawa, however, it serves to further clarify the relationship of Gilgameš and Enkidu to one another. With a goddess as his mother, Gilgameš can easily be seen as greater than humanity, as indeed kings were often considered in Mesopotamian culture. However, his companion Enkidu is a mortal entirely of the earth (literally made from clay), as are the fifty soldiers who accompany them. While it might not be surprising, then, that Gilgameš can travel such great distances, the presence of Enkidu and the citizens of Uruk anchor his strength, showing that all of Uruk has these abilities. This journey further unites Gilgameš and Enkidu, making them equals in strength just as the cause of Sumerian civilization made them cultural allies.

A reliance on civilization and the bonds of friendship is certainly the overarching moral for the warriors, but that does not mean that the differences of their origins are wiped away. Likewise, the myth is not a narrative in which Gilgameš is already a flawless and heroic leader, but one in which he learns to become a just king and soldier. It is because of this that Gilgameš and Enkidu again come into conflict with one another as the monster Huwawa finally approaches them. Having spent the day cutting down the cedar forests, both the leaders and their men fall asleep in exhaustion. Yet Enkidu, as someone who came from the wilderness, is intuitively aware of the dangers there. As night sets in, he tries desperately to wake Gilgameš and to convince him that the army must return to safety. Gilgameš, however, has become too obsessed with his own mission and too enamored with the strength of his army to heed Enkidu's warning. For Gilgameš, to return to the city without having finished his quest would be a devastating failure; as he says, it would be "as if I were slumbering still on the lap of my own mother Ninsumun" (line 91). Gilgameš is not here concerned with whether he actually lives, but rather with whether his legacy is secured. To die in battle would ensure that his renown is established and that his name will live on, while returning to the city (even if it were the only way to ensure survival) would instead result in the end of his legend. As someone with a greater connection to his own mortality and earthly nature, Enkidu can see beyond the egotistical goals of the battle, but as a subservient to Gilgameš, he cannot prevent his master from entering into battle.

Gilgameš appears fully and sincerely committed to the ideals of his civilization, even if that commitment comes across as dangerously hubristic. He even stresses this logic in his argument with Enkidu, insisting that "two people together will not perish!" (line 107). However, when Huwawa actually approaches the warriors, Gilgameš's confidence and his moral grounding waver. He trembles before the giant, a symbol of the untamed nature that exists outside of humanity, and despite all of his grandstanding, he does not immediately move into battle. Instead, while Huwawa shows respect to Gilgameš, saying that his mother and his nurses raised him well, Gilgameš does not show the same respect to Huwawa. Rather, he immediately begins to lie, saying that he has only come to the forest in order to learn where the monster lives. Further, he swears on his mother and father (a goddess and a former king) and offers up his sisters to be a wife and a concubine to Huwawa. These are on the surface signs of great respect and of civilization, with Gilgameš

HISTORICAL CONTEXT

While relatively little is known today of the history of the Sumerian city of Uruk, it thrived as one of the largest and most powerful urban centers in the world for almost two millennia. It was located in modern-day Iraq. The combination of waterways and farmable land allowed people to settle there, so that during the fourth millennium BCE (known as the Uruk period), the Sumerian civilization first emerged. Like most Sumerian cities, Uruk was built when three distinct social classes came together: agricultural workers who had developed irrigation, sheep and goat herders, and people who fished in the nearby marshes. As these people settled in essentially the same area, they constructed two large temples to a powerful god and goddess, further anchoring the city and establishing two "neighborhoods" within it. From here, over hundreds of years, the people of the cities developed workshops, a canal system, a defensive wall, and other advancements that solidified their role as a stronghold of Sumerian civilization.

The development of urban areas is inseparable from the development of language and the arts, with the stratification of labor allowing people greater amounts of leisure time in which to explore aesthetics, philosophy, and entertainment. When the Sumerian language developed, however, it was not primarily used to craft poetry or song; it was put to practical ends, recording debts and other economic transactions. While lists of the gods and of former, often mythological kings were common, copies of Sumerian literature and mythology were rare and came to modern readers primarily through the Akkadian Empire, which eventually bordered and shared culture with Sumer. These records, scant as they might seem, still stand as evidence of the first human civilization, the approximately eighty thousand people of Uruk who initiated the start of recorded history.

even declaring, "I want to become your kinsman!" (144). However, because Gilgameš is actually lying to Huwawa, the signs are stripped of their meaning and become instead cheap tricks, disrespectful for the mighty king to use.

The process by which Gilgameš defeats Huwawa in battle is a long game of deceit, with Gilgameš repeating his first oath ("by the life of my mother Ninsumun and of my father, holy Lugalbanda," line 148) and his last promise ("I want to become your kinsman," line 144) seven times. With each promise and each offer of a different gift, Huwawa is welcomed further into the civilization that Gilgameš represents; as such, the giant loses some of his terrible aura to the warrior. Much of Huwawa's power seems to come from his legend and the fear surrounding him, his connection to the untamed wilderness; when he is offered pacts and bargained with in a civilized manner, then, that power is effectively destroyed. While this is clever on Gilgameš's part, it does not reflect his original intentions, and the conniving oath breaker he becomes is hardly recognizable as compared to the heroic, mighty warrior he has been. This contrast is made even more obvious when Gilgameš finally confronts Huwawa physically after pretending to offer him a kiss.

Throughout the myth, Gilgameš is in a constant struggle between his role as a just and generous leader and his inclination to conquer and exploit. In facing Huwawa, who represents the greatest danger of the natural world, Gilgameš is at his weakest, and so it is unsurprising that he resorts to his less admirable qualities. This failure is more than just Gilgameš's failure; it is also a failure of the civilization he represents. Huwawa pleads for mercy not just from Gilgameš, but from Utu, the powerful god of the sun, declaring to the god that Gilgameš has made false promises to him in the name of the mountains that Utu protects. As Huwawa makes these pleas, Gilgameš is given the choice between offering the giant respect and ending his life, a choice that parallels the moment early in his rule when he learned to offer his own subjects mercy and protection rather than violent exploitation. This is a pivotal moment in the development of the myth—while the quest to establish a legacy had previously been centered on killing Huwawa, Gilgameš is now given an opportunity to establish his legacy through kindness and a peaceful relationship with the outside world.

Gilgameš does not, however, have the opportunity to actually make his decision, as Enkidu slaughters Huwawa in a willful moment, placing the giant's head in a leather bag. Just as Gilgameš has resorted to his lesser nature when confronting Huwawa, Enkidu regresses to his uncivilized ways, acting out of impulsive violence. This final moment of the quest highlights the constant back-and-forth that occurs between the two warriors and friends, a relationship in which each challenges the other to become more civilized or more kind despite the fact that they constantly run the risk of regressing to their baser qualities. Importantly, however, while the death of Huwawa represents something of a failure, Gilgameš and Enkidu have in fact completed their original quest. Gilgameš has displayed tactics seemingly beneath a king and Enkidu has lashed out with forbidden violence, but together the two succeed in slaughtering the giant of the cedar forest. Their legacy ultimately is established, the cedar secured for the city of Uruk, and the value of civilization affirmed. Despite this glory, however, the warriors and rulers of the civilization remain flawed, failing even as they strive for nobler purposes.

The full explanation of Gilgameš's failure does not become explicit until he and Enkidu bring the head of Huwawa to the god Enlil, the god of the wind and one of the most powerful deities in Sumerian mythology. Enlil was also the primary god worshipped in the temples of Nippur, another early urban center associated with political and cultural power. When Gilgameš and Enkidu drop the head of Huwawa in front of Enlil, they do not receive praise but are scolded. Enlil states that Huwawa "should have eaten the bread that you eat, and should have drunk the water that you drink" (line 190). Their failure is not that they traveled to the cedar forest and sought Huwawa but that, once there, they treat him with violence instead of welcoming him as a friend into their civilization. This final condemnation of Enkidu and Gilgameš is a surprising twist from what precedes it; the majority of the myth is given over to celebrating the might of the warriors. However, as is always the case with Gilgameš, brute strength is not enough to secure his, or his people's, legacy. The myth of Gilgameš and Huwawa is a myth in which individuals fail and meet their mortal deaths while those who come together in community succeed, crafting legacies and legends that will transcend their physical death. It is fitting, then, that the myth does not end by celebrating the force of the military or the sheer strength of one warrior. Instead, it offers an ambiguous lesson, with the seemingly impossible quest completed through the interdependence of Gilgameš and his people, but also with a denunciation

from one of the most powerful gods. The power of civilization is affirmed; it is now up to the people of that civilization to live up to their own ideals and to show respect for the world that sustains them.

CROSS-CULTURAL INFLUENCE

The history of *The Epic of Gilgamesh* is markedly different from most other surviving ancient myths in one important way: while the majority of myths were actively preserved—enduring for centuries through both their retellings and translations into new languages—the myths of Gilgameš were instead "lost" somewhere around the beginning of Christianity. Of course, this loss followed many thousands of years during which the myths were told and retold, going through the process of translation and inscription necessary to maintain literary traditions. However, the interest in Gilgameš eventually faded, and the myth seems to have never been translated into Greek or Latin. Instead, it survived on lost tablets in an ancient language and through its influence on later works of literature—primary among them the Bible, the eighth-century BCE *Odyssey*, and the fifteenth-century CE *Arabian Nights*. For thousands of years, however, the actual story of Gilgameš remained essentially unread.

All of this changed in conjunction with a rise in archaeological research during the nineteenth century. The excavation of ancient palaces in Iraq uncovered some fragmented versions of the myth, while linguists studying the ancient Akkadian language slowly began to translate previously indecipherable tablets of literature. At first, these tablets were considered lost accounts of biblical events, and early scholarship was unable to link together anything resembling the full Gilgameš story. However, by the end of the nineteenth century, large sections of the myth had been pieced together through a massive collective effort. What followed was a rush of academic and popular debate, often focusing on the implications of the text as a piece of lost Christian literature but increasingly approaching it for what it was: a pre-Christian epic that seems to have had a massive influence on the ancient world and the development of human culture.

This history has a direct influence on the way the story of Gilgameš has been interpreted in modern times. Whereas most ancient texts come to modern readers through centuries of close study and with the heavy influence of Western culture and philosophy, *The Epic of Gilgamesh* manages to avoid that fate to a large degree (even as the narrative was nestled at the very start of

Western civilization). As such, it was appealing to many writers and philosophers who were interested in examining human consciousness outside of the context of ancient civilization and Judeo-Christian values. To these writers, the epic seemed fresh and unspoiled, a text that could be approached for what it was rather than for what it had come to represent. Especially by the middle of the twentieth century—a time when classic modes of thought had been upset by modernism and during which experimentation dominated many artistic and literary scenes—the myth of Gilgameš became a topic of widespread fascination.

The poet Charles Olson was one of the first modern American poets to take on Gilgameš as a large theme in his work. Olson founded a school of poetry called objectivism, a type of writing that seeks to emphasize the written word and literature as objects rather than as symbols to which meaning can be added. Olson believed that modern people had become so overwhelmed by the Western traditions of thought that they were unable to truly engage with the world or with their own relationship to nature. To remedy this, Olson sought to create a type of poetry that upset those literary traditions and taught people to see themselves as only objects in a world of other objects (other people, the nature world, and physical things). As can likely be surmised based on his rather heady philosophy, the poetry that Olson created is some of the most complex in English literature. However, its core drive to overturn the traditions of Western literature remains accessible, especially to audiences familiar with subject matter such as *The Epic of Gilgamesh* that Olson favored.

Olson explains his own draw to Gilgameš in his essay "The Gate and the Center," saying, "As I read it, it is an incredibly accurate myth of what happens to the best of men when they lose touch with the primordial and phallic energies and methodologies which, said this predecessor people of ours [the Sumerians], make it possible for man, that participant thing, to take up, straight, nature's, live nature's force" (*Collected Prose* 173). Olson reads the epic, then, as instructional, showing audiences how to stay connected to their true natures and to be more fully a part of the world. The Gilgameš he sees invading the cedar forest is one struggling to "live nature's force," the pressures of civilization affecting his behavior. The most explicit uses of Gilgameš come through the poems "Bigmans" and "Bigmans II," both of which combine the character of Gilgameš with the invented character of "Bigman," likely a stand-in for

Olson. These poems recount the myths of Gilgameš, but only in slight ways, focusing on the philosophy rather than the narrative of what occurs. An event such as the slaughter of Huwawa, for instance, is not in "Bigmans II" a dramatic story of traveling into the cedar wilderness, but rather the question of "the ways / to use what is called strength after its misuse" (lines 3–4). In this way, Olson sees the myth as showing an ancient man struggling with the same questions with which modern people struggle, the same questions that dominate Olson's own life. The reality that Gilgameš must encounter in the cedar forest—the sense that "no strength / is good enough which turns on self alone" (lines 89–90)—and the insistence on the importance of community speak to Olson across the expanse of time.

While Olson saw in the myth of Gilgameš a route to "true" humanity that modern culture has denied, his contemporary Louis Zukofsky uses the narrative to slightly different ends. Zukofsky, like Olson, was a midcentury writer interested in complex forms and grand ideas. Of all his work, his long poem *"A"* is widely considered the most important. *"A"* is an attempt to objectively explore the reality of the twentieth century. Rather than overthrowing or upending conventional ideas, however, he was focused on taking all of the divergent components of his life in the twentieth century and viewing them together in the same work, so that the emotional life he shared with his family was treated similarly to a Johann Sebastian Bach concert. Because twentieth-century scholarship was as concerned with relics from the past as with the future, it is natural that Gilgameš finds his way into Zukofsky's work.

Like Olson, Zukofsky chooses to recreate Gilgameš by summoning only the scant details of the myth. Gilgameš himself is called "Strongest" and the giant Huwawa called only "It." These core components are recreated in a spare, almost ungrammatical language, emphasizing further the ancient nature of the myth. Despite these stylistic changes, because Zukofsky focuses on the most telling and narratively impactful details of the myth, it is still easily recognizable. By approaching the cedar forest, Gilgameš hopes that the quest will "make me so and my / friend brothers everlasting together," while the actual journey involves "12 leagues of treemountain" that he must pass (Zukofsky 542; A-23). In this way, the battle between Gilgameš and Huwawa is largely stripped of its historical context and brought instead into the twentieth century. Zukofsky recognizes the myth for what it is, a historical narrative that extols the values of civilization and of loyalty in the face of inevitable death. Rather than attempting to put a firm political or philosophical meaning behind the story, he instead presents it as a historical fact that has miraculously made its way into the modern era, existing as one of countless influences on the poet's life. Because the myth is free of so many Western literary influences, it is able to function on its own basic qualities; thus, readers are more likely to take it on its own terms.

For both Zukofsky and Olson, the allure of Gilgameš was inextricably linked to the ancient nature of the epic. The fight with Huwawa and the journey into the cedar forest were unique events in Western mythology and literature, full of potential because they were untouched for so many centuries. Many other writers were likewise attracted to the story, but instead of preserving something like the original meaning, they were instead concerned with retelling the narrative as a vessel for their modern ideas. The modern retelling *Gilgamesh* (2002) by Derrek Hines, for instance, presents readers with a soldier in the army of Gilgameš, angered that he has to travel into the cedar forest and risk his own life only to extend the glory of his king. The Hines version not only takes a differing perspective from the original but also inserts a new political slant (the disconnect between the working soldier and the glory of the hierarchical civilization) that would have been unfamiliar to ancient audiences. Likewise, the Spanish writer José Ortega envisions Gilgameš within a fantasy landscape in his popular Khol series of novels. There, the core of the story of Huwawa is undercut when Gilgameš, disillusioned with his quests, returns to the cedar forest and takes on the role of protecting the trees that the giant had previously held. For Ortega, the great journeys and quests of mythology are not simply suspect (as with the ancient Gilgameš, scorned for his murder of Huwawa), but instead are unambiguous failures.

Ortega and Hines both tell of the fight between Huwawa and Gilgameš (as well as the remainder of the epic) in manners that are drastic departures from the ancient myth. Their departures, however, are in line with the general trajectory of mythology, a tradition in which narratives are told repeatedly because of the seemingly endless meaning inherent in them. It is for this reason that the legendary battle between Gilgameš and Huwawa has been used in philosophical debates, in attempts to celebrate environmentalism and green politics, and as a foundational text in exploring the history

of gay and lesbian narratives in Western culture. While the above examples are far-reaching and diverse, they do not come close to giving a full account of Gilgameš's increasingly popular role in modern culture. Indeed, just as the modern interpretations of Gilgameš expand, the number of ancient fragments also continue to grow, with more tablets and aged inscriptions uncovered with relative regularity. The result is that modern scholars and artists have an ever-changing Gilgameš available to them. This rediscovery continues the process that so interested Olson and Zukofsky, by which Gilgameš is brought into the modern world almost untouched by the legacy of Western culture. As more fragments are discovered, modern society's connection to the early historic past is made richer, and people are likewise given more opportunities to combine these ancient narratives with modern philosophies and cultural concerns. In this way, the simple story of Gilgameš confronting Huwawa in the cedar forests becomes a timeless narrative, as much a part of the past as it is of the continuing present.

T. Fleischmann, MFA

BIBLIOGRAPHY

Abusch, Tzvi. "The Development and Meaning of the Epic of Gilgamesh: An Interpretive Essay." *Journal of the American Oriental Society* 121.4 (2001): 614. Print.

Freeman, Philip. "Lessons from a Demigod." *Humanities* 33.4 (2012): 34. Print.

"Gilgameš and Huwawa (Version A)." *Electronic Text Corpus of Sumerian Literature*. Faculty of Oriental Studies, University of Oxford, 19 Dec. 2006. Web. 1 Apr. 2013.

Jarman, Mark. "When the Light Came On: The Epic 'Gilgamesh.'" *Hudson Review* 58.2 (2005): 329–34. Print.

Olson, Charles. *The Collected Poems of Charles Olson.* Berkeley: U of California P, 1987. Print.

---. *Collected Prose.* Ed. Donald Allen and Benjamin Friedlander. Berkeley: U of California P, 1997. Print.

Spatt, Hartley S. "The Gilgamesh Epic." *Masterplots.* 4th ed. Ipswich: Salem, 2011. Print.

Ziolkowski, Theodore. *Gilgamesh among Us: Modern Encounters with the Ancient Epic.* Ithaca: Cornell UP, 2011. Print.

Zukofsky, Louis. *"A."* New York: New Directions, 2011. Print.

The Girl Who Pretended to Be a Boy

Author: Andrew Lang
Time Period: 1501 CE–1700 CE
Country or Culture: Romania
Genre: Fairy Tale

OVERVIEW

"The Girl Who Pretended to Be a Boy" is an intriguing fairy tale about a girl who cross-dresses in order to embark on a heroic quest. With the help of her faithful magic horse, the brave Fet-Fruners dresses and acts like a man to achieve astonishing deeds. Part of a long tradition of stories with cross-dressing women, this extraordinary Romanian tale nonetheless raises questions about gender that readers have only begun to explore in recent decades.

The story appears in *The Violet Fairy Book*, one of twelve anthologies of fairy tales that Scottish scholar Andrew Lang published between 1889 and 1910. Lang's version of the story tells of a magician-emperor who is asked to send a son to serve a conquering ruler for ten years. Having three daughters and no sons, the magician-emperor sends his youngest daughter dressed as a man, because she alone succeeds at his tests of courage. With her father's magic horse, Fet-Fruners embarks on a long series of adventures. She first defeats a genie and wins her horse's younger sibling, named Sunlight, after outwitting the genie's mother, who suspects she is actually female. She then discovers a golden curl, which belongs to the princess Iliane, whom Fet-Fruners's new lord wishes to marry.

The rest of the story recounts how this new lord commands Fet-Fruners to fulfill various deeds. First, she must bring Iliane to the emperor, which entails defeating the mother of the genie. Then, Fet-Fruners must capture Iliane's stud of mares, which she achieves by killing the genie who had first captured Iliane. Finally, when Iliane demands that the emperor deliver a flask of holy water from a church in Jordan, the emperor again commands Fet-Fruners to make the journey. After she steals

the flask, Fet-Fruners actually becomes a man when a hermit curses her. When Fet-Fruners returns with the flask, the emperor names him his successor, but Iliane murders the emperor and declares her intention to marry Fet-Fruners, her true love. He agrees but first playfully affirms his masculine dominance over his betrothed.

Although stories of cross-dressing women are common in fairy tales and folklore, this tale departs from the typical model in numerous ways. The most intriguing difference is the story's conclusion in which the heroine Fet-Fruners is transformed into a man, only to declare his role as "the man who wears the pants." This ending seems to reestablish a traditional gendered hierarchy, but close analysis of gendered behavior throughout the story suggests that "The Girl Who Pretended to Be a Boy" actually challenges conventional gender norms to a remarkable degree. Specifically, attention to all the characters' actions, not merely those of Fet-Fruners, and to the story's broad historical context reveals how the tale subverts traditional norms of gendered identity and behavior in various ways. An analysis of gender roles thus offers two benefits because it reveals this story's subtle messages and offers a general interpretive model for texts that present conflicting evidence.

SUMMARY

The story begins by introducing an emperor who conquers many countries. Upon each victory, the emperor grants peace by asking that the leaders of the conquered nations send a son to serve their new master for ten years. A certain neighboring emperor is a great warrior, but when he eventually grows old and must submit to the more powerful ruler, he begins to despair because he has three daughters but no sons. Explaining the situation to his children, he laments that they know only how to 'spin, sew, and weave" (Lang 321), but his oldest daughter immediately volunteers to serve. He reluctantly agrees, so the daughter departs dressed like a knight. However, her father is also a magician and tests her by

"When her father saw her mounted and curveting about the court, he gave her much wise advice, as to how she was to behave like the young man she appeared to be, and also how to behave as the girl she really was. Then he gave her his blessing, and she touched her horse with the spur."

"The Girl Who Pretended to Be a Boy"

changing himself into a wolf that attacks her along the journey. Frightened, she quickly returns to the castle, where her father affirms his initial doubts about her ability. The second daughter then attempts the deed but fails the same test, prompting her father's reprimand.

Next, the youngest daughter obtains her father's permission to undertake the journey. Unlike her sisters, she chooses her father's old warhorse after the magic animal tells her how to rejuvenate him. With only "some boy's clothes" (Lang 325) and a small amount of food and money, the princess departs. When her horse informs her of her father's impending test, she courageously draws her sword when the animal appears, causing it to retreat. The father then tests the princess twice more, appearing to her as a lion, which the princess drives away, and then as a twelve-headed dragon. The princess fears the dragon, but her horse encourages her. After fighting the dragon for an hour, she finally cuts off one of its heads. At this, the dragon falls down and transforms back into her father, who lovingly congratulates his daughter on her victory. Reminding her to heed his counsel and that of her horse, he grants his blessing and departs.

The princess then goes forth and reaches the mountains, "which hold up the roof of the world" (Lang 329), where she finds two genies who have been fighting for two years. Each genie asks for the help of the princess, whom they call Fet-Fruners, and they offer a reward. Fet-Fruners's horse advises her to defend the genie offering the horse named Sunlight, who is his younger sibling, so the girl kills the opposing genie. She then follows the first genie to his house, where he plans to deliver the new horse. However, the genie's mother suspects that

Fet-Fruners is female and attempts to reveal the girl's true sex through three tests. The first two tests involve magic flowers, which will wither only when held by a man. Alerted by her horse, Fet-Fruners evades the first test and is clever enough to outwit the genie on the second test. She is asked in the third test to choose a piece of weaponry, which she does successfully. She then announces her departure, and although the genie's mother is not convinced that Fet-Fruners is male, she has no choice but to allow her to leave. Fet-Fruners departs with Sunlight after bidding farewell to her first magic horse, who asks to return home and advises her to obey his brother. A few miles later, Fet-Fruners discovers a golden curl lying on the road. When she consults Sunlight about whether to take it, the horse declares that she will repent either way, so she should take it. Fet-Fruners places the curl around her neck "for safety" (332).

Fet-Fruners finally arrives at the palace of her new lord and is welcomed by his pages. Quickly establishing herself as an excellent cook, Fet-Fruners earns the emperor's respect, but when she is discovered to possess the golden curl, the pages tell the emperor that Fet-Fruners knows the golden-haired Iliane, whom the emperor desires for his wife. The emperor commands Fet-Fruners to either fetch Iliane or lose her head. Sunlight informs Fet-Fruners that a genie has captured Iliane, who has declared that she will only marry him if he presents the "whole stud of mares which belong to her" (Lang 334). As instructed by Sunlight, Fet-Fruners asks the emperor for twenty ships loaded with precious cargo. She reaches the palace of Iliane and gains entrance by impressing the slaves and Iliane herself with a tiny pair of bejeweled golden slippers. In this way, Fet-Fruners persuades Iliane to board her ship, and they set sail as Iliane admires the treasures around her. When Iliane realizes that she has been tricked, she secretly rejoices but pretends to lament her fortune.

Arriving at the emperor's shores, Fet-Fruners and Iliane discover that the captor genie's mother has pursued them. They quickly mount Sunlight and flee as the horse advises them to throw a rock, brush, and finally Iliane's ring behind them to create obstacles for their pursuer. Defeating the genie's mother, Fet-Fruners delivers Iliane to the emperor, but because Iliane does not wish to marry him, she sets him the task of capturing her stud of mares. When the emperor commands Fet-Fruners to carry out this deed or lose her head, she initially complains that he has asked too much, but the emperor insists. Once again, Sunlight instructs Fet-Fruners on how to achieve the deed and declares, "The emperor's desires will be his undoing" (339). To capture the stud, Fet-Fruners defeats in a fierce sword fight the genie who had first captured Iliane, while Sunlight battles one of the resistant mares. They gather the stud and bring them to the emperor, who immediately commands Fet-Fruners to milk the mares so that he and Iliane may bathe in the milk, which will keep them young forever. Fet-Fruners laments yet another task assigned but suddenly finds heavy rain falling. The rain rises to the horses' knees and immediately turns to ice, immobilizing the animals and allowing Fet-Fruners to milk them easily.

Having evaded the emperor's marriage requests as long as possible, Iliane sets him a final task of obtaining a flask of holy water from a church beyond the river Jordan. Once again, the emperor assigns the deed to Fet-Fruners. With the help of Sunlight, Fet-Fruners steals the flask, which is guarded by nuns, but when the nuns hear Sunlight's hooves, a hermit curses the thief with a spell that causes its victim to change sex. The spell thus changes Fet-Fruners into a man. Delighted at his sex change, he presents the flask to the emperor, who declares Fet-Fruners as his successor. Iliane, however, is angered at the emperor's endangerment of Fet-Fruners. She invites the emperor to bathe with her in the mares' milk and then has one of the animals breathe burning air onto him, which immediately incinerates him. Iliane then declares that because Fet-Fruners is the true hero, he "and none other, shall be my husband" (344). Fet-Fruners agrees to marry her but concludes the story with a promise: "But know that in *our* house, it will be the cock who sings and not the hen!" (344).

ANALYSIS

"The Girl Who Pretended to Be a Boy" is an action-packed adventure story that focuses on gender roles and how they arise. If gender roles in this tale are understood as the extent to which characters conform to traditional norms of male and female behavior prescribed by the story itself, readers can see that Fet-Fruners's cross-dressing enacts a major theme. From the father who repeatedly affirms and yet challenges his daughters' feminine limits, to the genie's mother who suspects that Fet-Fruners is actually female, to the pages who note a "strange" attraction to their comrade, to the heroine's final sex change, the tale relentlessly underscores the characters' gender roles as a primary topic. On the one hand, Fet-Fruners's cross-dressing challenges conventional attitudes about what it means to be feminine

and masculine when she proves that all it takes to be perceived as a man is to look and to act like one. On the other hand, when she is actually transformed into a man with all-too-typical attitudes toward his feisty fiancée, the story seems to ultimately reinforce conventional gender beliefs. These conflicting messages leave readers in a quandary as to how to understand the story: does it present subversive or conventional ideas about gender? An analysis of all the characters' behavior and attention to the story's historical context reveal that "The Girl Who Pretended to Be a Boy" indeed challenges traditional gender codes to an unusual degree, given the story's purpose and time period.

To understand the importance of gender roles in this story, one must first contextualize the cultural uses of fairy tales in the periods before and during the early twentieth century when Lang published his version of this story. Literary fairy tales such as those collected by Lang developed first in Italian Renaissance story collections and later flourished in seventeenth-century France, when aristocratic writers, including many women, collected and rewrote fairy tales specifically to reflect the culture of the nobility and to instruct young people. Many of the tales were not intended for frivolous amusement but instead were meant to "provide models of behavior for the rearing and schooling of upper-class children" (Zipes 30). Thus, aristocratic writers gathered in salons to share stories that were designed in no small part to inculcate the cultural values specific to a certain class. Jack Zipes portrays the fairy tales in this context as created by writers who sincerely intended to nurture good human beings. However, he also states that the tales have a darker side, as they function "to indoctrinate children so that they will conform to dominant social standards that are not necessarily established in their behalf" (34).

A well-known example of a story intended to indoctrinate social standards is "Beauty and the Beast," which tells of a girl who accepts the marriage proposal of a beast after she gradually realizes her love for him despite his ugliness. When Beauty finally accepts the beast as her husband, she is rewarded for her virtue by the beast's transformation into a handsome prince. Zipes discusses how this tale developed in seventeenth-century France to become a story used to teach children to accept prescribed social and sexual identities—in other words, how to become civilized adults. For girls, becoming civilized according to this tale meant learning to be submissive, patient, and humble like Beauty, whereas

HISTORICAL CONTEXT

Andrew Lang (1844–1912) was a prolific Scottish man of letters who worked in many genres, including poetry, prose fiction, and literary criticism. He also produced scholarship in various fields, including classics, religion, mythology, and anthropology. Today, Lang is best known for his twelve-volume collection of fairy-tale books, which he published serially from 1889 to 1910. The first volume, *The Blue Fairy Book*, was highly successful and prompted eleven additional volumes, each of whose title includes a color. This proved to be a successful marketing strategy as subsequent volumes were immediately recognizable as part of Lang's series. When Lang published his first fairy-tale volume, there were few previous collections in England, a country with conservative attitudes toward folktales and fairy tales as compared with Germany and France, which by the late nineteenth century had long established folklore traditions as part of nationalistic movements.

Lang's fairy-tale collections are very different in scope from those of his European counterparts and from those he inspired in England, such as the collections of Joseph Jacobs. Because Lang did not collect his tales directly from oral storytellers, he did not limit his tales to English and Scottish sources. Instead, using printed and secondary sources as well as translators, he was the first to create a multicultural collection of tales from all over the world. In his editorial practices, however, Lang sometimes followed conventional practice. He was careful to point out that he was the collector, not the writer of the tales he presented. Yet like other folklore and fairy-tale anthologists, he edited certain stories and defended the practice based on his intended audience of children.

greater control over their lives, Zipes notes. Fairy tales were a safe venue for women to explore new and challenging ideas because such tales were considered by many to be harmless children's stories, despite their obviously didactic purpose. Therefore, some of these female authors began to write fairy tales that include subtly subversive elements, such as stronger female characters or powerful fairies, which changed the tone or quality of the stories' didacticism. Over time, this subversive tendency developed throughout Europe among both male and female writers to produce markedly different versions of similar story types. For example, the "Beauty and the Beast" plot began to appear in tales such as the Norwegian variant, "East o' the Sun and West o' the Moon," in which the female protagonist is vested with significantly greater agency and independence than in earlier renditions. It is this didactic, yet experimental tradition that Lang inherited when he published his twelve volumes of fairy tales; Zipes even classifies Lang as one of the nineteenth-century writers who "opposed the authoritarian tendencies of the civilization process and expanded the horizons of the fairy-tale discourse for children" (170).

Cross-dressing characters were a popular motif used to enlarge this discourse. Such characters, who extend back to ancient literature in the West, became popular in fairy tales because they allowed writers to explore and challenge gender norms in a genre that, instructive value notwithstanding, was accorded less importance than the literary classics that comprised the canon used in formal schooling for boys. In her study of cross-dressing in children's literature and film, Victoria Flanagan notes that whereas cross-dressing for adults in Western culture most often evokes the idea of a man dressing as a woman, cross-dressing in children's literature appears most commonly as female characters dressing as males. According to Flanagan, this female-to-male pattern dominates in children's literature because the need for girls to cross-dress arises from repressive social contexts in the stories that limit

boys were to imitate the beast's self-control, rationality, and perseverance. The story's primary social message is that girls can only become civilized by humbly submitting to a male-dominated marriage, which was in fact a social requirement for most women. For boys, the story implies that they can become real human beings only when they tame disorderly female forces that represent a threat to male power. This and other fairy tales thus emerged to form a didactic genre for children throughout Europe, and by the nineteenth century, such stories were available to the lower classes as well.

However, in addition to the instructive and socializing functions of fairy tales, a competing tendency emerged from some female authors. Seventeenth- and eighteenth-century French literary fairy tales were often written by educated women, many of whom desired girls' freedom and opportunities. When girls disguise themselves as males in these settings, they gain access to experiences and liberties previously denied to them. The stories of cross-dressing, in turn, serve to question traditional gender categories, and they even define gender as a performance, not a natural or biologically determined trait (Flanagan 26). Fet-Fruners as a cross-dressing female thus represents, to a remarkable degree, a character type that partially stems from the history and status of such fairy tales as a children's genre informed by women.

"The Girl Who Pretended to Be a Boy" does not simply challenge traditional gender roles, however. Instead, the tale seems to relentlessly subvert and yet reinforce traditional ideas of femininity. Melanie Aron notes that Fet-Fruners's father embodies the story's ambivalent attitude towards women as he both encourages his two elder daughters and gloats over their failures. He initially circumscribes their learning to the realms of sewing and weaving, but then he readily allows each daughter to dress as a man and attempt the dangerous journey. He offers the first daughter extensive advice on how to appear as a man while maintaining her true feminine nature, only to turn himself into a savage wolf to test the bravery that he apparently does not quite believe that she possesses. When she fails the test and returns to the palace, he tells her, "Did I not tell you, my child, that flies do not make honey?" (Lang 323). He responds similarly when the second daughter also fails to stand up to the wolf. The father then tests Fet-Fruners not once but three times when he appears first as the wolf, then as a lion, and finally as a twelve-headed dragon. Only when she cuts off one of the dragon's heads does he return to human form and praise her for being "as brave as the bravest, and as wise as the wisest" (329), granting his blessing for the journey.

In the same scene, however, the father tells Fet-Fruners that she has "chosen the right horse, for without his help you would have returned with a bent head and downcast eyes" (Lang 329). This statement raises the question of how much Fet-Fruners's success lies in her own abilities as opposed to those of her two magic horses. The horses, first her father's warhorse and then Sunlight, advise and aid the princess at nearly every turn of events. The first horse warns her of her father's disguises, tells her which genie to defend so that she can win Sunlight, and informs her of the traps laid by the genie's mother who perceives Fet-Fruners's true sex. Sunlight then advises Fet-Fruners to take the golden curl,

provides crucial information on how to capture Iliane, offers the three magic objects that Fet-Fruners uses to defeat the second genie mother's attack, and again delivers crucial knowledge to allow Fet-Fruners to gather Iliane's stud of mares and to obtain the flask of holy water from the church beyond the river Jordan. Given how much the princess relies on the horses, is she a true hero or simply a fortunate one?

As Aron notes, the presence of a magic horse is a standard feature of heroic tales and thus does not necessarily undermine Fet-Fruners's abilities, which in fact often reflect remarkable independence. After fighting for an hour, Fet-Fruners cuts off the dragon's head with a "well-directed side blow" (Lang 329). When she attacks the first genie, she immediately "[cleaves] his skull" (330). For one of the genie mother's three tests, Fet-Fruners knows how to choose armor, and she is careful to protect her identity with the emperor's pages. To persuade Iliane to board her ship, Fet-Fruners cleverly presents the bejeweled golden slippers, and Iliane's secret joy at her second capture suggests her attraction to Fet-Fruners as a true masculine hero. The princess in disguise even stands up to the emperor when he demands too much, reminding his lord of the other "valiant young men" to whom he should assign such difficult tasks (339). The battle with the genie who first captures Iliane is fierce enough to cause wild beasts to flee "twenty miles round" (339) and culminates in Fet-Fruners beheading her enemy. Finally, the princess displays great skill in stealing the flask of holy water, being careful not to alert the sleeping nun who guards the precious liquid. With these heroic deeds, the princess proves herself to be a true and clever warrior, not simply a female character in disguise as sometimes occurs in the female-to-male cross-dressing motif in fairy tales (Aron 108).

Yet, as the story affirms Fet-Fruners's masculine abilities, it continually reasserts her femininity as well. The mother of the first genie suspects that Fet-Fruners is actually female, and even when Fet-Fruners passes the three tests, the mother is not convinced that the princess is male. When Fet-Fruners arrives at the palace of the emperor she is to serve, the pages immediately wonder "why they felt so attracted" to their guest (Lang 332), whose performance as a male nonetheless kindles the attraction of Iliane later in the story. In all these ways, from the father's attitude to various characters' perceptions of Fet-Fruners, to the inconsistent portrayal of her abilities as heroically masculine, the story presents contradictory views of femininity: women are sometimes incapable or require extensive help, but other times, they are better than men as warriors and problem solvers; women who dress as men might convince many but will never fool everyone, implying that gender is both a malleable performance that relies on appearance and behavior and yet is somehow just as fixed as biological sex.

The conclusion delivers what appears to be a final blow to the story's subversive aspects when the hermit curses Fet-Fruners so that she actually becomes male rather than merely performing as one. When Fet-Fruners perceives that she is "really the man she had pretended to be, she was delighted, and if the hermit had only been within reach she would have thanked him from her heart" (Lang 343). To Fet-Fruners, the sex change is thus no curse at all, and it enables the narrative to conclude in an appropriate way for a male hero: the emperor declares that Fet-Fruners's trials are over and names him successor to the throne. Iliane is able to act on her sympathy and attraction by murdering the emperor and declaring her intention to marry her true love. Finally, when Fet-Fruners agrees to marry her, he asserts his masculine dominance by literally having the last word, the message of which is to tell her in no uncertain terms that he will indeed dominate her.

The most obvious way to read these final events is that the story ultimately curtails and even shuts down its interrogation of gender as a flexible cultural performance. The ending implies that Fet-Fruners becomes a man because to perform masculinity as successfully as she does requires that she be a man—as if the narrator can no longer tolerate the idea of gender as culturally determined and therefore seeks to restore traditional gender norms. According to the dictates of such norms, behavior must match the sex to which it is believed to correspond in order to conserve society's power structures. The role of narratives in maintaining these structures is clear: only men can achieve the spiritual and material transformations that result from a successful heroic quest. Thus, while readers might expect a she-turned-he to be sympathetic to a strong woman, Fet-Fruners as a conventional man must ensure that the feisty Iliane knows who is boss.

In contrast, Aron argues that Iliane and other characters in relation to Fet-Fruners powerfully undermine the story's ultimate affirmation of traditional male dominance. Throughout the story, the female Fet-Fruners and Iliane are in fact the most heroic and active agents, in marked contrast to the passive emperor and other male characters (Aron 116). Despite the harsh tests set by her father, Fet-Fruners's deeds ultimately save him by fulfilling the conquering emperor's demand for a son. Iliane is initially captured but later manipulates the emperor and every aspect of her future, repeatedly demanding tasks as conditions for her marriage and ultimately murdering the emperor so that she can choose Fet-Fruners instead (114). Iliane is explicit about her desire for revenge on the emperor because of how he has endangered Fet-Fruners and because the emperor has been unmanly; he forces another man to attain the holy water when the emperor "ought to have fetched it himself, which he could have done without any risk at all" (Lang 343). The emperor in fact displays only passivity, forcing Fet-Fruners to capture Iliane and subsequently to carry out each of the tasks she sets.

Aron convincingly concludes that precisely because Fet-Fruners performs masculinity so well in comparison to the "real" men around her but also physically becomes a man, she totally usurps the masculine symbolism of chivalry. Her sex change is thus a diversion and a sleight of hand for the marriage proposal, or rather command, of Iliane, who largely controls the story's final outcome once Fet-Fruners becomes male (116). On this interpretation, despite the story's deep ambivalence toward Fet-Fruners's femininity, her gendered performance as both a cross-dressing woman and as a man in relation to Iliane and the emperor actually signals the overall dominance of women in the story. Flanagan supports this type of interpretation, noting that because female cross-dressers frequently prove to be better than the men around them, their behavior prompts a "reevaluation of both masculinity and femininity based on the heroine's lack of conformity with such categorizations" (22). The cross-dresser's masculine behavior is thus measured against other characters' gendered identities, prompting a "critical assessment of gender on all levels" (100). In this way, the meaning of Fet-Fruners's gendered behavior emerges most vividly in the context of the behavior of the characters with whom she interacts.

Lang published "The Girl Who Pretended to Be a Boy" at the turn of the twentieth century, when it was not permissible or even conceivable to present a fairy tale with an overtly feminist message. Aron argues that this story's dominant female power is extraordinarily subversive and that the ending simply makes the story acceptable to conventional society, thus ensuring its survival. Clever readers, however, would recognize the conclusion as something of a cover for the story's deeply transgressive values. Readers cannot know whether Lang actively intended to promote these values to his young readers, but there is no doubt that he contributed much to his own collection and to the larger fairy-tale corpus by preserving this fascinating Romanian tale.

CROSS-CULTURAL INFLUENCE

Fairy tales with cross-dressing females often challenge conventional gender roles, but what happens when women cross-dress in real life? Christian saints' lives reflect a strong narrative tradition in which female saints, such as Athanasia of Antioch and Pelagia, dress as men to evade marriage and pursue a spiritual life (Flanagan 64). Although many of these narratives cannot be verified, a notable exception is Joan of Arc, arguably the most famous cross-dressing saint in history. A fifteenth-century French peasant girl, Joan of Arc (Jeanne d'Arc) claimed to be inspired by God and led France to victory in several key battles during the Hundred Years' War but was later executed for heresy. Historians agree that Joan's cross-dressing played a central role in why she was brought to trial and eventually burned at the stake. However, although French culture has celebrated Joan's cross-dressing, and historians emphasize its importance, Flanagan shows that children's stories markedly downplay the role and meaning of Joan's decision to dress as a man. English writer Josephine Poole's 1998 *Joan of Arc*, a nonfiction story for children, is an engaging tale that nonetheless exemplifies this tendency. Her narrative raises the question of why cross-dressing is diminished in the case of a historical figure such as Joan of Arc, whereas fairy tales prominently explore cross-dressing as a theme to interrogate gender norms. More importantly, the relationship between Joan's history and its presentation to young readers underscores the narrative medium of history and the challenges such narratives pose.

For this analysis, Joan of Arc's life and accomplishments are necessarily summarized in brief. The Hundred Years' War between France and England began in 1337 when the English king Edward III claimed the right to the French throne through his mother's lineage. When Joan was born in 1412 in eastern France to a family of peasant farmers, the war was still raging. When she was seventeen, she presented herself to the dauphin (heir) to the throne of France, Charles VII, as a divinely inspired savior. At this point, France was nearly defeated due to dynastic infighting. The Duke of Burgundy had allied with the English after his father's death at the hands of Charles's supporters in 1419; in 1420, the English king Henry V named his heir, Henry VI, as future king of England and France. By the time Joan presented herself to Charles in February 1429, the Burgundian-English alliance held control of Paris and the territories north of the Loire River, and the town of Orléans was under siege. Joan was instrumental in leading the French forces to defeat the English at Orléans in May 1429 and in escorting Charles to his coronation soon after. The following year, in May 1430, she was captured by Burgundians during a skirmish in Compiègne. She unsuccessfully attempted to escape, and the Burgundians eventually sold her to the English, who turned her over to the Inquisition. After a politically motivated and irregular trial, she was condemned as a heretic, in part for violating the Bible's prohibition against cross-dressing. Burned at the stake in May 1431, she was later vindicated and was declared a Catholic saint in 1920.

Poole's story begins with a phrase that underscores the tale's claim to historical status, "This is a true story," which ensures that young readers will not take it as mere fiction. The narrator then summarizes the historical setting as more than five hundred years ago in France, when the French king faced "great danger" because his "cousin, the Duke of Burgundy, wanted the throne for himself, and had persuaded England to fight with him" (Poole 2). Joan is then introduced as a "farmer's daughter" who helps her mother and works in the fields. One day when Joan is thirteen and finds herself "alone in the garden, the air around her turned very clear and bright—much brighter than the sun could make it" (3), she begins to hear voices from heaven. The voices bring her immeasurable happiness, but Joan weeps when they speak of the conflict in her country. After listening to the voices for four years, Joan deeply desires that "her King should have his kingdom" (3). Wanting to help save Orléans, which was under siege by English soldiers, Joan heeds the divine voices she hears and sets off for the nearest military garrison. There, she is first ridiculed, but her persistence pays off when the captain finally gives her a horse and some guards. At this point, she "cut[s] her hair and dress[es] like a man so that she could travel more safely" (7).

When Joan first meets the king, he tests her by dressing as one of his lords to see if her divine powers are real. Joan passes the test by immediately identifying the king, and she later declares that her divine voices have commanded her to liberate Orléans and bring the king to be crowned in the city of Rheims. Initially reluctant because he thinks she might be a witch, the king sends Joan to Orléans, where she learns to fight. With her reputation as a divine maiden preceding her, Joan arrives to much acclaim and impresses a crowd when she easily extinguishes a burning standard while on horseback. The next day, she leads the French soldiers into battle and is wounded but keeps fighting, even persuading the French captain to continue the battle when he tries to stop. Panicked at the sight of Joan and her troops, hundreds of English troops attempt to retreat across a bridge and are defeated. That day, Joan eats nothing but toast and a small amount of diluted wine. The next day, the English retreat without a fight, ending the siege of Orléans. Acclaimed as a hero and accompanied by a large military company, Joan then brings the king to be crowned at Rheims.

After the coronation, Joan is asked by her captains to fight more battles. This time, the town of Compiègne must be liberated, and Joan agrees to help although her divine voices tell her that she will be captured there. When the French captain raises the town drawbridge, leaving the French forces to fend for themselves, Joan is captured and locked in a high tower. She jumps out but is caught and returned to prison, where she heals from her injuries and is comforted by the archangel Michael and other angels. The French king makes a "secret truce" with the Duke of Burgundy and the English, who "needed to get rid of [Joan], because to ordinary people, Joan was a heroine and a saint" (Poole 25). She is sent to Rouen to be tried for heresy, based on her claims of hearing divine voices and conversing with saints. To ensure a guilty verdict, the English pay the bishop presiding over Joan's trial. She withstands her inquisitors' relentless questioning but is condemned to death for heresy. Encouraged by her voices, Joan submits to the English, who burn her at the stake and throw her ashes into a river. The story concludes by stating, "But that was not the end. A saint is like a star. A star and a saint shine forever" (29).

It is clear that Poole's rendition is not intended to plumb the depths of Joan's history, but because it is presented as a true story, Flanagan correctly claims that Poole (and other authors of children's stories about Joan) denies a key part of Joan's history by glossing over her cross-dressing. As Flanagan notes, Poole mentions Joan's masculine clothing only once when she states that Joan cut her hair and dressed in men's clothing so that she could travel safely. Yet numerous scholars have

documented that Joan was forced to stand trial not for heresy per se, but rather for her cross-dressing. Marjorie Garber notes that at least five of the charges leveled against Joan pertained to her insistence on dressing like a man. Her inquisitors charged that her transvestitism and bearing of arms signified a lack of femininity, immodesty, and an unmerited sense of entitlement (Garber 215–16). Joan insisted that God had ordered her to wear men's clothing, which she refused to give up, declaring that she would rather die than do so (216). Thus, the Inquisition put her to death in 1431 partly for her insistence that "cross-dressing was a religious duty" (Flanagan 63).

These details tells us that Joan of Arc's cross-dressing was a crucial part of her identity and history, which is why French culture has celebrated her and historians have studied this aspect of her behavior. Yet Poole's narrative all but eliminates the centrality of Joan's cross-dressing in her life and death. In addition, Flanagan notes that Joan's military prowess and her subjectivity in general are "always presented in terms of her religious subjection" (67), such as when Poole narrates, "Joan simply did what God told her to do, and nothing, nobody could prevent her" (20). These strategies produce two effects. First, Joan appears as a heroic but distant and unknowable figure. Second, young readers lose the significance of her cross-dressing as a specific behavior that might have informed her identity and that successfully challenged patriarchal gender constraints (Flanagan 65).

Suppressing the importance of Joan's cross-dressing markedly contrasts with children's fairy tales that emphasize cross-dressing as a behavior that constructs gendered identities (Flanagan 66). What might account for this puzzling difference? Garber states that like other female saints, Joan refused to marry and "rejected male domination even as she assumed male privilege" (215). Unlike most female saints, however, Joan did not adopt the costume of a male monk, which, Garber notes, the church had tolerated in the case of certain female saints; instead, she chose the clothing and armor of a knight. Furthermore, Joan did not pretend to be a man but insisted that she was a true woman who had been directed by divine inspiration to dress as a man. In this way, she claimed masculine duties but rejected the male sex to imply an identity that was neither male nor female, like the divine angels whose voices she claimed to hear (216). Flanagan argues that this type of transvestitism was marked as violating class and gender norms in a way perceived to be very different and much more dangerous than simply a pious woman wearing the clothes of a monk for the sake of her spirituality. Such an ambiguous identity might be celebrated in a fictional character, but writers have reacted more conservatively to Joan, possibly due to her "iconic cultural status and the widespread popularity of her story" (Flanagan 71). Flanagan believes that in fictional stories, anonymous female characters have a "cultural invisibility" that makes possible a "radical interpretation" of their behavior, but for Joan as a real, culturally contextualized woman, such a radical interpretation is perceived as too dangerous (71). Thus, stories of Joan's life for young readers have emphasized the spiritual quality of Joan's inspiration and character while ignoring the historical complexities of the gendered identity she created as a human being.

If writers are more willing to reveal and challenge gender norms in fairy tales than in historical narratives for children, what might be concluded about the value of these respective genres? Critics should point out the revisionist nature of Poole's narrative and explore the reasons for crucial omissions when they occur. Yet perhaps more salient is to notice the contrasts and similarities between fairy tales such as "The Girl Who Pretended to Be a Boy" and historical narratives. On the one hand, precisely because such fairy tales candidly explore subversive themes, they provide counterpoints and interpretive models that help readers to examine historical narratives more critically. This is in fact part of Flanagan's method, as her awareness of the fictional treatments of cross-dressing partly allows her to unearth the historical writers' patterns of suppression.

On the other hand, as argued above, "The Girl Who Pretended to Be a Boy" also reveals complexities that are not so different from Poole's treatment. As noted, Lang's fairy tale negotiates its challenge of gender roles by presenting a conclusion that seems to curtail the story's subversive impulses, making the tale more palatable to traditional readers. Similarly, Poole's narrative omits cross-dressing as the central justification for Joan's execution, presumably to make her story somehow more acceptable, if not more accurate. To be sure, these narrative strategies are not equivalent, because fiction and history reflect different methods and purposes. Yet such strategies remind readers that both genres are constructed through narrative. As such, both fictional and historical narratives can and do offer much truth—truth that is never absolute because it emerges from the gifts and complexities of human memory, language, and culture.

Ashleigh Imus, PhD

BIBLIOGRAPHY

Aron, Melanie Sylvia. "Hero in Drag: Victorian Gender Identity and the Fairy Tales of Andrew Lang." MA thesis. California State U, Fresno, 2008. Print.

Flanagan, Victoria. *Into the Closet: Cross-Dressing and the Gendered Body in Children's Literature and Film.* New York: Routledge, 2008. Print.

Garber, Marjorie. *Vested Interests: Cross-Dressing and Cultural Anxiety.* New York: Harper, 1993. Print.

Lang, Andrew, ed. *The Violet Fairy Book.* New York: Dover, 1966. Print.

Poole, Josephine. *Joan of Arc.* New York: Knopf, 1998. Print.

Warner, Marina. *Joan of Arc: The Image of Female Heroism.* New York: Knopf, 1981. Print.

Zipes, Jack. *Fairy Tales and the Art of Subversion.* New York: Routledge, 2006. Print.

Heracles's Twelve Labors

Author: Pseudo-Apollodorus
Time Period: 999 BCE–1 BCE
Country or Culture: Greek
Genre: Myth

OVERVIEW

The great warrior Heracles (more commonly known by his Roman name, Hercules) is the subject of a large range of myths and legends. Carrying a wooden club and wearing the fur of a lion, he battles his way across Greek and Roman mythology, crushing poisonous snakes with his bare hands as a baby, sacking the great city of Troy, and adventuring in new lands with the legendary Argonauts. He seems to be in a continuous process of falling in and out love, fathering fifty sons at one moment and building a shrine to his fallen male lover in the next. Representing the heights of masculinity, heroism, and strength, Heracles and his myths are dominant forces in Greek mythology. It is the story of his twelve labors, however, that is most familiar to modern audiences.

The story of Heracles's twelve labors is an important component of both the life of Heracles and the progression of Greek mythology. Before the myth properly begins, Heracles is driven into a rage by the goddess Hera. Heracles is the son of Zeus and a mortal woman, and jealous Hera, the immortal wife of Zeus, makes a project out of tormenting the earthly hero. In that rage, Heracles slaughters his children. Seeking forgiveness, he visits the oracle of Delphi and is ordered to serve his cousin Eurystheus, the king of Tiryns. Hera and Eurystheus then set Heracles to his labors, which are designed to kill the hero, testing his strength, endurance, and wit in the most extreme of circumstances.

The myth is an engaging and thrilling read, as Heracles completes seemingly impossible tasks and encounters the greatest monsters and gods of all Greek mythology. However, the myth is most important on a symbolic level. Greek culture separated the realm of the earth and mortality (the chthonic realm) from that of the sky and immortality (the Olympian realm). The tale of Heracles's twelve labors is the story of the chthonic and mortal hero proving his might and elevating himself to the Olympian realm. He is a champion of Greek civilization and of the immortal Olympians who lord above it. Because of this, as he conquers the great beasts of the wilderness and vanquishes entire armies, he is demonstrating the power and value of the chthonic and Olympian realms both. When he completes his final task and returns from the underworld, he represents the ultimate triumph, moving beyond the confines of mortality and becoming a deity. The rare story of a chthonic hero overcoming his own nature, the myth of Heracles's labors speaks to the hopes of Greek civilization and to the belief that within one's earthly self might rest something heroic, legendary, and immortal.

SUMMARY

The son of the god Zeus and the mortal Alcmene, Heracles is both blessed and cursed from the start of his life. Incredibly mighty and heroic, he accomplishes feats of great strength at a young age. However, the goddess Hera, Zeus's wife, decides to punish Heracles in order to take revenge for her husband's infidelities. One day she drives Heracles into a frenzy, during which he kills his children. When Heracles then goes to the oracle of Delphi to seek forgiveness, Hera influences the oracle, who tells Heracles that he must swear allegiance to his mortal cousin Eurystheus for twelve years, after which he will be redeemed and gain immortality. Hera, who is in league with Eurystheus, plans to set Heracles to such great tasks during this time that he will meet his mortal death.

Eurystheus immediately orders Heracles to complete ten great labors, which Heracles attempts with legendary heroism. First, he slays the Nemean lion, an invulnerable beast born to the monster Typhon. When he brings the body of the beast back to Eurystheus, Eurystheus realizes how strong Heracles truly is and commands

"When Hercules [Heracles] asked Pluto [Hades] for Cerberus, Pluto ordered him to take the animal provided he mastered him without the use of the weapons which he carried. Hercules found him at the gates of Acheron, and, cased in his cuirass and covered by the lion's skin, he flung his arms round the head of the brute, and though the dragon in its tail bit him, he never relaxed his grip and pressure till it yielded."

Bibliotheca

that he never enter the city again and instead bring proof that he has completed each task to the city gates. Next, Heracles slays the Lernaean hydra, a nine-headed beast that had been killing cattle throughout the countryside. When he fights the monster, he realizes that for every head he cuts off, two more grow in its place, and so he instructs his nephew, Iolaus, to burn the necks to prevent new heads from growing back. Eurystheus, however, denies the success of this labor, as Iolaus had assisted Heracles in the battle.

For his third labor, Heracles captures the Cerynitian hind, a beast precious to the goddess Artemis, after chasing it for an entire year. Next, he goes to capture the Erymanthian boar. While this task is simple compared to the others, Heracles stops to visit the centaur Pholus and, after being convinced to drink the wine that belongs to the other centaurs, finds himself in a bloody battle when those centaurs return. For his fifth labor, Heracles is ordered to dispose of the dung of the cattle of King Augeas in a single day. The son of a god, Augeas has seemingly endless cattle. After convincing the king to pay him for the work, Heracles redirects mighty rivers into the cattle yards, washing the dung away. However, Eurystheus rejects this labor on the grounds that Heracles received payment for completing it.

For his sixth labor, Heracles chases away the birds of Stymphalus by clanging together castanets given to him by the goddess Athena. Next, he captures the Cretan

bull, showing it to Eurystheus before letting it go free again. For his eighth labor, he captures the man-eating mares of King Diomedes, the son of the god Ares. In addition to slaying Diomedes and taking the mares, Heracles founds a new city on the grave of Abderus, who had been the mares' caretaker before dying during the battle. For his ninth labor, Heracles goes to fetch the belt of Hippolyte, who is the queen of the Amazons, a community of fierce warrior women. On the way to Hippolyte, he slays a massive army that attacks his ships. Hippolyte at first offers the belt freely, but Hera, disguised as an Amazon, convinces the female army to attack Heracles, and so he is forced to kill them all. Next, Heracles travels a great distance and kills many people in order to fetch the cattle of Geryon, a monster with the body of three men.

Eight years and one month after the start of the labors, Heracles finishes the tenth task. However, because he received help with the second labor and payment for the fifth, Eurystheus requires two more tasks of him. For his eleventh labor, Heracles must fetch the apples of the Hesperides from the ends of the earth, where they are guarded by the Hesperides themselves as well as an immortal dragon. Rather than steal the apples himself, however, he convinces the Titan Atlas to do so for him. Because Atlas has been punished by Zeus and tasked with holding up the sky, Heracles takes his position temporarily and tricks Atlas into holding the sky when he returns. Finally, Heracles enters the underworld itself to capture Cerberus, a three-headed hellhound with the tail of a dragon. After successfully wrestling the beast without using weapons, Heracles is allowed to bring it to the gates of Eurystheus, though he returns it shortly after. With this final labor complete, Heracles concludes his obligation to Eurystheus, having done exactly as the oracle of Delphi asked of him years before.

ANALYSIS

The lyric poet Pindar, one of the most influential poets of ancient Greece, describes Heracles with the term *hereos theos*, meaning that he is both a hero and a god. This epithet captures the core of the myth that surrounds Heracles. Born to a mortal mother from her union with an immortal god, living as the greatest earthly hero before ascending to the heights of Mount Olympus, and at once cursed and blessed by the most powerful deities in the Greek pantheon, Heracles is the rare figure that transcends the divide between the realm of the mortals and that of the gods.

As Heracles's most famous myth, the story of the twelve labors offers a detailed exploration of how the mortal hero ascended to the heights of immortality. The world of Greek mythology was split between the chthonic realm and the Olympian realm. The term "chthonic" refers to things that are of the earth, which in Greek culture encompassed humanity, the underworld, death, monsters, and heroes. Temples were built to chthonic figures, particularly by cults devoted to heroes, and sacrifices were made at these locations prior to similar sacrifices to the gods. The Olympian realm, in contrast, was the fixed and relatively inflexible world of the sky, Mount Olympus, and the Greek pantheon. While mortals regularly entered the world of chthonic heroes after death, those worshipped in the Olympian realm never died, living on in the heights of the sky. The labors of Heracles, then, are the challenges that the mortal hero must overcome in order to become immortal, as declared by the oracle of Delphi. Because of this, the long list of battles and tribulations can be understood not as arbitrary wars with monsters and warriors but as one man triumphing above the chthonic realm, conquering earthly things with such might that he ultimately ascends as an Olympian deity.

Although Heracles is not fully mortal in lineage (Zeus, his father, is the god of the sky and the most powerful force associated with the Olympian pantheon), it is important that from the start of his twelve labors, he is firmly and unambiguously a chthonic hero and not an extension of the Olympic world he champions. This is almost always the case for a figure born to a mortal mother and an immortal father, but in the instance of Heracles, it is particularly important to understand his mortality and his connection to the earth. The fact of his mortality is made clear first by the oracle, who declares that he can only become immortal by completing his vassalage to Eurystheus, and second by the scheming of Hera, who intends to kill him through the extremity of the labors. It is also, importantly, because of his chthonic origin that Hera torments him in the first place, angered by the insult of her divine husband taking a mortal woman as a partner. Heracles, then, is entirely of the earthly realm and, as such, fits in the long tradition of folk heroes in Greek and pre-Greek culture. His masculinity, skill as a warrior, sexual appetite (he has hundreds of partners, both male and female), and adventuresome spirit identify him as a typical Greek hero whose role is to protect and champion Greek civilization in the face of the chthonic threats of monsters, the natural world,

and death. Through figures such as Heracles, the people of Greece could see their own triumph as the greatest people in the chthonic realm.

The labors of Hercules, then, are labors in which Hercules conquers the chthonic realm to which he belongs, facing the most dangerous elements and monsters the world has to offer. His first task, that of killing the Nemean lion, makes this clear. The Nemean lion is the child of Typhon, the greatest of all the monsters in Greek mythology, and the grandchild of Gaia, the goddess of the earth itself and one of the few immortal deities to be associated with the chthonic. By facing the Nemean lion, Heracles is directly battling the ideal of the chthonic monster. It is important also that at this time in Greek history, lions had likely not been brought to the Greek state and instead had only been learned about through travels. Therefore, the Nemean lion with its invulnerable pelt also represents the fear of the unknown in the natural world, the rumor of great beasts outside the protection of Greek civilization. When Heracles tracks down this beast and defeats it, his triumph represents the triumph of all Greek people over the mysterious beasts and threats of foreign lands. A similar interpretation can be applied to the Lernaean hydra, the beast of the second labor and also a child of Typhon.

The first labor also includes an important aside that helps define the meaning of Heracles's quest. Before approaching the Nemean lion, Heracles comes across a man who is preparing to make his regular sacrifice to the beast. Heracles stops him, however, and insists that the man wait. If Heracles dies in battle, he instructs, the man should make the sacrifice to him as a hero. If Heracles succeeds, the sacrifice should be made instead to Zeus. Had Heracles perished, he would have fit neatly into the tradition of hero cults that celebrated many historical and legendary figures from the chthonic realm. Put another way, in death, his mortality would be official, thus making Heracles a hero. However, in conquering the beast, Heracles instead directs the man's sacrifice toward Zeus and the Olympian realm. This is important in that while Heracles fulfills the trajectory of the hero and champions Greek society, he also transcends that role, directing the glory not to himself but to the gods. From the start, he is crossing the divide between the chthonic and the Olympian, acting as a champion of both realms at once.

The first two labors having proven that Heracles is mighty enough to conquer any dangerous beast, the next labors test a different set of skills. Instead of vanquishing a fearsome monster, Heracles must capture a hind (deer) and a boar. While Eurystheus selects mystical versions of these animals, with the hind being faster than an arrow and the boar fearsome and strong, they are both animals that are the common objects of hunts. In capturing the boar and the hind, Heracles represents the success of mortals in conquering the natural world to provide food and sustenance for themselves. This is stressed through the fact that the hind is the sacred animal of Artemis, the goddess of the hunt, while the boar likewise roams in the forests that Artemis sometimes calls home. In capturing the hind, Heracles angers Artemis, who comes to stop him accompanied by her brother, Apollo. However, Artemis hears Heracles's story and comes to approve, giving his mortal task the blessing of an immortal. This again blends together the chthonic and the Olympian, with Heracles's success dependent on both his earthly skills and the blessing of the gods.

The fourth and fifth labors involve side stories in which there is conflict between Heracles and centaurs, moments that heighten the tension between humanity and the natural world. Centaurs, in their half-human and half-horse form, often represent the link between civilization and wilderness. This dual nature makes centaurs seem monstrous to many humans in Greek mythology, especially as they seem to suggest that humans themselves might still have feral, unsophisticated elements to their being. Heracles encounters and, through violence, conquers this nature in both labors. In the fourth, he visits a centaur friend, Pholus, who in entertaining Heracles and offering him wine demonstrates that it is possible to overcome one's beastly nature and embrace civilization. However, the other centaurs succumb to their wild roots, attacking Heracles and meeting their death. The other centaur to whom Heracles expresses affection is Chiron, a legendary teacher and giver of wisdom in Greek mythology. When Heracles inadvertently injures Chiron with an arrow, he rushes forth to remove the weapon, which suggests that even as he conquers the animal instinct of some centaurs, he still respects the wisdom available through the natural world and humanity's own conflicted nature. Likewise, Heracles pauses during his fifth labor in order to kill a centaur who plans to take a human woman as a wife. This follows the labor in which Heracles cleans the massive stalls of a thousand cattle and demonstrates the dominance of domestication and farming over chthonic beasts. These two examples make clear the relationship between Heracles and the natural world: humans can gain wisdom from their own

animal natures, but only if they conquer those natures and take care not to indulge them too fully (as in the carnal relationship suggested by the marriage between centaur and human).

The risk of unleashing the wild nature of beasts within humanity is realized in the sixth, seventh, and eighth labors. In these tasks, Heracles captures first the violent Symphalian birds, then the legendarily fierce bull of Crete, and finally the man-eating mares of the warrior king Diomedes. In every instance, Heracles successfully captures or defeats the animals. However, other myths reveal that the birds of Stymphalian go on to pester the legendary heroes known as the Argonauts. Similarly, the story of the seventh labor mentions that Heracles eventually sets the Cretan bull free, after which it begins to harass the people of the city of Marathon. These instances show that the beasts, even once conquered, can again wreck havoc if they are unleashed within civilization. In contrast, the flesh-eating mares are likewise released but instead make their way to Mount Olympus, the home of the gods. The beasts are quickly destroyed by the animals of the mountains, suggesting that the Olympian realm (in contrast to the chthonic realm) has nothing to fear from untamed wilderness.

While the first eight labors pit Heracles against the beasts of the earth, the ninth and tenth labors amplify the danger and the level of his challenge. He has already, in diverse ways, proven his superiority over the greatest of monsters. However, he has not proven similar superiority over other humans, a necessary step if he is going to elevate himself to the status of the immortals. In the ninth labor, he battles the legendary Amazons, a group of fierce women warriors, as well as the armies of a number of other leaders and warriors. While at first Heracles's reputation is such that Hippolyte, the ruler of the Amazons, offers him the belt requested by Eurystheus freely, Hera spreads discontent among the Amazons, resulting in the battle. These battles do not represent Heracles turning against or conquering human civilization, but rather serve to demonstrate his godlike superiority in military matters. The armies he slaughters are massive, yet the hero does not tire, pressing on toward victory.

Heracles also challenges the core elements of the natural world in the ninth and tenth labors. Once again, this is a heightened conflict in comparison to what came before, emphasizing that Heracles is not only demonstrating superiority over untamed nature but also reaching total deification, which will separate him from the chthonic realm. During these labors, Heracles

MYTH INTO ART

Widely considered the greatest artist of the Italian Renaissance, Michelangelo frequently drew inspiration from the myths of Greek antiquity. His drawing "Three Labors of Hercules" depicts the hero fighting with the Nemean lion, with Antaeus, and finally with the hydra. The drawing does not include the intense attention to detail that characterizes Michelangelo's more famous works, such as the ceiling of the Sistine Chapel. However, it conveys the typically Renaissance sense of grandeur that defines the time period.

Like many of his contemporaries, Michelangelo was interested in large, expressive, ornate art that inspired awe in its audience. He was drawn to sprawling narratives and dramatic details, such as the biting heads of the hydra and the torn mouth of the lion depicted in his drawing. In this sense, classical antiquity was a fertile source of inspiration for the artist.

Stories such as the myth of Heracles's twelve labors are packed with action and grand themes, such as the struggle for immortality.

In "Three Labors of Hercules," Michelangelo draws not only from the narrative details of the Heracles myth but also from styles and poses from mythology. It was common in ancient times to carve sequences of drawings (often even of Heracles) onto sarcophagi or other objects or structures. The progression of poses Michelangelo selects here mimics many of those sequences as well as similar drawings of Heracles by other Renaissance painters and artists. While not rendered at the grand scale of some of his other works, Michelangelo's drawing shows that the legendary hero was thrilling enough to capture the eye of one of the most gifted and dramatic artists of all time.

comes into continual conflict with humans fathered and monsters formed by Poseidon, the god of the sea. Poseidon is associated with terrible floods and earthquakes, natural disasters that seemed to rise spontaneously from the earth to destroy civilization. When Poseidon sends sea monsters toward coastal cities during the labors, however, Heracles quickly destroys those monsters in battle. In a similar move, exhausted by the heat of the sun, Heracles turns his bow and arrow toward the sky. While he certainly cannot defeat the sun and the sky in battle, the god of the sun is pleased by Heracles's courage and rewards him with a golden goblet in which to sail safely.

With the original ten labors complete, Heracles has demonstrated his mastery over all aspects of the chthonic realm. He has killed the monsters of unknown lands, has domesticated the wildest beasts of Greece, has overcome the elements, and has vanquished entire armies. This mastery more than fulfills the qualifications for becoming a legendary hero and inspiring a chthonic cult. However, as the oracle has promised, Heracles is destined for an even greater place in mythology, and consequently, he must complete two more tasks that extend beyond the realm of the earthly hero.

For the eleventh task, Heracles must fetch the apples from the garden of the Hesperides. This garden, located in the distant west, far away from Greece, is the property of Hera herself. In it, she planted an apple tree given to her by Gaia on the day of her wedding to Zeus. The fruit of this tree gives immortality to anyone who fetches it, but it is also guarded by an immortal dragon and by the Hesperides nymphs themselves. By claiming these apples, Heracles is essentially entering the realm of the gods, both trespassing into Hera's sacred space and gaining for himself one route to immortality. However, as he is still a mortal hero, he cannot enter the garden himself. He seeks the assistance of Atlas, a Titan who has been condemned to spend eternity holding up the sky. Heracles momentarily takes the place of Atlas and symbolically becomes at once of the earth and of the sky, his body dividing the realms yet in contact with them both. It is by taking this position and acknowledging these dual roles that Heracles is able to obtain the apples. When Atlas returns, Heracles tricks him into resuming his position and is able to deliver the fruit to Eurystheus.

While Heracles has completed this task, he has not actually gained immortality, and the apples are returned to the garden out of respect. Instead, it is through his final labor that he truly conquers death. In this labor, he must go into Hades (the underworld or the realm of death) and retrieve Cerberus, a monstrous hellhound with the tail of a dragon that guards the gates. Many figures in Greek mythology attempt to enter the realm of the dead, but very few successfully return to the world of the living. In entering this realm, Heracles confronts the greatest power in the chthonic realm and proves that he, like the Olympian gods, is unaffected by this danger. This is the true divide between the chthonic and the Olympian: it is not that the Olympian gods are reborn after death but rather that they do not die. Likewise, even if a hero is memorialized in temples and worshipped at festivals, he still faces a mortal death and is still sent to the underworld. Heracles overcomes this threat, traveling with the secrets of the Eleusinian cult and wrestling Cerberus. Heracles's triumph over Cerberus suggests that even were he to find himself in Hades with the other mortal heroes, he would not be contained there, as his might is such that he could win his freedom at any time. To heighten this contrast, he comes across Theseus, the legendary chthonic hero and founder of Athens, who, unlike Heracles, is unable to escape the underworld.

His labors complete, Heracles is free to go on to other adventures with the promise from the oracle that he will one day become immortal. Indeed, in later legends, his earthly body is destroyed in a funeral pyre he built himself, while his godly form rises to the immortal realm of the Olympians. However, the labors of Heracles themselves end long before he meets this destiny. The labors, then, are not about the existence Heracles will share on Mount Olympus, nor are they about immortality and godliness, even as those rewards drive the story from the start. Instead, the myth of the labors is about the triumph of Greek civilization over the untamed and often frightening natural world. Heracles is the greatest hero to come out of antiquity, a legend born in the chthonic realm. His greatest feat, however, is not simply his brutish triumph over beasts and monsters. Rather, his glory is the glory of all Greece, of the earth and of the gods. In directing sacrifices to Zeus and obeying the command of the oracle of Delphi, Heracles offers the devotion and respect expected from the chthonic realm. Paradoxical as it may seem, it is by becoming an ideal of chthonic life that Heracles is elevated at last to the Olympian realm, indicating that perhaps the two realms are not be as separate as they seem.

CROSS-CULTURAL INFLUENCE

The ancient Greek Heracles was the pinnacle of the masculine hero, capable of conquering entire armies and slaughtering ferocious beasts. He fathered children with nearly a hundred women, traveled to the ends of the earth, and defended the entirety of Greek civilization on many occasions. However, the heights of Greek masculinity do not match up neatly with modern ideas of masculinity. The ancient Heracles was also a playful figure, enjoying leisurely games and spending time with his children when possible. In addition to his many wives, he took on countless male lovers to whom he expressed passionate, unabashed romantic love. In the ancient context, these qualities made him even more heroic and masculine, even if they seem incongruous with contemporary ideals of masculinity and heroism.

Primarily because of his role as the ultimate hero, the myths surrounding Heracles have had a significant legacy through the modern day. Countless European and American films revisit the Heracles story, including the 1997 animated Disney musical *Hercules* and a long series of popular Italian adventure films from the mid-twentieth century. Comic books, theatrical productions, and television series have also regularly featured Heracles. Almost without exception, however, these portrayals focus on a version of Heracles who fits comfortably into modern ideas of masculinity. He is presented as a stern or angry figure, quick to fight and lacking the playfulness and romanticism of the Greek myths. While he may rescue endangered strangers, as he does in the ancient stories of the twelve labors, the modern Heracles rarely falls in love with those strangers and even more rarely has his heart broken by them.

One of the few contemporary exceptions to these portrayals is found in the book *Autobiography of Red* (1998) by the Canadian-born poet and classicist Anne Carson. A novel written in verse fragments, the work is a retelling of the tenth labor of Heracles, during which he battles the monster Geryon. Carson takes some inspiration from the ancient poet Stesichorus (Stesichoros), whose long poem *Geryoneis* tells the myth from Geryon's perspective. While the *Geryoneis* is largely lost to time, existing only in a few fragments of text, those fragments inspired Carson to create a modern version of the myth that likewise tells the story from Geryon's point of view. However, while the *Geryoneis* focuses on the violence of Heracles arriving at Erythea, the island where Geryon resides, and killing the supposedly immortal monster with a poisoned arrow, Carson instead imagines Geryon and Herakles (in her spelling) as young lovers, with Herakles abandoning Geryon and breaking his heart. In presenting Herakles as causing emotional rather than physical violence, Carson focuses the reader's attention on a different aspect of the myths surrounding the legendary hero, highlighting the often romantic and sometimes tragic core of Greek mythology.

The narrative of *Autobiography of Red* begins when Geryon is a young, sensitive boy, interested in art and close with his mother. While the mythological Geryon is a fiery beast with three heads and three sets of arms who is typically accompanied by his two-headed hound, the Geryon of Carson's story is a slight boy with beautiful red wings, hardly someone to be feared. Geryon's early life is marked by tragedy when his older brother sexually abuses him, traumatizing the young boy and forcing him further into the seclusion of his mind. However, he begins to engage with the world again when a new boy, Herakles, arrives in town. Geryon almost immediately falls in love with Herakles, and the two have a brief affair until Herakles eventually abandons Geryon and leaves the town. The devastated Geryon retreats again into his mind. A few years later, he travels to Argentina, knowing that his lost love might be there. Geryon by chance encounters Herakles, who is accompanied by his new lover. The three men form a sort of love triangle, with the infatuated Geryon reaching out for brief moments of sexual contact and affection from Herakles. At the novel's conclusion, the three travel to a famous volcano and stand at its molten edge, uncertain what to do with the complicated love that exists among them.

The Carson version of the myth might seem, outside of a few telling details, nearly unrecognizable to audiences familiar with the tenth labor of Heracles. There is no violent battle, no command from Hera or promise of immortality to give the story a sense of importance or legendary inspiration. However, Carson is focused less on the narrative details of swordfights and monstrous hounds and more on the emotional core at the heart of much Greek mythology. In her own appended translation of the Stesichorus text, for instance, she includes a simple fragment announcing that "the red world And corresponding red breezes / Went on Geryon did not" (xv). These simple lines, presenting simply the information that Geryon has died, have an emotional and lyric intensity that makes that information into something deeply moving. Stesichorus, though engaged in a project very different from Carson's, still saw the sense of loss and sadness present in the myth. Geryon at once belongs to the world, a place in which even the breeze is as red as he is, and is separate from that world, brought to death by Herakles. There is romantic and emotional

depth to the myths of Heracles, Carson reminds the reader, even if modern versions of those myths rarely include those aspects.

This moment of lyric intensity in the *Geryoneis* is the dominant mode in Carson's modern version. Just as in Stesichorus's text, Geryon is red, although this red marks him as different from, rather than part of, the world. Because of this, the young boy becomes obsessed with volcanoes and other fiery landscapes, seeing in them a home that he does not find in daily life. What remains the same, however, is the sense that the world itself has gone on while Geryon has not and that it is the fault of Herakles that this separation exists. After Herakles has broken the red boy's heart, Geryon cries into the night, his voice "upcast to that custom, the human custom of wrong love" (75). Carson is deeply engaged with the sense that love itself, an experience so often idealized and treated as "right," can in actuality be wrong (just as Herakles, in his righteous quest, is actually leaving great destruction and sadness in his wake). More than this, however, Carson notes that the experience of wrong love is itself a "human custom," a tradition all humans experience. Because of this, the Geryon apart from the red world in the *Geryoneis* and the Geryon left heartbroken by Herakles in *Autobiography of Red* are in many ways one and the same, linked by that sense of abandonment and betrayal.

The shift from physical violence to emotional violence is also appropriate in light of the history of Stesichorus himself. Stesichorus wrote many centuries after the myth of Heracles had become common. The story of the twelve labors was popular enough that even though most audiences could recall the details on their own, writers such as Stesichorus were able to tell their own versions, remaking a myth that had been remade many times before. In this context, Stesichorus shifted the perspective of the myth from Heracles to Geryon while also shifting the sympathies of the audience. Geryon, a supposedly immortal figure, is slaughtered by the single-minded and uncompassionate Heracles. The monster, in no uncertain terms, becomes a sympathetic victim. Likewise, Stesichorus breaks apart the traditional metrical qualities of Greek poetry, creating a new rhythmic form in order to tell the myths in an unfamiliar and surprising manner. Carson, in writing a novel in verse, maintains this tradition. The Herakles and Geryon she creates are both familiar and unfamiliar, just as the poetic fragments of her novel are both recognizable and unusual. By basing this narrative off the Stesichorus fragments, she reminds her readers that such revision of classic myths is not a betrayal of the originals but rather a continuation of an ancient tradition in which writers keep stories alive by telling them in new ways.

This sense of connection through revision, of understanding the past by engaging with the contemporary world, resonates throughout *Autobiography of Red*. A large array of myths and legends have persisted through the centuries, and while figures such as Heracles seem to dominate these cultural traditions, unchanged after all that time, they are in actuality always remade, their narratives and meanings shifting. When the Herakles of *Autobiography of Red* brags that he is "a master of monsters" (129), the meaning of his declaration is heightened and complicated by humankind's many cultural legacies. What does it mean to hold power over another person, whether through physical strength or emotional dependency? How do humans make monsters out of one another, and when does the monster actually deserve sympathy and understanding? Who is the hero: the dashing and powerful warrior, the sensitive and kind monster, or both? Questions such as these, nestled at the heart of the labors of the Heracles, are deep and complicated enough that they draw readers in today just as they did thousands of years ago. As much as Heracles himself might seem a bundle of contradictions and Carson's version of the myth a departure from the intent of the original narrative, it is the availability of these different interpretations that makes the legendary hero so much more than a mighty warrior with a quest for immortality.

T. Fleischmann, MFA

BIBLIOGRAPHY

Burkert, Walter. *Greek Religion*. Cambridge: Harvard UP, 1985. Print.

Carson, Anne. *Autobiography of Red*. New York: Vintage, 1999. Print.

Curtis, Paul. *Stesichoros's* Geryoneis. Leiden: Brill, 2011. Print.

Genovese, E. N. "Hercules and His Twelve Labors." *Masterplots*. 4th ed. Ed. Laurence W. Mazzeno. Pasadena: Salem, 2010. Print.

Hirst, Michael. *Michelangelo and His Drawings*. New Haven: Yale UP, 1988. Print.

Miller, Geordie. "Shifting Ground." *Canadian Literature* 210–211 (2011): 152–67. Print.

Morgan, Pauline. "Hercules and His Twelve Labors." *Cyclopedia of Literary Places*. Ed. R. Kent Rasmussen. Pasadena: Salem, 2003. Print.

Murray, Stuart J. "The Autobiographical Self: Phenomenology and the Limits of Narrative Self-Possession in Anne Carson's *Autobiography of Red*." *English Studies in Canada* 31.4 (2005): 101–22. Print.

Pseudo-Apollodorus. *The Library*. Trans. J. G. Frazer. 1921. Cambridge: Harvard UP, 1996. Print.

Jason and the Theft of the Golden Fleece

Author: Apollonius Rhodius
Time Period: 999 BCE–1 BCE
Country or Culture: Greek
Genre: Myth

OVERVIEW

The myth of Jason the Argonaut and his theft of the Golden Fleece is told by numerous sources but is most cohesively recorded in Apollonius Rhodius's *Argonautica*. The four-book epic was written in the third century BCE during the Hellenistic period, when the famous Library of Alexandria flourished, and it is considered the only surviving epic from that period. Although written specifically for Ptolemaic Alexandria, Apollonius fashioned the *Argonautica* on the Homeric epic tradition that preceded it. While following the great epic tradition of Homer, Apollonius is also credited with doing much to add to tradition by incorporating studies of geography, phenomena, and peoples and religions. Perhaps because of his fusion of scholarship and storytelling, the *Argonautica* initially experienced a hostile reception by its audiences, but it eventually grew in success once it was translated into Latin. In translation, it influenced Roman writers Valerius Flaccus, Catullus, Ovid, and perhaps most important, Virgil. Appreciation of the *Argonautica* has also grown in modern scholarship, where the work and its author have received admiration for its unprecedented poetic and empirical techniques.

The story of the *Argonautica* begins in Jason's kingdom, Iolcus (Iolcos); however, when Jason was a young boy his evil uncle, Pelias, assumed power, and Jason was secretly whisked away by those who feared Pelias would try to kill him. After receiving a prophesy that a stranger wearing only one sandal would herald his destruction, Pelias is greeted by his long-lost nephew, Jason, who has returned to take back his kingdom, having lost one of his sandals along the way. Pelias tells Jason that he will return the kingdom to Jason only if he brings him the Golden Fleece, a sacred gift of Zeus that hangs in a tree in distant Colchis, where it is protected by a dragon. Jason accepts Pelias's challenge and assembles a crew of heroes, said to be the most famous crew there ever was, including Heracles, Theseus, and Orpheus. The crew departs for their journey on the ship named *Argo* (meaning "swift"), which is assembled with a plank of divine wood and thought by the Greeks to be the first boat to have both a name and a personality. Before reaching Colchis, the crew, captained by Jason, encounters many different peoples and endures different heroic trials. After successfully obtaining the sought-after Golden Fleece, Jason and the Argonauts are pursued by irate Colchians, experience many more difficulties, and finally return home to Iolcus.

Analysis of Jason and his crew reveals Jason to be a highly problematic hero, while Medea, the traitorous daughter of the Colchian king and later wife of Jason, proves a formidable female character.

SUMMARY

When the Argonauts finally reach Colchis, Jason decides that it would be most diplomatic of him to negotiate calmly for the Golden Fleece with the king, Aeetes. The king receives the strangers warmly and offers them a banquet; however, when Jason brings up the Golden Fleece, King Aeetes erupts with anger. Thinking the tasks impossible, Aeetes tells Jason that the fleece is his only if he ploughs the fields of Ares with fire-breathing oxen, sows dragon's teeth into four acres of land, and then cuts down the crop of armed men. With reluctance, Jason accepts the challenge. Meanwhile Aeetes's daughter, Medea, a young princess with magical powers, has been shot by Eros's arrow and fallen in love with Jason. Fearing the fate of her four nephews, whom the *Argo* has captured, and the fate of her love interest, Medea gives Jason the magical powers he needs to complete the tasks. On the day of the trial, Jason performs the impossible tasks with ease, and the third book ends with Aeetes in a state of disbelief, already speculating about

Jason's feats and scheming ways to prevent him from obtaining the fleece, which he has rightly earned.

The fourth book of the *Argonautica* begins with the invocation of the muse, who is asked to tell of the labor and wiles of Medea, who after treasonously assisting her love, Jason, in his quest to obtain the Golden Fleece, has made the hasty decision to flee her home with her four nephews. She approaches the camp of Jason and his Argonauts cautiously and asks that Jason help her escape, reminding him that she is in this precarious position because she helped him. Jason not only assures his assistance but also promises to marry her when they return to his home. The pair then goes about obtaining the Golden Fleece; Medea uses her magic to subdue the dragon, allowing Jason to attain the glorious fleece.

They return to the others and assemble to depart on the *Argo*, suspecting by now that the Colchians will be in pursuit. One of the two fleets chasing the *Argo* sails into the Propontis, while the other ship, captained by Medea's brother, Apsyrtus, tails the *Argo* up the Ister River. Apsyrtus eventually corners the *Argo* on the Brygean islands in the Sea of Cronos, where the two crews decide to make peace by allowing Jason to keep his rightfully earned fleece under the condition that Medea's fate be decided by a third-party mediator. Fearing the outcome of this, Medea devises a different plan and lures her brother into a trap in which he is murdered and then dismembered by Jason. Without their leader, Apsyrtus's crew does not put up much of a fight, and they decide that instead of returning home to announce their failure, they will reestablish themselves elsewhere. Zeus, enraged by this brutal murder, decides to delay the Argonauts' return home.

The Argonauts are blown north up the Eridanus River and then through to the Sardinian Sea, where they are met by the witch Circe (Kirkê), the daughter of Perse and Helios. There Jason, Medea, and the Argonauts supplicate before Circe, the only one capable of cleansing them from their bloodguilt and thus freeing them from Zeus's curse. Circe cleanses them from their guilt, but she notably scorns Medea, telling her that her crimes are intolerable and will likely be avenged and then asking her to leave.

Meanwhile on Olympus, Hera asks the goddess Iris to summon the nymph Thetis so that they might have a conversation. The two have an amicable chat during which Hera informs Thetis that her young son, the future hero Achilles, will eventually marry Medea in the Elysian Fields. After sharing this information with the

"And as a maiden catches on her finely wrought robe the gleam of the moon at the full, as it rises above her high-roofed chamber; and her heart rejoices as she beholds the fair ray; so at that time did Jason uplift the mighty fleece in his hands; and from the shimmering of the flocks of wool there settled on his fair cheeks and brow a red flush like a flame. And great as is the hide of a yearling ox or stag, which huntsmen call a brocket, so great in extent was the fleece all golden above."

Argonautica

water nymph, Hera asks her to protect Medea and the Argonauts by ensuring that the *Argo* makes it safely to the south.

The *Argo* successfully passes the treacherous Sirens, beautiful songstresses who are notorious for luring sailors to doom with their enchanting songs. One of the Argonauts, Butes, falls overboard and comes close dying, but he is rescued by the goddess Cypris. Next, the *Argo* encounters the dangerous Wandering Rocks that boom beneath the sea and cause great and powerful surges. At this point, the crew is assisted by the Nereids, who protect them from danger. After making it through these obstacles, the *Argo* lands at Drepane, where it encounters another fleet from Colchis. Intent on preventing any harm from occurring on his soil, the king of Drepane, Alcinous, offers to mediate the conflict. In private, he tells his wife, Aretê, that his plan is to surrender Medea to the Colchians unless he finds out that she is married. Aretê takes pity on Medea and reveals Alcinous's plan to her and Jason. The couple then secretly marry, preventing Alcinous's plan from coming to fulfillment. Unsuccessful in their attempt to capture Medea, the Colchians think better of returning home and, like the previous fleet, decide to settle there.

When the Argonauts depart from Drepane, another strong wind blows them off course to the southern sandbank called Syrtis. Trapped on the sandbank, which renders their ship essentially useless, the Argonauts are overwhelmed with feelings of helplessness. They assume they have met their ends in Syrtis and go about preparing for their doom. Medea and her maids huddle together and lament their dismal fates. When it seems that all is lost, Jason is encountered by three nymphs, who provide him with unusual instructions for survival. When Jason shares these instructions, Peleus interprets them as meaning that the crew must carry their ship across the desert. After twelve days of trekking, they arrive at the Garden of the Hesperides and Lake Triton.

While they are gathered with the Hesperides, the nymph Aegle tells them that Heracles had been to the garden and raided it only one day before their arrival. During the group's time with the Hesperides, Canthus encounters and is killed by a shepherd defending his flock. On the same day, Mopsus is bitten by a snake and is poisoned to death. Orpheus decides that it would be a good idea to offer libations to the gods and to fetch the tripod for Apollo from the *Argo*; when they arrive at the ship, Triton, the messenger god of the sea, is waiting for them. He tells them of a route from the lake that opens into the sea, and he offers Euphemus a magical piece of the earth that will be used to become the island Thera. The Argonauts take Triton's suggested route and land at the island Anaphe. The heroes set up worship to the god Apollo. They also found Aegina, where they have a festival and competitions. The story finishes here, and the heroes eventually make it home with no further adventures to report.

ANALYSIS

Drawing formally from the Homeric epic tradition, Apollonius's four-book epic narrative prompts inevitable comparisons with Homeric texts, which established the epic form and the archetype of the epic hero. Many scholars have noted the hallmarks of the Homeric tradition in the *Argonautica*: the invocation of the Muses, the heroic quest, the episodic narrative (particularly comparable with *The Odyssey*), the role of the gods, epic battle scenes, and the exploration of foreign lands and peoples. Yet despite the story's heroic and epic framing, beginning with the German classicist Hermann Fränkel in 1957 and likely even earlier, critics have been keen to criticize the epic's supposed hero, Jason. While the criticisms range from outright condemnations of Jason's unheroic behavior to less harsh analyses that attempt to understand Jason as a stoic hero or the Everyman hero,

they all seem to agree that as the protagonist hero of a formal epic poem, Jason is not up to snuff.

Jason's epic begins rather unconventionally. Probably assuming that his audiences would have been familiar with the myth of Jason and the Argonauts, Apollonius does not go into too much detail introducing the mythical premise of the ensuing epic journey. He spends less than twenty lines explaining that Pelias, Jason's uncle, has received a prophesy that warns him of a wandering stranger who will approach in only one sandal; that shortly after Jason appears to reclaim his kingdom, missing a sandal; and that Pelias then conspires to challenge Jason with the impossible task of capturing the Golden Fleece in exchange for his kingdom. Considering that these important details are the impetus for the entire narrative, Apollonius is rather hasty in his telling of them. Compared with the emotional drama that is invoked at the beginning of *The Iliad* (ca. 750 BCE), in which the muse sings the song of the rage of Achilles, Jason's epic conflict is introduced in a comparatively pallid way.

Aside from the insipid lack of emotional drama, another crucial difference between the opening of *The Iliad* and the opening of the *Argonautica* is that Jason is paid little attention from the outset of the narrative. Unlike the Homeric muse in *The Iliad*, who inspires the bard to tell the story of Achilles, Apollonius's muse is asked to help the poet "recount the famous deeds of men of old, who, at the behest of King Pelias, down through the mouth of Pontus and between the Cyanean rocks, sped well-benched *Argo* in quest of the golden fleece" (1.1–4). In Apollonius's invocation, no one is singled out as the central character of the epic tale. Despite his audiences' foreknowledge of Pelias's challenge to Jason to capture the Golden Fleece, Apollonius finds it seemingly unnecessary to draw specific attention to the singular nature of the challenge. Oddly, Apollonius describes the epic story as a journey that will be accomplished by a collective of heroes. Only Pelias, the story's initial nemesis, and the ship, *Argo*, are singled out as significant characters. Jason's name is not even mentioned until line 6 and then only briefly.

Jason's brief introduction is also contrasted by the introductions the narrator gives the other heroes. Apollonius's cursory introduction of Jason as the central character might be understood as his assumption that his audience was familiar with the character had he not formed a catalog of the *Argonautica*'s crew of other heroes. Many of these heroes, including Theseus,

Heracles, and Orpheus, are more heroic than Jason in the traditional sense. Beginning with Orpheus, Apollonius gives each hero introductions of more than two hundred lines. As Mary Margolies DeForest notes, "All the other characters have skills or character traits that make them stand out from all the rest. Idmon is a seer; Idas, a drunken bully; Telamon, a loyal friend; Polydeuces, a skilled boxer; and the Boreads have wings. Only Jason is undefined" (54). The introduction that Apollonius provides for each hero establishes something fundamental about the mythical history or their specific character traits that develop as the narrative unfolds. Because Jason lacks an introductory description, his character is undefined for the entire narrative.

Once the extensive catalog of heroes has assembled, Heracles, not Jason, is singled out as commander. Since the crew has assembled to assist Jason, he would seemingly be the logical choice to lead the expedition; however, "when Jason finally gets the attention of his comrades and invites them to choose the best man as their leader, they unanimously chose Heracles. Their enthusiasm goes beyond rejected Jason, whom they do not seem to have even considered" (DeForest 50). The unanimous choice of Heracles highlights Jason's comparative inadequacy. Heracles does resemble a Homeric hero in a way that Jason does not, and Apollonius and his crew of heroes all seem to recognize that. Although chosen, Heracles defers the role of commander to Jason. As a result, "Jason does not take command because of his inherent superiority to the other heroes or to any other hero. His insignificance is underscored when he is given the title of commander by the man the Argonauts have unanimously chosen to lead them" (50). Jason is not chosen to be the leader because he is inherently worthy but by default, for reasons external to his character.

The episode between Jason and Heracles calls into question exactly what function Heracles is to have in the epic narrative. By traditional epic standards, Jason would appear to be Heracles's foil. DeForest observes that:

> From the point of view within the poem, Heracles holds the central position. He is the central Argonaut in the catalogue. When the list of men comes to life, he sits at their center (1.342). Before they set off, the Argonauts assign him to the center rowing-bench (1.396–97, 531). Thus, he is consistently presented as having an equal number of Argonauts stretching out on either side. Within the story, he is the central hero. (50)

Heracles's decision to appoint Jason as the leader is reflective of his central role in the narrative. Ironically, if it were not for Heracles, Jason would not have been appointed leader in the narrative about his own specific mission. In denouncing his role as leader, Heracles simultaneously assumes it by taking decisive action and, in effect, making an appropriate and honorable decision. Jason does nothing to earn his position as leader; it happens to him, not because of him.

When the Argonauts reach the shores of Lemnos, despite Jason's position of authority, Heracles continues to occupy the role of the hero. Lemnos is an island occupied by women only. The women tell Jason and his crew that all the men abandoned them, but in actuality, they killed all of the men and threw their bodies into the sea. This fact, of which Jason and his men remain unaware, puts the Argonauts, except for Heracles and a few others, into a compromising position. Instead of joining the other Argonauts and sleeping with the women, Heracles opts for a more cautious behavior and guards the *Argo*. Jason's liaising on Lemnos seems to put the whole mission for the fleece in jeopardy. Not only does Jason put the crew into a potentially dangerous situation, but he also becomes utterly distracted by the women and seems to lose interest in completing his quest. In contrast, Heracles remains firmly committed to the completion of Jason's epic, never veering from his heroic tasks.

DeForest observes that even after Jason is granted the position as commander, circumstances at Lemnos reveal that he only arbitrarily occupies a position of leadership. She notes, "When the Argonauts have lingered too long on [Lemnos], Heracles is revealed as the one with real authority. Calling the men to order, he destroys any semblance of authority Jason might have imagined to have" (58). Once again, Heracles is willing to take decisive action, whereas Jason is passive, allowing circumstances to occur. "On Lemnos, it seemed that Jason could be detached from the story and that his loss would not make a major change," DeForest argues (60). Having called the men to the ship, Heracles lectures them about their behavior:

> Wretched men, does the murder of kindred keep us from our native land? Or is it in want of marriage that we have come hither from thence, in scorn of our countrywomen? . . . No fair renown shall we win by thus tarrying so long with stranger women; nor will some god seize and give us at our prayer a fleece that moves of itself. (1.868–71)

Although he does not directly chastise Jason, Heracles critiques the passivity that characterizes Jason, reminding them all that the mission will not complete itself. His speech reflects poorly upon Jason, who passively reacts to being lectured for his impassiveness: "For eleven lines after Heracles' speech, it is not clear that Jason is among the Argonauts who obey Heracles's command so promptly" (DeForest 58). Jason does not even take charge when his lack of authority is being called to attention.

Although Jason does not seem to mind Heracles's upbraiding, Heracles's presence becomes problematic when trying to establish Jason as the central hero of the tale. Although, as DeForest points out, Jason could have probably been left behind on Lemnos without dramatically compromising the mission, "Instead it is Heracles who will be left behind. The stories of antithetical heroes is incompatible; the poem can no longer revolve around two centers" (60). Heracles's presence not only prompts an unfavorable comparison between him and Jason, but Heracles actually calls to attention Jason's inadequacies. Apollonius's decision to get rid of Heracles so soon is significant: "By ousting Heracles at the end of the first book, the narrator makes a literary statement: the *Argonautica* is not a tale in which an epic hero can thrive—it is not, in fact, a true epic" (60). The actual narrative function of Heracles's character is befuddling; what is the purpose of having a hero, obviously superior to Jason, steal the spotlight in the latter's tale?

Either way, Heracles walks away from the story for a rather histrionic reason. After convincing the Argonauts to leave Lemnos, Heracles, Jason, and the Argonauts encounter the monstrous six-armed, earthborn men, and despite being kindly welcomed, they mistake each other for enemies and kill each other in the dark. Jason kills the king, Cyzicus, who had shown them hospitality. The Argonauts have fought their first battle, but it is a battle that is fought tragically because of its total lack of necessity. When they next land on Cius, Heracles, not Jason, is faced with heroic hardship. Much like Achilles's relationship with Patroclus in Homer's *Iliad*, Heracles is accompanied on the journey by his young squire and lover, Hylas, whom he cares for passionately. Filling an urn in a spring on Cius, Hylas is abducted by the nymphs who admire his beauty. In the meantime, an argument breaks out among the Argonauts regarding who is the best oarsman. They decide to have a contest in order to determine who can row for the longest, and naturally, Heracles wins the contest:

The departure of Heracles is signalled when he breaks his oar. Eager to put the debacle at Cyzicus behind them, the Argonauts hold a contest to see who can row the longest. When furious winds arise in the evening, all except Heracles stop, exhausted. Though Heracles has won, he continues to row the ship single-handedly in a burst of frenzied competition. His effort is heroic, but absurd. Not content to be the central hero, he has to be the only hero. (DeForest 61–62)

After winning the contest, Heracles learns from Polyphemus about Hylas's mysterious disappearance. Evocative of Achilles's powerful wrath, which resulted in the Greek troops' revival during the Trojan War, Heracles throws down a pine tree and is filled with sadness and rage. Heracles and the few around him recognize that the time has come for him to abandon Jason's mission and to go on his own heroic conquest. The *Argo* sails off without its most authoritative epic hero. Thus, "Heracles' departure puts Jason in undisputed control and defines the literary nature of the poem" (DeForest 66).

With Jason no longer having to contend with Heracles as a heroic rival, one would imagine that Jason would rise to the task and more assertively assume his heroic role. With the loss of the *Argonautica*'s most obvious epic hero, readers "look at his Jason, expecting to find an Achilles or an Odysseus" but instead find "at best a supple diplomat, overshadowed as a character by Medea" (Hainsworth 72). Jason remains in a position of undisputed authority for a short time in the epic. Once Medea is introduced in book 3, Jason's passivity and lack of heroic fortitude is highlighted again by the juxtaposition of the two characters. Medea's unprecedented feminine heroics essentially put Jason to shame. All of the potentially heroic deeds that Jason performs are accomplished neither by his inherent brute strength nor by his intellectual shrewdness, but instead through the assistance of a woman who equips Jason with magical powers. When Jason finally embarks upon the mission to attain the Golden Fleece, the scene in which he does so is marked by Medea's bravery, rather than his: "Hereupon Jason snatched the golden fleece from the oak, at the maiden's bidding; and she, standing firm, smeared with the charm the monster's head, till Jason himself bade her turn back towards their ship, and she left the grove of Ares, dusky with shade" (4.162–65). Jason's heroic action is spurred by Medea's bidding, while Medea bravely fends off the dragon. The oddness of this situation is enhanced by the fact that Medea is referred to as a maiden, further establishing the inversion of roles performed throughout their relationship.

Exactly why Jason is portrayed as an anti–epic hero has been the subject of much critical speculation. Jason Joseph Clauss argues that "at a time when greater-than-life heroes like Heracles no longer existed in the collective mind, Apollonius created for his *Argonautica* a real-life hero, vulnerable, dependent on the help of others, even morally questionable, but successful" (2). Clauss is right to assert that despite Jason's apparent lack of vigor, he is ultimately successful in accomplishing his mission. Perhaps, as Clauss suggests, Apollonius's construction of Jason is reflective of a collective recognition that the great epic heroes of the past, such as Achilles, Odysseus, and Heracles, had somehow lost their appeal or their relevance. Heracles's swift departure in the first book might attest to this suggestion. Either way, Jason's character is a perplexing one. His subsequent mythological fate, imagined by many, might pronounce the final authoritative verdict on Jason's mythological portrayal, since he is eventually fated to an utterly passive end, waiting for death alongside the landed *Argo*, which finally kills him when a rotting beam falls and hits him in the head.

CROSS-CULTURAL INFLUENCE

Apollonius's *Argonautica* has been, and continues to be, admired for its innovative and original storytelling, but the story of Jason and his quest for the Golden Fleece was already well known by the Greeks at the time that the epic was composed. While the *Argonautica* seems to end rather inconclusively, the myth about Jason and his Colchian wife, Medea, had inspired many writers and storytellers long before Apollonius to imagine the mythical continuation and ending of the story. Perhaps the most popular imagining of Jason and Medea's homecoming is Euripides's fifth-century Attic tragedy *Medea*. Despite finishing in last place at the Dionysia in the year of its production, 431 BCE, *Medea* has inspired

MYTH INTO ART

Jason and the Argonauts Disembark at Colchis was completed by the French painter Charles de Lafosse in 1672 and is on display at the Palace of Versailles in the Salon of Diana. As the title suggests, the painting depicts Jason and his troop of heroes after landing in Colchis, where they are greeted by King Aeetes, Medea's father. The scene portrayed occurs in book 3 of Apollonius Rhodius's *Argonautica*, where most of the climactic action that occurs in the final book of the epic is established. In the painting, Jason has disembarked from the *Argo*, and he offers his hands to Aeetes. Jason leans toward Aeetes—a gesture that is seemingly returned by the king who welcomes him. These peaceful gestures elucidate Jason's diplomatic intention to discuss the potential of obtaining the Golden Fleece.

Born in Paris in 1636, Lafosse was one of the most renowned decorative painters during the reign of Louis XIV. After receiving training from Charles Le Brun, Lafosse assisted him at the Palace of Versailles. Lafosse was also highly influenced by the Italian painter Pietro da Cortona, with whom he stayed in Italy from 1658 to 1663. It is likely that while there, Lafosse was exposed to the rich colors and warm style of the Italian baroque painters. In 1689, Lafosse traveled to England and took up residence in London, where he worked for the former English ambassador to France, the first Duke of Montagu. In 1692, he returned to Paris, where he decorated the church of Les Invalides. Many art historians assert that Lafosse's work on the church's dome and the pendentives portrays is a clear antecedent to the rococo movement that became popular shortly afterward.

numerous adaptations and has contributed to making its titular character arguably more infamous than her heroic husband.

Medea was written and performed within a specific context of Athenian theater, a tradition that is rather different from modern theater. The golden age of Athens coincided with a flourishing arts and culture in the city. The performance of plays centered on an annual festival called the Great Dionysia that took place in March. As the name suggests, the festival was held in honor of the Greek god Dionysus. Although there were a variety of competitions, including large choral performances called the dithyramb, the main two genres in which playwrights competed were tragedy and comedy. Tragedies were composed in tetralogies consisting of three connected plays concluded by a shorter satyr play that was not especially connected thematically to the trilogy. The plays were performed in a large, open-air theater that was located on the southwestern side of the hill of the Acropolis and was capable of seating up to seventeen thousand people.

Unlike the Attic comedies, the stories told in the tragic plays were not directly current; instead, the content of tragedies was made up by the mythic past. Thus, much like Apollonius's audience, the audiences at the Dionysia would have already been somewhat familiar with the stories, including that of Jason and Medea. Often the plays involve famous family dynasts, such as the House of Atreus in Aeschylus's *Oresteia* (458 BCE) or the Oedipal house of Cadmus. As subjects of the tragic genre, these families are portrayed as dysfunctional, having been cursed by the gods or having incurred punishment for a family member's wrongdoings. Usually, the play would center on a main character, either male or female; however, all the actors on stage would be men wearing masks. Apart from the lead protagonist, there were few additional supporting actors, accompanied by a chorus of twelve to fifteen people. Rarely taking any action, the chorus was portrayed as a homogenous group of societal onlookers that, through song, provided context for the audience, expressing what lead characters could not say and commenting on themes and developments throughout the play.

Among Euripides's eighteen extant plays (although he is said to have written at least ninety), *Medea* is perhaps his best known and most popular. The play essentially begins where Apollonius concludes the *Argonautica*, with Jason and Medea's arrival in Corinth. Prior to arriving in Corinth, Jason and Medea had returned home to Iolcus after fetching the Golden Fleece; however, Pelias still refused to give up the throne to Jason as he had promised. According to most mythical traditions, Medea then schemed to have Pelias killed by his two daughters. She tells the daughters that through her sorcery she could turn an old ram young by chopping it up and burning it in a pot. After demonstrating this, the daughters are convinced and decide to do the same thing for their father; however, their attempt results in Pelias's murder. Some traditions say that following this, Jason and Medea flee to Corinth; others suggest that Medea kills the daughters too and the couple stay in Iolcus for some time until the Iolcians force them to leave, feeling suspicious and uncertain about Medea's magical powers.

Either way, the couple end up in Corinth with their two sons, which is where Euripides starts his play. After arriving in Corinth, King Creon (a different mythical Creon from the king of Thebes) offers Jason the hand of his daughter Glauce in marriage despite the fact that Jason is married to and has two sons with Medea. Jason thinks well of the offer and accepts it. The play begins with Medea standing outside of their house in Corinth despondent and furious over Jason's decision. She is accompanied by her nurse and watched by the women of Corinth, who are all fearful about what she might do. Creon, who is content knowing his kingdom might be passed on through his daughter's marriage with the Greek hero, also feels concerned about Medea and arrives at her house to send her into exile. She manages to persuade Creon to give her a day to prepare to leave. In the following scene, Jason arrives and attempts to explain his decision to Medea. He tells her that he could not give up the opportunity to marry a Greek princess and that he eventually plans to unite his two families and have Medea as his mistress. Medea reminds him of all the sacrifices she has made for him and how she assisted him in attaining the Golden Fleece. After betraying her father and killing her brother, she cannot return home, and as a barbarian, she cannot find a home in Greece. Jason assures her that he will support her, but Medea angrily dismisses him.

Medea is then unexpectedly visited by King Aegeus of Athens, who tells her that he and his wife are distressed over their inability to conceive. Recognizing the situation as one that could potentially benefit her, Medea promises to concoct a spell to help them get pregnant as long as the king promises to offer her refuge in Athens. King Aegeus agrees and departs, leaving Medea to scheme over ways to kill Creon and Glauce. She decides that she will poison golden robes and offer them to Glauce as a wedding gift. She also resolves to kill her children as a punishment to Jason. She fetches him and coyly pretends to apologize, giving him the robes as a gift of concession. She tells him that she thinks it right that she should go but begs for the children to be able to stay. Jason accepts her request and her gift and then leaves to offer the gift to Glauce and Creon, both of whom are poisoned by the clothes and killed offstage. After learning of their deaths from a messenger, Medea plans the horrific filicide of her sons and leaves the stage with a knife. While the chorus laments her actions, the terrifying sounds of her sons' screams are heard from offstage. When Jason returns to castigate her for murdering Creon and Glauce, he finds his sons have also been murdered by her.

Medea appears before Jason, in the chariot of the sun god, Helios, from whom she is descended. She revels in Jason's pain and misfortune, explaining to him that he will never be able to make a new family. She tells him that she intends to take the bodies of the boys from him as well, so that they can be buried in Hera's domain, and then she prophesizes an evil doom for him. Once she leaves, the chorus reacts to the horrible events of the play that have ensued. The play ends under the premise that Medea successfully escapes to Athens. Although Jason's fate is addressed no further, audiences watching the play would have been familiar with the story of Jason's death. As the myths recount, following Medea's departure, Jason wanders around aimlessly, a ruined man. Apparently he wastes his days on the shores perched beside his loyal ship, the *Argo*, which eventually kills him when a beam comes crashing down from it, hitting him in the head.

Following its performance, Euripides's play was not received warmly by Athenian audiences and was given last place in the contest of the Great Dionysia. There are numerous reasons why the Athenians would not have liked the play. Apart from the horrific filicide, Athenians may have taken issue with the unflattering portrayal of their city throughout the play. Describing their mythical king Aegeus as infertile was probably not taken too kindly, but more important, the idea that the murderous barbarian woman could extort and then be granted refuge in Athens was likely to have been extremely problematic for the Athenians, who were concerned with democracy and justice. Also, that Medea purportedly evades prosecution through her partially divine lineage would have not gone over well either. According to Edith Hall, "Medea stands alone amongst tragic felons in committing her offence with impunity. In extant Greek tragedy no other kin-killers reach the end of their plays unpunished" (xvi). Medea's lack of a verdict is a far cry from Orestes's trial for the vengeful murder of his mother in Aeschylus's first prize–winning *Oresteia*, in which Orestes is prosecuted and eventually acquitted by the Areopagus.

Even apart from the issues that the Athenians might have found in Euripides's play, the notoriously controversial playwright is also thought to have made some provocative alterations to the already-tragic myth. According to Eumelus, the eighth-century BCE poet attributed with writing *Korinthiaka*, Medea's murder of her children is recorded as being accidental. Alternately, the legendary Greek poet Creophylus of Samos attests that Medea's sons are killed not by Medea, but by the people of Corinth. Most scholars attribute Euripides with the invention of Medea's calculated murder of her sons, a decision that has been criticized by many as being too drastic. Yet, despite this criticism, Euripides's supposed alteration was largely accepted as the standard ending of the myth, which would be imitated and used many times in different adaptations.

Despite its lack of success during Euripides's lifetime, *Medea* went on to be celebrated as one of the greatest tragedies in the Western canon. The play experienced a Roman revival and was rewritten by the likes of Ennius, Lucius Accius, Ovid, Seneca the Younger, and Hosidius Geta. It also experienced a resurgence in popularity in Europe in the sixteenth century and has more recently received interest from feminist critics who have sought to understand the play as the story of an abandoned woman seeking vengeance in a patriarchal world. *Medea* is largely credited with preserving the story of her ill-fated husband, Jason, and for that reason, many critics have noted that Medea's dominant personality tends to eclipse or highlight the insipidness of Jason's character in the play and throughout his mythical legacy.

Katherine Sehl, MA

BIBLIOGRAPHY

Apollonius Rhodius. *Apollonius Rhodius, the Argonautica*. Trans. R. C. Seaton. Cambridge: Harvard UP, 1961. Print.

Clauss, James Joseph. *The Best of the Argonauts: The Redefinition of the Epic Hero in Book One of Apollonius's* Argonautica. Berkeley: U of California P, 1993. Print.

DeForest, Mary Margolies. *Apollonius' Argonautica: A Callimachean Epic*. New York: Brill, 1994. Print.

Euripides. *Medea and Other Plays*. Trans. James Morwood. New York: Oxford UP, 1997. Print.

Hainsworth, J. B. *The Idea of Epic*. Berkeley: U of California P, 1991. Print.

Hall, Edith. Introduction. *Medea and Other Plays*. By Euripides. Trans. James Morwood. New York: Oxford UP, 1997. Print.

Hunter, Matthew L. *Jason and Medea: A Whirlwind of Ruin*. New York: IUniverse, 2005. Print.

King Arthur and the Sword in the Stone

Author: Thomas Bulfinch
Time period: 501 CE–1000 CE; 1851 CE–1900 CE
Country or Culture: England
Genre: Legend

OVERVIEW

The classic saga of King Arthur and his knights has endured in Western literature since it was first told by Geoffrey of Monmouth in his twelfth-century pseudo-historical work *Historia regum Britanniae* (*History of the Kings of Britain*). Because Geoffrey included many fanciful events based on English, Cornish, and Welsh folktales in his account of Arthur's life and reign, there has been much debate regarding whether the fabled king was a historical figure. Some scholars believe that King Arthur is based on a Roman British *dux bellorum*, or warlord, who fought against Anglo-Saxon forces at the battle of Mount Badon in the late fifth or early sixth century CE (Day 15). Others have suggested that Arthur never existed and is simply a heroic figure in the rich folklore of the Britons and Celts. Another theory posits that the character of Arthur is based on a Celtic deity. Whatever Arthur's historical or literary origin, his story has appeared in various incarnations across cultures for more than nine hundred years and remains just as compelling to modern-day readers.

American writer Thomas Bulfinch's nineteenth-century retelling of the story of Arthur in *The Age of Chivalry* (1858), one of three books later combined and published as *Bulfinch's Mythology*, portrays events common to Arthur's story since it first became popular in the Middle Ages. Arthur is the son of a king and queen but is unaware of his heritage. After his birth, he lives an anonymous life in the care of his foster father, Sir Ector, on a rural English estate. Since the death of Arthur's biological father, King Uther Pendragon, the kingdom has been plagued by civil war as competing lords fight each other for the crown. The nobles know that the former king's heir is alive, but they have no idea who he is.

The defining moment for Arthur comes when the unwitting teenager easily draws an enchanted sword out of a stone—an action that identifies him as the true king of England. Thereafter, Arthur goes on to win battles, the nobles' allegiance, and eventually the hand of the beautiful princess Guenever.

Although the events of the story remain relatively constant, the social, political, and spiritual aspects of the legend change in the hands of accomplished storytellers from different eras. For example, Bulfinch's emphasis on courage, courtesy, and spirituality resonated with his nineteenth-century readers because those ideals were tightly woven into the fabric of Victorian society. *Le Morte d'Arthur* (1485; The death of Arthur), penned by fifteenth-century English knight and adventurer Thomas Malory, became a source book for subsequent Arthurian retellings and mirrors Malory's own experience as a soldier and noble in a war-torn country. T. H. White's Arthurian fantasy *The Once and Future King*, of which *The Sword in the Stone* is a part, is a mid-twentieth-century exploration of the relationship between power and justice. Because each of these works is the product of a particular era, comparisons between them serve as useful lenses through which to view Western social and literary history.

SUMMARY

After Roman rule ends in Britain, Saxon tribes from what is now Germany invade the island during the fifth and sixth centuries CE, waging a war of conquest against the Celtic inhabitants. According to Geoffrey of Monmouth, King Constans, one of the primary sovereigns of the late sixth century, has three sons: Moines, Ambrosius (or Uther), and Pendragon. When the king dies, Moines takes the throne. His conniving seneschal, Vortigern, plots against him, and Moines is overthrown by the invaders. Vortigern becomes king, but Uther and Pendragon dethrone him. Pendragon succeeds Vortigern and names the powerful magician Merlin his chief counselor.

When another conflict erupts between the Saxons and the Britons, Merlin insists that the two brothers swear fealty to one another—and also predicts that one brother will be killed in battle. Pendragon is slain, and Uther, who takes his dead brother's name in addition to his own, becomes king. Uther, like his brothers before him, has great confidence in Merlin's abilities, and he asks the magician to transport huge stones from Ireland to Salisbury Plain. The resulting collection of standing stones marks the tomb of Pendragon and forms what becomes known as Stonehenge. Merlin also conceives the idea of the Round Table, around which selected nobles and their ladies gather once a year to profess their loyalty to the king and one another. The companions also promise to embark on individual adventures, lead a life of chastity when called upon to do so, and tirelessly defend the realm against enemy attacks.

During one of the Round Table's annual meetings, Gerlois, Duke of Tintadiel, brings his beautiful wife, Igerne, to the king's court. Uther falls in love with her and presses her to return his affection. She is put off by his impropriety and tells her husband. Enraged, Gerlois takes Igerne and escapes to his fortified castle at Tintadiel, on the Cornwall coast. The king demands that he return, but when Gerlois refuses, Uther declares war on the duke. Consumed with passion for Igerne, Uther asks for Merlin's help. The magician obliges by transforming the king's appearance into that of the duke. While Gerlois is fighting Uther's troops, the disguised king slips into Tintadiel to visit the duchess. When the duke is killed in battle, Uther makes Igerne his queen, and she later gives birth to a son, Arthur.

Secretly raised by Sir Ector, Arthur becomes the foster brother and squire of Ector's son, Kay. Arthur's rise to power after Uther's death is not "without opposition, for there [are] many ambitious competitors" (Bulfinch 374). Seeking to identify the legitimate king, Bishop Brice preaches a Christmas Eve sermon in which he asks his congregation to pray for a sign from God. When the service ends, the worshippers discover a mysterious sword lodged in a stone outside of the church. Words engraved on the sword's pommel read, "I am hight Escalibore, unto a king fair tresore" (374). The bishop declares that the man who draws the sword out of the stone will be declared Uther's successor. Renowned knights try to remove the sword, but it does not move.

When the spring tournament season begins, Sir Kay attends along with his squire, Arthur, who is unaware of his heritage. Kay breaks his sword during a joust and

> *"A miraculous stone was discovered, before the church door, and in the stone was firmly fixed a sword. . . . Bishop Brice, after exhorting the assembly to offer up their thanksgivings for this signal miracle, proposed a law, that whoever should be able to draw out the sword from the stone, should be acknowledged as sovereign of the Britons; and his proposal was decreed by general acclamation."*
>
> "King Arthur and His Knights"

commands Arthur to ride home and retrieve a new one from his mother. Arthur obeys his master but cannot find Kay's mother. Remembering that he had ridden by a church where he saw a sword stuck in a stone, he returns to the spot, easily draws the sword, and brings it to Kay. The older boy recognizes the weapon and decides to claim the throne for himself. When the blade is again placed in the stone, however, Kay cannot pull it out—only Arthur is able. Thus Arthur is "decisively pointed out by Heaven as their king" (375).

After Arthur's coronation, he seeks to consolidate his rule and goes to war against eleven kings and a duke. The forces arrayed against him are so overwhelming that Merlin casts a spell to collapse the tents of the opposing army, allowing Arthur and his soldiers to fall upon and rout the enemy. After cementing his power among his own people, Arthur defends his lands against the Saxon invaders at Mount Badon. He arms himself and, "calling on the name of the Virgin, rushes into the midst of his enemies, and destroys multitudes of them with the formidable Caliburn [Escalibore], and puts the rest to flight" (375–76). His victory breaks the Saxon yoke and ushers in a golden age.

After this victory, Merlin again directs the course of Arthur's life, this time acting as a matchmaker. Arriving incognito at the court of King Laodegan, Merlin, Arthur, and thirty-nine knights find Laodegan attempting to defend his kingdom from Irish invaders. Merlin, serving as leader of Arthur's retinue, volunteers their services on

MYTH INTO ART

In 1969, performers John Cleese, Graham Chapman, Terry Gilliam, Michael Palin, Terry Jones, and Eric Idle, collectively known as Monty Python, created *Monty Python's Flying Circus*, a comedy program that ran on British television until 1974 and subsequently aired on American television. Their trademark anarchic style, known for its stream-of-consciousness format, lack of punch lines, and use of surreal animations, overturned traditional models of comedy. After Monty Python's successful stint on television, the troupe turned to movies. Their second film, *Monty Python and the Holy Grail* (1975), is a hilarious send-up of the Arthurian legend and mocks familiar themes, including the chivalric code and the institution of the monarchy.

Commanded by God to search for the Holy Grail, King Arthur, the squire Patsy, Sir Bedevere the Wise, Sir Lancelot the Brave, Sir Robin the Not-Quite-So-Brave-as-Sir-Lancelot, and Sir Galahad the Pure embark on the quest and encounter trials along the way. For example, Arthur and Bedevere meet strange knights whose favorite word is "Ni" and who demand shrubbery for safe passage. Lancelot answers a call from a maiden in distress and single-handedly destroys a wedding at Swamp Castle. Galahad sees what he thinks is a vision of the Grail above Castle Anthrax and discovers that the castle is inhabited by beautiful women who want to seduce him. Other adventures include an absurd battle between Arthur and the Black Knight, who insists that he and Arthur continue fighting even though the king has chopped off all his limbs.

In the decades since its premiere, *Monty Python and the Holy Grail* has become a revered part of pop culture. It was named the second-best comedy of all time in a 2011 poll conducted by the ABC television network and *People* magazine. In 2005, Idle's *Spamalot*, a Broadway musical based on the film, won three Tony Awards.

---

the condition that they remain anonymous. A few days later, the enemy masses for an attack. Merlin, Arthur, and the knights march to defend the city. When Merlin commands the porter to open the gates, he refuses, so Merlin instead takes "up the gate with all its appurtenances of locks, bars, and bolts, and direct[s] his troops to pass through, after which he replace[s] it in perfect order" (381). Again the Britons find themselves outnumbered, so Merlin enchants the enemy, which leads to a victory for the Britons.

Laodegan's beautiful daughter, Guenever (or Guinevere), witnesses Arthur's exploits on the battlefield and wishes that he become her husband. After the battle, Guenever and her maids wait on the warriors as they bathe and feast. Over the next few days, the attraction between Arthur and Guenever deepens. When Merlin finally confesses that the purpose of the group's visit to Laodegan's court was to find a wife for Arthur, Laodegan offers Guenever to the young king. Arthur reveals his true identity, and he and Guenever are married.

ANALYSIS

Bulfinch's retelling of Arthur's youth, call to kingship, and early reign reinterprets centuries of literary traditions to present the story of Arthur from the perspective of nineteenth-century Victorian morality and spiritual ideals. The well-known events of Arthur's heroic tale remain intact. Similar to preceding versions, Bulfinch's account includes the unusual circumstances of Arthur's birth, brief mention of his obscure childhood, the crucial test that legitimizes his claim to the throne, tales of his prowess as a warrior, and his marriage to Guenever. The concepts of chivalry and courtly love—two ideals developed by medieval authors that resonated with the Victorians—illuminate the plot and serve as the motivation for the characters' behavior.

The Victorians' attraction to classical and medieval themes in literature had its roots in the romantic movement, which developed during the late eighteenth and mid-nineteenth centuries. The romantics' emphasis on individual heroism, the forces of nature, and passion as well as their interest in medievalism survived in the art and literature of the Victorian era (1837–1901), although in a more restrained form. Depictions of dashing knights, fair ladies, and heroic battles were fairly common in the visual arts during the period. Artist such as James Archer, Thomas Woolner, and John William Waterhouse explored Arthurian subjects, although they did not depict content they found morally objectionable (Lacy 603–4). Paralleling the revival of Arthurian subject matter in painting and other visual arts, British prose and poetry of the period also featured elements of Arthurian legend. Writers such as Matthew Arnold, William Morris, and Algernon Charles Swinburne contributed to the growing body of Arthurian literature. The cycle of poems *Idylls of the King*, composed by Alfred, Lord Tennyson and quoted on several occasions in *Bulfinch's Mythology*, was perhaps most influential in sparking a renewed interest in Arthur's story in England and the United States. Influenced by Malory's *Le Morte d'Arthur*, Tennyson sought to create an epic that would draw on the past to speak to the present about the need for morality and spirituality in the Victorian era.

The chivalric code is especially central to Bulfinch's account because the values of chivalry were consonant with living a moral life. The word "chivalry" derives from the French word *chevalier*, which denotes a mounted soldier, and was first used in a military sense in medieval times (Lacy 103). Subsequently, the concept of chivalry became synonymous with a behavioral ideal that shaped and was used to judge the character of knights. The virtues at the heart of chivalry were many and included physical prowess, loyalty, generosity, piety, chastity, and fidelity. The ideal knight would keep his pledge to fight for good and destroy evil, protect the weak, strive to be honest and trustworthy, and adhere to Christian principles. He was also bound by the ideal of courtly love, a complex concept that has generally come to be understood as faithfully serving a woman one loves from afar.

The chivalric qualities of strength, fairness, honor, and faith informed the ideal of manhood among the middle and upper classes in the Victorian era. The ideal Victorian man took pride in his work; protected women, who were viewed as the weaker sex; was well mannered; strove to attain material success; and adhered to Christian teachings. Women were likewise expected to conform to certain models of behavior. The ideal Victorian woman was an industrious homemaker and subordinate to her husband. Motherhood was a sacred responsibility regarded as the truest path to female spiritual fulfillment, and young Victorian women spent their lives preparing for marriage. These contrasting gender roles in Victorian society played into the medieval concept of courtly love. Women in both medieval and Victorian societies were idealized, and both Victorian men and medieval knights strove to serve and protect their ladies with devotion, honor, and courtesy. The Victorian

custom of sexual restraint only served to intensify this view of romantic love.

Bulfinch's narratives concerning Uther and Igerne and Arthur and Guenever promote the ideals of chivalry and courtly love as the Victorians understood them and call attention to the contrasts between an honorable knight and a dishonorable one and between a legitimate love and an illegitimate affair. In some ways, Uther fits the medieval and Victorian image of the ideal ruler and man. In other ways, he fails to live up to the code he has promised to preserve. Uther's strength in battle enables him to outlive his brothers and become high king over the Britons. He is an able leader who seeks the counsel of wise men, especially that of the renowned magician Merlin. Uther is not afraid of innovation; his institution of the Round Table is revolutionary and binds his nobles to him through their oath to "assist each other at the hazard of their own lives, to attempt singly the most perilous adventures, to lead, when necessary, a life of monastic solitude, to fly to arms at the first summons, and never to retire from battle till they had defeated the enemy, unless night intervened and separated the combatants" (Bulfinch 373).

There are honorable knights among the king's company of nobles, but Uther is not one of them. Instead of respecting the marriage of Gerlois and Igerne, he allows his passion to get the better of him and tries to lure the duchess into adultery. Her refusal reveals her to be an honest woman who is faithful to her husband. In contrast, Uther goes against the ideals he has instituted and betrays one of his own knights by trying to steal his wife. He further compounds his missteps by asking Merlin to transform his appearance into that of Gerlois so that he can enjoy "stolen interviews" with Igerne while the real Gerlois is fighting against the king's army (374). Uther's deception does not impugn the honor of Igerne, as she remains unaware of Uther's real identity. Her ignorance allows her to remain a loving wife, thus sparing her reputation and nullifying any suggestion that she was a willing accomplice in adultery.

In an attempt to avoid offending Victorian sensibilities concerning illicit affairs, Bulfinch sidesteps the question of when Arthur is conceived. In Geoffrey of Monmouth's account of the relationship between Uther and Igerne, Arthur is conceived on the night Gerlois is killed by Uther's troops, which makes Arthur illegitimate. Bulfinch takes another approach. Instead of identifying Arthur as the product of Uther's adulterous union with Igerne, he merely states, "At length the duke was killed in battle, and the king espoused Igerne. From this union sprang Arthur" (374). In approaching the relationship of Uther and Igerne in this vague manner, Bulfinch turns away from the opportunity to highlight the bitter irony and injustice inherent in the circumstances surrounding the birth of the heir to the throne. In addition, reinterpreting the circumstances of Arthur's conception eliminates the possibility of foreshadowing later tragedy. Uther's affair with Igerne parallels and presages the adultery of Lancelot and Guenever years later, which is the major cause of the dissolution of the Round Table and the subsequent war between Arthur and Lancelot. The idea that Arthur was conceived through an adulterous relationship, even if the woman was an unwitting participant, would have shocked the very audience Bulfinch was trying to reach.

In contrast to Uther's duplicitous and treacherous character, Arthur is portrayed as an honest, good, brave, and faithful young man. His innocence and humility are apparent in the story of the sword in the stone. Although Bulfinch says nothing about Arthur's early life, the fact that Arthur serves as squire to his foster brother, Sir Kay, indicates that he is a knight in training. As a squire, Arthur is required to carry his master's shield and sword, run errands for the knight, and replace his sword if something happens to it. In Bulfinch's story, Arthur faithfully and eagerly performs all of these tasks. He is completely ignorant of his royal lineage, as is Kay, who commands his young squire to go home and retrieve a new sword when he breaks his old one during a joust.

Arthur's royalty is soon revealed through the test of the sword in the stone, which not only demonstrates his right to the throne but also emphasizes the spiritual element involved in his rise to power. The sword is placed in front of a church, which is a central gathering place for the community. In some versions of the tale, Merlin magically causes the sword in the stone to appear. Bulfinch, however, presents a Christianized version in which a bishop has full knowledge of the oddity and its purpose. Instead of an enchanted artifact, the sword is a sign to the people that "should manifest the intentions of Providence respecting their future sovereign" (374). The monarchy and religion were intertwined during the Middle Ages and remained so into the Victorian period. If a country lacked a king, the church often took the lead in determining the right of succession. In Bulfinch's version, the bishop, as God's representative, not only declares the sword in the stone a miracle—and thus an act of God—but also announces that the person able

to draw the sword out will be declared the heir to the throne by divine right. Arthur pulls the sword from the stone and is "thus decisively pointed out by Heaven" as God's choice to rule (375). The concept of the divine right of kings was a familiar one in Bulfinch's time. Just as Queen Victoria was considered by the British to be defender of the faith, Arthur is cast as a Christian king.

After his coronation, Arthur must establish that he is worthy of wearing the crown by proving his manhood. Like his father before him, he takes to the battlefield and, with Merlin's help, wins decisive victories over his rebellious lords. After he unifies his country, his next task is to defend it by beating back the Saxon invaders, which he does at the famous battle of Mount Badon. However, Arthur is no ordinary warlord. To emphasize Arthur's sacred authority, Bulfinch quotes from Geoffrey of Monmouth's account:

> Arthur himself dressed in a breastplate worthy of so great a king, places on his head a golden helmet engraved with the semblance of a dragon. Over his shoulders he throws his shield called Priwen, on which a picture of the Holy Virgin constantly recalled her to his memory. Girt with Caliburn [Escalibore], a most excellent sword, and fabricated on the Isle of Avalon, he graces his right hand with the lance named Ron. This was a long and broad spear, well contrived for slaughter. (375)

Geoffrey's description of Arthur is both mythical and spiritual. His armor and weapons reveal him to be a mighty warrior, charged by God to save the Britons from the Saxon hordes. Instead of paying court to a mere woman, Arthur adorns his shield with the image of the Virgin Mary. She—not an earthly love—is his inspiration as he charges into the fray. Uther was an able though flawed leader, but Arthur is godlike. It is clear that he is a superb specimen of ideal manhood, a strong leader who courageously serves God and others, and a worthy example for every man to follow.

As heroic and godlike as Arthur is, he is incomplete. A true knight serves his lady, and a king needs a queen to produce an heir. Merlin takes on the task of shaping Arthur's destiny and, just as he did with Uther and Igerne, engineers a match between Arthur and Guenever. Although Guenever, like Igerne, is unaware of Arthur's true identity, there is no stealth, deceit, or dishonesty involved in bringing about a meeting. As Merlin leads Arthur and his companions against the invaders,

Guenever's father, King Laodegan, is carried off by his enemies while Guenever watches from the sidelines, pulling out her hair in distress. However, Arthur's brave exploits—including holding off the enemy, killing a giant, and saving the king—convince the princess that she wants the knight for her husband, although she has no idea who he is. Their relationship is both an arranged marriage and a love match, much like the marriage of Queen Victoria and Prince Albert. Arthur and Guenever are equal partners in a match that promises to make a positive difference in the realm they will rule together. Their partnership parallels that found in the Victorian home, in which husband and wife took on complementary roles. The ideal husband was the provider and protector, and the ideal wife was keeper of the home. Together with their children, they formed an essential social unit that passed Victorian values on to succeeding generations.

While Bulfinch's story of the beginning of Arthur's reign shines with hope, subsequent events such as Lancelot and Guenever's affair are inherently pessimistic and, to Victorian readers, sinful. Bulfinch addresses these events later in his account but does not focus on them. Instead, he adheres to his high-minded purpose—to promote the virtues of goodness, service, faithfulness, courage, respectability, and duty in order to inspire moral behavior and strengthen spiritual values in Victorian society.

CROSS-CULTURAL INFLUENCE

Published by printer William Caxton in England in 1485, Sir Thomas Malory's *Le Morte d'Arthur* is the text on which most modern adaptations of the Arthurian legend are based. The familiar images of bold knights, fair ladies, pitched battles, friendly jousts, and dreadful monsters are all found in Malory's compilation, as are the dramatic stories of the institution of the Round Table, the quest for the Holy Grail, and the sword in the stone, among others. Malory was the first to select episodes from well-known Norman and English sources and organize them into a recognizable narrative that follows Arthur's life from his birth to his death. Subsequent writers have used Malory's book as a source text for their own versions of the Arthurian legend.

Malory's fifteenth-century world was not very far removed from the medieval society of *Le Morte d'Arthur*. At that time, war was common, nobles were expected to defend their lands and people, and the code of chivalry was still viewed as the standard by which knights should live their lives. Although Malory was a nobleman and was expected to live up to chivalrous ideals, according to writer Robert Graves's introduction to *Le Morte d'Arthur*, his conduct fell far short of the expectations of the time. Born to Sir John Malory and Lady Phillipa Malory likely within the first two decades of the fifteenth century, he inherited his mother's estate in Newbold Revel (sometimes spelled Revell) in 1433. A professional soldier, he served under the Earl of Warwick and became a member of Parliament for Warwickshire in 1445, but his respectable life was eventually derailed by his criminal inclinations. He is believed to have ambushed and attempted to murder the Duke of Buckingham in 1450 and was also accused of rape, cattle theft, and highway robbery. Malory was apprehended and sent to Coleshill Prison and Colchester Castle, escaping both of them. During the Wars of the Roses, he fought for the house of York and then switched his allegiance to the house of Lancaster. Because of his desertion, he was incarcerated in Newgate Prison, where he penned *Le Morte d'Arthur*. Malory is thought to have died in 1471.

Malory's checkered career as an adventurer, soldier, mercenary, and criminal afforded him a perspective from which to write Arthur's story that differs greatly from the genteel Victorian perspective of Bulfinch. In "The Tale of King Arthur," the first section of *Le Morte d'Arthur*, Malory, like Bulfinch, covers Uther's adultery with Igerne (whom he calls Igraine), the political unrest resulting from Uther's death, the test of the sword in the stone, and Arthur's succession to the throne. At the time Malory was writing, England was engulfed by the Wars of the Roses, a series of civil wars, taking place over several decades, in which the rival Yorks and Lancasters fought to gain control of the throne. Thus, the preoccupation with the right of succession in the first book of *Le Morte d'Arthur* mirrors the political and social discord in Malory's era. In addition, Malory's account is rooted in the real world and is characteristic of one who has actually experience the violence of war. He writes, "Both parties dressed their shields, leveled their spears, and charged. The fighting was grim and furious. Kings Arthur, Ban, and Bors galloped into the thick of it, and soon their horses were up to their fetlocks in blood, and trampling the wounded" (34). Malory's gritty description of the horrors on the front lines seems more historical than fictional. Bulfinch's idealized treatment of a messianic king in shining armor pales in comparison to the disturbing image of a battlefield awash in blood and muck and littered with the trampled bodies of the dead and dying.

Although the miraculous nature of the sword in the stone is highlighted in *Le Morte d'Arthur*, the episode reflects Malory's concern with the role of power and authority in the right of succession rather than Bulfinch's concern with the spiritual aspect of kingship. In both accounts, the church plays a key role in the incident. Bulfinch focuses on Bishop Brice, who seeks God's will concerning Uther's successor. In Malory's version, the archbishop of Canterbury colludes with the magician Merlin to manipulate circumstances in Arthur's favor. The alliance between the supreme representative of the English church and the heathen enchanter, who is reputedly the son of a human woman and an incubus, reveals an ambiguous attitude toward Christianity (Lacy 383). In Bulfinch's account, Arthur is God's clear choice. In Malory's version, Arthur becomes king as a result of paganism's influence on the church.

Malory also portrays Arthur as a sometimes morally corrupt and ruthless ruler, a portrayal that is unlike Bulfinch's image of him as a noble defender of chivalry. For example, in Malory's narrative, the appearance of the beautiful lady Lionors at the king's court leads to a one-night liaison that produces a son, Borre, who becomes a knight of the Round Table. Likewise, Arthur's adulterous affair with his sister Margawse (Morgause) produces Modred (Mordred). In response to Merlin's prophecy that Modred will bring down Arthur's kingdom, the king orders all noble children born on May Day be set adrift in a boat to drown. His order is reminiscent of the biblical king Herod's command, recounted in the Gospel of Matthew, that all male infants in Bethlehem be killed to prevent the prophesied future king from coming to power. Like Herod, Arthur does not hesitate to use force to get his way, even if it means killing innocent children.

English writer T. H. White addresses the issue of might versus right in his version of the Arthurian legend, *The Once and Future King*, first published in 1958. Based on events in Malory's work, the book takes its title from a quotation from *Le Morte d'Arthur*: "And inscribed on his tomb, men say, is this legend: *Hic iacet Arthurus, rex quondam rexque futurus*" (502). Translated, the phrase means "Here lies Arthur, king once and king to be." White pays further homage to Malory when he introduces twelve-year-old page Tom of Newbold Revell, who serves Arthur just before his death.

White wrote his masterwork against a backdrop of worldwide turmoil. Led by dictator Adolf Hitler, Nazi Germany began its conquest of Europe in the late 1930s. Germany invaded Czechoslovakia in March of 1939 and in September of that year attacked Poland, which caused Britain to declare war on Germany. As the Nazi threat increased, it seemed entirely possible that might would triumph over right. Although White employs humor, anachronisms, and endearing characters to engage his readers, his Arthurian fantasy explores serious themes that still resonate with contemporary audiences, including communism versus democracy, the evils of a fascist regime, justice versus injustice, and the malignant side of human nature that takes pleasure in oppressing others.

The Once and Future King is actually a collection of four novellas: *The Sword in the Stone* (1938), *The Queen of Air in Darkness* (1939), *The Ill-Made Knight* (1940), and *The Candle in the Wind* (1958). Although White draws from Malory for much of his tetralogy, he offers an almost entirely original view of Arthur's childhood in *The Sword in the Stone*, which was adapted into a popular animated film by Walt Disney Productions in 1963. White's narrative of Arthur's early life includes his education as a knight as well as his experiences learning important lessons designed to help him become a wise ruler. The story opens as Arthur, called the Wart, and his foster brother, Kay, are hawking in the forest. Their bird escapes, and Arthur goes in search of him. Along the way he meets the befuddled King Pellinore, who is searching for the Questing Beast. Finally, he encounters Merlyn, an old man with a long white beard and a pointed hat. Arthur returns home to Sir Ector's castle with Merlyn in tow. When the magician demonstrates his powers, Sir Ector is unimpressed but hires him as Arthur's tutor anyway.

Merlyn proves to be a wise and unconventional teacher. One of his favorite pedagogical techniques involves using his magical powers to turn Arthur into various animals. One summer's day, Merlyn and Arthur dive into the moat and become fish. There they meet an enormous pike, ruler of the watery underworld, whose face is "ravaged by all the passions of an absolute monarch" (51). His Machiavellian words of wisdom are typical of dictators: "There is nothing except the power which you pretend to seek. . . . and only Might is Right" (52). On another occasion, Arthur becomes a merlin and spends the night in the mews with other hunting birds, where he learns about the snobbery of the military elite and their preoccupation with ancestry. He also passes a test of courage, a necessary personality trait for a warrior king. When he is transformed into an ant, Arthur becomes part of a mindless, militaristic society, the members of which are identified only by numbers. The residents of the nest are bombarded by patriotic lectures and slogans that justify aggressive behavior against a competing nest. His experience in the ant colony reveals to Arthur the ridiculousness of war. In contrast to the repressive communist culture of the ants, Arthur observes the freedom of an ideal democratic society when Merlyn turns him into a goose. The flock has no laws, and its leader is whichever goose can best navigate for the group. A female, Lyolyok, is surprised when Arthur wonders why the geese do not protect themselves against possible attacks by competing flocks and comments that geese find the idea of two groups of the same species fighting each other repellent. For his final lesson, six years later, Merlyn turns Arthur into a badger. During this adventure, Arthur has a philosophical conversation with an old badger about the benefits and drawbacks of evolution. Their conversation ends with a discussion about the mixed benefits of man's domination of animals.

Merlyn's lessons prepare Arthur for his last test before he is declared king. A sword inscribed with the words "Whoso Pulleth Out This Sword of This Stone and Anvil, is Rightwise King Born of All England" appears in an anvil in front of a London church (197). White's version of this episode includes the same plot elements that are in Bulfinch and Malory. However, no church representative takes part in Arthur's final test. Instead, fantasy comes into play as time stops and past and present merge. When Arthur tugs at the sword, unearthly music plays, and all of Arthur's animal teachers spiritually surround him, encouraging him to pull out the sword. It is a mystical moment, but there is no mention of God's will, the authority of the church, or pagan influences, the absence of which reflects the humanist philosophy that informs the novel.

From the early appearance of Arthur in Geoffrey of Monmouth's seminal work to twentieth- and twenty-first-century retellings of Arthur's adventures, the Once and Future King returns not physically but in spirit through various literary incarnations. That the Arthurian legend lives on in literature as well as in film and theatrical productions is a testament to the fascination past and present generations have with myth, mystery, and magic. Arthur's heroic story offers a window into the deepest human emotions and continues to speak of hope and the possibility of better days to come.

Pegge Bochynski, MA

BIBLIOGRAPHY

Barber, Richard. *King Arthur: Hero and Legend*. New York: St. Martin's, 1986. Print.

Bulfinch, Thomas. *Bulfinch's Mythology*. New York: Modern Lib., 2004. Print.

Day, David. *The Search for King Arthur*. New York: Facts on File, 1998. Print.

Lacy, Norris et al., eds. *The Arthurian Encyclopedia*. New York: Bedrick, 1986. Print.

Malory, Thomas. *Le Morte d'Arthur*. Ed. Keith Baines. Introd. Robert Graves. New York: Mentor, 1962. Print.

Monty Python and the Holy Grail. Dir. Terry Gilliam and Terry Jones. Perf. Gilliam et al. Python Pictures, 1974. Film.

White, T. H. *The Once and Future King*. New York: Ace, 1987. Print.

Penelope and the Suitors

Author: Homer
Time Period: 999 BCE–1 BCE
Country or Culture: Greek
Genre: Myth

OVERVIEW

The story of Penelope and the suitors is one of the many popular episodes in Homer's epic tale *The Odyssey* (ca. 725 BCE). Chronologically, *The Odyssey* begins at the end of the Trojan War, which, as recounted in Homer's *Iliad* (ca. 750 BCE), lasted ten years and was finally won by the Greeks through Odysseus's cunning trick of the famous Trojan horse. Spanning an additional ten-year journey, *The Odyssey* describes Odysseus's drawn-out and eventful homecoming. The first four books of *The Odyssey*, often referred to collectively as the *Telemachy*, relate the unfortunate state of Ithaca, Odysseus's kingdom, in his absence. While Odysseus is away, his palace has been occupied by a reported 108 suitors for his wife, Penelope, who while vying for her hand in marriage have been perverting the valued Greek custom of hospitality and plundering the inheritance of Odysseus's son, Telemachus.

From the sixth book onward, *The Odyssey* is divided between Odysseus's return and his revenge. His return plot begins on the island of Ogygia, where Odysseus, having lost all of his men, has been held captive by the goddess Calypso (Kalypsô) for seven years. Taking pity on him, the gods agree to let Odysseus journey home; however, Poseidon, who was not consulted and hates Odysseus, sees him escaping the island and causes a storm, leading him to lose his ship and wash up on the shores of the Phaeacians. Odysseus is welcomed by the Phaeacians, who treat him with great hospitality; after telling them the sensational story of his journey home—including the famous episodes with the Cyclopes, the Sirens, and Circe—they offer to help him return to Ithaca. Having been restored to Ithaca by the Phaeacians, Odysseus plots his revenge. Assisted by Athena,

Odysseus is disguised as a beggar so that he will be able to enter his palace undetected by the suitors, whom he eventually massacres.

While Odysseus is famous for his wily maneuvers and clever machinations, critics have often noted that Penelope, more than merely the devoted wife of the Greek hero, is his intellectual match. In her efforts to keep the unruly suitors at bay, Penelope devises a clever plan of her own in which she tells the suitors that she will not consider their offers until she has woven a robe for Odysseus's father, Laertes. Each day she weaves, and each night she unravels most of the work that she has performed, prolonging the completion of her project. Her plan holds off the suitors for years until her act is discovered and she is betrayed by one of her maidservants. Feeling fairly certain that Odysseus will never return and knowing that she can no longer delay the suitors, Penelope presents them with the challenge of stringing a bow and shooting an arrow through twelve axes, a feat that only Odysseus has been able to accomplish. She is kind yet cautious, challenging characters with tests in order to ensure that she can trust them.

The suitors are presented as a group of entitled, rowdy, and troublesome men. Perhaps the most arrogant of the suitors, Antinous, leads a campaign, assisted by the manipulative Eurymachus, to have Telemachus killed. While the suitors inhabit the palace, they not only squander Telemachus's birthright but also are downright mean and violent. Their complete disregard for the Greek custom of hospitality is repeatedly shown both to heighten their despicable ingratitude and to justify the gory massacre that awaits them at the end of the epic poem.

SUMMARY

As a subplot in Homer's *Odyssey*, the story of Penelope and the suitors comes at the end of Odysseus's epic journey, when Odysseus, after a ten-year journey from Troy, finally returns to Ithaca. The goddess Athena disguises Odysseus as an unidentifiable stranger so that he will be better able to discover those who have betrayed him in his absence. Returning home from Sparta, Telemachus encounters Odysseus, disguised as a wandering beggar, who eventually reveals himself to be Telemachus's father. After briefly reuniting, they resolve that the suitors, who have been inhabiting the palace while vying for Penelope's hand in marriage, must be killed. Deciding that it would be best to launch a surprise attack from within the castle, Odysseus reassumes his disguise as a beggar and enters the castle, and Telemachus returns to the castle in order to hide the palace's weapons from the suitors.

Odysseus finds himself in the palace among the suitors and the maidservants, who all treat him with little courtesy. Inspired by Athena, Penelope appears before the suitors, who shower presents upon her. Meanwhile, a brawl nearly breaks out between Odysseus and a suitor who throws a chair at him, but Telemachus diffuses the situation and the suitors retire for the night. Following Odysseus's instructions, Telemachus uses the opportunity to hide the palace's weaponry. Left alone in the hall, Odysseus is insulted by the maidservants as they tidy up the dinner mess. One of the maidservants, Melantho, is particularly ruthless as she insults him, and Odysseus scolds her for belittling the unfortunate, ironically warning her of the potential of her own impending misfortune.

Overhearing Odysseus's exchange with Melantho, Penelope chases her off and asks to have a conversation with the beggar by the fire. Asking of the beggar in the traditional way, Penelope questions who he is, where he is from, and who is parents are, but with cunning, Odysseus evades having to answer the question directly and merely informs her that his history is too sad to share. Penelope responds by sharing her own sorrows, telling the stranger of how her husband has been gone for twenty years and, in the meantime, she has had to fend off the interests of brash suitors who obnoxiously overstayed their welcome in the palace. Initially, she had warded off the suitors by telling them that they must wait until she had woven a robe for her father-in-law, Laertes.

After sharing her own story, Penelope probes the beggar once again for his history, and Odysseus is prompted to fabricate a narrative. He reluctantly tells Penelope that his name is Aethon, son of King Decalion and the younger brother of Prince Idomeneus, and that he is from the island of Crete. Being the younger brother, he did not go to Troy to fight the war, but his brother did; before the war began Odysseus stopped at

"Stranger, all excellence of mine, both of beauty and of form, the immortals destroyed on the day when the Argives embarked for Ilios [Troy], with them went my husband, Odysseus. If he might but come, and watch over this life of mine, greater would be my fame and fairer. But now I am in sorrow, so many woes has some god brought upon me. For all the princes who hold sway over the islands—Dulichium and Same and wooded Zacynthus—and those who dwell around in clear-seen Ithaca itself, all these woo me against my will, and lay waste my house."

The Odyssey

Crete on his way to Troy, where Aethon took him in until the winds calmed down and it was safe to set sail again. While he tells this story to Penelope, she weeps at the name of her husband, and Odysseus is filled with sorrow seeing his wife this way. Wanting to be sure that the beggar's story is indeed true, Penelope tests him by asking him to describe the nature of Odysseus's raiment that he wore when he visited Crete. The beggar tells Penelope exactly what he had been wearing in great detail, including tokens that she is sure to recognize, and after he finishes, Penelope commences her weeping, knowing that the beggar is speaking the truth.

In his beggar disguise, Odysseus tells Penelope the comforting news that he has heard from Pheidon, king of the Thesprotians, that Odysseus is nearby and will be making his return with many treasures soon. He tells her truthfully about the loss of Odysseus's men and Odysseus's rescue by the Phaeacians. He assures her that King Pheidon is a trustworthy source since Odysseus had in fact stopped at his palace and left him some treasure. Penelope tells him that she wishes to believe what he says, but she feels that her heart is too weak to be that optimistic. She offers him a luxurious bed, cloaks, and a footbath, all of which the beggar humbly declines, except for the footbath, which he says he will only accept from a truehearted old lady.

Impressed by the beggar's humility, Penelope summons Eurycleia, an old servant who had taken care of Odysseus as a young boy, to wash his feet. As she approaches, Odysseus remembers the large scar on his leg, stemming from being gashed by a boar during a family hunting expedition that he went on as a boy. He shrouds himself in as much darkness as he can so that Eurycleia might not notice the scar, but as soon as she feels it with her hands, she knows that the beggar is Odysseus in disguise. She tries to make eye contact with Penelope in order to tell her what she has realized, but the goddess Athena distracts the latter to help Odysseus hide his identity from her. Odysseus grabs Eurycleia by the throat and threatens her, making her promise not to betray him. She assures him that she has never betrayed him and never would and that she will assist him in extricating all of the traitors from his household. Odysseus assures her that he will need no help with that.

Eurycleia leaves to refill the water basin, and Penelope turns to the beggar, asking him to interpret a dream that she had. In her dream, there were twenty geese in the house eating wheat when an eagle descended upon them and killed them all. During the onslaught, Penelope watched and wailed, but the eagle assured her in a human voice not to worry and that her dream would be fulfilled. The beggar tells her that the dream is clearly a prophetic vision of Odysseus's return home, that the geese are the suitors and Odysseus is the eagle. Penelope wistfully brushes off the beggar's good news once again and tells him that she has set forth a challenge for the suitors on the following morn, in which they are required to string a bow and shoot an arrow through twelve axes, the winner taking Penelope as their prize. The beggar persists that Odysseus will be there the next day to attempt the challenge himself. With sadness, Penelope leaves the beggar and retires for the night.

ANALYSIS

Book 14 of *The Odyssey* begins with the anticipation of the contest of the suitors in books 20 and 21, followed by their brutal slaying in book 23. For modern readers, or those unfamiliar with the Greek custom of *xenia* ("guest-friendship"), Odysseus's massacre of the suitors appears unreasonably savage and harsh. However, with a better understanding of *xenia*, it is easier

to understand the severity of the suitors' misbehavior and abuse of hospitality. Throughout the epic poem, the suitors' abuse of *xenia* is contrasted with ideal examples of the guest-host relationship. In the *Telemachy*, Telemachus is offered great hospitality by the people he visits, as is Odysseus when he visits the Phaeacians, Eumaeus, and, finally, the halls of his great palace, where he is dressed in the disguise. In book 19, the abuse that the disguised Odysseus incurs from the suitors and the maids is in direct contrast to the hospitality he receives from Penelope. Without a presiding male figure in the household, the hospitality that Penelope offers Odysseus reveals the distinctively feminine way in which women participated in the custom of *xenia*.

The custom of *xenia* was of indispensible value for a vast population of separate city-kingdoms connected by a network of islands in the Mediterranean Sea. Travelers and seafarers would often journey for days, having to stop in numerous places where they would be dependent on the hospitality of strangers, since they had no rights outside of their own polis (city-state). *Xenia* enabled the Greeks to travel more freely and establish bonds that would be generationally inherited throughout the Greek world. As explained in *Ancient Greece: A Political, Social, and Cultural History* (1999), "'Guest-friendship' (*xenia*) was a reciprocal relationship in which xenoi [plural of xenia] were pledged to offer one another protection, lodging, and assistance whenever they traveled to each other's demos [people]. The relationship was handed down from generation to generation between the families of xenoi" (59). Not only was the bond of *xenia* a form of common hospitality, but also, as is the case for Odysseus in many instances throughout *The Odyssey*, it was used to help travelers in trouble.

Although important across the Greek world, the custom was notably important for the Ithacans. Using archaeological evidence, scholars such as Catherine Morgan have effectively argued for the importance of *xenia* in Ithaca, pointing out that geographically, Ithaca was the likely stopping place for many people traveling throughout the Greek world; in fact, the earliest recorded inscription for *xenia* was found in Ithaca in the main sanctuary of Aetos (Malkin 24). Perhaps Ithaca's geographical position and the heightened importance of *xenia* for Ithacan culture are partially why the custom plays such a prominent role in *The Odyssey*. As Elizabeth Vandiver observes, "Particularly in the *Odyssey*, *xenia* ranks among the moral imperatives that humans cannot violate without bringing down divine vengeance upon themselves; as Nausicaa and Eumaeus both put it, 'all strangers are from Zeus'" (144). As the unruly suitors exhibit in *The Odyssey*, *xenia* is violated not only by those unwilling to provide hospitality but also by those who take advantage of someone's hospitality.

As guests in Odysseus's city-kingdom, many of the suitors who travel to Ithaca initially qualify as *xenoi*. However, as suitors, rather than travelers or visitors, these men problematize the amount of hospitality they might be worthy of receiving. Important to remember is that although Odysseus has been gone for a long time, there has been no confirmation of his death; therefore, the suitors are not typical or ideal recipients of *xenia*. One might argue instead that their presence is actually threatening or encroaching. Regardless of their intentions, the suitors are nonetheless received by Penelope and Telemachus and offered the kindness customary to travelers because of *xenoi*, a practice that included a huge feast and a place to stay. Yet, the kindness of Penelope and Telemachus is exhausted long before Odysseus returns home; the suitors have certainly overstayed their welcome.

Having stayed in the household of Odysseus for an impressive twenty years, the suitors push the boundary between being mere visitors and instead assume a liminal status as occupants or almost residents. Thus, at the time that Odysseus enters his household disguised as a beggar, the suitors could almost be expected to pay him some of the kindness that a host might offer a traveling *xenos*. Instead, they do just the opposite: they abuse him verbally and entice him to enter a physical fight with another beggar. The maidservants, who have been traitorously assisting the suitors, also treat the disguised Odysseus terribly. As they clean up the hall, one of the maidservants says to Odysseus: "Stranger, wilt thou even now still be a plague to us through the night, roaming through the house, and wilt thou spy upon the women? Nay, get thee forth, thou wretch, and be content with thy supper, or straightway shalt thou even be smitten with a torch, and so go forth" (19.68–69). Instead of providing traditional hospitality, the maidservant offers the disguised Odysseus the opposite, slandering him and suggesting that he wander the rest of the night. The suitors and the maidservants not only abuse the custom of *xenia* for themselves but also spoil the possible experience of *xenia* for others staying at Odysseus's palace.

The severity of the suitors' and maidservants' abuse of *xenia* seems to be one of the primary reasons for the severity of their punishment. After having slandered Odysseus the beggar, the maidservant is rebuked by Penelope, who overhears what she says: "Be sure, thou bold and shameless thing, that thy outrageous deed is in no wise hid from me" (19.90–93). Penelope's opinion of the maid's behavior is clear. Her use of adjectives like "bold" and "shameless" reveals the serious nature of her behavior. The maidservant is not merely mean or unkind; rather, she is insensible to the disgrace she brings upon herself and the household. Penelope continues to foreshadow the maidservant's impending doom, saying, "And with thine own head shalt thou wipe out its stain" (19.94–95). Although Penelope does not yet know that Odysseus will soon slaughter the suitors, have the maidservants clean up their dead bodies, and then hang the maidens, she prophesies this looming fate. Penelope's language in response to the maidservant's abuse of *xenia* seems to suggest that maidservant's crudeness to the disguised Odysseus and the brutality of her death are inextricably bound.

Odysseus's return home in disguise as a poor beggar is reminiscent of an earlier scene in *The Odyssey* in which Odysseus finds himself stranded on the shores of the Phaeacians, unrecognized and with nothing. Although briefly taken aback at finding Odysseus naked on the beach, Nausicaa (Nausikaa) takes in Odysseus, clothes him, and brings him to her home without questioning him about who he is. He is then treated by Alcinous and Arete (Aretê) to a huge feast and series of games in his honor, still without them knowing who he is. On discovering his identity and listening to the tale of his treacherous journey, Alcinous tells Odysseus: "Raiment for the stranger lies already stored in the polished chest, with gold curiously wrought and all the other gifts which the counsellors of the Phaeacians brought hither. But, come now, let us give him a great tripod and a cauldron, each man of us, and we in turn will gather the cost from among the people, and repay ourselves" (13.13–15). As Alcinous explains, before knowing Odysseus's identity, he had offered him impressive gifts, but upon learning that the stranger is actually the heroic Odysseus, Alcinous adds a tripod, cauldron, and a gift from each man to be included in Odysseus's parting gift. The contrast between the hospitality Odyssey receives with the Phaeacians and the lack thereof in his own home is ironic and stark. Alcinous's servants, staff, and populace all contribute to improving Odysseus's visit. On the other hand, in his own house, the maidservants and suitors work to undermine the *xenia* that Penelope attempts to offer the stranger.

Without a presiding male figure, Penelope is not capable of offering the disguised Odysseus the same protection that Alcinous offers. Although Odysseus is insulted by the suitors and pushed to participate in a contest, Penelope is not able to prevent this from occurring. She is only able to intercede when the female maidservant insults him. In contrast, when Odysseus is insulted in the halls of Alcinous, the latter comes to his defense and forestalls the contest in favor of song and dance: "So spoke Alcinous the godlike, and the herald rose to fetch the hollow lyre from the palace of the king. Then stood up masters of the lists, nine in all, men chosen from out the people, who in their gatherings were wont to order all things aright" (8.256). Penelope cannot offer Odysseus the same level of security that Alcinous can; however, she is does offer him the same type of hospitality provided by Arete and Nausicaa.

Notably, the nature of the hospitality that is rendered by the female characters in *The Odyssey* pertains to distinctively feminine domains of the house. As Melissa Mueller observes in her 2010 article "Helen's Hands: Weaving for *Kleos* in *The Odyssey*," "When a guest is ready to depart, the standard protocol in the *Odyssey* is for female hosts to offer gifts that represent their own role within the domestic sphere" (6). With the Phaeacians, after the feast has ended and Alcinous has protected Odysseus from abuse, Arete intercedes to provide him with the comforts of her home: "So he spoke, and Arete bade her handmaids to set a great cauldron on the fire with all speed. And they set on the blazing fire the cauldron for filling the bath, and poured in water, and took billets of wood and kindled them beneath it" (8.433–36). Penelope's offerings to Odysseus are nearly identical, as are the sequence of events in which they are offered:

> But still, my maidens, wash the stranger's feet and prepare his bed—bedstead and cloaks and bright coverlets—that in warmth and comfort he may come to the golden-throned Dawn. And right early in the morning bathe him and anoint him, that in our house at the side of Telemachus he may bethink him of food as he sits in the hall. And worse shall it be for any man among them who vexes this man's soul with pain; naught thereafter shall he accomplish here, how fierce soever his wrath. (19.317–29)

Much like Arete, Penelope ensures that Odysseus is bathed in warmth and comfort. Penelope offers as much protection to the beggar as she is capable of, ensuring that he be seated by the lead male figure in the household, Telemachus.

If, as Mueller argues, the gifts that the women offer are representative of their role in the domestic sphere, then Penelope's offering of raiment could not be more appropriate. Throughout *The Odyssey*, weaving and clothing have been of fundamental importance to Penelope. Her use of her weaving is often communicative of her level of hospitality. With the completion of Laertes's funeral shroud—an act that presumably would not occur unless Laertes did in fact die and therefore require the shroud—not only would Penelope have communicated that she was ready to accept the offer of one of the suitors, but she also would have little choice *but* to accept one of the suitors. The raiment that Penelope offers to the disguised Odysseus has communicative functions for Penelope as well. After offering him comforts, she explains to him, "For how shalt thou learn of me, stranger, whether I in any wise excel other women in wit and prudent counsel, if all unkempt and clad in poor raiment thou sittest at meat in my halls?" (19.330–31). Penelope recognizes that her feminine gifts of hospitality speak for her kindness in the same way that a man's offering of *xenia* affects his reputation.

The communicative capacity of the robes and the act of women weaving in *The Odyssey* also enable both to function as tokens of recognition. When Odysseus enters the hall of the Phaeacians, Arete immediately recognizes the robes that Nausicaa has given him and questions who he is: "Then white-armed Arete was the first to speak; for, as she saw it, she knew his fair raiment, the mantle and tunic, which she herself had wrought with her handmaids" (7.233–39). Odysseus's garb communicates to Arete more about the stranger than Alcinous might have recognized on his own. Recognizing the robes as something she made, Arete is justifiably suspicious and asks Odysseus to identify himself or at least explain how he has come to be dressed in the robes, much earlier than the conventions of *xenia* usually allow. Once Odysseus explains how he has come to be clothed in the garments, Arete is satisfied and does not question him any further since, had she come across him first, she would have probably offered the clothing to him herself.

When the disguised Odysseus tells Penelope that Odysseus visited his island on the way to Troy, Penelope knows that because of the conventions of *xenia* it is likely that the beggar will remember what Odysseus had been wearing. As Odysseus describes the garments in which he was clothed with great detail, Penelope reacts strongly and weeps, recognizing his description as clothing she had made herself and given to him as a parting gift. In this particular exchange with the beggar, given the description of the woven purple tunics, not only does Penelope know for certain that Odysseus visited the stranger's native land, but more importantly, it is through her recognition of the clothing that Penelope realizes that the beggar is not lying (although, ironically, he is) and that she can trust him. Much like when Alcinous discovers Odysseus's identity and offers a more generous gift of hospitality, Penelope offers the beggar more when she recognizes his honesty: "Now verily, stranger, though before thou wast pitied, shalt thou be dear and honored in my halls, for it was I that gave him this raiment" (19.256–58).

Thus, the gifts of hospitality that the women in *The Odyssey* offer not only function as gifts but also extend their reputations and serve as a mode of communication and recognition. The hospitality that Penelope offers to Odysseus in book 19 not only reveals both the feminine nature of *xenia* and the extended networks that women are able to achieve from their homes through weaving, but also her *xenia* is juxtaposed with the disgraceful behavior of the suitors. Penelope's encounter with the disguised Odysseus foreshadows the impending doom of the suitors, contributes to the suspense of the dramatic action, and justifies the poetic justice Odysseus will shortly claim through the bloody massacre of the suitors and the maidservants. The custom of *xenia* was used to protect strangers so that anyone, including the disguised Odysseus, would be entitled to the kindness of room and board; yet ironically, the suitors' abuse of this custom prevents Odysseus from receiving these entitlements in his("own home.

CROSS-CULTURAL INFLUENCE

As with most of the myths from classical antiquity, the episodes of Homer's epics, *The Iliad* and *The Odyssey*, have influenced Western culture widely and have been the choice material for many appropriations, adaptations, and retellings. However it is probably fair to say that the episode of Penelope and the suitors is more often overlooked for the fantastical adventures of her heroic husband; although there are artistic treatments and responses to Penelope's story, they are fewer and lesser known than the adventure tales. This noteworthy absence from the critical and artistic world is what

inspired the Canadian writer Margaret Atwood to set about revising Penelope's life story and her role in the tale of *The Odyssey* in her aptly named novella *The Penelopiad: The Myth of Penelope and Odysseus* (2005).

Atwood's impetus for writing *The Penelopiad* came from a series of factors. A considerable portion of her body of work takes interest in feminine mythological subjects. Her novel *The Robber Bride* (1993) appropriates Homer's *Iliad* in a modern Toronto. The short story "The Elysium Lifestyle Mansions," written for *Ovid Metamorphosed* (2000), retells the myth of Apollo and the immortal prophetess Sibyl. Also, an early poem called "Circe/Mud Poems" is Atwood's first literary appropriation of Penelope's character. In the long series of poems, Atwood gives Penelope's character a voice, much as she does in *The Penelopiad*; in doing so, she also complicates Penelope's character, questioning the degree to which she remains emotionally loyal to Odysseus and tarring her dignified image.

Atwood's interests in mythological material and her renown as a popular Canadian author made her an ideal candidate for the project of the Canongate Myth Series. Conceived by Jamie Byng in 1999, the series asked contemporary authors each to write a short novel that would reimagine ancient myths from any culture. Initially, Atwood had intended to write an interpretation of the Norse creation myth and an American Indian story, but she struggled to find the right inspiration for these projects. Just as she was about to cancel her contract with Byng, it occurred to her that she could write about Penelope and the twelve hanged maids in *The Odyssey*.

The idea of appropriating the end of *The Odyssey* was appealing to Atwood, who felt haunted by Homer's story and the unfortunate fate of the twelve hanged maids. As she explains in her introduction, "The story as told in *The Odyssey* doesn't hold water: there are too many inconsistencies. I've always been haunted by the hanged maids; and in *The Penelopiad*, so is Penelope herself" (xv). Many of the inconsistencies Atwood found in the closing scenes of the epic were the unanswered questions, a result of the mostly silenced female voice and perspective. To remedy this, Atwood explains, "I have chosen to give the telling of the story to Penelope and to the twelve hanged maids. The maids form a chanting and singing Chorus which focuses on two questions that must pose themselves after any close reading of the *Odyssey*: what led to the hanging of the maids, and what was Penelope really up to?" (xv). Thus, Atwood's speakers in the novella are exclusively

MYTH INTO ART

Ulysses and Penelope, painted by Francesco Primaticcio around 1560, depicts one of the more domestic and intimate scenes of Homer's epic poem *The Odyssey*. Primaticcio was born in 1504 in Bologna, where he developed his skills as a painter, draughtsman, architect, and stuccoist. He was also given the appointment of overseeing the decoration of the Palazzo del Te. His experience and the quality of his work led him to secure a position as a resident painter at Francis I's Palace of Fontainebleau in France in 1532. Along with Florentine Rosso Fiorentino, Primaticcio's work at the palace classed him among the so-called First School of Fontainebleau. Between 1541 and 1560, Primaticcio worked on an extensive decoration of the palace called the Galerie d'Ulysse, which included sixty scenes from *The Odyssey*. Although this entire work has been lost, his painting *Ulysses and Penelope*, which drew inspiration from the gallery, attests to the work's incredible achievement.

As one of the principle mannerist painters of the late Italian High Renaissance, Primaticcio was largely responsible for introducing the artistic movement to the French. Primaticcio's interests in classical subject matter coincided with a renewed interest in the artistic and intellectual communities in Greek and Roman history and philosophy. *Ulysses and Penelope* depicts a scene from the end of Homer's *Odyssey* (book 23) in which Odysseus and Penelope are pictured nude, reunited in bed. The extraordinary connubial fidelity between these two mythological lovers is expressed through their fixed gaze upon each other and the delicate way in which Odysseys cups Penelope's chin in this hand. The expressiveness of Penelope's hands suggests that the pair is engaged in telling each other of their adventures over their twenty-year separation.

life and marriage, and the scandalous rumours circulating about her" (xiv–xv). Reportedly, Atwood consulted E. V. Rieu's version of *The Odyssey* and *The Greek Myths* (1955) and *The White Goddess* (1948) by Robert Graves, who adhered to Samuel Butler's theory that *The Odyssey* was written by a woman.

The novella begins in Hades in the twenty-first century. All of the events in *The Odyssey* have taken place thousands of years ago, and its characters, including Penelope, find themselves in Hades. In the first chapter, "A Low Art," Penelope is reflective, opening with the line "Now that I'm dead I know everything" (1). She confesses to having learned secrets and factoids that she had not known when living. She also admits to knowing that Odysseus rigged the competition that her father used to determine who would marry her when she was fifteen. Despite the fact that she considers storytelling a "low art"—explaining, "Old women go for it, strolling beggars, blind singers, maidservants, children—folks with time on their hands" (4)—she resolves to recount her story.

Starting with her childhood, Penelope reminisces over her unusual relationship with her father and mother. After explaining and partially sympathizing with her father's early attempt to kill her, Penelope explains that her father became too affectionate, and her feelings toward him oscillated between mutual affection and fear for her life. On the other hand, her mother seemed to lack maternal instincts and was essentially absent for much of Penelope's life. After marrying Odysseus at the young age of fifteen, Penelope is reasonably happy, even though she is mocked by everyone, including her own sister, Helen, who denigrates Odysseus over his short stature and his modest home in Ithaca. Neither Odysseus's mother, Anticleia, nor his nurse, Eurycleia, like Penelope at first, but eventually Eurycleia becomes more friendly and helps Penelope more often.

Just after Penelope gives birth to Telemachus, Odysseus is called to fight in the Trojan War, leaving Penelope

female, alternating between eighteen chapters narrated by Penelope and eleven interludes provided by the chorus of the maids.

Despite Homer's noted scrupulousness in recording the lineage of his male characters, Atwood found that there was insufficient context in *The Odyssey* for the female characters, which is partly why she consulted other sources in her research. Atwood's project sought to undermine the prevalence of the heteronormative narrative. Homer's version of *The Odyssey* is undeniably the most popular, but as she explains to her readers it "is not the only version of the story" (xiv). Thus, Homer was not Atwood's only source; as she tells her readers, "I have drawn on material other than *The Odyssey*, especially for the details of Penelope's parentage, her early to raise Telemachus on her own and to run the kingdom of Ithaca. Not long after Odysseus leaves, Penelope begins to be approached by various suitors who are selfishly optimistic that Odysseus will not return from Troy. Penelope stalls the suitors, but her reasons for doing so are not exclusively out of loyalty for her absent husband. Instead, she stalls the suitors primarily because she thinks that they are more interested in running her kingdom than being her lover. In the chapter "The Suitors Stuff Their Faces," the suitors pressure her by consuming her resources and by being a nagging presence, to the point that Penelope eventually fears that they may cause violence or unmanageable chaos. To prevent this from ensuing, Penelope proposes to marry one of them when she has finished weaving a funerary robe for her father-in-law. She delays the completion of the shroud by having her maidservants assist her in unraveling it at night.

Penelope's account supplies many more details involving the unfortunate fates of her maidservants. Along with enlisting their help in unweaving her shroud, Penelope asks the maidservants to hang around the suitors and spy on them. In retrospect, she learns that this is a terrible idea since the suitors rape the maids and harass them into giving up the secret of the shroud. Eventually, Odysseus returns to Ithaca in disguise, and Penelope confesses to having recognized him immediately (although she goes along with Odysseus's rouse and instructs her maidservants not to reveal his identity). Odysseus massacres the suitors. After having the maidservants clean up the gory mess, Odysseus orders Telemachus to have the maidservants executed by hanging, assuming that they had been treasonous accomplices of the suitors. Penelope sleeps unknowingly while all of this happens. Afterward, Penelope and Odysseus are reunited and tell each other stories about their time apart, but Penelope, haunted by the deaths of the murdered maids, cannot bring them up in conversation. Penelope, and her story, remains eternally haunted by them in Hades.

Throughout the novella, as Penelope reminisces over her past, her story is broken up by interludes spoken by a chorus of maids. Although not a feature of ancient Greek epics, the chorus is a well-known and standard technique from tragic Attic drama. All of the well-known tragedies by the playwrights Aeschylus, Euripides, and Sophocles involved choruses, a cast of non-individualized characters that function in contrast to the heroic protagonist. The chorus usually consisted of the general population of the drama and would interrupt the dialogue of the play's main characters in order to offer insights or to express what the main characters could not say on their own. Although in *The Penelopiad*, Penelope needs no assistance in expressing herself from the underworld, the chorus of maidservants functions in a similar way to the choruses of Greek drama. The maidservants' interludes are expressed by various generic modes of expression: jump-rope rhyme, lament, idyll, ballad, lecture, judicial trial, and many types of songs.

Atwood's alterations to the Homeric telling of the story reveal what many critics have characterized as her feminist agenda. By granting the maidservants voices, Atwood supplies a sympathetic and miserable context for the maidservants' lives. Through their interludes, readers learn that the maidservants were slaves as children and had no parents and no playtime. They dream of freedom and of being princesses, contrasting their own fates with the life of Telemachus, their eventual murderer. They blame Penelope and the nurse Eurycleia, for their deaths, since both women knew how loyal and innocent they had been. In Hades, they haunt Penelope and Odysseus, perpetually reminding the couple of the injustice they faced at their hands. Unlike Homer's maids, Atwood's appear to have a clean record. Although Atwood indifferently allows one of them to disclose Penelope's secret of the robe, in her telling the maids are loyal and good to Penelope, whereas Homer's maids are deceitful and crude (perhaps not deserving of execution, but certainly not innocent). By clearing their records, Atwood makes the deaths of the maids more tragic. Also, by providing the maids with a chance to tell their story, Atwood's story suggests that the repression of the feminine voice by the heteronormative male perspective is an injustice in itself.

Katherine Sehl, MA

BIBLIOGRAPHY

Atwood, Margaret. *The Penelopiad*. New York: Canongate, 2005. Print.

Bassett, Samuel E. "The Suitors of Penelope." *Transactions and Proceedings of the American Philological Association* 49 (1918): 41–52. Print.

Fiorenza, Giancarlo. "Penelope's Web: Francesco Primaticcio's Epic Revision at Fountainebleau." *Renaissance Quarterly* 59 (2006): 795–827. Print.

Foley, Helene P. "Penelope as Moral Agent." *The Distaff Side: Representing the Female in Homer's Odyssey.*

Ed. Beth Cohen. New York: Oxford UP, 1995. 93–116. Print.

Heitman, Richard. *Taking Her Seriously: Penelope and the Plot of Homer's* Odyssey. Ann Arbor: U of Michigan P, 2005. Print.

Homer. *The Odyssey.* Trans. A. T. Murray and George E. Dimock. Cambridge: Harvard UP, 1995. Print.

Malkin, Irad. *The Returns of Odysseus: Colonization and Ethnicity.* Berkeley: U of California P, 1998. Print.

Mueller, Melissa. "Helen's Hands: Weaving for *Kleos* in the *Odyssey.*" *Helios* 37.1 (2010): 1–21. Print.

Pomeroy, Sarah B., et al. "The Late Dark Age (Homeric) Society." *Ancient Greece: A Political, Social, and Cultural History.* New York: Oxford UP, 1999. 53–66. Print.

Reece, Steve. *The Stranger's Welcome: Oral Theory and the Aesthetics of the Homeric Hospitality Scene.* Ann Arbor: U of Michigan P, 1993. Print.

Vandiver, Elizabeth. "'Strangers Are from Zeus': Homeric Xenia at the Courts of Proteus and Croesus." *Myth, Truth, and Narrative in Herodotus.* Ed. Emily Baragwanath and Mathieu Bakker. New York: Oxford UP, 2012. 143–66. Print.

Quetzalcóatl

Author: Traditional Aztec
Time Period: 501 CE–1000 CE
Country or Culture: Mexico
Genre: Myth

OVERVIEW

When Aztec mythology was chronicled in written accounts during the sixteenth century, it offered a diverse spiritual and religious tradition, populated by a range of deities and competing beliefs. It was a mythology carried forth by visual art and oral narratives, morphing from city to city and from one century to the next. Within all of this, the god Quetzalcóatl was one of several figures who consistently arose as an important and powerful founder, even as the specifics of his representation evolved over time. As often as not, however, the roots of the Aztec Quetzalcóatl were grounded in Toltec culture. The Toltecs were seen as the spiritual predecessors of Aztec civilization, having previously occupied the land on which Aztec cities were to one day flourish. Aztec society idealized Toltec life, with perhaps the most dramatic idealization coming through the story of Quetzalcóatl and his founding of the city of Tollán.

In the myth, Quetzalcóatl is a powerful god who assumes the role of founder and leader of Tollán. Prior to his rule, the people of Tollán had lived in the wilderness, scrounging for food and barely supporting themselves. When he arrives, he fetches the maize of the mountains for them, and with this agricultural knowledge, they are able to build the city-state. There, Quetzalcóatl continues to impart cultural lessons, sharing the knowledge of arts and crafts that allows the city to thrive, utopian in its peace and prosperity. This continues for many years until the arrival of Tezcatlipoca, a god of war and destruction. Tezcatlipoca tricks Quetzalcóatl and drives him from the city, ending the blessed period of an idealized Tollán and initiating a period of warfare and sacrifice. Quetzalcóatl, exiled from his own city, goes on a long journey to the sea, promising to return one day and to reestablish the paradise that Tollán offered.

Tollán was a real Toltec city during the tenth century, and its peaceful ruler, Topiltzin, assumed the name of Quetzalcóatl during his legendary reign. The myths of Quetzalcóatl and of Tezcatlipoca were popular before Topiltzin's rule, but for Aztec civilization, the line between this historical fact and the ancient myths often blurred. The centuries that mark the height of Aztec culture were a time when warfare and violent sacrifice defined the dominant cities. In this civilization, Quetzalcóatl and Topiltzin were both powerful myths, suggesting that the impossible dream of peace might have one day been made real. In the years following the invasion by the Spanish and the colonization of Mesoamerica, the promise of Quetzalcóatl gained even greater prominence, becoming a favorite myth among writers and artists in the seventeenth, eighteenth, and nineteenth centuries. Quetzalcóatl has become the most recognizable Aztec deity, his mythology more familiar to modern audiences than that of any other Aztec figure. Both real and imagined, historically present and remembered through fantasy, Quetzalcóatl offers an important point of access to the complex and varied spiritual traditions of the ancient Aztecs.

SUMMARY

The god Quetzalcóatl lives in the great city of Tollán. There, he teaches the people all manner of crafts that had previously been unknown, including the building of statues, the painting of symbols into books, and astrology. The only craft that Quetzalcóatl does not teach is the craft of war. Because of this, Tollán is a peaceful place, and the people there make their offerings to Quetzalcóatl with bread and perfumes rather than sacrificing human lives, as is the practice in other cities.

Quetzalcóatl himself lives in a splendid house, built out of precious metals with chambers of gold, emerald, seashell, and jasper. About the house, birds chirp

> *"'One has come who will drive me hence; perhaps it were better that I went before he drives me, and drank from a fountain in the Land of the Sun, whence I may return, young as a boy.' So he [Quetzalcóatl] said, and his servants saw him burn down his house of silver with its green precious stones and its thatch of bright plumage, and its door-posts of white and red shells."*
>
> "Quetzalcoatl"

melodious songs. Outside the house grows gigantic maize, so big that the people of Tollán are never hungry. Alongside the maize grow giant pumpkins and cotton in splendid colors so that the people of Tollán never even have to dye it. The maize itself had not always been there but was brought by Quetzalcóatl years before. Before that, people knew the grain to be deep in the mountains, and other gods had even tried to fetch it for them. None succeeded until Quetzalcóatl took the form of a black ant in order to find it, laboring hard to bring the grain back to the people. With this grain, they were able to plant their first crops, build their city, and learn their first crafts. It is because of this that the people honor Quetzalcóatl.

The people live in peace until one day Tezcatlipoca arrives at the city, lowering himself down upon them with spider webs. Tezcatlipoca is a wicked god who spends his time spreading deceit and warfare among humans. As he descends, Tezcatlipoca blows a freezing breath across the city, killing all the flowers in it. When Quetzalcóatl feels this wind, he knows that someone is coming to drive him out of the city. Instead of staying and resisting, he decides to leave for the Land of the Sun, where he can drink from a fountain of youth. As he burns down his home in Tollán and sends away his beautiful birds, he makes a promise to return one day as a young man and to then protect his people.

Before Quetzalcóatl can leave, however, Tezcatlipoca challenges him to a ball game. While they play with all of the city watching, Tezcatlipoca transforms himself into a jaguar and attacks Quetzalcóatl, humiliating him. Quetzalcóatl has no choice but to flee from the city, unable as he is to overpower the fierce jaguar god. As Quetzalcóatl runs, the magical dwarfs who often accompany him join by his side, allowing him to run even faster. Eventually, deep in the mountains, he collapses under a tree. Resting there, he looks into a mirror and sees that he is an old man, unable to defend himself or his city. He tosses the mirror aside in frustration and angrily throws rocks at the tree that shelters him.

As Quetzalcóatl continues his journey, his dwarfs kept him company, playing music in an attempt to lift his spirits. However, he soon grows weary again, collapsing by a creek. Looking down upon his distant city, he weeps. Both his tears and his wringing hands permanently imprint the stones there. Rising and continuing on his way again, he meets some of the men from Tollán on the path, and he teaches them new crafts, revealing the last skills that he had kept secret from them. Still, he keeps on, abandoning his precious gems into a fountain where they rest to this day. He eventually crosses mountains of snow and fire so intense that his companions all die. Totally alone, he composes a sad song in their memory.

Finally, Quetzalcóatl comes down from the mountain and arrives at the sea. Some people believe that at the shore he crafts a raft out of snakes and, climbing onto the raft, sails away toward the sunset. On this journey, he eventually reaches the Country of the Sun, where he drinks the Water of Immortality, which returns him to his youthful state of strength and power. As such, he will someday return to challenge Tezcatlipoca, reclaiming his city. Others, however, say that at the shore he throws down his bright robe and colorful mask, heaving himself into a fire so that he is consumed into ashes. Many birds fly out of those ashes, and his heart rises into the sky, becoming the Morning Star. These people say that Quetzalcóatl is now the Lord of the Dawn.

ANALYSIS

The myth of Quetzalcóatl cannot be separated from the myth of Tollán, the city founded by the ancient god. Tollán is the name of several historical cities in Mesoamerica, all of them holding positions of relative prominence at one time or another. In addition, the name Tollán was sometimes added onto the name of an already powerful city, likely as a way to announce its influence over neighboring cultures. Of these cities, the Tollán at the heart of the Quetzalcóatl is likely an analogue to the city of Tollán that was ruled by Ce Acatl Topiltzin, a man who was himself often conflated with Quetzalcóatl, even taking on Quetzalcóatl's name at times to announce his connection to the god's traditions and the peaceful way of living that he championed. Tollán was the center of Toltec culture, the Toltecs being the people who preceded the Aztec civilization in the Valley of Mexico and who were considered the cultural ancestors of the Aztecs. A great majority of the historical information about the Toltecs is lost to time, so much so that there is academic debate over whether or not it is even possible to speak of a Toltec civilization as having existed as a unified culture. However, it remains relatively clear that Ce Acatl Topiltzin successfully ruled Tollán in the tenth century and that while in power he brought an end to the tradition of human sacrifice and replaced it instead with a cult that worshipped snakes (Quetzalcóatl is often portrayed as a feathered serpent). Following Topiltzin's rule, both his name and the name of Tollán were passed on to future generations, slowly becoming integrated into various mythological traditions—most notably, those of the Maya and Aztec peoples.

Myths surrounding Quetzalcóatl and Quetzalcóatl-like figures precede the historical figure of Topiltzin in oral literary traditions, and later cultures, such as the Maya, would eventually claim a mythological Tollán as their founding city, dating it back centuries before the Common Era. It is exactly this blurring of myth and history that helps in understanding the myth of Quetzalcóatl. Throughout Mesoamerican mythology, Quetzalcóatl is part-man and part-feathered serpent, a powerful figure who traverses the realms between the earth and the sky. In the myth of the founding of Tollán, this god-like figure is woven into the history of a benevolent and powerful ruler, just as the mythological understanding of a glorious, utopian city becomes inseparable from the peaceful and prosperous historical city of the Toltecs. Tollán itself came to represent the promise that urban centers offered in Mesoamerica, rich with the possibility of harmony and plentitude, sheltered from the harsh landscape of rural life. By latching this promise onto Quetzalcóatl, that promise became something at once possible and mystical, established in the distant past but remembered like a dream. Through his battle with Tezcatlipoca and the myth's ambiguous conclusion, Quetzalcóatl enacts the struggle of ancient Mesoamerican cities, powerful centers of unified culture that, through sacrifice and war, fell tragically short of their utopian promise.

From the start, the myth roots the utopian nature of the city of Tollán in a clear definition of its cultural and artistic achievements. Tollán is a place where "all the arts and crafts that we know of were first practised" (Colum 298). These arts—focusing on the making of ornate and decorative crafts, on language, and on astrology—are integral to the idealized nature of the society. In focusing on art, the city also becomes a city that does not practice the craft of war and, by extension, offers its gods sacrifices of luxury items like perfumes rather than violent human sacrifices. Most Mesoamerican cities practiced some form of human sacrifice, with the Aztec society being perhaps more extremely dedicated to the practice than any other. Major rituals sometimes included the deaths of hundreds of slaves at a time, while more private rituals and ceremonies often at least included the death of an animal or nonfatal bloodletting from a human. This practice seems to have developed alongside the formation of the cities themselves. Mesoamerican cities were the geographic center in which culture and civilization came to form, with people from rural areas moving into urban areas at a greater rate than perhaps anywhere else in the world. While this growth occurred, a large number of spiritual traditions competed for influence within the city, and those in power used human sacrifice in part to enforce the dominance of their own beliefs. This was true both before the rule of Topiltzin and in the centuries following his decline. Tollán, however, is presented in the myth as a rare exception, a place where culture itself is unified through the arts and human sacrifice is rendered unnecessary, outlawed within the city walls.

The description of the city as utopian is dependent not only on the lack of sacrifice and war, but also on the abundance of resources there. Several times throughout Mesoamerican history massive droughts, floods, and famines wrought widespread death and destruction on the civilizations, sometimes contributing to major declines in population and weakening cities to such a degree that they fell to outside invaders. The abundance of the resources in Tollán signals not only the luxury of material objects but also the security and cultural unity that come along with such resources. Importantly, this abundance is explicitly linked to Quetzalcóatl himself. The maize (a foundational crop for all Mesoamerican civilization) that grows so high it can barely be carried is not a naturally occurring crop but something that must be laboriously harvested from a nearby mountain, a task so difficult that other gods had failed at it before. Likewise,

Quetzalcóatl's silver home, the colored cotton, and the splendid songbirds are all mystical manifestations of real, mundane resources. These descriptions make clear that the presence of Quetzalcóatl is concomitant with the luxury and wealth of Tollán, which itself is responsible for the peace the citizens enjoy. A step further, the very existence of urban centers is tied to this material gain, with the people of Tollán living "upon roots and on what they gained in the chase" before Quetzalcóatl introduces maize (Colum 293), the agricultural advancement enabling the city's founding and everything that follows.

The utopian nature of Tollán cannot last long, however, and is soon shaken through the introduction of Tezcatlipoca. One of the major deities in Aztec mythology, Tezcatlipoca is the god of destruction and warfare and is often portrayed as either a rival to or counterpart of Quetzalcóatl, with the two even defined as brothers in several mythological traditions. On a broader scale, Aztec mythology teaches that the earth is regularly destroyed and remade in a new form, with the current earth set during the fifth cycle of this creation and inevitable destruction. In this tradition, Tezcatlipoca was the creator of the first cycle, only to have Quetzalcóatl destroy that earth and initiate the second cycle. While Tezcatlipoca is then a figure of destruction and chaos, destruction is treated as an integral part of the universe in Aztec cosmology and, as such, is neither inherently beneficial nor tragic. Tezcatlipoca is not necessarily evil in this view, even if his actions cause sorrow and pain in the world. Instead, his role is fundamental to the universe itself, with Quetzalcóatl even referred to as the White Tezcatlipoca or the Tezcatlipoca of the West in some myths.

The introduction of Tezcatlipoca into the myth of Quetzalcóatl is the introduction of a natural element of the universe into the utopian society. Tezcatlipoca is a god "who can go into all places" (Colum 299), indicating that there is no location safe from his meddling. The myth makes clear that Tezcatlipoca's entrance into Tollán is a disaster, signaled by his ominous arrival on spider webs and the accompanying cold wind that destroys the beautiful flowers of the city. While the god of destruction will quickly come to directly challenge Quetzalcóatl's rule over Tollán, Quetzalcóatl does not need to experience this challenge in order to know that it is time for him to leave and that his rule is incompatible with the rule of the destructive god. Sensing that Tezcatlipoca has come to force him out of his home, he instead decides to leave on his own accord, intending to seek a magical fountain in the Land of the Sun

that will revive him to his youthful strength. This plan is significant to the myth in that it suggests the necessity of the cycle of life in order for the god to succeed. Quetzalcóatl knows that his cycle is ending and that his body has entered old age, and he recognizes that he cannot sustain his utopian city unless he can also begin a new cycle of life, just as the universe itself must always begin again. Tezcatlipoca initiates just such a cyclical change, although he brings about that change by initiating warfare and conflict rather than through the bounty Quetzalcóatl seeks. By fleeing the city and destroying his palace, Quetzalcóatl is not acting like a coward and running away from the challenge, but rather hoping to find a peaceful alternative, advancing into the next cycle while avoiding the death that Tezcatlipoca heralds.

Before Quetzalcóatl can begin his quest, however, Tezcatlipoca tracks him down and challenges him to a ball game in the middle of the city. The ball game in Mesoamerican traditions was both a common recreational activity in the countryside and a ritualized spectacle in major urban areas. Hardly a city existed that was not centered around large ball courts with ornate decorations and stadium seating, the historical Tollán being no exception. In these courts, citizens and slaves would play a violent game involving large rubber balls, although the details of the rules have been largely lost to time. The games served as entertainment during festivals and religious holidays, but also as forums to dramatize the cycles of life and to re-create historical battles. The courts themselves were even considered to be symbolic links to the underworld, so that as the players fought one another, they represented the link that connected life and death, with one team often sacrificed (whether these were the winners or losers is debated). When Tezcatlipoca challenges Quetzalcóatl to such a ball game, he clarifies his role in the city, announcing that he is there to initiate the inescapably violent cycle of life and death, present now even in the utopian city of Tollán.

Quetzalcóatl's decision to enter the court and accept the challenge of Tezcatlipoca is a major moment in his eventual downfall. By doing so, he validates the violent tradition of ritualized sacrifice that the ball game symbolizes. While he acknowledges early on that life is cyclical and that he must be rejuvenated to continue leading his city, the tradition of the ball game, linked so closely to the rituals of war and conflict, is ultimately the wrong venue to access that cycle. This becomes evident when Quetzalcóatl walks onto the court; rather than actually engaging in the spiritual ritual of the competition,

Tezcatlipoca instead transforms himself into a jaguar, attacking Quetzalcóatl and chasing him out of the city. The jaguar is a symbol of the warrior class in Mesoamerican history, and jaguar warriors were a common motif in Aztec spirituality and the artwork associated with warfare. By taking on this form, Tezcatlipoca solidifies the link between the sacrifice of the ball game and the political tradition of warfare and cultural violence. The two are reliant upon one another, and for Quetzalcóatl to step onto the ball court provides an invitation for that violent culture within his utopian city.

Once chased out of his city, Quetzalcóatl is forced into the shame of exile. He has no choice but to slowly shed the accoutrements and symbols of the very civilization he founded, his cycle of rule having come to an end and his body weakened in its elderly state. He parts ways with his material wealth, the ornate symbols of prosperity that allowed for the city to grow and thrive in its security. He also loses the dwarves that accompany him, signaling the loss of his spiritual following. Dwarves and hunchbacked figures were common in Aztec mythology, often as the companions and helpers to mystically powerful leaders and gods. When Quetzalcóatl's dwarves perish in his exile, he is stripped of this symbol, suggesting that the worship he had enjoyed from Tollán is likewise faltering as the religion of Tezcatlipoca takes hold. He also offers the last of his artistic knowledge to the people of Tollán, several citizens having followed him on his path. While these divestments all signal the loss of Quetzalcóatl's cultural and spiritual power, they also suggest that it is possible for people to once again connect with those gifts. The god marks stones with his tears, allowing the citizens of Tollán to trace his path. He also leaves his jewels at the bottom of a pond and writes a mournful song to memorialize the dwarves that served him. All of these small actions suggest that Quetzalcóatl's rule and the peaceful life he championed are not lost forever, but instead remain somewhere in the landscape of Mexico, able to be tracked down by someone with the persistence to do so.

Once Quetzalcóatl reaches the end of his journey, the myth likewise provides an ambiguous conclusion, suggesting at both times his failure and the possibility of his eventual return. In one ending, he forms a raft that brings him to the mythical Country of the Sun. There, he restores himself to his youthful state and heads once more for the city of Tollán, where, in a new cycle, he will once again establish a culture of peace and of artistic wealth. In the other ending, however, he strips himself

of his last material marks, leaving on the shore the robe and mask that indicate his role as a spiritual leader. Completely abandoning his connection to the culture of the city, he then burns himself into ashes, his heart rising into the sky as the planet Venus, called the Morning Star by the Aztecs. These are markedly different endings, and by offering both conclusions at once, the myth leaves open the possibility that the culture of warfare initiated by Tezcatlipoca will come to an end and that the Mesoamerican people will again live in prosperity and peace. While the conclusions are different, however, it is important to also note that both strongly emphasize the importance of the cycles of culture. In one, the cyclical nature of the universe is affirmed by Quetzalcóatl's youthful return and the reestablishment of the culture of Tollán. In the other, that cycle exists through the daily rise and descent of Venus. Moving always between the realm of day and the realm of night, the Quetzalcóatl of the sky may not return himself, but he remains visible to all people as a reminder that cyclical change is at the core of the universe itself.

Just as Quetzalcóatl is driven from the city by Tezcatlipoca, the historical ruler Topiltzin was ultimately defeated during an invasion by the Chichimec people. Little information survives to this day to describe the origins of these particular Chichimec people or of the conflict between them and the city of Tollán, although it remains fairly likely that the invasion itself was inspired by a famine in the land north of Tollán, the invaders drawn to the agricultural resources of the city. Following the conflict, and likely primarily because of it, Tollán itself fell and the people of the urban area scattered, integrating into new cities and new civilizations across Mesoamerica. Once again, the myth of Quetzalcóatl merges with historical reality. Rather than seeing them as direct analogues to one another, however, it is important to remember that stories of Quetzalcóatl and Tezcatlipoca had flourished for centuries before the rule of Topiltzin and, likewise, that as many Tolláns existed in mythology as they did in reality. It is through this diversity of traditions and histories that the myth of Quetzalcóatl can best be understood. He and his city were an impossibly utopian dream—a thriving center of culture splendored with multicolored cotton and precious metals—that at moments seem to have become real (or at least possible) in the long history of Mesoamerican people. Just as Quetzalcóatl crossed freely between history and mythology, the promise of his return also remains tantalizingly prophesized and impossible. Warfare and

MYTH INTO ART

Drawn on animal skins sometime before the Spanish colonization of Mesoamerica, the Codex Borgia is a rare document, describing in depth some of the religious traditions associated with Quetzalcóatl and other gods.

One of the most famous images from the codex presents Quetzalcóatl alongside Mictlantecuhtli, the Aztec god of the dead. The two gods are back to back, their images mirroring one another as they kneel on a pile of bones. These bones reference the Aztec creation story in which Quetzalcóatl travels to the underworld in order to fetch the bones of previous gods. Mictlantecuhtli wrestles with Quetzalcóatl to stop the theft, and in their struggle, the bones are shattered, eventually brought to earth, and made into humans. The gods are linked in this image just as they are in mythology, representing life and death not as distinct realms but rather as similar aspects of existence. In that fashion, Mictlantecuhtli is adorned with skulls and human bones. While these decorations remind modern audiences of death, however, in Aztec mythology they are symbols of fertility and wealth, and the morbid decorations hanging from the god's body are reminders that life itself will come again from death. Quetzalcóatl also adorns himself with the human body, although rather than taking on bones as his symbol, he wears a mask that shows his human face, hiding his true form as a feathered serpent. This mask is made from maize, and it highlights the god's own connection to fertility and growth. Together, Quetzalcóatl and Mictlantecuhtli are both powerful rulers, their ceremonial sandals and scepters distinguishing them as leaders of men. One a god of death and one of life, kneeling over the bones they destroyed, they are ultimately two aspects of the same cycle, as endlessly similar as they are distinct.

sacrifice would become defining factors of Aztec culture in the centuries that followed the downfall of Tollán, with city-states in constant competition for influence and resources. Within this reality, however, the Morning Star of Venus would daily ascend and fall as a reminder that all things must end and that in that cycle remains Quetzalcóatl's promise of something better.

CROSS-CULTURAL INFLUENCE

While many diverse gods populated Aztec mythology prior to Spanish conquest and colonialism, from the sixteenth century onward, Quetzalcóatl emerged as the most popular of all the ancient deities. In modern art and writing from Mexico and from other regions of the world, Quetzalcóatl has come to stand out as a representative of the Aztec past, a figure symbolic of an idealized pre-Columbian life and the promises of Mesoamerican culture. Tied with the myth of idyllic Tollán and the prophecy of Quetzalcóatl's return, modern depictions of the ancient god are often driven by contemporary political interests as well as by misunderstandings of the Aztec and Toltec cultures. The diversity of traditions associated with Quetzalcóatl—as well as the common lack of access to historical information about Mesoamerica—has resulted in a modern version of the god that often has much more to do with contemporary issues than with Aztec history and spirituality.

One of the most dramatic examples of the use and misuse of Quetzalcóatl's myth came immediately with Spanish invasion. Some scholars claim that Hernán Cortés, the Spanish conquistador who led the invasion of Aztec civilization, was believed by the Aztec leaders to have been Quetzalcóatl, returned as prophesized to bring about a golden age of prosperity and peace. This belief was bolstered by the fact that Cortés first arrived in the year associated with Quetzalcóatl's return through some Aztec spiritual traditions. This idea was commonly promulgated for years, with many Spanish writers emphasizing that the Aztecs had believed them to be gods, and the story was used to justify the colonization of Mesoamerican land and people. However, contemporary research suggests that it is unlikely the Aztecs actually supported this belief and that instead the link between Quetzalcóatl and Cortés was a fabrication of European invaders, emphasized in the years following the invasion. The difference between the Quetzalcóatl of sixteenth-century Aztec culture and the Quetzalcóatl of post-invasion period is dramatic, with the myth radically reinterpreted by the invading government to justify oppression and violence.

This conflicted relationship with Quetzalcóatl extends through several cultural traditions, with some modern religions even viewing Quetzalcóatl as an incarnation of Jesus Christ, come to set the roots of Christianity in the Mesoamerican world. At the same time, however, Quetzalcóatl has become a symbol of Mexican independence and the rights of indigenous people to develop their civilization and culture free from European influence. This Quetzalcóatl, while also sometimes depicted in ways inconsistent with Aztec cultural history, shares little in common with the Quetzalcóatl crafted by Spanish invaders. He is instead the god as depicted by the artist Diego Rivera, who featured Quetzalcóatl in his 1929 painting *La leyenda de Quetzalcóatl* (*The Legend of Quetzalcoatl*).

Rivera's work is part of a much larger fresco titled *The History of Mexico*. It is painted on the walls of the National Palace in Mexico City, a sprawling building that has been host to the Mexican national government since 1821. Centuries before that, the same land had been the seat of power of the final Aztec rulers who were conquered by Cortés, the buildings left burned and destroyed after his violent invasion. As a leading national artist, Rivera was invited to create his painting following the Mexican Revolution (1910–28). The years after the revolution were marked by widespread cultural and economic growth, with the new government supporting the arts and interest in Mexican heritage, especially when that heritage had become obscured by time and by European influence. For this site, Rivera chose a painting that emphasized the diversity of myths and interpretations surrounding Quetzalcóatl, avoiding any singular narrative or interpretation. Instead, Quetzalcóatl appears in four different forms within the same piece. He is a serpent breathing fire out of a volcano, a priest peacefully leading his city from within his temple, a godlike figure departing into the sea on his raft of snakes, and the face on the Morning Star arriving once again. Surrounding these four Quetzalcóatls, Rivera depicts a large number of active scenes set during indigenous times. While some people peacefully worship the priest, warriors on the outskirts defend their land against invaders; others actively and passionately practice their drumming and dance. As a whole, the painting is flourishing with action, the sad reality of war occurring alongside a thriving culture and spirituality. Rivera's painting carefully reminds viewers that the myth of Quetzalcóatl, like the culture that created him, should not be simplified into easy

narrative or political points, but rather celebrated for all of its complexities and contradictions.

Around the same time Rivera was completing this celebrated fresco, the American novelist and poet D. H. Lawrence was abandoning his life in the United States in order to explore Mexico and Mexican history. Lawrence's interest in Quetzalcóatl is both similar to and very different from Rivera's. Like the painter, Lawrence saw in Aztec mythology and culture a way of life that should be celebrated, recovered from the expanse of time and the tragedy of colonialism. Lawrence was particularly interested in finding ways of life that offered alternatives to modern American society and the realities of industrialism, which he believed were poisonous to both the earth and to human consciousness and spirituality. While Rivera included a strong dose of Mexican nationalism and independence in his portrayal of Quetzalcóatl, Lawrence saw the god more as representing an idealized spirituality free of the context of nation or politics, a pure way of life that that been lost, much to the detriment of the modern spirit.

Lawrence's depictions of Quetzalcóatl often lacked the subtlety of interpretation and the emphasis of diverse traditions that Rivera foregrounded. Instead, the idealization came through novels like *The Plumed Serpent* (1926), which depicts an American tourist traveling to a Mexican bullfight, where she encounters a small group of men who worship Quetzalcóatl and try to bring the ancient god back to his rightful place of power. This Quetzalcóatl is entirely the idealized god, his religion holding the potential to transform Mexico into Tollán once again, filled with riches and art and prosperity for all people. While this tradition fascinated and excited Lawrence to no end, however, he just as often despaired over the possibility that it could become a reality. While the characters of *The Plumed Serpent* try to revive the lost tradition, his poem "Quetzalcoatl Looks Down on Mexico" offers a very different story.

In the poem, Lawrence describes the ancient god returning to the modern state. The return of the god is initiated by the departure of Jesus, who abandons Mexico and calls to Quetzalcóatl that he should return the Christian traditions that had become the dominant religion in many regions. Jesus no longer wants "the images of my mother, and the images of my saints" to reside in Mexico (line 4) and instead decides he shall sleep, leaving the opportunity for Quetzalcóatl's return. From the start, this seems to offer the idealized situation for Lawrence's utopian society, the Western tradition having been outcast and the ancient ways of life able to rise once more. This moment is the prophesized return from the end of the ancient myth, with the god at last arriving from the Country of the Sun to establish a new Tollán. When he reaches the top of the mountain and glances down at Mexico, however, he sees "the men that worked in the fields, with foreign overseers" and "the hearts of them all, that were black, and heavy, / with a stone of anger at the bottom" (20, 24–25). The people of Mexico that he encounters are not people hungry for culture, the arts, and peace but are instead wrapped up in the toil of capitalism, angry with one another and with the world itself. Quetzalcóatl even attempts to call after them, but all except a very few appear to be deaf to his voice.

From this moment of disappointment and despair, Lawrence inverts the optimism of the poem's start. Quetzalcóatl is no longer the god returning to establish the golden age of the old Tollán, revived and peaceful from his ancient journey. Instead, he is the god that ends the cycles of the worlds, initiating new periods in Aztec mythology. Looking on the people of Mexico, he declares that "the earth is alive, and ready to shake off his fleas" (line 83). He prophesizes death and destruction and claims that he will bring about war with the sound of his voice. Quetzalcóatl explicitly links this death with the actions of men, whom he sees as spoiling the earth with their industry, unworthy of the idyllic existence he has promised. For Lawrence, it seems the promise of ancient ways of life might be unrecoverable, the trappings of modern culture so damaging that civilization itself must end for a new cycle to begin. While this appears to be an inversion of what is expected from the start of the poem, it is not an inversion but a return to a more ancient tradition of the Quetzalcóatl myth. Even as Lawrence idealizes the history of Mexico, he ultimately recognizes some of the complexity Rivera celebrates, knowing that humanity itself is as likely to worship Tezcatlipoca as it is to accept the gifts of Quetzalcóatl.

Among the many gods celebrated by the Aztecs, Quetzalcóatl remains the most popular. While he represents entirely different concepts and histories depending on the artist or writer depicting him, the core of his popularity is always rooted in his unique connection to history. Just as the ancient Aztecs celebrated him to celebrate their own idealized past, so too do modern artists and writers champion Quetzalcóatl as a figure who links them to an ancient Mexico that is utopian in its independence and culture. For Spanish invaders, this meant manipulating the myth in order to convince others that the colonizing government was the best possible world. For Rivera, celebration of the god meant celebration of Mexican national and cultural history, complete with all its complexities, the warrior existing alongside the artist just as they always had. For Lawrence, Quetzalcóatl's root in precolonial Mesoamerican culture meant that he could represent life outside of modern warfare and industrialization, even if that life might ultimately be lost forever. Quetzalcóatl remains a god of many traditions, a symbol of both optimism and failure. Quetzalcóatl was exiled from his own city, but the promise of his return remains, allowing modern artists to celebrate the richness of Mesoamerican culture while also mourning for what has been lost.

T. Fleischmann, MFA

BIBLIOGRAPHY

Carrasco, David. *Quetzalcoatl and the Irony of Empire.* Chicago: U of Chicago P, 1982. Print.

Colum, Padraic. "Quetzalcoatl." *Myths of the World.* New York: Grosset, 1930. 298–300. Print.

Florescano, Enrique. *The Myth of Quetzalcoatl.* Trans. Lysa Hochroth. Baltimore: Johns Hopkins UP, 1999. Print.

Harris, Wilson. "Quetzalcoatl and the Smoking Mirror (Reflections on Originality and Tradition)." *Review of Contemporary Fiction* 17.2 (1997): 12. Print.

Kleiner, Fred S. *Gardner's Art through the Ages: A Global History.* Boston: Wadsworth, 2011. Print.

Lafaye, Jacques. *Quetzalcóatl and Guadalupe: The Formation of Mexican National Consciousness.* Chicago: U of Chicago P, 1976. Print.

Lawrence, D. H. "Quetzalcoatl Looks Down on Mexico." *Selected Poems.* Ed. Kenneth Rexroth. New York: Viking, 1959. 122–25. Print.

Sir Gawain and the Quest of the Sangreal

Author: Traditional
Time Period: 501 CE–1000 CE
Country or Culture: England
Genre: Legend

OVERVIEW

Questing knights, fair maidens, bleeding swords, and the mysterious fisher king—these are the features of the Holy Grail (or Sangreal) legend, which was born in medieval Europe and still enchants audiences today. Although there is no single authoritative text of the Grail story, numerous versions and fragments remain, often with conflicting details, including which knight fulfills the quest and the nature of the Grail itself. In most surviving accounts, King Arthur's nephew Sir Gawain does not succeed in the quest, although he does achieve it in an early German version written by Heinrich von dem Türlin around 1220.

Türlin's account of the legend, an epic poem called *Diu Crône* (*The Crown*), begins with Gawain traveling to the Grail castle. After entering a paradisiacal garden and passing by a strange glass-walled dwelling with a sword suspended over its entrance, Gawain reunites with his fellow knights Lancelot and Calogreant (Calogrenant). They reach the Grail castle, where the aged host welcomes them. A youth places a sword before the host, and a banquet follows. During the banquet, Lancelot and Calogreant accept wine and immediately fall asleep; Gawain refuses, allowing him to remain awake to witness the marvelous Grail procession. A series of maidens and youths enter, carrying a spear, a golden platter on a silk cloth, and a precious container resembling a reliquary. They walk before the host and place the objects on the table. The spear produces drops of blood, which the host consumes along with bread in the reliquary. Gawain recognizes one of the maidens, who had previously instructed him to ask about such actions if he ever encountered them. He inquires about the meaning of the mysterious procession, which immediately causes great

rejoicing because his question releases all of the people in the paradisiacal land from a curse of living death sent by God. Soon after, the host and most of his company vanish. The maidens proclaim that Gawain has achieved the quest and bless him for his virtue. Gawain and his two companions depart.

The reputation of Gawain, the winner of the Grail in this version and an upstanding knight in many other medieval tales, declines markedly in later accounts of the Grail quest. A comparative analysis reveals these changes and shows that Gawain's reputation for both virtue and vice often centers on his interactions with women. Stories such as his marriage to Dame Ragnelle (Ragnell) and his interactions with Lady Bercilak (Bertilak) in the Green Knight legend exemplify his close link with ladies, which scholars believe to be related both to his status as Grail winner early on and his less stellar reputation in later versions. In addition to the intriguing problem of Gawain's shifting status, a comparative analysis further reveals what is at stake in defining the Grail winner, whose success signifies nothing less than the power to restore life. For this reason, readers have viewed the identity of the knight who fulfills the quest to be crucial to the meaning of the Grail's mysterious healing ritual, which represents a hybrid of pagan and Christian traditions.

SUMMARY

Heinrich von dem Türlin's story of the Grail castle, as translated by Jessie L. Weston, begins with Gawain traveling on horseback. He comes upon a rich and fertile land that seems like the earthly paradise. Within this garden appears a glass-walled dwelling, but blocking the entry is a fiery sword. Believing this to be a dangerous omen, Gawain passes by the dwelling. He journeys for twelve more days in the land until he happily discovers his fellow knights Lancelot and Calogreant sleeping beneath a tree. They reunite and travel together, meeting a squire who directs them to the next town. The knights

"Sir Gawain might scarce trust his senses, for of a truth he knew the crowned maiden well, and that 'twas she who aforetime had spoken to him of the Grail, and bade him an he ever saw her again, with five maidens in her company, to fail not to ask what they did there—and thereof had he great desire."

Sir Gawain at the Grail Castle

next discover a castle where many knights practice horsemanship in a meadow nearby. These knights greet the newcomers warmly and bring them inside the castle to meet their lord, who also welcomes the men and invites Gawain to sit beside him. They become acquainted until evening, when many knights, ladies, minstrels, and servants enter for a banquet.

Next, a "wondrous fair youth, of noble bearing" enters the hall with a sword and places it before the aged host (Weston, *Sir Gawain* 39). Wine is then served, first to Gawain and his companions, but the host refrains from eating or drinking, so Gawain abstains as well. Lancelot and Calogreant, however, quench their thirst with the wine, which immediately causes them to fall asleep. The host frequently invites Gawain to drink, but he refrains, not wanting to fall asleep, too. A procession then begins: first come four seneschals, or stewards, followed by two maidens carrying two candlesticks. Behind the maidens are two youths who hold a sharp spear between them. Next, two more maidens arrive carrying a "salver [tray] of gold and precious stones, upon a silken cloth" (40). Walking behind these maidens is another woman surpassingly lovely and richly dressed. She holds a piece of samite cloth, on which lies a red-gold jewel that serves as a base for another golden container resembling a reliquary on an altar. The woman wears a gold crown and is followed by another maiden who weeps. The procession advances to the host to bow before him.

Gawain recognizes the maiden wearing the golden crown as one who had once told him about the Grail and "bade him an he ever saw her again, with five maidens in her company, to fail not to ask what they did there"

(Weston, *Sir Gawain* 41). The youths then lay the spear on the table with the salver underneath. Amazingly, the spear sheds three drops of blood onto the tray, and the host immediately drinks them. The golden-crowned maiden then places the reliquary on the table, and the host removes from it a piece of bread, which he eats. At this point, Gawain can no longer contain his curiosity: "Mine host, I pray ye for the sake of God, and by His Majesty, that ye tell me what meaneth this great company, and these marvels I behold?" (42).

As soon as Gawain utters these words, the knights and ladies in the hall cry out and rejoice, but the host commands them to be seated. Hearing the noise, Lancelot and Calogreant awaken briefly but quickly fall back into a slumber. The host then tells Gawain that the wondrous thing he has seen may not be revealed to everyone, but because Gawain has asked, the host responds that he has indeed seen the Grail. The host congratulates Gawain for displaying both "manhood and courage" because his question has liberated many from "sorrow they long had borne" (Weston, *Sir Gawain* 42, 43). The host states that he and his people had hoped that Perceval would liberate them, but he failed to question the meaning of what he saw. The host then explains that their sorrow began with a man who killed his brother to gain his land, prompting God to punish the man and "all his kin" (43). The punishment, he explains, was to banish life from the people, who only appear to be living. The only resolution for this curse was for a man to ask about the marvelous procession as Gawain has done. The host states that he is also dead, but because he is not guilty of the original crime, the spear and bread were able to nourish only him once each year. Only the maidens, he claims, are not dead by God's command. Both the penance and Gawain's quest are now complete.

The host gives the sword to Gawain and tells him it will never break, commanding that he carry it with him always. The host then continues to explain the Grail procession, stating that God had given the responsibility of the Grail to the maidens because of their "unstained purity" (Weston, *Sir Gawain* 45). However, the maidens are now saddened because they know that the Grail will no longer be witnessed, given that Gawain has "learned its secrets" (45). Mortals can behold the Grail only by God's grace, and no one is allowed to speak of its mysteries any longer. After these words, dawn approaches, and suddenly the old man, the Grail, and all the knights and ladies in the hall vanish, leaving only the maidens and Gawain with his two companions. Gawain is saddened at the host's disappearance, but one of the maidens again tells him that he has achieved everything necessary in the quest for the Grail, which had been present only in that land. Previously wasted, the land and the people are now healed, bringing them great joy. When Lancelot and Calogreant awaken, they celebrate the good news but regret having missed the Grail procession. The knights find hospitality in the town, and the maidens bless Gawain, wishing him a long and prosperous life. Gawain then departs.

ANALYSIS

The legend of the Grail is both amazingly popular and unusually varied, with no single authoritative version or text. Instead, the Grail legend as it is known today developed in northern Europe in the late twelfth century as one of many stories associated with King Arthur and his Knights of the Round Table. For approximately fifty years, numerous versions of the Grail legend proliferated, presenting myriad conflicting details that have prompted much scholarly debate, particularly regarding who achieves the quest and the meaning of the mysterious Grail itself, which is sometimes portrayed as a chalice, a platter, or a cauldron. Most versions portray not Gawain, but Perceval or Galahad as the knight who achieves the quest. Yet some scholars have been intrigued by Heinrich von dem Türlin's German version with Gawain as the winner in part because of his fame in other medieval narratives, a fame that markedly degrades as the Grail narratives evolved. Part of Gawain's early glory involves his prowess as both warrior and as lover, but his character as a "ladies' knight" appears to be his downfall in later Grail legends. A comparative analysis examines Gawain's roles in different versions of the Grail story and in other medieval tales to determine how they relate to the early account in which he fulfills the quest. More importantly, a comparative reading reveals the significance of the Grail, which might well symbolize a pagan fertility ritual signifying the renewal of life, a ritual that eventually came to be Christianized during the Middle Ages.

The Grail legend belongs to a large body of work known as Arthurian literature, which are stories associated with the figure of King Arthur, a legendary Briton king who may have defeated Saxon invaders in the sixth century. The twelfth-century scholar Geoffrey of Monmouth wrote in his *Historia regum Britanniae* (1130–38; *History of the Kings of Britain*) that Arthur established an empire and ruled over Gaul, Britain, Ireland, Iceland, and Norway. Other writers developed stories called "romances," based on the Knights of the Round Table, a chivalric society of knights dwelling in Arthur's court. These romances frequently feature knights other than Arthur as the protagonist, and the Grail story exemplifies this pattern.

Perceval: The Story of the Grail is an early text that is nonetheless not the origin of the Grail story, which had already developed in Celtic and oral sources, as Nigel Bryant points out. Written in the 1180s by the poet Chrétien de Troyes, the story tells of the knight Perceval who witnesses a mysterious procession that includes a precious vessel called the Grail, but the knight does not ask the proper question to understand the mystery. Chrétien died before completing the poem, prompting several anonymous authors to write different and often conflicting continuations. At the same time, other writers began to offer entirely new versions of this story that enthralled twelfth- and thirteenth-century audiences. Between 1220 and 1225, an anonymous writer offered *The Quest of the Holy Grail*, a totally new version with a new winner named Sir Galahad, while yet another version called *The High Book of the Holy Grail* kills off the fisher king—the host or lord of the Grail castle—before he is ever healed (Bryant 3). Further continuations of Chrétien's work appeared in the 1230s with still different endings.

Even before the thirteenth century, the Grail legend became distinctly Christian in character. Robert de Boron penned *Joseph of Arimathea* likely around the time of Chrétien de Troyes, a prequel that identifies the Grail as a spear accompanied by "a vessel used by Christ at the Last Supper and by Joseph of Arimathea" (Bryant 3), who according to the New Testament offered his own tomb to bury Jesus Christ after his crucifixion. Joseph's descendants guarded these objects until one of them sinned by gazing lustfully on a maiden and was immediately wounded by the spear. This sinner is the frail fisher king of most Holy Grail stories, who can only be healed by a virtuous knight who asks the right question. There also appeared *The High Book of the Grail* around 1200, which connects the Grail quest with the crusades that Western Europeans were conducting in the Holy Land in the twelfth century. Thus, even before 1250, the legend had already spawned an impressive number of inconsistent texts, offering different heroes and underscoring pagan or Christian elements. For this reason, there is no authoritative text or coherent narrative tradition. Modern readers frequently know the Grail legend from

Thomas Malory's fifteenth-century *Le Morte d'Arthur* (*The Death of Arthur*), an English compilation of popular French and English romance tales. By this time, Gawain is firmly established as an unrepentant sinner and failed seeker. Galahad becomes the true Grail winner.

Particularly intriguing, however, are Gawain's renowned character in other medieval legends and his prominence even in Grail stories in which his quest fails. First, John Matthews cites numerous texts, such as Geoffrey of Monmouth's history, that firmly establish Sir Gawain as King Arthur's brave nephew; one twelfth- or thirteenth-century account called *The Rise of Gawain* characterizes him as a great hero whose many valiant deeds include the rescue of a besieged lady at a castle of maidens. Second, although Gawain's Grail quest fails in most surviving versions, he nonetheless plays a major role in these stories, as David Leeming notes. Many Grail narratives begin with the Knights of the Round Table gathered at Camelot, the court of King Arthur. Sitting together, the knights suddenly hear a clap of thunder and see an intense light, followed by a vessel covered by white samite, a silken cloth. The vessel passes through the hall and vanishes. Following this vision, Gawain is the first knight to dedicate himself to the Grail quest, which he promises to undertake for twelve months and a day. The other knights follow suit.

Furthermore, Chrétien de Troyes's above-named incomplete poem and a thirteenth-century version named *Parzival* present Perceval as the protagonist but give far more attention to the adventures of Gawain. In Chrétien's story, Gawain appears after Perceval has failed to ask the right question at the Grail castle. Gawain then undertakes a series of adventures, the highlights of which include meeting a mysterious proud lady, who leads him to the Castle of Wonders, where he fights bravely to liberate many other ladies imprisoned there. Once he achieves this, he is introduced to three queens, who turn out to be his grandmother, his mother, and his sister. Gawain is told that as liberator, he must remain forever at the Castle of Wonders, but instead he leaves to fight another foe at the proud lady's behest, finally returning to the castle and sending a message for Arthur and Guinevere to join him there. Chrétien's narrative ends at this point. Wolfram von Eschenbach's *Parzival* completes the story by having Gawain marry the proud lady after fulfilling all of her commands and receiving the Arthurian court at the Castle of Wonders, where he is now lord, earning the title Knight of the Maidens. Gawain thus serves as a foil to Perceval, who is left

to complete the Grail quest, a contrast that becomes a pattern in other Grail narratives as well. Nonetheless, Matthews argues that these and other narratives grant Gawain such prominence because he was known as an important and virtuous character, so that medieval authors felt the need to explain his failure to justify the success of Sir Galahad, a newer character who lacked an established history (120–24).

Other continuations of the Grail story reveal that Gawain fails at the quest due to his "fatal attraction to the opposite sex" (Matthews 126). In one typical version, Gawain meets a maiden in a tent who, not knowing his identity, instructs him to protect her at all costs. When Gawain reveals his name, the maiden offers her love freely. Gawain then must fight both the maiden's father and brother, who accuse him both of destroying their family honor and of previously killing their uncle. The matter is eventually settled peacefully, and Gawain proceeds to a series of adventures that lead him to a castle where he encounters what is clearly a Grail procession, including a broken sword that must be reunited. Gawain is unable to rejoin the sword; he asks about the sword and lance that he sees but falls asleep during the explanation, waking the next morning on the seashore and lamenting his failure. The stories thus present him as a well-meaning but feckless character who is particularly unable to resist temptation in matters of love (129).

Interestingly, Gawain's relationships with women mark his virtue in two of the best-known stories about him, as Matthews demonstrates. The first is the famous fourteenth-century poem *Sir Gawain and the Green Knight*. The story opens at Camelot, where Arthur's court prepares to celebrate Christmas, when an enormous knight bursts into the hall. The knight is dressed all in green, has green skin, and even rides a green horse. Bearing a large axe and a bough of holly, he challenges the court to an ostensibly friendly Christmas game entailing an exchange of blows: someone must strike the giant with his axe, and he will return the blow after a year and a day. The challenger will win the axe as a reward. When no knights come forward, Arthur nearly accepts, but Gawain agrees at the last moment. He beheads the green giant, who simply picks up his head, reminds Gawain to meet him at the Green Chapel in one year's time, and departs.

At the end of the year, Gawain seeks out the Green Chapel and happens upon the castle of Lord Bercilak, who receives him kindly and assures him that the chapel is close by. Gawain meets Bercilak's lovely wife and an old, ugly woman who is treated with great respect. Bercilak goes hunting the next day while Gawain rests at the castle, where the host's wife attempts to seduce Gawain. He resists her advances but agrees for the sake of courtesy to accept one kiss from her. When Bercilak returns, he offers to exchange his hunting spoils with whatever Gawain has won that day, so the latter delivers one kiss to his host. The wife persists in her seduction for the next two days, but Gawain continues to resist her, accepting two kisses on day two and three on the final day, along with a green girdle (or belt), which the wife says will preserve him from all danger. That evening, Gawain delivers three kisses to his host but says nothing of the belt.

The following day, Bercilak's guide accompanies Gawain to the Green Chapel, and Gawain refuses the guide's offers to lead him to safety. Gawain meets the Green Knight, who twice pretends to strike him with the axe and mocks Gawain for flinching. The third time, he merely nicks Gawain's neck, and Gawain immediately declares that he has fulfilled the agreement. The Green Knight then reveals himself as Bercilak and says that the old woman at his court, who is really the sorceress Morgan le Fay and Arthur's sister, enchanted him to test Arthur's knights. Gawain has passed the test; his only failure is that he accepted the girdle from Lady Bercilak, who was also commanded by Morgan to test Gawain. Gawain is ashamed, but the Green Knight readily forgives him. They part ways, and Gawain wears the belt as a sign of his error. The Knights of the Round Table, however, wear similar belts as a symbol of Gawain's honor.

Somewhat less known is the fifteenth-century story *The Wedding of Sir Gawain and Dame Ragnelle*. This tale is a version of the loathly lady, a popular motif in the Middle Ages. It begins with King Arthur out hunting when he encounters Gromer Somer Jour, a churlish knight who accuses him of wrongfully granting land to Gawain; the knight promises to behead Arthur unless he can tell him in one year's time what women most desire. Arthur returns to Carlisle and reports the task he has been given. Gawain offers to assist him and suggests that they each travel the country separately to seek answers. Over the course of the year, the knights compile books full of answers until finally, with the year's end fast approaching, Arthur meets an ugly old woman in the forest who declares that she will grant the true answer on condition that Sir Gawain agrees to marry her. Dejected, Arthur returns to court, where Gawain immediately accepts the challenge. Arthur then goes to meet Gromer, finding the hag on the way; she tells him the answer and promises to claim her husband soon. When Arthur encounters the knight, he first tries to no avail all the answers in the books he and Gawain have compiled. As a last resort, he offers the old woman's answer, which is that women most desire sovereignty. At this, Gromer is enraged because only his sister could have told Arthur the correct answer. He promises to take revenge on her.

Arthur returns to Gawain with a heavy heart. The marriage proceeds, and the bride's ugliness and bad manners offend all. On the wedding night, Gawain reluctantly kisses the hag—or, in some versions, simply agrees to treat her as his wife—at which point she suddenly transforms into a beautiful young woman. She explains that she has been under an enchantment and that Gawain may now choose whether to enjoy her beauty only at night or during the day when they are with others. When Gawain defers the decision to her, he breaks the spell permanently because he has given her sovereignty, the answer to Gromer's question. Gawain's wife is now completely free of the enchantment. The court rejoices, and Ragnelle lives for five years and bears Gawain a son.

What do the stories above reveal about Gawain's encounters with the opposite sex? In a thorough study briefly summarized here, Matthews demonstrates that nearly all women encountered by Gawain are sorceresses or goddesses who test him in some fashion. The story of the besieged lady whom Gawain rescues in *The Rise of Gawain* also exists in more than ten other texts; scholars have identified the lady as Morgain (an incarnation of whom is Morgan le Fay), an otherworldly figure related to the pagan Irish goddesses Macha and Morrigan (Matthews 48–51). In Chrétien's *Perceval*, the mysterious proud lady who commands Gawain to fulfill several quests is a goddess who guides him through an otherworld so that he may liberate the castle of ladies and meet the three queens. Matthews argues that these queens represent the "triple aspected goddess" (123), a well-known common archetype of pagan goddess figures throughout the world. Lady Bercilak in the Green Knight tale is an aspect of Morgan, who is actually called a goddess in the text and both tests and protects Gawain with her magic green girdle. The story itself descends from a pagan Irish "beheading" tale in which the hero ultimately wins and serves a goddess figure, according to Matthews. The story of Dame Ragnelle is a parody of medieval romance tales but is highly significant for understanding Gawain. She represents the

MYTH INTO ART

Jessie Weston's scholarly treatise *From Ritual to Romance* (1920) sparked intense debate over the roots of the Grail legend and deeply inspired T. S. Eliot's *The Waste Land* (1922), arguably the most important poem of the twentieth century. According to Weston, the link between the wasted land and the wounded fisher king make them the central elements of the legend. She traces this link to universal pagan nature rites, arguing that the Grail, described variously in the legends as a cup, a cauldron, a platter, and so forth, represents renewed fertility for both the king and the land. In his notes to *The Waste Land*, Eliot names Weston's work as having defined his poem's title, structure, and symbolism. His theme is a modern land laid waste by the psychic disillusionment of modernity, which is plagued by failed progress and persistent war.

Eliot's poem is difficult, with obscure allusions, symbols, and shifting voices, but the language powerfully evokes sterility, beginning with the famous first lines denying spring as a sign of renewal: "April is the cruelest month, breeding / Lilacs out of the dead land" (1–2). The speaker claims that none can say "what branches grow / Out of this stony rubbish" (19–20), because the only things known are "A heap of broken images, where the sun beats / And the dead tree gives no shelter" (22–23).

The poem invokes the fisher king near the end, but in Eliot's hands, this figure is powerless: "I sat upon the shore / Fishing, with the arid plain behind me" (424–25), says the king, but then he asks, "Shall I at least set my lands in order?" (426). The question echoes the command in the biblical verse Isaiah 38:1, "Set thine house in order: for thou shalt die and not live." Eliot thus powerfully transforms the symbolism of the fisher king to evoke the frustration of life in a fatally sterile landscape.

loathly lady, a figure who appears in many Grail stories to chide and instruct the knights. Yet, according to Matthews, she descends from the Celtic goddess of the land, who was believed to grant kings sovereignty over their land through a symbolic ritual in which the king mated with her mortal representative. In the Dame Ragnelle story, the goddess figure grants human fertility.

The ritualistic connection between kings and their land turns out to be crucial for understanding the Grail legend. In Heinrich von dem Türlin's version, Gawain clearly enters an "otherworldly realm" when he discovers the garden of paradise with the glass-walled structure inside (Matthews 151). When Gawain and his companions enter the castle, the lord who greets them is not the frail fisher king of most Grail stories, but he is nourished by the blood and the bread. Gawain liberates all of the land's people from "death," the state of suspended life in which they live, and restores the wasted land to fertility. Furthermore, Gawain succeeds because he recognizes the crowned maiden, whom he had previously encountered and who had instructed him to ask about what he saw her doing with five maidens. Matthews claims that this maiden in the original German is called a "lady" and a "goddess," making her yet another incarnation of the supernatural queens that Gawain continually encounters in so many stories (152). Matthews concludes that Gawain, who himself descends partly from a Celtic hero named Gwri Gwallt Euryn (Gwri Golden Hair), represents an archetypal hero who serves ladies that descend from the great pagan goddess of sovereignty. In the legends, the different aspects of this goddess are represented by the otherworldly sorceress ladies whom Gawain frequently serves.

This interpretation partly rests on a reading of the poem that Jessie Weston offers in her seminal study *From Ritual to Romance*, published in 1920. Weston argues that the largely Christianized Grail legend descends from a pagan fertility ritual that links the wasted land with a king who is ill. When a hero asks the right question, he can restore the king and the land to health. The Grail is a cup, platter, cauldron, or other type of serving dish because it symbolizes the nourishment and renewal that both the king and the land require. The Grail procession refers to a ritual originally practiced in a religious cult that was suppressed by the rise of Christianity in the Middle Ages. Thus, according to Weston, the narrative that accompanied this fertility ritual gradually became separated from the practice of the religion and instead became a romance heavily overlaid with Christian symbols. Such symbols are present in Heinrich von dem Türlin's account, most notably the bleeding spear and the reliquary containing the bread, which refer to the Eucharist, the symbolic wine and bread that

Christians receive to signify the crucifixion of Christ and the redeeming power of his death.

Weston's work initiated an intense debate over the extent to which the Grail legend was originally pagan versus Christian. Yet both pagan and Christian versions show that achieving the Grail quest signifies the power to renew not simply human life but all natural life—thus the high honor attached to the Grail winner. Weston also argues that Gawain's female consorts are consistently otherworldly creatures, which explains his seemingly promiscuous behavior in some narratives, an idea that later scholars such as B. J. Whiting would refute. Still, Matthews and others have revived and built on Weston's ideas to argue for Gawain as an archetypal hero whose powerful link with the pagan sovereign goddess makes him the likely original Grail winner. However, his subservient relationship with the goddess could not be incorporated into Christianity, which posits a male deity and emphasizes male dominance. For this reason, Gawain was eventually displaced as the Grail winner, and his reputation gradually shifted in the legends from an honorable knight of maidens to a lascivious failure. Nevertheless, strong hints of Gawain's relationship with the goddess remain, though scholars will likely never fully know the nature of Gawain's role and other details of the Grail story. Perhaps the greatest value of these debates is their preservation of narratives that might otherwise be long forgotten.

CROSS-CULTURAL INFLUENCE

The Grail legend blossomed most intensely in the first half of the thirteenth century, but the story has continued to evolve and is known to many readers in Alfred, Lord Tennyson's *Idylls of the King*, a series of twelve idylls, or narrative poems, published between 1856 and 1885, that retell various Arthurian tales. A renowned English poet of the Victorian era, Tennyson (1809–92) was poet laureate of the United Kingdom, and the *Idylls of the King* is considered one of his highest achievements. With its celebration of medieval legend and its spiritual values, the poetry cycle belongs to the literary movement known as romanticism. The twelve idylls, written in blank verse, narrate the rise and fall of Arthur's exemplary society to suggest an allegory for the moral disintegration of Victorian society. The Grail legend appears as the eighth idyll and presents the quest as a mostly failed journey that weakens the society of Arthur's court. Notably, Gawain in Tennyson's account is the least virtuous knight, and Perceval (whom Tennyson

calls Percivale) is not the Grail winner. Instead, he becomes the protagonist and the narrator of the poem, which prizes social loyalty and upholds the importance of spiritual virtue.

Tennyson's eighth idyll, titled "The Holy Grail," opens with Percivale living in a monastery. His fellow monk Ambrosius sits with him beneath a yew tree and asks why he left the company of Arthur's knights to follow a religious life. Was it earthly passion that drove him away from the Round Table? Percivale replies that it was not passion but the vision of the Holy Grail that spurred him to a virtuous life away from the "vainglories, rivalries, / And earthly heats" (lines 32–33) that arise from jousts witnessed by women, who "waste the spiritual strength / Within us, better offer'd up to Heaven" (35–36). Ambrosius then asks about the nature of the Grail. Percivale replies it is Jesus's cup from the Last Supper and was passed down by Joseph of Arimathea, who eventually brought it to Glastonbury, where it displayed magic healing powers to any faithful soul who touched or saw it. Because of the world's sin, the cup eventually "was caught away to Heaven, and disappear'd" (58).

Ambrosius then asks if anyone living in their times has seen the Grail, to which Percivale replies that his own sister, a devout nun, had a vision of the Grail. She entreats Percivale to fast and pray so that he too might behold it. Percivale does so, but since Galahad is a surpassingly virtuous knight, Percivale's sister cuts off her hair for him and uses it to make a plaited sword belt with an interwoven image of the Grail. She gives Galahad the belt and encourages him so that he too might witness the holy cup. One day, the knights are at the Round Table, and Galahad sits in a magic chair of the sorcerer Merlin. The chair causes whoever sits in it to "lose himself" (line 174), but Galahad proclaims that if he loses himself, he will save himself. The moment that Galahad is seated, the Grail, shrouded in mist, passes through the hall in a beam of light. Percivale claims that he was the first to vow to seek the Grail for a year and a day, followed by Galahad, Bors, and Lancelot. Gawain commits last "and louder than the rest" (202). Arthur returns to find his hall in tumult, with some knights vowing to go forth and others protesting the idea. Percivale explains what has happened, and Arthur first objects to their vows, especially when the knights—with the exception of Galahad—confess they have not actually seen the Grail because it was shrouded in mist. Preferring that his knights remain with him to defend the innocent, Arthur proclaims that the quest is only for Galahad, but he nevertheless honors their vows and arranges a final tournament, in which Galahad and Percivale prevail.

Percivale then recounts the adventures of his quest, which include a series of phantoms, a babbling brook and apples, a welcoming woman, a knight in golden armor, and so forth, that turn to dust upon his approach. He finally meets a hermit in a chapel who tells him that he lacks humility. Galahad then appears in the chapel, prays with Percivale, and reports that he has seen the image of the Grail during his travels while "Shattering all evil customs everywhere" (line 477) and defeating pagans. The two knights leave the chapel to climb a hill, where a thunderstorm rages over a black swamp filled with the bones of men. The swamp includes piers that only Galahad may cross, while an image of the Grail hovers above his head. Percivale eventually finds himself back at the chapel, where he decides to return to Arthur's court. Ambrosius then asks if Percivale encountered anyone else besides Galahad, and Percivale confesses that he was diverted from the quest when he found a town full of maidens. The maidens lead him to a castle ruled by a beautiful widow whose people urge Percivale to marry, but the knight resists and departs in shame at his weakness.

Ambrosius persists with his questions, asking if Percivale met any other knights. Percivale recounts how the other knights fared in the quest. Along his way, he discovers Bors, who in turn had briefly encountered Lancelot riding madly and claiming to flee from a lion. Grieving over Lancelot's apparent insanity, Bors loses motivation and comes to a town where the people scoff at his quest. They imprison him, but through a loose stone in his prison wall, he miraculously views the Grail image, after which a maiden secretly frees him. Returning to the court and facing Arthur's questioning, Percivale announces his wish to become a monk. Arthur responds by asking Gawain about his adventures. Gawain states that the quest was "not for such as I" (line 738), so he consulted a holy man, who confirmed that he was unfit for the quest. He states that he was tired of the quest but discovered "a silk pavilion in a field, / And merry maidens in it" (742–43). He entertains himself there and is only disturbed when a gale destroys the pavilion and "blew my merry maidens all about / With all discomfort" (745–46). Otherwise, he states, "my twelvemonth and a day were pleasant to me" (747).

Bors then enters and declares to Arthur that he did indeed see the Grail. Asked to speak, Lancelot recounts

a long journey in which he feels overcome by sin, so he consults a holy man who reports that his journey is in vain. Then his madness causes him to wander in "waste fields far away" (line 785), where he is defeated by lesser knights. Encountering a storm on a beach, he throws himself into the sea to wash away his sins and miraculously floats to a castle built on a rock. He enters the castle, and a voice beckons him to ascend a tower to witness the Grail. He climbs to the tower, where he finds a fiery room in which he thinks he glimpses the Grail veiled in red samite. Nonetheless, he concludes, "this quest was not for me" (849).

Gawain then condemns the quest and claims that he has never before failed Arthur. He further declares that by introducing the Grail, Percivale and his sister have "made our mightiest madder than our least," and he promises that he will subsequently ignore "holy virgins in their ecstasies" (lines 860, 863). Arthur condemns Gawain, admonishing him not to take idle vows and accusing him of "being too blind to have desire to see" (868). In contrast, he states, Bors, Lancelot, and Percivale are praiseworthy because they "have seen according to their sight" (871). Nonetheless, Arthur confirms his original view of the quest, that it would lead most of his knights to "follow wandering fires, / lost in the quagmire" (887–88). He laments that Galahad, the most successful, has not returned, whereas Lancelot hardly believes he saw the Grail and Percivale will leave the Round Table for a religious life. He declares that all kings belong at home to guard what they rule, whereas visions "come, as they will" (907) without the need to seek them. Percivale concludes by stating, "So spake the king: I knew not all he meant" (916).

The *Idylls of the King* belongs to the period of English literature known as romanticism, which began in the late eighteenth century and peaked in the first half of the nineteenth century. In part, romanticism was a response to the Industrial Revolution, which brought undeniable progress but also population growth, sprawling cities, and a new level of materialism. Romanticism also reacted against the Enlightenment, an eighteenth-century movement that emphasized reason as the highest principle of intellectual and creative life. In contrast, romanticism celebrated human emotion and nature as sources of creativity. The movement embraced ancient folk customs and themes and did much to develop the idea of the inspired, individual artist. This embracing of ancient narratives meant that romantic poets were deeply interested in medieval stories, including the Grail legend.

In Tennyson's hands, the Grail story is part of a larger moral allegory, or extended metaphor, in which he comments on the moral and spiritual degeneration of the Victorian era in which he lived. This allegory functions by making Arthur represent the human soul: when Arthur's knights are loyal to him and fulfill their knightly ideals, "all is well in Camelot," but when they are disloyal or sinful, they represent destructive human passions. Indeed, as Jerome Buckley says in his foreword to Tennyson's *Idylls*, "the whole Arthurian order is threatened by a ruthless, self-seeking individualism, the assumption that each man can be his own law unto himself, which leads ultimately to the destruction of all social values" (x). Each of the twelve idylls, or stories, can stand on their own, but they also serve the overarching structure of the work, which documents the rise and fall of Arthurian society, an exemplary culture that stands in for Tennyson's Britain.

As the eighth idyll, the Grail story demonstrates social disintegration but also the value of spiritual life, which Tennyson achieves in two ways. The first is his use of Christianity, which was already a prominent element in many Grail stories. Tennyson, however, makes Percivale a monk who has left King Arthur's court to live a wholly spiritual life. In his narrative, Percivale emphasizes the Grail as the cup of Jesus at the Last Supper, and he states that the Grail image appears in modern times first to his sister, a devout nun. Furthermore, throughout the knights' adventures, holy men repeatedly advise them, such as when one man informs Percivale that he lacks humility, and a holy man confirms Gawain's unsuitability for the quest. Tennyson does not make use of the Grail procession as found in medieval accounts but focuses instead on the spiritual and moral worth of each knight. The story presents a clear moral hierarchy, with Galahad pegged as the best knight and Gawain as the unequivocal worst. Here, Tennyson follows the tradition that had gradually developed over the course of the Grail legend, which assigns Galahad as the winner while degrading Gawain. However, Tennyson's Gawain is especially lax as he casually recounts how he entertains himself with "merry maidens" and then blames Percivale and his sister for endangering the knights, prompting Arthur's stinging rebuke. The knights who see the Grail are consistently described as virtuous Christians, particularly Galahad, who is the most celebrated and most supported by Percivale's nun sister.

Tennyson's second notable technique is his creation of Percivale as the narrator. Galahad is the Grail winner, but as the narrator, Percivale effectively becomes the protagonist and hero of the story; he tells the story from his point of view and emphasizes his own role, claiming that he was the first to swear to undertake the quest. He also underscores Arthur's high regard for him, such as when he states that Arthur preferred to rank him closely with Galahad. Percivale comments parenthetically on how "reckless and irreverent" Gawain was (line 853), which further bolsters his own reputation. Furthermore, Percivale tells the story in retrospect, with his own decision to live a holy life presented as the point from which he speaks and as the proper ending. Arthur makes it clear that even though the knights who witnessed the Grail deserve praise, the quest was actually fruitless because it was not worth the trouble and has weakened the society of the Round Table.

In this sense, the quest in Percivale's story seems to serve two purposes. On the one hand, it represents a foolish journey because it leads the knights to failure and even madness. The good knight, Arthur makes clear, remains with his king. On the other hand, the quest proves to be a valid spiritual test that reveals Galahad as the most devout, Gawain as the least, and the others somewhere in between. In this way, Tennyson focuses on Arthur as the moral center holding society together. However, by privileging both the Grail quest and Percivale's reformed life as signs of virtue, he creates tension between the idea of social cohesion and spiritual strength. Thus, at least in the eighth idyll, the allegory of social disintegration seems to be at odds with the emphasis on a devout Christian life. Nonetheless, like many prior versions of this legend, Tennyson's engaging poem attests to readers' enduring fascination with the elusive and mysterious Grail.

Ashleigh Imus, PhD

BIBLIOGRAPHY

Borroff, Marie, trans. *Sir Gawain and the Green Knight*. New York: Norton, 1967. Print.

Bryant, Nigel. *The Legend of the Grail*. Rochester: Brewer, 2004. Print.

Buckley, Jerome. Foreword. *Idylls of the King*. By Alfred, Lord Tennyson. New York: Houghton, 1963. Print.

Eliot, T. S. *The Waste Land and Other Poems*. New York: Penguin, 1998. Print.

Leeming, David Adams. *Mythology: The Voyage of the Hero*. 3rd ed. New York: Oxford UP, 1998. Print.

Matthews, John. *Sir Gawain: Knight of the Goddess*. Rochester: Inner Traditions, 2003. Print.

Tennyson, Alfred. *Idylls of the King*. New Haven: Yale UP, 1983. Print.

Weston, Jessie L. *From Ritual to Romance*. 1920. Garden City: Doubleday, 1957. Print.

---, trans. *Sir Gawain at the Grail Castle*. Vol. 6 of *Arthurian Romances, Unrepresented in Malory's* Morte d'Arthur. London: Nutt, 1903. Print.

Whiting, B. J. "Gawain: His Reputation, His Courtesy, and His Appearance in Chaucer's Squire's Tale." *Gawain: A Casebook*. Ed. Raymond H. Thompson and Keith Busby. New York: Routledge, 2006. 45–95. Print.

Tales of Odysseus
(Lotus-Eaters, Cyclops)

Author: Homer
Time Period: 999 BCE–1 BCE
Country or Culture: Greek
Genre: Myth

OVERVIEW

A renowned hero of Greek myth, Odysseus is the wily protagonist of Homer's *Odyssey*, an epic poem likely composed in the eighth century BCE that tells of his arduous homecoming after the Trojan War. Odysseus is a brave warrior and adventurer but is best known for his cleverness, having devised the scheme of the Trojan horse that ensured Greek victory in the war. A lesser-known but crucial part of his character is his masterful storytelling ability, which is most evident in the stories he tells about himself. His tale of evading the Lotus-eaters and others who seek to hinder him on his journey and escaping Polyphemus (Polyphêmos) the Cyclops particularly illustrates his narrative genius.

This tale begins in book 9 of *The Odyssey*, after Odysseus has been washed up on the shore of the Phaeacians. When he finally reveals his identity to his hosts, Odysseus first tells of his battles with the Cicones and the Lotus-eaters before moving on to his encounter with the fearful Cyclops, who eats several members of the hero's crew. When he and his crew are trapped in Polyphemus's cave, Odysseus lulls the giant to sleep with wine and then blinds him with a giant wooden stake. Polyphemus begs the other Cyclopes for help, but they reject him when the giant tells them that "Nobody," the name Odysseus claims for himself, has wounded him. Odysseus and his men then escape by hiding beneath sheep so that blind Polyphemus cannot use his hands to locate the men as the animals transport them out of the cave. Once the men are safe at sea, Odysseus cannot resist twice taunting Polyphemus. The giant reacts by throwing enormous boulders at the ship, nearly recapturing

the men the first time but ultimately propelling their ship farther away and by asking the god Poseidon, his father, to sabotage Odysseus's journey. Odysseus and his men safely reach an adjacent island and continue their adventures the following day.

A traditional interpretation of Odysseus's meeting with Polyphemus regards the encounter as the hero's process of becoming recivilized after enduring the savagery of war: Odysseus becomes trapped within the cave of the uncivilized Cyclops and must use his human ingenuity, rather than his military prowess, to save himself and his men. In this reading, the challenge of the Cyclops represents the hero's psychological rebirth. However, the ways in which Odysseus represents himself and his adventures to the Phaeacians and to other characters is a key aspect of his psychology. A narratological analysis focusing on Odysseus's stories about himself reveals that his behavior with the Phaeacians and his stories of his own past are crucial tools that he uses to fashion his character and reputation to win fame. His narratives reflect masterful strategies that include withholding and selecting key pieces of information, creating suspense, lionizing himself, and employing sophisticated techniques of anticipation. These tactics reveal that Odysseus is not simply a clever hero of wily stratagems. Rather, part of his intelligence and his psychological motivation lies in his ability to construct his identity and reputation deliberately through narrative. A narratological interpretation uniquely reveals how the fame of Odysseus relies deeply on both his actions and his masterful storytelling.

SUMMARY

Odysseus's narrative to the Phaeacians begins in book 9 when he first identifies himself by name and explains that he is the "son of Laertes, known to all men for [his] stratagems" (*Od.* 317). He mentions his experiences

"Cyclops, you ask me of my glorious name, and I will tell you it; and do you give me a stranger's gift, even as you promised. Nobody is my name, Nobody they call me—my mother and my father, and all my comrades as well." So I spoke, and at once he answered me with pitiless heart: "Nobody will I eat last among his comrades, and the others before him; this shall be your gift."

Odyssey

with Calypso (Kalypsô) and Circe (Kirkê), women who unsuccessfully tried to ensnare him, and proceeds to a more detailed account of his wanderings prior to his arrival in the land of the Phaeacians.

After departing from Ilium (Troy), Odysseus and his crew sail to the land of the Cicones and sack and loot their city, but they remain too long and are attacked by the Cicones and their allies, who kill some of the men. Embarking again, they are caught in a storm but eventually reach the land of the Lotus-eaters, who serve magical lotus food that causes some of Odysseus's men to "forget their homecoming" (323). Odysseus himself must drag the men back to the ships to free them from the influence of the enchanting flowers.

Next, Odysseus tells of his encounter with the Cyclopes, "insolent and lawless folk" who live as savages, practicing neither agriculture nor any type of social government (*Od.* 323). After landing on a nearby island at night, Odysseus and his crew spend the following day exploring the land and feasting on the goats they find there. Odysseus then takes a smaller crew to explore the Cyclopes' adjacent island. He and his men enter the cave of Polyphemus, one of the Cyclopes, and find abundant milk and cheese. Wishing to meet the creature, Odysseus and his men remain there until Polyphemus returns with his flocks and blocks the entrance to the cave with a giant boulder. After he milks his ewes and goats, Polyphemus discovers the intruders and inquires about their

identity and purpose. Odysseus identifies himself and his men as "Achaeans" and "the men of Agamemnon, son of Atreus," who have wandered the sea in search of home (335). He invokes Zeus several times and begs Polyphemus for hospitality and generosity.

Polyphemus responds by scorning the gods, proclaiming himself and all Cyclopes better than any deity, and he then asks Odysseus the location of his ships. To this, Odysseus responds falsely that he and his men have been shipwrecked. The Cyclops promptly kills and eats two of Odysseus's men and then falls asleep, at which point Odysseus plans to kill the giant but quickly realizes that he and his men would be trapped in the cave by the boulder. Instead, they spend the following day sharpening an enormous stake of olive wood, and when Polyphemus returns in the evening with his flocks and feasts on two more men, Odysseus offers him three bowls of strong wine. As he drinks the wine, Polyphemus demands to know his guest's name, and Odysseus responds by telling him that his name is "Nobody." After Odysseus and his crew drive the stake into the sleeping giant's eye, blinding him, Polyphemus cries out for help. Yet when the Cyclopes who live in the surrounding caves ask what has happened, Polyphemus states, "My friends, it is Nobody that is slaying me by guile and not by force" (*Od.* 345). The other Cyclopes respond that if nobody is hurting him, Polyphemus must be afflicted by Zeus and should pray to their father, Poseidon. The anguished Polyphemus then removes the boulder from the mouth of his cave and sits in the entryway to prevent the men from departing.

Having blinded Polyphemus, Odysseus now plans the Achaeans' escape from the cave. He binds three sheep together side by side and instructs a man to hide underneath by grasping the middle sheep's belly, repeating this process until the entire group is hidden. When Polyphemus touches the animals to determine whether they are his flocks or his human prisoners, he does not discover the men. After the sheep have all left the cave, Odysseus unties himself and his men, and they flee to their ships, taking the sheep with them. Odysseus forbids his crew from mourning the lost men, instead urging them to embark quickly. When they are within shouting distance, Odysseus taunts Polyphemus, telling him that the man who defeated him was evidently "no weakling" and that Zeus and other gods have punished the giant. Enraged, Polyphemus hurls a "peak of a high mountain" at the ship, which causes the backflow of the sea to return Odysseus and his men to the Cyclopes' shore (*Od.* 351).

They quickly row back out to safety, and although his men urge him to keep silent, Odysseus once again cannot resist calling out to Polyphemus. This time, the hero names himself, "Odysseus, the sacker of cities," as the blinder of the Cyclops (*Od.* 353). Polyphemus laments his fate and recounts that a prophet had foretold that a man named Odysseus would one day rob him of his sight. He begs Odysseus to return so that he may bestow gifts and pray to Poseidon for Odysseus's safe passage. Odysseus responds by wishing that he could send the soul of Polyphemus to Hades, the underworld. Polyphemus then prays to Poseidon, asking that Odysseus never reach home, or if he does, that he lose his ship and crew and meet misfortune in Ithaca. Polyphemus then throws a boulder even larger than the first. Fortunately for the Achaeans, the boulder hits the water and propels the ship toward the island where the rest of Odysseus's men wait. The men divide the sheep among themselves, and Odysseus sacrifices a ram to Zeus. They spend the rest of the day feasting and embark the next morning, continuing their long journey home.

ANALYSIS

Heroes of ancient myth often have epithets, or linguistic tags that identify their most eminent features. Odysseus's epithet is "resourceful," and he displays his resourcefulness in both *The Iliad* and *The Odyssey*, two ancient epics attributed to the poet Homer. Odysseus is an important Greek warrior in *The Iliad*, the story of the Trojan War, but he is the main character of *The Odyssey*, which recounts his long and difficult journey home to the island of Ithaca. The first four books of *The Odyssey* tell the story of Telemachus (Telemakhos), the son of Odysseus, and his attempts to discover the whereabouts of his father and protect his mother, Penelope, from the suitors who have come to her palace in the hope of usurping Odysseus's wife and legacy. Book 5 begins the story of Odysseus, who has spent seven years with the nymph Calypso after a shipwreck on her island left him the sole survivor of his crew. By the command of Zeus, Calypso finally releases Odysseus, who builds a raft and floats at sea, barely escaping another storm generated by Poseidon and finally arriving in Scheria, the land of the Phaeacian people. Prompted by Athena, the goddess who protects Odysseus throughout the story, the Phaeacians welcome and entertain Odysseus in books 6 through 8. In books 9 through 12, which make

up one-sixth of the entire poem, Odysseus tells of his adventures prior to his arrival in Scheria. A narratological analysis of this long story within a story reveals that Odysseus's tales of his adventures serve as a central part of his character development. His account of his meeting with Polyphemus vividly reveals his talent for crafting a favorable self-image and his profound need to justify his insatiable and perilous desire for knowledge and adventure. To create his intended effects, Odysseus carefully selects and omits crucial bits of information and celebrates his individual role while diminishing the roles of his men. A narratological reading thus recognizes Odysseus's encounter with Polyphemus as a tale crafted by a complex personality who continually reinvents himself for his audience.

Narratology is the study of how stories are crafted to inform an audience's perceptions. One way of reading stories involves focusing on the action, or the events themselves, whereas a narratological reading examines how the events are presented, or narrated. For this reason, such a reading is especially appropriate for stories that draw attention to the act of narration, often through a technique known as a frame narrative. A frame narrative is a story that includes more than one narrator. In *The Odyssey*, the poet creates a narrative voice when recounting the story's events. However, when Odysseus tells his own stories within the larger story, he becomes a separate narrator with strategies and interests that are unique to him as a character, even though the poet ultimately creates all stories in the poem. A frame narrative thus creates the illusion of distance between the author and the characters that he or she creates. Because the ways in which Odysseus tells stories about himself reveal key aspects of his character, a narratological analysis focusing on both how and what he narrates is especially fruitful. Numerous theories exist regarding how to implement narratological analyses. In this case, a narratological interpretation emphasizes the strategies Odysseus uses to justify his actions and shape his reputation as resourceful Odysseus.

To appreciate Odysseus's narrative fully, one must first understand the context of his relationship with the Phaeacians, with whom he spends two days in books 5 through 8 before beginning his narrative in book 9. Book 6 opens with Odysseus washed up on the shore of Scheria after his raft is destroyed in a storm. Athena orchestrates events so that Nausicaa (Nausikaa), daughter of the Phaeacian king Alcinous (Alkinous) and his wife, Arete (Aretê), discovers Odysseus and directs him to her parents. In book 7, Odysseus proceeds with Athena's assistance to the palace of Alcinous, where he is kindly received by the king and queen. Book 8 describes the feasting and celebration that occur at Alcinous's command the following day. When the minstrel Demodocus (Demodokos) sings of the Trojan War and Odysseus in particular, the hero, who has not yet revealed his identity to his hosts, cannot hold back his tears. He covers his face to hide his sorrow, but Alcinous observes his weeping and cuts short the song, initiating competitive games so that his guest can witness the Phaeacians' athletic excellence. Odysseus refuses to participate until he is taunted by Euryalus, at which point he angrily proves his strength with the discus. Alcinous breaks the tension by ordering his people to perform dances, and Demodocus once again sings. Alcinous then orders his people to prepare rich gifts for Odysseus, and another banquet ensues, after which Odysseus specifically requests that Demodocus sing of the Trojan horse. When the minstrel complies, Odysseus again weeps and is again observed by Alcinous, who commands the minstrel to stop singing. This time, however, Alcinous commands Odysseus to reveal his identity and explain why he grieves at the minstrel's song. Odysseus complies at the opening of book 9.

Several details of these interactions with the Phaeacians contribute to an understanding of Odysseus's subsequent narrative. First, Odysseus carefully evades the Phaeacians' questions about his name and origins for two days. In book 7, Arete directly asks Odysseus about his identity on the first day, when he appears in her palace wearing the clothes that Nausicaa has given him. In response, Odysseus withholds his name and instead laments, "Hard it would be, my queen, to tell to the end the tale of my woes, since the heavenly gods have given me many" (*Od.* 263). He proceeds to tell her of his long imprisonment by the nymph Calypso, his eventual escape, and his arrival in Scheria, but he never states his name or birthplace. Second, as classicists Frederick Ahl and Hanna Roisman argue in *The Odyssey Re-Formed*, Odysseus likely orchestrates the revelation of his identity when he specifically asks Demodocus to sing about the Trojan horse, even mentioning his own name (which he has not yet revealed as his own) in his request. When Demodocus sings of Odysseus's actions during the war, the hero has a logical reason to weep, and his tears prompt Alcinous to ask him who he is precisely when the hero has decided it is advantageous to reveal himself. This tendency to withhold crucial information is

a key trait in Odysseus's story about the Cyclops. Finally, in book 7, the Phaeacians reveal their ancestry from giants as well as their divine origin, which they state is similar to that of the Cyclopes (Ahl and Roisman 48). Odysseus, then, may focus at length on his defeat of Polyphemus because, believing the Cyclopes exist, the Phaeacians are likely to accept and admire Odysseus's story of ingenious conquest as well as to grasp their visitor's implicit message that he is perfectly able to defend himself against strange and potentially hostile hosts (48).

Odysseus sustains his careful self-presentation in his brief accounts of the Cicones and the Lotus-eaters, in which he casts himself as a highly individual hero. He builds this portrait from the moment that he finally reveals himself to the Phaeacians as "Odysseus, son of Laertes" in book 9 (*Od.* 317). Odysseus describes his home in Ithaca and briefly mentions his escape from both Calypso and "the guileful lady" Circe in order to underscore his individuality and his love of home: even those two enchanting women could not sway him from his desire to return to Ithaca. Odysseus casts himself as a dedicated family man, perhaps to soften the savagery of his attack on the Cicones. Upon arriving in the Cicones' land, Odysseus and his crew "[sack] the city and [slay] the men; and from the city . . . [take] their wives and much treasure," but he offers no explanation for this brutal and evidently unprovoked attack (319). Instead, he emphasizes his wisdom in contrast to the folly of his men, who disobey his order to flee after the attack and instead feast and drink wine on the shore, giving the Cicones time to retaliate. Likewise, when several of Odysseus's men eat the enchanted flowers of the Lotus-eaters, which cause them to forget their desire to return home, Odysseus alone must rescue them: "I myself brought back these men, weeping, to the ships under compulsion, and dragged them beneath the benches and bound them fast in the hollow ships" (323). With these two anecdotes, Odysseus implies that his crew's repeated disobedience and weakness cause problems that he must single-handedly resolve (Ahl and Roisman 89).

This image of Odysseus as a hero who acts alone prepares his audience for his similar role in the Polyphemus episode. Indeed, the hero is careful to distinguish his actions from those of his crew, as indicated by his shifting use of the pronouns "I," "we," and "they" (Ahl and Roisman 90–91). For example, he crowds his speech with "I" to underscore his agency, such as when he tells of preparing and sharpening the stake used to blind

MYTH INTO ART

Odysseus has inspired not only ancient and medieval writers but also more recent artists such as the twentieth-century Russian poet Joseph Brodsky, who settled in the United States after being forced out of the Soviet Union in 1972. Brodsky was an accomplished writer and translator of many genres but focused primarily on poetry and essays. He taught at several American universities, won the Nobel Prize in literature in 1987, and was named United States poet laureate in 1991. Published in his acclaimed volume *A Part of Speech* (1980), his brief poem "Odysseus to Telemachus" is a psychological probing of a father-son relationship that adopts the form of a letter written by Odysseus to his son Telemachus, whom he has not seen for many years.

In Brodsky's hands, Odysseus is a sad, diminished figure who repeatedly declares his memory loss and laments the futility of war. He begins by noting, "The Trojan War / is over now; I don't recall who won it" (lines 2–3) and states in the second stanza that he does not know where he is: "It would appear some filthy island, / with bushes, buildings, and great grunting pigs. / A garden choked with weeds; some queen or other" (10–12). He attempts to communicate the numbing effects of war, his endless wanderings that make all islands seem alike, and age, which has robbed him not only of his renowned cleverness but also of his ability to recall "how the war came out" and his son's age (18).

In the third and final stanza, Odysseus first offers a glimmer of hope by telling his son to "grow strong" (line 20), but he ultimately considers that perhaps Telemachus has been better off without him: "away from me / you are quite safe from all Oedipal passions, / and your dreams, my Telemachus, are blameless" (26–28). Brodsky thus transforms the negative post-Greek view of Odysseus into a modern portrait rooted in the complexities of family psychology.

Polyphemus. Sometimes he even speaks of himself as if he were alone even when he is clearly traveling with a group, such as when he chooses twelve men to accompany him to the cave of Polyphemus: "I chose the twelve best of my comrades and went *my* way" (*Od.* 331; emphasis added). Such statements position Odysseus as an exalted leader while diminishing his comrades' actions. On the other hand, Odysseus reverts to "we" when he wishes to avoid revealing himself. When Polyphemus first notices the men in his cave and asks who they are, Odysseus carefully avoids stating his name: "We, you must know, are from Troy, Achaeans, driven by all the winds there are over the great gulf of the sea" (335). However, after he and some of his men escape from Polyphemus, Odysseus cannot resist taunting him not once but twice because he wants the Cyclops to know exactly who has conquered him. Notably, Odysseus neglects to give his men any glory despite their heroic role in defeating Polyphemus.

Odysseus sometimes acknowledges the wisdom of his men, such as when they urge him not to taunt the Cyclops a second time and when he admits that "it would have been far better" if he had listened to his comrades and abandoned the cave of Polyphemus sooner (*Od.*

333). As Ahl and Roisman argue, Odysseus occasionally acknowledges his bold behavior in part because by the time he reaches the Phaeacians, he has lost his entire crew and must justify this loss. Part of his strategy, Ahl and Roisman assert, is to blame the crew for their frequent mistakes, but as a clever storyteller, he also knows that he must claim some responsibility for his very unheroic failure to bring even one crew member back from the war (109). Yet as leader, Odysseus does not take responsibility for his failures as much as he vaunts his genius for getting himself out of trouble and blames others for his misfortunes. His taunting of the Cyclops creates a dangerous situation but concludes with safe arrival back at the ships. After Polyphemus prays for Odysseus's destruction, the hero sacrifices a ram to Zeus but then retrospectively blames the god for his subsequent misfortunes: "he did not heed my sacrifice, but was planning how all my well-benched ships might perish and my trusty comrades" (*Od.* 357).

A primary strategy that Odysseus uses to lionize himself and demonize the Cyclopes is the careful selection and omission of information. As a storyteller, Odysseus is a master at drawing the audience into his own perspective, such as when he characterizes the Cyclopes as uncivilized savages and conveniently neglects to mention their widely known mythological role as blacksmiths for the gods. Ancient Greek poets such as Hesiod portray the Cyclopes as skilled artisan blacksmiths who contribute much to civilization (Ahl and Roisman 116). By omitting this fact and focusing on the Cyclopes' savagery, Odysseus presents himself as a civilized, ingenious man who defeats a savage, useless giant. Furthermore, in his story, Odysseus does not initially reveal that Polyphemus eats humans, even though he knows this in retrospect. Instead, when Achaeans approach the cave, Odysseus simply calls Polyphemus a "monstrous man" (*Od.* 329), effectively recreating his own perspective for the audience by providing the limited information that he had at the time of his experience.

Odysseus also invents information or outright lies, sometimes to protect himself, as when Polyphemus asks the location of his ships and Odysseus wisely responds that he and his men are shipwrecked. Other times, however, the lies are not strictly necessary, such as when Odysseus claims to be called "Nobody" as Polyphemus drinks his powerful wine. This withholding of identity recalls Odysseus's similar behavior with the Phaeacians, but the trick of calling himself "Nobody" proves to be ingenious when Polyphemus cries out to the other Cyclopes that "Nobody" has wounded him, prompting them to turn their backs on their neighbor. We also learn at the end of book 9 that Polyphemus had previously learned through an oracle that a man named Odysseus would one day blind him, which further justifies Odysseus's use of the false name. If Polyphemus had heard Odysseus's actual name in the cave, he surely would have killed the hero immediately to try to avoid his fate.

Yet it is important to remember that when Odysseus claims to be named "Nobody," he does not yet know that Polyphemus will later call for help or that the Cyclops had been told the name of the man who would blind him. The use of "Nobody" only becomes a clever trick in retrospect, yet Odysseus presents himself as acting on information that he could not possibly have had at the time of his experience (Ahl and Roisman 113). This is a frequently used strategy that allows Odysseus to create the illusion of ingenuity and perspective. Even when he describes Polyphemus as monstrous (but not cannibalistic), Odysseus relies on information that he learns later in his encounter with the Cyclops. A revealing example of this technique, which is called prolepsis, occurs when Odysseus explains his reason for taking a rare and powerful wine with him to the cave: "my proud

spirit told me that very soon a man would come upon us clothed in tremendous strength, a savage man that knew nothing of rights or laws" (*Od.* 331). As Ahl and Roisman point out, wine is not generally the weapon of choice when one anticipates an enemy. Here, Odysseus boasts of extraordinary foresight that he simply could not have had, but it makes for a great story.

Indeed, these narrative techniques reveal Odysseus to be a gifted storyteller. As Paul Murgatroyd points out in *Mythical Monsters in Classical Literature*, when Odysseus initially describes the Cyclopes as uncivilized but not as monsters accustomed to eating humans, he employs prolepsis subtly but also creates suspense, building up to the horrible truth rather than giving it away all at once. He creates a similar effect by delaying action, such as in his long description of the island where he and his companions harbor their ships before proceeding to the home of the Cyclopes and the delay between the planning of the escape and the blinding of Polyphemus. Similarly, when Odysseus hides beneath Polyphemus's favorite ram, the giant addresses the animal as it leaves his cave, noting that "Nobody . . . has not yet escaped destruction" and wishing that the ram could speak "to tell [him] where [Nobody] skulks away from [his] wrath" (*Od.* 349). The irony here is that Odysseus is both right in front of Polyphemus and escaping him, but in dramatic terms, Odysseus creates a moment of hair-raising suspense as his audience wonders whether the hero will truly escape unharmed.

Odysseus clearly appreciates his own genius for storytelling, but more important is what his narrative reveals about his character and psychology. Odysseus's narrative strategies at best complicate the traditional reading of his encounter with Polyphemus as a psychological rebirth, a process of becoming newly civilized after the ravages of war, for Odysseus's stories show that he is not simply a man reborn. He is in fact highly skilled in crafting his image to protect and especially glorify himself. Ahl and Roisman go so far as to argue that Odysseus is more like than unlike the Cyclopes. The hero emphasizes that he himself heats the giant stake in the fire, recalling the conventional portrait of the Cyclopes as skilled smiths, and he then uses it to blind the giant rather than to dislodge the boulder blocking the entrance or carry out some other less-violent escape method. For this reason, instead of viewing the encounter with Polyphemus as a rebirth into civilization, one might read it as a narrative performance in which Odysseus reveals the complexity of his resourcefulness, a trait encompassing both deeds and an imagination that ancient audiences likely perceived as heroic yet deeply self-interested.

CROSS-CULTURAL INFLUENCE

Ancient Greek audiences celebrated Odysseus's ingenuity and insatiable desire for adventure, but the hero did not fare so well in later times. Because the Greeks defeated the Trojans, whom the Romans viewed as their ancestors, Odysseus has markedly less valor in the hands of Roman poets such as Virgil and Ovid. The Christian Middle Ages followed this Roman tradition and viewed Odysseus, known by his Latin name, Ulysses, as a man whose thirst for knowledge and adventure represented unbridled desire. An exceptional portrait of this type appears in Dante Alighieri's *Divina Commedia* (*Divine Comedy*), a stunning fourteenth-century Italian poem that chronicles Dante's spiritual crisis and visionary journey through hell, purgatory, and heaven. As a character, Ulysses appears in the twenty-sixth canto of the *Inferno*, in which he is punished for fraud, specifically for providing false counsel in various ways during the Trojan War. Just as Odysseus narrates his adventures in *The Odyssey*, Ulysses recounts his exploits, but his story is unique and without parallel in the classical world, culminating not in safe homecoming but in death by shipwreck. It is likely that Dante invented this conclusion, but he did not do so merely to condemn the failings of a pagan adventurer whose desire overcame his virtue. Dante's unique story of Ulysses represents the Christian poet's awareness of his imaginative kinship with the Greek traveler, who, like Dante, desired to transcend all human limits of knowledge and experience.

The *Divine Comedy* comprises one hundred brief cantos grouped into three parts, which are known as *cantica*, or canticles: *Inferno*, *Purgatory*, and *Paradise*. The poem is narrated by the poet Dante, who recounts his own prior journey as Dante the pilgrim through the afterlife. This structure creates two distinct voices in the poem: that of the pilgrim and that of the poet. The *Inferno* begins with Dante the pilgrim in spiritual crisis because he has failed to follow the path of virtue, clinging stubbornly to the love of earthly things rather than the more virtuous and reliable love of God. The pilgrim stumbles upon the poet Virgil, Dante's greatest poetic inspiration and author of the *Aeneid*, an unparalleled Latin poem celebrating the founding of Rome, which Dante viewed as the legitimate source of earthly power. A "virtuous heathen," Virgil resides in Limbo but serves as Dante's guide through hell and purgatory at the

command of Beatrice, a woman whom Dante loved on earth and whom he views as an aspect of God. Dante's hell takes the shape of a conical helix and is divided according to different types of sins. The sins of incontinence (lust, anger, and so forth) are less severe than and distinct from the sins of violence. The worst sins are those of fraud and betrayal, as they involve the abuse of reason, a uniquely human quality. Dante places Ulysses among the fraudulent sinners, specifically those who gave false counsel in life.

In *Inferno* 26, Dante the pilgrim comes upon the souls of the false counselors when he notices what initially appear to be fireflies dwelling in the eighth crevasse, or subsection, of the eighth circle of hell. Virgil explains that the lights are in fact flames, each of which contains a sinner. Dante asks about an especially active flame, and Virgil tells him that it contains the souls of the Greek warriors Ulysses and Diomedes, who "are paired / in God's revenge as once they earned his wrath" (lines 56–57). Their sins of fraud, Virgil explains, are essentially three: they devised the stratagem of the Trojan horse; they persuaded Achilles to join the war against Troy, which caused Deidamia (his lover) to die of grief when Achilles perished in the war; and they stole the Palladium, or wooden image, of Athena and then presented the Trojan horse as a fraudulent peace offering. Dante begs Virgil to speak with the flame if he can. Virgil assents but instructs Dante to keep silent and allow the Roman poet to communicate with the Greek souls. Virgil then requests that the souls speak and recount how they met death.

In response, the flame begins to flicker, and Ulysses offers his narrative of his final fateful journey before he and his men perished at sea. He begins from the point at which he escaped the witch Circe, who had kept him for more than a year. He states,

> not tenderness for a son, nor filial duty
> toward my aged father, nor the love I owed
> Penelope that would have made her glad,
> could overcome the fervor that was mine
> to gain experience of the world
> and learn about man's vices, and his worth. (*Inf.* lines 94–99)

This insatiable desire, he says, drove him after all his trials to set sail once again with only one ship and the few men who had not deserted him. With these loyalists, he journeyed throughout the Mediterranean and eventually reached the limits of the known world, "the narrow strait / where Hercules marked off the limits / warning all men to go no farther" (107–9).

Ulysses then reports the astonishing speech that he delivered to his men at this point, urging them not to waste their final brief lives without seizing "the chance to know— / following the sun—the world where no one lives" (*Inf.* lines 116–17). He told them, "Consider how your souls were sown: / you were not made to live like brutes or beasts, / but to pursue virtue and knowledge" (118–20). His words spurred the desire of his men so much that he could not have restrained them had he wished to do so. They pursued their "mad flight," turning "oars to wings" for five months until they reached a mountain towering higher than any he has seen (125). The joy of Ulysses and his men was brief. A whirlwind from the "unknown land" destroyed their ship (137), turning it and the waters around until "the prow went down—as pleased Another— / until the sea closed over" them (141–42).

From the beginning of this masterful speech, Ulysses reveals himself as a failed hero in Christian terms. Like Homer's Odysseus, Ulysses focuses obsessively on himself, using the pronoun "I" no less than ten times in his fifty-two-line speech, celebrating his travels with "I set forth" (*Inf.* line 100), "I saw as far as Spain" (103), and "I and my shipmates had grown old and slow" (106). Yet in Dante's hands, Ulysses's desire for adventure destroys all devotion to family and community; his lust for knowledge is almost wholly individual, as he is willing to continue even with only one ship and a few men. When he and his crew reach the Strait of Gibraltar, the limits of the known world in Dante's time, Ulysses delivers a speech that effectively becomes his ultimate false counsel as he convinces his men not to squander what remains of their lives on anything less than worlds yet unknown, which he cleverly mischaracterizes as virtue and knowledge.

In Dante's terms, what Ulysses truly desires is adventure, glory, and knowledge that transcends proper human limits. The poet indicates this transgressive desire through the image of flying, as Ulysses states, "in our mad flight we turned our oars to wings" (*Inf.* line 125). This metaphor signals the speed of their ship but also recalls the Greek myth of Icarus, who flew using wings made of feathers and wax but ventured too close to the sun, resulting in his tragic death. The most important sign of transgression, however, is the mountain that Ulysses and his crew nearly reach. According to

Dante's medieval Christian cosmology, this mountain is purgatory, at the top of which lies the earthly paradise, the Garden of Eden, where Adam and Eve lived before they were expelled by God for committing the first sin of humankind. Dante believed that no humans had visited this realm since the time of Adam and Eve. Thus, in Christian terms, Ulysses's attempt to turn this divine realm into another one of his exploits is vainglorious and rightly punished by the whirlwind with which God ("Another") destroyed the ship. Ulysses spends all of eternity trapped within a flame resembling the ingenious tongue he used in service of his devious tales and schemes.

Dante's Christian view motivates his unique story of Ulysses, which has been the focus of intense scholarship partly because of its striking similarities to the poetic and spiritual project of Dante himself. Virgil states that Ulysses is punished for providing false counsel, and we see this in action as Ulysses recounts how he manipulated his men into risking the final journey. Yet it is the nature of Ulysses's desire that truly interests Dante and drives him to invent an entirely new story for the classical hero. Ulysses's speech highlights most prominently his deepest wish, which overcame even love of his family: to learn of the world and to "learn about man's vices, and his worth" (*Inf.* line 99). He urged his shipmates to spend their final waking moments "pursu[ing] virtue and knowledge," which eventually led them to glimpse Mount Purgatory itself. Readers have noted that these desires are also shared and undertaken by Dante: he too wishes and desperately needs to learn of men's worth so that he might repair his own before it is too late. He too visits the world where no one lives, the Christian afterlife, in pursuit of virtue and knowledge, and he too reaches Mount Purgatory, at the top of which Virgil pronounces Dante's will healed and prepared to experience paradise. The difference, of course, is that Dante's journey is successful, which makes it clear that Dante uses the story of Ulysses as a spiritual foil for his own. Ulysses is the failed pagan version of Dante the pilgrim himself, who believes that desire for virtue and knowledge alone are not sufficient; one must also have faith in God.

As Teodolinda Barolini argues in *The Undivine Comedy: Detheologizing Dante*, however, Ulysses is not simply a one-dimensional foil because Dante also understands that the Greek hero is his poetic alter ego. For Dante, Ulysses in fact is a highly complicated figure who embodies the very grave risks that Dante undertakes as a poet. It is one thing to claim to have had a spiritual vision, but it is quite another to broadcast it in arguably the boldest, most imaginative, and controversial poem in Western civilization. Dante's astonishing poetic audacity in representing his journey through the afterlife thus makes him the ultimate Ulyssean figure, a poetic traveler and hero whose desire deeply risks transgression and depends on spiritual discipline and the grace of God. In this sense, Dante the poet is well aware that the difference between him and Ulysses is perilously small, and he signals this awareness in several ways. First, Ulyssean flight and nautical imagery appear throughout the *Divine Comedy*, and Dante uses this imagery to represent the risks of writing the poem. For example, in the second canto of *Paradise*, Dante warns those readers whose boats (that is, intellects) are too small to follow his own, which traverses waters never yet traveled. Second, Ulysses is the only character in the *Divine Comedy* whom Dante mentions in all three canticles, a strategy by which the poet deliberately recalls the shared risks of his and Ulysses's journeys. Finally, the poet echoes the transgressive "mad flight" theme of Ulysses in other ways, such as when he acknowledges in canto 1 of *Paradise* that he has no choice but to trespass against language, signs themselves, if he is to describe the inherently ineffable realm of heaven.

Ulysses in the *Divine Comedy* thus represents a Christian interpretation of the quest for knowledge but also a quest for glory that Dante consciously shares. What makes Dante's Ulyssean journey so fascinating is that he does not take this transgressive quest for granted. Precisely because he has chosen to write the poem, Dante knows that he too is subject to the Ulyssean risk of failed enlightenment. Rather than simply assert his spiritual and poetic superiority, Dante continually recalls the risk he takes as a way of negotiating it. In the process, he gives the world a Ulysses no less complex and intriguing than his Greek ancestor.

Ashleigh Imus, PhD

BIBLIOGRAPHY

Ahl, Frederick, and Hanna M. Roisman. *The Odyssey Re-Formed*. Ithaca: Cornell UP, 1996. Print.

Barolini, Teodolinda. *The Undivine Comedy: Detheologizing Dante*. Princeton: Princeton UP, 1992. Print.

Brodsky, Joseph. *A Part of Speech*. New York: Farrar, 1980. Print.

Dante. *The Inferno*. Trans. Robert Hollander and Jean Hollander. New York: Anchor, 2002. Print.

Homer. *Odyssey*. Vol. 1. Trans. A. T. Murray. Ed. George E. Dimock. Cambridge: Harvard UP, 1995. Print. Loeb Classical Lib. 104.

Murgatroyd, Paul. *Mythical Monsters in Classical Literature*. London: Duckworth, 2007. Print.

Powell, Barry B. *Classical Myth*. 3rd ed. Upper Saddle River: Prentice Hall, 2001. Print.

Third Voyage of Sindbad

Author: Traditional
Time Period: 501 CE–1000 CE
Country or Culture: Arabia; Persia
Genre: Myth

OVERVIEW

The Thousand and One Nights—originally translated as *The Arabian Nights' Entertainments*, from the fifteenth-century *Alf layla wa-layla*, and also known as *Arabian Nights*—has become a classic of world literature, a collection of stories from the Islamic golden age that centuries later found popularity in Europe, the United States, and Japan. Beginning in the eighth century, the Islamic golden age was a period of incredible learning and artistic production, bringing together knowledge and traditions from North Africa to India. The stories of *The Thousand and One Nights* are sourced primarily from oral literary traditions throughout the Middle East and South Asia, and they reflect the diversity of style, literary content, and culture of the region. Among the many stories, one of the most enduring myths is that of Sindbad (Sinbad) the Sailor, the heroic adventurer of an epic story cycle.

Sindbad's third voyage takes place in the middle of his larger narrative. When it begins, he has already completed two dangerous quests, bringing untold riches back to his home in Baghdad. Unable to retire into a life of luxury, however, he is drawn again to the sea to seek more wealth and more adventure. On the third voyage, he finds his ship stranded on an island inhabited by a cannibalistic giant, whom Sindbad stabs through the eye in order to make a panicked retreat with his companions. One of only a few to survive, he faces violent storms and giant pythons, eventually being rescued by a friendly captain. The last surviving member of his original crew, he manages to return to Baghdad, richer than ever before, boasting of his incredible strength and wit.

The story of Sindbad overcoming monsters and facing great odds has become a classic of adventure literature and films. His narrative is familiar to children all around the world, and depictions of his great accomplishments are regularly made into popular films, video games, and comic books. However, as the myth of Sindbad left its original Persian context in the Islamic golden age and entered the literary canon of the Western world, the great sailor changed considerably. The original myth is a complicated layering of stories, with Sindbad coming across hardheaded and foolish as often as heroic and adventurous. His quest for wealth comes at the expense of hundreds of lives, and his relationship to the city of Baghdad is much tenser than modern versions of the story typically present it. The story is also inextricably linked in its various forms to the larger narrative of *The Thousand and One Nights* and to the specifics of Persian literary traditions. While the disparity between the Sindbad of the eighth century and the Sindbad of the modern day seems great at times, taken as a whole, the history of his third voyage offers an opportunity to study mythology not as a fixed art with permanent meanings but as a dynamic force, its influence too powerful for any one culture to contain.

SUMMARY

Although Sindbad the Sailor is young, he has already acquired great wealth through two long voyages, and he lives in Baghdad at the beginning of the story. While he remembers the many dangers of those voyages, he is not one to rest idly and decides after a short time that he should set sail again. At first, this new expedition goes well, and he gathers a great number of goods from distant ports. After some time, however, a large storm upsets the route of his ship, bringing him to an island inhabited by monstrous creatures.

Beastly men, most only two feet high, swim out to Sindbad's ship. The captain warns everyone that, although the men are small, they are so many in number that they could easily overpower the sailors. Because of this, the men of the ship watch helplessly as the creatures lower their sail, swim the boat to an island, and abandon the men there, departing with their ship and their wealth. Sindbad and his men know that this island is dangerous, but resigned to their situation, they spend the afternoon searching for fruit and herbs. In this search, the men come to a large palace with gorgeous gates. Walking into the courtyard, they immediately see a pile of human bones scattered beside roasting spits. This gruesome sight, along with the men's fatigue, causes them all to collapse where they stand, lying motionless before the palace as night sets in.

That evening, a horrible giant emerges from the palace. He towers above the men, his one eye glowing red and his terrible talons hanging above their heads. The men all play dead, and while they do, the giant looks among them, inspecting each one. At last, he picks up the fattest man, the captain, and devours him. Satiated, he returns to his porch and falls asleep. The men spend the evening listening to his monstrous snoring.

When the day comes and the monster leaves, the men try to devise a plan, but they realize there is no way they can overcome the monster. They spend the day searching for food, and when night comes, surely enough, the giant once more devours one of the men. The next morning, they are so distraught that several are ready to throw themselves into the sea. However, Sindbad persuades them that it is better to try. At his advice, they spend their day building small rafts and hiding them by the shore. When evening comes, they watch as another of their men is roasted alive and devoured. Then, when the giant falls asleep, nine of them pick up the roasting spits, light the ends on fire, and plunge them into the giant's only eye.

The giant runs into the distance howling, and the men hope that he will die there. By morning, however, he emerges from the woods accompanied by a number of other giants. The sailors all flee, quickly boarding their rafts and rowing away. As they depart, the giants hurl rocks at them, sinking nearly every raft but sparing the one that carries Sindbad and his two companions. The sea tosses that raft about, eventually landing it on another island.

This new island seems to offer a chance to recover. Sindbad and his companions eat the fruit they find there and fall asleep by the shore. That evening, however, a gigantic snake emerges, eating one of the men as he sleeps. The next evening, Sindbad and the other sailor climb a tree, hoping it will offer them protection, but the snake simply climbs after them, devouring Sindbad's

> *"As soon as we heard him snore, according to his custom, nine of the boldest among us, and myself, took each of us a spit, and putting the points of them into the fire till they were burning hot, we thrust them into his eye all at once, and blinded him."*
>
> "The Third Voyage of Sinbad the Sailor"

companion. The final evening, desperate, Sindbad makes a fire around the base of the tree he climbs. While this keeps the snake away, Sindbad climbs down the next morning exhausted and fearful.

Feeling that he is out of options, Sindbad decides to throw himself into the sea to die. Once he reaches the shore, however, he sees a ship in the distance and hails it with the linen from his turban. The ship sends a small boat to shore, rescuing Sindbad. Once aboard, he tells his story and receives food and fresh clothing. He stays with the ship as it travels to several ports, gathering more wealth. When they reach the port of Salabat, the captain of the ship comes to Sindbad with several large parcels. The goods in these parcels, he tells Sindbad, belong to a sailor that he had tragically lost on a previous voyage, accidentally abandoning the man on an island. If Sindbad sells them, the captain promises him a small commission, the bulk of the profit being promised to the abandoned sailor's family.

Sindbad is shocked, suddenly realizing that he was that sailor, having fallen asleep beside a brook on his second voyage. Sindbad and the captain are overjoyed to recognize one another at last, and the captain gives Sindbad the parcels to sell and keep the profit. His wealth and health both restored, Sindbad stays with the ship through several more ports. When he returns to Baghdad, he has so much wealth that he buys a beautiful estate and gives the remainder of his money to the poor.

ANALYSIS

The myth of Sindbad's third voyage is a double-framed story—that is, a story told within a story told within yet another story. On a broad scale, Sindbad's adventures are recounted within the book *The Thousand and One Nights*, recorded somewhere around the tenth century during the Islamic golden age. The origins of Sindbad likely rest in oral literary traditions and, like most of *The Thousand and One Nights*, were adapted and retold in order to be included in the text. The book tells of a king who discovers that his bride has been unfaithful and, concluding that all women are evil, decides to take a new bride every evening, murdering her in the morning. This continues until a woman, Shahrzad (Scheherazade), spends her wedding night telling the king an enchanting tale. The story is so engrossing that the king spares her life so that he can hear more stories, and she spends the next thousand nights entertaining him until at last he agrees to stay with her forever. Within these stories, Shahrzad tells of Sindbad, a legendary sailor. When Sindbad is introduced, he is a rich and retired sailor who encounters a poor porter, also named Sindbad. Sindbad the Porter is complaining to Allah about all his great misfortunes, and Sindbad the Sailor takes the opportunity to tell of the seven voyages that brought him his riches, attempting to justify his lavish lifestyle to the impoverished porter. All seven of the tales highlight the danger of the voyages and the incredible strength and will Sindbad the Sailor has demonstrated in earning his fortune.

The framing of the story of Sindbad provides some important cues in understanding its meaning. The narrative of the third voyage, like all the voyages, is told through Sindbad's voice. The Sindbad telling this story is not an impartial narrator recalling the story exactly how it happened. Instead, he is a narrator with an agenda, attempting to convince Sindbad the Porter (and the rest of his audience) that his fortune has been justly earned and that the world is not a place where the poor are arbitrarily left to suffer while the rich luxuriate. While Sindbad often describes himself as heroic and adventurous, if one looks a bit deeper, in reality, he often behaves with unnecessary violence and greed. There is a firm split between the ethics that Sindbad the Sailor claims and the reality of his actions, just as there is a firm split between the actions of the wife-murdering king and the ethics he proclaims, seeing all women as traitorous liars. While Shahrzad is never explicitly present in the narration of the tale, it is important to recall that she is in fact the voice behind it all, speaking for Sindbad as she entertains the king on one of those thousand and one nights. Like almost all of the famous tales in that book, the tale of Sindbad's third voyage works

as a tool for Shahrzad, who uses the myth in a subtle effort to show the king that he, just like the legendary sailor, pursues his own happiness and self-interest at the expense of others.

From the moment Sindbad conceives of his third voyage, it is clear that the pursuit is unnecessary at best and dangerously foolish at worst. As he says, "the pleasures of the life which I then led soon made me forget the risks I had run in my two former voyages" (Dixon 85). Sindbad had, in his first and second voyages, encountered gigantic birds, snakes, and whales; his body was thrown about the sea, and his life was constantly in danger, yet he emerged both times with vast riches. Now, it is the life of leisure and pleasure that those riches ensure that has brought him to a restless place. Sindbad's decision to embark again on an adventure and to seek greater treasures is without doubt an extravagance, the journey itself existing for its own sake rather than for the sake of riches (no man could need more than Sindbad has). That he frames the voyage this way to Sindbad the Porter shows how disconnected Sindbad the Sailor is from the realities that face impoverished people, the quest for material wealth being for him a game rather than an act of survival.

In order for Sindbad to prove that he deserves the wealth he has acquired, then, it is necessary for him to begin each adventure from a point of absolute destitution and poverty. In all of his voyages, the myth offers a reset of financial gain, with Sindbad beginning the journey with inestimable riches only to encounter disasters that strip him of that wealth. In the third voyage, this occurs when the small, monstrous people overtake the boat. The scene is presented as one in which Sindbad and his fellow sailors have absolutely no power—in Sindbad's words, they stand "without daring to offer to defend ourselves, or to speak one word to divert them from their mischievous design" (Dixon 85). By taking the ship and all the wealth and supplies that the sailors have acquired, the monstrous people strip Sindbad and the sailors of more than just their economic privilege. The loss of wealth is equated in many ways with the loss of civilization and the loss of security; the sailors are abandoned on an island and forced to survive and defend themselves without the benefits of Islamic civilization, scrounging for wild fruit and vulnerable to whatever creature might wish to attack them. This disparity between civilization and the islands is further heightened by the description of the monstrous people, who are an "innumerable multitude of frightful savages"

(85). While these descriptions will strike modern readers as problematic, based on racial bias and ignorance, in the myth, they serve to highlight the divide between the civilized and prosperous Baghdad from which Sindbad came and the destitute, frightening world of the island to which he is abandoned. This state is necessary, however, as it gives Sindbad the opportunity to rise once more from nothing, proving that he earned his place in Baghdad after all.

Once abandoned on the island, Sindbad and the sailors face a physical threat through the giant. Again, as with the rest of the voyages, Sindbad must not only lose his material wealth but also confront death in one form or another. On this voyage, death takes the form of the one-eyed giant, a beast that both exhibits primal, monstrous strength and represents civilization (because of both his palace and his kinship with the other giants of the island). Readers first encounter the giant not through images of his terrible form but through images of his palace. His home is "well built, and very lofty, with a gate of ebony with double doors" (Dixon 86), implying that perhaps a kind and sophisticated person might live there. However, that scene of civilized domesticity and of wealth is betrayed by the pile of human bones scattered over the lawn. The violent nature of the palace's inhabitant is confirmed when the giant at last emerges; his physical appearance is likened to that of an elephant, a horse, and a terrible bird. Like many descriptions in Sindbad's voyages, the description of the giant borders on racism, reflecting an ignorance and fear of unknown lands and people that was common in premodern times. For the purposes of Sindbad's quest, the giant represents exactly that fear, tied as he is to a foreign civilization advanced enough to build the palace, yet practicing cannibalism, an act that marks him as outside of civil society. Facing this threat, Sindbad is stripped of the benefits of his own civilization, allowing him once more to prove that his individual values earn him a place in the elevated society of Baghdad.

Up to the encounter with the giant, the majority of the myth focuses on Sindbad's misfortune, the sailor an unfortunate victim of circumstance and bad luck. However, it is important to remember that these circumstances can be directly traced back to the opening of the voyage, when Sindbad was already wealthy and safe in Baghdad but elected to go on an additional adventure out of boredom and greed. In this regard, the ill fate that befalls him and the other sailors is not unavoidable, as the narrator Sindbad describes it, but rather a direct consequence of that greed. His selfishness and brash nature are made more evident when he plans the escape of the sailors. They spend a day successfully building escape rafts, and because Sindbad recognizes that some of the rafts might not hold up at sea, the vessels remain on the shore. Rather than use this option of escape, however, Sindbad considers the rafts part of a backup plan and instead attempts to kill the giant. The assault on the giant involves the inevitable death of another sailor (as the giant only sleeps after eating), and the plan includes the false promise that they might be able to live peacefully in the giant's palace once they have killed it; in effect, Sindbad decides to sacrifice one of his own men and risk all of their lives on a gamble for the palace. The risk is proven foolish when the giant, blinded by hot spears, returns with a large number of other giants, all throwing rocks and intent on slaughtering the sailors. In the end, almost every sailor dies in the attempted escape, with only those on Sindbad's raft surviving.

The story of Sindbad's escape from the giant offers the greatest moment of disconnect between the ethics the sailor believes he demonstrates and the real-life effect of those actions. In presenting his plan to the sailors, he describes them as "brethren" (Dixon 87). He likewise presents the sacrificial death as a tragedy, as they are "forced to see another of our comrades roasted" (87). All of the actions, despite how noble Sindbad wishes to make them seem, result in a cowardly attack on a sleeping enemy and a failed war between civilizations, the sailors from Baghdad fleeing while the gathered giants defend their land. If Sindbad truly does consider himself a bold leader and an exemplary man, worthy of his fortune, then this story would represent a spectacular failure. He could hardly have failed his men on a greater scale, given that all but those on his raft perish. He is not simply a poor strategist; he is a failure at the contract of civilization, as he selfishly elects for a heroic plan that serves his own interests rather than a plan that takes into account the needs of all the sailors. In contrast, the giant summons the strength of his entire civilization, relying on others in order to support him while injured and to avenge his attack. Much more than Sindbad, then, the giant reflects the values of camaraderie by which the sailor claims to live. By seeing this escape as an example of his greatness rather than as a failure, Sindbad echoes the greater story of *The Thousand and One Nights*, with the murderous king slaughtering his wives while telling himself that he is championing the good of his realm.

Through the ordeal with the giant, Sindbad recognizes that the other sailors often wish to give up—to throw themselves into the sea and to die rather than carry on through the hardships he has brought upon them. Sindbad largely manages to avoid this temptation until he faces the last catastrophe. Washed ashore after escaping the giant, he and his two surviving companions find themselves on an island populated by man-eating snakes that emerge only in the evening. The snakes quickly take the lives of both of his friends, leaving Sindbad alone and more despondent than ever. It is in this state that he at last contemplates suicide. However, as he has it, "I was going to throw myself into the sea; but nature prompting us to a desire to live as long as we can, I withstood this temptation to despair, and submitted myself to the will of God, who disposes of our lives at His pleasure" (Dixon 89). The moment when Sindbad is most terrified and brought closest to absolute despair is the moment when the other sailors are gone—that is, the moment when he is most cut off from the civilization that sustains and rewards him. The entirety of Sindbad's sense of self-worth is inextricably linked to the civilization centered in Baghdad: his wealth is reliant on the trade networks of the great city, and his social stature dependent upon the approval of the other citizens. Separated from both his wealth and other citizens, he sustains himself by turning his attention to Allah. Sindbad's Baghdad was an Islamic city thriving during the Islamic golden age, and like nearly all major civilizations from that period, religious beliefs were at the foundation of cultural and political activity. In turning to Allah at this moment, then, Sindbad is not only turning to his religion but also calling upon the core of the culture of Baghdad to keep him alive in his time of greatest need.

With Allah invoked, Sindbad is rescued from the island and slowly restored to his previous place in society. Just as his fall from material and physical comfort is presented as being beyond his control, so too his salvation is treated as almost preordained, a gift from Allah meant to remedy the unfortunate circumstances of his voyage and to reward his perseverance. The ship arrives when Sindbad is at his lowest moment, the sailors miraculously sighting him from a great distance; the captain overwhelms Sindbad with his generosity, offering "the best of what they had to eat" as well as one of the captain's own fine suits (Dixon 90). While this rescue is linked to Sindbad's prayer to Allah and his reliance on Baghdad culture, Sindbad describes his restoration as the effect of own abilities and resilience. As the ship continues on

its trade route, Sindbad and the captain slowly come to realize that they had known one another in the past, this being the ship that Sindbad had traveled on in his second voyage. Because of his past connection to the ship, Sindbad is not simply given a great amount of wealth as a reward from Allah but instead is reconnected with the wealth he had already earned. Similarly, because the captain of the ship believed Sindbad to be deceased, the rescue is akin to Sindbad coming back from death, miraculously surviving the sea as a result of his own attributes and strength only. By the time of his complete restoration, then, Sindbad has risen from a starving, abandoned man on an isolated island and become a wealthy sailor, capable of overcoming death itself.

For Sindbad's own purposes (convincing Sindbad the Porter that he has earned his place in Baghdad society), this is a convenient story, the drama of the adventure securing Sindbad's right to his wealth and stature. Especially when combined with the heavy reliance on fate and Sindbad's deep connection to the culture of Baghdad, Sindbad the Sailor is clearly persuaded by his own tale. However, it is important to remember the culture and the city are what Sindbad the Porter doubted from the start, lamenting the unjust structure of the society and the impossibility for those of lower classes to succeed. Because of its class structure, for Sindbad the Porter, Baghdad would not represent a shining example of moral righteousness or something glorious to which the sailor could be restored. Sindbad the Sailor links Baghdad culture with the hard work and tribulations he has faced at sea, so that the expansive trade routes that fund the city prove that it is a just place, while the just nature of the city proves the worth of the trade routes. However, Sindbad the Sailor ends the story of his third voyage on an ambiguous and perhaps self-deceptive note. He concludes his narration by saying, "I gave a great deal to the poor, and bought another great estate in addition to what I had already" (Dixon 91). This final act of charity (which itself might imply a guilty conscience) is tied to a final act of extravagance, suggesting an uneasiness about both the wealth and the social responsibility that are attached to such riches.

Despite the death of his entire crew and the loss of his ship, Sindbad remains convinced of his success and the righteous nature of his voyage. A headstrong hero with an insatiable appetite for riches, he will return repeatedly to the sea, amassing an even greater fortune and watching countless sailors and friends meet their violent deaths along the way. He never quite comes to accept his own flaws, even with the constant presence and critique of Sindbad the Porter. However, the disparity between the virtuous Sindbad he describes and the greedy Sindbad of the voyages remains clear, if also subtle.

Within the larger context of *The Thousand and One Nights*, this is exactly the type of story Shahrzad needs. Over many evenings, she slowly brings the king to understand his own failings and to realize that he, too, may not be as moral as he would like to believe. A story folded into a story, the myth of Sindbad's third voyage contains as many meanings layered on top of each other as there are speakers reciting the narrative. Perhaps most striking, however, is that the complexity of this myth is skillfully woven throughout a straightforward story of danger and adventure. As Sindbad gathers his courage and heads into danger once more, the myth encourages us to cheer for the conquering hero only to slowly realize his flaws, Shahrzad deftly leading readers to an insight that Sindbad himself would never dare to admit.

CROSS-CULTURAL INFLUENCE

There is an often tense relationship between the story of Sindbad in its original written context of Arabic culture and the story as it was made popular in the Western world (and, subsequently, as it is commonly read by diverse global audiences). The roots of this tension and the multiple interpretations often brought to Sindbad and his adventures can be seen in the first European translation of *The Thousand and One Nights*. This translation, *Mille et un nuits* (1704–17), was compiled by Antoine Galland, a French scholar of Arabic literature and culture. In assembling the book, Galland included the story cycle of Sindbad within the larger narrative as told by Shahrzad. However, it seems likely that the Sindbad myths had historically existed on their own, free of the larger context of *The Thousand and One Nights*. In addition, Galland edited the texts through the translation process, and he describes the Arabic world as a place of exoticized beauty and heightened mysticism, while the original texts were often much more grounded in everyday life. Despite this historical discrepancy, Galland's version became immensely popular in the early eighteenth century, and later translations into English, German, and even Arabic were often based on his work. From the moment of Galland's translation, the myth of Sindbad, and the entirety of *The Thousand and One Nights*, has straddled the line between Western and Eastern cultures, with historical or cultural authenticity blurred in the process.

Once Sindbad's myth entered Western literature, it was a huge success, capturing the popular imagination. As a piece of children's literature, the myth was an exciting adventure set in distant lands and populated by magical creatures. Illustrated versions of Sindbad's voyages were some of the most popularly read children's stories throughout Europe and, into the nineteenth and twentieth centuries, in Japan, the United States, and other regions as well. At the same time, the myths became the primary object of focus for Western scholars interested in studying the cultural and literary legacy of the Arabic world during the Islamic golden age. While the literary community outside of the Arabic world somewhat obsessively turned its attention to the text, within Arabic culture, *The Thousand and One Nights* did not receive the same attention. Instead, critics and the public celebrated a large range of other writings and myths, and only once Sindbad's stories were filtered through the translations and interpretations of Western culture did they again arrive to a point of prominence within the Arabic literary community, sometime around the early twentieth century.

This cultural back-and-forth is somewhat unique in world literature, and the story of Sindbad's voyages through literary traditions has received detailed study by contemporary critics and scholars. Looking back, a few examples from Western culture stand out as particularly impactful interpretations of the Arabic myths. Among these is the writer Edgar Allan Poe's short story "The Thousand-and-Second Tale of Scheherazade." Writing in the middle of the nineteenth century, Poe was influenced equally by the romantic movement in poetry and art and by his own interest in engaging plots and entertaining storytelling. The romantic poets often took inspiration from Arabic culture, which they saw as representing a style of life more fully connected to the earth, spirituality, and art than the often austere culture of the Western world since the time of the Enlightenment. The age of Enlightenment had tried to advance society by focusing on reason and scientific logic, and romantic writers and artists (many of whom had celebrated *The Thousand and One Nights* in their youth) sought sources that instead privileged emotion, subjectivity, and self-expression. It is in this tradition that Poe penned his own addition to the narrative of Sindbad.

"The Thousand and Second Tale of Scheherazade" begins by placing an additional frame around the story of Sindbad. This time, Poe claims to have come across an additional, undiscovered text that tells of Sindbad's

MYTH INTO ART

The account of Sindbad blinding the giant is not a unique story in world literature but instead offers a direct parallel to the ancient Greek epic poem *The Odyssey*.

In *The Odyssey*, the sailor Odysseus journeys for ten years to reach his home of Ithaca following the end of the Trojan War. Like Sindbad, Odysseus encounters many monsters during his journey, prime among them the Cyclops Polyphemus. The gigantic Polyphemus captures Odysseus and his men, eating several of them for every meal. Desperate, Odysseus sharpens a giant stick and convinces the Cyclops that his name is No One. When Polyphemus gets drunk that evening, Odysseus and his men light the stick on fire and plunge it into Polyphemus's only eye, causing Polyphemus to run around screaming that "no one" has blinded him. Making their escape, Odysseus calls back to the island that the Cyclops was not blinded by "no one," but rather by the great adventurer Odysseus. However, this boasting comes at great expense, as Polyphemus then tells his father, the sea god Poseidon, what has occurred.

The parallels between the story of Odysseus and that of Sindbad are many, with both sailors eventually meeting great misfortune because of their hubris. Similar stories were prominent in a large number of mythological traditions in the Western and Eastern worlds, with the particular narrative of Polyphemus spreading throughout the Greek Empire. While it remains impossible to trace directly the route between Sindbad and Odysseus, the obvious connection serves as a reminder that many ancient stories—like Sindbad himself—refuse to remain in only one literary tradition.

the text. This layer makes evident the disconnect between the original myth (something that has been lost to translations) and the myth as nineteenth-century audiences understood it. The disconnect is further heightened through the footnotes, with Sindbad coming across the Mammoth Caves of Kentucky and telegraphs as well as a host of other features with which Poe's audience would have been familiar. The king, however, reacts with disbelief to all of these wonders. The only story he believes is the story that describes a continent resting on the back of a cow, and he bases that belief on the fact that he has previously heard the story (it being taken from the Qur'an). Throughout his short story, then, Poe makes fun of both his own audience and the audience of the king. No one, he seems to suggest, has access to a "true" story or an original myth of Sindbad; instead, everyone becomes wrapped up in her or his own ideas, only believing those things that are familiar.

While Poe pokes fun at the history that brought Sindbad's myths to the modern world, the writer James Joyce includes Sindbad in his masterpiece novel *Ulysses* with a different goal in mind. Written in 1922, *Ulysses* is widely considered to be the most important modern novel in English literature. In it, Joyce tells the story of Leopold Bloom, an advertising executive who lives in Dublin, Ireland. The entirety of the long novel takes place within a single, somewhat uneventful day of Bloom's life and focuses on his social world and his relationship with his wife. Confined within this day, however, Joyce makes the story of Leopold Bloom one as sprawling, energetic, and great as the epic stories of ancient mythology. This is made particularly clear through the direct connections between Homer's *Odyssey* (ca. 725 BCE; English translation, 1614) and Joyce's modernist novel. Leopold Bloom can be understood as a stand-in for Homer's Odysseus, and Bloom's wife is treated as a parallel to Penelope. Rather than heading on a grand adventure across seas, however, the action of *Ulysses* takes place largely within the heads of the characters, with Joyce developing a stream-of-consciousness narration.

actual final voyage, a story that had previously been lost to Western audiences. The final voyage includes the typical elements, with Sindbad encountering grave danger and horrible monsters only to use his own wit and strength to overcome them. As Sindbad sails across the world, Shahrzad describes countless wonders and oddities that he discovers. These wonders are all taken from the real world of the nineteenth century, and through footnotes, Poe details the actual locations of every amazing thing Sindbad comes across. However, they are also wonders that were not known in the ancient world, and as Shahrzad describes Sindbad encountering them, the king becomes increasingly agitated. At last, frustrated with her exaggerations, he interrupts the story and declares that she will be killed in the morning after all.

Poe's story is in many ways a satire of the history of Sindbad's myths. The story-within-a-story is exaggerated, with Poe adding another layer through his own finding of

The journey of Leopold Bloom not only parallels the journey of Odysseus but also is made analogous with several other great literary travelers, among them Sindbad the Sailor. Sindbad's name comes up at several points throughout the novel, most notably when Leopold is falling asleep at the end of his long day. His final, jumbled thoughts before sleep overtakes him are a list of puns on Sindbad's name, with Leopold rambling, "Sinbad the Sailor and Tinbad the Tailor and Jinbad the Jailor," among a number of other variations (qtd. in Irwin 279), and even recalling faint (if confused) details from the sailor's epic voyages. This jumble of words comes as Leopold reflects upon the day that dominates the novel, and through the variations, he aligns himself with the ancient hero, perhaps seeing himself for a moment as the champion of a quest. However, he also indicates the ease with which a person is made different, as by changing only one letter he is able to alter the sailor's name and his profession. In this way, Leopold is enacting the process of translation that marks this history of Sindbad's voyages. He is familiar with the stories and even recognizes himself in them, but at the same time, he cannot make that connection without altering the meaning (and even the names) of the myths' main characters. A similar connection is made at several other moments throughout his day—most obviously, Leopold names a sailor that he happens to meet "Sinbad" and considers writing a song that tells the story of the voyages. Again, however, Joyce both establishes a connection across literature (Leopold is Odysseus is Sindbad) while showing that connection to be tenuous, suggesting difference as much as it does similarity.

It is an incredibly complex act for a writer to take a myth from one culture and transplant it into her or his own society. For Poe and Joyce, two of the most accomplished writers in English literature, the decision to adapt the myth of Sindbad and his voyages was made in full consideration of the complicated past between Western and Eastern literary traditions. Both were well aware that writers constantly misread other cultures, changing details and altering plots in order to serve their own interests. Rather than ignoring this reality, they highlight it, emphasizing the uneasy practice of translation while still recognizing the possibility for connection and communication that myths offer different cultures.

Treatments such as these have become increasingly common, with modern writers in a large variety of languages attempting to portray Sindbad's ancient story as accurately as possible. At the same time, however, the Sindbad of children's adventures and easy thrills still dominates popular culture. Movies, comic books, and video games regularly feature the sailor as a swashbuckling hero, overpowering monsters and winning great riches in faraway lands. This version is a far cry from the original Sindbad, a character who, however heroic he might have been, represents a complicated moment in the development of Islamic society and international trade, his own story told in defense of his often foolish behavior.

Within this flurry of translations and interpretations, scholars continue to explore the historical texts that preserve the oldest known versions of *The Thousand and One Nights* and its related myths, with restored versions based on "original" Syrian texts made widely available for the first time at the end of the twentieth century. As with so many mythological characters, it becomes impossible to talk about a singular, recognizable Sindbad, a definite character who can be easily understood. Instead, the Sindbad from medieval Syria and the Sindbad from twenty-first-century Japan, for example, are so different as to become unrecognizable. Across those representations, however, endures the strength of the culture and arts of the Islamic golden age, which remains as exciting and fascinating to contemporary audiences as it has ever been, even as the particulars of the great sailor change with every additional voyage.

T. Fleischmann, MFA

BIBLIOGRAPHY

Denuccio, Jerome D. "Fact, Fiction, Fatality: Poe's 'The Thousand-and-Second.'" *Studies in Short Fiction* 27.3 (1990): 365. Print.

Dixon, E., ed. "The Third Voyage of Sinbad the Sailor." *Fairy Tales from* The Arabian Nights. London: Dent, 1910. 85–91. Print.

Irwin, Robert. The Arabian Nights: *A Companion*. New York: Tauris, 2005. Print.

Joyce, James. *Ulysses*. New York: Vintage, 1990. Print.

Makdisi, Saree, and Felicity Nussbaum, eds. The Arabian Nights *in Historical Context: Between East and West*. New York: Oxford UP, 2008. Print.

Marzolph, Ulrich, ed. The Arabian Nights *in Transnational Perspective*. Detroit: Wayne State UP, 2007. Print.

Poe, Edgar Allan. "The Thousand-and-Second Tale of Scheherazade." *The Complete Stories and Poems of Edgar Allan Poe*. New York: Doubleday, 1984. Print.

THE HOST OF HEROINES

Athena and the Contest of Arachne

Author: Ovid
Time Period: 1 CE–500 CE
Country or Culture: Roman
Genre: Myth

OVERVIEW

The myth of Athena and Arachne (Arakhnê) was a late addition to the large canon of classical Greek mythology. The story is told in works by the Roman writers Ovid and Virgil, although Ovid's account is much more substantial. Both of these poets were writing at the beginning of the Roman Empire, during the reign of Augustus. Although the myth is very rarely represented in statues or on Greek pottery, most scholars agree that it bears all the features of a myth of Greek origin, and it is just by chance that the earliest extant record of the myth is Roman. Ovid's account of Arachne's unfortunate tale is recorded in book 6 of his Latin narrative poem *Metamorphoses*. Along with recording classical myths of transformation, the *Metamorphoses* has the ambitious project of describing the history of the world from its formation to the deification of the Roman sovereign Julius Caesar. Interestingly, in Ovid's version of the Arachne story, Athena is referred to as Pallas; elsewhere in the *Metamorphoses*, Athena is identified by the Roman name Minerva.

Arachne's complicated story is about many different things. It fits into Ovid's *Metamorphoses* as a tale of transformation, but perhaps more importantly, it is a cautionary tale that is meant to warn against the perils of hubris and the blasphemy of challenging the gods. The story depicts the severe wrath of Athena, a warrior-maiden goddess who, like other Olympians, is not immune to feelings of jealousy and spite. Athena's jealous wrath is well documented in other myths; during the Trojan War, the goddess sided with the Greeks after Paris selected Aphrodite as the most beautiful goddess in a contest among several goddesses.

Yet Athena's awful wrath is encouraged by the hubris of Arachne, a young girl from Lydia who is renowned for her skill in woolwork. While hubris in any respect was looked down upon by the Greeks, hubris against the gods was regarded much like a cardinal sin. Many other characters who have exhibited hubris in myth, such as Ajax, Icarus, Oedipus, and Antigone, have suffered equally terrible fates. Although enraged, Athena meets Arachne in disguise and gives her an opportunity to make amends with the dishonored goddess, but Arachne remains brash and indignant, and instead of accepting the disguised goddess's advice, Arachne further insults her. The fact that Arachne actually wins the contest against Athena is of little consequence; because of her hubris, her fate is, in some regards, already sealed.

The myth may also have an etiological function, as it is believed by some to explain the origin of spiders. From the name Arachne, Greek for "spider," comes the modern scientific term "arachnid," which is used to refer to spiders as well as scorpions, mites, and ticks. The myth of Arachne has also gone on to influence a variety of adaptations in popular culture. Her character and her transformation into a spider can be found in several movies, television shows, video games, novels, and illustrations and paintings.

SUMMARY

In Lydia, there is a young girl named Arachne who has no distinction or pedigree but who has achieved renown for her unprecedented skill at woolwork. She is so good that her skill is said to rival that of the patron goddess of woolwork, Athena. Her widowed father, Idmon of Colophon, makes his livelihood by dyeing the wool purple. Both of her parents were lowborn, and Arachne lives in a modest town and a modest house, but these details hardly matter when the people in the towns of Lydia encounter Arachne's remarkable skill with wool. The nymphs who live on the mountains of Tmolus and in Pactolus's stream come to watch the grace with which she weaves the wool. As they and others watch her, it is obvious that Arachne has received her training from none other than Athena herself.

Yet despite how obvious this is, Arachne denies it—a blasphemous thing to do and an insult to the great goddess. The notion that Arachne's talent is owed to Athena hurts her pride, and she often proposes to challenge Athena in a contest of skill. Angered by Arachne's irreverence, Athena dresses herself in the guise of an old woman and goes to visit the girl. Sitting with Arachne, the disguised goddess tells her that because she is wise in years, she has learned that it is necessary to give the gods their due credit. She suggests that Arachne seek pardon from Athena and assures her that Athena would receive it warmly. Arachne cannot believe the audacity of the old woman and is so enraged that she almost strikes her. She insults the woman's age and tells her that she does not need her advice. Once again, she goads Athena to the contest, questioning why Athena has not yet come to meet the challenge.

With that, Athena throws off her cloak and reveals herself to the defiant girl, causing the watching Lydian women and nymphs to bow down in reverence. But Arachne, who is fearless and determined to beat Athena in the contest, stands boldly. With all speed, Athena and Arachne prepare their looms by tying the warp to the crossbeam, and "a cane divides the threads; / The pointed shuttles carry the woof through . . . The comb's teeth, tapping, press it into place" (122; bk. 6). They both work quickly with excellent poise and skill, weaving beautiful purple and gold threads into their tapestries. Athena chooses to depict her own mythical contest with the sea god (Greek Poseidon, Roman Neptune) for Athens and, into the four corners of the tapestry, weaves four examples of the transformative nature of the punishment that awaits her opponent. Arachne depicts different examples of the gods seducing mortals while disguised as animals, with flowers and ivy wrapping around the edges.

Regarding Arachne's work, Athena can find no fault and is so enraged that she rips up her tapestry and strikes the girl four times on the head with a wooden shuttle. Unable to endure the torture of the goddess, Arachne ties a noose around her neck in order to hang herself. As she hangs, Athena begins to pity her and calls upon the girl to live for all of posterity and to be remembered for her wicked blasphemy. Before leaving to go,

"And as she turned to go, she sprinkled her / With drugs of Hecate, and in a trice, / Touched by the bitter lotion, all her hair / Falls off and with it go her nose and ears. / Her head shrinks tiny; her whole body's small; / Instead of legs slim fingers line her sides. / The rest is belly; yet from that she sends / A fine-spun thread and, as a spider, still / Weaving her web, pursues her former skill."

Metamorphoses

Athena sprinkles some of Hecate's magic powder on the girl, causing her to transform into a spider. As a spider, Arachne's fate is to weave her web for all eternity, and her story becomes known through all of Lydia.

ANALYSIS

The most well-known and extensive source for the myth of Athena and Arachne is Ovid's *Metamorphoses*, a narrative poem composed in Latin and completed in 8 CE. *Metamorphoses* has since been canonized as a fundamental text from the so-called golden age of Latin literature. Apart from its own impressive stature, the classic text has gone on to influence important writers such as Geoffrey Chaucer, who adapted a myth for *The Canterbury Tales*, and William Shakespeare, who used Ovid's work as source material for many of his plays, including *Romeo and Juliet* and *A Midsummer Night's Dream*. As such a popular text, Ovid's *Metamorphoses* was known to educated people for quite some time in Latin and French, but it was not until around the sixteenth century that translations started to appear in English. Shakespeare is thought to have read Arthur Golding's English translation repeatedly. Yet while translation enables a text to achieve notoriety through a more wide-ranging dispersion, the translation of a text can also be viewed as a violent act. The deeply imbued metaphors, lyrical cadences, and poetic tropes, or even just the polyvalence of particular words, can be lost by the translator's choice of words or interpretation of their meaning. It raises the question: how intimate was Shakespeare's relationship with Ovid's text? How is "Englished" Ovid different from the Ovid written in original Latin? The popularity of Ovid's work and the many translations that followed have led the story of Athena and Arachne to be told in a variety of different ways, perhaps none more judgmentally than George Sandys's translation.

It is impossible to determine a distinctive "Latin Ovid" from a distinctive "Englished Ovid" because the different English translations of his work are inevitably different from translation to translation. Ovid composed *Metamorphoses* in a period that is difficult for historians, scholars, and translators alike to be sympathetic with, and trying to understand exactly what Ovid was attempting to accomplish in his work is somewhat fallacious. In his book *The Motives of Eloquence: Literary Rhetoric in the Renaissance*, Richard Lanham describes the *Metamorphoses* as a narrative that describes a world filled with anger, terror, and violence. Often described as a mock epic, Ovid's work is ambitious to say the least. While darting between different myths of transformation, Ovid also takes up the task of narrating the history of the cosmos to the founding of the Roman Republic. Assuming the meter of grand heroic and epic poems, dactylic hexameter (used by Homer and Virgil, the latter Ovid's contemporary), Ovid presumably had a sense of the meaningful import that might be available from his work; however, exactly what he wanted it to be is not obvious.

Many critics note the inversions of Ovid's poem, which finds many of the gods humiliated and dishonored; however, despite many efforts and interpretations, Ovid's voice is characteristically not didactic. In the case of the mythic dispute between Athena and Arachne, critics are divided with regard to their interpretation of Ovid's judgment. It is essentially not there. As Liz Oakley-Brown remarks in her book *Ovid and the Cultural Politics of Translation in Early Modern England* (2006), "the narrative voice [of] Ovid's poem, a 'diffuse authorial self,' does not offer these violent episodes in a didactic mode of address; 'the point is not to hierarchise—there are no hierarchies here, and no perspectives either'" (72). While the episode between Athena and Arachne appears to be a moralizing tale about the due reverence one should offer the gods or the poetic justice that is inevitable for a character exhibiting too much hubris, Ovid does not provide the moral. His tale ends not, as typical moralizing tales do, on a note of judgment but rather on the dispersion of the tale itself:

"All Lydia rang; the story raced abroad / Through Phrygia's towns and filled the world with talk" (125; bk. 6). Any interpretation of the moralizing nature of this ending would have to be inferred. Perhaps being the subject of rumors is negative and just cause to worship the gods with humility. Then again, perhaps it is not, and Arachne's legendary fame as a marvelous spinner is simply preserved for all time. Either inference is available for those who are willing to search for them.

Thus, Ovid's decidedly perspectiveless speaker more easily enables critics and translators alike to gloss over his works with perspectives and interpretations suited to them and their historical contexts. When Ovid's poem began to be translated into English in the sixteenth century, this is exactly what happened: "The translator's voice, most apparent in the paratextual material that often accompanies the work, considerably alters the political agenda of the *Metamorphoses*" (Oakley-Brown 72). Arthur Golding's 1567 translation remained preeminent for most of the sixteenth century and is regarded by many to have been a faithful, nearly literal rendering of Ovid's original work. Yet, Golding's loyalty to the original text was in some ways his own undoing. As Mark P. O. Morford and Robert J. Lenardon note, Golding's "fourteen-syllable lines do hardly justice to Ovid's swift-moving energy" (720–21). In order to translate Ovid literally, Golding compromised the poetic virtues of his own work and lost the quick cadence and rhythm that is present in the original.

Consequently, when Sandys's neatly rhythmic iambic pentameter translation appeared in 1626, it largely replaced Golding's translation as the authoritative and more popular version. While in translation there is already room for interpretation, Sandys's choice to apply the metric restriction of iambic pentameter to what once was dactylic hexameter Latin provided him with room to interpret the original text more liberally. Sandys translates the 11,995 lines of Ovid's poem into 13,210 lines in English, revealing that although his translation has the guise of being terser through its rhythm, it has obviously been expanded upon (Oakley-Brown 81). Yet, Sandys's translation goes beyond obvious expansion; scholars such as Oakley-Brown have even noted that "when Sandys renders corporeal violence into English there is a reduction in detail" (81). Sandys's agenda, apparently, was motivated by more than just poeticizing his English translation of the *Metamorphoses*.

Sandys's 1626 translation of the *Metamorphoses*, which he aptly titled *Metamorphosis Englished*, is largely considered the first work of English verse completed in the New World. He began to work on the *Metamorphoses* during his voyage from England to Virginia, where he took up his post as the treasurer of the Virginia Company. Parts of the unfinished translation appeared in Sandys's *Relation of a Journey Begun Anno Domini 1610* (1615), a travelogue that chronicles his earlier journeys throughout the eastern Mediterranean. He probably completed his translation during his stay in Jamestown from 1621 until late in 1625, since upon his return to England in 1626, he saw to the publication of the completed *Metamorphosis Englished*. The 1626 version of Sandys's translation was shortly followed by a second, revised edition in 1632. Printed by John Lichfield of Oxford, the second edition was a more impressive version of the first and also included fifteen full-page woodcut illustrations by Francis Clein and Salmon Savery, thorough commentary provided by Sandys, and "An Essay on the *Aeneid*" placed after Ovid's poem.

From his father, Archbishop Edwin Sandys, who reputedly helped translate the Bishop's Bible, Sandys inherited not only a knack for translation but also ideologies that were inherently Christian and conservative. Sandys's translation of Ovid lives up to these associations despite the fact that Ovid's *Metamorphoses* was composed before the Christian religion was founded and thus patently does not identify with it. According to Oakley-Brown, Sandys's *Metamorphosis Englished*, "produced within a context of intellectual and religious sobriety, is the epitome of a conservative text" (73). As further evidence of this, Oakley-Brown points to the second edition's publisher, Lichfield, whose chosen works established his reputation as a notoriously pious publisher only interested in works of the "moralized Christian tradition" (73). The fact that Sandys's translation of Ovid's work was thought to belong within Lichfield's library of moralizing works is a telling sign of the amount of interpretation Sandys undertook in its creation.

Knowing Sandys's Christian predilections makes his slant on the Arachne story fairly predictable. Despite winning the weaving contest against Athena, Arachne is found guilty by Sandys. Her primary sin is her offense against the goddess. For Sandys, Arachne's brashness in challenging a goddess and asserting her skill over divine power is so audacious that he actually alters the outcome of the contest in his translation: "He revises Ovid's remark that Envy found nothing to reproach in the tapestry ("non illud carpere Livor / possit opus,"

"Envy could find no fault in that work," 6.129–30) by assigning a new motive to Envy: the goddess rightfully censors an act that typifies underlings' pleasure in hearing gossip about their superiors" (Jones and Stallybrass 98). Sandys justifies Athena's response to Arachne's work by describing it as rightful censorship: "Minerva [Athena] teares in peeces what envy could not but commend, because it published the vices of great ones, and beats her with the shuttle to chastise her presumption" (221). For Sandys, Arachne's craftsmanship could not have been superior to Athena's, and if anything, she is essentially disqualified for choosing to depict such sacrilegious content. "Profane Arachne," he writes, "sets forth the rapes and adulteries of the Gods" (220).

Yet, for critics such as Oakley-Brown, Ann Rosalind Jones, and Peter Stallybrass, Sandys's moralizing of Arachne's profanity is not his only agenda; Sandys also sought to deliver a moral of political ordering that sees Arachne as a political agitator and outlaw. Tellingly, on the frontispiece of Sandys's 1632 edition of *Metamorphosis Englished* is the dedication "To the most High and Mightie Prince Charles, King of Great Britaine, France, and Ireland." For Oakley-Brown, Sandys's translation of Ovid's poem is "inscribed with an acute awareness of the domestic political and cultural issues at stake for fashioning and sustaining Caroline subjectivity" (72). Thus the neutral closing to Ovid's narrative—"All Lydia rang; the story raced abroad / Through Phrygia's towns and filled the world with talk" (125; bk. 6)—is interpreted by Sandys to be evidence of Arachne's disturbance of established political boundaries and "evidence of the inconstancy of the common people" (Jones and Stallybrass 98). Sandys commentates, "The common people who envy the eminent, and pitty those whom they envyed in adversity, storme at the ruine of so excellent an artisan" (221). Sandys's gloss is indeed a melodramatic embellishment of Ovid's incidental conclusion to the episode. Arachne's unruly strides toward eminency are read as threatening by Sandys, who views them as inciting a mob and disrupting necessary social hierarchies held in place by his dedicatee, King Charles.

For Sandys, Arachne's insolence is best demonstrated through her tapestry. While her representation of the gods and their amorous misadventures with mortals is profane, the ivy frame she weaves around the central images is evidence of her unwarranted political ambitions: "These personages, with the places, being woven to the life by Arachne, she incloseth the web with a

HISTORICAL CONTEXT

The importance of women's weaving and the manufacture of textiles in domestic life probably influenced the significance of women weaving in myth. In ancient homes, women's quarters included rooms devoted exclusively to performing woolwork, which was performed exclusively by women. Although the manufacture of textiles was a gendered task, it was done by free women and slaves alike. The textiles produced by women in ancient homes were used for the household or, if made by an unmarried woman or slave, sold in shops. Women also engaged in weaving for important religious festivals. For the Panathenaea, a festival held every year in Athens for the city's patron goddess, Athena, the women of Athens worked on a large garment that would be paraded through the streets and eventually adorn the impressive statue of Athena in the Parthenon.

As the goddess of skill and crafts, Athena was regarded as presiding over this aspect of the household and usually plays a prominent role in myths that involve weaving. As an art form and a rare expressive outlet for women in Athenian society, the textile arts often function as analogy and metaphor in myth. Like the wise and clever goddess Athena, women in Greek myth are often portrayed as using woolwork with cunning and resourcefulness. Perhaps the most famous example of this is Penelope in Homer's *Odyssey*, who stalls her rowdy suitors by promising to accept one of their offers once she has completed a shroud that she weaves by day and secretly unravels by night. In myth and society alike, weaving was a woman's resource for accomplishing *arête* (virtue and respected glory).

traile of Ivy; well suiting with the wanton argument and her owne ambition. [Ivy is] Worne in garlands at lascivious meetings; and climbing as ambitious men, to compasse their owne ends with the ruine of their supporters" (221). Sandys's associations with ivy are heavily inferred from his own historical context. Intent on reading Arachne's tapestry as a "wanton" offense to political and divine order, he ignores the fact that ivy was the decoration attributed to Dionysus (Dionysos) and therefore associated with immortality and resurrection. Apart from his insistence on reading political and divine agitation into Arachne's motives, many commentators have acknowledged that Sandys's ignorance of her apparent talent in weaving is likely the result of a misogynistic ideology that rejected weaving as "trivial female fiddling" (Jones and Stallybrass 97).

In his commentary, Sandys provides an historical anecdote in order to justify the outcome of the contest but also to illustrate the particular threat that women pose to the political order. Sandys relates the mythical contest between Athena and Poseidon, in which they each vie to be the patron divinity of Athens. In describing the outcome to the contest, Sandys provides an ending to the story that is not well known:

The Athenians therefore put it to the Balloting: when the men were for *Neptune* [Poseidon], and the women

for Minerva [Athena]; who carried it only by a pebble. Whereupon incensed *Neptune* surrounded most of their territories. . . . but after, appeased by thus punishing the women; That they should have no voices in the publique decrees, that their children should not carry their names, nor themselves be called *Athenians*. . . . *Neptune* was more easily reconciled to *Minerva*; both having in *Athens* one Temple, wherein an Altar was erected to Oblivion. (218)

Here, political order is solidified and established by the erasure of women's rights in the political and even domestic sphere. Ironically, the goddess's victory is only granted to her through the complete abolishment of her own gender's rights. Jones and Stallybrass argue, "In contrast to Arachne's tapestry, which assures that posterity will remember gender injustice in the form of male gods' rapes of mortal women, the chapter Sandys adds to Athenian history paradoxically justifies the denial of the women citizens' vote as the basis of harmony for the 'democratic' city" (97). Arachne is viewed as a disrupter not only of social hierarchies but also of gender hierarchies.

For Sandys, Arachne's character epitomizes threatening behavior as read through her tapestry, which portrays profanity toward divinity, impudence of social hierarchies, and disregard for gender boundaries; yet paradoxically, as Jones and Stallybrass argue, Sandys asserts the inevitable futility of her craft through his endorsement of her punishment to weave perpetually. He writes, "And [Arachne] is by the Goddesse converted into a Spider: that she might still retaine the art which she had taught her, but toile without profit. For uselesse and worthlesse labors are expressed by the spiders web" (221). By describing Arachne's labors as "uselesse" and "worthlesse," Sandys effectively undoes his argument about Arachne's tapestries presenting a menacing threat to social order. But perhaps even more alarmingly, Sandys reads Arachne's tapestry depicting the sexual misdeeds of the gods into as an admission of her own lascivious character. Such readings, as Jones and Stallybrass point out, have dangerous repercussions: "His treatment of the mortal weaver repeats the strategy of the kind of judge who, in rape trials, interprets a woman's accusation of a man as proof that *she* is prey to indecent fantasies" (99). While Arachne's tapestry is condemned and censored by Athena under Sandys's premise that it threatens worldly order and Arachne is thus punished as the creator of this threat, Sandys simultaneous holds the view that weaving is essentially a meaningless and trivial endeavor.

Recognizing the bias perpetuated by a translator is of fundamental importance. While Sandys's translation of Ovid's poem did much to disseminate and preserve the popularity of Ovid's *Metamorphoses*, it also perpetuated the notion that Sandys's ideological class, social, and gender politics were historical views of the world. Sandys's reading of Arachne as a wanton agitator of political and divine order could have been read as a view intended by Ovid and thus a classical and historically substantiated view on the world. Translations are generally differentiated from critical interpretations of literature, but as is evidenced by Sandys's *Metamorphosis Englished*, translations can often be violent in themselves, operating as interpretations but under the guise of neutrality.

CROSS-CULTURAL INFLUENCE

The myth of Arachne's unfortunate contest with the goddess Athena has served as inspiration for many artists. Gustave Doré's illustration of Arachne for Dante's *Purgatorio* is so popular that the band the Mars Volta has used it as a recurring image on album artwork and merchandise. While Doré's dark and moody sketch of Arachne as a large spider impressively captures Dante's imagining of Arachne's unfortunate fate, Diego Rodríguez de Silva y Velázquez's 1657 painting *Las*

Hilanderas (The spinners) captures the dramatic tension of the weaving contest between Athena and Arachne. Unlike Doré, who illustrated Arachne for Dante's epic, Velázquez was likely inspired by the classical Roman myth as found in Ovid's *Metamorphoses* or Virgil's *Georgics*. Its probable source material having only recently been identified, the painting has had an extensive and mysterious archival history. As scholar Jonathan Brown has noted, Velázquez's painting "attracts interpretations like flypaper" (qtd. in Georgievska-Shine 179).

Although *Las Hilanderas* is generally regarded as Velázquez's most impressive and admired work, it is surrounded by a great deal of mystery. The painting's vague title, which literally means "the spinners," is now often accompanied by the subtitle "the fable of Arachne," although this subtitle has only recently been added to the painting. In fact, up until very recently, it was thought that the subject matter of the painting was not the mythical spinning contest between Athena and Arachne but instead a traditional scene of women working on tapestries in Santa Isabel. It was not until 1948 that archivist María Luisa Caturla published an inventory of the original owner of the painting, Pedro de Arce, dated 1664 (Martínez Alfaro para. 21). With the inventory of the painting now in the public domain, a complicated history of naming and renaming has been revealed, enabling art historians to consider different possible subjects for the painting.

For a period of more than two hundred years, the painting was never connected with the myth of Arachne. In 1711, when entered into the Spanish royal collection, the painting was accompanied by an inventory that described it with the title *Mujeres que trabajan en tapicería*, translating as "Women working on tapestry" (Martínez Alfaro para. 20). A different title, *Una fábrica de tapices y varias mujeres hilando y devanando*, was used for it in 1772, yet the new title adds little detail, translating loosely as "A tapestry factory where women spin and wind." Two years later, it was referred to by yet another title, *Quadro llamado de las hilanderas*, describing the four prominent women depicted in the painting as "the spinners," the short name by which the painting is now most commonly known. The most telling title, however, can be found in Pedro de Arce's 1664 inventory of the painting, which includes the title *La fábula de Aragne* (The fable of Arachne). Subsequently, the painting's subject matter was confirmed by art historians Diego Angulo Iñiguez and Charles Tolnay, who identified it as a scene from the Arachne myth told in Ovid's *Metamorphoses*.

Las Hilanderas was originally commissioned for a palace official, Velázquez's friend Pedro de Arce (whose inventory unlocked the mystery of the painting's subject), and was completed by 1657. By this time, Velázquez was already renowned as a portrait artist in Spain, having painted many portraits of the Spanish royal family and other notable figures. Although renowned for his skills at portraiture, Velázquez also took to painting scenes of historical significance. Apart from *Las Hilanderas*, which has generated a great deal of attention due in part to the recent revelations regarding its subject matter, *Las Meninas* (The ladies in waiting), probably completed one year before *Las Hilanderas*, is perhaps Velázquez's most famous composition. He spent most of his career in Spain but made a notable journey to study and practice in Italy, then the center of the predominant baroque art movement of which Velázquez was an important exponent. In line with this art period, Velázquez's paintings are clear and intelligible scenes of grandeur and decadence that, through their dark tones, convey a heightened sense of tension and drama.

The painting depicts a generic scene of women weaving in a large but crowded room. The perspective of the painting divides the room into the two distinctive areas of foreground and background, with two separate scenes occurring. In the foreground are five women of varying ages dressed in a traditional and modest working garb from the seventeenth century. On the left is an older woman seated at a spinning wheel while a younger woman sitting to her right winds the yarn. On the right, three other women bring additional wool and appear to be sorting through materials. The foreground is dark and shadowy, and the women are dressed in mostly dark or pale hues. In the background is an illuminated alcove that is slightly raised and filled with five women who, in to contrast the women in the foreground, are more elegantly dressed. Behind these woman hangs a tapestry that is reportedly Titian's *Rape of Europa* (1562). Although it is in the background, the alcove is somewhat prominent, as it is centered in the composition and maintains the most light.

Although most art historians agree that *Las Hilanderas* depicts the myth of Arachne, there is a fair amount of disagreement regarding which figures represent the goddess Athena and the unfortunate maiden, Arachne. Because of the significant differences in the staging of the two scenes, the implications vary depending upon

which women are identified as the two central characters. In *Renaissance Clothing and the Materials of Memory*, Ann Rosalind Jones and Peter Stallybrass poignantly ask, "Is she [Arachne] the woman in the middle of the group of five women in the background scene? If so she is presented at her moment of triumph, having equalled the skill of Minerva. She stands in front of one of her own tapestries, depicting the crimes of the gods" (101). This interpretation is possible. The tapestry, allegedly depicting the rape of Europa, corresponds with Ovid's account, which attests that Arachne chose to portray in her weaving the seduction of mortals by gods. Following this interpretation, Arachne stands toward Athena, who stands to her right. Athena has her arm partially raised, but the gesture is not obviously intelligible. If, indeed, this scene depicts the moment when Arachne presents her flawless tapestry, it can be inferred that Athena's arm is probably raised with fury.

However, other interpretations assign two of the figures in the foreground with the roles of Athena and Arachne, an interpretation that drastically alters the situation the painting depicts. As Jones and Stallybrass continue, a few of these women could be identified as Arachne:

> But Arachne could equally be identified as the woman spinning in the left foreground of the painting. . . . Or should we identify Arachne with the woman in the right foreground, upon whom the light falls as she turns away from us, winding finished thread into a ball? Or are Arachne's labors split between these figures, so that she is both part of the foreground world of manual labor and part of the background world of courtly display? (101)

If Arachne is indeed one of the figures depicted in the foreground, the scene being depicted might be the actual occurrence of the contest. It is possible then that the older figure on the left is in fact Athena, still disguised, though this would not corroborate with Ovid's account, which describes Athena as revealing herself before the contest takes place. An additional problem with this interpretation is that it raises the question of who the women are in the background.

Some argue that it is more difficult to accept that higher-ranked women would commiserate in the background, apparently indifferent to the divine contest taking place in the foreground. Although Ovid emphasizes Arachne's modest origins, the woman who could be identified as Arachne in the courtly scene is portrayed in a way that Jones and Stallybrass describe as identifying with the "plebeian" women in the foreground: "The rolled-up sleeves of her smock mirror the rolled-up sleeves of the smock of the woman winding the thread in the right foreground" (101). As Jones and Stallybrass muse, perhaps these two figures are the same woman, possibly Arachne, at different moments during the contest, though others regard this interpretation as being unlikely, citing the fact that apart from the rolled-up sleeves, the clothing on each figure is distinctive.

To some scholars, the notion that a definitive interpretation can ever be found is a fallacy. An authority on Spanish painting and the interpretive history of Velázquez's *Las Hilanderas*, Jonathan Brown, explains:

> By virtue of his original conception of the antique text, the artist raises questions which both demand and frustrate attempts to answer them. Who are the women in the foreground? Who are the elegantly-dressed females who accompany Minerva and Arachne? Why did Velazquez reverse the logic of the composition, placing the climactic moment of the story in the distance instead of in the foreground? And what is the purpose of the quotation from Titian's *Rape of Europa*? ("Minerva, Arachne and Marcel")

He goes on to remark that a "myriad of interpretations . . . have been inflicted" on the painting since the 1948 discovery and notes that while "authors assert with absolute conviction, on the basis of the assembled evidence, that they have unlocked the 'secret' of this masterpiece," these interpreters actually (and unintentionally) demonstrate the converse: "no single interpretation can possibly be sufficient."

For Brown and others, such as Martínez Alfaro, identifying the figures that represent Athena and Arachne is somewhat beside the point. Others argue that more important is the thematic intent of the painting. For Aneta Georgievska-Shine, in her article "'I Repair My Work That Was Left . . .': Velázquez and the Unfinished Story of Arachne," Velázquez's work is about the artfulness of the artist's efforts toward perfection and the simultaneous lack of finitude that is accomplished by such a venture.

Regardless how Velázquez's *Las Hilanderas* is interpreted, the amount of attention and critical work that the painting has inspired is a testament to the remarkable talent of the artist and the longevity of Arachne's myth, which, at its core, is about the perils of artistic undertaking. As Georgievska-Shine has astutely noted, the subject matter of the painting—and the subsequent controversy that has been associated with it—is somewhat ironic. The mystery of Velázquez's painting is reminiscent of the mystery that was associated with woman's work in classical literature and that the myth of Arachne partially illuminates.

Katherine Sehl, MA

BIBLIOGRAPHY

Barber, Elizabeth Wayland. *Women's Work: The First 20,000 Years*. New York: Norton, 1994. Print.

Brown, Jonathan. "Minerva, Arachne and Marcel." *Tout-Fait: The Marcel Duchamp Studies Online Journal* 2.5 (2003): n. pag. Web. 1 May 2013.

---. *Painting in Spain: 1500–1700*. New Haven: Yale UP, 1998. Print.

Dundas, Judith. *Pencils Rhetorique: Renaissance Poets and the Art of Painting*. Newark: U of Delaware, 1993. Print.

Georgievska-Shine, Aneta E. "Velazquez and the Unfinished Story of Arachne." *Subject as Aporia in Early Modern Art*. Ed. Alexander Nagel and Lorenzo Pericolo. Burlington: Ashgate, 2010. 175–93. Print.

James, Sharon L., and Sheila Dillon. *A Companion to Women in the Ancient World*. Malden: Wiley-Blackwell, 2012. Print.

Jones, Ann Rosalind, and Peter Stallybrass. *Renaissance Clothing and the Materials of Memory*. Cambridge: Cambridge UP, 2000. Print.

Lanham, Richard A. *The Motives of Eloquence: Literary Rhetoric in the Renaissance*. New Haven: Yale UP, 1976. Print.

Martínez Alfaro, María Jesús. "A Tapestry of Riddling Links: Universal Contiguity in A. A. Byatt's 'Arachne.'"*Journal of the Short Story in English* 45 (2005): 145–61. Web. 1 May 2013.

Morford, Mark P. O., and Robert J. Lenardon. *Classical Mythology*. 8th ed. New York: Oxford UP, 2007. Print.

Oakley-Brown, Liz. *Ovid and the Cultural Politics of Translation in Early Modern England*. Aldershot: Ashgate, 2006. Print.

Ovid. *Metamorphoses*. Trans. A. D. Melville. Oxford: Oxford UP, 1998. Print.

Sandys, George. *Ovid's Metamorphosis Englished, Mythologized, and Represented in Figures by George Sandys*. 1632. Whitefish: Kessinger, 2003. Print.

The Ballad of Mulan

Author: Traditional
Time Period: 1 CE–500 CE
Country or Culture: China
Genre: Legend

OVERVIEW

Fifth- and sixth-century China, immediately preceding the founding of the Tang dynasty, was a period of warfare and political upheaval. As groups vied for power and political boundaries were established and broken, the Northern Wei dynasty managed to unite a large area of northern China for nearly 150 years. Toward the end of this period, however, the constant power struggles erupted in the dynasty itself, splitting into the Eastern Wei dynasty and the Western Wei dynasty, both of which would fall soon after.

It was during this period that the legend of Hua Mulan was first recorded. A brief poem, "Ode of Mulan" was written in a book of popular songs, although it is likely the story, variants of which are called "The Ballad of Mulan," existed for some time before that. While scholars do not know the author of the ballad or even whether Mulan was a real person, the brief narrative of "Ode of Mulan" does remain extant today. In it, readers are told the story of a young woman who disguises herself as a boy in order to join the army of the ruling khan in her father's place. Mulan heads to war and survives for twelve years, winning great honor and eventually earning a place in the government of the khan himself. Rather than taking this position, however, Mulan declines and returns to her hometown, where she lives again as a woman in the company of her family. The poem is filled with rich images and deep emotions as the young woman risks her life and innocence in a cruel war, all motivated by the deep love and devotion she feels toward her father.

As the tale of Mulan has been told again and again through the modern day, it has become a favorite text for feminist scholars. Mulan is a powerful figure, a female warrior who excels above men and who rejects the lifestyle of military conflict and violence in order to live a peaceful existence with her family. While these details have made the story appealing to many modern audiences, the actuality of the original legend is more complicated. Mulan certainly defies stereotypes of gender roles and familial obligations, but she is also positioned at a complex intersection of loyalties. On the one hand, she feels obligated to risk everything in order to demonstrate devotion and loyalty to her father, who holds all the power in her patriarchal family. On the other, she is commanded by the khan—a cold and cruel figure, interested in warfare but not in the lives of his people—to enter into a bloody battle that robs her and thousands of others of their youth, if not their lives. In this context, the "Ode of Mulan" is primarily concerned with a critique of the culture of warfare prominent during the Northern Wei dynasty, all the while focusing on a character brave enough and wise enough to transcend the boundaries of her role in life, beginning to see the possibility of different worlds.

SUMMARY

A girl named Mulan sits in her parent's home, facing the door to the outside world as she weaves and sighs sadly to herself. Her sadness is not brought on by the typical concerns of young women, such as romantic heartbreak. Indeed, she cannot even think of romance, for the night before, she saw the scrolls recently posted around town announcing a draft for the army. The khan, in order to defend their land from outside invaders, needs a large number of troops, many more than are currently available. On every one of the twelve scrolls posted in the town, the name of Mulan's father is listed. While most families can send a strong young son, Mulan's father has only his daughters, a young boy, and a wife, and so he would have to go himself despite his elderly age. Mulan, thinking about this as she weaves, realizes she must purchase a horse and go in her father's place, pretending to

"Her comrades are all amazed and perplexed. / Traveling together for twelve years / They didn't know Mu-lan was a girl. / 'The he-hare's feet go hop and skip, / The she-hare's eyes are muddled and fuddled. / Two hares running side by side close to the ground, / How can they tell if I am he or she?'"

"Ode of Mulan"

be a boy in order to meet the requirements of the khan's decree.

Mulan heads immediately to the four markets of the town, buying a horse and the supplies needed to join the army. Wasting no more time, she leaves town and camps on the bank of the Yellow River. There, she sleeps to the sound of the rushing water, which is loud enough to block out the calls of her mother and father, who are begging her to return. The next morning, she travels to the Black Mountain; there, the neighing of the wild horses of Mount Yen is loud enough to block out the sounds of her parents, whom she loves as dearly as they love her.

Away from her family, Mulan joins the powerful army, pretending to be a man so that the other warriors will accept her. She travels thousands of miles, battling and waging war with the men of the army the entire time. She travels as quickly as the wind and seems to fly across the mountain as part of the fierce, ironclad army. The years pass this way, with Mulan taking part in many battles. While many generals and other fierce warriors die, she manages to stay alive, continually proving herself a strong warrior. Countless battles later, she is finally able to return home, one person among many men who have been changed by their many years away. First, however, she stops to visit the khan, called the "Son of Heaven," in his Splendid Hall. Here, the leader of the state gives out favors and promotions to the powerful warriors who have defended his land. He raises people to positions of power and bestows upon them riches and gifts. When Mulan approaches, however, she declines the official government post that is offered to her,

instead asking only for a fast horse that can take her to visit her family as quickly as possible.

Mulan's family is thrilled to hear that she is returning. Her father and mother wait outside the wall to their home. Meanwhile, her elder sister fixes her makeup in order to look as nice as possible, while her younger brother, now older, readies his knife so that he can slaughter a pig and a sheep for a feast celebrating Mulan. When she comes home, she opens the doors of her room, takes off the clothing of war, and relaxes at last on her couch in her old attire. In almost no time at all, she transforms herself back into the beautiful young woman she was before the war. She fixes her hair so that it is as gorgeous and soft as a cloud and dabs the powder of a yellow flower on her face as makeup. Looking like this, she rises again and greets the soldiers who had fought beside her in the war, then passing by outside.

Her comrades, of course, are shocked to see Mulan. They had spent twelve years together, traveling across the mountains of China and battling fiercely, living in close quarters and sharing supplies, yet none had suspected that Mulan might actually be a woman. They ask Mulan to explain herself, and she simply says that just as a female rabbit and a male rabbit might appear different when resting beside one another, when they are running together in a blur of movement, no one would be able to tell which is a "he" and which a "she." Likewise, Mulan, in the movement of battle, was indistinguishable from any man and certainly just as strong.

ANALYSIS

From the start of her recorded history, the figure of Hua Mulan has sat at the intersection of Chinese history and Chinese legend. It remains unclear to modern scholars if she was a real woman, a fabrication of literature, or some combination of both. The roots of her legend, likewise, remain blurry, with academics disagreeing on the exact cultural and historical beginnings of the story. Moreover, the legend of Mulan has remained a popular topic in literature, opera, song, dance, visual arts, and film, both in China and abroad. The end result is that there is not one story of Mulan, but countless contradictory stories of countless contradictory Mulans.

Regardless of how different artists and writers interpret the figure of Mulan, however, they all trace their origins back to a relatively brief Chinese poem entitled "Ode of Mulan." This poem contains the core details of Mulan's life that appear in most all subsequent retellings, with the young woman dressing as a man and taking the place of her father in war. The author of the poem remains unknown, and the earliest version available is a copy that was transcribed sometime around the twelfth century. The original version, from what can be gathered, was first written down in the sixth century, although that copy has been lost to time. Because of this scant information, most scholars consider the "Ode of Mulan" to likewise take place around the sixth century, with the appropriate cultural and political contexts of that period.

Whether or not one knows these contexts, the emotional core and narrative suspense of the poem remain powerfully in place. A young woman who should have a secure and happy future ahead of her, Mulan instead sacrifices everything—especially her safety—in order to protect her father and her family. In contrast to the devotion and love Mulan expresses for her family, the commands of the state and of the khan come across as cruel and arbitrary. While Mulan fulfills both her filial and state duty despite the additional challenge of being a woman in a patriarchal society, the different ways the poem represents the family and the state stand in stark relief to one another. It is this exploration of loyalty and duty that rests at the heart of the many versions of Mulan.

From the very start of the ballad, readers are asked to understand Mulan as a character torn between her potential life as a happy young woman in the company of her family and the obligations put upon her family by the khan. As the poem opens, she sits in the doorway of her family home, weaving a piece of fabric and sighing to herself. This is a typical domestic image, with Mulan fulfilling her role as a daughter in the household by weaving. The concern she expresses, sighing and "tsieking," is not, however, a typical one for a girl her age. As the poem ensures us, "No one is on Daughter's heart, / No one is on Daughter's mind" (lines 7–8). Neither romantic woes nor the concerns of young adulthood weigh her down, but rather the decrees of the khan that she has seen about town. A khan is a type of military and political leader, and khans often vied for power in this historical period. In seeing her elderly father's name on the draft scroll, Mulan is suddenly thrust into a position in which two loyalties and two types of power in her life come into direct conflict: the orders of the khan cannot be ignored, and her father's obligation to serve cannot be eschewed; yet for him to head to war would mean his certain death and the downfall of her family.

While this conflict is carefully explained throughout the first stanza, with considerable time in the brief poem given over to describing Mulan in her domestic position, she makes a quick and unambiguous decision to join the army herself in her father's place. Neither the poem nor Mulan herself ever directly criticizes the khan or the state he leads. Instead, the contrast between the family and the state is made clear through the actions of each entity in relation to Mulan herself. Mulan's enthusiasm for joining the army, her quick decision to buy a horse and to pretend to be a boy, should not be understood as enthusiasm for the military or for the interests of the khan. Instead, she sublimates her duty to her father into her duty to the state. She is taking on great personal risk and likely facing death as a member of the army. Yet, as the first stanza makes clear, her actions should never be considered as actually supporting that army, but rather as facing the danger of the military in order to save her family.

The risks that Mulan faces, primarily implied instead of being made explicit, also deserve a close reading. By dressing as a young man and fraudulently taking her father's place in the khan's service, Mulan is not simply taking on the typical risks one associates with military service, such as death and dismemberment. Instead, as the only woman in service with an army of men, she faces the possibility of violence from her fellow soldiers as well as from the enemies. She risks her innocence, faces the glaring possibility of sexual violence, and is in danger of legal consequences should her true identity be discovered. She also sacrifices her potential life from the poem's start, as in the twelve years of her service she ceases to be a young woman possibly sighing over love and becomes aged, robbed of that romantic time period. That she takes on all of these risks in the service of her father largely undermines the feminist possibility some readers see in this original text, although the possibility for feminist retellings of the legend remain fruitful. Mulan, in taking on the role of a man and defying the expectations placed upon her gender, is not exactly upsetting social norms and arguing for the worth of all women. Rather, she is putting herself at great risk for the sake of her loyalty to her father, the man who holds the power in her household. That Mulan is a woman disguised as a man is significant to the legend; its significance, however, rests in the heightened danger her gender adds to her sacrifice to a patriarchal figure more than to any feminist consciousness or politics.

While the reality of the patriarchal family in the ballad remains glaring obvious, there is also a strong tenderness that exists between Mulan and her mother and father, a tenderness that is once again in contrast to the relationship between the young woman and the state. Mulan, with her horse and new equipment, takes off away from her home and toward the battle. When her father and mother realize what she has done, they call after their lost daughter. The poem repeats this information twice, stating that "she doesn't hear the sound of Father and Mother calling" (lines 23, 27). Here, Mulan is placed between two directives. On the one hand, the father and mother are lovingly calling after her, concerned with her safety and urging her to come home. On the other, the khan is demanding her service, but only through the impersonal and demanding scrolls nailed about the town, none of which take into account the daily realities of Mulan's family.

This moment offers a tension that would be familiar to people living in the Northern Wei dynasty of sixth-century China. While the northern region of China had been unified by the Wei in 439, by the end of the dynasty, internal unrest and war had become common. This violent period included many demands on common people to provide supplies and soldiers for war, while for many of those people (like Mulan's family), the war itself represented little to no promise of security or wealth. Even the locations where Mulan rests during her journey recollect the conflict of this period; the dams of the Yellow River, for instance, were constantly destroyed to flood the regions of rival states. Mulan, with her family calling her sweetly on one side and the heartless demand of the ruling party on the other, captures an experience that was increasingly common when the story was first popular.

As with her choice to enter the army of the khan in the first place, the success of Mulan while in battle can be understood as an expression of her extreme filial loyalty. Mulan herself is never directly described as slaying any enemies, but rather as someone who "crosses paths and mountains like flying" (30). She has an almost superhuman strength, the distances she travels becoming legendary, especially considering the arduous nature of such travel in the time period. Knowing that such strength is impossible, the implication remains strong that Mulan is succeeding in war because of her love for her family, and more specifically because of the duty she feels to her father. In contrast to the relatively peaceful (if still powerful) image of Mulan flying across the mountains, readers are given the details of actual war, in which "generals die in a hundred battles" (line 33). The majestic image of the filially devoted daughter is

contrasted with her surroundings, a place in which those with loyalty to the state are perishing in vast numbers. Once more, although she and her fellow soldiers fight beside each other in the same conflicts, their motivations and loyalties diverge, resulting in a mythically safe Mulan and the nameless deaths of her commanders.

While Mulan never directly confronts the khan for his mistreatment of her family, she does receive the opportunity to deny him, albeit only in a subtle way. Following the war and her great success, she is offered a position in the government, an official job that would have provided her with great power and wealth for the remainder of her years—assuming the government remained in control. This scene is presented in a way that heightens the glory of the position, with the khan residing as a "Son of Heaven . . . in the Splendid Hall" (36). He is freely giving out incredible wealth and treasures to the people who have shown him loyalty during battle, a group in which he includes Mulan. However, this ultimate reward of loyalty to the state is entirely uninteresting to the young woman, and she instead only requests a fast horse so that she can return home to her mother and father. This moment, undramatic as it may seem, in actuality demonstrates a clear dismissal of the state itself. The loyalty that Mulan has demonstrated was not, after all, a loyalty to the state, for if it were she would have gladly taken the due reward in that system. Instead, she makes clear that it was loyalty to her family, and she uses the privilege she has earned only to hasten the return to her mother and father.

That return home, in contrast to the tribulations of war, is idealized just as the opening domestic scene presents an idealized and seemingly tranquil moment in Mulan's life. The mother and father wait expectantly outside, the sister makes herself beautiful, and the brother prepares a feast for the entire family. What matters most here, however, is not the romantic state of this domestic family, but rather Mulan's immediate reintegration into it. Although she still wears the masculine clothing of war and falsely presents herself as a person loyal to the state of the khan, upon entering the domestic bliss offered by her family, she immediately transforms back into her feminine self. She takes "off [her] wartime gown / And puts on [her] old-time clothes" (lines 51–52).

This is a transformation into a beautiful, feminine self, with her hair long and soft and makeup from flowers on her face. While this description paints a comfortable image of a young woman, the reality of these clothing items is more complicated than the bliss they first imply. The wartime clothes are false in the sense that Mulan never feels true loyalty to the khan, although she certainly has the strength and courage to wear such armor. Likewise, the old feminine clothes are also not entirely true representations of her. In putting them on, she is fulfilling the role of loyalty to her father, taking on the feminine attributes required of her place in the family. Yet, knowing the bravery she has exhibited for twelve years in battle, this demure and passive presentation also rings false. Both outfits are costumes, each representing a different loyalty; Mulan herself, however, does not truly fit comfortably into either any longer, the demands of each loyalty restricting a different aspect of her life.

Although Mulan returns to her family and reclaims her position as a daughter—a role she has fought to achieve for twelve years—she also seems to realize the failings of this prescribed loyalty with the last lines of the poem. Seeing her fellow soldiers and at last revealing her true identity to them, she recites a brief parable, declaring:

> The he-hare's feet go hop and skip,
> The she-hare's eyes are muddled and fuddled.
> Two hares running side by side close to the ground,
> How can they tell if I am he or she? (59–62)

This exploration of her position, although very brief, is the only moment in the ballad when Mulan directly describes her own take on her situation. While at the start of the poem she is a deeply loyal daughter, willing to put herself at extreme danger to fulfill the loyalty of her role and to protect her family, now she seems to take a more nuanced appraisal. On one hand, readers are given the characterizations of the male hare, a figure associated with movement and action. On the other, readers are given a female hare who has "muddled and fuddled" eyes, implying that she is unable to see what is going on around her. This contrast implies a world in which the men take action and make decisions, while the women are kept from seeing the reality that unfolds in front of them. When both the male and female hare are engaged in similar movement, however—when they run together—it becomes impossible to tell which is the male and which the female.

Mulan, in telling this tale, does not prescribe herself to the female role. Instead, she keeps the masculine and feminine figures in the distanced realm of the hares. It is only in the last line, the line in which ambiguity is introduced, that she mentions herself. "How can they tell if I am he or she?" she asks, implying that she herself may not have an answer to that question. While not a rejection of the feminine and masculine roles outright, this does mark a shift in Mulan's awareness. Neither the masculine role of the military nor the feminine and subservient role of the household seems to fully capture her any longer. That final question can be read not so much as a rhetorical move meant to challenge the other soldiers' understanding of Mulan, but rather as sincere, Mulan herself unsure where she can now fit.

While Mulan herself ends the ballad in an uncertain state, changed by her experience at war, as a whole the poem does not go so far as to offer a direct critique of the patriarchal family structure or of filial loyalty. Readers can still assume that Mulan, in the safety and luxury of her home and away from the danger of war, is relieved, grateful to return. Much stronger than this subtle critique of the family structure, and much more in line with the culture of the Northern Wei dynasty, is the critique of the warlike khan, which resonates as Mulan abandons the treasures of the Splendid Hall in favor of the simpler comforts of her family. In a period in which warlords and leaders of state constantly challenged one another for power, destroying the lives of thousands of innocent people in the process, tensions ran high between the joys of the household and domestic life and the tragedies of military power.

Questions related to gender roles, while hinted at it in this early version, would only be teased out and expanded upon in later versions of the story, told during time periods when the state was at relative peace as compared to the Northern Wei dynasty and when writers and artists were more able to turn their attention to the concerns of the household. At the core of all of this, however, Mulan remains a figure courageous enough to transcend the boundaries of her culture and to take on powerful positions that would have traditionally been denied to her. Whether she uses her courage to challenge the dominance of the state or to critique the role of women in the patriarchal family, her character remains inspiring as someone willing to sacrifice everything in order to accomplish what she believes needs to be done.

CROSS-CULTURAL INFLUENCE

The legend of Mulan first persisted across centuries primarily as an oral tradition. While some versions of the story or song were written down, most people have learned the narrative by hearing their family and friends sing it in times of celebration or of leisure. As with many

Historical Context

During the politically turbulent period of the Sixteen Kingdoms in ancient China (303 CE–439 CE), the Northern Wei rose to briefly unite the northern regions of the land. It was under this rule that the story of Mulan seems to have first flourished.

The Northern Wei were originally vassals of the Later Yan, another powerful state at the time, but they eventually rebelled and established their own rule. Under the Northern Wei, peasants were organized into strict systems of communal living, regularly facing extortion from their government rulers, and forced to defend the borders against outside invaders. While these rulers established their hold of power in China, however, they were not ethnically Han Chinese but instead descended from the nomadic Xianbei aristocracy. The Northern Wei subsequently went through a slow process of adapting Chinese cultural traditions, largely in order to better hold power. In this context, Buddhism replaced Taoism (Daoism) as the official religion, and temples to the Buddha were constructed on a massive scale, even as Confucian ideals thrived elsewhere in the region.

The Northern Wei seemed to have a strong hold on the land, regularly expanding and taking new territories. However, as was often the case in the Sixteen Kingdoms, power rarely lasted for long. After around 150 years of steady Northern Wei leadership, two rival generals fought for the throne to the dynasty, and the government soon collapsed into the Eastern Wei dynasty and the Western Wei dynasty. Other dynasties would take and lose power in the region over the next century, with warfare taking a constant toll on citizens, regardless whether they were involved in politics or not. It was not until the Tang dynasty took power in 618 that a period of relative peace and cultural growth began again.

the legend of Mulan naturally traveled with them. Separated from the landscape and immediate cultural context of China, the story took on new meanings and acquired new resonances as parents told their children—born in the United States, in France, in Germany, and elsewhere—this narrative that has been passed down in oral and written traditions for generations. This history is one of the launching points for Maxine Hong Kingston's 1975 memoir *The Woman Warrior: Memoirs of a Girlhood among Ghosts*. The text is a mixture of different genres and forms, with Kingston drawing freely from her own autobiographical experience, from the stories of her relatives, and from Chinese cultural myths. Upon its release, the memoir won the prestigious National Book Critics Circle Award and became a popular seller, eventually becoming a standard text in university education across the United States.

The Woman Warrior is primarily concerned with the tension that exists in Kingston's life as a Chinese American, tied to the cultural legacy of China while living in Stockton, California—a world very different from that of her parents. In addition, Kingston is concerned with what it means to be a woman in this context, with the strict gender roles and expectations of her traditional parents butting against her own experiences as a girl craving a more liberated and self-determined life. In exploring both national identity and gender identity together, she focuses her attention squarely on the legend of Mulan in the second section of the memoir, "White Tigers." There, Kingston's mother recites to her the story of Fa Mu Lan (as Kingston renders the name), the traditional warrior woman of the legend. In hearing the story, Kingston blurs the distinction between imagination and reality, between myth and truth, by imagining herself into the narrative. What follows is a retelling of the legend with Kingston at its center.

oral literary traditions, the story traveled first throughout China and finally throughout the world, and as it entered different contexts of time and geography, the people remembering the song would revise it to reflect their own circumstances. Over time, the story became significantly longer, with writers expanding especially upon the specifics of Mulan's time at war and the details of her training to become a warrior. During the late sixteenth century under the Ming dynasty, the story was expanded into a popular novel, and Mulan herself was fleshed out as a complex character sensitive to the concerns of her time.

In the twentieth century, as global migration became increasingly common and Chinese people moved to other geographic regions in numbers greater than ever before,

As Kingston imagines it, a white crane comes to her as a young girl and leads her away from her childhood home and to the top of a mountain. There, an elderly brown man and an elderly gray woman offer her two options: either she can return home, where she will live as a traditional girl is taught to live and grow to become a wife and mother herself, or she can stay with them for fifteen years, studying to be a warrior woman. They tell her that the life of a warrior woman is filled with hardship and difficult labor, but Kingston accepts anyway. Her training begins and she learns to fight her way through the mountains, living like an animal and capturing her own food. The hardship goes on and on until at last the old couple returns. They bring Fa Mu Lan/Kingston to a water gourd, and inside she sees her father and brother being drafted into the army. Furious at their fate, she causes a giant sword to fall from the sky and is released from her training. Back home, her parents demand that she stay with them, even carving their names into her back. She then defiantly takes on her role as the warrior woman: she fights a massive giant, forms an army out of other women she has saved, rebels against the emperor, and defeats a baron who had stolen the sons of her village. Throughout all of this, she marries and bears a child but sends her husband away to raise the child on his own until she is done with her battles.

The story, rich with drama and fantastical battles, comes eventually to an end. Kingston concludes her fantasizing and instead compares the legend of Fa Mu Lan to her own time in the United States. Her parents and other members of her family constantly devalue her life, telling her that she will not amount to anything, unlike the mythical figure who defends her entire village. She longs for the magical powers and legendary strength Fa Mu Lan finds in the Chinese tradition; in actuality, Kingston is dismissed by her boss when she tries to stand up to his racist comments. Beyond that, Kingston also realizes that she is opposed to the violence of the military, even if she enjoys the fantasy of overpowering evil inherent in the legend of Fa Mu Lan. And while her mother tells her the story of a liberated and strong woman, she also tells her to practice obedience, insisting that Kingston live the repressed life associated with her traditional gender role. These conflicting ideas form a flurry of contradictions in Kingston's mind, so that she both realizes there is nothing she can do to liberate her relatives in China, yet still identifies strongly with Fa Mu Lan. She decides that it will be words rather than swords that she uses in her battle against the mistreatment of women.

When Kingston draws upon the story of Fa Mu Lan, she is in many ways drawing upon her broader cultural heritage as a Chinese American as well. It is for this reason that the many contradictions and divergent ideas she sees within the story are, in some ways, appealing to her. It would be perhaps easier to dismiss the legend altogether, either for the violence Fa Mu Lan champions that Kingston eschews, or because, after all the time she spends disguised as a male warrior, Fa Mu Lan ultimately does return to her domestic role as a mother and wife. However, Kingston, in her bicultural identity as a Chinese American, sees herself trapped in similar contradictions. She strives to be strong, to defend herself and her family, yet she sees herself reverting to a shy, quiet, and stereotypically feminine role in the classroom and at work. She finds solace and inspiration in this story of a warrior woman, especially as it comes through the voice of her repressive mother, although the other myths and legends she learns tell of women who are punished and castigated for their independence. In this way, the legend of Fa Mu Lan is an ideal narrative for Kingston to explore her own complex relation to her Chinese American identity. There are no easy answers or simple motivations, just a clear need to explore her history while living an independent, empowered life.

These qualities of Kingston's retelling of Mulan have made the memoir somewhat controversial. Many fellow writers have criticized the text, in part seeing Kingston as relying on an American view of the legendary figure rather than on a traditionally Chinese view. The Fa Mu Lan that Kingston constructs is a departure from the traditional Mulan, a figure who is typically rooted firmly in the historical conditions of feudal China. By taking Mulan out of that context, some critics argue, Kingston strips the legend of its historical Chinese roots. Related to this, some see the representation of Chinese culture as patriarchal and oppressive to women as being a stereotype rather than a common reality. At the very least, the culture of the United States in the 1970s was itself also a place in which women faced many oppressions and social obstacles. For these reasons, the Fa Mu Lan of *The Woman Warrior* is read by some as an American construction of a Chinese legend and, as such, a distortion of that original legend rather than another faithful retelling.

While the critical debate around these considerations has continued, *The Woman Warrior* itself is perhaps less concerned with historical veracity and cultural critique than it might first appear. Kingston draws deeply from Chinese and American cultures, even using both English and Cantonese within the text. However, rather than attempting to make an "authentic" Chinese American Mulan, she instead attempts to understand her own personal history and the family legacy that has been given to her. Not all Chinese people hold onto strictly traditional ideas about gender roles and the obligations of marriage, but Kingston's family did present those expectations to her, and they were reinforced by the cultural legacy of mythology, language, literature, and storytelling.

In this way, the figure of Mulan is even more appropriate to the exploration that Kingston undertakes. The "historical" Mulan is torn between an obligation to the state of the khan and to the love of her family. Kingston, likewise, is torn between the love and obligation she feels for her own family and the cultural legacies of two states (China and the United States). When she imagines herself as Fa Mu Lan—raising an army of women and overcoming an emperor, freeing children from an evil baron, and slaying monsters—she is in part also imagining the contemporary Kingston freeing the women of her family from oppressive traditions and ensuring that new generations of Chinese children will have greater opportunities. That she anchors this desire so firmly to the Mulan narrative only heightens her own conflicted relationship with her past.

The oppressions and expectations attached to gender and nationality intersect in complex ways. This is the case in the modern United States, as presented by Kingston, just as it was in the ancient Chinese landscape of the Mulan legend. While it is often tempting to look for easy conclusions and optimistic readings—to see Mulan as a woman overcoming patriarchal powers or as a peasant rebel defying the state—in actuality, there are a wide range of cultural legacies affecting every person's life and an even wider range of possible reactions to those legacies. Legends like that of Mulan and its retelling in *The Woman Warrior* allow us to approach these realities for what they are, asking us to better understand the paradoxes inherent in our lives as part of our process of making a better world. For this reason, Kingston's text continues to offer a powerful lesson on how we might add one more voice to the chorus reciting our legends.

T. Fleischmann, MFA

BIBLIOGRAPHY

Bolaki, Stella. "'It Translated Well': The Promise and the Perils of Translation in Maxine Hong Kingston's *The Woman Warrior*." *Melus* 34.4 (2009): 39–60. Print.

Edwards, Louise. "Transformations of the Woman Warrior Hua Mulan: From Defender of the Family to Servant of the State." *Nan Nü: Men, Women, & Gender in Early & Imperial China* 12.2 (2010): 175–214. Print.

Feng, Lan. "The Female Individual and the Empire: A Historicist Approach to Mulan and Kingston's *Woman Warrior*." *Comparative Literature* 55.3 (2003): 229–45. Print.

Kingston, Maxine Hong. *The Woman Warrior: Memoirs of a Girlhood among Ghosts*. New York: Vintage, 1989. Print.

Mair, Victor H., and Mark Bender, eds. *The Columbia Anthology of Chinese Folk and Popular Literature*. New York: Columbia UP, 2011. Print.

"Ode of Mulan." *The Flowering Plum and the Palace Lady: Interpretations of Chinese Poetry*. Trans. Hans H. Frankel. New Haven: Yale UP, 1976. 68–72. Print.

Stanley, Sandra K. "The Woman Warrior." *Masterplots II: Women's Literature Series* (1995): 1–3. Print.

Yuan, Shu. "Cultural Politics and Chinese-American Female Subjectivity: Rethinking Kingston's *Woman Warrior*." *Melus* 26.2 (2001): 199–223. Print.

Personal Recollections of Joan of Arc

Author: Mark Twain
Country or Culture: France
Time Period: 1001 CE–1500 CE
Genre: Legend

OVERVIEW

Although better known for authoring the American classic *The Adventures of Huckleberry Finn*, Mark Twain considered *Personal Recollections of Joan of Arc* his greatest literary accomplishment. After having already established himself as a writer with a rather wry and witty personality, Twain thought it best to publish the book under a pseudonym, Sieur Louis de Conte, since the story of Joan of Arc is decidedly not humorous. In fact, Sieur Louis de Conte would be the pseudonym for what was already a pen name; Twain was born Samuel Langhorne Clemens in 1835. *Personal Recollections of Joan of Arc* was initially published in 1895, serially printed in *Harper's Magazine* under the mysterious pseudonym. It took a while for the public to discover that *Personal Recollections* had actually been authored by Twain (the initials SLC match both Samuel Langhorne Clemens and Sieur Louis de Conte), a discovery that confused an audience familiar with his fictitious and more humorous literary endeavors. Regardless of the authorship, *Personal Recollections* was largely received with negative reviews and was defended by only a few, including Twain's daughter, Clara Clemens, and Twain's biographer, Albert Bigelow Paine.

Twain, who had reportedly become obsessed with the historical figure of Joan of Arc (Jeanne d'Arc) after discovering an article about her in a textbook, spent a great deal of time researching for this novel, in which he intended to tell a historically based biography of the legendary woman under a fictitious premise. After Jules Quicherat published her trial records in a five-volume series between 1841 and 1849, a great deal of interest was revived in Joan of Arc. The narrator of Twain's novel is the invented author of the tale, Sieur Louis de Conte, whom Twain imagines to have been good friends with Joan since childhood. Since de Conte would have recorded the recollections in French, Twain invented a fictional translator, Jean François Alden, who is attributed with a translator's preface in which he notes: "The Sieur Louis de Conte is faithful to her [Joan of Arc's] official history in his *Personal Recollections*, and thus far his trustworthiness in unimpeachable; but his mass of added particulars must depend for credit upon his own word alone" (11). The question of how much confidence should be invested in the historical loyalty of the fictitious translator, the fictitious author, or even Twain is up for debate; however, most agree that the account conveys a generally accurate narrative of what is known about Joan of Arc's life.

Yet there is only a certain level of accuracy that is possible to attain in recounting the life of the exceptional historical figure turned legendary heroine. While a great deal is known about Joan of Arc's life, especially through the transcripts of her trials, a significant amount of detail is either missing or has likely been obscured or embellished, depending on the source. Known as the peasant girl who, under divine guidance, led the French army to significant victories during the Hundred Years' War and enabled the coronation of King Charles VII, Joan is hailed as both a French national and religious heroine. After being captured in 1430 and executed the following year, Joan of Arc's extreme devotion to her Christian faith resulted in her being appreciated as a religious martyr; she was beatified in 1909 and canonized in 1920. Joan's figure is one of undeniable importance in Western culture, and she has served as an inspiration for many political figures, artists, and devotees. Many artists besides Twain have been inspired by Joan of Arc, including William Shakespeare, Voltaire, Friedrich Schiller, Pyotr Ilyich Tchaikovsky, Bertolt Brecht, George Bernard Shaw, and Leonard Cohen, along with many others.

SUMMARY

Personal Recollections of Joan of Arc is divided into three major sections (books 1–3) as well as an introduction and a conclusion. The introduction is preceded by a translator's preface and a note titled "A Peculiarity of Joan of Arc's History," written by the fictitious translator. The translator comments on the extraordinary figure of Joan of Arc and, for the most part, assures the veracity of Sieur Louis de Conte's ensuing account. The account then opens with an introduction written from Domrémy, France, by de Conte in 1492. The eighty-two-year-old narrator tells readers that he is about to relate the story of something that he experienced in his childhood. He explains that as a childhood friend of Joan of Arc and then later as her page and secretary, he was with her for her whole life. Thus, he feels confident enough to tell her story, which he believes should be told since she was the noblest person ever to be born after Christ.

Born two years earlier than Joan, Sieur Louis de Conte begins life in a small town called Neufchâteau in France. His childhood is characterized by the misfortunes brought on by the Hundred Years' War, which has been fought by the French against the English and Burgundian armies for the past seventy-five years. France has not been faring well at this stage and is losing morale. When de Conte's family dies at the hands of the Burgundians, the five-year-old boy is sent to Domrémy, where he lives with a priest and is mothered by the priest's housekeeper.

In Domrémy, de Conte meets the young Joan of Arc who, although leading a relatively simple and quiet life, shows early signs of the greatness that lies ahead of her. He describes a number of episodes that exhibit her sagacity and clear-headed judgment, from which the town benefits. He is so close with Joan that when she reaches fourteen years of age, he notices a peculiar change in her constitution and in her behavior, resulting in her assuming a much more serious air. A year and a half later, de Conte is told that Joan has been visited on a regular basis by messengers of God. On May 15, 1428, she is told by God that she has been chosen to lead France's armies back to glory and to assist Charles, the dauphin (heir) of France, in claiming his kingship. Initially, Joan is hesitant to act upon this message, but she soon becomes overwhelmed with the compulsion to answer her calling. The first book concludes with Joan facing the challenge of the governor of Vaucouleurs, who refuses to provide her with the necessary escort of men-at-arms that she needs in order to complete her mission.

Committed to her mission, Joan eventually is provided with an escort and journeys to the Castle of Chinon. There, she intends to share her mission with the dauphin. Before she is granted access, however, she is challenged to identify the future king, who has changed into layman's clothes. Joan easily identifies Charles and even gives him an additional sign, thoroughly convincing him that she truly is on a divine mission. He appoints her the general of the armies of France, and she sets about organizing her campaign. She begins her campaign by sending a letter to the English at Orléans, ordering them to abandon their siege of the city. She then establishes policies with her troops, banning gambling and the frequenting of prostitutes, and orders that they make confession and attend a divine service twice daily. Joan also dresses androgynously, fully clad in armor and wearing her hair cropped short.

Joan and her army march across France and have great success, as Joan is consistently encouraged by her spiritual messengers. They do not always have good news; in one instance, they warn her that she will be shot in the neck with an arrow, a prophecy that comes true the next day. Joan sustains the injury and her army goes on to have many more successes, giving the French army their first major advantage in ninety-one years. The coronation of King Charles occurs on July 5, 1429, but Joan is unsatisfied and insists on continuing on to Paris. She receives permission to march on Paris, but then the king ends the campaign, calling a truce instead. On May 24, 1430, Joan is captured by the Burgundians at Marguy and is held prisoner.

When the third book opens, Joan is still being held prisoner by the Burgundians, who have asked King Charles to pay a ransom for her release. She is held for five months while they wait for the ransom, which the king never provides. Eventually, Joan is sold to the English, who hold her prisoner. Led by Bishop Pierre Cauchon of Beauvais, the English decide that in order to try to lessen Joan's influence over her countrymen, they will charge her with crimes against the faith. De Conte provides a meticulous account and a transcript of the three-month-long trial in which, despite the exhaustive attempts of the English and Burgundians to befuddle her, Joan rises to all of their questions with bold answers and a steadfast commitment to herself and to her faith. However, after being imprisoned and being treated so poorly for so long, the illiterate nineteen-year-old signs a document that confesses herself a witch, a liar, a blasphemer, and a messenger of the devil. The document

"As she said those last words a sudden deep glow shone in her eyes, which I was to see there many times in after-days when the bugles sounded the charge and learn to call it the battle-light. Her Breast heaved, and the colour rose in her face. 'But today I know. God has chosen the meanest of His creatures for this work; and by His command, and in His protection, and by His strength, not mine, I am to lead His armies, and win back France, and set the crown upon the head of His servant that is Dauphin and shall be King.'"

Personal Recollections of Joan of Arc

also binds her to dress like a woman, which she does. She soon breaks this promise, however. According to de Conte, one night while she sleeps, a guard steals her feminine apparel and leaves in its place her masculine attire. De Conte reports that knowing what will happen if she puts on the masculine attire, Joan dresses herself in it on nonetheless, exhausted by the English attempts to see her guilty. Having broken her commitment to the document she signed, Joan is sentenced to death. She is burned at the stake on May 30, 1431.

Sieur Louis de Conte concludes the story by returning once again to his present year of 1492, reflecting on the great heroics of his remarkable friend.

ANALYSIS

Twain's interest in Joan of Arc is simultaneously understandable and surprising. Regarded as the father of American literature for having written the "great American novel," *The Adventures of Huckleberry Finn*, along with many other American classics, Twain also wrote a semibiographical account of France's heroine of the Hundred Years' War. In many ways, *Personal Recollections of Joan of Arc* is completely uncharacteristic of Twain's literary interests; most of his novels

are set in contemporary America, center on young male protagonists, and do not focus on history. Yet, several decades before Twain began researching for and writing *Personal Recollections*, interest in Joan of Arc had been revived by the release of Quicherat's records of her trial in the 1840s. By the time Twain began to work on his version of Joan of Arc in the 1880s, opinions about the heroine were felt strongly enough in Europe and in America for Twain to have been impressed and inspired by this remarkable figure. Despite Twain considering *Personal Recollections of Joan of Arc* to be his best novel, most of his critics hardly came close to sharing the sentiment. Instead of pursuing interest in the work itself, subsequent critical debates have attempted to probe exactly what it was that interested Twain in Joan of Arc.

Twain's close friend and biographer, Albert Bigelow Paine, recorded the first moment Twain considered Joan of Arc as a potential inspiration for a novel. In his book, *Mark Twain: A Biography; The Personal and Literary Life of Samuel Langhorne Clemens*, Paine relates this moment in his sixteenth chapter, titled "The Turning-Point":

> There came into his life just at this period one of those seemingly trifling incidents which, viewed in retrospect, assume pivotal proportions. He was on his way from the office to his home one afternoon when he saw flying along the pavement a square of paper, a leaf from a book. At an earlier time he would not have bothered with it at all, but any printed page had acquired a professional interest for him now. He caught the flying scrap and examined it. It was a leaf from some history of Joan of Arc. The "maid" was described in the cage at Rouen, in the fortress, and the two ruffian English soldiers had stolen her clothes. There was a brief description and a good deal of dialogue—her reproaches and their ribald replies. (81)

Twain was apparently astonished by the story he read on the paper. He did not know if it was true, and initially he did not have very much historical awareness of the topic. He consulted his well-read brother Henry, who informed him that the story was indeed true. Twain then became obsessive about researching Joan of Arc, who inspired "within him a deep compassion for the gentle Maid of Orleans, a burning resentment toward her captors, a powerful and indestructible interest in her sad history" (81).

For Paine, Twain's fortuitous discovery of the stray leaflet about the heroine was the "turning point" in his life. After learning briefly about the historical character, Twain took up her history as his own personal mission. According to Paine, "He read hungrily now everything he could find relating to the French wars, and to Joan in particular. He acquired an appetite for history in general, the record of any nation or period; he seemed likely to become a student" (82). Twain's devotion to Joan of Arc and his literary project demanded much more diligence than any of his other works ever had. According to Twain himself, he spent twelve years preparing for the writing of the book and then two years writing it, whereas his other books needed little preparation. In a letter to an acquaintance H. H. Rogers, Twain shares how much work went into the book: "I have never done any work before that cost so much thinking and weighing and measuring and planning and cramming . . . on this last third I have constantly used five French sources and five English ones, and I think no telling historical nugget in any of them has escaped me" (Gerber 196). Instead of assuming his more usual and well-known style of the wry and imaginative storyteller, for *Personal Recollections of Joan of Arc*, Twain not only felt inspired by her story, but he felt compelled to adjust his regular approaches to writing. In order to tell Joan's story, Twain adopted the role of historian.

Although Paine addresses the moment that prompted Twain's fascination with Joan of Arc and describes the subsequent steps he took in order to prepare for writing about her, he provides little information on exactly what it is about Joan's story that was so compelling to Twain. He does share that Twain was filled with a "burning compassion for her" and resentment toward her captors and executioners. Yet the ways in which discovering Joan's story functioned as a turning point in Twain's life remain somewhat elusive. Paine additionally shares that the story "crystallized suddenly within him sympathy with the oppressed, rebellion against tyranny and treachery, scorn for the divine rights of kings" (82). Having struggled with finances all his life, Twain was likely to feel compassion for the modest peasant who championed the causes of her country and then was betrayed by those who stood in a position of power and wealth above her.

A few months before he passed away, Twain published an essay titled "The Turning-Point of My Life," but in it, he does not credit the stray leaflet as inspiration as Paine does in his similarly titled chapter. Twain did,

however, write another essay called "Saint Joan of Arc," in which he goes to great length to discuss the outstanding historical figure. In the essay, he comments on the unusual exceptionality of the young woman's character: "In the world's history she stands alone—quite alone. Others have been great in their first public exhibitions of generalship, valor, legal talent, diplomacy, fortitude; but always their previous years and associations had been in a larger or smaller degree a preparation for these things. There have been no exceptions to the rule" (*Complete Essays* 321).

For Twain, Joan of Arc represents an unprecedented figure in history. He compares her to the likes of William Shakespeare, Raphael Sanzio, Richard Wagner, and Thomas Edison. In the introduction to *Personal Recollections of Joan of Arc*, as Sieur Louis de Conte, Twain additionally compares her to the outstanding military figures Julius Caesar and Napoleon Bonaparte. Joan's lack of education and training makes her undertaking as the military savior of France completely unlikely, not to mention that she was also a petite teenage girl. Her exceptionality alone made her enticing to Twain.

Twain was utterly baffled by Joan's ability to master arts that she had not been trained in, but perhaps more remarkable to him was her ability to tell true and unbelievable prophecies. In his essay, he marvels over her predictions:

> Her history has still another feature which sets her apart and leaves her without fellow or competitor: there have been many uninspired prophets, but she was the only one who ever ventured the daring detail of naming, along with a foretold event, the event's precise nature, the special time-limit within which it would occur, and the place—*and scored fulfilment.* (*Complete Essays* 322; emphasis in orig.)

Successful predictions in and of themselves are worthy of admiration, but as Twain points out, the prophecies that Joan spoke of and then saw through to fulfillment seemed to most people to be impossible. Not only were her prophecies rather audacious at the time, but they were also quite specific. As Twain highlights in his essay, she not only foretold the crowning of Charles, but she also imparted the location of the crowning: Rheims. She told Charles that it would happen within the following year, and it did. Public records document her predictions of the injuries she would receive, and of course, she did receive them. According to Twain, she even foretold her death and her subsequent martyrdom correctly. There were many other prophecies that came true, all of which Twain notes specially in his appreciation of her.

For Twain, the young and exceptional woman had also suffered an extreme and tragic historical injustice that needed to be righted. He notes in the essay that prior to her rehabilitation trial in 1456, when Joan's initial proceedings were reexamined and she was subsequently found innocent and declared a martyr, Joan was perceived by many as being a witch and a source of evil. Despite her record being cleared in 1456, Twain was still indignant about the fate that she endured at the hands of those whom he deemed to be her enemies. Expressing his thoughts through the fictionalized friend and admirer of Joan, Twain writes, "And for all reward, the French King whom she had crowned stood supine and indifferent while French priests took the noble child, the most innocent, the most lovely, the most adorable the ages have produced, and burned her alive at the stake" (10). Historians still debate over what motivated Joan's execution and the degree of guilt that should be attributed to those responsible for her death. Even other writers contemporaneous with Twain were not as certain of the historical injustice. In his preface to the play *Saint Joan* (1924), George Bernard Shaw chastises Twain for what he perceives as being Twain's idealistic ignorance of the contextual circumstances of the trial.

Although Twain's essay on Joan of Arc provides a number of insights into what it was that inspired him about Joan's character, many critics think that Twain was interested in more than he suggested, or perhaps even more than he was consciously aware of. In her book *Gender Play in Mark Twain: Cross-Dressing and Transgression*, Linda Ann Morris argues that Twain, who had already written about and imagined characters who took to cross-dressing in his other books, was probably also intrigued by this peculiar aspect of Joan of Arc's story. In her research, Morris analyzes the marginalia that Twain left behind on the sources he consulted for his research. She reports that a "careful perusal of the many historical sources Twain researched in preparing to write Joan of Arc reveals that he made numerous marginal notes in the texts related specifically to how Joan dressed" (90–91). Within Clémentine de la Morre Chabannes's *La Vierge Lorraine Jeanne d'Arc* and Marius Sepet's *Jeanne d'Arc*, Morris documents, there are numerous instances where Twain took note and careful interest in their descriptions of Joan's dress; he

even translated a passage in which Sepet describes an instance of Joan wearing feminine clothing over her masculine clothing.

Indeed, as Morris points out, many of Twain's novels involve his characters cross-dressing for some purpose. Early on in Twain's career, before he encountered the historical Joan of Arc (if Paine was correct about the timing of Twain's discovery of her), Twain had already written a story that contains cross-dressing, "An Awful Terrible Medieval Romance" (1870). As Morris notes, in this story, Twain is not only interested in cross-dressing, but also connects the practice of cross-dressing with death:

> In this initial foray, Twain sets the stage for many of the episodes of the more embellished scenes and stories of cross-dressing that would follow: he creates a female cross-dresser who is accused of fathering a child, he further blends gender categories by playing with the pronouns he assigns his characters, and he links cross-dressing with the threat of death. (27)

Cross-dressing can be found once again in another story, "1,002d Arabian Night" (1883). Though present early on in these stories, cross-dressing takes a more prominent role in Twain's novels, especially *The Prince and the Pauper*, *Pudd'nhead Wilson*, *Those Extraordinary Twins*, and *The Adventures of Huckleberry Finn*. Following Morris's assertion, long before Twain had been inspired to write *Personal Recollections of Joan of Arc*, and even while doing his research and preparing to write it, he was already interested in cross-dressing and used it as a mechanism to explore gender instabilities.

Joan of Arc's story and her tragic fate are inextricably connected to her dressing as a man, an act viewed by the church as a transgression that could be used to justify her execution. Unlike Twain's other works that involve cross-dressing, Joan of Arc's decision to cross-dress was not an invention of the author, but is instead a well-documented fact. Morris notes that Joan's cross-dressing and its connection to her death is overemphasized in *Personal Recollections*: "Joan's gender disruptions are writ at large, and they are insisted upon by Twain" (90). Twain goes to great lengths not just to describe the attire of Joan of Arc throughout the narrative, but also to contrast her simple masculine clothing with detailed descriptions of the adornments of prominent male characters, such as King Charles. Beyond just paying special attention to the aesthetic effect

MYTH INTO ART

The subject of revived critical and artistic interest since the publication of her trial by Jules Quicherat in 1841, Joan of Arc inspired further interest after her canonization in 1920, Pierre Champion's republication of the trial transcripts in 1921, and George Bernard Shaw's successful production of his play *Saint Joan* in 1923. Yet, according to director Carl Theodor Dreyer, the decision to begin production on the movie *The Passion of Joan of Arc* was determined by chance in a game of matches, beating out the other options of Marie Antoinette or Catherine de Medici. The silent film, produced in France in 1928, stars the unlikely principle actress Renée Maria Falconetti as Joan of Arc. Despite the accolades she received for her exceptional performance, the stage actress—who had never before acted in a film—never performed in film again after playing that role.

Having closely studied Champion's republished transcripts, Dreyer decided to have the film depict Joan's experience in captivity. He shows her being brought before trial, being mercilessly tortured, signing a confession, recanting, and then finally being burned at the stake. The budget for the film reportedly had one of the most expensive sets ever built for European theater at the time, which was mostly used to build a large Rouen Castle. The cinematography is characterized by tight angles and close-ups. Dreyer did not allow his cast members to wear makeup and made use of lighting and close-ups to enhance warts and other physical imperfections. Falconetti wore her hair closely shaven at the behest of Dreyer, a decision many argue left an indelible impression on subsequent conceptions of Joan of Arc's image.

The film, which was immediately hailed as a masterpiece when it premiered in 1928, has gone on to be revered as one of cinematography's finest accomplishments. Although the original version of the film was lost for decades after being destroyed by a fire, it was rediscovered in 1981 in the janitor's closet of a mental institution in Oslo, Norway.

of Joan's cross-dressing, Twain also consistently acknowledges the repeated occasions in which her choice of attire offends people around her. He states, "There had been grave doubts among the priests as to whether the Church ought to permit a female soldier to dress like a man" (164). Although the transcripts hint at the reason why Joan insisted on cross-dressing, and historians have offered many plausible reasons, such as the virgin's fear of being raped, Twain does not seem interested in explaining what compelled Joan to insist on dressing as a man. Instead, he seems more interested in what the act of cross-dressing enables and the different implications that result from it.

Analysis of the scenes involving cross-dressing in Twain's most celebrated novel, *The Adventures of Huckleberry Finn*, provides some insight into exactly what Twain was interested in exploring through Joan of Arc's assumption of masculine attire. Morris notes that "cross-dressing and other forms of gender transgression in Twain's work clearly challenge the socially constructed nature of gender boundaries; this in turn both creates and reveals deep-seated anxieties about the corporeal body, the site upon which and through which gender is performed" (40). In *The Adventures of Huckleberry Finn*, Morris additionally notes that "cross-dressing is also firmly linked with racial crossings and racial transgressions" (28).

Cross-dressing is used as a way to negotiate racial boundaries within *The Adventures of Huckleberry Finn*, and in *Personal Recollections of Joan of Arc*, it works much to the same effect. Joan's decision to dress in masculine attire provoked deep-seated anxieties about women's bodies that were present at the time of her trial and persisted into Twain's historical context. According to some sources, Joan's body was examined at least once in order to ensure that she was female. Other sources even report that she was burned at the stake so that the public could have definitive proof about her physical sex. Such a death completely absolves the corporeal body that was responsible for provoking such anxiety. Along these lines, Joan of Arc's insistence on crossing gender boundaries preempted the crucial boundary that she would eventually cross: the boundary between life and martyrdom. For Twain, Joan of Arc's cross-dressing ostensibly marks her as an exceptional historical character and also enables her ultimate transcendence.

Morris's assertions about Twain's use of cross-dressing to explore gender boundaries and to enable him and his characters to cross social boundaries are thought provoking. Despite the critical failure of *Personal Recollections of Joan of Arc*, analyses like Morris's provide insights into Twain's interests beyond his writing of American classics. What is clear, and what Twain goes to great lengths to make clear, is that the story and the person of Joan of Arc are truly unprecedented and exceptional by all standards. As a champion of her greatness, Twain's voice is but a voice in the crowd of the many who praise the multifaceted and widely revered heroine.

CROSS-CULTURAL INFLUENCE

In the preface to his play, *Saint Joan*, which premiered in December 1923, George Bernard Shaw reflects on Mark Twain's *Personal Recollections of Joan of Arc* amid the extensive list of literary treatments of her. Among the many critics of Twain's take on the legendary and historical heroine, Shaw characterizes Twain's work as being much like the works of Voltaire and Friedrich Schiller, whom he accuses of romanticizing the heroine. He remarks that "Mark Twain was converted to downright worship of Joan directly by Quicherat" and that Twain "writes his biography frankly in the form of a romance" (25, 26). For Shaw, these romantic accounts of Joan's are not compelling because their worship-like description devalues what he deems to be an otherwise fair valuation. By writing *Saint Joan*, Shaw sought to reconstruct the narrative and character of Joan of Arc in what he conceived of as being a more historically conscious and solemn dramatization of her life.

According to Shaw, the common mistake he encountered among the romantic treatments of Joan's character is their failure to accurately account for her own historical context. He explains in his preface that "to see her in her proper perspective you must understand Christendom and the Catholic Church, the Holy Roman Empire and the Feudal System, as they existed and were understood in the Middle Ages" (26–27). Shaw attributes Twain's idealistic vision of Joan to his unconscious desire to imagine Joan by his own Victorian standards for women. Shaw finds Twain "determined to make Joan a beautiful and most ladylike Victorian" and describes the American writer as being "out of the court from the beginning" (26, 27), after describing what he perceived as Twain's inept attempt to be historically empathetic. For Shaw, Twain's *Personal Recollections of Joan of Arc* holds Joan in an esteem that the historical heroine

deserves but goes about it in a completely idealized and therefore uncompelling way.

Shaw, who is famous for having penned more than sixty plays, was also a critic, essayist, fiction writer, and socialist thinker. Despite his criticism regarding the romantic idealization of Joan of Arc, Shaw had long appreciated her and considered writing about her. With the great deal of popular interest in her following the release of the Quicherat records in the 1840s and her canonization in 1920—the latter of which occurred in his own lifetime—Shaw had the incentive he needed to write the play. His extensive preface that accompanies the 1924 publication of the play reveals that Shaw had thought at length about the historical character and on how he would not only go about portraying her in his drama, but also on how he might right some of the wrongs he found in earlier literary imaginings. Shaw meticulously researched Joan's historical context and anything related to Joan that he could find. He made himself extensively familiar with the literary renditions of her life—the antecedents to his play—and conceptualized where he thought his play would sit among them. He explains in his epilogue to the preface that he felt "it was necessary by hook or crook to shew the canonized Joan as well as the incinerated one" (53) and that as a result his drama "may give the essential truth of it" (51).

The truth that Shaw reached after his extensive research is that despite the tragedy of Joan's execution, her executioners may not have been as villainous as one might believe. According to Shaw, Bishop Pierre Cauchon of Beauvais, Inquisitor Jean Lemaître, the Earl of Warwick, and others who were concerned in the matter of Joan's execution acted in good faith and based their judgments on what they thought were the principles of their faith. Shaw explains, "To Shakespear as to Mark Twain, Cauchon would have been a tyrant and a bully instead of a Catholic, and the Inquisitor Lemaître would have been a Sadist instead of a lawyer. Warwick would have had no more feudal quality than his successor the King Maker has in the play of Henry VI" (49–50). Shaw did not find the situation so readily disposed to the traditional dichotomies of good versus evil or black and white; instead, the real tragedy of his play is found in the gray areas, the space between clear judgments. He explains, "There are no villains in the piece. Crime, like disease, is not interesting: it is something to be done away with by general consent, and that is all [there is] about it. It is what men do at their best, with good intentions, and what normal men and women find that they must and will do in spite of their intentions, that really concern us" (50). Thus, to treat any of Shaw's characters as archetypal arbiters of good or evil would be reductive.

The play, described by the playwright in a subtitle as "A Chronicle Play in Six Scenes and an Epilogue," begins in the year 1429 CE, on "a fine spring morning on the river Meuse" at the castle of Vaucouleurs (57). The first scene opens with military squire Captain Robert de Baudricourt complaining about his hens' inability to produce eggs, when he is told of the arrival of a young maid (Joan) who demands to meet with him and refuses to go away until her request is appeased. When Joan is given an audience, she tells him that she hears the voices of the archangel Michael, Saint Margaret, and Saint Catherine, who, sent by God, have told her that she must lift the siege against Orléans, accompanied by his men-at-arms. De Baudricourt initially derides the peasant girl, who also tells him that she will crown the dauphin, but he eventually feels inspired by her and decides to give her his consent. At the end of the scene, de Baudricourt's servant declares that the hens are laying eggs, which de Baudricourt believes is a sign from God.

Joan is then received by the dauphin, Charles, whom she also tells of her voices and her great mission. Through her flattery and her strong sense of leadership, she convinces him that she is destined to lead France to glory. Joan receives her support and sets about her mission, commiserating with Jean Dunois, the Bastard of Orléans, on the battlefield before successfully breaking the Siege of Orléans. The dramatic time allotted to her success is short lived, however, and Joan is soon betrayed and captured at Compiègne. Her trial begins immediately after her capture. Bishop John de Stogumber, a character Shaw created for the play, is forceful in his argument that Joan should be immediately executed, while Bishop Cauchon, the inquisitor, and other church officials are more prudent and carefully deliberate over the exact nature of her heresy. While on trial, Joan steadfastly holds to her conviction that she is visited by angels who speak to her as messengers from God.

Under the pressure of torture, Joan signs a document that renounces her assertion of hearing voices and is then told that in so doing she will be granted her life in permanent confinement. Hearing this, Joan decides that she would rather die than live such a life, and she faces her execution. Once again, de Stogumber demands her immediate execution while the bishop and inquisitor excommunicate her and then give her to the English.

The bishop and inquisitor acknowledge her naïveté and her fundamental innocence. After seeing her burned at the stake, de Stogumber, Joan's strongest opponent, appears shaken and confesses that he had not entirely understood the horror of the punishment he had demanded for her.

The epilogue occurs twenty-five years following Joan's execution. A nullification trial has just declared Joan's innocence. This news is brought to King Charles, who is then visited by Joan in a dream. Joan happily speaks with Charles in the dream, as well as with enemies and acquaintances, who enter the dream. The men discuss with Joan their fates and their feelings toward her. They are visited by an emissary from 1920 (a few years prior to present day at the time of the play's performance), who tells them that Joan will be canonized by the Catholic Church in 1920. Joan asks to be resurrected so that she can perform miracles, but she is slowly abandoned by everyone; they express that that world is not capable of receiving a saint like her. The play concludes with Joan left alone on stage bemoaning that the world and humanity are unable to accept saints.

Saint Joan was an international success and is likely the reason that Shaw won the Nobel Prize in Literature in 1925. However, his nonheroic treatment of Joan did lead to some criticism. After seeing the play, T. S. Eliot wrote in his review for *The Criterion* that Shaw's version of Joan of Arc "is perhaps the greatest sacrilege of all Joans: for instead of the saint or the strumpet of the legends to which he objects, he has turned her into a great middle-class reformer, and her place is a little higher than Mrs. Pankhurst" (1–5). Emmeline Pankhurst, though an important and commendable leader of the women's suffragist movement, was no Joan of Arc for Eliot. More contemporary critics of Shaw's play range from Harold Bloom, who describes the play as being overwhelmingly Protestant; to feminist critics such as J. Ellen Gainor; to drama critics Alexander W. Allison, Arthur J. Carr, and Arthur M. Eastman. The play has been reproduced and adapted numerous times and has even been painstakingly annotated by Arnold Jacques Silver, who gives a scene-by-scene analysis of the play's historicism in the book *Saint Joan: Playing with Fire*.

At the beginning of his prologue, Shaw anticipates the inevitable adaptations and modifications that would be made to the play. Despite whatever negative criticisms he may have received or suggestions for the play's improvement, Shaw, like Joan, remained steadfast to his earlier vision. Indeed, the vision of Joan of Arc was an important one in Shaw's life. When he died at the age of ninety-four in 1950, Shaw's ashes were scattered in his backyard gardens, along the footpaths and around his statue of Saint Joan.

Katherine Sehl, MA

BIBLIOGRAPHY

Eliot, T. S. "A Commentary." *Criterion* 3.9 (1924): 1–5. Print.

Gerber, John C. *Mark Twain*. Boston: Twayne, 1988. Print.

Holroyd, Michael. *Bernard Shaw: The One-Volume Definitive Edition*. New York: Norton, 2006. Print.

Morris, Linda A. *Gender Play in Mark Twain: Cross-Dressing and Transgression*. Columbia: U of Missouri P, 2007. Print.

Paine, Albert Bigelow. *Mark Twain: A Biography; The Personal and Literary Life of Samuel Langhorne Clemens*. New York: Harper, 1912. Print.

Shaw, George Bernard. *Saint Joan*. 1924. New York: Penguin, 2003. Print.

Silver, Arnold Jacques. *Saint Joan: Playing with Fire*. New York: Twayne, 1993. Print.

Twain, Mark. *The Complete Essays of Mark Twain*. Ed. Charles Neider. 1963. Cambridge: Da Capo, 2000. Print.

--—. *Sieur Louis de Conte: Personal Recollections of Joan of Arc*. Internet Medieval Sourcebook. Fordham University, n.d. Web. 1 Apr. 2013.

---. *Personal Recollections of Joan of Arc*. New York: Oxford UP, 1996. Print.

---. *What Is Man? and Other Essays*. New York: Harper, 1917. Print..

The Queen of Sheba

Author: Traditional
Time Period: 999 BCE–1 BCE
Country or Culture: Ethiopia; Southern Levant
Genre: Legend

OVERVIEW

The Queen of Sheba is most widely known through her brief but memorable appearances in the Hebrew Bible and in the Qur'an. She has been celebrated in story and song throughout Europe and the Middle East. It is, however, Ethiopian tradition that has most expanded the legend of this mysterious and elusive figure. According to Ethiopian lore, she ruled wisely at a time and in a place where women were hereditary rulers, until she broke the custom by relinquishing her throne to her son, Menelik I (also called Bayna-Lehkem and David II), believed to have been begotten by the fabled Israelite king Solomon. Though she is given no personal name in either the Bible or the Qur'an, Islamic oral tradition calls her Bilqis or Balqis, while Josephus, a Jewish Roman historian of the first century CE, identifies her as Nicaule in his *Jewish Antiquities*. Among the Ethiopian people, to whom she means the most, she is known as Makeda. In the New Testament, Jesus refers to her as the Queen of the South.

Outside the holy books of the Jews, Christians, and Muslims, the Queen of Sheba belongs to varying legends, not all of them in agreement. Her historical reality is also questioned by many secular scholars and archeologists, despite the persistence of her legend. Assuming she really did live and reign, even the land of her origin and the people over whom she ruled are open to conjecture, as the legends differ in where they locate her geographically. Josephus says that she is the queen of Egypt and Ethiopia. Nubia, south of ancient Egypt, was believed to have been ruled in ancient times by a series of warrior queens, and some have suggested Sheba was one of them. Another long tradition associates her with Saba, a monarchy in ancient Yemen. Still others have suggested that she may have been the ruler of a trading colony in northwestern Arabia.

The varying versions agree that her kingdom possesses great wealth and that she is well endowed with servants, camels, and other beasts of burden. Gold, silver, precious jewels, and valuable spices are plentiful in her realm. She is also a fiercely independent woman, often described as a virgin queen regnant, not a royal consort. Moreover, though she seeks advice from her counselors, she ultimately makes her own decision to embark on her famous visit to the court of Solomon.

Though the biblical account of Sheba's visit to Jerusalem makes clear that she sought wisdom, later embellishments proposed a romantic liaison between her and Solomon, who was known as much for his love of foreign women as for his wisdom. But because Solomon's kingdom was situated at a trade crossroad, a more pragmatic motive may have sent her traveling: a trade mission to promote the coveted spices produced in her realm.

The fullest account of the Queen of Sheba's visit to Solomon's court is found in the treasured Ethiopian document *Kebra Nagast*, which has been available in English since the 1922 publication of a translation by Sir E. A. Wallis Budge. The work is venerated by the Ethiopian people, considered proof of their association with the ancient Israelites and of the Solomonic line of their legitimate rulers, ending with Haile Selassie in the twentieth century. This last emperor designated himself the Lion of Judah and used the lion on his crest. The *Kebra Nagast* also addresses the patriotic longings of the Ethiopians by identifying their country as a new promised land. Because the majority of the Ethiopian people accepted Christianity from early times, their kinship with Jesus, a Jew, is also affirmed by the document.

Ethiopians believe the text was found in the library of St. Sofia in Constantinople (now Istanbul) in the third century CE, but European scholars believe it to be a fourteenth-century compilation of Abyssinian history and folklore. In it, King Solomon is reported to have made the prophecy that Ethiopia would usurp Israel as the Promised Land favored by God.

The third important figure in the Sheba legend is her son, Menelik (Menyelek), who, according to the *Kebra Nagast*, bore an extraordinary resemblance to his father, Solomon. He is credited with founding the royal dynasty, which lasted centuries, ending with Haile Selassie. Like his parents, he is remembered as a seeker after wisdom and is believed to have transported the Ark of the Covenant from Jerusalem to Aksum, where it is said to lodge to this very day.

The legends of the Queen of Sheba have been important to people of several nationalities and cultural heritages for a number of reasons. They not only support national aspirations and pride but also associate Sheba with the ancient wisdom tradition, which transcended tribal and national boundaries. Another reason the Queen of Sheba is venerated today is that she is, however shadowy her historical authenticity, one of the relatively few dominant female figures of ancient narratives. While other women have sought domestic security or prided themselves on their beauty, taking subservient roles to men, Sheba dominated her own court and was an equal in foreign ones. Though relatively little is known of the real woman, Sheba has cast a strong shadow down the ages and continues to speak with a pertinent message.

SUMMARY

The legend of the Queen of Sheba is one of the most pervasive of the ancient Near East. The Hebrew Bible mentions the queen's visit to Solomon rather briefly as part of the long saga of Israel's most majestic king. This episode is found in 1 Kings 10:1–13 and reiterated in 2 Chronicles 9:1–12. According to the Hebrew Bible, Sheba in her distant land hears rumors of the wisdom and wealth of Solomon. A lover of wisdom herself, she arrives in Jerusalem after a long trip with a large retinue. She comes to test the king with "hard questions" in order to find out if there is truth to the reports she has heard (1 Kgs 10:1). According to the second verse, "she communed with him of all that was in her heart." The more philosophical Jews of the first century CE believed these questions probed the nature of divinity and the meaning of life. But the oral tradition regarded them as clever riddles designed to leave Solomon speechless. All agree that whatever the questions are, he provides impressive answers. In his great

"And the Queen Makeda spake unto King Solomon, saying 'Blessed art thou, my Lord, in that much wisdom and understanding have been given unto thee. For myself I only wish that I could be as one of the least of thine handmaidens, so that I could wash thy feet, and hearken to thy wisdom, and apprehend thy understanding, and serve thy majesty, and enjoy thy wisdom. O how greatly have pleased me thy answering and the sweetness of thy voice, and the beauty of thy going, and the graciousness of thy words, and the readiness thereof.'"

Kebra Nagast

wisdom, Solomon is able to answer all her questions and resolve all her perplexities. After her dialogues with him, Sheba confesses that she had not believed the reports heard in her own land of his wisdom and prosperity. Now, having seen with her own eyes, she realizes that not even the half of it had been told. Somewhat enviously, she concludes: "Happy are thy men, happy are these thy servants, which stand continually before thee, and that hear thy wisdom. / Blessed be the Lord thy God, which delighted in thee, to set thee on the throne of Israel: because the Lord loved Israel for ever, therefore made he thee king, to do judgment and justice" (1 Kgs 10:8–9).

Sheba, herself from a wealthy land, is also impressed by the elegance and lavishness of Solomon's court. Many valuable gifts are exchanged between the sovereigns, and Solomon offers her everything her heart desires. When the queen finally departs for her own land, it is with a bit of wistfulness and an admiration for the god who has bestowed such wisdom and discernment in judgment on his anointed, Solomon. The biblical account does not suggest that either a sexual union or a religious conversion took place.

Josephus's tale largely follows the biblical account, though he had access to subsequent Jewish legends surrounding the queen and the Solomon of history and lore. In his *Jewish Antiquities*, Josephus writes that after building and dedicating the temple—a major achievement during the reign of Solomon and the fulfillment of a dream of his father, David—Solomon sets about constructing a sumptuous palace for himself, thirteen years in the making (140). Lined with columns, the palace is built of white marble and the cedars of Lebanon and decorated with much gold and silver. For himself, the king commissions an ivory throne.

Solomon also constructs "towers into the walls around Jerusalem to fortify it" (140). He builds several cities, complete with springs and wells in the desert, as well as a fleet of ships, presumably to carry fine goods for trade in foreign lands. Sheba, here named the queen of Ethiopia and Egypt, is described as both "a great lover of wisdom" and a woman of great wealth herself, who, hearing rumors about Solomon, decides to visit his realm herself and "test his wisdom" (140).

Although Josephus acknowledges Solomon's habit of marrying foreign women, there is no mention of any liaison with Sheba, a woman who, according to his characterization of her, would hardly take second place to any man. Likewise, though Josephus remarks on the impression the temple sacrifices make upon Sheba, there is no mention of any conversion to monotheism.

The Holy Qur'an provides additional information not found in earlier written sources. In the sura known as "The Ants," Solomon (or Suleiman) is described as conversant with animals. When a bird brings him news from the land of Sheba, where a woman is found ruling over the people, he is intrigued. She is wealthy and virtuous, he is told, but she and her subjects, unfortunately, are sun worshippers and do not know the true God. Satan, Solomon is assured, has seduced them from the straight path. The king sends a message to Sheba by the bird "in the Name of God, the Lord of Mercy, the Giver of Mercy" (Q27:30). She receives the message, which admonishes humility and extends an invitation for a state visit. There is an implied threat in Solomon's message, and the queen, fearing an invasion, decides to send a gift and await a reply. She also consults her nobles, who defer to her own judgment. But Solomon replies through her envoy. He suspects she intends to pacify him with gold and tells her that God has given him a gift far greater than riches. He instructs her

servant to return and warn her that her people will be humbled by the Israelites.

In the Qur'an, Solomon is harsher than in other versions. He orders Sheba's throne to be miraculously transported to him. Then he commands that it be altered and waits to see if she will discern the changes. When at last she arrives in Jerusalem in person, she recognizes her throne. Then, a curious detail enters the narrative. When Sheba arrives at the palace, it has been paved with polished glass. Because she thinks it is water, she lifts her clothing, exposing her feet.

As the visit progresses, Solomon concludes that admirable though Sheba may be, false gods have led her astray. She admits to having sinned but promises to submit with Solomon to Allah, the god of the universe. The message is clear: Allah alone controls the universe, and it is essential for all to acknowledge and worship him, just as the queen and Solomon do.

By far the fullest account of the legend of the Queen of Sheba comes from Ethiopia, the country that exalts her above all others. Her story is told at length in the *Kebra Nagast*, the national epic, which supports the Solomonic origin of the Ethiopian monarchy, locates the lost Ark of the Covenant at Aksum, and asserts that God transferred his earthly abode from Jerusalem to Aksum.

In its fuller portraits of both Solomon and Sheba, the *Kebra Nagast* makes several additions to their legend. A merchant named Tamrin, who had been on a trade mission to Jerusalem, returns to his native land and his queen, here called Makeda. Though Tamrin has left the luxury and comfort of Solomon's court with reluctance, duty to his own queen has called him. He returns not empty handed but laden with costly gifts for Makeda. She listens to his tales of the wonders of the land of Solomon the Wise. He speaks of the graciousness, authority, and fair judgments of its king. He tells her how generously Solomon treats even his servants and how he listens to them, just as they partake daily of his own wisdom.

Each morning, Tamrin tells the queen more and more about Solomon, until she is filled with a yearning to behold the mighty king for herself. But the journey to Jerusalem is long, difficult, and dangerous. It is God, in his own providential design, who increases the desire in Makeda's heart to behold Solomon in all his glory.

Speaking to her people of her thirst for wisdom, Makeda prepares for her journey to Jerusalem. She explains how wisdom surpasses gold, silver, and precious

MYTH INTO ART

With her glamour and mystery, it is not surprising that the Queen of Sheba has inspired many artistic representations. Though the oldest sources of her legend give no physical description, artists have concluded that she was a woman of youth, beauty, and allure. In an anonymous sixteenth-century drawing from Persia (now Iran), she is shown in lazy, luxurious recline, surrounded by motifs that represent her character and destiny in Islamic lore. Traditional Ethiopian depictions feature Sheba in active, stylized poses and vivid colors, while European Renaissance artists clothed Sheba and Solomon in the raiments seen in the royal courts of their time.

In Western Christian art, the work of Lorenzo Ghiberti (ca. 1378–1455) merits special attention. His gilded bronzes are a Renaissance treasure of the Duomo in Florence, Italy. The queen before Solomon is vividly depicted in one of ten panels from *The Gates of Paradise* (ca. 1426–52), which surround the cathedral baptistery. The panels commemorate events from the Hebrew Bible that were believed to have prophetic application to the Gospel story. Solomon and Sheba are elaborately arrayed in the style of a Renaissance court. They are accompanied by courtiers and attendants, some with horses and other fine animals. A few appear to be bearing gifts, while on Solomon's side, court musicians are playing. Arches and columns from the artist's own period form a background to the scene. Solomon and Sheba greet one another as equals, shaking hands, in contrast to other Renaissance renditions in which Sheba performs obeisance or curtsies to Solomon. The king and queen appear to be the same age, mature rather than in first youth, and are of comparable stature. Ghiberti's work is prized for its intricate detail, its stateliness, and the way in which the artist has brought together the central themes of the story, as interpreted by European Christians of his time.

stones in value, satisfies more than choice meat, gladdens more than wine, and offers protection and comfort. It is the best of all treasures, she concludes, and she loves wisdom as if it were her own child. Her nobles, slaves, handmaidens, and advisers all agree and bless her journey, finding it fitting that the wisest of queens should meet the wisest of kings.

The journey requires many preparations and is initiated with much pomp. Her retinue includes, in addition to many attendants, "797 camels and mules and asses innumerable" (Budge lxviii), all laden with treasures from her land.

After many days, she arrives in Jerusalem and presents her precious gifts to Solomon, who receives her as befits her station. He provides her with fine quarters in the royal palace, near his own apartments. Night and day, she and her servants are given the finest food and wine. Fifty singers, evenly split among men and women, are engaged to entertain her. She is presented with the finest clothes. Every day, she converses with Solomon, observing how justly he deals with his people. Never has she known a man so eloquent and graceful in all his movements. She is most moved by his reverence for God. In his supplications, he does not ask God for military victory, long life, riches, or renown. He asks instead for the wisdom and understanding that can only come from God.

Makeda agrees with Solomon that humans are worth nothing unless they learn to show kindness and love. Only fools live in sin and engage in magic, sorcery, and idol worship. Compassion, humility, and the fear of God give human beings their only majesty. Though some of her subjects still bow to graven images of stone and wood, the queen explains that she and most of her people worship the sun, sustenance of all life, a fit object of reverence until one learns of the true god. The queen tells Solomon that she has heard of the wonderful works of the Israelites' god. Solomon then instructs her in the worship of this true god, the lord of the universe, creator of angels and humans. The queen, easily persuaded, informs him: "From this moment I will not worship the sun, but will worship the Creator of the sun, the God of Israel" (Budge 29). Furthermore, she expresses her intention to instruct her kingdom to do likewise.

For six months, she remains in Jerusalem, according to the *Kebra Nagast*, conversing daily with Solomon as with an equal, marveling that even the birds and wild animals come to "hearken unto his voice" (30). But finally, somewhat sadly, duty calls, and it is time to return to her own land. When she so informs Solomon, he notes again her extraordinary beauty and concludes that God, for some purpose, has sent her to him from the ends of the earth. A collector of foreign women, Solomon wishes to add her to his harem. Already he had married four hundred women from surrounding nations and taken six hundred concubines, reasoning that together they will produce progeny loyal to God. Yet, so far, there have been no heirs.

The *Kebra Nagast* explains with delicacy that "those early people lived under the law of the flesh, for the grace of the Holy Spirit had not been given unto them" to institute the law of monogamy (Budge 31). Reluctant to see Makeda leave, Solomon concocts a seduction plan. He prepares splendid quarters for her, decorated with carpets, marble, and gems. Costly incense is sprinkled heavily about. For the feast of departure, Solomon sets out many dishes, all highly spiced, and drinks mingled with vinegar. Fish and other dishes are served, all seasoned with pepper. When Solomon bids her goodnight, he says, "Take thou thine ease here for love's sake until daybreak" (33). Probably knowing his reputation as a lover of women, she makes him promise that he will not force himself upon her, since she is a virgin and unprotected. Solomon gives his promise, but on one condition, that she take nothing that belongs to him. Makeda reminds him that her own kingdom has great wealth and there is nothing in his palace that she desires.

Solomon tells a servant to place a vessel of cool water not far from the queen's bed. He himself pretends to retire for the night. The queen, thirsty after her heavy meal, reaches for the water. At that moment, Solomon appears, seizing her hand. She has tried to consume his water without permission, thereby breaking her oath and freeing him from his, which she readily acknowledges. During the night Solomon then spends with Makeda, he has a brilliant dream in which a divine radiance leaves Israel and flies away to Ethiopia, where it shines ever more brightly.

Makeda had already reigned for six years in her own country and was a woman of excellent reputation, held deeply in the affections of her people. Solomon, knowing this, agrees to send her away, again with many fine gifts. But most important of all, he gives her a ring from his little finger as a token of remembrance. This ring, he says, will be a sign if a child is born of their brief union, and he hopes one day to see this child.

On her way back to her own land, after nine months and five days, the queen gives birth to a son. He does not learn the identity of his father until the age of twelve, but as a man, he visits Jerusalem and meets his father face to face. Everyone sees immediately that he has the likeness of Solomon. Assisted by an angel and the high priest Azariah, this son steals the Ark of the Covenant, moving it to Ethiopia where, many believe, it remains. Solomon at first angrily pursues the thief of the ark but, when informed by an angel that his own son is the culprit, concedes its loss.

Long after Solomon's reign was only the memory of a golden age, the Queen of Sheba would remain a symbol of wisdom and graciousness. In Matthew 12:42 (and repeated almost identically in Luke 11:31), Jesus says, "The queen of the south shall rise up in the judgment with this generation, and shall condemn it: for she came from the uttermost parts of the earth to hear the wisdom of Solomon; and behold, a greater than Solomon is here."

Medieval Christianity built Sheba's legend further, associating her with the much-sought-after true cross. According to Jacobus de Voragine's *Golden Legend* (seemingly influenced by the apocryphal Gospel of Nicodemus), during her visit to Solomon's court, she has a vision and venerates a tree whose wood is later used to fashion the cross on which Jesus is crucified.

Medieval Christians were also intrigued by the Song of Songs from the Hebrew Bible. From ancient times attributed to Solomon, this collection of seemingly secular, even erotic love lyrics became associated in the popular mind with the Queen of Sheba. "I am black, but comely, O ye daughters of Jerusalem" (1:5) is the self-description of the bride figure in the Song of Songs, and she describes her beloved as "fair" and having "doves' eyes" (1:15). Song of Songs 3:11 even states, "Behold King Solomon . . . in the day of his espousals."

In Jewish extrabiblical lore, additional details were added to the career of the Queen of Sheba. In the *Targum Sheni*, a hoopoe bird leads Solomon to contemplate the wealthy land of Sheba. The dust of that land, he is told, is more valuable than gold, and the silver is as plentiful as dirt. Trees growing there originated in paradise before the Fall of Man. The hoopoe becomes Solomon's first messenger to the queen, conveying the command that she visit him. Else, he threatens many misfortunes. To ward off possible invasion, she loads her caravan to make the journey. When she arrives, he receives her grandly in a glass house. Thinking that

Solomon is seated in water—so polished is the floor of his receiving chamber—she lifts her clothing as if to wade toward him. Thus, he notices that her feet are hairy like those of an animal. This is the only tarnish on her beauty, and the disfigurement features significantly in subsequent tales about Sheba. The *Targum Sheni* also records several riddles Sheba is said to have given Solomon to test his cleverness. They are much like the riddles solved by other figures of folklore and must once have been found amusing and challenging. Solomon answers them quickly and correctly.

ANALYSIS

The Queen of Sheba, as she is remembered in the Hebrew Bible and the Christian New Testament, takes her place in the wisdom tradition expressed in the thought and literature of the ancient world. According to the Bible, at the beginning of his reign Solomon was asked by God what he wished above all else. Instead of asking for riches, he asked for wisdom to judge his people rightly. God, pleased by his altruistic request, bestowed upon him both wisdom and riches. Considered the wisest of men, he is traditionally credited with the authorship of several books of the Bible that fall into the "wisdom" category: Proverbs, Ecclesiastes, and, in the Jewish Apocrypha, the Wisdom of Solomon.

Wisdom was prized in ancient Israel and neighboring lands and often personified in literature as a beautiful woman or an elderly sage. Wisdom books were created not only by the Israelites but also by the Sumerians, Babylonians, and Egyptians. Many of the similes, metaphors, allegories, and contrastive statements in these varying bodies of literature were similar, if not almost identical, because the pursuit of wisdom was not regarded as the unique attribute of a particular nation, and sages could come from any land, borrowing freely from one another. Rather than esoteric utterances, mystical rhapsodies, or systematic philosophies, the proverbs and admonitions found in wisdom literature are usually pragmatic and often especially mindful of youth, with the aged sharing their experience—and the wisdom gained from it—with the young.

Until later embellishments were added to her story, reflecting different preoccupations and cultural values, the Queen of Sheba remained a woman who prized wisdom above all. She sought Solomon not for love or for commerce but for wisdom. He respected her mind, finding joy in a woman who could converse with him as an equal. Although she is not an Israelite but a foreigner, not a man but a woman, she takes her place among the truly wise people of the Bible. Ethiopian lore gives her an especially exalted status as the bringer of true religion to that country. Wisdom and piety were closely associated in these ancient writings, because "the fear of the Lord is the beginning of wisdom" (Proverbs 9:10).

In the Qur'an, the queen accepts the worship of the one god; in the Hebrew Bible, there is only the hint that she might. But everywhere true wisdom leads to authentic religion, both Judaism and Islam agree. In several versions of her legend, Sheba gives up the worship of the sun (or pagan idols depending on the variant) for the true faith she learns from Solomon.

It is well known that in certain periods of Jewish history, as in the centuries after the Dispersion, higher learning and the study of theology have been considered unsuitable pursuits for a woman. But Sheba is one woman who is honored not for her domestic contributions or even her statecraft but for her thirst for knowledge. In the New Testament, she is invoked by Jesus, when he laments the inability of those around him to perceive truth, and he calls down the Queen of the South in judgment against their willful ignorance.

Feminist interpreters of sacred writings and ancient folklore also find reassurance in the life and career of the Queen of Sheba. According to one version of her story, she comes from a land where women have always ruled, a true matriarchal society. Whether from a matriarchal dynasty or not, she is a successful and wealthy ruler who, rather than send her ministers and messengers, plans an elaborate state visit herself. She is ready even to disregard the advice of her male counselors when her own judgment suggests otherwise. When she appears at Solomon's court, Sheba is extended all the proper courtesies, and more, due an important head of state. She determines the topics of conversation when she converses with Solomon and then decides when it is time for her visit to end.

Feminists who scrutinize these narratives and are aware of how easily praise of a strong woman can turn to condemnation are not surprised to discover that a minority interpretation of the character of Sheba has emerged from time to time. Here, a demonic Sheba has been introduced, a woman who uses her feminine wiles for evil ends, who arouses all ancient and modern revulsions and fears of the power of womankind.

There are hints even in the earliest legends that not all was always well with the queen. Although beautiful, she is said by some storytellers to have had hairy legs or hooves for feet, a sure sign of the demonic. Why would Solomon have polished the floor of his chamber so that it looked like glass or water if not to discover for himself, when she lifted her robes, whether the rumor of her disfigurement was true?

From the early seventeenth century, the darker side of the queen became more and more evident in imaginative literature, continuing into the operas of the nineteenth century and the films of the twentieth. She became, accordingly, a demon queen, almost a vampire.

Some scholars have found this darker Sheba rooted in Jewish mysticism, especially Cabala. Nicholas Clapp locates the emergence of this sinister side in the *Targum Sheni*, an Aramaic translation and jumbled, rambling commentary on the book of Esther dating from the late fifth century CE in which Sheba appears crass, mannish, and calculating, assuming the prerogatives considered rightfully belonging to men. Though a conniving shrew, she is not yet a witch in the *Targum Sheni*.

In the *Zohar*, the chief text of Cabala, Sheba becomes Solomon's opponent rather than his admirer. She feeds him riddles, hoping to trick him, and she urges him to teach her the art of witchcraft. She seeks to obtain the bones of magic serpents in order to cast spells. Cabala further associates her with Lilith, Adam's evil first wife, according to extrabiblical legend. While Cabala lies outside mainstream Judaism, its features have had some influence on both Jewish and Gentile popular ideas.

Although the book has not been widely disseminated, *Demonizing the Queen of Sheba: Boundaries of Gender and Culture in Postbiblical Judaism and Medieval Islam*, a 1993 publication by Jacob Lassner, professor of Near Eastern and Asian studies, brings together much of the lore of the dark Sheba and suggests its mythological and psychological underpinnings. Lassner believes that the popular traditions of both Judaism and Islam helped transform this biblical seeker of wisdom and politically skilled sovereign into a witch because her original characterization threatened the "time-honored rules of gender" (1). Her story, as it was retold through the ages, uncovered anxieties that strong women have long awakened. As early as the Middle Ages, according to Lassner, sexual politics had already entered into the retelling of her story. In her assertiveness, she was characterized as defying both nature and divine roles designated for her gender. New storytellers thus leveled the queen, putting her in her rightful place as a mere woman.

It is not difficult to see how the sketchy, tantalizing narrative of Solomon and the Queen of Sheba related in the Hebrew Bible and the Qur'an could, upon imaginative elaboration, speak to both feminist and antifeminist sentiments. Here is a strong, wise, beautiful queen who values learning above all and seems to be praised for it. Yet she is also a woman functioning all too successfully in a world many felt to be rightfully dominated by men.

CROSS-CULTURAL INFLUENCE

Fiction writers, dramatists, and composers of music throughout the centuries have been intrigued by Sheba. Giovanni Boccaccio, in the Middle Ages, included the queen, whom he calls Nicaula, in his *De mulieribus claris* (*On Famous Women*). Exaggerating the size of her domain, he makes her the queen not only of Egypt and Ethiopia but also of Arabia and describes her lavish palace on the island of Meroe. Christine de Pizan's *Le livre de la cité des dames* (*The Book of the City of Ladies*) built upon some lines in Josephus and was probably influenced by Boccaccio as well. During the English Renaissance, in Christopher Marlowe's play *Doctor Faustus*, Mephistopheles tempts Faustus by offering to present a courtesan as wise as the Queen of Sheba to him the following morning.

But flamboyant imaginations belong most spectacularly to nineteenth-century composers of opera and twentieth-century filmmakers. In Vienna, in the last quarter of the nineteen century, Karl Goldmark, who lived in the shadow of such musical geniuses as Felix Mendelssohn, Franz Schubert, and Johannes Brahms, was scraping together a living as a piano teacher and violinist in the local opera orchestra. In his time between lessons and performances, he composed music that even he acknowledged to be inferior. In fits of despondency, he would periodically destroy what he had composed. Inspired by the vocal career of a student with whom he had become infatuated, he composed *Die Königin von Saba*, an opera based on the Queen of Sheba. When he submitted his composition to the stage director of the court opera, where he was frequently employed, he was told that his work was ludicrous, violating all rules of harmony and propriety. However, his composition came to the attention of the opera's patron, Prince von Hohenlohe, who liked it and determined that it would be staged. Rehearsals were not encouraging, and even the cast was embarrassed by the opera. Nevertheless, when it was finally performed, the public loved it, and it became one of the most popular operas of its time, despite continuing disparagement by music critics.

Since *Die Königin von Saba* (1875) was a romantic opera, it is not surprising that the libretto bore little resemblance to the biblical story. Here Sheba is a seductress without conscience or morality. She has little interest in Solomon or his wisdom but rather pursues an Israelite nobleman who is betrothed to the high priest's own daughter. Assad, the nobleman who receives her attentions, nevertheless eventually dies in the arms of his betrothed during a sandstorm, before Solomon can gain control of the vixen wreaking havoc in his court. The music has been described as Wagnerian and Orientalist. Goldmark's opera served to inspire subsequent biblically derived operas and to further Orientalism in musical works.

In the middle of the twentieth century, films called "biblical spectaculars" were very popular with both American and international audiences. The overwrought style of filmmaker Cecil B. DeMille dominated, and several of these films were directed by him. Two films featuring the Queen of Sheba, one Italian and the other American, are still enjoyed by viewers and remembered by some cinema enthusiasts as prime examples of kitsch.

La Regina di Saba (*The Queen of Sheba*), made in Italy with Italian personnel, was released in black and white in 1952 and later distributed in the United States. Although advertised as "a monumental costume spectacle based on the events of the Bible," its torrid script bears little resemblance to the biblical story. The figures of King Solomon, the Queen of Sheba—here called Balkis—and Rehoboam, biblical son of Solomon, are almost all that remain of the original narrative. The rest is extravagant Italian romanticism. Directed by Pietro Francisci with music composed by Nino Rota, the production was promoted with a tagline describing its version of the Queen of Sheba: "Men were her slaves. Women her enemies." In this sword-and-sandal epic, the crown prince, Rehoboam (Gino Leurini), attempts to seduce the voluptuous Balkis (Leanora Ruffo), who is more interested in romance than wisdom. His father, King Solomon (Gino Cervi), plays a relatively minor role. The amorous situation of Balkis, who becomes queen on the death of her father, is complicated by a ritual marriage to her pagan god and the flesh-and-blood presence of the prince's betrothed, Princess Zymira. Although nations and rivals in love compete, Solomon, crafty as he is wise, is able to achieve some resolution of the impossibly complicated plot.

Solomon and Sheba was released in color in 1959. This American film by United Artists was a high-budget effort with a first-class cast, a major director, and sumptuous sets and costumes. King Vidor directed Yul Brynner, a veteran of biblical epics, as Solomon and Gina Lollobrigida, another sultry Italian actress, as Sheba. George Sanders, who was often cast as a villain, appeared as Solomon's angry brother Adonijah, a contender for the throne.

This biblical adaptation is filled with treachery and intrigue. Sheba, a highly spirited queen, is sent by her ally, the pharaoh of Egypt, to spy on Solomon. Instead, she is impressed by his character and falls in love with him. When her love is reciprocated, the Israelites become suspicious, disapproving of Solomon's involvement with a pagan queen. In the midst of marriage preparations, an orgiastic pagan ritual is performed, scandalizing the Israelites and precipitating the seemingly inevitable clash of the monotheistic Israelites against the polytheistic Sheba and Pharaoh. Two major conflicts dominate: brothers contend over the throne of Israel after the death of their father, King David, and a battle rages between the Israelites and the Egyptians. Like other biblical epics, this movie was filmed in Spain, which was believed to resemble the Holy Land.

As part of the action, Solomon does demonstrate his widely acclaimed wisdom in one episode taken directly from the Bible. Sheba is particularly impressed when two women come forth claiming the same infant, and the king finds an ingenious way of determining the true mother. Although Sheba is attacked and severely injured in the battle between the Egyptians and the Israelites, she recovers almost miraculously, swearing allegiance and devotion to Solomon and his god but vowing to return to her own land.

Nineteenth-century romantic opera and mid-twentieth-century biblical epics may have taken as their starting points personalities from ancient religious books. But the sensibility, the tastes, and the mores expressed in these dramas are definitely of their own time.

Allene Phy-Olsen, PhD

BIBLIOGRAPHY
Budge, E. A. Wallis, trans. *The Kebra Nagast*. 1922. New York: Cosimo, 2004. Print.

Clapp, Nicholas. *Sheba: Through the Desert in Search of the Legendary Queen*. New York: Houghton, 2001. Print.

Ginzberg, Louis. *The Legends of the Jews*. Vol. 4. 1913. Philadelphia: Jewish Publication Soc. of Amer., 1987. Print.

Grierson, Roderick, ed. *African Zion: The Sacred Art of Ethiopia.* New Haven: Yale UP, 1993. Print.

The Holy Bible. New York: Amer. Bible Soc., 1999. Print. King James Vers.

Maier, Paul L., trans. and ed. *Josephus: The Essential Works.* Grand Rapids: Kregel, 1988. Print.

Pritchard, James B., ed. *Solomon and Sheba.* London: Phaidon, 1974. Print.

The Qur'an. Trans. M. A. S. Abdel Haleem. Oxford: Oxford UP, 2005. Print.

Voragine, Jacobus de. *The Golden Legend; or, Lives of the Saints.* Vol. 3. Ed. F. S. Ellis. London: Dent, 1900. Print.

Qutulun

Author: Marco Polo; Rashīd al-Dīn
Time Period: 1001 CE–1500 CE
Country or Culture: Mongolia; China
Genre: Legend

OVERVIEW

Qutulun was a historical Mongol princess and great-great-granddaughter of Chinggis (Genghis) Khan. She became a legendary figure during her lifetime. Born around 1260 CE in what is now Kazakhstan, Qutulun lived during the heyday of the Mongol Empire. This empire was founded in 1206 and greatly enlarged by the conquests of Chinggis Khan in the beginning of the thirteenth century, before Qutulun was born.

Qutulun's outstanding beauty and extraordinary fighting strength made her the subject of legends early on in her life. In many of the martial arts contests held in her indigenous nomadic Mongol society, Qutulun consistently won victory over male opponents. When she became of marriageable age in her teens, Qutulun set the condition that the man whom she would consent to marry would have to beat her in a wrestling match. This laid the foundation of her ensuing legend as a headstrong, independent woman warrior.

The oldest existing written account of the life of Qutulun is found in the contemporaneous travel book of the Venetian merchant Marco Polo. In 1271, Marco Polo left Italy to travel across the Middle East through Central Asia to his destination at Qubilai (Kublai or Khubilai) Khan's capital of Dadu (now Beijing). After leaving China in 1291, Marco Polo arrived back in Italy in 1295. While imprisoned by Genoa, Venice's maritime rival, Marco Polo dictated his travel observations to fellow prisoner Rustichello (Rusticiano) of Pisa from the autumn of 1298 until their release in the summer of 1299. Marco Polo's travelogue was originally entitled *Il milione* (The million) and became known in English as *The Travels of Marco Polo*. The original copy of Marco Polo's book has been long lost, although some 150

initial, but sometimes varying, copies exist in various languages. In 1903, Henry Yule published his popular edition, *The Book of Ser Marco Polo*, based on a comparison of eighty initial copies. In this text, Marco Polo describes the history and legend of Qutulun in "Of the Exploits of King Caidu's Valiant Daughter" in book 4, chapter 4.

The second-oldest contemporary account of Qutulun's life and legend is found in the work of the celebrated Persian historian Rashīd al-Dīn, *Jāmi' al-tawārīkh* (ca. 1310–16; *A Compendium of Chronicles*, 1995). The section containing the story of Qutulun can be found in John Andrew Boyle's translation from the Persian, *The Successors of Genghis Khan* (1971). Rashīd al-Dīn's account of Qutulun's early life differs from that of Marco Polo, introducing a different legend. Al-Dīn continues Qutulun's story beyond where Marco Polo leaves off, shortly after 1280, and runs up to 1304. Qutulun's death in 1306 or 1307 is mentioned in other Persian historical works of her time.

An analysis based on new historicism, cultural criticism, and feminism will show possible reasons why the historical figure of a Mongol princess became the subject of popular legends. Combining a strong will, physical strength, and feminine beauty, Qutulun quickly entered the realm of popular narratives in Europe and Persia (now Iran). A literary history analysis will show how, through cross-cultural influences, the legends of the Mongol princess Qutulun were mixed later with elements from popular Persian and Afghan folktales before reaching the West in the early eighteenth century. By that time, Qutulun had become Turandot. Under this name, she was made immortal again through Giacomo Puccini's last opera, *Turandot* (1924–25).

SUMMARY

In the English tradition, the legend of Qutulun begins with the mystery of her name. In Mongolian, Qutulun's name is the female form for good fortune and happiness,

---

"Her father often desired to give her in marriage, but she would none of it. She vowed she would never marry till she found a man who could vanquish her in every trial; him she would wed and none else. And when her father saw how resolute she was, he gave a formal consent in their fashion, that she should marry whom she list and when she list."

"Of the Exploits of King Caidu's Valiant Daughter"

---

khutukh or *qutuq*. Depending on the English transliteration of this Mongolian name, written originally in the Old Uighur alphabet, her name has been spelled as Khutulun or Qutulun, the latter of which is preferred by contemporary scholars. John Boyle transcribes her full name, given by Rashīd al-Dīn, as Qutulun Chaghan. In Marco Polo's contemporary account, she is referred to by the Turkish name of Aijaruc or Aigiaruc. This name means brightly shining moon. In its spelling of Ai-Yárúk, this name was still given to Uzbek girls at the turn of the twentieth century, according to translator Henry Yule. It is no longer known why Marco Polo used the Turkish name for Qutulun, which may have been a nickname or a name used in a particular context.

The daughter of the historical Mongol leader Qaidu (rendered as Caidu by Marco Polo and Kaidu by some contemporary scholars), Qutulun develops into a teenager of remarkable beauty and even more remarkable strength. Marco Polo writes, "This damsel was very beautiful, but also so strong and brave that in all her father's realm there was no man who could outdo her in feats of strength" (463). Once Qutulun reaches marriageable age, her father wants to find a suitable husband for her. However, Qutulun insists on choosing her husband herself. Qutulun determines that her future husband must be able to beat her in a traditional Mongolian wrestling match. Remarkably for the age, Qaidu agrees to this condition of his daughter.

Qutulun specifies the consequences of each wrestling match with a potential suitor. If she wins, her suitor will have to pay a penalty of one hundred horses and withdraw. If he wins, she will become his wife. According to her legend, Qutulun wins ten thousand horses in these matches. This would amount to her winning an impressive hundred wrestling bouts against various men.

According to Marco Polo, in 1280, when Qutulun is nineteen or twenty, an outstanding suitor appears. He is described as "a noble young gallant, the son of a rich and puissant [powerful] king, a man of prowess and valiance and great strength of body" (464). In different versions of Marco Polo's book, the young man is sometimes defined as the son of the king of Pumar, a historically unidentifiable local kingdom. Confident of his victory, the prince raises his wager to one thousand horses in return for a chance to beat Qutulun at wrestling.

Qutulun's father, Qaidu, and her mother, the queen, both implore Qutulun to throw the match and let the prince win. This is because they like him immensely as a future son-in-law. However, Qutulun insists on a fair tournament. She tells her parents that she will not lose deliberately. On the other hand, she is willing to accept any outcome and marry her opponent in case of his victory.

The day of their match becomes a local holiday. In addition to king and queen, many spectators are in attendance. Qutulun enters first, dressed in a jacket of velvet. Next, the prince appears, dressed in similar outfit of silk. The two contestants take position in the middle of the hall appointed for the venue. They "grappl[e] each other by the arms and wrestl[e] this way and that" (464), without a conclusive outcome. Suddenly, Qutulun manages to throw the prince to the ground, winning the match.

Stunned, the prince sees the victorious Qutulun standing over him. He leaves immediately, feeling great shame at being beaten by a woman. He leaves behind his forfeit of one thousand horses. However, Marco Polo tells that Qutulun's parents are "greatly annoyed" at their daughter's victory (465). They had wished the prince to become their son-in-law. They feel spited by Qutulun and consider her victory a sign of her intransigence, rather than her wish to uphold her honor as a sportswoman.

Marco Polo reports that after winning this match, Qutulun accompanies her father on all his military campaigns. He values her greatly because she exceeds all his knights in valor. Qutulun's specialty in battle becomes rushing into the melee. There, she often captures a single opponent "as deftly as a hawk pounces on a bird," bringing her captive to her father before rejoining battle (465).

Marco Polo's account of Qutulun ends here. The Persian historian Rashīd al-Dīn, who does not mention Qutulun's wrestling matches, writes instead that Qutulun falls in love with Mahmūd Ghāzān, the historical Mongol ruler of Persia at her time. Ghāzān was born in 1271 and thus was about eleven years younger than Qutulun. He ruled the Mongol Il-khanate state based in Persia from 1295 to his death in 1304. However, nothing comes of this relationship, which is most likely purely legendary.

The twentieth-century French editor of Marco Polo's work, Paul Pelliot, and al-Dīn provide more information about Qutulun's fate after the famous wrestling match of 1280. According to Pelliot and al-Dīn, the closeness of Qutulun and her father, Qaidu, leads to the spread of ugly rumors of an incestuous relationship. To put an end to these rumors, Qutulun chooses a Mongol noble from among her father's men and marries him, bearing two sons. A variant copy of al-Dīn's history identifies Qutulun's husband as Abtaqul of the Qorulas (27 n74).

According to al-Dīn and Persian historian Al-Qāshānī, after her father dies of wounds incurred in battle around 1301, Qutulun supports her brother Orus as successor against his older half brother Chapar. She also seeks an active political role for herself. Chapar, who was firstborn but son of a concubine of Qaidu, rejects Qutulun's interference and becomes khan. Qutulun, according to both Al-Qāshānī and al-Dīn, is a guardian of Qaidu's tomb.

Historical accounts indicate that in 1305, Chapar fell out with his previous supporter, the Chaghataid khan Du'a (Duwa). In 1306, Chapar was defeated. While sparing Chapar himself, Du'a had Chapar's relatives killed. Qutulun was murdered by Du'a's followers in 1306 or early 1307. Du'a himself died in 1307 of natural causes.

ANALYSIS

Qutulun's extraordinary combination of a strong will, great physical strength, remarkable beauty, and the unusual fact that she fought alongside her father in his battles turned this historical Mongolian princess into a legendary figure during her lifetime. An analysis grounded in new historicism illustrates that the legend of Qutulun was triggered in part by the historical coincidence that two influential authors lived during Qutulun's lifetime and wrote about her remarkable exploits. Cultural criticism reveals that the legend of Qutulun was aided by the great difference between Mongolian women and women in the vast territories conquered by the Mongols before her birth, particularly in Persia and Central Asia, as well as traditional Western noblewomen. Feminist criticism analyses how the legend of Qutulun both illustrates an alternative role for women in the thirteenth and subsequent centuries and contains clear limitations for this role and the heroine. This is true especially when grounding the legend in its historical reality. The interplay of history and legend in the depiction of the Mongolian princess Qutulun reveals some fascinating insights on how a remarkable life can be turned into a popular legend enthralling audiences from vastly different cultures.

In the West, it was Marco Polo who disseminated the legend of Qutulun. Marco Polo actually traveled through the realm ruled by Qutulun's father when she was a young teenager. This was rather exceptional for a Westerner to do in the thirteenth century. However, he sets the climax of Qutulun's legend in the year 1280. Then, Qutulun was nineteen or twenty, and Marco Polo had been serving Qubilai Khan, the Mongol great khan, in China for five years already. This meant that Marco Polo must have relied on other contemporary reports of Qutulun for this later period.

It is important to note that when Marco Polo was serving Qubilai Khan, Qutulun's father, Qaidu, had developed into a formidable opponent of the khan. Reports from Qaidu's realm were thus considered intelligence from a hostile state at Qubilai Khan's court, where Marco Polo was working. The more outrageous the news from Qaidu's lands was, the more they were welcome to put this opponent in a critical light. There was therefore an incentive to make Qutulun's story as outlandish as possible. This incentive contributed to the shaping of a distinct legend of this remarkable historical woman.

It is no longer known why Marco Polo chose to name her Aijaruc ("brightly shining moon") in his travel narrative. From a direct comparison of Marco Polo and Rashīd al-Dīn's accounts, as well as comparison with several other Persian historical sources, it is clear that Qutulun and Aijaruc are the same person. One possibility for the name choice of Marco Polo is that his original source of her story came from the Turkish-speaking community of Central Asia. There, the legendary Mongol princess may have been given a local name more resonant with Turkish-speaking audiences. This appears likely especially since Ai-Yárúk (a variant spelling) long remained a popular girl's name in the region where Qutulun lived.

In Persia, which corresponds to contemporary Iran, al-Dīn compiled the core of his magisterial *Compendium of Chronicles* during the lifetime of Qutulun. In this chronicle, Qutulun is mentioned in detail as the remarkable daughter of Qaidu. Again, she is seen from a hostile perspective. This is because her father was an enemy of the Mongol ruler of Persia, Mahmūd Ghāzān, a descendant of Chinggis Khan. Ghāzān commissioned al-Dīn to write a history of the Mongols up to Ghāzān's time. This work was enlarged later to become a history of the world as known to the Mongols. Since Qaidu was considered a rebel against the great khan, Qubilai Khan, who was allied with Ghāzān, Qaidu's family members were viewed with some suspicion.

Al-Dīn adds his own spin to the legend of Qutulun. Most likely to please his patron, Ghāzān, al-Dīn writes that Qutulun repeatedly wrote to Ghāzān asking to become his wife. According to al-Dīn's history, Qutulun was quite enamored with Khan Ghāzān: "On several occasions when Qaidu's ambassadors came to the Lord of Islam [Ghāzān] . . . she sent greetings and *biligs* [recorded sayings] and said: 'I will be thy wife and do not want another husband'" (26).

However, Qutulun's crush on Ghāzān is almost certainly purely legendary. Not only was Ghāzān eleven years younger than Qutulun, but her father was Ghāzān's mortal enemy. Rather than depict a political plot to forge an alliance through an unlikely marriage, it appears that al-Dīn chose to flatter his ruler by making the legendary Qutulun fall in love with him. This interpretation is made even more likely by the fact that no other contemporary sources mention such a proposal on Qutulun's part. Quite to the contrary, Ghāzān married the Mongol princess Kokachin from the court of his ally Qubilai Khan.

Through the irony of history, Marco Polo was able to leave the court of Qubilai Khan because he won the commission to escort Kokachin to Persia in 1291. Originally, the seventeen-year-old Kokachin was intended for Ghāzān's widowed father, Arghun. However, Arghun died in 1291, before Kokachin and Marco Polo arrived in Persia in late 1293. Ghāzān married the princess before winning a civil war and becoming Il-khan of Persia in 1295. It is most unlikely that Ghāzān was interested in Qutulun, or she in him. He obviously preferred a princess from the court of an ally rather than an enemy.

For both Marco Polo and al-Dīn, Qutulun's great strength and her participation in exclusively male activities of her time, such as wrestling and warfare, gave birth to her legend. Both writers helped shape the legend of Qutulun from a historical base inspired by Qutulun's life. As historian Morris Rossabi has pointed out, traditional Mongol women were generally as tough as men. They had to support the arduous nomadic lifestyle of Mongolian society before and after the founding of the Mongol Empire. This included a variety of domestic chores but also caring for the domesticated animals, driving carts, and making and breaking camps of yurts. During peacetime, men tended the animals, which included horses, oxen, camels, and sheep. However, during war campaigns, women had to assume these chores, as almost all adult men participated in warfare. Even aristocratic Mongol women were expected to follow this pattern. For these historical reasons, Mongolian noblewomen stood out from their European, Central Asian, and Chinese counterparts. Some of this astonishment at cultural differences in the role of noblewomen in Mongol society found its way into the legend of Qutulun, where it was exaggerated to legendary proportions.

Marco Polo's physical description of Qutulun is full of awe at her prowess. His account highly elevates her strength to reach legendary proportions, stating, "The lady was so tall and muscular, so stout and shapely withal, that she was almost like a giantess" (463).

From the point of view of cultural criticism, it is clear that Qutulun's physical strength, based on the traditions of Mongol nomadic culture, strongly impressed both European and Central Asian audiences. Qutulun appears a far cry from a dainty Western or Persian princess. In her legend, the otherness of the Mongolian woman in comparison to her European and other Asian counterparts is concentrated in distilled form and given rich, detailed expression.

As Rossabi states, it was not uncommon for Mongol girls to be given some military training. As the Mongol Empire expanded through naked aggression and brutal warfare in the thirteenth century, women were trained to support the war campaigns of the men in many ways. Many Mongol women became expert horsewomen and able to shoot their bows with accuracy on horseback. While it was relatively rare for women to join men in actual battles, one of Chinggis Khan's daughters is known to have assisted in leading the final assault against the Persian town of Nīshāpūr and even dictated which citizens would be executed and which kept alive. European and Persian amazement at this influenced the legend of Qutulun.

Qutulun grew up among many brothers. Apparently, she joined them in activities traditionally reserved for boys in Mongol culture. Historically, Qaidu had as many as fourteen sons by various women. He also had daughters, two of whom, foremost Qutulun, are still known by name. In this environment, Qutulun apparently moved deep into the boy's sphere of martial education. Al-Dīn mentions that Qutulun "used to behave like a young man, frequently taking part in campaigns and performing acts of heroism" (26).

Marco Polo focuses his account of Qutulun on her participation in Mongolian wrestling. There, in an athletic discipline still reserved for boys and men in contemporary Mongolia, Qutulun excelled. According to Marco Polo, Qutulun remained undefeated. This perfect record is most likely a legendary touch. He states, "In all trials she showed greater strength than any man of them" (463).

The rules of Mongolian wrestling have remained relatively unchanged since the thirteenth century. In Mongolian wrestling, opponents grapple with each other without any time or spatial limit. The wrestling bout goes on until any part of the opponent's body—with the exception of the feet, or sometimes the hands—touches the ground. When this occurs, the wrestler whose body part touches the ground loses the match.

Rossabi states that wrestling was part of the overall military training in traditional Mongolian nomadic culture, and other scholars have noted that the wrestling component of Mongolia's annual Naadam festival, held in July each year, has its origins in that warrior tradition. Every year, during the Naadam festival, some 512 male wrestlers typically compete in nine or ten elimination bouts against opponents of varying ages and weights. (No female wrestlers are allowed to compete in modern Naadam bouts; in fact, all the wrestlers wear special jackets that expose their chests in order to ensure that participants are male.) The outcome is open, and victory is determined by the individual athletic skills of the two wrestlers.

It is significant that only Marco Polo refers to Qutulun's wrestling matches. In fact, Marco Polo makes these matches the core and climax of her legend. This narrative choice can be traced back to the fact that both Qubilai Khan, at whose court Marco Polo served, and Qaidu in Central Asia promoted Mongolian wrestling. This promotion was supported by the fact that both

realms contained a large number of Mongol subjects. This was in addition to the conquered people over whom they ruled, such as the Chinese in the east and indigenous Central Asian people in the realm of Qaidu. In Persia, even though the Mongols had established their Il-khanate empire there, Mongolian culture never permeated the indigenous people's cultures as much as in Central Asia and China. Most likely because Mongolian wrestling was far less widespread in Persia, al-Dīn's account of Qutulun does not contain any reference to it.

Given the prominence of Mongolian wrestling at Qubilai Khan's court, emphasizing Qutulun's legendary exploits in this sport gave her story great significance among the China-based Mongol society. According to Marco Polo, Qutulun did not limit her challenges to Mongolian wrestlers, having instead "distributed her challenges over all the kingdoms, declaring that whosoever should come to try a fall with her, it should be on these conditions, *viz.*, that if she vanquished him she should win from him 100 horses, and if he vanquished her he should win her to wife" (463).

Qutulun's conditions appear rather fantastical but have a strong kernel of historical truth. Traditional nomadic Mongolian society greatly valued horses. The Mongolian horse was and is a prized breed, as it is of relatively small size and astonishingly sturdy. They endure temperatures as low as −40 degrees Fahrenheit (−40 degrees Celsius), can handle rough terrain, and can travel great distances without needing to rest. As such, Mongols have relied on their horses both in peace and war, where they supported the Mongolian cavalry.

Qutulun's stake of one hundred horses resonated well with the original Mongolian audience of her legend that Marco Polo recorded. A Mongolian family relied on its horses. Most horses were kept in a semiwild free-ranging style, with only a few selected as regular riding mounts. Indeed, as a boy, Chinggis Khan faced near starvation when his widowed mother, Hö'elün, lost the family's horses to thieves. Possession of horses was thus especially prized in the empire he founded.

As historian Michal Biran has pointed out, one military advantage of Qaidu in his battles with Qubilai Khan was Qaidu's easier access to horses. Qaidu raised more horses on the steppes of his empire compared to Qubilai Khan in the Far East. For this reason, wagering a considerable sum of horses and winning ten thousand horses through her successful wrestling matches made Qutulun a formidable, if hostile, figure at Qubilai Khan's court. The round number of ten thousand horses,

HISTORICAL CONTEXT

The Mongol minor noble Temüjin established the Mongol Empire in 1206 when he united the Mongol tribes through warfare and diplomacy. Elected khan of the Mongols, he took the name of Chinggis (Genghis) Khan.

In a series of fierce, brutal, and successful campaigns, Chinggis Khan vastly expanded the Mongol Empire. In the east, he defeated the Chinese Western Xia and Jin dynasties. Turning west, Chinggis Khan's Mongol armies conquered Central Asia and advanced as far as the Aral Sea.

When Chinggis Khan died in 1227, the Mongol Empire was divided among four different khans. Among them, his third son, Ögödei (Ögedei), won the title of great khan. He ruled over the Mongol Empire from 1229 to 1241. Ögödei continued expansion of the Mongol Empire by force, conquering what is now Afghanistan, Persia, and Korea. His armies also invaded Poland, Hungary, and Romania.

One of Ögödei's sons was Qashi. Qashi's son Qaidu (or Kaidu) carved out an independent khanate in Central Asia around contemporary Kazakhstan, Tajikistan, and Uzbekistan. Qaidu was born around 1235. In 1260, his daughter Qutulun was born. Throughout his life, Qaidu opposed the new great khan, Qubilai Khan, who reigned in China from 1260 to 1294.

After Qaidu died following a victorious battle in 1301, his son Chapar became his successor against Qaidu's original wishes. Chapar allied himself with another khan, Du'a, and opposed his sister Qutulun's alliance with Orus, Qaidu's intended heir.

Qutulun, her husband, and Orus tended to Qaidu's grave until Du'a had Qutulun killed in 1306 or 1307. The Mongol Empire collapsed in 1368 with the fall of the Mongol Yuan dynasty in China.

Marco Polo describes him as "young and handsome, fearless and strong in every way, insomuch that not a man in all his father's realm could vie with him" (464). Immediately, the foreign prince raises the stakes tenfold to the extraordinary number of one thousand horses. True to form, Qutulun refuses to fix the match. She will not lose deliberately so she can be married to this desirable man. Defying her parents who wish her to do so, Qutulun insists on an open match. However, she concedes that by her own rules, "if, indeed, he should get the better of her she would gladly be his wife" (464).

Qutulun's victory over her most favored opponent marks the legend's climax and her fading out of Marco Polo's narrative. No further wrestling matches of Qutulun are recorded after this victory. This climactic end of her wrestling career follows closely the narrative structure of a legend, even though it may have been historical fact.

Marco Polo records that Qutulun next joins her father in his military campaigns. Al-Dīn confirms this. As mentioned previously, a daughter of Chinggis Khan had done the same for her father, so this turn in Qutulun's life is most likely historical. As Jack Weatherford has pointed out in his *Lapham's Quarterly* assessment of Qutulun, winners of Mongolian wrestling bouts were considered blessed by the spirits. Their presence in battle was considered auspicious. This reason, too, made Qutulun an ideal companion in her father's military expeditions.

Marco Polo ends his narrative of Qutulun with a description of her valor in battle. From there, he turns his historical account to a description of Qaidu's battle with Arghun of Persia. Ironically, Arghun was the father of Mahmūd Ghāzān, whom al-Dīn mentions as Qutulun's sole romantic interest in his version of her story. Even though Marco Polo did not leave Mongol-controlled China until 1291 and left Persia sometime between 1293 and 1295, he does not mention Qutulun again in his narrative. Her story is continued by al-Dīn and other Persian sources. For Marco Polo, Qutulun's legendary

corresponding to one hundred matches won at one hundred horses each, is clearly legendary. Yet given the fact that the winner of a major wrestling tournament would have to win about nine to ten matches in elimination rounds, a high number of victories by Qutulun is not entirely improbable.

It is not known why Marco Polo chose the exact year of 1280 for Qutulun's climactic wrestling match. As she was about nineteen years old, she was certainly at peak marriageable age in her community. As such, the year lent itself to a final showdown with a strong potential suitor.

In keeping with the formal requirements of a legend, Qutulun's final recorded suitor is given an appropriately high status. He possesses extraordinary strength himself.

life ends with her roaming the steppes in battles at the side of her father.

From a feminist and historical perspective, the legend of Qutulun points also to the limits of female power, encountered even by such a warlike princess as Qutulun. At first, Qutulun successfully gains the power to choose her own husband. However, in the end, she is reintegrated into patriarchal society. This Marco Polo only hints at but al-Dīn and other sources show in detail.

Qutulun's legendary feats of valor and independence are particularly remarkable when contrasted with the fate of her younger sister, Qutuchin. Against the backdrop of her sister's fate, Qutulun enjoyed far more independence and heroic female self-determination. Qutuchin was married early in her life to a Mongol noble, Tübshin. He was a descendant of Chinggis Khan and belonged to the Il-khanate line ruling Persia. According to a Persian contemporary quoted by Biran, Tübshin fell in love with a slave girl when Qutuchin was pregnant. When Qutuchin found out, she confronted Tübshin, who bit her, and she died. Rather than give in to his sons' request to avenge their sister, Qaidu responded that Tubshin's death would not benefit Qutuchin. Instead, Qaidu sentenced Tübshin to one hundred lashes. Then, in a stunning display of the Mongol tradition of keeping widows and widowers within the close family, Qaidu ordered Tübshin to marry another of his daughters. This was done so that the widower of Qutuchin would remain bound to her family. As Rossabi points out, Mongol custom sometimes forced a son to marry his stepmother if his father died, leaving her a widow. According to al-Dīn, however, Tübshin remained in love with the slave girl and tried to defect to Qubilai Khan. Learning of this, Qaidu put Tübshin to death. Al-Dīn does not report Qutuchin's ultimate fate in his history.

From a feminist perspective, Marco Polo's end of the story of Qutulun leaves a somewhat bitter aftertaste as well. Qutulun's valor in battle was superior, and regarding her support of Qaidu, Marco Polo reports that "not a knight in all his train played such feats of arms as she did" (465). Yet her specialty in battle was to pounce on a single opponent, seize him like a hawk seizes a bird, and "carry him to her father" (465). In a contemporary feminist reading, this action makes Qutulun resemble a falconer's trained bird rather than an independent warrior woman.

With some partisan glee, al-Dīn's account of Qutulun shows her and her father's eventual submission to the patriarchal rules of their society. These traditions ultimately limited even the freedom of an extraordinary, headstrong Mongol princess. In al-Dīn's history, Qaidu, who was the enemy of al-Dīn's patron, Ghāzān, is shown as shamed by his unusual relationship with his warrior daughter. Pressured by his people, he ends it. Al-Dīn writes, "Qaidu, out of excess of shame and the reproaches of the people, gave her in marriage to a Khitayan" (26–27). Even worse, when Qaidu dies, Qutulun is severely rebuked for her attempts to participate actively in the administration of his realm and her support for his son and heir Orus, rival to Chapar. Al-Dīn quotes Chapar and his foreign ally Du'a rebuking Qutulun in a voice dripping with misogyny: "Thou shouldst be working with scissors and needle. What concern hast thou with the kingdom and the *ulus* [tribe]?" (27).

The end of Qutulun's historical life is less than legendary. Living with her husband and her two sons, Qutulun dutifully tended the grave of her father after his death in 1301 until she was killed on Du'a's orders in 1306 or 1307. Yet the legend of the marvelously strong, independent, and beautiful Qutulun lived on in the West and in Persia. In much-altered form, it would reach the twentieth century.

CROSS-CULTURAL INFLUENCE

By the time the legend of Qutulun reached the West again in the eighteenth century, her story had changed considerably under the cross-cultural influence of Persian and Central Asian folkloric traditions. A new version of Qutulun's legend was compiled by French Orientalist François Pétis de la Croix. De la Croix published the story in the first volume of his five-volume collection of Persian tales, *Les mille et un jours* (*Persian Tales; or, The Thousand and One Days*).

According to de la Croix, he received a manuscript of the tales from a Persian dervish, or ascetic, named Moqlas. This occurred around 1675, while de la Croix was living in Isfahan in Persia. De la Croix copied parts of the manuscript in Persian and translated parts into French when he returned to France around 1692. De la Croix published his collection between 1710 and 1712. It was first translated into English in 1714 and published in subsequent editions with modernized English spelling.

In de la Croix's collection, the legend of Qutulun is contained, in a cross-cultural transformation, in "The History of Prince Calaf and the Princess of China." This tale shows quite diverse folktale influences. There are three key changes to the original legend. The first concerns the name of the heroine, which has been changed from Qutulun to Tourandocte or Turandot, meaning "Turkish daughter." The second is the replacement of the wrestling match with a series of riddles. A potential suitor has to agree that if he fails to answer these riddles correctly, he will be beheaded. The third change is that after he answers all of Turandot's riddles, Calaf proposes a riddle of his own to her. If Turandot can answer it, she will be free to have him killed after all; if she fails, she will marry him. In the end, although she obtains Calaf's name, Turandot decides to marry him, letting love triumph over tragedy.

Reasons for the cross-cultural transformation of Qutulun's legend as it becomes the story of Turandot are quite diverse. Moqlas based his Persian tales in part on an older Indian source called *Al-faraj ba'da al-shidda* (joy after sorrow), indicating that Qutulun's legend had spread quite far from Central Asia to South Asia and Persia.

The heroine's new name of Turandot conflates the past Mongol empires of Central Asia and China. In "The History of Prince Calaf and the Princess of China," Turandot's father is Altoun Khan, a Mongol king of China. The story takes place in Peking (Beijing), to which Prince Calaf travels. Mongol rule of China under the Yuan dynasty founded by Qubilai Khan lasted from 1271 to 1368. During that period, Mongols were the emperors of China. By naming the heroine "Turkish daughter," the new story acknowledges that she belongs to the Mongol realm of Central Asia, exactly where the historical Qutulun lived. In essence, the new tale takes Princess Qutulun from her native land and away from her historical father, Qaidu. It gives Qutulun a new father, ironically modeled after Qubilai Khan, her real father's bitter enemy. In fact, Qutulun's historical origin from among the steppes of Central Asia is only alluded to in her new name.

The change from Qutulun's wrestling matches to Turandot's riddles is the result of a significant cross-cultural transformation of the original legend. Folklore scholar Christine Goldberg has suggested that the idea of riddles, with a lethal consequence if they failed to be answered, can be traced back as far as the riddles of the Greek Sphinx that are finally answered rightly by Oedipus. The tale of Oedipus was first recorded by the Greek poet Homer around the ninth century BCE, giving it sufficient time for widespread travel and impact on later folktales.

However, a more direct, Persian source for the riddles is contained in the romantic epic poem *Haft paykar* (1197; *The Seven Beauties*, 1924) by Persian poet Nizāmī Ganjavī (pen name of Abu Muhammad Il-yas ibn Yusuf). This epic poem features the legendary king Bahrām, who is modeled after the historical king Bahrām V, who ruled the Sassanid Empire in Persia from 420 to 438 CE. Incidentally, Bahrām also features in the traditional Punjabi folktale *The Faithful Prince*. In *The Seven Beauties*, Bahrām builds a palace with seven domes for his seven princesses. The Slavic inhabitant of the Red Dome tells a story in which a Russian princess is reluctant to marry and builds a magic castle. The princess puts four challenges into the path of any potential suitor. They range from him being beautiful (the first condition) to him being able to answer correctly some learned questions (the fourth condition). If a suitor failed at any of these conditions, he would be put to death. Eventually, a prince manages to meet all four conditions and marry the reluctant princess.

According to comparative literary history, it appears that this Persian element of riddling questions, with their lethal consequences for failure was incorporated in exchange for Qutulun's wrestling matches in the adapted version of her story. This exchange made her legend more appealing to a later Persian audience. First, Mongolian wrestling was never popular in Persia, even under Mongol rule. For Persian tastes, a princess wrestling with her potential husband was not very appealing. Secondly, the stakes of horses, while very important and significant to Mongols, were obviously considered too low for Turandot's challenge.

Similar to the replacement of the riddles for the wrestling match, the new story took other elements from folktales popular in the region and integrated them in the transformed tale of Qutulun as she became Turandot. As Prince Calaf enters Beijing, he takes up lodgings at the home of a kind old widow, who introduces him to Turandot's challenges. This story element is apparently taken from the traditional Afghan folktale of Moghol-Dokhter and Arab-Bacha, which dates from the sixteenth century CE but incorporates some much older narrative elements. In the story of Moghol-Dokhter and Arab-Bacha, an Arab boy takes lodgings with an old woman. She shows him a Moghol (or Mongol) girl at her morning dressing table through the window of her home, which is adjacent to the princess's palace. This incorporation of diverse elements from other regional folktales shows how cross-cultural influence worked to transform the legend of Qutulun to a popular Persian tale of the seventeenth century. As such, the new tale made its way to the West, where it underwent further transformations.

In de la Croix's "History of Prince Calaf and the Princess of China," Calaf answers three riddles correctly. His answers are the sun, the sea, and a year. With this, Calaf not only saves his life but also wins Turandot's heart and hand in marriage. He is able also to redeem his own parents, who have fallen on hard times, adding the element of the dutiful son to the original legend.

It is interesting that Calaf is a prince of the Nogaïs, a Tartar tribe. His tribe's name obviously derived from that of the historical Nogai, a descendant of Chinggis Khan's oldest son, Jochi, who established the Golden Horde. While he lived during Qutulun's lifetime and died in 1299, Nogai had no known connections with her. His name is just another remnant from the age of the original legend that made it into the later cross-cultural version of the story.

In the West, the story of Turandot became very popular. In 1762, Italian playwright Carlo Gozzi wrote the comic play *Turandotte*. Gozzi changed the answers to the sun, the year, and St. Mark's lion. He also incorporated elements of the Italian *commedia dell'arte* and wrote sarcastic scenes for laughs. In 1801, the German dramatist Friedrich Schiller adapted Gozzi's play to create his own, much more serious version in German. In Schiller's *Turandot, Prinzessin von China* (1802; Turandot, princess of China), Turandot is portrayed as a captive of her own high moral and ethical standards. She is finally released from her cruelty by Calaf's true and deep love for her.

It was Schiller's play that influenced Italian composer Giacomo Puccini to write his world-famous last opera, *Turandot* (1924–25). In March 1924, Puccini was still struggling with his ending. All that remained to be written was the final duet between Calàf and Turandot, and he searched for a successful finale for his work. Puccini died of a heart attack following treatment for throat cancer on November 29, 1924. Franco Alfano was chosen to complete the opera, but he ran into difficulties with Puccini's publisher, who forced him to write a second ending. Finally, the opera premiered on April 25, 1925, but stopped at the point in act 3 where Puccini's work ended due to his death. A few days later, the opera was performed with Alfano's second ending. It quickly became popular, eventually becoming one of the most played operas in the twentieth century.

Puccini's *Turandot* begins act 1 with the impending execution of a failed suitor, the prince of Persia. The act features the sudden reunion of Prince Calàf with his blind father, Timur, who has lost his kingdom. The slave girl Liù is his father's sole companion. She tells Calàf this is because Calàf once smiled upon her while his family was still in power. While the crowds plead for mercy for the prince of Persia, Turandot appears and orders his execution to proceed. Despite Turandot's imperious cruelty, Calàf falls in love with her. Against the pleas of his father, Liù, and Turandot's three ministers, Calàf speaks her name and strikes a gong three times, announcing his quest to try Turandot's riddles the next day. Turandot accepts his challenge. Here, the opera sets the scene by featuring an apparently cruel and heartless Asian princess. However, all her suitors come to her of their own free will. They are dazzled, perhaps, by her beauty, but their ultimate decision to try the challenge is their own.

Before sunrise, in act 2, Turandot's ministers bemoan her cruelty. At sunrise, Emperor Altoum receives Calàf. Turandot reveals revenge as the motive for her apparent cruelty. She believes that she must avenge her ancestor, an ancient princess who was raped and murdered by a foreign invader from Central Asia. This adds a touch of what Palestinian American literary critic Edward Said has termed Orientalism: it is a vision of Asia corresponding to Western prejudices and preconceptions of Asian incomprehensibility and strangeness.

Calàf manages to answer all three riddles correctly. Puccini fine-tuned the answers to make them poetically and symbolically meaningful. They are hope, blood, and Turandot. When Turandot loses, she pleads with her father not to require her to marry Calàf. Now, Calàf raises the stakes after winning. He allows Turandot to kill him if she does not learn his name before sunrise the next morning.

Act 3 opens at night. A furious Turandot threatens all citizens with death if they fail to learn the prince's name. In a strange reversal of the original legend of Qutulun, it is the three ministers who beg the prince to throw the match and let go of Turandot. Calàf refuses to do so. Meanwhile, Turandot captures Timur and Liù. She has Liù tortured to reveal her master's name, but Liù refuses. Instead, she commits suicide just as Calàf enters. (It is here that Puccini's work ends due to his death.)

As Liù's body is carried away, Calàf confronts Turandot for her cruelty. Suddenly, he kisses her against her will. In Alfano's conclusion, Calàf tries to win Turandot's heart. She begs him to leave. He, however, reveals his name to her, putting his fate in her hands. In the last scene of act 3, Turandot and Calàf go before the emperor. Turandot says she knows Calàf's name: Love. He has truly won her heart, and the two are engaged to be married.

Puccini's *Turandot* stands out as one of the few classic Western operas with a happy ending for the protagonists. However, many critics and audience members have felt that the love of Liù for Calàf outshines that of Turandot.

For many decades, the People's Republic of China frowned upon *Turandot* as anti-Chinese. Finally, in 1998, the opera was performed in Beijing's Forbidden City. Acclaimed Chinese filmmaker Zhang Yimou was director, Chen Weiya the choreographer, and Zubin Mehta the conductor. The story of a fierce, strong-willed, powerful, and independent Mongolian princess from the Central Asians steppes, Qutulun, was finally performed in a cross-culturally transformed version in Beijing. There, about seven hundred years ago, Qubilai Khan, the enemy of Qutulun's father, had ruled over Mongol and Chinese subjects. Then, Marco Polo learned about Qutulun and wrote down her remarkable story, uniting history and legend.

R. C. Lutz, PhD

BIBLIOGRAPHY

Al-Dīn, Rashīd. *The Successors of Genghis Khan.* Trans. John Andrew Boyle. New York: Columbia UP, 1971. Print.

Biran, Michal. *Qaidu and the Rise of the Independent Mongol State in Central Asia.* Richmond: Curzon, 1997. Print.

Goldberg, Christine. *Turandot's Sisters: A Folktale Study.* New York: Garland, 1993. Print.

Ganjavī, Nizāmī. "Bahrām Sits on Tuesday in the Red Dome." *The Haft Paikar (The Seven Beauties).* Trans. C. E. Wilson. London: Probsthain, 1924. 171–87. Print.

Pelliot, Paul. *Notes on Marco Polo.* Vol. 2. Paris: Adrien-Maisonneuve, 1963. Print.

Pétis de la Croix, François. "The History of Prince Calaf and the Princess of China." *Persian Tales; or, The Thousand and One Days.* Vol. 1. Trans. Ambrose Philips. London: Lane, 1800. Print.

Polo, Marco. "Of the Exploits of King Caidu's Valiant Daughter." *The Book of Ser Marco Polo.* Vol. 2. 3rd ed. Trans. Henry Yule. Ed. Yule. London: Murray, 1903. 463–65. Print.

Puccini, Giacomo. *Turandot. Seven Puccini Librettos.* Trans. William Weaver. New York: Norton, 1971. Print.

Rossabi, Morris. "Khubilai Khan and the Women in His Family." *Studia Sino-Mongolica: Festschrift für Herbert Franke.* Ed. Wolfgang Bauer. Wiesbaden, Germany: Steiner, 1979. 153–80. Print.

"Turandot." *Operapaedia.* San Diego Opera, 2013. Web. 8 Apr. 2013.

Weatherford, Jack. *The Secret History of the Mongol Queens.* New York: Crown, 2010. Print.

---. "The Wrestler Princess." *Roundtable.* Lapham's Quarterly, 3 Sept. 2010. Web. 10 Apr. 2013.

Tomoe Gozen, Samurai Warrior

Author: Traditional
Time Period: 1001 CE–1500 CE
Country or Culture: Japan
Genre: Legend

OVERVIEW

As a female samurai warrior, Tomoe Gozen is a rare and exceptional person and a legendary character. Her given name is Tomoe; Gozen is an honorific title best translated as "lady" or "dame" in English. Most Japanese and international scholars believe Tomoe is a historical person who lived for ninety years in the tenth and eleventh centuries CE. Even though there is no irrefutable proof for Tomoe's historic existence, the evidence suggests she was a real person around whom a powerful legend was built. Her legend stems from her unusual status as a female samurai and as an accomplished warrior. In her early twenties, Tomoe Gozen fought for her lord, Kiso no Yoshinaka, during the Genpei War of 1180 to 1185 CE. She fought alongside Kiso no Yoshinaka at his last, fateful battle of Awazu in 1184. Thereafter, she relinquished the way of the warrior to become a wife, a mother, and, later, a nun.

The historic and legendary account of Tomoe Gozen is given in two primary Japanese sources. The most accessible one to an English reader is *The Tale of Heike*, translated in full by Helen Craig McCullough in 1988. It is used as source text for this discussion.

In Japan, *The Tale of Heike*, or *Heike monogatari*, originated as an oral tale generally told by blind monks. They chanted the tale to the accompaniment of the *biwa*, a Japanese musical instrument similar to the lute. Japanese tradition has it that it was a former governor of the province of Shinano, birthplace of Tomoe Gozen, who transcribed *The Tale of Heike* in the thirteenth century CE and read it to a blind monk to chant the text. The oldest existing copy of *The Tale of Heike* is the 1371 version named after its author, Kakuichi, a biwa storyteller who composed the standard text of the legend. This served as the basis for generations of biwa storytellers continuing into the twenty-first century.

The second, more detailed source of Tomoe Gozen's life and legend is the fourteenth-century Japanese work *Genpei jōsuki*, transcribed also as *Genpei seisuki* or *Genpei seisuiki*. It comprises forty-eight volumes, expanding on the subject covered by *The Tale of Heike*. By 2013, the *Genpei jōsuki* has not been translated into English in full. However, passages referring to Tomoe Gozen have been translated by Royall Tyler in his biography of Tomoe Gozen in Chieko Irie Mulhern's 1991 anthology, *Heroic with Grace: Legendary Women of Japan*.

An analysis grounded in new historicism and cultural criticism illustrates how Tomoe Gozen has captured the imagination of Japanese audiences since the thirteenth century CE. This popularity elevated her person to legendary status. Her life as a female samurai warrior has proven fascinating, and it has permeated and influenced what was told as historical record. In addition, a Noh play was created based on her story, translated into English by Tyler. A feminist critical analysis reveals how the extraordinary life of Tomoe Gozen stands out against the backdrop of traditional Japanese attitudes toward both women and the warrior caste of the samurai. Here, Tomoe Gozen's career as a female warrior does not serve as a general model. She is seen as a fascinating exception, and her character is ultimately reconciled with the beliefs of traditional society concerning the status of a highborn woman.

SUMMARY

Female samurai warrior Tomoe Gozen enters the narrative of *The Tale of Heike* just before the climactic last battle of her lord, Kiso no Yoshinaka. According to this text, Kiso brings along "from Shinano two female attendants, Tomoe and Yamabuki" (McCullough 291). In this case, "attendant," or *binjo* in the original Japanese, means a warrior woman attending to her lord.

"Tomoe was especially beautiful, with white skin, long hair, and charming features. She was also a remarkably strong archer, and as a swordswoman she was a warrior worth a thousand, ready to confront a demon or god, mounted or on foot. She handled unbroken horses with superb skill; she rode unscathed down perilous descents."

The Tale of the Heike

It is the *Genpei jōsuki* that provides more background about Tomoe's life. In the absence of a complete English translation of this Japanese chronicle, Tyler has translated or paraphrased the passages relating to Tomoe Gozen in his biography of the female samurai. Because of the details about Tomoe's life given in *Genpei jōsuki*, especially before and after her last battle at Kiso's side, most Japanese and international historians believe that Tomoe was a real person. Her prowess in battle became the source of her legend.

According to the *Genpei jōsuki*, Tomoe was born around 1157 to Gon no Kami Nakahata Kaneto, a warrior, and the wet nurse of her future lord, young Kiso no Yoshinaka. Yoshinaka was born Minamoto no Yoshinaka. However, after his father was murdered, the infant Yoshinaka was raised by the Nakahara clan in Kiso. For this reason, Yoshinaka changed his last name from Minamoto to Kiso (family names come first in Japanese). Tomoe's two brothers, Imai no Shirō Kanehira and Higuchi no Jirō Kanemitsu, were so-called milk brothers of Yoshinaka because they were breast-fed by the same woman (Tomoe's mother). Another medieval Japanese chronicle, the *Genpei tōjōroku*, states that Kanemitsu was Tomoe's father. However, this appears unlikely.

In the *Genpei jōsuki*, Tomoe, given the honorific title of Gozen, grows up with Kiso, who is three years older. Because it was a historical Japanese custom of the time, Tyler suggests that, as teenagers, they entered a casual, temporary marriage. For this reason, Tomoe is sometimes referred to as the concubine of Kiso. However, by the time Tomoe appears as a samurai warrior at Kiso's side, their relationship seems less romantic and more like that of lord and vassal.

After Kiso reconciles with the Minamoto clan, he is ordered to attack the rival Taira clan. Tomoe, like her brothers, accompanies Kiso on his campaign. According to the *Genpei jōsuki*, at the Battle of Kurikawa (also called Battle of Tonamiyama) on June 2, 1183, Tomoe "personally command[s] a force of one thousand mounted warriors" (Tyler 137), an extraordinarily rare feat for a female samurai. Kiso wins the battle and conquers the imperial capital of Kyoto. Tomoe moves to Kyoto as Kiso occupies the city.

In the fall of 1183, Kiso's relationship with his cousin Minamoto no Yoritomo sours to the point that both men try to destroy each other. Kiso's wild and barbarous behavior in Kyoto estranges him from the household of the retired emperor, Go-Shirakawa, who appoints Kiso as his shogun (military governor) nevertheless. In early 1184, Kiso is attacked by the two brothers of Minamoto no Yoritomo, Yoshitsune and Noriyoro. Kiso orders Tomoe's brother Kanehira to defend access to Kyoto in the east and sends her brother Kanemitsu on a raid to the south. The Minamoto brothers circumvent Kanehira's blocking troops and ford the Uji River to the south of him and advance toward Kyoto.

On March 4, 1184, which corresponds to the twenty-first day of the first month of the year 1184 in the traditional Japanese calendar (and often mistakenly transcribed as February 21), Kiso faces certain defeat. Outnumbered, Kiso lingers at the home of his sixteen-year-old girlfriend until it is nearly too late for an escape. Accompanied by Tomoe, Kiso performs a fighting retreat. It is at this point, according to the *Genpei jōsuki*, that Tomoe is tested in battle again. One of Minamoto's captains, Hatakeyama no Shigetada, believes Tomoe to be Kiso's mistress and seeks to capture her alive. Hatakeyama catches up with Kiso and Tomoe. Kiso does not want Tomoe to fight Hatakeyama in personal combat and drives his horse between him and her. Eventually, Hatakeyama is able to seize "the left sleeve of Tomoe's armor" (Tyler 142). On her strong battle horse, Harukaze (Spring wind), Tomoe breaks free of Hatakeyama, letting her sleeve be torn off. Convinced that Tomoe is a demon woman, at whose hands it would be extremely shameful to die, Hatakeyama gives up his pursuit of her.

Numbering only seven surviving warriors, Tomoe and Kiso's group reaches Awazu Plain south of Lake Biwa, east of Kyoto. Here, in preparation for a final battle, Tomoe takes off her helmet, lets fly her long hair, puts an ornamental band across her forehead, and dons an elegant white hat. She encounters the boisterous enemy samurai Uchida Ieyoshi, who appears confident of victory over her. Instead, Tomoe kills Uchida with her long samurai sword, the *naginata*.

Even though Kiso reunites with the surviving forces led by Tomoe's brother Kanehira, he is outnumbered and prepares to die in battle with Kanehira. Before this, as *The Tale of Heike* reports, Kiso wants Tomoe to leave the battlefield, saying, "It would be unseemly to let people say, 'Lord Kiso kept a woman with him during his last battle'" (McCullough 292).

Anguished but obedient, Tomoe looks for one last worthy opponent. This she finds in enemy samurai Onda no Hachirō Moroshige. Riding up alongside Onda, she "seize[s] him in a powerful grip, pull[s] him down against the pommel of her saddle, [holds] him motionless, twist[s] off his head, and [throws] it away. Afterward, she discard[s] armor and helmet and [flees] toward the eastern provinces" (McCullough 292). Obedient to the wishes of her lord, who indeed is killed in battle and followed in death by the suicide of Tomoe's brother Kanehira, Tomoe disappears from *The Tale of Heike*. However, the *Genpei jōsuki* chronicles her subsequent fate.

After the battle of Awazu, Tomoe is ordered by the victorious Minamoto no Yoritomo to report at his capital, Kamakura, near Edo (modern Tokyo). Tomoe complies. At Kamakura, she is originally sentenced to death as Minamoto's enemy and placed into the custody of his samurai Mori no Gorō. Another samurai, Wada no Kotarō, impressed by her valor as samurai warrior, falls in love with Tomoe. He wins her pardon and marries her. Together, they have a son, Asahina Saburō Yoshihide. When Tomoe's husband is killed by the rival Hōjō clan, Tomoe becomes a nun. She dies in 1247, at ninety years old (or ninety-one years by traditional Japanese account).

ANALYSIS

An analysis utilizing the approach of new historicism and cultural criticism reveals how female samurai warrior Tomoe Gozen has maintained a long-lasting and widespread hold on the popular Japanese imagination. The aspects of her story that turned her into a legendary character include her extraordinary singularity as woman participating in combat as an equal to male antagonists. In fact, Tomoe commanded a considerable number of cavalry soldiers. Her legend is also kept alive because of the general Japanese fascination with her era, characterized by the samurai-borne battles of the Taira and Minamoto clans, which ended the rather peaceful and cultured Heian period and led to the military dictatorship of the Kamakura shogunate. Tomoe Gozen has been seen as a paragon of samurai virtues, which included her absolute loyalty to her lord, Kiso no Yoshinaka. In addition to being mentioned in near-contemporary historical records, Tomoe Gozen became a revered subject of a Noh play titled after her in the fourteenth century. Interestingly, however, Tomoe Gozen's life after her legendary exploits on the battlefield ended in a more traditional fashion. Saved from execution by the love of a Minamoto warrior, Tomoe changes from a warrior to a mother and a nun. This indicates that the legend eventually grounds the exceptional female warrior in a traditional social life.

During the ancient period up to the tenth century CE, Japanese women of the aristocracy and warrior classes often possessed arms, among which straight daggers were most common. The purpose of these arms was twofold: for self-defense and for committing suicide when facing imminent capture by an enemy.

In the Heian period, during the latter part of which Tomoe Gozen was born, knowledge acquired from the Chinese led Japanese swordsmiths to design a new class of forged weapons. For women, a special dagger was invented called *kaiken* ("pocket knife"). The kaiken drew its inspiration from the smallest of the new swords, the *tantō*, and was even smaller at just eight to ten inches long. Women of the aristocratic and warrior classes could wear a kaiken either in a kimono sleeve or in a special pouch called a *futokoro*. Again, the purpose of the kaiken, in the use of which women were instructed, was either self-defense or suicide. Unlike the male ceremonial suicide involving disembowelment and decapitation by a companion, women were expected to kill themselves more quickly. This was done by cutting the left jugular, leading to nearly instant death.

Like Tomoe, as soon as the weapon was invented in the late Heian period, exceptional women from samurai families began to train with the *naginata*, a long, curved sword that was mounted on a pole. In fact, the naginata is said to be Tomoe's favorite and most effective weapon. The curved blade of the naginata is from about one to two feet long and is commonly mounted on a long shaft of about four to seven feet long. This length gives its wielder a considerable range and obviates the need for close hand-to-hand combat. For this reason, it became the weapon of choice of women, foot soldiers, and warrior monks. The naginata proved particularly effective in dismounting an enemy either through a direct stroke or by incapacitating the horse.

In addition to her prowess with the naginata, as described in *The Tale of Heike*, Tomoe Gozen had unusual skill with the bow and arrow, the traditional weapon of choice of the samurai of her period. One passage describes her equipment and skill as follows: "Whenever a battle was imminent, Kiso sent her out as his first captain, equipped with strong armor, an oversized weapon [the naginata], and a mighty bow; and she performed more deeds of valor than any of his other warriors" (291). This passage contains some hyperbole in celebrating Tomoe's legendary fighting skills and success on the battlefield. Yet it makes Tomoe stand out as a remarkable samurai warrior who both led male samurai and fought bravely herself.

While Tomoe Gozen was perhaps the most famous female samurai warrior of her age, she was not the only one who is still known. *The Tale of Heike* mentions her fellow female samurai warrior Yamabuki Gozen, who also served Kiso no Yoshinaka. However, during the Minamoto brothers' attack on Kyoto in February 1184, "Yamabuki had fallen ill and stayed in the capital" (291). She did not join Tomoe and Kiso at the final battle of Awazu, even though she had fought as a samurai before. Yamabuki's grave still exists, unlike that of Tomoe. This proves that Yamabuki was a historical person. It heightens the circumstantial evidence that her companion Tomoe was a real person, too.

On the side of the Taira—the common enemy of Kiso, Tomoe, and Kiso's cousin and nemesis Minamoto no Yoritomo—was Hangaku "Itagaki" Gozen. Daughters of a warrior, even after the utter defeat of the Taira in 1185, Hangaku and her warrior sister, Sukenaga, contributed to a violent uprising that many believe destroyed the Kamakura shogunate. In 1201, Hangaku, like Tomoe, not only personally yielded her naginata but also commanded three thousand warriors defending a fort at Torisakayama against a reported ten thousand attackers. As her defense collapsed, Hangaku was wounded and captured. Like Tomoe, she was presented to the Minamoto ruler and spared execution when the samurai Asari Yoshitō married her. They had a daughter and dropped out of recorded history.

The existence of female samurai warriors like Tomoe and her female counterparts in eleventh- and twelfth-century Japan owes something to the kind of combat fought in that era. Despite the thousands of warriors involved in a campaign, whose numbers may be inflated to some extent, basic samurai combat still consisted of a person-to-person armed duel. In battle, samurai of renown would challenge each other. The outcome of their personal battles would be observed and recorded by their audience. This type of battle placed great emphasis on personal skill and valor. A few exceptional women warriors, such as Tomoe, stood out and had a chance to perform their valiant feats, which were noted and embellished to legendary proportions.

A turning point in Japanese combat tactics occurred as a result of the two Mongol invasions of Japan in 1274 and 1281. The Mongol invaders, relying on masses of Chinese and Korean recruits, fought in tactical groups of men against the samurai, who were used to single combat. Samurai adjusted to this new kind of tactical warfare. Aided by two typhoons that destroyed the invaders' fleet and became known as *kamikaze* ("divine winds"), Japan repulsed both invasions. Yet the invasions led to a change in Japanese military tactics away from hand-to-hand duels to mass combat.

By the time of the Sengoku period (or Warring States period), ranging from about the beginning of the Ōnin War in 1467 to the climactic Battle of Sekigahara in 1600, warfare had changed drastically since the Heian and Kamakura periods. From the beginning the Sengoku period, there were more massive armies. The individual daimyo, or great lords, locked in a fight for supremacy over all of Japan increasingly augmented their ranks with foot soldiers. As professional warriors ran out, soldiers were drawn from the local peasantry, who were armed with spears and swords in the beginning.

The advent of firearms, in the form of locally copied and manufactured Portuguese muskets beginning in 1543, changed battlefield tactics even more drastically. Personal combat among renowned samurai became a quaint sideshow of the campaigns. The Battle of Nagashino of 1575 proved the deadly efficacy of firearms. Oda Nobunaga deployed three thousand samurai musketeers behind wooden stockades. Their volley fire broke his enemy's mass cavalry charge, leading to between three and ten thousand enemy dead. Importantly, the dead included eight valiant samurai generals participating in the charge against the defenders' guns.

On these early modern battlefields, a single female samurai warrior would have had little chance to prove her valor as Tomoe Gozen had done about four hundred years before. Indeed, as scholar Noel Perrin tells, in a 1584 battle, a single samurai leader, Lord Mori Nagayoshi, rode out in front of his battle line. He was dressed in similar splendor as Tomoe was for her last battle. Whereas Tomoe wore an elegant white hat, Mori wore a white silk cloak over his armor. Mori presented a conspicuous target at close range, and a plain soldier "knocked him off his horse dead" with his musket shot (Perrin 26). Firearms took classic battle heroism out of modern warfare.

Given the relative anonymity of Japanese warfare soon after the Heian period, Japanese popular imagination in the subsequent centuries became nostalgic and fascinated with the individual samurai warfare of a bygone era. Already in the fourteenth century, after the Mongol invasions, Tomoe's exploits as an exceptional and singular female samurai warrior fascinated audiences. People loved to listen to the tale of Tomoe's exploits when respective passages of *The Tale of Heike* were recited, generally by blind storytellers accompanied by the biwa.

The absolute loyalty shown by Tomoe to her lord, Kiso no Yoshinaka, has facilitated her legendary status throughout the centuries in Japan. Tomoe's obedience to Kiso's wishes is shown through her abnegation of her own desires, ambitions, and possible romantic feelings. If Tyler and other historians are correct that Tomoe was romantically and sexually involved with Kiso in their teenage years and early twenties, the fact that Kiso took a wife appropriate of his social standing cannot have passed without leaving a wound in Tomoe's heart. However, true to the classic samurai spirit and code of conduct enshrined in *Bushidō*, the way of the warrior, Tomoe is not known to have lamented her situation at all in any of the historical records of her life. Even more challenging for her must have been the fact that at the height of crisis on March 4, 1184, with the enemy closing in on them in Kyoto, Kiso lingered at the home of his latest girlfriend.

Again, according to the record, Tomoe does not express misgivings about this. In contrast, according to the *Genpei jōsuki*, two of Kiso's male samurai commit ritual suicide to show their objection to his behavior. With their suicides, they sought to admonish him, through the most extreme way given to a samurai vassal, to assume a proper course of action.

When Kiso faces certain defeat, despite Tomoe's and the esteem he has for her, Kiso gives in to old, culturally inscribed traditions of misogyny. In no uncertain terms, Kiso orders Tomoe to depart the battlefield. His final invocation is recorded in *The Tale of Heike*: "'Quickly now,' Lord Kiso said to Tomoe. 'You are a woman, so be off with you; go wherever you please. I intend to die in battle, or to kill myself if I am wounded'" (292). Kiso does not want to die in the company of a woman, no matter how brave she has shown herself to be. In alignment with his traditional culture, Kiso considers such a death deeply shameful.

The *Genpei jōsuki* gives a somewhat more nuanced reason why Kiso orders Tomoe off the battlefield. In the respective passage of this chronicle, translated by Tyler, Kiso releases Tomoe from her duties because he does not want to be seen as dying in her company. Yet Tomoe is resistant and responds, "I have served you ever since you and I were children . . . . Wherever you fall, my lord, I would lay my head besides yours" (Tyler 144). In response, Kiso gives a different reason for his decision. He acknowledges that ideally Tomoe's wish would be his own. Yet he left his wife and children in his hometown in Shinano and worries about them. Tomoe should inform them—and, by extension, posterity—of Kiso's death. He says, "I wish you to go now and carry the news of my death, and pray for my afterlife. Quickly, escape from here and go back to Shinano. Tell those there what has happened" (Tyler 144).

Here, Kiso is concerned about leaving behind an eyewitness who can attest to his heroic end. Differing from the version of *The Tale of Heike*, Tomoe obeys and stops fighting, not killing her last enemy, Onda. Instead, she observes the Battle of Awazu from the top of a hill. At its end, after Kiso has been killed by the enemy and Tomoe's brother Kanehira has committed suicide, Tomoe fulfills Kiso's wish. She discards her armor, goes to Shinano, and tells his family of his death.

Indeed, Tyler believes that the account of Kiso's and Kanehira's deaths was recorded by Tomoe and from her reached the official chronicles of the events. This version is not mutually exclusive with that of *The Tale of Heike*. Tomoe may have slain Onda first and then lingered to watch and ultimately report the final outcome of the last battle of Kiso.

The two historical accounts, *The Tale of Heike* and the *Genpei jōsuki*, raised Tomoe Gozen's status to near-legendary proportions, but her story is turned fully into a legend by the popular, anonymous Noh play *Tomoe*. In his biography of Tomoe Gozen, Tyler offers a full English translation of this Japanese play.

In *Tomoe*, the action takes place at the fictional Shintō shrine to Kiso no Yoshinaka at his death place

MYTH INTO ART

The female samurai warrior Tomoe Gozen has been a popular subject in Japanese art, particularly in the ukiyo-e genre that flourished from the seventeenth century to the nineteenth century. One of the most spectacular pieces to capture Tomoe's fierce battle spirit is *Tomoe Gozen with Uchida Ieyoshi and Hatakeyama no Shigetada* (1899), by celebrated Meiji period woodblock artist Yōshū Chikanobu (pseudonym of Hashimoto Naoyoshi).

For his print, Chikanobu takes some artistic license. He depicts Tomoe's adversaries from two different battles within the same scene on the fateful day of March 4, 1184. The picture, colored pigment on paper, consists of three panels. Occupying the center panel, Tomoe is riding full speed atop her black horse, Harukaze (Spring Wind). Tomoe wears traditional samurai body armor over her light green kimono with red borders, which covers her legs to the point where her feet emerge in her stirrups.

As described in the *Genpei jōsuki*, in the print, Tomoe has taken off her samurai helmet, revealing her long, flowing, gray-and-white hair held together by her white headband. The speed of her charge is visually represented by the bold flow line from her hair over her billowing dark bluish purple overcoat and by the curled strands of Harukaze's tail.

Tomoe wields her favorite weapon, the Heian period *naginata* (curved long sword), with her right hand. On her left side, facing the viewer, is a Heian *tachi* (long sword), tied to the *obi* (belt) of her armor. Chikanobu correctly depicts Tomoe wearing the tachi with the blade facing downward, as was done in her time.

The headless body of a samurai is shown lying behind the hooves of Harukaze. This samurai, felled by Tomoe, still holds his tachi in his right hand in a death grip.

Behind Tomoe on the right side, the torn left sleeve of her armor is held high by her pursuer, Hatakeyama no Shigetada, which follows the *Genpei jōsuki* account of her near-capture at the Kamo River. Hatakeyama is depicted as a fierce mounted samurai warrior in full battle dress. His open helmet sports two long golden horns on the front. Hatakeyama's frustration at seeing Tomoe riding away from him is starkly evident in his angry face.

On the left stands the samurai Uchida Ieyoshi. Dismounted and helmetless, he brandishes his tachi against Tomoe, who advances against him with her naginata drawn. Although Tomoe's historical encounter with Uchida happened later in the day on the Awazu Plain, Chikanobu's painting artistically captures the drama and fight of Tomoe of her last day as a female samurai warrior.

---

on Awazu Plain about two hundred years before the play was written. There, a wandering monk, functioning as *waki* (witness), encounters the *shite* (principle personage) of Tomoe, a ghost who has assumed the form of a village woman. Fittingly, the time of the year is the first month of the traditional Japanese calendar, corresponding to the day of the Battle of Awazu, which fell into the first month of the Japanese year in 1184.

The wandering monk passes by the shrine, where he encounters Tomoe. She appears in the mask of a young woman and weeps. As the monk inquires about the reasons for her tears, Tomoe and the chorus reveal a legendary version of the Battle of Awazu Plain. Their recollections are aided by a local man, performing the Noh role of the *kyōgen* (commoner essential to the plot).

Tomoe uses historical information from both *The Tale of Heike* and the *Genpei jōsuki*, indicating their widespread circulation in fourteenth-century Japan. Passages

such as a description of Tomoe's beauty combined with her fighting prowess are taken almost straight from *The Tale of Heike*. Kiso's farewell speech combines elements from both chronicles. The speech voices both his horror and shame at dying next to a woman in his last battle and his injunction to Tomoe to tell his family of his death. There are other, purely invented details, including the idea that fellow female samurai warrior Yamabuki Gozen died in the Battle of Tonamiyama (or Kurikara), where Tomoe commanded a thousand samurai. However, the historical Yamabuki was still alive, albeit sick, in the spring of 1184. *Tomoe* conflates two victims of Tomoe's last day of fighting into one person for greater narrative effect and unity of action.

To heighten Tomoe's legendary reputation, in the play, Tomoe lingers in battle dress as Kiso's horse becomes mired in the lakeshore mud and he is wounded. With his last strength, Kiso gives Tomoe his amulet and his robe and orders her to depart. To do so, Tomoe has to fight for her life as enemy samurai suddenly descend on her. The chorus tells the dramatic event from Tomoe's perspective: "I thrust out the halberd [that is, the naginata] full length, and swept it round. That circle of men fell like autumn leaves, like a rain of petals torn loose by storm winds" (Tyler 160).

After this poetically rendered legendary account of her final actions as warrior, Tomoe returns to find Kiso has committed suicide, unlike the historical reality. She takes his amulet and robe and returns to Shinano. The play ends in its present day, when a sacred rite is just about to be performed at the shrine to Kiso.

As a drama about the legend, Tomoe highlights well how Tomoe's exploits on her last day as a samurai warrior have captured the imagination of generations of audiences. Dramatically exalted, the female samurai's unyielding loyalty to the wishes of her lord, with whom she is given more time in his final moments than she was in history, is celebrated in high style. In the play, Tomoe's brother Kanehira, who did stay with Kiso to the end, is completely erased as an impediment to her legend. The female warrior coming to the dead body of her slain lord, after escaping her enemies in lethal combat, proved a lastingly popular image.

A feminist critical analysis illustrates that for all her exceptionality and valor in a male-dominated society and her prowess in the traditionally male domain of warfare, Tomoe Gozen is reintegrated into a traditionally female role. Ironically, it is exactly this reintegration that has convinced many scholars that Tomoe Gozen was a historical person around whom a legend formed. For the purpose of her legend, shown dramatically in the Noh play Tomoe, her subsequent fate as a warrior's wife, a mother, and a nun is not only irrelevant but also detracts to some degree from her legendary status. Historically, as a woman who had fought as a samurai against the alliance of victorious Minamoto no Yoritomo, Tomoe was spared execution because of her gender. By contrast, her second brother, Kanemitsu, surrendered but was bound in ropes and sent to Kyoto. There, on the sixth day after the Battle of Awazu, Kanemitsu was beheaded.

CROSS-CULTURAL INFLUENCE
Across the centuries, Tomoe Gozen has continued to be a popular character in Japanese mass culture, even into the early twenty-first century. Her persona has been featured in Japanese television series, manga, anime, and computer games. Tomoe Gozen has also made an appearance in American culture.

In the United States, one of the first texts featuring Tomoe Gozen was in the Hugo Award–winning science-fiction novel To Your Scattered Bodies Go (1971) by Philip José Farmer. In this novel, some humans and some aliens are resurrected on an earthlike planet, Riverworld. There, they face numerous challenges, foremost among them how to organize their society. Tomoe Gozen makes an appearance, as do other historical persons, such as the Nazi war criminal Hermann Göring and the novel's protagonist, English explorer Sir Richard Burton. Farmer created the Riverworld trilogy from his concept.

In 2010, a television movie was created by Stuart Gillard. The Riverworld film featured Tomoe Gozen as a positive character, played by Canadian actress Jeananne Goossen. Tomoe is resurrected with Kiso no Yoshinaka, played by Peter Shinkoda. Kiso is her husband in the movie and supports the film's good characters. Tomoe's trademark weapons are a long sword like a katana and a shorter one, modeled after an elongated tantō dagger. However, critics have pointed out that she employs a style of sword fighting popularized by Japanese swordsman Musashi Miyamoto, who flourished during the Edo period, about four hundred years after the historical Tomoe. For her character to follow his teachings is therefore anachronistic. Her character represents a form of cultural borrowing, or appropriation. However, she is on the side of good and does not conform to a prevalent Western cultural stereotype of an evil Asian character.

In the early 1980s, American fantasy author Jessica Amanda Salmonson used Tomoe Gozen as central character in her fantasy trilogy. The first novel in the series, Tomoe Gozen (1981), uses the character in a pure fantastical setting in an alternate universe. While the island nation of Naipon is a thinly disguised Japan, monsters, demons, and gods there interact with human characters much as in Japanese mythology.

The story line of the American fantasy novel Tomoe Gozen has little to do with any events from the Japanese legend. In Salmonson's novel, even though Tomoe Gozen is a female samurai warrior, she is killed in the beginning while fighting for her lord, Shojiro Shigeno. Her male friend Ushii persuades the evil Chinese monk Huan to resurrect Tomoe. The price for her resurrection is that Tomoe will be controlled by Huan's magic. Huan instructs Tomoe to do his nefarious bidding, including ordering her to kill her former master, Shojiro. After Tomoe carries out this grim task, the society of Naipon shuns her. Tomoe breaks free of Huan's magic mind control and roams the fictional island as a *rōnin* (masterless samurai).

As a *rōnin*, Tomoe takes part in a series of adventures. These include two lesbian liaisons, one with an aristocratic woman and one with a ninja priestess. Finally, Tomoe confronts the samurai Ugo Mohri, the champion of the reigning shogun. Defeating him restores Tomoe's honor and ends her time as a *rōnin*. Throughout the novel, Salmonson carefully depicts a realistically drawn classic Japanese feudal warrior society combined with the magic elements of fantasy. The novel won the 1981 World Fantasy Award for Amazons.

The editors of the original version of *Tomoe Gozen* asked Salmonson to tone down the lesbian story elements. In 1999, Salmonson offered a revised version entitled *The Disfavored Hero*. It draws its title from the action of the novel after Tomoe Gozen falls out of favor with the ruling aristocratic leadership of Naipon for killing her former lord, Shojiro. In this revised version, the lesbian subplot is fully developed in graphic detail. A few minor changes have been made to the overall story of the novel.

The second novel of Salmonson's Tomoe Gozen trilogy is *The Golden Naginata* (1984). The middle and end of this novel follow the actual legend of Tomoe Gozen more closely than the first volume does. In the middle of *The Golden Naginata*, Tomoe Gozen marries the warlord Kiso Yoshinake, obviously modeled after the historical Kiso no Yoshinaka. Why Salmonson makes a slight change to his name has not been revealed. The same is true for Tomoe's brother and Yoshinake's trusted friend Imai Shirō Kanehira. He is named Imai Kanchiro in *The Golden Naginata*. At times, these minor name changes, such as Naipon for Nippon, appear somewhat mannerist in the trilogy. This is true especially because Tomoe Gozen's name is not altered.

In Salmonson's *The Golden Naginata*, Tomoe is formally married to Lord Kiso. This is an invention of the American fantasy trilogy and is absent from the Japanese legend. As Tyler has argued, Tomoe and Kiso most likely shared an informal, temporary marriage-like relationship as teenagers and in their early twenties. In the Japanese legend, only enemies, such as Tomoe's would-be captor Hatakeyama, refer to Tomoe as Kiso's mistress at the time of the 1183 campaign and the 1184 Battle of Awazu. Both the historical chronicles, albeit sometimes

with legendary exaggeration, and the Noh play *Tomoe* stress instead the warrior bond between Kiso, the lord, and Tomoe, the vassal.

In the American novel, in addition to being legally married to her lord, Tomoe retains her personal independence after marriage. Salmonson undertakes this plot point to a degree that Tyler, who discusses *The Golden Naginata* in his biography of Tomoe Gozen, has called "unimaginable in Japanese song or story" about Tomoe (132). Tyler credits Salmonson for her "integration of genuinely Japanese motifs into contemporary American fantasy" (132). However, Tyler points out that in Salmonson's hand, Tomoe's American feminist character traits are far removed from the historical and legendary Japanese character.

Magic elements permeate Salmonson's story of Tomoe and Yoshinake as well. Tomoe is given a magic golden naginata. This naginata blinds anybody who sees it, unless the weapon has been covered by the blood of the magic *kirin* dragon. While the kirin is an authentic Japanese mythological beast, the golden naginata and the use of kirin blood are Salmonson's own invention. This mixture of authentic myth and authorial invention indicates the typical fashion in which the author borrows Japanese elements to combine with her own ideas for her fantasy tale.

The stark incongruity of a Tomoe Gozen who looks authentically Japanese but acts like a modern American woman is apparent in the episode of Yoshinake's death in *The Golden Naginata*. As Yoshinake plans to commit suicide on the battlefield, he forbids Tomoe from following him into death herself. In the American novel, Tomoe reasons that because Yoshinake forbade her to commit suicide with him, their souls would be estranged in the afterlife if she defied his orders. For this reason, Tomoe decides to formally obey Yoshinake. As in the Noh play *Tomoe*, but unlike in the historical record, Yoshinake does commit suicide. In *The Golden Naginata*, a whole group of his samurai follows him into death, not just Tomoe's brother, as in the historical records.

After Yoshinake's death, Salmonson's Tomoe continues her ways as a fiercely independent woman. Salmonson concludes her story in the last novel of the trilogy, *Thousand Shrine Warrior* (1984). The trilogy's dark ending leaves the original Japanese historical and legendary texts far behind.

The cross-cultural American adaptations of the legend of Tomoe Gozen, in the Riverworld trilogy and its 2010 filmic version and in the Salmonson's fantasy trilogy, show a large degree of creative freedom concerning characterization and the fate of the protagonist. Perhaps because the legend of Tomoe Gozen is not as familiar to American audiences as to Japanese audiences, American writers and directors have felt free to appropriate the Japanese female samurai warrior and give her a character largely of their own imagining.

In *Riverworld*, for example, Americanization extends to Tomoe Gozen's weapons. Her legendary naginata, which was wielded by Japanese women of Tomoe Gozen's historical period, has been replaced in favor of the katana, or long sword, more widely known in the United States. This change in weaponry subtly shifts her portrayal away from the original Japanese Tomoe. Indeed, even in contemporary Japan, martial arts involving the use of nonlethal naginata with bamboo blades are primarily a woman's sport. This indicates the long legacy of this weapon among Japanese women that the *Riverworld* version loses in its adaptation of Tomoe Gozen's character. In the process of coming to America, the legendary Tomoe Gozen did not escape substantial transformation to modern American tastes and preferences. In Japan, her authentic spirit is still widely respected and celebrated.

R. C. Lutz, PhD

BIBLIOGRAPHY

Farmer, Philip José. *To Your Scattered Bodies Go*. New York: Putnam, 1971. Print.

Faure, Bernard. *The Power of Denial: Buddhism, Purity, and Gender*. Princeton: Princeton UP, 2003. Print.

Gillard, Stuart, dir. *Riverworld*. Perf. Jeananne Goossen and Peter Shinkoda. SyFy Channel, 2010. Film.

Jones, David E. *Women Warriors. A History*. Washington: Brassey's, 2000. Print.

McCullough, Helen Craig. *The Tale of the Heike*. Stanford: Stanford UP, 1988. Print.

Oyler, Elizabeth. *Swords, Oaths, and Prophetic Visions: Authoring Warrior Rule in Medieval Japan*. Honolulu: U of Hawaii P, 2006. Print.

Perrin, Noel. *Giving up the Gun: Japan's Reversion to the Sword, 1543–1879*. Boston: Godine, 1979. Print.

Salmonson, Jessica Amanda. *The Disfavored Hero*. Boulder Creek, CA: Pacific Warriors, 1999. Print. Rpt. of *Tomoe Gozen*. 1981.

---. *Thousand Shrine Warrior*. New York: Ace, 1984. Print.

---. *The Golden Naginata*. New York: Ace, 1982. Print.

Turnbull, Stephen R. *The Samurai: A Military History*. New York: Macmillan, 1977. Print.

Tyler, Royall. "Tomoe, the Woman Warrior." *Heroic with Grace: Legendary Women of Japan*. Ed. Chieko Irie Mulhern. New York: Sharpe, 1991. 129–61. Print.

Vietnamese Rebels: The Trưng Sisters and Triệu Thị Trinh

Author: Traditional
Time Period: 501 CE–1000 CE
Country or Culture: Vietnam
Genre: Myth

OVERVIEW

Near the beginning of the Common Era, Vietnam was a state ruled by conflicting sources of power. Several forms of government and unified culture existed within the borders of what is today called Vietnam, with the northern Dong-Son culture being perhaps the most powerful. In 111 BCE, however, an invading army and accompanying government from the Han dynasty of China took control of that region. The Han dynasty brought with it a steady influence of Chinese culture and political ideas, sometimes strictly enforcing those cultural attitudes and Confucian beliefs. As the Han rulers increased taxation and amplified their efforts to convert the Vietnamese people to Chinese cultural traditions, however, the Vietnamese still maintained control over local governments, even if regional officials were also reporting to the Chinese government.

Within this context of political struggle arose two powerful stories of women rebelling and claiming their cultural autonomy. Around 40 CE, the Trưng sisters gathered an army of women and drove the Chinese forces first out of their home villages and then out of Vietnam all together. The sisters, Trưng Trắc and Trưng Nhị, were born into a military family and trained in the martial arts from a young age. Their rebellion was sparked when Thi Sách, the husband of Trưng Trắc, was executed by a powerful Chinese official. The sisters ruled as queens of Vietnam for two years until the Chinese army returned, more powerful than ever, and conquered the state once again. Their story remained popular, however, and two centuries later, it served as inspiration for the myth of Triệu Thị Trinh (sometimes called Triệu Ẩu,

or Lady Triệu). A rebellious and powerful woman, Triệu Thị Trinh likewise gathered an army and attacked the Chinese directly, charging into battle on the back of a war elephant. Her rebellion also failed, however, and the Chinese army is said to have entered the battlefield naked in order to disgust Triệu Thị Trinh and shame her into defeat.

The stories of the Trưng sisters and of Triệu Thị Trinh are both historical realities, their rebellions documented in Vietnamese and Chinese history. Following their deaths, however, the stories entered into the realm of mythology. Villagers built temples to the Trưng sisters and carried on the names of the fierce women warriors, praying to them in times of need. The mythology of Triệu Thị Trinh also grew over time, and centuries later, poems described her as a gigantic and gorgeous leader who haunted the Chinese army in their dreams and cursed them with plagues after her death. Both mythologies served as powerful examples of the fight for Vietnamese independence through the centuries. They also came to reflect the conflicted relationship many Vietnamese men had with the idea of powerful women, regardless of the important roles those women held in their country's independence.

SUMMARY

For several hundred years, Vietnam has existed under Chinese rule, with Chinese officials often exercising oppressive power over the Vietnamese citizens. The Trưng sisters, named Trưng Trắc and Trưng Nhị, are born in a rural area. Their family teaches them the military arts throughout their childhood and expects them to carry on the military tradition of their father. One day, Trưng Trắc meets and falls in love with a young man named Thi Sách, who is visiting from a nearby village. As the Chinese rulers increasingly try to force their culture onto the Vietnamese people, Thi Sách take a defiant and public stand against them, for which he is ultimately executed. This death so moves the Trưng sisters that they decide to lead a revolution for Vietnamese independence, vowing that such a death will never happen again.

The Trưng sisters begin by forcing the Chinese rulers out of their village. Following their success, they drive the Chinese government out of more and more villages, eventually gathering an army that consists primarily of women. This female army manages to win a succession of important battles until at last the Trưng sisters rule an independent Vietnam as its queens. After only a few years, however, the Chinese generals gather a massive army and descend upon Vietnam to reclaim control over their former province. The Vietnamese women defend themselves bravely, but when defeat appears inevitable, the Trưng sisters decide to drown themselves rather than face the shame of conquest. With the sisters dead, the Chinese reclaim power over Vietnam.

Although the Trưng sisters are gone, their legend remains and inspires the story of Triệu Thị Trinh several centuries later. Triệu Thị Trinh is portrayed as a powerful woman who stands over nine feet tall and is said to have gigantic breasts. As strong as she is beautiful, she is able to travel great distances while surviving on very little food. One day she gets in a fight with her evil sister-in-law, killing her in battle and then exiling herself to the woods. There, she gathers a small army of women and men intent on forcing the Chinese rulers out of their homeland. The army hides in the wilderness as they gather supplies and recruit more warriors. Triệu Thị Trinh's brother begs her to behave in a way that is more fitting for a woman, although she declares that she only wishes to be free and to help her people. Her brother is so moved by her words that he decides to join her army.

Riding atop a gigantic war elephant, Triệu Thị Trinh leads her army into battle, and the very sight of her causes the Chinese soldiers to tremble in fear. Her breasts slung over her shoulders and her war clothes glistening, she appears superhuman, her frightening image reminding some of the legend of the Trưng sisters before her. The Chinese army takes refuge inside their defensive walls, and Triệu Thị Trinh's untrained army grows impatient during the siege. Finally, the Chinese army emerges, charging into battle naked and kicking up dirt. They know that Triệu Thị Trinh is offended by anything filthy, and on the sight of the dirty and naked men, she turns and leaves the field in disgust, which causes her army to lose the battle. Furious with their commander, the Vietnamese army surrounds Triệu Thị

"I only want to ride the wind and walk the waves, slay the big whale of the Eastern sea, clean up frontiers, and save the people from drowning. Why should I imitate others, bow my head, stoop over and be a slave? Why resign myself to menial housework?"

"The Question of Women"

Trinh and forces her to commit suicide rather than live on as a defeated commander.

Even in death, however, Triệu Thị Trinh does not give up. Through dreams, she continues to haunt and terrorize the Chinese commander who defeated her on the battlefield, even creating a plague that devastates his army. In an attempt to end this curse, the commander orders his soldiers to carve penises out of wood and to hang them outside their homes, warding off the easily offended Triệu Thị Trinh.

Triệu Thị Trinh recurs throughout Vietnamese history, and as the Chinese continue their rule over Vietnam, she comes to Vietnamese warriors in their dreams, inspiring them to fight for independence. Likewise, villagers throughout Vietnam build temples to her and to the Trưng sisters, continuing their stories and passing on the names of their generals. While the Chinese maintain rule for hundreds of years, and while many male Vietnamese rulers attempt to quiet the stories of women acting in ways that are culturally inappropriate, the legends of the Trưng sisters and of Triệu Thị Trinh continue, to inspire women and men alike for centuries more.

ANALYSIS

The stories of the Trưng sisters and of Triệu Thị Trinh are firmly rooted in historical fact as actual military leaders, and their biographies and the rebellions they led have been well documented in Vietnamese and Chinese history (although each culture has a distinctly different version of the events). In the centuries following their deaths, these stories became mythologized and infused with a spirituality and mystical tradition built around the documented facts, translating the historical figures into legendary heroes. Like the documented facts of their lives, these mythologies can only be understood when placed in the context of Vietnamese history and the long struggle for power between Vietnam and China.

The Trưng sisters were born in the beginning of the first century, somewhere around 12 CE, approximately a century after the Han dynasty of China had invaded Vietnam and established a level of political control there. The Han Chinese had a large military and viewed the cultures outside of Chinese borders to be barbarian states. As such, a large part of their conquest involved the forced implementation of Confucian culture in Vietnam. Most Vietnamese people, however, were fiercely resistant to these changes, trying instead to preserve the Dong-Son culture that preceded the Chinese invasion and to continue their own traditions, an act that was most effective in villages and rural areas. By the time of the birth of the Trưng sisters, the Chinese leaders had increased their efforts to develop a strong tax base within Vietnam and impart a patriarchal power structure within the region. Both actions helped the Chinese to pass on their own culture to the Vietnamese while benefiting economically from the state. The end result was a rapid spread of Chinese cultural and political ideas with local Vietnamese governments being incorporated into the foreign system and a growing resistance movement taking hold within some segments of Vietnamese society. While the Trưng sisters ultimately lost their battle for independence, they did inspire other Vietnamese citizens by spreading the belief that independence was possible. By the time Triệu Thị Trinh initiated her rebellion, the cultures and governments of Vietnam and China were tied up in a complicated play for power, manipulating economic and military forces in their struggle for cultural dominance.

While the stories of the Trưng sisters and Triệu Thị Trinh have many historical and narrative similarities, they have been mythologized in markedly different ways. For example, in looking at the portrayals of gender and feminine responsibilities within the myths, the Trưng sisters are motivated by the death of the husband of Trưng Trắc, and their entire rebellion can be traced back to her loyalty to him and to the cultural loyalty the women feel toward men and the state. In contrast, Triệu Thị Trinh acts outside patriarchal expectations, even disregarding familial obligations by murdering her sister-in-law. Additionally, the Trưng sisters are portrayed as quietly beautiful and dutiful, while Triệu Thị Trinh is portrayed as a giant of a woman with almost supernatural physical proportions. It is unlikely that these women's motivations would be interpreted purely by gender expectations, but as the patriarchal culture of the Han dynasty struggled to overcome the Dong-Son culture, which had been more inclusive of women in positions of power, the Trưng sisters and Triệu Thị Trinh became examples of the polarizing relationship between gender and state power.

In the years following their rebellion, the mythology of the Trưng sisters was increasingly seen through the lens of their economic and social class. The sisters were part of a military family that owned land within rural Vietnam, giving them access to far greater power and economic resources than most other Vietnamese people. This access to power and wealth placed the sisters' family in a direct power struggle with Chinese officials, especially following the marriage of Trưng Trắc to Thi Sách, whose family was also involved in local government. For Thi Sách to stand up to Chinese power and argue for the sanctity of local Vietnamese culture, then, was not entirely a spiritual act or a rebellion arguing for cultural autonomy, but instead was an act equally motivated by the increasing pressure Chinese taxes were placing on his family and other wealthy families in the region. The myth presents Thi Sách and Trưng Trắc as figures driven equally by their love for their culture and their concern for financial stability, which are so closely linked that they are seen as indistinct from one another.

Family honor and economics collide in the myth when Thi Sách is executed by Su Ting, a Chinese official who was directly responsible for the increase in the region's taxes. While most myths present the Trưng sisters as defiantly anti-Chinese throughout their life, it is not until Thi Sách dies that they are portrayed as motivated to take action, which is then tied to the traditional role of the wife and her duty to her husband. This blending of female subservience with female power and leadership is unique to this point in Vietnamese history, which saw the patriarchal structure of Chinese society colliding with the Dong-Son traditions that were known to at times place women in positions of leadership. As Vietnamese society increasingly enforced stricter gender norms and placed women in inferior social positions, writers and artists began to focus on Thi Sách's execution as one of the key elements of the myth: the Trưng sisters were not depicted as rebellious women stepping outside of their prescribed societal role and inappropriately assuming military and political power. Rather, they were women avenging the death of a family member and protecting their family from foreign influence. The perception and portrayal of the sisters was that the further they stepped outside of their prescribed societal role, the greater their devotion to family and therefore the greater their connection to the patriarchal power structure.

Once the Trưng sisters defeat the Chinese army and briefly establish an independent Vietnam, however, they take on a role of unambiguous power within that society. They become queens and political and military leaders who exercise a freedom that is rivaled by no other person within the state. That the sisters were able to rule in such a fashion is indicative of two important facts: Vietnamese culture was more comfortable with female leaders than it would become in the following centuries, suggesting an ease with matriarchal power structures that Chinese influence would eventually suppress in most regions. Also, the sisters were supported by the ruling and rural classes of Vietnam since independence resulted in greater liberties and wealth for almost all people within its borders. Their rule was made particularly popular by the outlawing of all taxation, and in the years following their victory and eventual defeat, these aspects of the Trưng sisters would come to define their role in spiritual and mythological traditions. In temples and cults devoted to their legacy, they are celebrated for their feminine beauty as well as their might in battle, both of which are seen as symbols of patriotism for an independent nation. Charging into battle and motivated by the death of Thi Sách, they were women fulfilling their duty to family and nation, defending a tradition that would remain under assault for centuries.

In contrast to the Trưng sisters, the story of Triệu Thị Trinh presents a form of female power and independence that sits uneasily with notions of family and nation. While the Trưng sisters begin their rebellion because of the death of a husband, Triệu Thị Trinh begins her story by killing her sister-in-law and exiling herself into the forest. This action marks a dramatic separation between the individual and family and state (just as the action of the Trưng sisters connects them more fully with those entities). To murder a member of one's own family is a mark of disrespect and a deed appropriate for a husband to commit, not a woman. The myth does some work to explain away the inappropriate nature of this action by describing the sister-in-law as "evil," which provides enough justification that Triệu Thị Trinh can still function as a hero even as the action itself remains in conflict with the culture she champions. At once, then, Triệu Thị

Trinh takes on the form of male power and then uses that power to damage her family—because of this, she has no choice but to voluntarily exile herself into the wilderness, which serves to further break her away from society and societal norms.

As an exile from the traditions of the culture she will champion, Triệu Thị Trinh is an unlikely hero at the beginning of her narrative. The tension created by her inappropriate behavior is directly addressed by her brother, the man whose wife she has murdered and the person who, in the traditional family structure, would have held some power over Triệu Thị Trinh as well. He approaches her in the wilderness and tries to encourage her to lead a life that is appropriate to her gender and take husband of her own, thus reintegrating herself into the structures of the family and the state. However, since the family structure and state are ruled by Chinese leaders and are not independent in Vietnamese traditions, Triệu Thị Trinh declares, "I only want to ride the wind and walk the waves, slay the big whale of the Eastern Sea, clean up our frontiers, and save the people from drowning. Why should I imitate others, bow my head, stoop over and be a slave? Why resign myself to menial housework?" (qtd. in Marr 198–99). This speech is an impassioned declaration of freedom and a denunciation of the Vietnamese nation and family structure, as they existed under Chinese rule. To live freely in the world means that Triệu Thị Trinh (and by association Vietnam) cannot "imitate others" (meaning the Chinese), just as she cannot complete the "menial housework" traditionally assigned to wives. Instead, she dedicates herself to saving her people from that foreign influence. Her brother is moved by this speech to such an extent that he decides to join her battle, thus giving the rebellion the blessing of the family. Because of this, Triệu Thị Trinh ceases to be a fugitive from a false family structured by Chinese ideals and becomes instead the champion of an idealized Vietnamese family, even as she must fight to ensure that family exists at all.

The physical descriptions of Triệu Thị Trinh further reflect her conflicted relationship as a hero and as a woman behaving "inappropriately" in her societal role. She is stunningly beautiful, so much so that men are awestruck when they see her, and her voice rings out like a bell whenever she speaks. Within this stereotypical femininity, however, Triệu Thị Trinh is also incredibly tall and strong, indicating the masculine characteristics that allow her to succeed in battle. By contrast, the Trưng sisters were described as exhibiting a standard beauty that

HISTORICAL CONTEXT

When the Chinese army began to assert control over Vietnam around 250 BCE, they faced a dynasty that had thrived there for nearly three millennia.

The Lạc dynasty was the first dynasty to rule the area now called Vietnam, taking power around 2879 BCE. The last ruler of the Lạc dynasty, King Hùng Vương XVIII, was defeated by a Chinese general associated with the Qin dynasty, the first major Chinese dynasty to claim power. This general, Thục Phán, held power for a brief period of time, but soon lost control of his new state during political struggles for power within the Chinese government. The Qin dynasty itself soon fell, and new Chinese rulers conquered the northern lands of Vietnam, incorporating the state into the newly risen Han dynasty. The incorporation of Vietnam into the Han dynasty did not entirely take place on the battlefield, however, as the Vietnamese emperor, recognizing the dramatic difference in military strength between the two states, requested that his land become a tributary state of China rather than risk the loss of thousands of lives and the destruction of Vietnamese cities and villages. This decision is indicative of the relationship between China and Vietnam that would evolve over the following thousand years, with varying levels of autonomy given to local Vietnamese governments while tribute through taxes and other goods were consistently paid to the Chinese state. Despite this sometimes tenuous official agreement on the part of the ruling classes, citizens of Vietnam often vehemently opposed the Chinese rule, and the legendary rebellions of the Trưng sisters and of Triệu Thị Trinh were only two instances in a long history of Vietnamese resistance and independence movements.

fit their traditional roles as good wives. Triệu Thị Trinh is clearly beautiful, but her feminine characteristics are exaggerated to an almost unnatural degree. The most obvious example of this is her three-foot-long breasts, which she has to swing over her shoulders in order to enter battle. Seeing only Triệu Thị Trinh's feminine characteristics, her enemies are confused, and they refuse at first to take her seriously. Then, as Triệu Thị Trinh's masculine characteristics take over, they cower from her gaze. These descriptions have more to do with the mythmakers' own cultural uneasiness than with Triệu Thị Trinh herself. In making Triệu Thị Trinh gigantic and otherworldly, she becomes unconnected to women living in their own time, suggesting that while it is possible for the mythically heroic Triệu Thị Trinh to break away from society and lead a rebellion, it is unlikely that any woman who does not share those same physical attributes would be able to achieve such an extraordinary feat.

Likewise, Triệu Thị Trinh's ultimate defeat occurs because of the cultural tensions surrounding her gender. She is not willing to take on her traditional subservient role, and because of that, she is also not married. Her disassociation from the male body becomes a tool the Chinese army can use against her, and once in battle, they charge at her "naked, yelling, and kicking up dust like wild animals" (Marr 199). Triệu Thị Trinh's strength (her disassociation from society and traditional femininity) is now her weakness, which is symbolized in her extreme reaction to the Chinese army. No longer the towering, fierce warrior woman on an elephant, she is transformed into a disgusted and offended woman fleeing in irrational terror. She is later surrounded and forced to commit suicide. This final defeat allows writers in later centuries to undermine her role as a leader and to reinforce the importance of patriarchy and traditional gender roles.

The legend of Triệu Thị Trinh sustained itself well beyond her death and the historical moment in which a female warrior and leader might be celebrated; as such, male writers interested in preserving their patriarchal culture had to twist that story, altering it to suggest that strong women will not ultimately succeed as leaders.

The conclusion of the myth moves Triệu Thị Trinh fully out of historical reality and into the realm of mythology and spirituality. As a ghost, she haunts the Chinese general who defeated her, inspires male warriors to fight for Vietnamese independence, and curses the Chinese army with pestilence. This version of the female warrior is reduced to her core components with her own attributes exaggerated. She cares only about the independence of the Vietnamese state and the downfall of

China, yet by supporting male warriors, she is divorced from her original role championing a culture and a family unit that included power for women. She is no longer a fierce warrior who signifies a return to a Vietnamese culture rooted in gender equality, but rather she symbolizes a military force that can be manipulated in order to support a Vietnam that, while independent, maintains a division of power along gender lines. Her inferiority is further exaggerated when the Chinese armies hang wooden penises on their doors to fend off Triệu Thị Trinh and her curse. Even in death and as a mystically powerful force that arrives in dreams, she can still be disarmed and exiled by the suggestion of masculine force and the male body.

In the centuries of Chinese rule that followed the failed rebellion of Triệu Thị Trinh, her myth and that of the Trưng sisters thrived, especially in rural villages. The names of their generals and the legends of their strength were sanctified, and throughout Vietnamese history, the women were prayed to in times of emergency and hardship. As writers and artists in later centuries turned to these historical figures, however, they mythologized the warriors in ways that reflected their own ambivalence toward women holding military and political power. For the Trưng sisters, this meant interpreting their power and success as a by-product of their devotion to their husbands. Triệu Thị Trinh, however, is portrayed as ultimately weak and unsuccessful because of the flaw of her feminity and her dissassociation from a patriarchal family. For many, especially those in rural villages who felt the weight of oppression from the Chinese government, the rebellious women continued to offer inspiration and proved that any person could rise and demand independence. For many men who claimed power during this time, however, acknowledging Vietnamese independence came easier than acknowledging the potential for independence and strength in Vietnamese women, despite the mythology of these warrior women.

CROSS-CULTURAL INFLUENCE

Vietnam declared independence from China by 1000 CE. While China occasionally regained power over the region and the Chinese government often maintained a strong relationship with the ruling Vietnamese government, the centuries that followed were marked by a greater independence and self-rule than Vietnam had experienced since the fall of their first dynasty. This came to an end, however, when the French government slowly took control of Vietnam through military campaigns in the nineteenth century. Once France secured their power, Vietnam became a part of French Indochina, and colonial rule led to the rapid and often forced spread of Roman Catholicism and other cultural imports from the West.

In the newly colonized Vietnam, the stories of the Trưng sisters gained a new significance. Spirit cults devoted to the sisters had thrived for centuries, and their mythology was a popular source in poetry and drama and was often treated as emblematic of Vietnamese independence, nationhood, and pride. For writers and artists opposing French colonialism, these themes could be easily translated to their modern circumstances. Especially in the climate of censorship and the suppression of Vietnamese resistance movements, the ancient stories of the Trưng sisters and of Triệu Thị Trinh could sometimes be safely recalled even when more blatant anticolonial statements would have been suppressed by the French government.

Phan Bội Châu (1867–1940), Vietnamese activist and revolutionary, told the story of the Trưng sisters in a drama he composed in 1911 titled *Tuồng Trưng Nữ Vương* (Drama of the Trưng monarch). Phan was a forerunner in Vietnamese nationalism, having spent his early life forming independence movements in Vietnam before going into exile in Japan, Hong Kong, and other regions. By 1913, he was a highly sought-after target of the French government as well as a source of inspiration for the Vietnamese and for other independence movements within the colony. While he focused much of his energy on politics and securing foreign aid for his movement, he also believed firmly in the cultural and artistic value of drama as a tool in achieving his patriotic principles and nationalistic goals.

In Phan's version of the story, the Trưng sisters wear first-century clothing, pointing to the historical accuracy of their narrative, yet their language and actions are clearly analogous to modern colonial Vietnam. Phan believed that anticolonial struggles were pointing toward a quickly approaching revolution for independence and that, as had often been the case in Vietnamese history, it was necessary to include women in that revolution. Because of this, Phan broke away from the understanding of the Trưng sisters that had become common at that point in history. While he still includes the death of Thi Sách, Phan emphasizes that the sisters go to war because of their patriotism and their fierce devotion to Vietnamese independence. Phan downplays the women's sense of duty to husbands and family and does away with any sense of stereotypical female characteristics of servitude and obligation. Instead, the death of Thi Sách is one of many sacrifices the sisters must make in order to fight for independence. They give up their connection to their family just as they give up their comfortable existence, their safety, and eventually their lives for the cause. The Trưng sisters, as Phan saw them, were figures devoted to self-sacrifice, and while they certainly display deep love for their family, it is secondary to their love of country and patriotic principles and their core motivation for their briefly successful rebellion.

While Phan created a contemporary drama of political struggle against a colonial invader, he employed centuries-old characters and retained their femininity and stereotypical beauty. The women weep openly at the death and destruction they frequently encounter, often to the detriment of their ability to lead and potentially compromising their end goal. For Phan, these characteristics both heightened the sisters' sacrifice and made their characters more relatable and realistic to the culture within French Indochina that rarely encouraged women to behave outside of their prescribed gender roles. However, this choice also had the unfortunate effect of transforming their femininity—which had been viewed as a strength in earlier myths—into something more like a weakness. At one point, the younger sister even encourages Trưng Trắc by saying, "Come now, we can't give way to ordinary female emotions. We've got to get out and take care of military matters" (qtd. in Marr 201). Although Phan's intent in dramatizing the myth as he did was to encourage women to join the independence movement, he also folded into that narrative a sense of misogyny and a false stereotype of female weakness. The Trưng sisters thus became warriors who also had to overcome, or rise above, their inherent feminine flaws rather than be the fierce, unabashedly female warriors that prior versions of the myth had depicted them to be.

French Indochina was officially dissolved in 1954, bringing an end to colonial rule in Vietnam. However, this did not mark the beginning of a period of peaceful self-rule for the region, but instead initiated another long series of wars and power struggles. From 1954 until 1975, Vietnam was split along the seventeenth parallel north, effectively creating two separate nations, North Vietnam and South Vietnam, each with their own rulers, government systems, and cultural beliefs. For many citizens of the new nations, this split meant that they were forced to relocate based on their political or religious beliefs, with nearly a million people crossing the new border. The split also led to a number of insurgencies, assassination attempts, and invasions, including the military conflict with the United States that is referred to as the Vietnam War.

The constant violence and conflict that Vietnamese citizens faced in the twentieth century had massive and often devastating effects on the nation's culture. Within light of this history, fewer people saw Phan's version of the Trưng sisters' myth and their call to war as inspirational. Rather, the story was reshaped by later generations who oftentimes viewed the legacy of violence and rebellion with skepticism.

One example of this skepticism comes through in the 1989 memoir *When Heaven and Earth Changed Places: A Vietnamese Woman's Journey from War to Peace*, by Le Ly Hayslip. The memoir focuses on Hayslip's real-life experiences first in Vietnam and then as an immigrant to the United States.

Hayslip was born in a small village along the seventeenth parallel that divided North and South Vietnam. As constant war raged around her, Hayslip at a young age became a spy for the Vietcong of North Vietnam. As a result of the tensions surrounding the two nations, she was imprisoned at age fourteen and was sentenced to death and subjected to torture and sexual violence. After being released from prison, she fled to Saigon in South Vietnam (now Ho Chi Minh City) with her mother. She became pregnant at fifteen and later married an American who relocated her and her son to California. Hayslip did not return to Vietnam until 1986, when she traveled back to see the devastation the war brought to the family and friends she had left behind.

In telling this story, Hayslip makes prominent use of the Trưng sisters as well as the other Vietnamese traditions she had learned in her youth, telling her readers that "My father taught me to love god, my family, our traditions, and the people we could not see: our ancestors" (ix). Although she is taught to love traditions, which readers assume include traditional stories, she is skeptical of them, particularly stories such as that of the Trưng sisters, which "called us to war" just as "our myths and legends called us to war" (xiv). While this criticism is made abstractly at first, by the time Hayslip begins her story in earnest, the exact usage of the Trưng sisters becomes clear. The leaders of both North and South Vietnam repeatedly recall the myth of the sisters in an explicit attempt to rally young girls to their cause. The actions of the two nations, regardless of how violent or seemingly cruel, were instead painted as patriotic extensions of the tradition begun by the Trưng sisters so many centuries before. Especially for young children like Hayslip who were taught early on that respecting ancestors and traditions is a moral act, the manipulation of the Trưng sisters and their mythology became a powerful tool of propaganda. This tool is effective for much of Hayslip's life, and she is even told that by dying in battle she would have the opportunity to become an immortal hero, just as Trưng Trắc and Trưng Nhị had. The Vietcong in particular drew on the traditional understanding of the myth as a tale of family loyalty and avoided the more modern interpretations that Phan and others had put in place in order to paint Trưng Trắc once more as a wife fulfilling her duty to her husband.

Hayslip's narrative does not reach an easy conclusion. Instead, she becomes disillusioned with the ruling governments. Self-exiled in the United States, she sees the use of the Trưng sisters and other mythologies as a corruption of the original Vietnamese culture. While she had been taught to respect her ancestors and their cultural stories, she sees instead a government that abuses those traditions, manipulating them in order to achieve their own selfish and often cruel goals. The role of the woman warrior, idealized by the stories of the Trưng sisters and of Triệu Thị Trinh, ceases to represent the idealized life Hayslip might one day enjoy. Instead, forced to live in the United States, she is unable to celebrate her own cultural history and is therefore unable to respect her ancestors, having traded that connection for the relative safety of a new country. In the end, however, she still believes that a better way of life is possible, and she concludes her memoir with a plea to both the Vietnamese and the citizens of the United States, asking all people to leave behind the violent traditions as exemplified by the Trưng sisters and instead fight for understanding and compassion across cultures.

The Trưng sisters and Triệu Thị Trinh myths are inextricably linked to the history of war and rebellion within Vietnam. As such, interpretations of these warrior women change as quickly as the political context does. In times when popular opinion supports a rebellion as righteous and necessary, the women stand as shining examples from the past, exemplifying what is always possible. When the governments instead turn against their people and when conflicts such as the Vietnam War devastate communities, however, the example of mythical military leaders ceases to offer easy lessons or moralistic inspiration. Regardless whether one sees these myths as being violently manipulated or as representing pure ideals, however, their enduring popularity through centuries of diverse regimes, upheavals, and wars speaks to their significant power. Even today, statues and temples of the legendary women warriors populate Vietnam, making the myths available for future generations to use as they will, rising to the ideals of their ancestors or succumbing to similar downfalls.

T. Fleischmann, MFA

BIBLIOGRAPHY

Dong, Lan, ed. *Transnationalism and the Asian American Heroine: Essays on Literature, Film, Myth and Media*. Jefferson: McFarland, 2010. Print.

Hayslip, Ly Le. *When Heaven and Earth Changed Places*. New York: Plume, 1993. Print.

Hood, Steven J. *Dragons Entailed: Indochina and the China-Vietnam War*. New York: East Gate, 1992. Print.

Lockard, Craig. *Southeast Asia in World History*. New York: Oxford UP, 2009. Print.

Marr, David G. "The Question of Women." *Vietnamese Traditions on Trial, 1920–1945*. Berkeley: U of California P, 1981. 190–251. Print.

Taylor, Keith Weller. *The Birth of Vietnam*. Berkeley: U of California P, 1983. Print.

Wrath of Artemis

Author: Pseudo-Apollodorus; Pseudo-Hyginus; Homer
Time Period: 999 BCE–1 BCE; 1 CE–500 CE
Country or Culture: Greek; Roman
Genre: Myth

OVERVIEW

Ferocious yet beautiful, untouched yet nurturing, the goddess Artemis captivates readers with her strange contradictions. A primary deity in the Greek pantheon, Artemis (known as Diana in Roman myths) is the daughter of Zeus and Leto and the sister of Apollo. In ancient Greece, she was worshipped as a virgin goddess associated primarily with hunting and animals but also with major life transitions for women, particularly adolescence and childbirth. Nonetheless, some of the most popular myths about Artemis illustrate her punishing, wrathful nature. Three of these myths include the stories of Actaeon, Niobe, and Callisto as related in the *Bibliotheca* (*The Library of Greek Mythology*), once attributed to the Greek grammarian Apollodorus. The story of Callisto also appears in the *Poetica Astronomica*, formerly attributed to the Roman poet Gaius Julius Hyginus. Both texts are dated in the first century BCE and are now believed to be of uncertain authorship.

Actaeon is a hunter who gazes at Artemis while she bathes, so the offended goddess transforms him into a deer, prompting his own hunting dogs to devour him. Niobe is a mother graced with numerous children, but when her maternal pride gets the better of her and she declares herself more blessed than Leto, the mother of Artemis, Leto commands Artemis and Apollo to kill nearly all of Niobe's children. The aggrieved mother ultimately prays to be turned to stone, in which form she nonetheless weeps continually. A virginal devotee and Artemis's favorite, Callisto (Kallistô) becomes pregnant after she is raped by Zeus. When Callisto can no longer hide her pregnancy from Artemis, the goddess cruelly punishes her by changing her into a bear and even killing the animal according to some sources, but Zeus takes pity and places the animal among the constellations, calling it Arctos.

These stories raise puzzling questions about the nature of Artemis. What is the relationship between her various roles, specifically her connections with hunting and with women's rites of passage? Why does a virgin goddess provide protection for women in childbirth? Furthermore, what is the meaning of Artemis's wrath in these stories, particularly her punishment of Callisto, whom one might expect to receive protection from a goddess who presides over childbirth? These questions are best addressed by examining the prehistoric origins of Artemis, which numerous scholars identify in the Neolithic age of Europe. An anthropological analysis examines both archeological and textual evidence, which traces Artemis to the ancient European goddess of life and death, a deity that flourished for thousands of years prior to the arrival of Indo-European people in Europe.

Believed to be the source of life and death, this prehistoric goddess embodies a radically different view of the life cycle and accounts for the animalistic ferocity and maternal nurturing that Artemis continued to represent in ancient Greece. An anthropological interpretation thus demonstrates how Artemis evolved as a goddess from prehistoric times through classical Greek culture, revealing that although patriarchal cultures diminished the goddess in important ways, many of her core characteristics remain intact in Greek myths. In this way, an anthropological approach allows us to trace the history of Artemis and to comprehend her ruthlessness as only one facet of her manifold nature.

SUMMARY

Pseudo-Apollodorus begins his brief story of Actaeon by naming his parents, Autonoë and Aristaeus, and the centaur Cheiron, who raised Actaeon and trained him as a huntsman. Mentioning one version of the story in which Zeus punishes Actaeon because he courted

Semele, Pseudo-Apollodorus claims that the more common reason for Actaeon's death is that "he saw Artemis bathing" (61). When Actaeon spies the goddess bathing, she transforms him immediately into a deer, driving "his fifty hunting dogs into a frenzy so that they unintentionally ate him" (61). Then, lacking their master, the dogs howl and bay as they begin to search for him. The search leads the dogs to the cave of Cheiron, who produces a "likeness" of Actaeon to soothe the dogs.

Pseudo-Apollodorus also tells the story of Niobe, daughter of Tantalus and wife of Amphion. Niobe is blessed with fourteen children, seven sons and seven daughters, but Pseudo-Apollodorus points out that accounts differ regarding the precise number of her children, with Hesiod claiming that she bore ten sons and ten daughters, Herodotus stating she had five children in total, and Homer asserting that she had six sons and six daughters. Exceedingly proud of her fertility, Niobe "claim[s] to be more blest with children than Leto" (63), daughter of the Titans and the mother of Artemis and Apollo. Niobe's arrogance offends Leto, who "urge[s] Artemis and Apollo against Niobe's children" (64). Artemis uses her arrows to kill the female children of Niobe, and Apollo kills the males. According to Pseudo-Apollodorus, Amphion is spared among the males, and the daughter Chloris (Khlôris) is also not killed. The grief-stricken Niobe then departs from Thebes and returns to her father. After she prays to Zeus, she is metamorphosed into stone, but even in this form, she weeps continually.

Both Pseudo-Apollodorus and Pseudo-Hyginus recount the story of Callisto. Pseudo-Apollodorus states that Callisto, who is reported as a mortal by some sources and as a nymph by others, is "a hunting companion of Artemis" (71), who dresses like the goddess and swears an oath to maintain her virginity. Zeus, however, falls in love with her, disguises himself as Artemis or, according to some sources, Apollo, and rapes her. Wishing to elude the suspicions of his wife, Hera, Zeus transforms Callisto into a bear, but Hera convinces Artemis to hunt down and kill the animal. Other sources claim that Artemis shoots Callisto because the latter fails to protect her virginity. Callisto had become pregnant by Zeus, so he delivers her baby, Arcas, to be reared by Maia. He transforms Callisto into a star and names it Arctus. Pseudo-Hyginus provides a longer version of the story in book 2 of his *Poetica Astronomica*. There, he names Hesiod as his source and states that Callisto was the daughter of Lycaon, ruler in

> *"Out of her zeal for hunting she [Callisto] joined Diana, and was greatly loved by the goddess because of their similar temperaments. Later, when made pregnant by Jove, she feared to tell the truth to Diana. But she couldn't conceal it long, for as her womb grew heavier near the time of her delivery, when she was refreshing her tired body in a stream, Diana realized she had not preserved her virginity."*
>
> Poetica Astronomica

Arcadia. Dedicated to hunting, she follows Diana (the Roman name for Artemis), who grows to love Callisto because of their "similar temperaments" (181). After Jove (Zeus) impregnates Callisto, she is afraid to disclose the truth to Diana, but the goddess eventually discovers it when the signs of Callisto's pregnancy become obvious. When Callisto bathes in a stream "near the time of her delivery" (181), Diana realizes that her devotee has broken her oath of virginity. "In keeping with her deep distrust" (181), Diana punishes Callisto severely by changing her into a bear, and Callisto gives birth in her animal form to Arcas.

Pseudo-Hyginus then offers various sources to elaborate the story and to offer alternate versions. First, he states that Jupiter (Zeus) tricks Callisto by disguising himself as Diana and by pretending to assist Callisto in her hunt. In this way, he is able to overpower her when they are separated from their group. Later, when Diana asks about Callisto's swollen belly, Callisto states that it is "the goddess' fault" (181), which angers Diana and provokes her to transform Callisto into a bear. As a bear, Callisto wanders in the forest, and she and her son are captured by some Aetolians, who present the two as a gift to King Lycaon. Unaware of the law, she and her son charge into a temple, prompting the Arcadians to try to kill both mother and son. Jupiter then saves them by placing them among the constellations, naming Callisto Arctos and her son Arctophylax.

Pseudo-Hyginus reports other sources claiming that Juno, wife of Jupiter, becomes angry at her husband's betrayal and thus transforms Callisto into a bear. Later, Diana is hunting and kills the bear but places it among the constellations after recognizing the creature. Still other sources report that Jupiter himself changes Callisto into a bear to hide his infidelity from Juno, who rushes to the scene in an attempt to catch her husband in the act. When Juno discovers a bear instead of a mortal woman, she directs Diana to kill the animal. Saddened, Jupiter "put[s] in the sky the likeness of a bear represented with stars" (181).

ANALYSIS

In Greek mythology, Artemis is best known for being a virgin huntress and the sister of the god Apollo. She is frequently portrayed as a pure and beautiful goddess who lives away from civilization, shunning men and hunting in the wild with her band of female devotees, from whom she demands strict loyalty. Yet twins Artemis and Apollo resulted from a union between the father god Zeus and Leto, who first bore Artemis and then Apollo, with Artemis assisting in the birth of her brother, which signals another important trait of the goddess: her responsibility for assisting women in childbirth. In fact, Artemis was widely worshipped in ancient Greece as a goddess who assisted girls and women in transitional periods related to sexuality, from girlhood to adolescence to motherhood. Yet in many myths, Artemis is represented not only as a virgin but also as a cruel, punishing deity, raising puzzling questions about her nature and behavior. Why does she transform Actaeon, a fellow hunter, and allow his dogs to kill him? Why does a goddess who presides over maternal matters kill the children of Niobe and punish (rather than protect) Callisto, especially given that her pregnancy results from rape? An anthropological analysis tracing the history of Artemis back to her prehistoric origins allows us to address these questions. Such an investigation reveals that the Greek Artemis is a hybrid of patriarchal religious myth and a much older prehistoric religion in which she was a powerful goddess linked to animals and was believed to control the entire life cycle, from birth to death to regeneration. Both archaeological and textual evidence strongly suggest that this supreme goddess of life and death ruled for many thousands of years prior to the incursions of patriarchal Indo-European tribes into Europe and specifically into Greece. These Indo-European people brought with them a new religion in which

a male sky god reigned supreme. Interestingly, this new pantheon significantly diminished the ancient goddess of life and death but preserved many of her key traits in the figure of Artemis. This history helps to explain the apparently contradictory behavior of Artemis in some of her best-known Greek myths.

Anthropology is a very broad field that is defined most generally as the study of humanity, with roots in disciplines ranging from the natural and social sciences to the humanities. Anthropologists study diverse topics such as how human beings relate to each other and organize societies in biological, social, cultural, linguistic, and material terms, to name a few prominent categories in the field. Because of the breadth of topics and questions that anthropologists address, scholars from numerous disciplines use many diverse techniques to conduct research, including archaeological fieldwork, linguistic decoding, and religious studies. Addressing the meaning of Artemis in religious and mythical terms both in historic ancient Greece and in prehistoric times, the analysis in this article falls under the rubric of cultural anthropology and makes use of research in the fields of archeology, religious studies, and mythology. By examining evidence from prehistoric cultures, such as temple frescoes, bits of text on stone tablets, and clay figurines, as well as texts written by historical ancient Greek and Roman writers, one can begin to decipher the meaning of an older goddess who survives most vividly as the Greek deity Artemis.

One of the earliest Greek accounts of Artemis appears in the *Homeric Hymns*, an anonymous collection of thirty-four poems that celebrate the attributes of the Greek gods and goddesses, with some recounting stories that illustrate the deities' powers. The hymns are called "Homeric" because their meter, dialect, and style match that of the epic poems *The Iliad* and *The Odyssey*, which are attributed to a poet named Homer (Rayor 1). The collection contains two hymns to Artemis, both of which focus mainly on her status as graceful virgin, her link to hunting and wild animals, and her sibling relationship with Apollo. Hymn 27 begins with "I sing of Artemis, goddess with baying hounds / and golden distaff, revered virgin, deer hunter / who rains arrows, sister of gold-bladed Apollo" (lines 1–3). She is described as "delighting in the hunt" and shooting "deadly arrows" as she roams through mountains and valleys (4, 6). The poem emphasizes her power as a huntress as she strikes fear into wild beasts ("animal cries / echo horribly in the dense forest," 7–8) and causes earth and sea to tremble. The second part of the hymn portrays the beauty and grace of Artemis when she unstrings her bow and visits the "great house" of her "dear brother Phoibus Apollo in rich Delphi" to lead the Muses and Graces in dancing (13–14). As she leads the dance, the other goddesses celebrate how Leto bore children "far the best of all the gods in counsel and deeds" (20). The poet then bids farewell to the "children of Zeus and lovely-haired Leto" (21), promising to remember them.

By including the goddess's link to hunting, wild animals, her ferocity, virginity, beauty, and her relation to Apollo, the hymn corresponds to Artemis's key traits in some of the most popular Greek myths about her. The myths of Actaeon, Niobe, and Callisto all focus on the goddess's hunting prowess and on her merciless, punishing nature, which is frequently linked in some way to her virginity. In the story of Actaeon, Artemis punishes her fellow hunter, because she is a virgin and by observing her bathing, Actaeon has violated her remoteness and divine purity. Likewise, Artemis transforms and banishes (or kills) Callisto, who is also a huntress, because her pregnancy reveals that she has broken her oath of virginity. That Callisto becomes pregnant against her will does not move Artemis to pity, but she mercilessly punishes her devotee, who is ultimately spared only by Zeus when he transforms her and her son into constellations. Finally, directed by Leto to kill the children of Niobe, both Artemis and Apollo show marked ruthlessness as they use their bows and arrows to punish a mother's swollen pride.

Interestingly, the Homeric hymn omits one of Artemis's most important functions: assisting girls and women in key life transitions. In ancient Greece and other Mediterranean cultures, there were many cults of Artemis, Diana (her Roman counterpart), and other goddesses with different names but similar functions. In these cults, Artemis was widely established not only as goddess of the hunt but as one who presided over girls' transformation from virgin to "fully acculturated and fully tamed woman" and over childbirth and child rearing (*Oxford Classical Dictionary* 182–83). In one well-documented ancient ritual, girls between the ages of five and ten dressed as bears and served Artemis in preparation for their subsequent passage into adolescence and marriage (182). The story of the birth of Artemis and Apollo hints at Artemis's role as maternal protector because she is said to assist her own mother in delivering her twin, Apollo, who was born after her. Some scholars connect her ferocity with this influence over childbirth.

Powell, for instance, describes her as "a hunter of human prey who uses her bow to strike down women in childbirth or those who transgress against her terrible law. When a woman died suddenly without explanation, she was said to be 'struck by the arrows of Artemis'" (204–5). In one sense, then, Artemis can be viewed as a typical Greek deity who wields terrible and merciless power over humans. Like Zeus, who thoughtlessly rapes mortals and strikes them down with his thunderbolt, Artemis is just as likely to harm her worshippers as to help them. Nonetheless, puzzling questions remain about the relationships among her identities as hunter, virgin, and protector of female rites of passage related to sexuality.

Answers to these questions begin to emerge from the archaeological evidence of prehistoric religions that flourished long before ancient Greek culture, whose archaic period is dated approximately 750 BCE. Archaeologists such as Marija Gimbutas have discovered that prior to the arrival of Indo-European people in western Europe, cultures existed that worshipped what she calls the Great Goddess of Life and Death. These cultures flourished in Neolithic Europe and Asia Minor roughly between 7000 and 3000 BCE and are described by Gimbutas as the cultures of Old Europe (*Living* 3). The material remains of these cultures, including sculptures, rings, seals, frescoes, and images from temples and tombs, reflect female divinities modeled on various animals, particularly birds and other winged creatures, bees, snakes, bears, and deer. Human goddess figures are also frequently shown with these animals and clearly represent fertility, death, and regeneration. Gimbutas and others have interpreted these ubiquitous artifacts and images, which span large geographical areas and many millennia, as evidence of a goddess signifying not simply fertility but life, death, and regeneration in a way that implies the full circle of life. This representation was possible because these prehistoric religions apparently did not divide life and death as opposing events in the way that later historic religions did by worshipping life-givers while dishonoring those who bring death (xvii). Instead, these religions view birth as part of a cycle that includes death and regeneration, a connection made clear, for example, by prehistoric funerary themes in architecture and symbolic objects whose designs incorporate images of female genitalia and the womb (55).

When Indo-European tribes migrated into Old Europe in waves beginning in approximately 4300 BCE, they brought a very different culture of male domination, but they infiltrated various regions at different

HISTORICAL CONTEXT

The ancient cults of Artemis were numerous and powerful. The goddess was venerated not only in ancient Greece proper but also in Lydia, Crete, and Italy. According to archaeologist Marija Gimbutas, she was often called Artemis in these cults but also had other local names, such as Diana in Rome, Diktynna (or Diktynnaia), Pasiphaê, Europa («the wide-glancing one»), Britomartis («sweet virgin») in Crete, Laphria in Aetolia, Callisto (Kallistô) in Arcadia, and Agrotera («the wild») (*Goddesses and Gods* 198). These cults frequently involved rituals related to the transitions of girls and women, particularly the passage from childhood to womanhood and childbirth. However, there is also evidence of her worship in relation to initiation rites for boys and to warfare in Sparta and Athens. The most prominent cult center of Artemis was in Ephesus in Asia Minor, where a famous second-century CE marble statue shows her with bulls, griffins, and sphinxes adorning her body, along with dozens of breasts representing her link to fertility.

According to scholar Barry Powell, when the Christian apostle Paul visited Ephesus to spread the new religion of Christianity, he met a crowd who drowned out his words for two hours with shouts of "Great is Diana of the Ephesians!" (204). Evidence such as this demonstrates that the cults of Artemis endured not only in patriarchal pagan religions but well into the Christian era.

The deeply rooted cults also attest to a belief in the goddess' benevolent nature, in contrast to her wrathful behavior in many Greek myths. Yet scholars such as Gimbutas have been careful to note that Greek myth did not entirely replace earlier belief systems; rather, the Greek deities emerged from the mingling of Indo-European and Old European cultures that went on for millennia (*Living* 154). Close study of the Greek myths reveals these fascinating processes of cultural shifts and negotiations.

times and with inconsistent effects (Gimbutas, *Living* 131). The Indo-Europeans were patriarchal, which means that men dominated in their social organizations, and the tribes who eventually invaded areas corresponding to Greece in the third millennium BCE brought a new religion that exalted a male sky god resembling Zeus. However, the Indo-Europeans appear initially to have been skilled on horseback but not in navigation, which means that certain Aegean islands remained free of Indo-European influence long after the first invaders had appeared on the mainlands (131). One such island is Crete, where a Minoan goddess religion flourished for nearly two thousand years after

other Old European cultures had disintegrated through contact with the Indo-Europeans (132). The remains of Minoan temple complexes in Crete reflect worship of a goddess very similar to the Old European snake and bird goddess of life and death. Another nearby island named Thera contains a sixteenth-century BCE Minoan fresco showing an enthroned life-giving goddess of childbirth, who also embodies the fecundity of nature itself (*Language* 109). This figure is shown elevated on a mountaintop and is surrounded by winged dogs or lions (109). She too greatly resembles the Old European goddess figure represented in older pre–Indo-European cultures on the mainland.

Many scholars believe that this mother goddess figure with her wild animals is the ancestor of Artemis, and the evidence for this view is strong. Artemis as goddess of hunting and animals corresponds to the wild animal iconography of the Old European goddess, whose maternal significance also helps to explain Artemis's role as protector of women in childbirth. In addition, the Old European goddess's role as the source of both life and death helps to explain Artemis's death-dealing behavior. Because birth and death were viewed as interconnected, Artemis's destructive ferocity and maternal protection are not contradictory but part of a life continuum that was once viewed as natural. Further evidence of Artemis's prehistoric roots includes her name, which is not a Greek word and appears on tablets found in Pylos that are written in a language known as Linear B, an early form of Greek that came into use in approximately 1450 BCE. These Linear B tablets reveal dedications to goddess figures, including Artemis. Linear B belongs to an early Greek culture known as the Mycenaeans, descendants of Indo-Europeans who became prominent in 1600 BCE and eventually conquered Minoan cities. Interestingly, the archaeological record shows widespread goddess worship among the Mycenaeans despite their Indo-European roots. For example, in addition to the evidence from the Linear B tablets, the Mycenaeans produced thousands of goddess figurines. In the words of Gimbutas, the Mycenaeans thus "represent an important transitional phase between Old European gynocentric culture and the classical Greek culture, where the male element came to dominate almost completely" (*Language* 152). The evidence of Artemis's worship and other goddesses among the Mycenaeans indicates the deep roots of goddess religions prior to and during the process of Indo-European infiltrations into Old Europe.

Ancient Greek culture as we know it arose later in the eighth century BCE from a more stringently patriarchal group of Indo-Europeans, who overthrew the Mycenaeans in approximately 1200 BCE (Gimbutas, *Language* 152). With the advent of patriarchal cultures and religion, the figure of Artemis underwent significant changes. Diminished status and fragmentation are two of the principal changes that affected goddess figures with the advent of patriarchal religions. As the patriarchal religion of the sky god Zeus increasingly dominated, it could not eliminate the deeply rooted ancient goddess figures, so it incorporated them as subordinates in the form of wives, daughters, and sisters (Baring and Cashford 302). In the new religion, Artemis thus became the daughter of Zeus and the sister of Apollo, who gradually overshadowed her importance. In addition, the powers of ancient goddesses tend to become fragmented or split among different characters, and the goddesses sometimes gain new attributes (302). Scholars point out that Artemis was not originally a virgin, but this feature was added to make her more acceptable to patriarchal culture (Wall 12).

Despite her later status as virgin, daughter, and sister, Artemis retained in Greek culture most of her ancient traits. As goddess of the hunt, she was still linked to sacred animals, with Homer describing her as "mistress of the animals," a clear connection to the prehistoric goddess of life flanked by wild or winged animals, which were primary sources of food before the establishment of agriculture (Powell 204). As a life-giving goddess, Artemis was still believed to aid women in childbirth and, as noted, was worshipped in cults that enacted rituals dedicated to young girls' passage into adolescence and motherhood. As a ferocious hunter and even punisher, the Greek Artemis retained her prehistoric symbolism of nature's wildness as the maternal source of both life and death. She was venerated widely throughout the Mediterranean and had many names; in Arcadia, she was called Kallisto, which means "the beautiful," and

according to Gimbutas, the Arcadian Kallisto was not only the "companion and double" of Artemis but "was said to have assumed the form of a bear" (*Goddesses and Gods* 198).

Callisto as a form of Artemis herself helps us to make sense of this highly puzzling myth as it has been passed down to modern times. First, one can dismiss Artemis's virginity as irrelevant because it is a later addition to her persona. Second, with their shared identities in ancient cults, Callisto and Artemis can be understood as one figure split into two (Wall 15). Callisto's pregnancy and transformation into a bear represents the symbolic maternal fertility that Artemis once prominently represented prior to her "purification" and transformation into a virgin. Callisto's rape by Zeus and her rejection by Artemis thus represent a patriarchal revision of what might originally have been a very different story. But if the myth is not really about rape and punishment, was it simply invented to diminish and fragment Artemis's power, or might it signify something else? Wall argues that the Callisto story actually represents a fertility ritual enacting a sacred marriage between the sky god Zeus and Artemis to renew the fertility of the land (15). As noted, Greek girls dressed as bears in rites dedicated to Artemis, and in some versions of the Callisto story, Zeus disguises himself as Artemis to trick Callisto. This disguise could make sense if one understands the myth as a deliberate sacrifice of Callisto's virginity to Artemis herself. In this sense, the union between Zeus and Callisto might not originally have signified a rape but a ritual "marriage" for the sake of celebrating and renewing fertility. When Callisto becomes a bear, she is symbolically like the goddess, which makes sense given the bear's link with Artemis and its prominent role in prehistoric representations of goddess figures. On this interpretation, Artemis did not originally reject Callisto but simply sent her back to the secular world with her newfound fertility, which signified wisdom (Wall 17).

Similarly, scholars have suggested the myth of Actaeon as a story of a sacred marriage, specifically a ritual union with and sacrifice of the goddess's consort. Artemis was known as both goddess of the hunt but also as "mistress of animals," the mother of all of nature (Baring and Cashford 324). She slays animals, but she also sometimes appears incarnated as an animal, suggesting a strange paradox in which the hunter and the hunted are somehow the same figure (324). Again, this paradox relates to the goddess as the source of both life and death. Because she gives and takes away life, her role as hunter and hunted symbolizes a necessary balance in the life continuum (324). In some paintings of the Actaeon story, Artemis is shown with a deerskin hanging from her back, suggesting that when she transforms Actaeon into a stag, she changes him into a version of herself—that is, her consort (331). Her interaction with him then comes to symbolize a type of union, a sacred marriage, followed by a ritual sacrifice that again signifies a fertility ritual but also signifies death in a dramatization of "the relation between infinite and finite life" (332) that Artemis represents.

Because these interpretations are reconstructions of the myths based on Artemis's prehistoric meaning, they are necessarily tenuous, but there is abundant evidence that the Artemis of ancient Greece descended from an older matriarchal goddess of life and death. If the Artemis that survives in historical records seems paradoxical, the remains of prehistoric religions are clear and offer compelling evidence that helps us to make sense of an apparently enigmatic figure. Artemis's contradictions are not surprising; what is astonishing is how much of her prehistoric meaning survived, with vestiges alive even today in certain Christian practices surrounding the Virgin Mary, the biblical mother of Jesus Christ. According to several sources, the Old European image of the goddess as a bear is so deeply entrenched in mythical thought that it survives in modern Crete in the Christian epithet "Virgin Mary of the Bear." In this and other myths, the ancient meaning of Artemis lives on.

CROSS-CULTURAL INFLUENCE

Artemis as the goddess of life and death reemerges not only in current religious practices but also in American twentieth-century poetry. An early example of this reemergence appears in Edith Wharton's *Artemis to Actaeon and Other Verse*, a volume of poetry she published in 1909. Wharton (1862–1937) was a celebrated American writer best known for her numerous classic novels, including *The House of Mirth* (1905) and *The Age of Innocence* (1920), for which she won the Pulitzer Prize. Yet Wharton also wrote poetry, including "Artemis to Actaeon," an unrhymed, elegant poem of ninety-four lines written in iambic pentameter. The poem radically challenges traditional interpretations not only of the Actaeon myth but of the Greek gods' significance, portraying them as desiring and even envying the warm essence of humans. In Wharton's hands, Artemis does not punish Actaeon but claims to love him and paradoxically rewards his greatness with

death, which signifies not an end to life but regeneration. Wharton's poem thus recalls ancient notions of Artemis as it reflects modern sentiments by granting Artemis a voice and the power to demand a new sort of engagement from the reader.

Wharton's poem begins with the speaker adopting the voice and persona of Artemis and offering a confessional monologue in which she describes the events of the Actaeon myth. Speaking directly to the transgressive hunter, the speaker's voice is complex as she initially describes how she thinks Actaeon interprets the story. Addressing him, she declares, "Thou couldst not look on me and live: so runs / The mortal legend" (lines 1–2). She proceeds to describe the myriad settings in which Actaeon envisioned her, "the cloud, the wave, the bough" (4), and so forth, and imagines that from his perspective, she mocked and deliberately lured him to his fate. She asks, "Mocked I thee not in every guise of life" (7), luring him into "the primal silences / Where the heart hushes and the flesh is dumb?" (10–11). She supposes that Actaeon was driven by relentless desire made stronger by the impenetrable barrier between him and a goddess, so that "thy feet / Refused their rest, thy hands the gifts of life, / Thy heart its losses" (19–21). Concluding the stanza, she makes it clear that she presents her impression of his perspective: "This was thy thought. / And mine?" (23–24).

This question allows the speaker's voice to segue into the next stanza, where she reveals her own perspective. She first laments the gods' immortal yet empty existence: "The gods, they say, have all: not so!" (line 25). What the gods have, she protests, is beauty, wealth, and worship, "the blue / Spirals of incense and the amber drip / Of lucid honey-comb on sylvan shrines" (26–28), pure white doves, and garlands of ivy "glaucous with the dew" (31). They have, in short, everything from man except man himself, and so they remain cold and distant, enviously gazing from afar at the depth of human experience. Paradoxically, the gods await most anxiously those humans who transgress against their law, those who "fling past the people and the priest" (44) to enter the "inmost shrine" (45), where they "Drop dead of seeing—while the others prayed!" (47). The gods most desire this audacity that

Incarnates us, pale people of your dreams,
Who are but what you make us, wood or stone,
Or cold chryselephantine hung with gems,
Or else the beating purpose of your life. (lines 49–52)

In this way, the deities dream of being "*disimmortalised / In giving immortality!*" (58–59). Artemis, however, acknowledges the gods' fickleness as they sometimes allow such transgressions to go unpunished.

Yet, addressing Actaeon again in the third stanza, she makes clear that his trespass would not occur without consequences partly because of his deep ambition. Artemis claims that she recognized his "questing foot" as one that "never / Revisits the cold hearth of yesterday / Or calls achievement home" (lines 70–72). Surprisingly, however, she does not condemn but admires this aspect of her rival, confessing that "Long, long hadst thou inhabited my dreams" (75) and that although she judged him "rash to reach the heart of life" (78) in his transgression against her divinity, her wrath was in fact a sign of love. She proclaims, "*Because I love thee thou shalt die!*" (80).

The concluding stanza elaborates this astonishing claim. Immortality, insists Artemis, is not to wander "Unlimited through vast Olympian days, / Or sit in dull dominion over time" (82–83) but "to drink fate's utmost at a draught" (84), "to scale the summit of some soaring moment" (86), and "to snatch the crown of life and seal it up / Secure forever in the vaults of death!" (88–89). Thus, according to her, her reaction to Actaeon was a gift in which she allowed him "to lose thyself in me" (90) and to

Relive in my renewal, and become
The light of other lives, a quenchless torch
Passed on from hand to hand, till men are dust
And the last garland withers from my shrine. (91–94)

This challenging poem achieves its effects in part through the skillful contrast of abstract language and concrete imagery. Wharton begins the poem with vivid imagery when she claims that Actaeon witnessed her among images of nature, such as the clouds, water, trees, and other natural elements. The poet contrasts these concrete images with abstract language, such as when Artemis suggests that like the tide drawing waves from the shore, she drew Actaeon from the land "Till I enveloped thee from verge to verge / And hid thee in the hollow of my being" (lines 16–17). Here, the concreteness suggested by "hollow" shifts to the abstract word "being" to suggest the goddess' divine and unattainable nature. The second stanza renews the vivid imagery in the lengthy portrayal of the gods' opulence and loveliness, the blue smoke of their incense, the amber honeycomb, and the immaculate doves with their "Twin-cooing in the osier-plaited cage" (30). Wharton then immediately deflates the splendor of these images by describing them in abstract terms such as "Man's wealth, man's servitude, but not himself!" (32), and she laments that the gods are "pinnacled on man's subserviency" (35). Whereas abstract language in the first stanza refers to Artemis's exalted divinity and concrete imagery renders the human world, the speaker uses abstract language in the second stanza to describe the gods' disadvantage in relation to humans and concrete images to render the best of the human world that the gods possess. In this way, the speaker enacts a formal reversal that begins to mirror the opposing perspectives of Artemis and Actaeon.

The rest of the poem shifts again by increasingly emphasizing abstract language to elaborate the speaker's surprising love for Actaeon and her subversive view of immortality. Artemis states that she recognized that Actaeon was "fashioned for one hour's high use, / Nor meant to slake oblivion drop by drop" and that he was "rash to reach the heart of life" (73–74, 78). In this section, the spare use of imagery refers to Actaeon's "questing foot" not content to return to yesterday's "cold hearth" or to drink the unsatisfying drops of oblivion. These images function to support the more prominent abstract concepts of achievement, oblivion, and dreams, such as when Artemis proclaims that by inhabiting her dreams, Actaeon had surprised the goddess "as harts surprise a pool" (76). This emphasis on abstraction prepares the reader for the speaker's startling proclamation of her love as the cause of Actaeon's death and her rejection of conventional notions of immortality. She explains in the final stanza that true immortality is not the eternal, dull life of "vast Olympian days" (82) but to seize the greatest moment one can find and to preserve it paradoxically "in the vaults of death" (89). The few images in this concluding stanza—the wine, the torch, and the garland decorating the goddess's shrine—serve to facilitate the difficult concept of life in death that the speaker posits.

This paradoxical notion of life in death is striking for how it recalls the ancestor of Artemis, the ancient goddess of life, death, and regeneration. Artemis's claim that "*Because I love thee thou shalt die*" is puzzling, as is her assertion that by seizing the highest moment, one can preserve it forever in death. What does it mean when Artemis states that Actaeon, by losing himself in her, is able to "Relive in my renewal, and become / The light of other lives," like a torch passed on through the generations until the goddess is no longer worshipped? The speaker redefines Actaeon's gaze not as a crime for which he is punished but as a bold and even heroic deed that merits immortality. As might be expected, this immortality demands physical death but does not result in the sort of eternal life one might expect. Immortality, according to Artemis, signifies renewal that is both enacted and represented by her to literally enlighten "other lives." The phrase "lose thyself in me, / Relive in my renewal" is especially intriguing as it presents a view of the goddess consistent with the full meaning of her prehistoric ancestor. Wharton's Artemis is thus not a cold and distant Olympian; she is a goddess who loves mortals precisely for their humanity and whose expression of love links death to the ideal of human greatness as the true achievement of life and immortality. Her claim of the gods' disadvantage in relation to humans serves to close the conventional gap between mortals and immortals that was posited in ancient Greek thought. In this way, the poem echoes and develops Artemis's prehistoric roles as hunter and hunted, the "mistress of animals" who embodies the very creatures she sacrifices.

Wharton presents this ancient meaning of Artemis in modern form through a first-person confessional account that gives voice to the goddess herself. Her monologue sustains the poetic form of iambic pentameter and simultaneously suggests a dramatic performance. This performance is a carefully crafted argument in which Artemis first presents the view of Actaeon, moves on to refute the conventional view of the gods' privilege, and concludes by redefining her relationship to Actaeon and the meaning of immortality itself. In this way, Artemis forges an interiority that reflects the emphasis in modern verse on individual emotion and experience. Yet she also becomes a confident orator, a female figure who claims the right to speak and define the meaning of life and death itself. This aspect of her performance reflects the growing emphasis in twentieth-century American poetry on women's voices and experiences. Written early in the century, the poem emerges as an early example of the feminist sensibility that blossomed in later years. As death-dealer and life-giver, Wharton's vocal Artemis recalls ancient truths and enacts her own symbolic renewal, anticipating the amazing proliferation of female power in art and life in subsequent decades.

Ashleigh Imus, PhD

BIBLIOGRAPHY

Baring, Anne, and Jules Cashford. *The Myth of the Goddess: Evolution of an Image*. London: Viking, 1991. Print.

Gimbutas, Marija. *The Goddesses and Gods of Old Europe, 6500–3500 BC: Myths and Cult Images*. Berkeley: U of California P, 1982. Print.

---. *The Language of the Goddess: Unearthing the Hidden Symbols of Western Civilization*. San Francisco: Harper, 1989. Print.

---. *The Living Goddesses*. Ed. Miriam Robbins Dexter. Berkeley: U of California P, 1999. Print.

Hyginus. *The Myths of Hyginus*. Trans. Mary Grant. Ed. Grant. Lawrence: U of Kansas, 1960. Print.

Oxford Classical Dictionary. 3rd ed. Ed. Simon Hornblower and Anthony Spawforth. Oxford: Oxford UP, 2009. Print.

Powell, Barry B. *Classical Myth*. 3rd ed. Upper Saddle River: Prentice Hall, 2001. Print.

Pseudo-Apollodorus. *The Library of Greek Mythology*. Trans. Keith Aldrich. Lawrence: Coronado, 1975. Print.

Rayor, Diane J., trans. *The Homeric Hymns*. Berkeley: U of California P, 2004. Print.

Wall, Kathleen. *The Callisto Myth from Ovid to Atwood: Initiation and Rape in Literature*. Kingston, ON: McGill-Queen's UP, 1988. Print.

Wharton, Edith. *Artemis to Actaeon and Other Verse*. New York: Scribner, 1909. Print.

MYTH AND MONSTROSITY

David and Goliath

Author: Traditional Jewish
Time Period: 2499 BCE–1000 BCE
Country or Culture: Southern Levant
Genre: Myth

OVERVIEW

The book of 1 Samuel in the Old Testament chronicles the rise and fall of the first Israelite king after the period of leadership by judges. The four main characters are Samuel, King Saul, David, and Goliath. The books of Samuel, named after the prophet who guides Israel through the period that serves as a transition between leadership by judges to kings, tell the stories of Saul and David, contrasting these two men's conquests, leadership, and kingdoms. The first half of 1 Samuel tells about the rise and fall of King Saul, who is appointed by Samuel under God's direction; it also shares the story of the ascent of King David.

As Saul falls into disfavor with God because of his own arrogance and disobedience, David, a shepherd from Bethlehem, emerges from the background. David is first mentioned halfway through the book when Samuel goes to Bethlehem upon an order from God to seek one of Jesse's sons as the future ruler. Samuel asks Jesse to allow him to see all of his sons and then rejects each one on God's orders until only the youngest, tending sheep in the field, remains. God immediately gives his spirit to David, empowering him to eventually take the role of leadership that he would fill for years to come.

David's battle with the Philistine champion Goliath is the first instance in which he displays his ability to fight. This battle showcases David's intention to follow God's orders in becoming king of Israel. The tale of the battle between a lowly shepherd boy and a giant became the focus of biblical commentary, literature, and art for centuries.

Analysis of the story can be centered on David's heroism from a historical and religious viewpoint as well as the way David as a character fulfills the role of a hero in both an epic fashion and an archetypal one. Since historical analysis focuses on the way a piece of literature fits into the culture from which it was born, it can include a clarification of the social, cultural, or religious environment that surrounds the time period of the story itself. However, the historical critic's main goal is to provide a clarification of the meaning to the audience that was contemporary to the piece itself. The archetypal interpretation adds a layer of complexity to the critique as it explains how a particular aspect of the story can be seen as a part of what psychoanalyst Carl Jung called the "collective unconscious." For this story, both David's heroism and the thematic idea of a battle between an untried youth and a seasoned or fearful opponent can be examined in light of the archetype of the hero on a hero's journey.

SUMMARY

The story of David begins when Samuel obeys God by going to Jesse the Bethlehemite in order to choose a replacement for King Saul. Jesse parades his sons in front of Samuel until all but the youngest have been seen by the prophet. When David is sent for and then introduced to Samuel, Samuel knows at once that the boy will be the next king of Israel.

Soon after Samuel chooses David to replace Saul, the king is struck by "an evil spirit" (1 Sam. 16:14). His advisors urge him to send for a musician to help soothe his spirits. David is recommended and called into service for Saul when needed. In the meantime, Saul and the Israelite army gather in the Valley of Elah to battle with the Philistines. The Philistines' most terrifying champion is Goliath of Gath, "whose height was six cubits and a span" (1 Sam. 17:4), which in modern measurements is approximately nine-and-a-half feet. The giant, commonly referred to simply as the Philistine, is also described by his military garb: "He had a helmet of bronze on his head, and he was armed with a coat of mail; the weight of the coat was five thousand shekels of

217

"'Am I a dog, that you come to me with sticks?' And the Philistine cursed David by his gods. The Philistine said to David, 'Come to me, and I will give your flesh to the birds of the air and to the wild animals of the field.' But David said to the Philistine, 'You come to me with sword and spear and javelin; but I come to you in the name of the Lord of hosts.'"

1 Samuel

---

bronze. He had greaves of bronze on his legs and a javelin of bronze slung between his shoulders. The shaft of his spear was like a weaver's beam, and his spear's head weighed six hundred shekels of iron" (1 Sam. 17:5–7). His size and strength emphasize his ferocity as a fighter, and his attitude increases the fear he instills in the Israelite army. He taunts the army with the bargain that the Philistines will be servants to the Israelites if an Israelite champion can defeat him.

Three of David's older brothers serve in Saul's army, so his father takes him out of the field where he is tending sheep to deliver food to them and their commanders. While David is speaking with his brothers, Goliath repeats his taunt, and the Israelite army runs from the giant in fear. In their terror, some members of the army discuss the king's reward among themselves. Hearing the potential reward, David asks for specifics and is assured that the prize consists of freedom from taxes for his family, marriage to one of Saul's daughter, and riches. As David asks for reassurance of this compensation, his oldest brother scolds him for presumption. Disregarding his brother's anger over his questions, David approaches Saul and volunteers to fight the giant. He pushes aside Saul's concerns over his age and lack of military experience by pointing out his previous victories over wild animals while guarding his father's sheep. He also claims God's protection. Saul accedes to David's desire to fight Goliath and dresses the boy in his own armor. David rejects the battle gear and takes only his staff, his slingshot, and five small stones to face the enemy.

Goliath mocks the boy, but David holds strong, once again claiming God's protection. He then rushes at the giant, pulls a stone from his bag, and places it in his sling. The stone flies from the sling with deadly accuracy, hitting Goliath in the forehead, and the giant falls to the ground. David finishes his task by taking Goliath's own sword and chopping off his head, ensuring an Israelite victory. The story ends with the defeat of the Philistine forces.

ANALYSIS

To truly understand the heroism David displays when he fights Goliath, it is necessary to consider the role this battle plays in both David's own biography and the history of Israel contemporary to the battle. Therefore, it is important to learn about the background of the story and the religious overtones that make the story integral to the biblical story. Once these aspects of the story are clarified, David can be examined as an archetypal hero.

In the biblical book of 1 Samuel, the nation of Israel is at war with the Philistines. God has continually interacted with the Israelites under the leadership of Samuel, but as Samuel grows old, the people demand that he anoint a king. God tells Samuel to tell the people that a king would take the best of what they have through required tithes, but the people do not listen and continue to demand a king. Eventually, to appease the people and Samuel, God sends Saul—"not a man among the people of Israel more handsome than he; he stood head and shoulders above anyone else" (1 Sam. 9:2)—to fill the role. The people are content with Saul because they choose to focus on exterior signs of power rather than on actual intellectual, political, or even emotional ability to serve as their king. This simplistic acceptance becomes problematic as Saul's reign progresses and he makes rash decisions that result in disfavor in God's sight. Even though his leadership varies in strength, Saul rules as king of Israel for forty-two years (1 Sam. 13:1).

During his reign, Saul is aggressive in his pursuit of the Philistines, who have once again begun warring against the Israelites. However, Saul does not follow God's ways as faithfully or wisely as he should, so after a series of unfortunate decisions, the Israelites are put into a position where the Philistines have the advantage. The result is that Saul loses God's favor and sinks into a self-involved depression and fear. Samuel also sinks into grief at Saul's failures until God sends him to anoint a new king: "The Lord said to Samuel, 'How long will you grieve over Saul, since I have rejected him from being king over Israel? Fill your horn with oil and set out'" (1 Sam. 16:1).

God's choice of a new king is the beginning of Saul's ultimate removal from power and David's introduction as Israel's new hero. As a result, David is set up as a champion before the battle with Goliath even begins. The heroism is first noted in light of the nation's relationship as God's chosen people. Because God is involved in the way the nation is evolving, his choice of David is significant. When David is around fourteen or fifteen years old, Samuel goes to Bethlehem upon God's order to anoint one of Jesse's sons as future king. In contrast to the people's choice of Saul, God points out that David, rather than one of his brothers, is the best candidate for king. When Saul is chosen as king, Samuel focuses on his physical appearance and prowess. However, when Samuel is sent to Jesse to choose one of his sons as a replacement for Saul, God rebukes Samuel for falling into the trap of looking only at the surface qualities. Upon seeing Jesse's oldest son, Eliab, Samuel thinks, "Surely the Lord's anointed is now before the Lord" (1 Sam. 16:6). God's answer to Samuel's shortsighted forgetfulness comes quickly: "Do not look on his appearance or on the height of his stature because I have rejected him; for the Lord does not see as mortals see; they look on the outward appearance, but the Lord looks on the heart" (1 Sam. 16:7). After viewing and hearing God's rejection of all of Jesse's sons who are present, Samuel inquires about other offspring, and David is presented to him. Though David is described as "ruddy" and "handsome," with "beautiful eyes" (1 Sam. 16:12), it is his spirit that wins him God's favor. Presumably, Jesse and his sons are required to keep David's appointment quiet, and they appear to do so since David is not heard from for several years following Samuel's visit to Bethlehem.

David appears next in the story when Saul's disobedience to God leads to problems for the king. After Saul arrogantly offers sacrifices to God, God sends an evil spirit to torture the king for his sins. Saul's aids feel that music would soothe the king's spirit, and David, whose musical skill is known by many, is recommended. One of the king's men says, "I have seen a son of Jesse the Bethlehemite who is skillful in playing, a man of valor, a warrior, prudent in speech, and a man of good presence; and the Lord is with him" (1 Sam. 16:18). David's connection to God, his gentle spirit, and his heroism are necessary requirements to help him fit into the king's household, and as a result of his spirit, he is able to soothe the depressed Saul. Furthermore, he keeps

Samuel's proclamation of him as the next king close to his heart. He does not become Saul's musician with a superior attitude despite the knowledge that he will eventually replace the monarch. Instead, he attempts to aid the king both as a musician and later as a soldier.

Scripture does not reveal how much time passes between David's anointing, his musical service to the king, and his introduction as a true warrior. Critics even suggest that this sequence of events is not chronological since the biblical story of David and Goliath seems to reveal a few contradictions in David and Saul's relationship. However, it is widely thought that the historical David was between eighteen and twenty when he met with Goliath. The battle between the boy and the giant itself is significant for several reasons, one being the simple practical need for control over important territory. The Philistines had set up camp in an area between Azekah and Socah, located on the boundary of the Israelite territory. The Israelites needed to halt the Philistines' progression before their enemy could grasp control of "two major east-west highways in Judah's hill country" (Arnold and Beyer 202). The Israelites, in contrast, had chosen to camp on a western mountain facing the Valley of Elah. In order to maintain the ownership of these important roadways, King Saul's army had to eliminate the Philistine threat.

In 1 Samuel, action has been halted, however, by fear of the Philistine champion, the giant Goliath. Not only is his physical size threatening, but so are his armor and weapons: "he had a helmet of bronze on his head, and he was armed with a coat of mail; the weight of the coat was five thousand shekels of bronze. He had greaves of bronze on his legs and a javelin of bronze slung between his shoulders. The shaft of his spear was like a weaver's beam, and his spear's head weighed six hundred shekels of iron" (1 Sam. 17:5–7). The possible connection between Goliath and the theft of Israel's Ark of the Covenant further establishes their fear of their enemy. Goliath's size, armor, and reputation are not the only aspects of his ability to terrorize the Israelite army. He is also unafraid of their god, and he threatens them and mocks their god for forty days before he is defeated.

David's arrival at the Israelite camp seems coincidental, and it is not apparent in the story that he knows what has been happening for the previous forty days. However, he clearly sees the battle as one that would glorify God. Goliath's boasts about the Philistine gods suggest that Israel's God is not capable of defeating the Philistines. It is this mockery of God that catches

David's attention and initiates his fury. The troops also discuss the king's offer of a reward between themselves as they cower before the enemy. David wonders at his countrymen's lack of initiative in fighting Goliath when God's honor is being challenged and a prize has been offered, so twice he confronts those who are talking: "For who is this uncircumcised Philistine that he should defy the armies of the living God?" (1 Sam. 17:26). In another heroic stand, David must specifically ignore his eldest brother because Eliab, whom Samuel had first perceived as God's choice for king based on his outward appearance, becomes angry with what he considers David's interference. Eliab rebukes David, saying, "Why have you come down? With whom have you left those few sheep in the wilderness? I know your presumption and the evil of your heart; for you have come down just to see the battle" (1 Sam. 17:28). William J. Deane suggests that Eliab has not forgotten Samuel's visit years before and calls Eliab "a man of a jealous disposition, narrow-minded and worldly" (15). This memory might have increased his irritation with David's queries. David responds to his brother's accusations in a calm tone, and then he continues to seek affirmation of the troops' cowardice. His religious fervor over the situation leads him to take on the challenge that Goliath has offered. Simplistic in his faith, he apparently has no doubt that God will defeat the giant.

The argument with his elder brother can also be seen as a foreshadowing of his battle with the giant. The biblical account says that Saul hears about David's questions and asks for the boy to be brought before him. Upon entering the king's presence, David immediately volunteers to take on the contest: "Let no one's heart fail because of him; your servant will go and fight this Philistine" (1 Sam. 17:32). Though the king tries to convince David that his youth and inexperience will not be enough for a victory, David points out that he has heroically protected his father's sheep from wild animals. David does not fear the battle, declaring instead that he trusts God to shield him from harm. Saul accepts his words and attempts to prepare the boy for the fight by dressing him in the king's own armor, but David knows his limitations and rejects the garb, which feels foreign. Instead, he carries only his own simple weapon, his staff, and "five smooth stones from the wadi" (1 Sam. 17:40). The rejection of the king's armor could symbolically represent a rejection of adulthood and a return to the role of a youth. It is partially his youth that helps him overcome Goliath. Because he is beneath the enemy's attention, he is able to descend into the ravine that separates the two groups and ascend the other side where Goliath waits, without being noticed. When Goliath does acknowledge him, it is with mockery for his youth and God. David replies with his own ridicule and announces assurance of victory. He loads a stone into his sling, lets it go, and watches it strike the giant in the forehead. The blow is enough to knock the giant to the ground, allowing David to seize Goliath's own sword to decapitate his enemy and end the battle. The Philistines take flight, but the Israelite army follows and conquers them.

Though the battle had historical significance for the people of Israel, there are religious implications as well, marking David as both a religious and a national hero. Many biblical commentators argue that the battle is most noteworthy in the way it fulfills God's promise to Samuel that he would choose a new monarch based on what is in his heart (1 Sam. 13:14, 16:7). It also opens David to recognition from the people. As the giant is defeated, David becomes a leader in Saul's military. He continues to win battles with God's help, and the people of Israel take notice. This acknowledgement of David's prowess leads to the people's admiration and preference for David over Saul, which in turn incites Saul's jealousy of the young man and leads to further heroic adventures that culminate in David taking the throne. David's ability to serve as king is evident in what Bill T. Arnold and Bryan E. Beyer contend "ushered in a period of stability that would become Israel's golden age" (52).

Not only does his heroism in his battle with Goliath show David as both a religious and a historical hero, but the story also follows comparative mythologist Joseph Campbell's description of the hero as warrior. As can be seen in the biblical tale of David's life before his battle with Goliath, his actual battle with the giant, and his career as a soldier for King Saul, the boy's reputation may be exaggerated by the tale. David's life, then, is a hero journey, and this interlude fulfills the beginning of the cosmogonic cycle. Campbell states, "If the deeds of an actual historical figure proclaim him to have been a hero, the builders of his legend will invent for him appropriate adventures in depth" (321). Some scholars claim that there is a controversy over whether David himself actually fought and killed Goliath or if another man named Elhanan did so, which suggests that the biblical tale may have been attributed to David as an afterthought (Kirsch 56). The confusion in the story line—with David anointed king at about age fourteen, then being called into Saul's service as a musician before the battle with Goliath, and then Saul's question about David's parentage when he should have known—could also link David with Campbell's description.

Campbell further argues that the hero of legend will "face a long period of obscurity" that can be seen as "a time of extreme danger, impediment" and that he may fill the role of "the squire of low degree" (326). David's role as a lowly shepherd fulfills both of these descriptions. When Samuel goes to Jesse and anoints David, he is called in from the fields and presumably sent back to the fields to continue his shepherding duties. He is called to adventure with the recognition of his future role as king but returns to anonymity until he is ready to fill the role. While he works as his father's shepherd, David encounters wild beasts that he must fight to protect the sheep. His assurances to Saul that he is capable of fighting Goliath support this idea: "Your servant used to keep sheep for his father; and whenever a lion or bear came, and took a lamb from the flock, I went after it and struck it down, rescuing the lamb from its mouth; and if it turned against me, I would catch it by the jaw, strike it down, and kill it. Your servant has killed both lions and bears" (1 Sam. 17:34–36). Further, Campbell claims that the "myths agree that an extraordinary capacity is required to face and survive such experience" (327). God's choice of David as Saul's replacement marks him as being unusually talented.

On an additional note, Campbell contends that the hero's childhood will be completed with a "return or recognition of the hero, when, after the long period of obscurity, his true character is revealed. This event may precipitate a considerable crisis" (329). Again, the period between Samuel's visit and the battle with Goliath functions as an exile, while the battle itself becomes a threshold crossing into adulthood and the duties that await David as king. Seen in this light, Goliath fulfills the role of threshold guardian who blocks the hero's path to a place of increased power. David must conquer this "watcher of the established bounds" before experiencing a time in which the menace grows weaker (Campbell 82) or he becomes more capable of handling that risk. The encounter with the Philistine champion takes David from a point of childhood to a point of maturity. In crossing the valley that physically separates the Israelite army and the Philistines, he symbolically descends into death to emerge into a new life. Both armies expect David to fail, so the idea of an imminent death is clear to both his own side and to the enemy's. No one has been able to defeat Goliath, and the idea that a youth would succeed where no one else has even found the bravery to try is beyond comprehension for either group. His victory launches him into the rest of the hero's journey, which evident from the continuation of his narrative beyond this interval. Whether one reads the story of David and Goliath as a historical document, as a religious script, or as a mythological hero's journey, it is evident that David fills the role of a hero.

CROSS-CULTURAL INFLUENCE

Biblical scholars point to David as one of the three most important heroic figures of the Old Testament, so it is not surprising that his exploits would be depicted in literature and film. The tale of David's battle with Goliath is particularly represented since it can be adapted to a variety of audience types. For example, numerous children's storybooks are based directly on the tale. Writers for adult audiences, however, have modified the tale in more subtle ways.

The Bible itself is the source of several literary versions of the ideas presented in the David and Goliath story. David is widely considered one of the authors of the Psalms. Thus, it has been argued that Psalm 144, in which the author praises God for his protection and provision, may have been written about David's battle with Goliath; however, since the poem is not specific in its reference to the Philistine champion, it may have been written about David's later conflicts with Saul. Psalm 151 is another song that is relevant to the battle that made David a hero. The authorship and content of this particular psalm is controversial, and it does not appear in most versions of the Bible, either Protestant or Catholic. It can be found in the Apocrypha of the Revised Standard Version of the Bible. The last two verses of this poem clearly connect to the tale of David's conflict with the giant: "I went out to meet the Philistine, and he cursed me by his idols. / But I drew his own sword; I beheaded him, and removed reproach from the people of Israel" (Psalms 151:6–7). One reason this particular psalm is divisive may be its focus on David's ability rather than on God's providence in the victory, thus making the clash more about human heroism than about religious fervor.

In another example of the Bible's integration of the story, noted by Raymond-Jean Frontain and Jan Wojcik, the Old Testament tale of David and Goliath foreshadows the New Testament story of Jesus Christ. Connections can be made between David and Jesus both as

MYTH INTO ART

Baroque painter Michelangelo Merisi da Caravaggio was part of the Neapolitan school of painters. He produced the painting *David with the Head of Goliath* in 1609, a year before his death. Caravaggio was known for his religious subject matter and was sponsored by many religious patrons. He attempted to attract ordinary people rather than the upper echelon of his society with his choice of topics.

In *David with the Head of Goliath*, the biblical theme is stressed partially through the painter's use of strong distinction between the light and dark, a method called "tenebrism" (or "chiaroscuro"), which Caravaggio used in much of his religious work. Tenebrism can be seen through the streak of light that slants across the middle of the painting, seeming to shower the hero David with a divine blessing. The light also highlights the look of surprise on the giant's face and the serene expression of confidence on David's. The shadowed areas of the work are particularly black, amplifying the darkness and bringing the light areas into a stronger focus. Further supporting the painting's relationship to the biblical story, David is depicted as a youth in the work, contrasting with the obviously mature visage of Goliath.

The 1609 painting was Caravaggio's second depiction of the David and Goliath story; the first painting, *David Showing Goliath's Head* (1605), also shows David holding the giant's decapitated head. The main contrast between the two is David's aggressive stance in the first painting, making it appear as though it captures the immediate moments after decapitating Goliath, while the later painting captures a moment of finality in which the hero has lowered his sword in a more relaxed attitude. In the first work, the sword is over David's shoulder and his lips are pursed in a grimace of anger.

shepherds and as unexpected heroes. While Jesus is not what the people expect their messiah to be, the untrained teenager is not the person that Saul's troops would have looked to as a hero against the giant. Also, both David and Jesus are passionate about their defense of God. The religious interpretation of David as passionately confronting Goliath based on the boy's desire to uphold God's honor can be symbolically seen in the story of Jesus upturning of the temple money changers' tables. Both figures stand up for their God. Further, the Goliath character in the New Testament story is Satan, whom Jesus must overcome in order for God's plan of salvation to work.

According to Frontain and Wojcik, the David and Goliath myth is also the focus of a number of British and American literary pieces. The authors comment, particularly, on a collection of Renaissance poems to consider, including Michael Drayton's "David and Goliath," Robert Aylett's "David's Troubles Remembered," and Abraham Cowley's "Davideis." In these poems, Frontain and Wojcik observe, "David's prowess is seen as the physical incarnation of moral energy which evokes a sense of wonder in the reader; he may, then, be seen as a sort of religious 'Herculean hero,' a superior mortal whose *virtu* and *élan* put him outside the common moral order"

(4). During the following few centuries, David remained a focus of literature, but more attention was given to his later exploits than the youthful conflict that brought him to prominence.

Twentieth- and twenty-first-century works can also be interpreted in light of the David and Goliath stories. The "Godliness" chapters in Sherwood Anderson's *Winesburg, Ohio* (1919) follow the life and descendants of Jesse Bentley, a man who falls into farming when his older brothers are killed in the Civil War, leaving him to carry on his father's legacy alone. Anderson focuses on the connection between his story and the biblical one by sharing that Jesse had been studying to become a preacher when he was called home. In the second piece of this section, Jesse's grandson David Hardy is introduced. The boy's presence in Jesse's home is further connected to the biblical story when the narrator shares: "For him [Jesse] the coming of the boy David did much to bring back with renewed force the old faith and it seemed to him that God had at last looked with favor upon him" (82). The symbolic connection between the Davids is especially shown in the last part of "Godliness." In this chapter, David is in the forest near his grandfather's farm, where he makes "a sling with rubber bands and a forked stick" (98).

The boy's relationship with his grandfather is primarily positive, but Jesse's obsession with what he considers God's denial of his supplications leads the old man to passionate behavior rooted in religious ceremony. In this last piece of the tale, Jesse attempts to sacrifice a lamb to God, but David misinterprets his intent and attempts to escape. As the old man runs after the boy, raising a knife for the lamb, David unhesitatingly "reach[es] down, select[s] a stone and put[s] it in the sling. With all his strength he [draws] back the heavy rubber bands and the stone whistle[s] through the air. It hit[s] Jesse . . . squarely in the head" (102). In an ironic contrast to the 1 Samuel version of David and Goliath, the youth runs away in fear of what he has done, leaving his larger-than-life grandfather alive but sunken into dementia and grief.

Two popular fantasy series also reflect the myth of David and Goliath. In J. R. R. Tolkien's Lord of the Rings series, for example, Frodo, a lowly hobbit, represents the shepherd boy, and Sauron, the ultimate evil, becomes Goliath. J. K. Rowling's Harry Potter series also pits a youthful hero against a foe of larger-than-life proportions when Harry battles Voldemort.

In the first half of the twentieth century, Bible stories began to be adapted for film. In 1956, *The Ten Commandments* became one of the greatest epic films ever produced. In the years following that film's popularity, several additional Bible stories were modified for film use. In 1960, *David and Goliath* was directed by Ferdinando Baldi and Richard Pottier. It stars Orson Welles as King Saul, Ivica Pajer as David, and Hilton Edwards as Samuel. This remake provides a disjointed variation of the story as it shifts between subplots and characters while taking artistic license with the dramatic events of the tale. The film starts in King Saul's court, emphasizing his wealth through both his material belongings and his courtiers. His son, his general Abner, and his daughter are particularly brought into focus. Samuel enters the court and expresses God's dissatisfaction with Saul's leadership, especially the loss of the Ark of the Covenant to the Philistines. Verses that are uttered in private between God and Samuel in the biblical account are shared aloud with Saul in the film, so the king, who appears emotionally weak, knows not only that God has abandoned him but also that Samuel has been commissioned to anoint a new king.

The film then progresses through a series of vignettes that center on a number of subplots. The first shows David as a young man in the field with his father's sheep.

The film attempts to appeal to its twentieth-century audience by adding a love interest for the young man in this scene. She gives him a sling, imparting a symbolic meaning to the weapon that is not in the biblical tale. A second subplot provides a glimpse into the unrest in Saul's own home. His military commander, Abner, is having an affair with his daughter, and the two are plotting for their own reasons. This subplot brings another relationship that stresses sensuality for a more modern audience that is less concerned with the religious meaning of the original story. A third subplot centers on the Philistine king and his troops as they plan to defeat Saul's kingdom.

David's role in the film is significantly different from his in the biblical story. At first, he is interested in a youthful romance, but when his lover is struck by lightning, he becomes angry with God and must be counseled back into a right relationship. When he is anointed by Samuel, he leaves home and goes to the capital city, where he observes signs of Saul's corrupt leadership everywhere. While in the biblical story David is integrated into Saul's home as a musical healer, in the film he stands in the city center and berates the king's rule, urging the people to stand up against the king. Saul soon turns to the boy for advice, further undermining any strength he might have as king and promoting David as an aggressive hero. In a strange twist of events, David ends up serving as Saul's musician, but Abner is concerned about David's influence on Saul. Though the biblical David marries Saul's daughter Michal years after his battle with Goliath, the film hero becomes interested in her before the battle, bringing yet another focus on sexual desire and another layer of meaning to the reward mentioned in 1 Samuel.

The series of events leading up to the actual confrontation between the shepherd and the giant is drastically different in the film. In an effort to stress the reason for David's heroism in killing the giant, the film leads into the battle by providing clear motivation. First, the political unrest is further stressed with the side stories of Abner and the Philistine king. Abner schemes to get rid of David, whose influence over the king worries him, by advising Saul to send the young man to the Philistine king, hoping that this will lead to the boy's death. Further, Saul tells David about Goliath while still in the palace, after which Samuel appears to David in a vision telling him to go to the Philistines and recapture the Ark of the Covenant. The desire to take back the seat of God becomes David's driving force, and David, rather than the king, leads troops to confront the Philistine army. The political motivation for the battle deemphasizes the religiosity of the biblical story. In addition, David is no longer the unknown shepherd launched into heroism by righteous anger over disrespect for God; instead, his reputation is known by the Philistine king, who offers him the bargain that he will not destroy Israel if David can defeat the giant. The conflict itself becomes less impressive as well since Goliath throws spears before David's strikes. When David does finally sling his stone, the giant falls, but David appears to be confused by his victory rather than confident in it.

The film ends with Abner attempting to assassinate David when the youth delivers Goliath's sword to the king. In a surprise move, Saul, who had ordered Abner to kill David, shoots an arrow into Abner's heart, killing him. The king openly acknowledges David's right to the throne, and David is welcomed into his home through the promise of marriage to Saul's daughter. Overall, the film is typical of its time period. There is a stress on romance and politics, rather than on the religious undertones found in the biblical account of David and Goliath.

Literature and film have borrowed the story of David's heroism for plot inspiration, allusion, and imitation for centuries. The story's appeal is universal in its portrayal of an unexpected and inexperienced hero whose internal qualities shine over brute strength and size.

Theresa L. Stowell, PhD

BIBLIOGRAPHY

Alter, Robert. *The David Story: A Translation with Commentary of 1 and 2 Samuel*. New York: Norton, 1999. Print.

Anderson, Sherwood. *Winesburg, Ohio*. 1919. New York: Penguin, 1960. Print.

Arnold, Bill T., and Bryan E. Beyer. *Encountering the Old Testament: A Christian Survey*. 2nd ed. Grand Rapids: Baker, 2008. Print.

The Bible. 3rd ed. Oxford: Oxford UP, 2001. Print. New Revised Standard Vers. with the Apocrypha.

Campbell, Joseph. *The Hero with a Thousand Faces*. Princeton: Princeton UP, 1949. Print.

David and Goliath. Dir. Ferdinando Baldi. Perf. Orson Welles. Echo Bridge, 1960. Film.

Deane, William J. *David: His Life and Times*. New York: Revell, 1889. Print.

Freund, Richard A. "Searching for King David and King Solomon." *Digging through the Bible: Understanding Biblical People, Places and Controversies through Archaeology*. New York: Rowman, 2009. 107–46. Print.

Frontain, Raymond-Jean, and Jan Wojcik. "Introduction: Transformations of the Myth of David." *The David Myth in Western Literature*. Ed. Frontain and Wojcik. West Lafayette: Purdue UP, 1980. 1–11. Print.

Kirsch, Jonathan. *King David: The Real Life of the Man Who Ruled Israel*. New York: Ballantine, 2000. Print.

Pinsky, Robert. *The Life of David*. New York: Nextbook, 2005. Print.

Li Chi Slays the Serpent

Author: Traditional
Time Period: 999 BCE–1 BCE
Country or Culture: China
Genre: Myth

OVERVIEW

"Li Chi Slays the Serpent" is a classic Chinese myth that tells how its heroine, resourceful and determined Li Chi, slays a serpent that has terrorized her community. For some time, a giant snake has made its home in a crevasse in the mountain range in Li Chi's home county. The serpent begins killing people and refuses to be appeased by animal sacrifices. Soon, the serpent demands and receives a young girl to devour, lest it kill even more people. After nine years of this dreadful occurrence, young Li Chi volunteers to the local authorities. Against the wishes of her worried parents, she prepares to be the tenth girl offered to the serpent. Rather than meekly submitting to her imminent death, Li Chi arms herself with a sword and takes other creative precautions to battle the monster.

The story of "Li Chi Slays the Serpent" was transcribed first by the Chinese historian Gan Bao (Kan Pao) in the fourth century CE. Gan Bao came from a family of military and civil leaders and studied classical Chinese literature and history. He secured an appointment at the princely court of Sima Rui (276–322 CE), who became Emperor Yuan of the Eastern Jin dynasty in 317 CE. Serving Emperor Yuan, Gan Bao compiled a collection of 464 myths, legends, and folktales published in twenty chapters under the title *Soushen ji* (*Sou-shen chi*; *In Search of the Supernatural: The Written Record*, 1996) before his death in 336 CE. His popular anthology includes the myth "Li Chi Slays the Serpent." The myth is set in Minyue Kingdom, which existed from 334 BCE to about 111 BCE. In Gan Bao's recorded form, the myth contains a reference to a heroine from the Han dynasty who offered to sacrifice herself in the second century BCE. This reference establishes these years as the oldest possible date for the myth in its final form.

The oldest surviving complete copy of the anthology is a Chinese print from 1603. In 1979, Moss Roberts offered an English translation of "Li Chi Slays the Serpent" in his anthology *Chinese Fairy Tales and Fantasies*. Roberts's translation is based closely on the tradition of the 1603 text. Since then, other English translations from this source, or from its variants, have appeared. Roberts uses the Wade-Giles transcription of Chinese and the traditional Chinese name order for his text, which is the source text of this presentation. Thus, the protagonist's family name, Li, precedes her personal name, Chi. The modern Pinyin transcription of her name is Li Ji; however, this name is shared by unrelated figures, and most mentions of Li Ji refer to them, not to the protagonist of this myth. Consequently, for clarity, the more familiar Wade-Giles spelling, Li Chi, will be used in this essay, while all other figures will be referred to by their Pinyin spellings, along with Wade-Giles upon first mention.

A literary historical analysis can trace the origin of the myth in ancient times. An analysis informed by cultural criticism and new historicism illustrates how the myth "Li Chi Slays the Serpent" addresses key social issues of its original audience that have remained relevant for over a millennium. In particular, the analysis covers the issue of local government response to a threat to the community. It addresses the conflict of the Confucian order of society and the question of ordinary local people developing their own resources to mitigate a common threat. A feminist analysis focuses on the remarkable character of Li Chi, who defies common cultural stereotypes and traditional prescriptions for the role of women in feudal Chinese society.

SUMMARY

The myth "Li Chi Slays the Serpent" is set in a mountainous region that is part of the contemporary southeastern Chinese province of Fujian (Fukien). The story takes place in the time of the bygone Minyue Kingdom

"The volunteer [Li Chi] then asked the authorities for a sharp sword and a snake-hunting dog. When the appointed day of the eighth month arrived, she seated herself in the temple, clutching the sword and leading the dog. First she took several pecks of rice balls moistened with malt sugar and placed them at the mouth of the serpent's cave."

"Li Chi Slays the Serpent"

(334 BCE–ca. 111 BCE), which was based in this region and was conquered by the Han dynasty of China.

As the myth begins, "a giant serpent seventy or eighty feet long and wider than the span of ten hands" has come to live in a cleft in the mountain range and has begun to kill people (Roberts 129). Initially, its victims are members of the local military and civil authorities. The offer of sacrificial animals such as oxen and sheep has not appeased the serpent. Instead, the serpent enters the dreams of people to make its wishes known. The serpent also voices its wishes through local mediums. It lets the people know that it will stop killing the officials, but in exchange, the serpent demands "young girls of twelve or thirteen to feast on" (129).

In helpless terror, the authorities agree to this demand. Every year, they select a sacrificial girl from "daughters of bondmaids or criminals" and keep the girl until the day of the annual sacrifice to the serpent (129). The sacrifice occurs on a certain day in the eighth traditional Chinese month of every year, which generally corresponds to the Western month of September. For nine years, annually, a young girl is placed at the front of the cave of the serpent. From within the cave, the serpent emerges to eat its victim alive.

In the tenth year, authorities look again for a suitable girl. Young Li Chi speaks with her parents, explaining her reasons for wanting to volunteer as the sacrificial victim. She tells her father, Li Tan, and her mother that they will have no one to take care of them when they are old. This is because the Li family has only six daughters,

of whom Li Chi is the youngest. In traditional Chinese society, young wives joined the families of their husbands. So, without a son, "it is as if [her parents] were childless" (129). Not daring to compare her own planned sacrifice to that of Han dynasty heroine Tiying, whom she mentions nevertheless, Li Chi proposes to volunteer so that her parents will at least get some money from the officials in exchange for her sacrifice. "Since I'm no use to you alive, why shouldn't I give up my life a little sooner?" she asks (130). However, her parents love her too much to agree. Defying them, Li Chi leaves secretly and approaches the officials. From them, she demands both a good sword and a dog trained in hunting snakes.

On the day of her impending sacrifice, Li Chi sits down in the temple built at the mouth of the cave of the serpent. Holding her sword and the leash of her dog, Li Chi takes out a large quantity of rice balls sweetened with malt sugar. She places the rice balls at the entrance to the serpent's cave and waits for the monster to appear.

Attracted by the smell of the food, the serpent emerges. Although the serpent's head is "as large as a rice barrel" and its eyes are "like mirrors two feet across" (131), the undeterred Li Chi lets her dog off its leash. It bites the body of the serpent. Li Chi approaches the serpent from behind and cuts several deep wounds in the serpent's body with her sharp sword. In pain, the serpent leaps out of the cave and dies.

Li Chi enters the cave herself. There, she finds the skulls of the nine young girls killed and eaten in the nine years before. Li Chi takes the skulls out of the cave. With pity, she addresses the remains of the victims: "For your timidity you were devoured" (133).

Li Chi returns home, and soon, even the king of Yue learns of her accomplishment. He marries Li Chi, taking her as his queen. He extends his magnanimous rewards to her family: Li Chi's father is appointed magistrate of her home county, while her mother and older sisters receive treasures. The myth concludes with the assertion that ballads and songs of Li Chi slaying the serpent have survived to the present day.

ANALYSIS

"Li Chi Slays the Serpent" is a classic Chinese myth featuring a smart and skilled young heroine who destroys an evil monster that threatens her community and particularly young girls like herself. A literary historical analysis can determine the period during which the myth is set. An analysis grounded in cultural criticism and new historicism illustrates how this myth addresses social and political issues regarding the relationship between common people and their authorities. These issues were of cultural concern in China in the fourth century CE, when the myth was transcribed, and remained relevant in Chinese society long after that. Issues include the evaluation of the local authorities' response to a threat to the community they govern and the challenge to the Confucian system of political and social order represented by the threat. The myth resolves these issues through a celebration of the resilience of the local community. Through the acts of one common girl who becomes a valorous young heroine, the community eventually saves itself. The analysis shows how Li Chi's heroic act reestablishes order and is rewarded appropriately by the highest authority of her land, the king himself. Through feminist analysis, the character of Li Chi can be seen as transcending the strict traditional limitations of patriarchy and Confucian social order. Li Chi's disobedience to her parents ultimately frees the community from a persistent threat. It is only after Li Chi's victory that she is reintegrated into the traditional Chinese feudal social order.

The myth of "Li Chi Slays the Serpent" developed in the ancient, historical kingdom of Minyue in southeast China. The final form transcribed by Gan Bao cannot have originated prior to 176 or 167 BCE, as Li Chi mentions the sacrifice made by the heroine "Ti Jung of the Han Dynasty" (Roberts 129). The story of Chunyu Tiying (Shun-yü T'i-jung) is told in the historical work *Shiji* (*Shih chi*, 104–91 BCE; *The Grand Scribe's Records*, 1961), composed by near-contemporary Chinese historian Sima Qian (Ssu-ma Ch'ien). In 176 or 167 BCE, Tiying's father, Chunyu Yi, was accused of misconduct by the Han emperor Wen. When he was arrested, he complained bitterly that he had no son, only five daughters, none of whom he expected could help him then. In response, his youngest daughter, Tiying, wrote a letter to Emperor Wen. In the letter, she offered to become an imperial slave in exchange for her father's freedom. Deeply moved by her filial loyalty, Emperor Wen pardoned her father.

The strong parallel between Tiying and Li Chi in this instance may indicate that this episode was incorporated into an older indigenous Minyue myth after the kingdom surrendered to the Chinese emperor and was incorporated into China around 111 BCE. The historical act of Tiying may have been adapted locally into the myth of "Li Chi Slays the Serpent" even before the fall of Minyue. Minyue had cultural, political, and economic contact with China during the Han dynasty. There were also Chinese immigrants living in Minyue already. Alternatively, a Minyue storyteller may have added this reference to show a historical model for Li Chi's brave decision. Finally, the reference to Tiying may have been added to the original Minyue myth in the three intervening centuries before Gan Bao came across this myth and recorded it in his anthology of 464 tales of the supernatural. Regardless, 111 BCE is the latest year in which the myth could be set. After Minyue surrendered to China in that year, there were no more independent kings of Minyue, and Li Chi thus could not have been made queen. Consequently, the year 111 BCE presents the terminus for the time period during which the myth takes place.

The fact that the serpent begins its attack on humans by devouring top local military and civil officials represents a clear challenge to authority. It is interesting to note that the serpent does not prey on the common people but kills members of the leadership. Emerging from its cave in the mountain cleft, the serpent has "already killed many commandants from the capital city and many magistrates and officers of nearby towns" (Roberts 129). Rather than preying on farmers, villagers, or townspeople, the serpent chooses to destroy the military and civil leadership of the region it has infested. This choice of targets may mean that the narrative of the myth gives voice to the hope of the people that those in power, rather than the common people, would bear the brunt of an enemy's attacks.

Faced with an apparently invincible threat, local officials rely on common traditional remedies in their attempts to come up with a solution. They offer the serpent "oxen and sheep" as animal sacrifices (129). Yet this does not appease the evil creature. Through the dreams of men, it makes its desires known, demanding an annual human sacrifice of a girl as young as twelve or thirteen.

As the whole myth relies on a supernatural threat, the modus through which the escalation of the serpent's appeasement is justified does not appear all too critical. However, if the serpent's threat is extrapolated to mean a general threat to the leadership of the community, it is interesting to note how the idea of the need for human sacrifices is introduced. It is not only through the collective unconscious revealed in dreams but also "through mediums" that the serpent's wish is revealed (129). This could indicate that the ruling authorities avail themselves of collaborating instruments, willing mediums, to justify escalating the appeasement that deflects the focus of the threat from them. This idea of manipulating the spirit mediums is not explored in the myth as it is told, however.

The authorities react to the serpent's demand in a pragmatic fashion that runs counter to contemporary Western ethical ideas. "The commandant and the magistrates" decide to choose sacrificial victims from among the lowest members of society, selecting "daughters of bondmaids or criminals" and holding them captive "until the appointed dates" of sacrifice (129). These actions conform to the idea of doing the least harm to the social order of the community. If a painful choice must be made, the magistrates reason, they will make the choice that is most in harmony with their social values. From a contemporary Western point of view, this is of course highly unethical. Yet the narrative of "Li Chi Slays the Serpent" does not directly criticize the officials' actions.

After nine years of this procedure, which has taken on almost the status of an emerging ritual, change finally occurs through the intervention of the resilient, combative young girl Li Chi. As shown, Li Chi likens her sacrifice, in a very modest way, to the sacrifice performed by the historical Tiying, who saved her father from the emperor's wrath by offering herself as an imperial slave. Cultural criticism cannot fail to see the socially subversive side of this analogy. Through Li Chi's invocation of Tiying as a model, Emperor Wen's wrath is linked to the brutal demands of the monstrous serpent. This link of emperor and serpent, a rather rebellious analogy, must not have been lost on the myth's original audiences, who were also familiar with the story of Tiying.

The logic of Li Chi's appeal to her parents to let her sacrifice herself for their benefit follows Confucian ideology and tradition. It is built also on the basis of traditional Chinese marriage norms. To lead up to her plan, Li Chi outlines her parents' dilemma: "Dear parents, you have no one to depend on . . . having brought forth six daughters and not a single son" (129).

The reason for this dilemma, which renders Li Chi's parents as good as childless, in her own words, lies in traditional Chinese marriage conventions inspired and upheld by Confucian philosophy. As Roberts illustrates in his introduction to the anthology that contains "Li Chi Slays the Serpent," Confucianism is deeply concerned with fixed social order. Beginning with the emperor and his subjects, Confucianism sets a series of regulated relationships that define the superior party's obligation of wise rule and good care and the subordinate party's obligation of loyalty and obedience. The relationship between emperor and subjects is mirrored in other binary pairs, including parents and children, especially father and son; husband and wife or wives, as polygamy was part of traditional Chinese society; local authorities and the people under their command; and, finally, humans and animals. Adopting these Confucian philosophical prescriptions reinforced the traditional Chinese custom that a bride would leave her own family. After her marriage, a young wife would sever almost all bonds with her own family and become a member of her husband's family. This meant that parents could not rely on the help of their married daughters, as their undivided loyalties as wives were reserved exclusively for the families of their husbands. Disallowing a remaining bond between a wife and her own parents was perceived as necessary to uphold social order.

To convince her parents to agree to her plans, Li Chi mentions Tiying's noble sacrifice. She expands on the fact that she will not be able to provide for her parents once they are unable to fend for themselves due to their advanced age. She argues, "I cannot take care of you in your old age; I only waste your good food and clothes" (130). Very meekly and with utter self-depreciation, Li Chi sums up the conventional view of the value of daughters in traditional Chinese society. From the view of cultural criticism, Li Chi voices the extreme consequences of China's Confucian-reinforced marriage conventions. By holding up this stark mirror to the society of the audience of the myth, the text allows for a modicum of criticism of this philosophy to emerge.

This critical element is reinforced by Li Chi's parents' adamant refusal to accept her planned sacrifice. In the myth, the father and mother are said to have "loved her too much to consent" (130). This sets up an alternate model for parental relations with their daughters and an alternate valuation of the daughters' worth as well. As Roberts states, this implied criticism of strict Confucian philosophy and morality occurs quite often in tales and myths similar to "Li Chi Slays the Serpent." Roberts sees here the influence of the universal, egalitarian Daoist (Taoist) view that has conflicted with Confucianism ever since both philosophies emerged in the sixth and fifth centuries BCE. Another countercurrent to Confucian doctrine revealed in the parents' refusal to let Li Chi sacrifice herself could be that of Buddhism. Buddhism teaches compassion foremost. Compassion and love are what Li Chi's parents show her in response to her Confucian argument.

Strict Confucian doctrine is compromised further by Li Chi's disobedience. When they disallow her to do so, Li Chi rebels against her parents and goes "in secret" to the authorities to present herself as a sacrifice to the serpent (130). Perhaps for dramatic storytelling reasons, Li Chi does not tell her parents of her plans to fight the serpent. This could have made their consent somewhat more likely, though they may have still objected if they doubted her ability to fight the monster. However, from the point of view of cultural criticism, it appears as if the text of the myth does want to voice the most extreme position of Confucian family order, expressing the utter worthlessness of a daughter, in order to criticize it. By having Li Chi go in secret and overcome the serpent, "Li Chi Slays the Serpent" offers an alternative to strict Confucian behavior. The myth's conclusion rewards this alternative with success.

Li Chi's decision to fight the serpent represents the self-assertion of her local community in the face of a mortal threat that authorities appear helpless to eliminate. This represents another departure from Confucian principles. In exchange for the community's loyalty and obedience, it would have been the duty of the military and civil authorities to exterminate the monster. Instead, authorities have settled on a path of least resistance and shown their willingness to appease the serpent with a sacrificial girl every year. This behavior is especially shameful because the serpent has killed members of those very authorities before. Now, the elite members of society save themselves at the expense of those they deem most expendable in their community. As Roberts states in his introduction, by depicting these less-than-ideal actions of the officials, the myth integrates popular social criticism into its narrative.

The authorities do not impede Li Chi's plan, signaling their cooperation with a member of the community. Accordingly, the authorities comply with Li Chi's request that she be given "a sharp sword and a snake-hunting dog" (130). On the appointed day of her anticipated sacrifice, Li Chi carefully arranges the ground where she will battle the serpent. This shows her resilience, creativity, and autonomy as a young community member. Rather than meekly resigning herself to her fate, Li Chi shows a willingness to fight for her life and contest the outcome of her encounter with the serpent. Here, Li Chi's decision represents a deviation from ritualistic behavior and a willingness to oppose conventions.

Her preparations, stemming from her own creative battle plan, serve Li Chi well in ensuring a decisive victory. Distracted by the sweet food and opening its mouth to devour the rice balls, not Li Chi, the serpent is attacked by both dog and girl. Li Chi's strokes, delivered from behind the serpent, have a dramatic effect: "The wounds hurt so terribly that the monster leaped into the open and died" (131).

Just before finally reestablishing traditional order, "Li Chi Slays the Serpent" voices one last criticism of conventional behavior. When Li Chi enters the serpent's cave and discovers the skulls of the nine previous victims, she criticizes their behavior. Even though Li Chi's critique is born out of compassion and is voiced with empathy, her charge that the nine girls died because of their timidity is a challenge to conventional Confucian society, in which meekness, acceptance of fate, and self-abrogation are prescribed behaviors for women, young and old. By showing that this behavior that traditional Chinese society deemed admirable led to the pointless death of the nine girls, the myth invites a sharp critique of these social prescriptions. It appears ironic that one brave, skilled, and resourceful armed girl, with a trusted dog as her aide, succeeds in killing a monster that has killed many elite soldiers and officials and cowed them into appeasing it with an annual human sacrifice. In the end, through Li Chi, the community rids itself of the threat posed by the vicious serpent.

Finally, however, "Li Chi Slays the Serpent" reestablishes conventional order. The king, as the ultimate and highest authority of the land, appears unaffected by the impotence and disgrace of his county officials. He recognizes Li Chi's heroic feat and rewards her in the only fashion that narrative logic and cultural circumstances strongly invite, making her his queen. Perhaps recognizing, and correcting, the poor performance of the local authorities, the king "appoint[s] her father magistrate of Chiang Lo county" (131). Ironically, this turn for the better would not have happened had Li Chi not disobeyed her parents. Then again, had they agreed with their daughter's Confucian logic and given her permission to go to the authorities, she could have performed her feat as well. Thus, toward the end, "Li Chi Slays the Serpent" strongly recuperates Confucian values and ideas. The narrative allows the king to reorder society so it represents an ideal state with wise leadership and a heroine rewarded for saving her community.

From a feminist critical point of view, Li Chi is a remarkably autonomous character. Her eventual action of fighting the serpent instead of merely becoming its next annual victim allows the reader to view her plea to her parents in a new light. When her community, and in particular young girls like herself, is threatened by a serpent the local authorities have given up on fighting, Li Chi decides to end this plague herself. Looking at the myth from its end, it is clear that Li Chi appropriates the patriarchal, feudal discourse of Confucian ideology only to further her own ends. Her true purpose she relates to no one, not even her parents.

In a feminist critique of Li Chi, she merely masquerades as a dutiful Confucian daughter. This she does by requesting parental permission to follow through with her private heroic plan. Indeed, when her parents do not agree with her Confucian logic because of their non-Confucian compassion for her, Li Chi must defy and disobey them. As the local authorities comply with her wishes for a weapon and a dog, Li Chi can embark on her own ambitious plan to rid her community of the serpent.

As shown, Li Chi's bravery and success in defeating the serpent indirectly shame the local authorities who decided to appease, not fight, the monster. In a feminist view, the young woman Li Chi proves more resourceful, brave, committed, and skilled in defending her community than the officials designated by feudal society to carry out such a task. Her address to her nine dead sisters in spirit is similarly critical.

In the myth, Li Chi represents an alternative female action in the face of mortal danger. This alternative is much more in keeping with an autonomous female heroine than Confucian prescriptions for female behavior. Through her victory, Li Chi vindicates female resistance and self-reliance in the face of lethal danger. However, even "Li Chi Slays the Serpent" ultimately recoups proper Confucian order. For all her valor, Li Chi is reintegrated into feudal, patriarchal, and Confucian order. From a feminist position, it is the king who is given the right to act, and Li Chi becomes his loyal subject. The text is clear in highlighting the king's agency in "ma[king] Li Chi his queen" (131). Even though he may be a most desirable marriage partner, the action is his. He does not ask Li Chi if she wants to become his queen; rather, he exerts his royal prerogative to make it so. Yet given the myth's era of origin and social context, this final feudal reintegration of its remarkably resilient heroine appears a necessary concession to the myth's original audiences.

The enduring popularity of "Li Chi Slays the Serpent" in China since its publication in Gan Bao's anthology indicates a strong sympathy for its heroine. The myth permits Li Chi to step for a decisive moment outside the role prescribed by Confucian social doctrine. Her mythical character offers an alternative for autonomous female action that saves Li Chi's community from danger. As an imaginative and strong teenage heroine, Li Chi has continued to enrapture audiences in China well into contemporary times.

CROSS-CULTURAL INFLUENCE

In the West, "Li Chi Slays the Serpent" has been noticed and translated but not adapted as frequently as Chinese stories such as the legend of Mulan, for example. There are quite a few English translations of the myth available, as well as some creative retellings of the story. The translations are generally based on the text transcribed by Gan Bao, which exists in an authoritative version and some variants. The retellings add details and plot elements that are tailored more to an American audience.

Roberts's 1979 translation of "Li Chi Slays the Serpent" captures the original version very well. He presents the myth in accessible English, using the Wade-Giles system to transcribe Chinese names. Roberts offers the myth in the context of other myths, legends, and fairy tales in his anthology *Chinese Fairy Tales and Fantasies*. "Li Chi Slays the Serpent" has also been translated into English by Kenneth DeWoskin and James Irving Crump. Their "Li Chi Slays the Great Serpent" is presented in the two translators' edition of the complete anthology by Gan Bao, *In Search of the Supernatural: The Written Record* (1996). Their version demonstrates that different translations of one original text will always show some variation. It is interesting to compare DeWoskin and Crump's English text to that of Roberts and note the different nuances. DeWoskin and Crump use Wade-Giles as well. Like Roberts, they give the heroine's name in the traditional Chinese order of family name first. As this may prompt an English-speaking reader to believe mistakenly that Li is the protagonist's first name, DeWoskin and Crump primary refer to her by her personal name alone.

Working from a different variant of Gan Bao's original text, Carol Kendall and Yao-wen Li offer their translation of the myth in "The Serpent-Slayer" in their anthology *Sweet and Sour: Tales from China* (1978). The protagonist is here said to be older (fourteen years old) and the Li family's eldest daughter, but the most important variation is the addition of a venal sorceress. When the serpent begins its reign of terror, it attacks the livestock and villagers first. Then, the people ask the local

HISTORICAL CONTEXT

In what is now China's Fujian Province, where "Li Chi Slays the Serpent" is set, Minyue Kingdom was established in 334 BCE. The original inhabitants of the area, who may have created the oldest form of the myth, were people whom the Chinese called the Baiyue. In 334 BCE, the Chinese kingdom of Yue fell to the kingdom of Chu during the Chinese Warring States period. The nobility of Yue fled south and established the kingdom of Minyue, bringing a small number of upper-class Chinese to rule the indigenous population there.

During the Chinese Qin dynasty of the second century BCE, the kingdom of Minyue was conquered and administered as Minzhong Commandery. As the deposed Minyue king Wu Zhu supported the Chinese rebel Liu Bang, who destroyed the Qin dynasty and replaced it with his own Han dynasty in 202 BCE, the kingdom of Minyue was reestablished. During that time, it enjoyed cultural, economic, and political relations with its Chinese neighbor to the north.

Eventually, the kingdom of Minyue submitted to its powerful southern neighbor, the kingdom of Nanyue, from 183 to 135 BCE. When Minyue's vassal king tried unsuccessfully to fight the king of Nanyue in 135 BCE, this brought the intervention of Han China. In the end, the Han emperor dissolved the kingdoms of Minyue and Nanyue in around 112 or 111 BCE and incorporated both territories into China.

In the fourth century CE, Gan Bao (d. 336) served as historian at the Eastern Jin dynasty court of Emperor Yuan. Gan Bao included the myth "Li Chi Slays the Serpent" in his collection of 464 tales, *Soushen ji* (*In Search of the Supernatural: The Written Record*, 1996). The oldest and most authoritative existing copy of his work dates from 1603, in the Ming dynasty, and is the basis of contemporary English translations of the myth of "Li Chi Slays the Serpent."

magistrate for help in combating the serpent. Basically helpless, the magistrate relies on a sorceress to tell him what to do. After telling him to send animal sacrifices, which prove unsuccessful, the sorceress claims that only the annual sacrifice of a virgin girl will appease the serpent. Colluding with the magistrate, the sorceress then collects lavish bribes from well-to-do villagers in exchange for not selecting their daughters.

The rest of the myth as told by Kendall and Li follows Gan Bao's authoritative version. In this version, the plot element of the sorceress underlines the basic incompetence of the magistrate. It also illustrates corruption at the heart of selecting girls for sacrifice. Yet Gan Bao's authoritative version delivers its social criticism more directly and without the use of additional agents supporting the local authorities. In the authoritative version, the independent decision of the local authorities to begin with the daughters of outcasts, bond servants, and criminals is more haunting. It displays chillingly the outcome of the officials' desperate quest to minimize the damage to social order while protecting their own interests in not being targeted by the serpent.

Katrin Tchana's rendition, "The Serpent Slayer," follows Kendall and Li's version. However, Tchana changes the gender of the sorceress, turning her into the evil

and corrupt sorcerer Qifu. Tchana's text amounts to a creative retelling of the myth for an American audience. Original story elements are expanded on, and new ideas are introduced. Most important is that Tchana's "The Serpent Slayer" presents right away Li Chi's motivation to save young women like her before she addresses her parents. The text renders her thoughts on the issue: "The longer she thought about how these young, innocent girls were required to sacrifice their lives before they had even begun to live, the angrier she became. At last she decided that it was time somebody did something about this snake, and . . . she realized she must take action herself" (2).

While this rendition of the myth conveys immediately the idea of Li Chi as a brave and determined young woman, this adaptation to American tastes takes away something of the subtle surprise of the Chinese original. Similarly, in Tchana's retelling, Li Chi does not portray herself as a model Confucian daughter and does not state her gendered worthlessness to her parents in the traditional Chinese system. Tchana's text does not indicate the number or gender of children in the Li family, and Li Chi merely informs her parents that by allowing her to offer herself, they will get some money as reward and have "one less child to feed" (2). The only concession made by Tchana to the Confucian spirit of the original reasoning of Li Chi is her assertion to her parents that they "won't have to pay [her] dowry" (2). Tchana clearly does not want her heroine to speak of a daughter's worthlessness, even when this is used as a logical ruse to persuade her parents to agree to her secret plan, as in Gan Bao's original. Since the issue of filial duty is never raised in the text, Tchana's ending does not include Li Chi chiding the previous victims for their lack of defiance.

When Tchana's Li Chi approaches Qifu with her offer and her request for sword, dog, food, cooking utensils, and fire-making flint stone, the text outlines Qifu's reasons for agreeing to both her offer and her requests. Whereas the original text does not comment on the motivation of the local authorities to equip Li Chi, Tchana fills in her readers with a logical-sounding explanation. Qifu is grateful for a volunteer and willing to give her what little she wants, and he expects her to perish anyway. In giving Qifu's reasons, Tchana's text is more elaborate than the original, but it also limits the audience's self-discovery of possible motives of the authorities.

Occasionally, Tchana's (and Kendall and Li's) text displays its distance from the Chinese original and its social and cultural context. When the sorcerer (sorceress in Kendall and Li's version) agrees to lead Li Chi to the serpent's cave, for example, he walks halfway up the mountain with her before turning back as this physical effort becomes exhausting. In Chinese society of the time in which the myth takes place, a person of such rank would have requisitioned a palanquin or some locals to carry him or her on their backs up the mountain. This is a small but telling detail indicating the difference in the cross-cultural adaptation of the myth.

A very creative cross-cultural adaptation of the tale, told from the serpent's point of view, was posted online in April 2010. Called "Chi Li Slays the Serpent," this web entry by an American author calling herself "egogindustries" provides an elaborate background story of the serpent prior to its arrival in Chi Li's home district.

Acknowledged as a free, amateur retelling of the myth, this variant begins with the birth of the snake. Here, the author borrows from the very popular Chinese legend of the white serpent, which was published first by Feng Menglong as chapter 28 in his anthology *Jingshi tongyan* (1624; *Stories to Caution the World*, 2005). As in Feng Menglong's rendition, a human scholar, Xu Xian, marries a snake demon, Bai SuZhen, who has transformed herself into a human woman. Whereas they have a human son in the original Chinese legend, in this American version they have a snake daughter named Xu Feng. Her personal name, Feng, is probably an allusion to Feng Menglong, collector of the legend of the white serpent.

In the American tale, Feng suffers bullying and ostracism at the hands of the villagers because she is different, being a snake who cannot assume a human shape. This clearly carries a moral message against bullying and in favor of diversity, both contemporary American concepts. Eventually, Feng's father suggests she meet the emperor and offer her services to him. Her mother gives her a magic compass to aid her. Feng meets hatred in every village she enters, so to avoid human rejection, she travels at night only.

Feng's much-anticipated meeting with the emperor ends in failure, indicating that authorities are hostile to this special girl. The emperor is aghast and revolted by Feng's presence, calling her a "monstrosity," "fiend," and "freak." Angry herself, Feng slithers out of his palace and into the forest. Using her mother's magic compass to find a place that suits her, she finds a cave in the Yung Mountains. This is the location where the serpent dwells in the original myth of "Li Chi Slays the Serpent."

This turn of the plot brings the tale to the beginning of the Chinese myth. Feng next kidnaps a village girl out of loneliness and desire for a human companion. When the first girl, Lu Xia, escapes from Feng's cave to return to her village, Feng inadvertently kills her in her attempt to bring her back. Thereafter, Feng demands a new girl from the village every year. Inevitably, the girls try to escape and are killed by the serpent.

Finally, Feng learns that Chi Li has volunteered as the tenth girl to be given to her. Initially, Feng hopes for a real human companion and is encouraged to hear that Chi will come of her own free will. She bathes and cleans her cave in anticipation before taking a brief nap. Awakened by the smell of rice balls sweetened with malt sugar, a detail from the original story, Feng begins to devour this special food. Suddenly, she notices Chi standing over her with her sword and a big, ferocious dog at her side. Feng looks at Chi and sees in her face a mixture of emotions: "fear, mutiny, determination, nervousness, and, lurking beneath it all, a certain sadness."

In this retelling, Chi Li strikes the serpent first. Feng manages to kill the dog but is struck by Chi's sword. Wounded, Feng rolls atop the bones of the girls she has killed. She realizes her own death at Chi's hands is imminent. No longer resisting her fate, Feng accepts Chi's final blow. This the girl delivers while telling the snake, "I'm sorry."

In combining the tale of the white serpent and "Li Chi Slays the Serpent," the American retelling creates a sympathetic view of the serpent as an outcast. For all her good intentions, and the sympathy created for her by the narrative, the serpent Feng is doomed by her inability to establish a lasting friendship with a human companion. The tale carries the message that for all of Feng's sad loneliness, her attempt to force young girls to be her friends brings their deaths and ultimately Feng's own. Chi appears as an executioner who must show Feng the error of her ways, even though Chi can sympathize with her adversary and feel sorry for her situation. By placing Feng atop the skeletons of the girls she has killed at the moment of her own death, the American retellings expresses the view that the serpent's acts, understandable though they may be, are morally wrong. Realizing this, Feng accepts Chi's final blow without resistance.

R. C. Lutz, PhD

BIBLIOGRAPHY

"Chi Li Slays the Serpent." *egog-industries.deviantart. com*. deviantART, 29 Apr. 2010. Web. 1 Feb. 2013.

Feng Menglong, comp. "Madam White Is Kept Forever under the Thunder Peak Tower." *Stories to Caution the World: A Ming Dynasty Collection*. Vol. 2. Trans. Shuhui Yang and Yunqin Yang. Seattle: U of Washington P, 2005. 474–505. Print.

Gan Bao. "Li Chi Slays the Great Serpent." *In Search of the Supernatural: The Written Record*. Trans. Kenneth J. DeWoskin and James Irving Crump. Stanford: Stanford UP, 1996. 230–31. Print.

Kendall, Carol, and Yao-wen Li. "The Serpent-Slayer." *Sweet and Sour: Tales from China*. New York: Clarion, 1978. 33–38. Print.

The Legend of the White Serpent. Dir. Shirō Toyoda. Frank Lee International, 1956. Film.

Roberts, Moss. "Li Chi Slays the Serpent." *Chinese Fairy Tales and Fantasies*. New York: Pantheon, 1979. 129–31. Print.

Ssu-ma Ch'ien. *The Grand Scribe's Records*. Vol. 2. Trans. Tsai-fa Cheng et al. Ed. William H. Nienhauser Jr. Bloomington: U of Indiana P, 2002. Print.

Tchana, Katrin. "The Serpent Slayer." *The Serpent Slayer and Other Stories of Strong Women*. New York: Little, 2000. 1–5. Print.

Perseus and Medusa

Author: Hesiod; Aeschylus; Ovid; Pseudo-Apollodorus
Time Period: 999 BCE–1 BCE; 1 CE–500 CE
Country or Culture: Greek; Roman
Genre: Myth

OVERVIEW

For centuries, the myth of Perseus and Medusa (Medousa) has thrilled readers with its famed hero who conquers the Gorgon and harnesses the force of her petrifying gaze. Showcasing a mysterious quest, high adventure, and even romance, the story evolved in ancient versions and continues to fascinate audiences, with countless representations in poetry, prose, and especially the visual arts.

Originating in ancient Greece around 700 BCE, two of the story's most developed versions survive in the *Bibliotheca* (*The Library of Greek Mythology*), once attributed to the Greek grammarian Apollodorus and now credited to a writer known as Pseudo-Apollodorus, and in the Roman poet Ovid's *Metamorphoses*. Both writers lived during the first century BCE, and they tell of how Perseus embarks on a quest to find the snake-haired Medusa, one of the three Gorgons, when Perseus's friend Polydectes (Polydektes) commands him to bring back her head. With the help of a diverse cast of gods, crones, and nymphs as well as the magic objects they bestow, Perseus decapitates the Gorgon by gazing only at her reflection in his shield. Then, he defeats his enemies in other exploits—most notably the rescue of Andromeda, a beautiful maiden whose father sacrifices her to a savage sea monster sent as divine punishment after his wife offends the sea nymphs. In exchange for her rescue, Andromeda is given to Perseus in marriage, and when her abandoned fiancé Phineus (Phineas) opposes the union, Perseus uses Medusa's head to petrify him and his crew. The hero also turns Polydectes to stone when the ruler turns corrupt.

The story in the *Bibliotheca* is chronological, beginning with Perseus's birth and ending with the accidental death of the hero's father, which an oracle had initially predicted. In contrast, Ovid begins with the rescue of Andromeda, after Perseus has already defeated Medusa, telling the story of the Gorgon's defeat in retrospect when a wedding guest asks the hero to describe the deed. Ovid's version also includes the story of Medusa's transformation into the Gorgon and provides a different ending regarding Perseus's father.

Remarkably, monstrous Medusa has come to overshadow Perseus even though he is the story's nominal hero. This shift partly results from how Ovid's version diminishes the heroism of Perseus. Ovid is also unique in evoking sympathy for Medusa by telling the story of her rape, for which the goddess Minerva unjustly transforms her into the hideous Gorgon. Partly as a result of this important detail, Medusa in modern feminist interpretations has become, among many other things, a fascinating symbol of female power in the context of patriarchal cultures. A thematic interpretation explores how Ovid embeds the myth within a series of tales about the power of snakes, which emphasize the fascinating duality of the Medusa figure and snakes in general as sacred life givers and yet vicious destroyers. This thematic approach in turn invites readers to view Medusa within larger contexts of myth and anthropological studies, which demonstrate her likely ancestry in several ancient deities and show how she became linked increasingly with violence and death in ancient Greek culture.

SUMMARY

The story of Perseus in the *Bibliotheca* begins with the hero's birth. Acrisius (Akrisios), father of Danaë, learns from an oracle that his daughter will bear a son who will kill him, so he locks her in an underground bronze chamber. Nonetheless, Danaë becomes pregnant, either because she is seduced by Acrisius's twin brother, Proteus, or because Zeus transforms himself into a shower of gold that penetrates her womb. When Danaë gives birth to Perseus, Acrisius casts them both out to sea in an ark, which drifts to Seriphus (Seriphos). There, the fisherman Dictys finds and raises Perseus. Polydectes, the ruler of Seriphus, loves Danaë but is "unable to have sex with her, now that Perseus was a grown man" (34), so he pretends to want to marry Hippodameia and asks his friends for contributions so that he may obtain her hand. He requests horses from his friends but receives none from Perseus, who had claimed that he "would not deny Polydectes even the Gorgon's head" (34), so he accepts Perseus's brave offer.

Assisted by Hermes and Athena, Perseus first goes to Enyo, Pephredo, and Deino, the three daughters of Phorcus (Phorkys) and Ceto (Keto). The sisters of the Gorgons, these three crones possess one eye and one tooth, which they share and which Perseus takes, promising to return them once the sisters lead him to certain nymphs. The nymphs give Perseus winged sandals, a special knapsack, and the helmet of Hades, which causes whoever wears it to become invisible. In addition, Hermes gives him a harpé (curved sword). With these magical objects, Perseus flies to the ocean and finds the three sleeping Gorgons, Euryale, Stheno, and Medusa. The only mortal Gorgon, Medusa is Perseus's target. The three creatures, whose gaze turns humans to stone, are described as having heads "entwined with the horny scales of serpents . . . big tusks like hogs, bronze hands, and wings of gold on which they flew" (35). Looking into Medusa's reflection on his bronze shield rather than directly at her, Perseus cuts off her head with the aid of Athena, who guides his hand. Immediately, the winged horse Pegasus (Pêgasos) and his brother, Chrysaor (Khrysaôr), spring from her headless body; Poseidon is said to be their father. Perseus flees with Medusa's head in his special knapsack, and with his helmet, he evades the pursuing Gorgons.

Perseus then proceeds to Ethiopia, where he rescues Andromeda from a sea monster sent by Poseidon as punishment after the boastful wife of King Cepheus (Kepheus) challenges the beauty of the Nereids (sea nymphs). Cepheus ties Andromeda to a rock after he receives a prophecy declaring her sacrifice necessary to resolve the offense. Smitten, Perseus promises to free her if her parents will give the girl to him in marriage. Perseus then kills the sea monster and weds Andromeda, but then he must defeat Phineus, brother of Cepheus and former fiancé of Andromeda. Perseus uses Medusa's head to petrify Phineus and his supporters. Upon his return to Seriphus, Perseus likewise turns Polydectes and company to stone when the hero learns that his mother

"Her beauty was far-famed, the jealous hope / Of many a suitor, and of all her charms / Her hair was loveliest. . . . / She, it's said, / Was violated in Minerva's shrine / By Ocean's lord. Jove's daughter turned away / And covered with her shield her virgin's eyes, / And then for fitting punishment transformed / The Gorgon's lovely hair to loathsome snakes. / Minerva still, to strike her foes with dread, / Upon her breastplate wears the snake she made."

Metamorphoses

and Dictys have fled the ruler's violence. Perseus then makes Dictys ruler, returns his magical items to Hermes, and gives Medusa's head to Athena, who places it on her shield. The story also mentions that some report that Athena is responsible for Medusa's beheading when the latter allows herself to be compared to Athena's beauty. The story concludes with the hero returning to Argos with Danaë and Andromeda to "get a look at Acrisius" (34). Acrisius flees to the Pelasgian land but is nonetheless killed by his grandson, as the oracle had predicted, when Perseus takes part in a pentathlon and accidentally strikes his grandfather with a discus. Perseus buries him and refuses to inherit Argos, instead reaching an agreement with Megapenthes, who allows him to rule the two realms of Tiryns as well as Mideia and Mycenae.

Ovid's version begins quite differently, with Perseus's rescue of Andromeda after he has already defeated Medusa. As Perseus flies over Libya with the Gorgon's head, drops of her blood fall on the sand below and become deadly snakes, accounting for the prevalence of snakes in that region. Flying among the stars, Perseus is wary of flying at night and lands on shores belonging to Atlas, a wealthy giant. Boasting of his divine lineage, Perseus requests lodging, but Atlas rejects him because he recalls an oracle predicting his downfall. When both words and arms fail, Perseus petrifies Atlas with Medusa's head. The giant first becomes a mountain and then grows "beyond all measure" so that "on his shoulders rest[s] the whole vault / Of heaven with all the innumerable stars" (4.664). The next morning, Perseus proceeds to Ethiopia, where he discovers Andromeda chained to a rock and is so astonished by her beauty that he nearly forgets "to hover in the air" (4.676). Perseus condemns the chains and persuades the modest Andromeda to recount her plight, but soon the terrifying sea monster appears. Perseus presents himself to Andromeda's cowering parents and offers to rescue her if they agree to promise her as his wife. The couple agrees, and Perseus promptly kills the monster. Meanwhile, Medusa's head, resting on a rock, transforms the fresh seaweed into coral, engendering a new species.

After Perseus sacrifices to the gods, he and Andromeda enjoy a royal wedding, and the hero then learns of his new wife's country. In turn, Cepheus asks Perseus to recount his defeat of Medusa. Perseus then briefly describes how he cunningly stole the single eye from Phorcys's daughters, after which he arrived in the land of the Gorgons, where he witnessed many petrified figures. Looking at only the reflection of Medusa's head on his shield, he decapitated her, at which point Pegasus and his brother sprang from her body. After recounting other adventures, Perseus falls silent. When another guest asks why Medusa is the only sister to have "snake-twined hair" (4.793), Perseus then tells of how Medusa was once famous for her beauty, particularly for her lovely hair. As Medusa worshiped in Minerva's temple one day, Neptune raped her, and the offended virgin goddess shielded her eyes but then punished Medusa by turning her hair into snakes. Then, she placed the head on her breastplate "to strike her foes with dread" (4.803). Perseus's story concludes in book 5 as Phineus interrupts the wedding party to reclaim his "stolen bride" (5.10). When Cepheus cannot persuade Phineus to back down, an epic battle follows, running for nearly two hundred lines, in which Perseus slays many warriors. Ultimately outnumbered, Perseus resorts to Medusa's head, turning everyone to stone and mercilessly refusing to spare the defeated Phineus. Perseus and Andromeda then return to Argos and use Medusa's head to avenge Acrisius, his grandfather, who had been expelled by his brother. When Polydectes denies Perseus's heroism and his defeat of Medusa, he too is turned to "bloodless stone" (5.251).

ANALYSIS

The myth of Perseus and Medusa has all the essential ingredients of a classic heroic quest: a brave protagonist who endures a long journey through strange realms; magical objects granted by wise, mysterious creatures; a hideous foe to be conquered; and a beautiful maiden to be won. The best-known version of this particular tale, however, has something else that makes the quest anything but classic. Medusa has proved to be a complicated enemy for Perseus, refusing to serve neatly as the chief object of his victory. Underlying this complexity is Ovid's unconventional portrayal of both hero and foe in his *Metamorphoses*, a collection of myths that presents stunning cycles of creation and transformation with irony and sophistication, reflecting the poet's subtle interest in human psychology. Heightening the antiheroic tendencies of Pseudo-Apollodorus's text, Ovid also presents a unique account of how Medusa becomes a snake-haired Gorgon, presenting her as a beautiful maiden cruelly victimized by Neptune and unjustly punished by Minerva. Yet even as a Gorgon, Medusa proves to be more powerful than Perseus, who repeatedly uses her petrifying gaze when his own prowess fails. Furthermore, Medusa is strangely productive, generating new species from her broken flesh and protecting Perseus's marriage to Andromeda. A thematic interpretation rooted in the larger context of Ovid's version reveals that the Perseus and Medusa story is embedded in a cluster of snake tales that reveal the poet's interest in the animals as both sacred and ruinous. This context invites an understanding of Medusa through a wider mythological lens that accounts for the various deities that inform her. This perspective reveals her sacred origins and the ways in which the ancient Greeks increasingly diminished her dichotomous nature to associate her with death alone, a trend that did not entirely prevail.

Medusa is linked to Perseus relatively late in the mythological tradition. Descriptions of the terrifying Gorgon appear in Homer's *Iliad*, composed in approximately 750 BCE, when her image appears on the aegis of Athena, Greek goddess of war and many other qualities, and on the shield of the warrior Agamemnon. As Miriam Robbins Dexter points out, Gorgon images were quite common in Greek iconography at this time, but while Perseus appears in both *The Iliad* and *The Odyssey* (the latter composed in approximately 725 BCE), he is not depicted in connection with Medusa at all. The earliest sources linking the pair are two poems written in approximately 700 BCE and originally attributed to the Greek poet Hesiod. The first is *The Shield of Herakles*, now no longer attributed to Hesiod, which describes Perseus fleeing with the Gorgon's head as her enraged sisters pursue him. The second is Hesiod's *Theogony*, a genealogy of the Greek gods and an important source for subsequent mythology. This poem describes Medusa in more detail, naming her parents as Phorcys and Ceto, her sisters as Pemphredo and Enyo and the Gorgons. Medusa alone of the Gorgons is mortal, and the poem suggests that Poseidon "lay . . . in a soft meadow among the spring flowers," such that when Perseus decapitates Medusa, the winged horse Pegasus and Chrysaor spring forth from her headless body (Hesiod 12–13). By about 500 BCE, writers such as the poet Pindar describe the Gorgons' heads as snaky and endow their gaze with the power to petrify those who meet it. The fifth-century playwright Aeschylus penned the *Phorcides*, part of a trilogy recounting Perseus's quest for the Gorgon's head, which survives only in fragmented descriptions in later sources. The dramatist Euripides, also of the fifth century BCE, describes in his play *Ion* the dual power of Medusa's blood, which can both cause death and heal illnesses. Thus, the story of Perseus and Medusa survives from roughly 700 to 400 BCE, with the various accounts already suggesting the Gorgon's complex powers and the theme of her seduction and violation that subsequent authors developed.

The *Bibliotheca*, now attributed to Pseudo-Apollodorus, develops some of these early hints of Medusa's complexity and suggests that Perseus is a less-than-ideal hero. In this account, Perseus receives magic objects and divine aid to an extent that, Stephen Wilk argues, undercuts his heroism. Two deities, Hermes and Athena, guide him to the daughters of Phorcus and sisters of the Gorgons. He steals their one eye and tooth to learn the whereabouts of the nymphs, who give him the winged sandals, the special knapsack to contain Medusa's head, and Hades's helmet of invisibility. Hermes then bestows "a sickle made of adamant." If this were not enough, Athena further aids Perseus by "guiding his hand" as he beheads Medusa (35). He escapes Medusa's sisters not because of his own skill but because his helmet makes him invisible. After he defeats the sea monster and marries Andromeda, he uses the Gorgon's head as a weapon to conquer both Phineus and Polydectes. The conclusion, in which Perseus accidentally kills his grandfather with a discus and thus refuses to inherit Argos out of shame, further diminishes the hero's status.

The *Bibliotheca* does not include the account of Medusa's coupling with Poseidon but does imply her beauty and links her with fertility and wisdom. When Athena places the Gorgon's head on her shield, the text relates that some people claim that Athena caused Medusa's decapitation because the girl had allowed her beauty to be compared to that of the goddess. This detail implies Medusa's original beauty and establishes the theme of punishment that Ovid transforms so compellingly. In this account, Medusa's headless body produces Pegasus and Chrysaor, suggesting her fertility. Furthermore, the entire story is framed in the context of marriage, albeit not always in a genuine fashion. Polydectes asks Perseus to bring back Medusa's head on the ruler's pretext of wanting to marry Hippodameia. Having conquered Medusa, Perseus wins Andromeda as a wife after he defeats the sea monster, but it is the Gorgon's head that he uses to defend his own marriage when he turns Phineus to stone. Then, Perseus petrifies Polydectes, who had caused Perseus's mother to flee. In these ways, Medusa is repeatedly associated with fertility throughout the story as she produces offspring and protects Perseus in his marriage and family conflicts. Finally, it should be noted that Medusa's one-eyed sisters, who direct Perseus to the nymphs, also link the Gorgon to wisdom.

With characteristic originality, Ovid magnifies Perseus's antiheroism and Medusa's complexity mainly by altering the story's structure and adding details both narrative and stylistic. Most notably, he changes the order of events to present Perseus's defeat of Medusa as an afterthought, possibly an embarrassing one at that. As noted previously, Ovid's account of Perseus begins as he proceeds to rescue Andromeda, which becomes the focal point of the story. Readers only learn of his encounter with Medusa when Cepheus, father of Andromeda, asks him about it. The hero responds with a brief account relayed, as Paul Murgatroyd notes, "in retrospect and in reported speech," which minimize the deed (108). Ovid also has Perseus tell the story of Medusa's rape only when another guest asks why she alone has snaky hair, suggesting that Perseus initially avoids the story because he is aware that it casts his own behavior in a bad light. The detail of Medusa being the only sister with snakes for hair is uncommon, and the story of her rape by Neptune is unique to Ovid, as Murgatroyd points out. In describing Medusa's famed beauty, Ovid focuses on her hair, thereby linking it to her punishment and heightening the poignancy of her plight. Furthermore, the effect of Medusa's victimization is particularly brutal given

MYTH INTO ART

It is easy to understand why visual artists have been irresistibly drawn to Perseus and his dramatic victory over the snake-haired Medusa. Among the most celebrated sculptures of the hero is that of Benvenuto Cellini (1500–1571), a Florentine multimedia artist who is considered a key figure of mannerism, an artistic movement that followed the Renaissance. In addition to creating sculptures, Cellini was a painter, goldsmith, musician, and even an entertaining autobiographer, but his sculpture of the ancient Greek myth is considered one of his most important achievements.

Commissioned by the grand duke Cosimo I de' Medici, the bronze statue, *Perseus with the Head of Medusa*, was completed in 1554 and still stands in the Piazza della Signoria in Florence. The statue celebrates Perseus's victory, displaying the hero at the moment he has beheaded the Gorgon. His muscled figure stands with one foot on Medusa's headless body. In his right hand he holds a sword, while his left arm raises her head high. The scene is meant to celebrate Perseus's triumphant dominance over the Gorgon, and it was also intended to convey the political power of its patron, Cosimo I de' Medici. With this rendering, Cellini casts the story differently from the ancient myth as recounted by the Roman poet Ovid, who mocks the heroism of Perseus and presents Medusa as a suffering victim with mysterious powers of both destruction and fertility. In his autobiography, Cellini recounts the great challenges he overcame to create his Perseus, and this renowned text is an important early example of an artist's celebration of individual genius and achievement.

that Neptune rapes her as she, ostensibly a virgin, worships the virgin goddess Minerva in her temple. She is thus both raped and deflowered. Yet instead of defending her devotee, Minerva cruelly punishes Medusa by turning "the Gorgon's lovely hair to loathsome snakes" and wearing Medusa's image on her armor "to strike her foes with dread" (4.801–2). Here, Ovid turns the tables by making the gods rather than Medusa seem monstrous and hateful, evoking the reader's sympathy for Medusa and further deflating Perseus (Murgatroyd 108–9).

Ovid also undercuts Perseus by portraying him as pompous and by mocking other aspects of his heroism. Nervous about flying at night, Perseus nonetheless brags about his divine lineage and his bravery when he meets Atlas, promising that Atlas will admire his deeds. Likewise, when he bargains with Andromeda's parents to slay the sea monster, he exalts himself with repetitive phrases: "I, Perseus, / The son of Jove . . . I, Perseus,

/ The snake-haired Gorgon's victor; I, who dared / On soaring wings to ride the winds of heaven" (4.693–98). He assures them that "none for sure / Could be [his] rival as [their] son-in-law" and graciously offers "to dower so glorious" (that is, himself!) his "service" (4.699–703). Such vaunting is in fact a habit, as is evident when Perseus describes "what stars on soaring pinions he had touched" during his winged journey (4.789). Yet Ovid contrasts Perseus's words with other touches that mock, rather than celebrate, the hero. In addition to mentioning Perseus's fear of night travel, Ovid pokes fun by making him nearly fall down when he is thunderstruck by Andromeda's beauty. His battle with the sea monster is hardly a challenge, as the rather stupid creature first attacks its own shadow and is slow to realize when he has been struck. His most threatening act is to throw up on Perseus's wings, making them too soggy to fly (Murgatroyd 160–61). Later, Perseus defends his marriage to Andromeda in a ridiculously long mock-epic battle that opens book 5 and drags on for nearly two hundred lines. Here, Ovid spoofs the epic mode as he describes an extended and grisly bloodbath not on a battlefield in a war but at a wedding reception. Perseus slaughters his enemies as the bride and guests stand by. Ultimately outnumbered, however, he must resort to using the Gorgon's head to petrify Phineus and company.

Indeed, Ovid repeatedly draws attention to Perseus's reliance on Medusa's head. Yet he does so in a way that underscores not her defeat but her powers of destruction and of regeneration and protection. With the exception of the lackluster sea monster brawl, Perseus does not win a single battle through his own might. Instead, he uses the Gorgon's head to defeat Atlas, Phineus, and Polydectes as well as to avenge Acrisius. Ovid, however, is interested in more than simply taking the wind out of Perseus's sails. The poet dwells on the strange duality of Medusa's powers. The first description of her appears as Perseus transports her head over Libya; when drops of her blood fall on the sand below, they immediately generate "smooth snakes of many kinds, and so that land / Still swarms with deadly serpents to this day" (4.622–23). The conflict with Atlas allows Ovid to describe the stunning transformation in which the petrified giant nonetheless grows until the vault of heaven itself rests on his shoulders. As a woman unfairly punished for her mother's crime, Andromeda implicitly recalls the innocent Medusa, but the Gorgon makes another appearance in this episode when Perseus places her head on a seaweed-covered rock. Here again, Medusa produces new life as her contact with the vegetation changes it to coral, delighting the sea nymphs. Ovid thus intensifies the mystery of Medusa's dual powers by magnifying both her destructive and her regenerative/protective roles.

Attention to the larger context of this story within the *Metamorphoses* begins to reveal Ovid's particular interest in the Gorgon and her ophidian force. As he often does, Ovid has deliberately situated this myth as part of a larger structure. In this case, several other myths involving snakes frame the Perseus and Medusa story and echo the paradox of her deadly life. The first part of book 4 demonstrates the power of the god Bacchus when the daughters of Minyas spurn him by refusing to participate in his festival. Instead, they remain indoors to tell stories until they suddenly find that Bacchus has transformed them into bats. The goddess Juno, wife of Jupiter, becomes enraged at Bacchus's display of power because he is the result of Jupiter's dalliance with Semele. Because Ino, Semele's sister, raised Bacchus, Juno directs her rage toward Ino and her husband, Athamas. The goddess commands the Furies, goddesses of vengeance who, like Medusa, have "black snakes hanging in their hair" (4.456), to make Ino and Athamas go insane. Girded with serpents, the Furies achieve this by attacking the couple with vicious snakes that breathe the venom of madness into them. Frenzied, Athamas promptly murders his baby son, provoking Ino to jump with their other son off a cliff into the ocean. Pitying them, Venus persuades Neptune to turn them into deities, so that Ino becomes Leucothoe and her son Palaemon.

Cadmus, founder of Thebes and the father of Ino, despairs over her death and abandons Thebes, wandering with his wife to Illyria. There, he wonders aloud whether his misfortunes result from an earlier incident in which he killed a possibly sacred snake and scattered its magic teeth over the soil. Here, Cadmus refers to an episode in book 3. Unable to find his sister Europa after Jupiter abducts her, Cadmus wanders as an exile until an oracle tells him to found a new city. In the process, he slays

a giant snake after it kills his men, but he immediately hears a voice pronounce that he too will one day become a snake. Minerva then appears and tells him to plant the serpent's teeth to found a new race of people. From the planted teeth spring warriors, most of whom kill each other, but the five survivors become Cadmus's partners in founding the city of Thebes. Recalling these events, Cadmus declares, "If it is he [the snake] the jealous gods avenge / With wrath so surely aimed, I pray that I / May be a snake and stretch along the ground" (4.574–76). Speaking these words, Cadmus immediately becomes a serpent, and in a poetic tour de force, Ovid describes how Cadmus and his wife both become peaceful snakes. The poet then follows this saga with the story of Perseus and Medusa.

These preceding myths thus create a thematic frame for the Perseus and Medusa episode not only by including snakes but also by featuring serpents that, like Medusa, are sometimes deadly and sometimes life giving. The Furies represent pure destruction, but the lethal, sacred snake defeated by Cadmus produces a new race of humans. Cadmus himself then becomes a snake, providing a thematic link to Ovid's unique account of Medusa's serpentine change. These details show that Ovid was interested in snakes as more than simply a general theme. Rather, he was fascinated by their power because it is precisely rooted in the paradox of metamorphosis as initiating both death and life. As a poet deeply invested in the theme of transformation, Ovid was fixated on snakes as deadly yet transformative beings and Medusa as the human incarnation of this creative paradox. Changed from a beautiful woman into a snaky creature, Medusa continues to spawn new transformations even though she is technically dead. Ovid's version of her story is the first to grasp the astonishing import of her creative, symbolic potential—a potential that subsequently blossomed with particular force in the twentieth century.

Yet why does Ovid center this paradox on snakes, and what is the origin of Medusa's representative role? The first question is easier to answer than the second. As the archaeological work of Marija Gimbutas has demonstrated and scholars such as Dexter have confirmed, the Neolithic period (roughly 10000–4500 BCE) in Europe and the Near East reflects widespread evidence of snake and bird goddesses as deities that likely represented the endless cycle of life, death, and regeneration. As Dexter notes, these creatures are logical choices for such mythological symbols because they both shed skin or feathers, suggesting regeneration, and inhabit multiple realms: birds inhabit the air, land, and sometimes water, while snakes live on the earth, in water, and underground. In addition, similar deities from early historic religions in Egypt and Mesopotamia have also persuaded scholars such as Dexter to interpret the Neolithic figures as divine representations. Gimbutas argues for the snake in particular as "stimulator and guardian of the spontaneous life energy" (95) in these Neolithic cultures, which consequently anthropomorphized serpents and also birds as goddesses. Ancient Greece inherited these goddess figures, traces of which Gimbutas believes survive in the Greek goddesses Hera, Athena, and Aphrodite, who are linked with birds or snakes in ancient representations. Because such mythological beliefs and images survive for thousands of years, it is not surprising that snakes with paradoxical powers appear in the myths of Ovid.

Regarding the origin of Medusa, however, scholars do not agree. Gorgon images are widespread in Greek iconography long before Medusa's characteristics and story had fully developed. Some scholars believe that the Gorgon is simply a death mask with an apotropaic function, designed to ward off evil (Wilk 190). This explanation, however, does not account for Medusa's twin abilities to produce and destroy life. Gimbutas finds representations of Medusa on pottery from the Bronze Age (3300–1200 BCE) and argues that she is linked specifically to the dual figure of Hekate-Artemis, a powerful virgin goddess representing life and death and descended from the earlier goddess figures. Dexter argues that even though Medusa gains her snake and winged attributes rather late in narrative history, she is a synthesis of the Old European bird/snake goddess figure and the Near Eastern demon spirit of Humbaba, whose image and beheading in the epic poem *Gilgameš* may be a prototype for Medusa's similar fate in Greek narratives. Medusa also sometimes appears in early artistic representations as a horse figure, which, as Dexter states, could help explain why she produces the horse Pegasus in later myths.

These various figures might help to explain the origin of Medusa's mysterious powers, which became increasingly linked to death in ancient Greek culture. Because this culture was patriarchal (that is, male dominated) and viewed life and death as linear, rather than a circular regenerative process, fear of death was a prominent cultural trait. Medusa thus became increasingly disconnected from the life continuum and characterized as deadly and dangerous, according to Dexter. Nonetheless, Greek

and Roman renditions of her story, particularly that of Ovid, retain strong hints of her creative and protective power. For Ovid, Medusa with her serpentine powers became a sort of muse, perfectly embodying his enchantment with metamorphosis as both the theme and method of the poem that ensured his own immortality.

CROSS-CULTURAL INFLUENCE

Medusa's duality and compelling force have captivated readers since ancient times. As Nancy Vickers and Marjorie Garber demonstrate, poets beyond Ovid have portrayed her as a muse figure, with many praising her beauty and condemning her petrifying gaze. Visual artists have likewise rendered her as both lovely and terrible, anthropologists have theorized about her apotropaic role, and political theorists have interpreted her as a symbol of revolution. In the twentieth century, Medusa took on an entirely new meaning when Sigmund Freud, the pioneer of psychoanalysis, proclaimed her as a symbol of the fear of castration. Later in the century, some female artists and feminists began to reclaim Medusa as a symbol of female power and rage, with numerous writers reviving her story. Two notable modern efforts are those of Sylvia Plath (1932–63) and May Sarton (1912–95). Plath was an American poet and novelist whose poem "Medusa" appears in her final acclaimed volume of poetry, *Ariel*, which she wrote shortly before her death in 1963. Both terrifying and masterful, "Medusa" is addressed to Plath's mother, whose name, Aurelia, is similar to the Latin *aurela*, the genus name of the Medusa jellyfish, a snaky-tentacled species named for its likeness to the Gorgon. With stunning precision, Plath transforms the imagery of the jellyfish to interrogate and detonate the suffocating maternal bonds that tormented her, renewing the ancient regenerative role of Medusa only to engulf it in a cold rage of broken ties. May Sarton, the pen name of Eleanor Marie Sarton, who was born in Belgium and immigrated with her parents to the United States as a child, offers a very different reading, defining the Gorgon as poetic inspiration in "The Muse as Medusa." Imagining a personal encounter with the Gorgon, this lyric rejects conventional portrayals of Medusa as petrifying to redefine her in poetic terms as part of the speaker's psyche. Radically different in tone, both poems nonetheless revive the notion of Medusa as a fertile power even as they affirm her destructive nature.

As noted, Plath explores her relationship with her mother in "Medusa," a free-verse poem of forty-one lines divided into five-line stanzas, by capitalizing on the similarity between her mother's name and the Latin term for the Medusa jellyfish. The poet uses the imagery of the sea creature to represent her mother's boundless and stifling control over her psyche, positing the mother as a Medusa figure but ultimately claiming the Gorgon's destructive power for herself. The poem achieves this by skillfully alternating precise imagery with chilling direct address, producing highly original and intensely unsettling lyrics. The poem begins with such imagery, suggesting first a landscape "off that landspit of stony mouth-plugs" (line 1), where the Medusa figure dwells:

> Eyes rolled by white sticks,
> Ears cupping the sea's incoherences,
> You house your unnerving head—God-ball,
> Lens of mercies. (2–5)

Here, Plath uses marine imagery to situate her mother (who lived across the Atlantic Ocean when Plath was in England) as a threatening presence. "God-ball" is the first of a series of religious references suggesting Plath's furious rejection of her mother's Christian piety. The second stanza presents an image of the mother's Gorgon/jellyfish agents pursuing the speaker in a ship, "plying their wild cells in [her] keel's shadow" (7). The third stanza picks up the religious theme again, describing these maternal creatures as "dragging their Jesus hair" (11).

At this point, the speaker presents the first direct address, posed to herself as a question: "Did I escape, I wonder?" (12). The next line implicitly answers in the negative: "My mind winds to you / Old barnacled umbilicus, Atlantic cable, / Keeping itself, it seems, in a state of miraculous repair" (13–15). Here, the speaker makes explicit the linked imagery of the mother and jellyfish in the phrase "barnacled umbilicus" as well as her own prison of dependence, trapped as she is by the mother's psychological umbilical cord, miraculously intact despite the distance of an ocean. The addresses turn to the mother figure and become increasingly menacing as the speaker declares, "You are always there" (16), and later, "I didn't call you. / I didn't call you at all" (21–22). Interspersed with these accusations are images of a suffocating and even predatory figure: the mother is a "tremulous breath at the end of [her] line" (17) and is "fat and red, a placenta // Paralysing the kicking lovers" (25–26) and stealing the speaker's breath. The addresses become attacks in the seventh stanza when the speaker

returns to religious allusion, demanding, "Who do you think you are / A Communion wafer? Blubbery Mary" (32–33).

Until this point, the speaker has portrayed herself as a victim of the Medusa mother figure, but in line 38, she reverses the roles by refusing to feed off of the creature who imprisons her, stating, "I shall take no bite of your body, / Bottle in which I live" (lines 34–35). The shocking conclusion sustains the refusal:

> Ghastly Vatican.
> I am sick to death of hot salt.
> Green as eunuchs, your wishes
> Hiss at my sins.
> Off, off, eely tentacle!
> There is nothing between us. (36–41)

In lines 32–41, the speaker builds her disdain into a cold fury, finally rejecting piety but also pity in the form of tears and the marine environment of the jellyfish, "the hot salt" of line 37. The final declaration of "nothing between us" plays on the possible meanings of no connection versus no separation whatsoever between mother and daughter, leaving the final interpretation open as to whether the speaker has truly escaped her mother's control. The speaker's astonishing control, however, clearly indicates that she has usurped Medusa's force. No longer wanting or needing the mother's choking presence, the speaker appropriates through sheer economy of image and deadly tone the paralyzing effect of her mother's power. Plath in fact achieves the apotropaic effect of the ancient Gorgon, but she presents it as a psychic process. Instead of Medusa warding off the evil she already embodies, the tone of Plath's speaker comes to adopt the Gorgonian threat she perceives in her mother. It is this poetic mastery and psychological force that have rightly earned Plath her place in literary history.

Sarton was born two decades before Plath but published "The Muse as Medusa" in 1971, nearly a decade after Plath's "Medusa." In her work, Sarton imagines the speaker's encounter with the Gorgon, who becomes both muse and part of the speaker's psychic struggle. The poem, consisting of twenty-eight lines arranged into quatrains, or four-line stanzas, begins by contrasting the speaker's benign encounter with Medusa with the legendary reputation preceding her. The speaker declares that she has seen Medusa and looked her "straight in the cold eye, cold" but was not petrified (2). She then asks, "How to believe the legends I am told?" (4). The speaker develops her response over the course of the poem. First, she likens herself in the second stanza to "any little fish, / Prepared to be hooked, gutted, caught" (5–6), but Medusa surprises her by not only sparing her life but also allowing her to leave "clothed in thought" (8). Subsequent lines develop the idea of the speaker's contact with the Gorgon producing a new realm of experience. After gazing at Medusa, this new pensive swimmer is permitted to roam throughout the deep, "flashing wild streams" (11) and daring to escape "to many a magic reef" (13).

In the fifth and sixth stanzas, the speaker shifts to explore her view of Medusa's meaning based on their unexpected encounter. She introduces two provocative ideas, that Medusa chose her fate by resigning herself to "lack of motion" (19) and that this resignation did not really work because "nothing really froze" (20). In the next stanza, the speaker articulates this claim, which she describes as a "world of feeling / Where thoughts, those fishes, silent, feed and rove" (21–22). But it is also a world "full of healing, / For love is healing, even rootless love" (23–24). With these words, the speaker portrays the fish specifically as her own thoughts and emotions—in other words, her psyche, itself cold, that has encountered and survived the Gorgon's "cold eye" (2). The reference to "love" in line 24 hints at both the speaker's possible losses in love and Medusa's suffering at the hands of Poseidon. The final stanza specifies what Medusa really means for the speaker's psyche:

I turn your face around! It is my face.
That frozen rage is what I must explore—
Oh secret, self-enclosed, and ravaged place!
This is the gift I thank Medusa for. (25–28)

These lines make it clear that Medusa is a metaphor for the speaker's rage; no dreaded creature to be vanquished, Medusa is part of the speaker herself. The poem thus enacts a psychic encounter that gradually pinpoints the meaning of the Gorgon's "frozen rage" as poetic and emotional inspiration but also as the locus of healing that the speaker must "explore" (26). Sarton's achievement is to reclaim Medusa to a certain degree as a positive regenerative force, an experience of female rage that nonetheless offers hope. The poet communicates this hope partly through her use of the *abab* rhyme scheme, which she uses to forge a light tone and stable movement, a formal technique that effectively uplifts the intensity of Medusa as a symbol of psychic anger. In

this way, the tone of Sarton's poem is radically different from the chilling menace of Plath's "Medusa."

Both Plath and Sarton's treatments arise in part from the influence of American feminism, which enabled many female writers in the second half of the twentieth century to speak and write in ways that had previously been socially forbidden. However, both writers to some degree ultimately emphasize the patriarchal view of Medusa as a vicious destroyer. Plath's maternal Gorgon strangles through her overwhelming filial connection. Her force is thus purely destructive and something the speaker ultimately usurps to try to escape, as the speaker's voice takes on Medusa's deadly power. In contrast, Sarton's Medusa is not entirely destructive because she denies its annihilating power and links it with her psyche, suggesting a vital spirit. Nonetheless, the poem concludes with anger as the defining characteristic of this psyche. On the one hand, expressing this anger in connection with Medusa as a victimized woman represents a breakthrough, particularly for feminist readers who wish to reclaim and redefine Medusa's legendary rage as just or, in Dexter's words, to provide "an ancient locus for modern rage" (41), as Plath and Sarton do. On the other hand, Dexter is right to criticize this modern critical tendency as limited because it continues the erosion of Medusa's "beneficent aspects: the fact that one-half of her blood is healing and that images of her head are used to protect buildings of multiple functions within the Greco-Roman sphere" (41). Dexter argues that modern artists and critics should remember these essential features of the Gorgon, suggesting that the long dismantling of Medusa's dual nature is not so easily repaired. For this reason, whether one regards the treatments of Plath and Sarton as feminist interpretations of Medusa depends on the values one assigns to Medusa herself. In any case, both poets produce fine work that invites readers to reclaim the full significance of the ancient Gorgon.

Ashleigh Imus, PhD

BIBLIOGRAPHY

Cellini, Benvenuto. *Perseus with the Head of Medusa*. 1890. *Image Collection*. Web. 24 Sept. 2012.

Dexter, Miriam Robbins. "The Ferocious and the Erotic: 'Beautiful' Medusa and the Neolithic Bird and Snake." *JFSR* 26.1 (2010): 25–41. Print.

Garber, Marjorie, and Nancy Vickers, eds. *The Medusa Reader*. New York: Routledge, 2003. Print.

Gimbutas, Marija. *The Goddesses and Gods of Old Europe*. Berkeley: U of California P, 1974. Print.

---. *The Language of the Goddess*. San Francisco: Harper, 1989. Print.

Hesiod. "From *The Shield of Herakles* and *Theogony* (c. 700 B.C.E.), translated by Richmond Lattimore: Medusa and Perseus." Garber and Vickers 11–13.

Homer. "From *The Iliad* (c. 750–725 B.C. E.), translated by Richmond Lattimore: Medusa as Shield and Sign." Garber and Vickers 9–10.

Murgatroyd, Paul. *Mythical Monsters in Classical Literature*. Cornwall: Duckworth, 2007. Print.

Ovid. *Metamorphoses*. Trans. A. D. Melville. Oxford: Oxford UP, 1986. Print.

Plath, Sylvia. "Medusa." Garber and Vickers 102–3.

Pseudo-Apollodorus. *The Library of Greek Mythology*. Trans. Keith Aldrich. Lawrence: Coronado, 1975. Print.

Sarton, May. "The Muse as Medusa." Garber and Vickers 107–8.

Wilk, Stephen R. *Medusa: Solving the Mystery of the Gorgon*. Oxford: Oxford UP, 2000. Print.

Saint George and the Dragon

Author: Jacobus de Voragine
Time Period: 501 CE–1000 CE
Country or Culture: Eastern Europe
Genre: Legend

OVERVIEW

The tale of Saint George and the dragon is part of a collection that Jacobus de Voragine, the archbishop of Genoa, assembled in the late thirteenth century as *The Golden Legend*. First published in Latin in 1470, it was quickly translated into Bohemian, French, Low German, and Italian, and an English translation was commissioned by the Earl of Arundel and printed by William Caxton in 1483. Gutenberg's printing press had been developed only a few decades prior, in 1450, thus the work was clearly held in great esteem. It remains in print.

Voragine was born near Genoa, Italy, in 1228. He became a Dominican priest in 1244, assuming the responsibility of provincial of Lombardy and then becoming archbishop of Genoa. He attempted to be a peacemaker in the feud between the two powerful parties of Guelphs and Ghibellines; for this work, he was canonized as a saint in 1816. He entitled his collection of saints' lives *Legenda Sanctorum* (*Legends of the Saints*), but because it was considered such a valuable resource, it became widely known as *Legenda Aurea* (*Golden Legend*). The book was divided into five periods of the church year, from Advent to Christmas, Christmas to Septuagesima, Septuagesima to Easter, Easter to the Octave of Pentecost, and from the Octave of Pentecost to Christmas. The work contains nearly two hundred chapters. As hagiography, it has been both reviled for gross inaccuracy and praised as a devotional text. In addition to writing a history of Genoa and a defense of Dominicans, Voragine also compiled 307 of his sermons.

In this version, the legend includes only a handful of characters. They include a king, his daughter, and her protector, along with unnamed townspeople. The star of the tale is the dragon—a serpent with an apparently insatiable appetite—that consumes sheep and human children daily. The king has capitulated to the will of the people, who demand the princess's death as decreed by lot, following the deaths of their own children. Unlike some rulers, this king has fatherly feelings and pleads for the life of his daughter, to no avail; instead, he wins a week to mourn her. Saint George fortuitously appears on the scene as the consummate soldier, determined to rescue the king's daughter, which he does. In this version, he is offered money as a reward, while in other variants, he is given the princess in marriage.

The story has been interpreted in a variety of ways. During the Protestant Reformation, it became an allegory of the triumph of Protestantism over the Roman Catholic Church. Other allegorical constructions include the dragon as sin (specifically sexual sin) and Saint George as the virtuous (and chaste) triumphant male.

A feminist reading brings interesting aspects of the narrative into relief and will be implemented below. Feminist literary critics began writing during the 1960s and 1970s in an attempt to question commonly accepted definitions of terms such as "female" and "feminine." Feminist criticism later began to reclaim and study texts written by women, in an attempt to construct a female literary tradition. A number of feminist critics also have embraced the insights of post-structuralists such as Jacques Derrida, Michel Foucault, and Jacques Lacan. The analysis below will rely on feminist Samantha Riches's study of the cult and imagery of Saint George.

SUMMARY

Jacobus de Voragine begins his retelling of the tale of Saint George and the Dragon with several potential etymologies of the name George, together with their allegorical meanings. These possibilities include *geos* (earth) and *orge* (tilling), referring to George tilling his own flesh and bringing forth "the wine of gladness" and "the wheat of good works." That imagery is symbolic of the Eucharist and thus links his martyrdom to that of Christ. Alternatively, the word may be a compound meaning "holy wrestler," referring to combat against the dragon. It may also be construed as meaning "pilgrim and counselor." Voragine is also candid that this narrative was rejected for inclusion in biblical scripture at the Council of Nicene. By that time, several versions of the story conflicted as to the location and the time of Saint George's martyrdom.

The story begins with George's birth in Cappadocia, in modern Turkey. As is common in stories of heroes, the narrative skips his childhood and jumps ahead to his arrival as a knight in Libya. In a pond outside the city of Silene lives a frightening dragon with breath that foul enough to kill people. To placate the dragon, the citizens of Silene offer him two sheep daily. When the sheep are nearly gone, a lottery is devised to select one person to accompany a single sheep.

When the lottery is held and the lot falls on the king's daughter, he begs the people to take his silver and gold instead, but they refuse. If the girl is not offered, they threaten, they will burn both the king and his house. After eight days that are granted to mourn their impending loss, the king and his daughter come forth for the sacrifice, the young woman wearing bridal finery.

Saint George arrives in time for the sacrifice, asking why the girl is weeping and how he might help. Despite the princess's injunctions to him to leave so that he will not perish, the knight vows to slay the dragon in the name of Jesus Christ. George spears the dragon when the creature rushes them and tells the princess to place her girdle around the dragon's neck. They lead the beast into the city, where he frightens the people. George tells them that he will slay the dragon if they agree to believe in Jesus and be baptized. In all, the king and about fifteen thousand men are baptized, with no count made of women and children. The slain dragon, whose head is cut off, is taken outside the city in four carts and thrown into the fields.

In his gratitude, the king builds a church dedicated to the Virgin Mary and to Saint George. A healing fountain appears at the church as well. Although the king offers him money, the knight refuses it, telling the king to give it to the poor instead.

This segment of the legend is a later addition to the tale of martyrdom that Voragine includes, admitting that there are discrepancies as to the location and ruler. In his telling, he prefers the event to have occurred during the reign of the Roman emperors Diocletian and

"Thus as they spake together the dragon appeared and came running to them, and S. George was upon his horse, and drew out his sword and garnished him with the sign of the cross, and rode hardily against the dragon which came towards him, and smote him with his spear and hurt him sore and threw him to the ground."

The Golden Legend

Maximian in the late third century CE. In light of the martyrdom of twenty-two thousand in a single month, many Christians recant their faith and sacrifice to idols, as requested. Upon seeing this defection, George sets aside his knightly garb, sells his possessions, and distributes his proceeds to the poor. He then courts martyrdom, proclaiming the pagan gods to be devils and his God the true God and creator of the heavens.

George survives several forms of torture, including hanging on a gibbet, beatings with both wooden and iron staves, branding, and imprisonment. God appears to encourage him in prison. Next, George drinks strong poison that does not harm him but leads instead to the conversion of the magician assigned to kill him. When George is placed on wheels to break his body, the wheels break instead. Next, he is dipped in hot lead, which has no effect.

The frustrated emperor (whose name changes to Dacian from Diocletian during the telling of the tale) offers George honor if he will only offer sacrifice to the pagan gods. George agrees to this, and a public show is planned. However, rather than offer sacrifice, George prays for God to destroy the temple. Fire descends and burns the temple, and the earth opens and swallows the ashes.

A conversation between the emperor Dacian and his wife leads to her admission that she has also become a Christian. Dacian beats her almost to death; when she consults George about dying without being baptized, he assures her that she will be baptized in blood. Dacian also has George beheaded. On Dacian's way home, however, the ruler and his servants are consumed by fire. Voragine dates the event to the year 287. Subsequently, when Christians from Antioch go up to defend Jerusalem, George goes before them and gives them victory. The narrative includes mention of the Order of the Garter and of a college at Windsor said to contain the heart of the martyr. Voragine concludes by saying that Saint George is the patron and protector of England and his name the cry of men in battle.

ANALYSIS

Women have been writing about the place of women in society and in literature for centuries, beginning with such notable works as Mary Wollstonecraft's *A Vindication of the Rights of Women* (1792). Feminist literary theory is a direct outgrowth of the so-called second wave of feminism, which occurred during the 1960s and 1970s in the larger context of an international women's movement. Kate Millet, Sandra Gilbert, Susan Gubar, and other writers concerned with both the representation of women in literature and new analyses of the largely male-produced classics began publishing their critiques of the status quo—from identifying the misogyny in extant criticism to rediscovering texts by women to broadening to include the insights of French feminism. Feminist theory is not a monolithic construct, however. Feminist writers interact with other critical theories, such as Marxism and postmodernism. Nor do all feminist scholars agree as to the emphasis of their work, with French feminism sometimes privileging *l'écriture feminine* (female writing) and African American theorists, such as bell hooks (the pen name of Gloria Jean Watkins), differing from white feminists in their approach.

The analysis below takes a feminist approach to the legend of Saint George and the dragon, considering the female characters and the roles that they play within the narrative. Following the work of medievalist scholar Samantha Riches, attention will be given to the images that portray the dragon as female. This in turn will lead to a historic survey of dragon myths, uncovering the misogynistic bent of early religions, as well as of medieval Christianity. In addition, consideration will be given to the portrayal of Saint George as a male virgin martyr.

The cult of Saint George focuses on his successful battle with the dragon, rather than on his martyrdom, which is the oldest part of the legend. However, the dragon presents more interesting opportunities for the saint's iconography. A variety of artworks using this imagery have been documented throughout Europe and the Middle East. They vary in specifics but share common elements. At the very least, the characters of Saint George and the dragon appear. Saint George is most frequently mounted and carrying a lance or sword. It is the dragon's imagery that permutates.

Most of the images, whether painted or carved, do not reveal any sexual characteristics, although a few do include male genitalia. In some fifty images from the fifteenth and sixteenth centuries that critic Samantha Riches has observed, the dragon is clearly female. The dragon's sex is indicated by the presence of breasts, a woman's head, a genital slit, or dragonets. In these images, the dragon appears lying down on her back, the slit clearly exposed. This gendered dragon appears in a variety of media in several countries, including England, France, Germany, Italy, and the Netherlands.

Riches suggests that the female imagery is used to indicate an allegorical interpretation to the legend that would be in harmony with medieval thought. She notes that the dragon's pudendum is consistently revealed, often with a broken lance or other phallic imagery to lead the eye of the viewer to that spot. Further, Saint George is depicted as being in the process of attacking the mouth or throat of the dragon, a covert sexual image, with the mouth standing for the vagina.

The dragon may have been a stock image in medieval culture; a late fifteenth-century English translation of *The Golden Legend* uses a woodcut of Saint George and a female dragon, despite the fact that the text refers to the dragon as male. The use of a woodcut suggests that the printer had a block made for use whenever the image was needed, thus perpetuating the idea of a female dragon.

Early religions and myths provided a template of conflict between a champion and a dragon as indicative of the dualities of light and darkness, good and evil, reason and nature. For example, the *Enuma Elish* of Mesopotamia includes the account of the struggle between Tiāmat, a sea goddess associated with dragons and chaos, and her son Marduk. To bolster her own strength, Tiāmat spawns monsters such as dragons, serpents, and centaurs to aid her in vengeance for the slaying of her consort, Apsû, the god of fresh water. The gods select Marduk to face Tiāmat in single combat and agree that if he is victorious, he will become king of the universe. When Tiāmat opens her mouth to swallow Marduk, he sends a great wind to keep that orifice open and then stabs her. Thus, he triumphs over Tiāmat, killing her and her brood. From her body he then creates the heavens and earth, and from her pierced eyes stream the Tigris and Euphrates Rivers. Marduk also kills her second husband, from whose blood he creates humankind. The myth introduces the trope of dragons and water, which appears in several different cultures. This contest can be read not only as a creation myth but also as a battle between patriarchy and the older fertility goddess religions.

The fertility cults generally included myths that enacted the triumph of spring over winter. The Greek story of Demeter, the corn goddess, and Persephone, her daughter captured by Hades, is just one example. In this myth, Persephone returns to her mother and the earth during spring and summer but spends the fall and winter with Hades as queen of the underworld.

Saint George's feast day is April 23 in the liturgical calendar of the Christian church, linking him with the return of spring. The placement of the saint's feast day occurred prior to the addition of the dragon story. Riches suggests that the dragon was added to incorporate elements of Celtic deities. To support this idea, she cites place names such as Ogbourne St. George in Wiltshire, which combines the Celtic sun god Og with Saint George. In addition, during the medieval period, people held parades through the fields on days when those fields were blessed. People carried dragon figures in these processions, their control of the figures symbolizing the triumph of spring. Although this custom was not directly linked to Saint George, the association may have been present in the minds of the rite's participants.

Ancient Greek philosophers, such as Aristotle, and mythographers, such as the playwright Aeschylus, taught that women were inferior to men. Early Christian thinkers such as Saint Thomas Aquinas regarded women as imperfect men. Aquinas's theories would perhaps matter less than any other disproved medieval ideas, except that the Roman Catholic Church declared him a doctor of the Church, enshrining his theology. The Hebrew Bible (which Christians refer to as the Old Testament) includes the monsters Leviathan and Behemoth, the latter being gendered female. In addition, some artistic depictions show the serpent that tempted Adam and Eve in the Garden of Eden as having a female face and long hair. The Christian church inherited these scriptures and teachings and incorporated the prevailing attitudes of the larger culture when codifying the behavior of women.

In the book of Revelation, the last book of the New Testament, dragons appear in both the sky and the water. The champion Saint Michael, with the aid of angels, defeats the sky dragon. The water dragon, which is associated with Satan, is finally chained for a thousand years. The dragon is thus placed as a symbol of evil and bestial female sexuality in opposition to the humans, who are chaste and good.

For many in medieval European culture, women were regarded in one of two ways: evil, sexual, and bestial, or good, virginal, and saintly. This bifurcation was a consequence of early Christian misogyny present in sermons and writings of the early church. Regarding Eve, not Adam, as the blameworthy agent of the Fall in the Garden of Eden, church leaders passed that blame upon all women, considering them inferior to men. The attitude of women as weaker and lesser people permeated the early church, which adopted and perpetuated the familiar patriarchal patterns of the larger Greco-Roman world. With the importance of the Church in medieval European society, women continued to be regarded as second-class citizens.

Riches makes the argument that Saint George functions as a male virgin martyr. This idea sets up the contrast between the ideal chaste male knight and the bestial, sexually intemperate female monster. Riches sees the dragon as a symbol of the dreaded female sexuality. Saint George refuses the offer that a female lying on her back, genitals exposed, would be making; perhaps the posture was assumed in an attempt to avoid being slain. By attacking the mouth of the dragon with his sword, he is sublimating sexual desire.

Saint George thus becomes a virgin martyr, even though most commonly those martyrs were women who faced multiple tortures rather than submit to marriage with a nonbeliever. Male martyrs, in contrast, are generally associated with one specific torture motif. Examples of the former include Saint Margaret, who was not only beaten and burned with torches, but also faced a dragon. Saint Sebastian, by contrast, faced a single agent of death, arrows. The case may be made that Saint George must also surmount multiple tortures to borrow the trope of virgin martyrdom. In fact, some of his tortures are identical with those suffered by female virgin martyrs. Like Catherine, he is to be broken on a wheel, although in both cases, the wheel falls apart before torture can take place. Like Margaret, he too is beaten and burned. This idea of Saint George as virgin martyr is further strengthened by his refusal to accept the princess

MYTH INTO ART

The Renaissance painter Raphael created a small painting of Saint George and the dragon in 1506. Unframed, it is about the size of a sheet of notebook paper, approximately eleven inches by nine inches, and was done on wood. The twenty-three-year-old artist signed his name across the horse's bridle. The other word in the painting is *Honi*, which is the beginning of the phrase *Honi soit qui mal y pense* ("Disgraced be he who thinks evil of it"), the motto for the Order of the Garter, of which Saint George was the patron saint. The Duke of Urbino, who had become a member of the order, commissioned the painting. It may have been a gift for an envoy from the English court.

The work is notable for the imagery within the painting. The dragon is serpentine, recalling the serpent that tempted Eve in the Garden of Eden. Its mouth is open in threat or pain, as Saint George pierces it with a long lance, set at an angle that gives the composition movement. It seems to be near the entrance of a cave, perhaps its home. Saint George is wearing the full body armor of a soldier, with a cloak flowing behind. These appear to be green, which could be conflating Saint George with Green Man imagery. A gold circlet above his helmet indicates his sainthood. He is mounted on a white horse. A lady in red, her hands folded as in prayer, is at the right side of the painting. In the distance, the towers of the city appear. The near landscape is a blend of forest and rock.

The landscape of this painting is similar to the work of Hans Memling, a Dutch artist. Paintings from the Netherlands were popular in Italy in the early sixteenth century and may have influenced Raphael's depiction. In addition, the posture of Saint George is reminiscent of Leonardo da Vinci's cartoon sketch for the fresco *The Battle of Anghiari* (1505).

Previously owned by Charles I of England and Catherine II of Russia, the painting has been in the collection of the National Gallery of Art since 1937.

---

in marriage when she is offered to him as a reward (in Alexander Barclay's 1515 version), as well as by his slaying the female dragon.

In addition, Saint George is identified with the Virgin Mary as her champion. By extension, the ultimate virgin would require a champion who was also chaste. According to *The Golden Legend*, the king of Silene, where the dragon was vanquished, built a church to honor both the Virgin Mary and Saint George. This dual dedication also occurs in several iconic motifs in British churches. Furthermore, it is present in the lyrics of some medieval Christmas carols. Edmund Spenser uses this identification with Mary in the epic poem *The Faerie Queene*, whose hero in book 1 is the Redcrosse Knight of Holiness, Saint George, who protects the Virgin. The poem can also be read as Anglicanism triumphing over Roman Catholicism to uphold Queen Elizabeth I's reign following that of her Catholic sister, Mary.

An interesting aside to the legend is the power of Saint George to aid barren women. Those who visited shrines in northern Syria dedicated to the saint became magically impregnated by him. This provides a further link to the Virgin Mary, who gave birth to her son without a human agent.

The role played by the only human female character in the legend thus reflects medieval sensibilities about the virtuous woman. The princess is a pawn in the game between the people of the kingdom and the dragon. Despite his kingly status, her father—in patriarchy, the one designated to protect her—is powerless before the dragon and the people alike. Like the children of the peasants, she is about to be offered to the dragon to save the rest of the community. She is helpless and weeping over her fate, powerless to save herself. Although she is doomed to obedience, she urges Saint George to save himself; it apparently does not occur to her (or to him) that she could go with him to safety. She is the ideal woman of patriarchy: submissive to her father and ready to sacrifice herself for another. However, she does play a role in the defeat of the dragon by placing her girdle around its neck, albeit at a man's direction, and leading it into the city.

Feminist theory looks at the speech as well as the actions of the characters in a literary work. The unnamed princess has two direct speeches and one summarized speech. Both of her direct speeches are warnings to Saint George. She first says: "Go ye your way fair young man, that ye perish not also." Following George's affirming that he would help her, she responds: "For God's sake, good knight, go your way, and abide not with me, for ye may not deliver me." She has no speeches either when she is chosen by lot to be sacrificed, nor on the day she is to die. Nor does she have anything to say in the Barclay version when her father offers her as a reward to the knight. She speaks only words of warning to Saint George. His disregard of these warnings, not once but twice, increases his heroic status.

Saint George embodies the stereotypical male chivalric hero: he is fearless, he rescues the damsel in distress, and he slays the dragon. In *The Golden Legend* and several other versions, he is offered—and refuses—a monetary reward. Other texts present the offer of a city or kingdom.

In Alexander Barclay's text *Life of St George* (1515), the king offers the princess in marriage to her rescuer. From this retelling comes the legend of Princess Sabre and the subsequent marriage of the saint and the princess. The artists William Morris and Dante Gabriel Rossetti incorporated that aspect of the legend into at least two pieces of nineteenth-century art.

Saint George is also linked to the Greek hero Perseus, who rescues the princess Andromeda from a sea monster. Her father, with somewhat less feeling than the king in *The Golden Legend*, has tied her to a rock as an offering to the monster, in hopes that it will stop menacing the region. Perseus rescues Andromeda, by pulling the head of Medusa, whom he has just slain, from a bag. Still potent in death, Medusa's head turns the sea monster into stone when he looks at it. Perseus marries Andromeda, providing a contrast to Saint George in nearly all of the written versions of the legend.

In applying feminist concerns to the legend, it is clear that Saint George's narrative is male-focused. Not only does the saint protect the city by slaying the dragon, but he also has more spoken lines than any of the other characters. The iconography that portrays the dragon as female further enforces the male prohibition against unbridled female sexuality and sets up the dragon as a foil against the chaste human princess. This is a text about male power and heroism, in which to be female is to be either in danger or dangerous.

CROSS-CULTURAL INFLUENCE

Saint George is a patron saint in several countries and cities. Aragon, Catalonia, Georgia, Germany, Greece, Lithuania, Palestine, and Portugal claim him, as do the cities of Genoa, Istanbul, Moscow, and Venice, where he is second only to Saint Mark. He also is the patron saint of many different groups of people—archers, cavalry, chivalry, farmers and field workers, riders, and soldiers. In addition, he is the helper of those suffering from leprosy, the plague, and syphilis.

However, it is with England that Saint George is most clearly identified, although he probably never set foot in that land. The saint's multivalent uses throughout centuries of British history and literature will be considered here. Some believe that he became popular through the melding of his stories with those of an earlier pagan or Celtic hero. In any case, soldiers returning from the Crusades brought Saint George's story to England. They claimed that he had appeared to lead the men into battle, a claim that would be repeated in subsequent conflicts until World War II. In 1222, April 23 was named as his saint's day.

In about 1348, King Edward III founded the Order of the Garter, placing it under the protection of Saint George. It was the most important order of knights in England. Saint George slaying the dragon is pictured on the order's badge. Saint George's Chapel at Windsor, completed in 1528, is the Order's official seat. Members include the monarch and the Prince of Wales, along with twenty-four others and twenty-six knights or ladies companions. Thus, from the fourteenth century on, the saint became associated with England. His flag, a red cross on a white background, is incorporated into the design of the British flag. At the Battle of Agincourt, the English king Henry V invoked Saint George in his speech to the troops before the fighting began, as so famously reenacted in William Shakespeare's 1599 play *Henry V*.

Another great English writer, Edmund Spenser, used Saint George as his model for the Redcrosse Knight in his epic work, *The Faerie Queene*, published in 1589. The knight travels with Una, who represents True Religion (Anglicanism) and Truth; clearly, she is meant to signify the princess. Some critics believe that, in light of Sir Thomas Malory's Arthurian epics, Spenser reenvisioned the legend of Saint George as a quest. In the early part of Spenser's poem, the dragon is a living enemy, not a conquered one, and Una serves as the guiding heroine. The Redcrosse Knight is the champion of Gloriana, referring to Queen Elizabeth I (the Virgin Queen, as she was known) and/or the Virgin Mary (often called the Queen of Heaven).

The first battle that the Redcrosse Knight faces is against the Error Monster, depicted as half woman and half snake. As is true in some of the iconography of Saint George, she has spawned monsters and snakes.

She also wraps her tail around the Redcrosse Knight's body, as the dragon wraps itself around Saint George's leg. The knight attacks the monster's throat with his bare hands, while Saint George similarly attacks the dragon's mouth with a lance.

One of the most curious appropriations of Saint George came as a result of the Boer Wars between British and Dutch settlers in South Africa. One of the famous soldiers from the second Boer War was British colonel Robert Baden-Powell. Distressed by the fact that the British Army required seven months to defeat the Boers, Baden-Powell became convinced that the English youth needed a training program to make them better soldiers of the British Empire and to protect England from future invasion. Beginning in 1884, he published works on skills for scouts, believing that well-trained and skilled groups of young men would make excellent spies and informants and be invaluable as message-bearers. After reading Ernest Thompson Seton's "Birch-Bark Roll," a work designed to encourage outdoor skills in young Canadians, Baden-Powell developed his own Boy Scouts. Seton and Baden-Powell met in 1906; the following year, the latter led his first group on a camping trip to Brownsea Island. The experience is generally used to date the beginning of the Boy Scout movement. The movement began in the United States in 1910, the year after William Dickson Boyce visited the Boy Scout headquarters in London.

The Boy Scout exemplar was none other than Saint George, who not only personifies chivalry but is also its patron saint. One chapter in the highly popular *Scouting for Boys* (1908) is entitled "The Chivalry of Knights" and presents nine elements of the "Knight's Code." *Scouting for Boys* would remain second in sales only to the Bible throughout the English-speaking world for many years.

Around 1914, Alice Brewster published a work specifically for the Boy Scouts: *The Life of St. George, the Patron Soldier-Saint of England*. She acknowledged drawing from a work published in 1907, *Saint George, Champion of Christendom and Patron Saint of England*, written by Elizabeth O. Gordon. According to both Baden-Powell and Brewster, Saint George had inspired King Arthur to found the Round Table. Brewster also created further layers to the legend, giving 207 CE as the date of Saint George's birth and asserting that he became friends with the Roman emperor Constantine, with whom he had gone to England. There they visited Constantine's mother, Queen Helena of York and

Glastonbury. According to Brewster, Saint George also visited the tomb of his supposed ancestor, Joseph of Arimathea, who had given the tomb in which Jesus was buried. In Brewster's account, the lesson to be drawn in Saint George's slaying of the dragon was the need to stand up and face whatever confronted one, rather than shirking one's duty.

The early years of the scouting movement also witnessed the image of Saint George being utilized, along with his flag, a red cross on a white field, and the Union Jack. In one illustration, a Boy Scout rolls up a khaki shirtsleeve as if preparing for work. He is looking at a statue of Saint George, mounted on a white horse and piercing the dragon's mouth. The cover of the 1916 work *The Young Knights of the Empire*, also by Baden-Powell, shows a young knight looking at a caged and decidedly dejected dragon. On the bars of the cage are written ideals such as kindness, obedience, and courtesy.

In England, the Boy Scouts and Saint George remain linked, with annual Saint George's day parades in some parts of the nation. (Saint George's Day was fixed as April 23 in 1222.) Color guards carry the British flag along with banners as the troops process to church for a special service.

Another Edwardian appropriation of the Saint George legend occurred in 1911 with the publication of the children's novel *Where the Rainbow Ends*, by Mrs. Clifford Mills. Mills also adapted the work into a stage play with the aid of the actor Reginald Owen, under the pseudonym John Ramsey. Owen first acted the role of Saint George in the play, which opened December 21, 1911.

According to the novel, two young people have lost their parents, who were returning from India by sea. Seeking the "Land Where All Lost Loved Ones Are Found," about which they have read in a book, the children are aided by a genie granting them each a wish. The daughter, Rosamund, asks for the aid of Saint George. To her surprise, the knight who appears is initially gray and explains that he has been neglected. When Rosamund asks for his protection, he is transformed into a knight in shining armor. Saint George defeats the Dragon King, and the children are reunited with their parents.

Such was the popularity of the tale that it became an annual Christmas tradition into the 1950s, with an estimated twenty million people having seen it by 1960. The subtexts of patriotism and nobility of character created a demand that led to several editions of the novel, now almost forgotten.

More recently, during the Luftwaffe's bombing of Britain during the Second World War, King George VI created the George Cross for acts of great heroism or courage in great danger. The medal is generally presented to civilians and carries an honor second only to the Victoria Cross. On the medal itself is an image of a mounted Saint George slaying the dragon. The entire island of Malta received the George Cross for its resistance to attack during the war.

For hundreds of years, the legend of Saint George and the dragon has permutated in British culture to suit the needs of the time. As a figure of chivalry, patriotism, and heroic action, this Cappadocian soldier has inspired generations of hearers and readers.

Judy A. Johnson, MLS, MTS

BIBLIOGRAPHY

Barry, Peter. *Beginning Theory: An Introduction to Literary and Cultural Theory*. 3rd ed. Manchester: Manchester UP, 2009. Print.

Clark, Elizabeth. *Women in the Early Church*. Collegeville: Liturgical, 1983.

Jacobus de Voragine. "St. George." *The Golden Legend: St. George*. American Buddha, n.d. Web. 12 Mar. 2013.

Morgan, Giles. *St. George*. Edison: Chartwell, 2006. Print.

Riches, Samantha. *St. George: Hero, Martyr and Myth*. Phoenix Mill: Sutton, 2000. Print.

--- "Saint George as Male Virgin Martyr." *Gender and Holiness: Men, Women and Saints in Late Medieval Europe*. Ed. Samantha Riches and Sarah Salih. New York: Routledge, 2002. 65–85. Print.

---. "Virtue and Violence: Saints, Monsters and Sexuality in Medieval Culture." *Medieval Sexuality: A Casebook*. Ed. April Harper and Caroline Proctor. New York: Routledge, 2008. 59–78. Print.

Showalter, Elaine. "The Feminist Critical Revolution." *The New Feminist Criticism*. Ed. Showalter. New York: Pantheon, 1985. 3–17. Print.

Theseus and the Minotaur

Author: Diodorus Siculus; Hyginus; Ovid
Time Period: 999 BCE–1 BCE; 1 CE–500 CE
Country or Culture: Greek; Roman
Genre: Myth

OVERVIEW

The myth of Theseus and his triumph over the captive Minotaur (Minôtauros) has fascinated writers and visual artists for centuries. The artists who designed ancient Greek vases and twentieth-century artist Pablo Picasso both depicted the Minotaur. The stratagem of Ariadnê, who gave Theseus a thread to unwind as he entered the labyrinth, has been a symbol of psychoanalytic thinking. The labyrinth itself can be seen to represent the mystery of the human mind and soul.

Several sources of the myth exist, including the texts by Diodorus Siculus, Gaius Julius Hyginus, and Ovid. The Greek historian Diodorus Siculus, who was originally from Sicily, lived during the first century BCE. His most famous work was the *Bibliothēkē* (also known as *Bibliotheca historica* or *The Library of History*). It was composed of forty short books covering different areas of the world, with the first book containing legends. He relied on older sources for much of the work, including prehistoric mythology. Little is known of Hyginus, a Roman who may have lived during the first century CE and may have been acquainted with Ovid. His work is of value largely because it draws on material from Greek dramas that have subsequently been lost. Publius Ovidius Naso, known as Ovid, was a prolific Roman writer who lived from 43 BCE until around 17 CE. Ovid's *Metamorphoses* (8 CE), a long poem written in hexameter and retelling a number of Greek and Roman myths, has influenced numerous later writers, including William Shakespeare and John Milton.

Several major characters play roles in the story of Theseus and Ariadnê. Theseus is the young prince who defeats the monster in the maze. Aegeus is the king of Athens and father of Theseus. King Minos of Crete precipitates the need for a labyrinth and ritual victims by his refusal to sacrifice a fine bull, angering the gods. Minos's daughter Ariadnê is a prime actor in the drama, making it possible for Theseus to succeed in killing the beast. The Minotaur is her half brother, the son of her mother, whom the gods made to fall in love with a prize bull as a rebuke to Minos. The creature has the head of a bull and the body of a man. Daedalus is the noted court architect who constructs the labyrinth that houses the Minotaur. The main god who acts in the myth is Dionysius (Dionysios), who takes Ariadnê as his own, either by force or after she is abandoned, depending on the version being read.

Archetypal literary theory is based on the work of twentieth-century Swiss psychologist Carl Jung and will be applied to the myth. The term "archetype" refers to a pattern, conscious or subconscious, that underlies and directs human behavior. The word is a compound Greek word formed from *arkhe*, alluding to what is original or first, and *typos*, referring to a mold or a seal. The term appeared in Hellenistic religious and philosophical writings of authors such as Philo and Plotinus.

Centuries later, Jung referred to an archetype as an "inherited mode of psychic functioning," comparing it to the innate knowledge that a bird has in building a nest (qtd. in Moon 381). He believed that a person's thoughts and actions are determined by unconscious patterns. Folklorists Aarne Anti and Stith Thompson further adapted and used archetypes in their study of folklore and literature. The analysis will include a look at some of their categories as well.

SUMMARY

Several Greek and Roman writers, each of whom emphasizes a different place within the narrative, penned fragments of the myth of Theseus and the Minotaur. Each has his own slant on the tale, but they agree in the basic outline of events. The story begins with Minos, the king of Crete, or his wife, Pasiphaê, offending the gods. In some accounts, Minos is to sacrifice an especially fine bull to Poseidon (according to Diodorus) or Jupiter (Ovid), but instead he offers other bulls. According to Hyginus, Pasiphaê neglects to honor Venus with sacrifices. To punish the offense, the gods cause Pasiphaê to fall in love with a bull. All variants relate that with the help of Daedalus, the court architect, she has intercourse with the bull. The child born of the union has the head of a bull and the body of a man.

The king is outraged and commands Daedalus to construct a labyrinth in which to hide the Minotaur. Daedalus himself has difficulty retracing his steps out of the maze, so intricate is its design. The creature demands sacrifice, however, and Minos offers young men and women sent in tribute from Athens. Sent into the labyrinth, they cannot find the way out and are devoured. According to Ovid, this offering occurs three times a year for nine years; other sources say the sacrifice occurs once every nine years.

Determined to end the slaughter, Theseus, son of Aegeus, king of Athens, volunteers to be part of a group bound for sacrifice, intending to kill the Minotaur. Concerned for the fate of his son, Aegeus asks that the ships be outfitted with black sails. If Theseus prevails, the sails are to be changed to white. In this way, Aegeus will be informed of the success or failure of the quest before the fleet's arrival into port.

When Theseus arrives in Crete, Ariadnê, daughter of Minos and half sister of the Minotaur, falls in love with him. She gives him a thread to carry into the labyrinth and unwind as he goes, thus allowing him to retrace his steps after slaying the monster. As Diodorus Siculus puts it, "When they had landed in Crete, Ariadnê, the daughter of Minos, became enamoured of Theseus, who was unusually handsome, and Theseus, after conversing with her and securing her assistance, both slew the Minotaur and got safely away, since he had learned from her the way out of the labyrinth" (4.61.4).

After his triumph, Theseus takes Ariadnê with him, planning to marry her in reward for her loyalty to him. Hyginus relates that en route to the Greek mainland they are stranded on an island because of a storm. Despite his promise of marriage, Theseus abandons Ariadnê on the island of Dia (also called Naxos). He is fearful that if he were to take her to Athens, he would be rebuked because Athens is a vassal state of Crete. Dionysus (Liber or Bacchus in the Roman versions) finds her there on the island. In a version told by the Roman poet Catullus,

"When Theseus came to Crete, Ariadne, Minos' daughter, loved him so much that she betrayed her brother and saved the stranger, for she showed Theseus the way out of the labyrinth. When Theseus had entered and killed the Minotaur, by Ariadne's advice he got out by unwinding the thread. Ariadne, because she had been loyal to him, he took away, intending to marry her."

"Theseus and the Minotaur"

more emphasis is placed on Ariadnê and her plight after being abandoned on the island.

According to Hyginus, it is Liber who marries her. In Diodorus Siculus's version, it is Dionysius who finds her and takes her from Theseus for himself. This action is deemed the cause of Theseus's depression and forgetfulness. Both Diodorus Siculus and Ovid explain the constellation Ariadnê's Crown as a result of Dionysius (Bacchus to the Romans) resolving to grant her fame. Hyginus and Diodorus Siculus relate that Theseus later marries Ariadnê's sister, Phaedra.

Theseus, sailing back to Athens, forgets to change the color of the sails. When Aegeus sees the black sails, he is certain that the Minotaur has slain his son. The grief-stricken father leaps into the sea, which is then named Aegean in his honor, according to Hyginus. By contrast, Diodorus Siculus relates that Aegeus leaps from the Acropolis to his death.

These versions of the myth follow the plot analysis of fights with monsters set forth by scholar Paul Murgatroyd. There are three distinct episodes: a prelude of events that will affect the confrontation, the actual combat itself, and the aftermath of the combat (Murgatroyd 133–34). It is noteworthy that each of these three retellings minimizes the actual combat. Each relates only that Theseus "slew the Minotaur" or "killed the Minotaur." This may be related to the Greek dramatic convention of having violence occur offstage. Rather than emphasizing the battle, the writers focus on the prelude and aftermath. This contradicts another insight Murgatroyd posits—that the Greek and Roman myths featuring battles with monsters offered audiences a safe scare or thrill (2). However, he suggests instead that the short shrift given to the battle in this case is to highlight how easy it was for the hero to overcome the monster (135).

ANALYSIS

The myth of the monster in the labyrinth is told in both Greek and Roman literature. Several features of the myth coincide with aspects of archetypes and myth that the Aarne-Thompson tale type classification analyzes. These aspects will be considered below. Formulated in the late nineteenth and early twentieth centuries by two prominent folklorists, the tale type categories enable readers to spot aggregates of motifs that appear in myth and folklore across cultures. For example, beast-men (a category that also includes beast-women) were common characters throughout Greek mythology. The Minotaur is not the only example of these monster hybrids but a member of a larger category.

The story of Theseus and the Minotaur continues to fascinate modern readers, possibly due to the features of the myth that are amenable to Jungian analysis. Using the dreams that his patients brought to their sessions, the twentieth-century Swiss psychologist Carl Jung identified several key components that can help humans in the quest to understand themselves. Although a contemporary of Sigmund Freud, Jung took a different approach. His archetypical insights will also be explored in this section.

In the eighteenth century, the romantic movement in Europe gave rise to an interest in folklore, along with other aspects of so-called peasant culture. Building on the work of early folklorists and mythologists, later researchers discovered that myths were not limited to a single culture and that certain types of tales appeared in both Eastern and Western literature.

By the mid-nineteenth century, interest in classifying the various types of tales had grown. Finnish father-son team Julius and Kaarle Krohn were key in organizing their nation's collected runes, proverbs, and written folklore. In 1910, the Finnish folklorist Antti Aarne, who had studied with the Krohns, published *Verzeichnis der Märchentypen* (Tale type index). American Stith Thompson translated and expanded the index, which was published in English in 1928 as *The Types of the Folktale*. The work, which has been twice updated, does not limit itself to folklore, discussing motifs found in myth as well.

The Aarne-Thompson classification scheme is similar to the arrangement of the Dewey decimal system, another late nineteenth-century development. Letters A to Z are assigned to broad subject categories, followed by numbers that have decimal points to allow for expansion. So, for example, B is "Mythical Animals," and "Mythical Birds" are classified as B30.

"Beast-men" are cataloged in B20–29. The category includes not only the Minotaur (B23.1) but also other creatures familiar from Greek myth, such as the centaur and satyr. Beast-men may have the body of a man and the head of a beast, as does the bull-headed Minotaur. Centaurs, in contrast, have the body of a beast (horse, in this case) and the trunk and head of a man. Although the Minotaur does not appear specifically in other myths, it is useful to recognize that the category of man-beast does contain other creatures, such as centaurs, lamias, and satyrs. Centaurs are generally portrayed as savage and warlike. Lamias are unusual in that they have a woman's upper body and vampiric tendencies. The satyrs, of whom Pan is god, are noted for their lustful nature. The Minotaur has aspects of all of these hybrid creatures.

FitzRoy Richard Somerset, the fourth Baron Raglan, published the definitive volume *The Hero: A Study in Tradition, Myth, and Drama* in 1936. In "Tradition," he examines the characteristics of the hero cycle throughout multiple cultures and overlaps with the hero cycle of the Aarne-Thompson classification scheme. Raglan distills those attributes into a list of twenty-two aspects that a hero might exhibit. No hero has all of these aspects; for example, King Arthur has sixteen of them, while Oedipus has twenty. Theseus embodies several of the elements. He is of a kingly line and also held to be a son of a god, and he marries a princess and becomes a king.

Theseus also follows the pattern of a hero in going on a quest to destroy the enemy of his people—in this case, the Minotaur, who demands regular human sacrifice. He is thus in company with other heroes such as Gilgameš (Gilgamesh) and the Knights of the Round Table. Also like Gilgameš, he slays a monster, an event classified in the Aarne-Thompson classification scheme as A531, "Culture-hero (demigod) overcomes monster." Another aspect of the hero cycle is the hero's death, descent to the underworld, and resurrection. Although Theseus later in his life does descend to the underworld, this entrance into the labyrinth is also a form of death. He follows a path he cannot see to slay a monster at its center.

Jung's psychoanalytic approach was rooted in the study of dreams rather than of myth; however, Jung's work can be applied to myth as well. Jung wrote of the "collective unconscious," the concept that humans involuntarily inherit a vast system of symbols, myths, dreams, and images. These are at the root of the recurrent types found in folklore, fairy tales, and mythology.

One of Jung's primary concepts is that of the shadow side, or the latent aspect, of a person. Most people push aside this version of the self, which is perceived as flawed, and prefer not to deal with it. Jung believed that this ignored shadow side nevertheless operates at a subconscious level of which a person might not be aware. In the myth of the battle with the Minotaur, the labyrinth then functions as an analogue of the subconscious. One interpretation of the Minotaur is that he is a perfect example of a hidden-away, shadow aspect of personality; he is Theseus's double. To be completely human, Theseus must enter the labyrinth and thus confront this shadow side. As scholar André Peyronie puts it, "Who is the Minotaur and what does Theseus do when he kills it? Is it possible to become oneself by eliminating or recognizing the monster? The central episode of the story of Theseus places us within a dialectic of 'other' and 'same,' and it is easy to understand that it is a powerful evocation of the issue of identity" (1121).

Myths are by nature multivalent. It is impossible to assign one-to-one correspondences to the characters or actions of a myth. Another interpretation could be that the Minotaur symbolizes the irrational (and sometimes violent) desires of the subconscious mind. The creature lives in the labyrinth, which could stand for the mind's fathomless depths. The Minotaur can also represent the duality of the conscious and subconscious, which creates conflict. Theseus then stands for the conscious mind and intelligent awareness and exploration of these mysterious paths. For some artists, the Minotaur also stands for creativity, which arises from a dark and unknown source, in contrast to—and yet complementary to—the lighted world of the conscious intellect. The journey of an artist into the human soul and mind is fraught with danger, no less than is Theseus's travel into the labyrinth.

After tracing the development of the Minotaur myth through Western literature, Peyronie concludes that for modern readers, the Minotaur is Other, the inverted image of Theseus. By descending to the heart of the labyrinth, Theseus can confront and slay the shadow. The challenge then for modern archetypal critics is to find a way to transform the beast in all of us so that it can complete us, bringing the shadow side to full awareness.

Régis Boyer, a professor at the Sorbonne, identified three aspects of the archetype. The first, in which the archetype serves as a prototype or example, is most closely related to the Greek meaning of the word. This meaning certainly fits Greek myths, which are among the oldest surviving examples of Western literature. The myth of Theseus and the Minotaur belongs in this category. The second aspect of an archetype is to consider it as the perfect model of something. In this realm, Theseus stands as the model of a human daring to do battle against dark forces, whether physical or psychological. The final aspect is that of being the absolute type. Boyer cites the medieval mystic Meister Eckhart's idea that there is an ideal world in which only archetypes develop. From that world, the Creator then sends the archetypes into the material world, where they inhabit objects and people. Everything is thus attached to the Creator, giving it significance. Ariadnê then becomes the archetype of a woman who is so in love that she will betray her own family members—the Minotaur is her half brother and her father the king is Theseus's enemy—for her beloved. As the myth relates, this action and its consequences bring her into a relationship with Bacchus, suggesting that the myth, as was frequently the case in Greece, may have been connected to religious ritual.

The roles that Ariadnê assumes within the myth of the Minotaur combine to form a picture of what to the Greek mind was an archetype of the woman in love. She guides the hero in his quest, she is abandoned by him, and she marries a god. She has knowledge that Theseus needs to survive, yet she suffers at his hand and is ultimately vindicated by merging with the transcendent.

Of all the writers to portray Ariadnê's abandonment, Ovid does so most fully. Even before writing about the myth in *Metamorphoses*, he addressed Ariadnê's suffering in earlier works. In *Heroides*, he includes a letter to Theseus from Ariadnê. He also writes of her in book 1 of the *Amores* (*The Loves*) and in book 3 of *Ars Amatoria* (*The Art of Love*). So moving is his account of Ariadnê abandoned on the island of Naxos that for many years her role as weeping lover overshadowed that of guide to Theseus. He is restrained in his portrayal in his *Metamorphoses*, however:

Without delay the victor fled from Crete,
Together with the loving maid, and sailed
For Dia Isle of Naxos, where he left
The maid forlorn, abandoned. Her, in time,
Lamenting and deserted, Bacchus found
And for his love immortalized her name.
He set in the dark heavens the bright crown
That rested on her brows. Through the soft air
It whirled, while all the sparkling jewels changed
To flashing fires, assuming in the sky
Between the Serpent-holder and the Kneeler
The well-known shape of Ariadne's Crown.
     (Ovid 344; bk. 8)

The thread that Ariadnê gives to Theseus she obtained from Daedalus, who had also constructed both the covering disguise that allowed Minos's wife to mate with the bull and the labyrinth that imprisoned the result of that union. To find his way back out of the labyrinth, Theseus has to tie himself to Ariadnê; later, however, he breaks the tie. One way to read this action is that humans cannot be held back from their destiny.

For one of Jung's interpreters, comparative mythologist Joseph Campbell, the journey of the hero was of paramount importance. Campbell spent his adult life as an academic, teaching at the prestigious Sarah Lawrence College in New York and writing such landmark works as *The Hero with a Thousand Faces* (1949). In Campbell's formulation, the hero is separated from the tribe or group. He then undergoes a trial or test, often in another, previously unknown location; after emerging victorious, he returns to his civilization with increased wisdom to share.

As a hero, Theseus follows this pattern. The son of the king of Athens (a state that has paid human tribute to the king of Crete for the Minotaur), he volunteers for the dangerous task of slaying the beast. With the other youths intended as an offering, he journeys by boat to the island of Crete. He meets the princess, the daughter of his enemy, who assists him. Curiously, there is no indication of precisely how Theseus triumphs over the monster. Ancient Greek vases depict him naked before the Minotaur, a short sword in hand, but none of the narratives that have survived mention a weapon. In some versions of the myth, Theseus kills the beast as it sleeps, hardly a heroic action. Diodorus Siculus briefly tells of the trial Theseus undertakes: "Theseus, after conversing with her [Ariadnê] and securing her assistance, both slew the Minotaur and got safely away,

since he had learned from her the way out of the labyrinth" (4.61.4).

Psychologically, this journey is from the outer, conscious awareness to the unknown, Jungian subconscious. At the heart of the labyrinth, the unknown awaits. The hero must return with new knowledge for the tribe. Theseus does return to Athens and become king after the suicide of his father. He was reputed to be a good king, suggesting that he had indeed gained wisdom on his quest. For Jung, this sharing of wisdom corresponded to the tasks of the second half of life. The first half of life was devoted to more external events, such as career and family, while the second half of life called for skillful navigation of the labyrinth of one's own mind and subconscious for wisdom.

In some respects, Theseus fails as a hero. Although he slays the Minotaur, he becomes so entrapped in his own gloomy thoughts that he forgets the important task of changing the color of the sails on his return home. Thus, he inadvertently causes the death of his father, who is watching for the return of his son and in his grief on seeing the black sails takes his own life. This death of the father is a recurring theme in Greek myth, most famously in the Oedipus story. (Interestingly, as king, Theseus later offers refuge to the blind Oedipus at Colonus.)

Theseus also fails in his conduct toward the woman who gave him the tools to navigate the labyrinth. In some versions of the myth, he abandons Ariadnê on the island of Dia or Naxos, after taking her with him and promising her marriage. He later marries her sister. In some versions of the myth, Ariadnê is stolen from him by one of the gods, apparently without a fight.

Subsequent Greek writers give Theseus a place of honor in their work. Mythographers, such as Homer in both *The Iliad* and *The Odyssey*, make reference to Theseus as a hero. Thucydides, in book 2 of the *History of the Peloponnesian War*, considers Theseus to have been a historical and exemplary king and credits him with instituting many features of Athenian life. The playwrights Aeschylus, Sophocles, and Euripides all wrote dramatic works that give prominent roles to Theseus.

From ancient Greece through the medieval period, the Renaissance, and beyond, the myth has been revived in multiple forms. Modern writers have also continued to find this myth a source of inspiration, using the Minotaur as a metaphor and creating fantasy series that feature the beast. This ancient myth remains for modern readers a mirror into the self.

HISTORICAL CONTEXT

Beginning in 1900, British archaeologist Arthur Evans excavated the palace at Knossos on the island of Crete, one of the largest islands in the Mediterranean. He named the island's early civilization, which flourished between 2500 BCE and 1500 BCE, Minoan after the legendary King Minos. The evolution of Minoan culture was initially seen as falling into three periods, according to pottery type, but archaeologists later designated it based on differences in palace architecture.

Timber was a major Minoan export and, as a result, contributed to the island's deforestation. Other exports included purple dye, wool cloth, wine, honey, and fruit. Imports were mainly raw materials such as tin, precious stones and metals, and ivory. Trade may have extended as far as Spain in the west and India in the east, though the Minoans' chief trade partners were Mesopotamia and Egypt. Interaction with the latter two cultures resulted in a mutual cultural influence.

Minoan government remained decentralized until about 2000 BCE, when a king controlled the region. Palaces were built and became the centers of urban settlement. This period also saw the beginnings of social hierarchy, with peasants, artisans, nobles, and perhaps slaves.

The palaces were destroyed about 1700 BCE. Archaeologists do not know whether this was the result of invading forces or natural disaster. They were quickly rebuilt, however, and the civilization continued to prosper. A paved network of roads expanded during this time period, furthering trade and the enriching of an affluent upper class. Women played important roles in Minoan society.

This culture mixed with the Mycenaean civilization of the Greek mainland, which eventually challenged the Minoans and their powerful navy. Once again the palaces and villas in Crete were destroyed, around the mid-fifteenth century BCE. The cause of this second destruction also remains unknown, though archaeologists have posited volcanic ash, tsunami, or invasion as possible explanations. Knossos suffered destruction in 1375 BCE. Early writings suggest that the Mycenaeans controlled the island by this time. In 67 BCE, the island became a Roman province.

CROSS-CULTURAL INFLUENCE

Pablo Picasso was arguably the most significant figure of the twentieth-century art world. His prolific genius allowed him to create paintings, etchings, and sculptures from his earliest years. Born in Málaga, Spain, in 1881 to an art teacher, he received his early artistic instruction from his father, later enrolling in an art school where he was trained in the traditional European style.

During his famous blue period, which began in 1901 and prominently featured blues and grays, Picasso painted the first of many harlequin portraits. The harlequin, a figure from the world of pantomime, always wore a diamond-patterned outfit, with ruffles at the neck and wrists. Picasso saw this stock character—part clown, part rogue—as emblematic of himself, painting it as a surrogate self-portrait. Many years later, he would also paint his son Paulo as harlequin. Picasso's artistic style evolved over the course of the ensuing decades, moving from traditional realism to primitivism to cubism to neoclassicism to surrealism. Among his artistic influences were early Spanish sculpture, African art, Paul Cézanne, geometric shapes, and fellow cubist pioneer Georges Braque.

Along with his postwar surrealist and cubist works, Picasso also painted large-scale human figures in a neoclassical style. *Three Women at the Spring* (1921) and *The Pipes of Pan* (1923) suggest Picasso's interest in the mythology of Greece and Rome, which began to emerge in prints and drawings from 1920 onward. Beginning in the late 1920s, Picasso began to depict the Minotaur in sketches. The beast came to replace the harlequin as Picasso's self-portrait image. Picasso's identification with the Minotaur can be seen in two photographs taken by Dora Maar. In one, the artist holds a bull's skull in front of his face to become the Minotaur. In another, he dons a straw mask of a bull's face that he received from a bullfighter.

The surrealists chose the Minotaur, which they associated with passion, as their major symbol. For surrealists, the Minotaur in the maze could be equated with the human subconscious, a place ruled by passion rather than reason. When the surrealists began to publish a journal in 1933, they entitled it *Minotaure*; Picasso designed the cover of the first issue, perhaps in acknowledgement that many of the articles were about him and his work. Other artists, including Salvador Dalí and Diego Rivera, also illustrated *Minotaure* covers.

For his cover, Picasso used the medium of collage, drawing the Minotaur facing the viewer with a short Roman sword clutched in his right hand. The image is slightly off-center of the overall design, which also includes ribbon, foil, wallpaper, linen leaves, and a paper doily. All this is tacked to corrugated cardboard cut in the shape of a window.

Picasso attended bullfights his entire life and depicted them in his early work. The violence and danger suggested to him an artistic motif—the Minotaur myth. In addition to bullfights, Picasso incorporated into his work the images of the women with whom he was involved. These three aspects of his life came together in a series of Minotaur-themed works, most of which were executed in the 1930s. That tumultuous period of Picasso's life was marked by marital discord, the birth of a daughter to his much-younger mistress, Marie-Thérèse Walter, and separation from his first wife, ballerina Olga Koklova. The works Picasso produced at this time form the basis for the collection of etchings that culminated with the richly symbolic *La Minotauromachie* (*Minotauromachy*) in 1935. It features a huge Minotaur figure in the right half of the print, looming over a dead pregnant woman lying across a horse in the center. On the left, a young girl holds a candle and flowers, two women look on from above, and a bearded man climbs a ladder. Sixteen of Picasso's Minotaur pieces became part of the Vollard Suite, one hundred prints named after Ambroise Vollard, the Paris art dealer who purchased them.

The Minotaur first appeared in etchings from 1928 and continued to occupy Picasso until 1937; only rarely did he portray the beast-man after that time. In addition to the upheavals in his personal life, Picasso was dismayed by all of the political disturbances in Europe. This found expression in his famous 1937 mural *Guernica*, which includes the figure of a bull.

Blindness is one of several repeated themes that are presented in the Minotaur engravings. For all visual artists, blindness is greatly dreaded; Picasso addressed the theme as early as 1903. In ten works from 1934, the Minotaur is shown as blinded, being led by a young girl carrying a candle. She is also shown with flowers or a dove. In these works, Picasso merges the Minotaur story with that of Oedipus, who blinded himself after the revelation that he had fulfilled the prophecy he desperately tried to escape and had killed his father

and married his mother. Antigone, Oedipus's daughter, served as guide on her father's journey away from Thebes. In Picasso's etchings, the Antigone figure has Marie-Thérèse's face and Oedipus has become the bullman. Clearly, Picasso views blindness as a punishment for the sin of adultery. At the same time, he may be referencing Tiresias, the blind prophet of Thebes, who "sees" clearly.

Another theme in the Minotaur collection is that of rape. Picasso again turns to Greek myth, this time the rape of Europa, a frequent subject in art. Zeus, who was in love with Europa, assumed the form of a bull to abduct her and take her to Crete. One of their three children is Minos, whose wife, Pasiphaê, couples with the white bull Poseidon has given Minos to be sacrificed. A common rendering of the rape of Europa is of the bull with the woman on his back, a motif Picasso uses as well.

Images of bullfights also appear in the group. In a couple of engravings, the Minotaur is dying in the bullring, observed by several women in the box above. One stretches out her hand as if to touch the dying creature. All is not violence in the sequence, however. In several engravings, the Minotaur is banqueting; sometimes he is with just one woman, while in other scenes, other characters attend the feast. Of particular note is the sculptor in his studio. After a hiatus of ten years, Picasso had returned to sculpting, which may explain the use of that artist. There are also tender scenes of the Minotaur watching his beloved sleep or of a woman watching a sleeping Minotaur.

Although most of the Minotaur works are etchings or engravings, Picasso did an oil painting that is dated November 4, 1938. In the near-dark segment on the right side of the painting, the Minotaur appears, lit by a candle glowing on the left side. Near the candle are a book, an artist's palette, and brushes. The painting appears to contrast knowledge and light with ignorance and darkness. The Nazi German forces had that autumn marched on Austria, to which the other European nations had turned a blind eye, in hopes of keeping peace. The preceding spring, Guernica, Spain, had been destroyed.

By the 1940s, however, the Minotaur appears in Picasso's work only rarely and seems to have lost any symbolic significance. It had served its purpose, and Picasso moved on to the next alter ago. Sylvie Vautier puts it well: "In delving into his inner self, he [Picasso] bequeaths his soul to the Minotaur while availing himself of the personality in the myth. The exchange is reciprocal and both come out of it enriched, rejuvenated, and renewed" (246).

Judy A. Johnson, MLS, MTS

BIBLIOGRAPHY

Boyer, Régis. "Archetypes." Brunel 110–17.

Brunel, Pierre, ed. *Companion to Literary Myths, Heroes and Archetypes*. London: Routledge, 1996. Print.

Diodorus Siculus. "Theseus and the Minotaur." *Library of History*. Vol. 3. Trans. C. H. Oldfather. London: Heinemann, 1993. 11–13. Print. Loeb Classical Lib. 340.

Garry, Jane, and Hasan El-Shamy, eds. *Archetypes and Motifs in Folklore and Literature*. New York: Sharpe, 2005. Print.

Freitas, Lima de. "Labyrinth." *Encyclopedia of Religion*. Ed. Mircea Eliade. Vol. 8. New York: Macmillan, 1987. 411–19. Print.

Hyginus. "Theseus and the Minotaur." *Myths of Hyginus*. Trans. Mary A. Grant. Ed. Grant. Lawrence: U of Kansas P, 1960. 54–55. Print.

Leal, Paloma Esteban. "Picasso/Minotaur." *Picasso: Minotauro*. Madrid: Museo Nacional Centro de Arte Reina Sofía, 2001. 223–38. Print.

Leslie, Richard. *Pablo Picasso: A Modern Master*. New York: SMITHMARK, 1996. Print.

Moon, Beverly. "Archetypes." *Encyclopedia of Religion*. Ed. Mircea Eliade. Vol. 1. New York: Macmillan, 1987. 379–82. Print.

Murgatroyd, Paul. *Mythical Monsters in Classical Literature*. London: Duckworth, 2007. Print.

Ovid. "Minos and the Minotaur." *Metamorphoses*. Vol. 2. Trans. Brookes More. Francestown: Jones, 1941. 342–44. Print.

Peyronie, André. "The Minotaur." Brunel 814–21.

---. "Theseus." Brunel 1110–23.

Vautier, Sylvie. "Picasso's Minotaur: A Myth Too Human." *Picasso: Minotauro*. Madrid: Museo Nacional Centro de Arte Reina Sofía, 2001. 238–46. Print.

Ziolkowski, Theodore. "The Minotaur: The Beast Within and the Threat Outside." *Minos and the Moderns: Cretan Myth in Twentieth-Century Literature and Art*. New York: Oxford UP, 2008. 67–116. Print.

THE CULTURE
HERO

Adventures of Monkey

Author: Traditional
Time Period: 1501 CE–1700 CE
Country or Culture: China
Genre: Myth

OVERVIEW

The adventures of Monkey, a cycle of mythical Chinese stories about a tricky monkey king with supernatural powers, is contained in its full, authoritative version in the Chinese novel *Xiyou ji* (*Hsi-yu chi*), known in English as *The Journey to the West*. The oldest existing version of this novel was printed in China in 1592. The character of the mischievous monkey king appears to be drawn from traditional Chinese folklore. Many scholars believe that the character of this Chinese monkey king was influenced also by the Indian monkey god, Hanumān. Hanumān is a prominent character in the Indian Sanskrit epic Rāmāyana, created perhaps as early as the fourth or third century BCE.

In *The Journey to the West*, Monkey's adventures are told in two distinct plots. The novel opens with the first plot as Monkey is born from a stone egg. Intelligent and playful, yet also ambitious, courageous, and rebellious, he becomes Handsome Monkey King of a monkey kingdom. As a disciple of the Daoist (Taoist) immortal Subodhi, Monkey is given the new, semireligious name of Sun Wukong. Gaining great supernatural powers, Sun Wukong is invited to heaven. As punishment for his wild mischief there, Buddha himself imprisons Monkey beneath a rock for five hundred years. In the second plot, Sun Wukong is freed by the Buddhist pilgrim Xuanzang (Hsüan-tsang), also known as Tripitaka. Xuanzang wishes to travel to India to bring Buddhist scriptures from there to China. On this perilous journey, Sun Wukong becomes guardian, protector, and the most powerful, effective, and loyal fighter for Xuanzang. Their ordeals typically involve supernatural and shape-shifting enemies, which test all of Monkey's powers and abilities.

With *The Journey to the West*, there is one definitive text of the novel but no final scholarly consensus about its author. The authoritative 1592 text was printed with a preface stating that the author is unknown. This was a strategy of literary authors in China at the time. They did not want their reputation as serious writers to be sullied by association with a piece of popular fiction officially held in low esteem. It is also clear that the novel incorporates many older myths and folktales, particularly concerning Monkey's support for the pilgrim Tripitaka, which can be found in texts dating to the thirteenth century. Since the early twentieth century, the Ming dynasty writer and minor official Wu Cheng'en (Wu Ch'eng-en) has been considered the anonymous author of *The Journey to the West*. However, the historical and literary evidence supporting this attribution have failed to persuade some scholars, and the matter remains under dispute.

An archetypal analysis looks at Monkey as a remarkably versatile and creative trickster hero. Both his rebellion against the gods and his loyal and resourceful support for Tripitaka are analyzed in light of his quality as archetypal character. This analysis shows that Monkey is richly imagined and well integrated into the many popular mythical stories contained in *The Journey to the West*. An approach from new historicism and cultural criticism shows how the relative peace, prosperity, and stability of the Ming dynasty gave rise to lengthy popular novels. Among them, *The Journey to the West* profits in reader popularity due to its masterful incorporation and presentation of the adventures of Monkey, which have become the true distinction of this novel. A feminist analysis reveals that occasionally Monkey must rely on the help of the female bodhisattva Guanyin (Kuanyin or Kwannon), balancing out male power in the story.

SUMMARY

In Anthony Yu's translation of *The Journey to the West*, the adventures of Monkey begin right after the novel opens with a retelling of the traditional Chinese myth

"He [Sun Wukong] strode right up to the tiger, crying, 'Cursed beast! Where do you think you are going?' Crouching low, the tiger lay down on the dust and dared not move. Pilgrim Sun aimed the rod at its head, and one stroke caused its brain to burst out like ten thousand red petals of peach blossoms, and the teeth to fly out like so many pieces of white jade."

The Journey to the West

of the origin of the world. Atop Flower-Fruit Mountain, a big stone is impregnated "with a divine embryo" (1: 67). The stone gives birth to an egg, which the wind transforms into a stone monkey. Stone Monkey leaps up with fully formed limbs and an adult monkey body. It mingles with other monkeys on the mountain. Soon, Stone Monkey jumps through a waterfall to discover Water-Curtain Cave. This is an ideal dwelling place for all monkeys. Because his discovery makes him their accepted leader, Stone Monkey appoints himself Handsome Monkey King.

After some three to four hundred years of carefree life, Monkey King realizes that his death will come eventually. After a farewell feast put on by the other monkeys, he leaves his cave and mountain to embark on a voyage to find immortality. Traveling across the ocean to a different continent, Monkey King meets the first humans on the shore. He strips one man of his clothes and begins to mingle with people: "With a swagger he walk[s] through counties and prefectures, imitating human speech and human manners in the marketplaces" (Yu 1: 75).

On the next continent, Monkey King finally finds the Daoist immortal Subodhi. Initially reluctant to take him on as disciple because he is a monkey, Subodhi eventually relents. Subodhi gives him a new name, Sun Wukong. The Chinese character for Monkey's surname Sun alludes to him being a monkey. Wukong has been translated as "awakening to vacuity" or "awakening

to emptiness," a Buddhist religious concept somewhat ironic for a monkey to represent.

Trained by Subodhi, Sun Wukong's "mind [becomes] spiritualized," and he gradually acquires supernatural powers (Yu 1: 88). These include mastery of the art of the seventy-two transformations into different animate and inanimate forms, as well as using any of his eighty-four thousand hairs to change into either a copy of himself or another object. Sun Wukong learns the art of cloud-hopping, traversing 108,000 *li* (33,554 miles) in a single leap. However, when Monkey shows off his prowess to other disciples, Subodhi dismisses him and Monkey returns home.

At Water-Curtain Cave, Monkey finds that Monstrous King of Havoc is harassing his monkeys. With his new powers, including the creation of a little monkey army from his hairs, Monkey King fights the monstrous king. Snatching his enemy's scimitar, Monkey brings it down "squarely on the monster's skull, cleaving it in two" (Yu 1: 97). Reestablished in Water-Curtain Cave, Monkey King arms his monkeys and goes on a quest to receive a mighty weapon for himself from the Dragon King of the Eastern Ocean. He successfully takes along a heavy iron staff, the "Compliant Golden-Hooped Rod" (1: 108). It is very heavy, over 17,800 pounds. It can shift its shape to become as little as a needle, which Monkey carries in his ear when he is not using his staff as a weapon. In a dream, Monkey journeys to the underworld. There, he wipes off his and his monkey friends' names from the ledger of souls to be summoned to die.

Eventually, the Jade Emperor of Heaven decides to offer Monkey a position in heaven to prevent him from running wild on earth. There, Monkey is made keeper of horse stables, called Bimawen (Pi-ma-wen). When he learns that this is a most menial position, he rebels and shouts, "I won't do this anymore! I'm leaving right now!" (Yu 1: 122). Returning to his mountain, Monkey names himself "Great Sage, Equal to Heaven" (1: 124) in open defiance. The heavenly imperial authorities persuade Monkey to return to heaven. There, he is put in charge of the Garden of Immortal Peaches. However, Monkey eats most of the peaches, gets drunk on the nectar, breaks into the palace of Laozi (Lao Tzu), and eats the elixir of immortality before returning to Flower-Fruit Mountain.

At first, Monkey defeats a celestial army of one hundred thousand warriors by himself. However, led by their divine general Erlang Shen (Ehr-lang), the gods finally capture Sun Wukong in concert. The Jade Emperor sentences Monkey to be burned to death in a crucible. However, Monkey emerges from this ordeal stronger than ever.

Finally, it is the Buddha himself who captures Monkey literally in his palm. Monkey is imprisoned underneath five mountains created from the five fingers of one hand of the Buddha. This ends the first part of the adventures of Monkey as told in *The Journey to the West*.

After punishing Monkey, the Buddha seeks one faithful Chinese pilgrim to travel to India, the cradle of Buddhism, and bring back Buddhist scriptures from there. The goddess of mercy, Guanyin, decides to find such a person. To aid this human pilgrim, Guanyin approaches four different beings that, like Monkey, are all punished for some transgression. In exchange for forgiveness and spiritual salvation, all four agree on Guanyin's terms. Monkey promises Guanyin "to practice religion" and to stop his rebellion in exchange for his release (Yu 1: 195).

The Journey to the West provides the story of the pious ascetic Xuanzang up to the point where he agrees to Guanyin's request to travel to India for Buddhist scriptures. He receives the name Tripitaka, meaning "collection of scriptures," by which he is often referred to in the novel. At the western border of China, Tripitaka encounters the first of his guardians, Monkey. Monkey is imprisoned in a stone box. He tells Tripitaka, "Get me out, and I'll protect you on your way to the Western Heaven!" (Yu 1: 298). Tripitaka complies. Monkey, now called Pilgrim Sun or Xingzhe ("ascetic"), proves true to his word. He kills six robbers attacking Tripitaka. Because he took their lives, the strict Buddhist Tripitaka dismisses Monkey. To discipline Monkey in the future, Guanyin gives Tripitaka a headband made from a hair of the Buddha. Once Monkey returns and is tricked into putting on the headband, he cannot take it off. When Tripitaka says a certain spell, the band tightens, causing unbearable headaches for Monkey.

Soon, Tripitaka and Pilgrim Sun are joined by other protectors of Tripitaka. A dragon prince becomes Tripitaka's White Dragon Horse. Then there is Zhu Wuneng (Chu Wu-neng), an immortal who was reborn in the body of a pig because he drunkenly accosted the moon goddess. Next to join is Sha Wujing (Sha Wu-ching), a celestial being turned into a sand monster for accidentally smashing a crystal goblet in heaven. With Monkey as the most valiant and resourceful, but also the most headstrong of Tripitaka's protectors, the group of pilgrims manages to survive one ordeal after another, encountering mostly superhuman enemies. These battles with shape-changing monsters and other hideous creatures make up the bulk of *The Journey to the West*. Monkey is in the lead when protecting Tripitaka. At times, when even his strength and ingenuity is insufficient, he is aided by Guanyin.

Finally, Tripitaka, Monkey, and the others receive the desired Buddhist scriptures upon their arrival in India. The scripture keepers play a final trick on them, handing them blank volumes at first. It is Monkey who realizes the problem. He explains to Tripitaka that this is "because we had no gifts for these fellows," meaning the greedy keepers of the scrolls (Yu 4: 393). The pilgrims return, complain, and finally receive real scrolls. After one final ordeal on the way home, the pilgrims arrive back in China, where they are welcomed by the emperor. The Buddha himself rewards all pilgrims. Monkey is honored for "scourging of evil and the exaltation of good . . . smelting the demons and defeating the fiends" (4: 425). He is made into the Buddha Victorious in Strife. This ends the adventures of Monkey in the novel.

ANALYSIS

An archetypal analysis of the mythical story episodes of the adventures of Monkey as rendered in the novel *The Journey to the West* reveals Monkey as the quintessential trickster hero. He is imaginative, resilient, ambitious, and rambunctious in his rise to become Monkey King. The same holds true in his rebellion against the gods of heaven, including the Jade Emperor himself, who represents ultimate authority. However, after his fall and punishment, Monkey shows genuine repentance. He becomes the loyal and protective guardian of the human Buddhist pilgrim Xuanzang. Without reservations, Monkey supports Xuanzang unquestioningly in the pilgrim's quest to travel to India to bring Buddhist scriptures back to China. An analysis grounded in new historicism and cultural criticism indicates how the period of stability of the Ming dynasty helped create a Chinese readership for long, carefully plotted popular novels. Among Ming novels, *The Journey to the West* was particularly popular. This is owed to no small extent to its multidimensional, creative trickster hero, Monkey. Feminist analysis highlights how the helplessness of Xuanzang puts him into a gendered position traditionally reserved for the helpless female of quest narratives. Feminist analysis shows further how the necessary intervention of Guanyin, the popular goddess of mercy, creates a balance to the male power of Monkey and his all-male companions.

The elemental nature of Monkey is established both by his birth from a stone egg and the recounting of the origin of the universe at the beginning of *The Journey to the West*. Monkey is born soon after the long creation of the world was finished, according to traditional Chinese legends. He comes from inanimate, basic matter. His birth is sufficiently special for an archetypal character. The stone that "the seeds of Heaven and Earth and . . . the essences of the sun and the moon" impregnate with a "divine embryo" is of considerable size and circumference (Yu 1: 67). It has existed since the world was created, and one day splits open to release a stone egg. This plot device means that the forces of the known universe themselves are the parents of Monkey, who has no biological parents, which thus reinforces his mythical status.

Right from the beginning, even with the best intentions, Monkey manages to disturb the realm of the gods with his actions. This will become a sustained theme throughout the first, rebellious half of his adventures. After his birth, Monkey "bow[s] to the four quarters" of the directions, paying homage to the universe that has created him (Yu 1: 67). However, "two beams of golden light [flash] from his eyes" and reach the heavens (1: 67–68). There, they disturb the Jade Emperor, who sends two celestial officers to check on the source of the light. They return, identifying Monkey's eyes, but state that his eyes are dim now as he is beginning to eat and drink. Involuntarily, in his primal state, Monkey manages already to upset the divine order of things.

As he becomes closer to the world of real animals and humans, Monkey loses some of the supernatural powers of his eyes. However, his golden shining eyes remain a characteristic of him throughout his adventures. In this allegory, seeing the world also becomes illuminating it. The more Monkey focuses on ordinary activities like feeding, the more his special powers of seeing and illumination are dimmed. By lessening a Daoist form of understanding the universe, this allegory hints at the price that becoming fully human, or a humanlike animal, will exert.

Combining trickery with an intrepid, pioneering spirit and bold actions, Monkey establishes himself as an archetypal charismatic leader. He does not hesitate to demand obeisance. When the monkeys on the mountain discover a waterfall, they promise to make king the one who boldly goes through it to the hidden other side. It is Stone Monkey who rises to the challenge. The narrative creates a direct sense of excitement at Monkey's first feat establishing his mythic reputation: "Look at him! He closed his eyes, crouched low, and with one leap he jumped straight through the waterfall" (Yu 1: 70). Behind the waterfall, Stone Monkey is rewarded for his boldness and leadership action. He discovers the Water-Curtain Cave, which turns out to be a perfect sheltered habitat for the monkey population.

Even though the cave houses a magically erected iron bridge and a stone mansion fully equipped with stone utensils ready for use, the myth also alludes to humans—and animals—finding shelter inside caves at the dawn of civilization. This may tie the myth back to the collective subconscious and makes Monkey a representative of a vaguely, collectively remembered human past as well.

Assuming a new position in the allegorical tale, Monkey takes on a new name. This pattern will be repeated throughout *The Journey to the West*. It will be followed not only by Monkey, but by every character who develops and takes on a new function or role in the narrative. Accordingly, Stone Monkey takes the new name Handsome Monkey King as he now rules from the Water-Curtain Cave over his newly founded monkey kingdom.

As archetypal trickster hero, Monkey King becomes restless after a few centuries of carefree and rule over a happy band of monkeys. Suddenly, Monkey King becomes worried about his own mortality.

The desire for immortality has deep roots in traditional Chinese culture. Historical emperor Qin Shi Huangdi, who unified China in 221 BCE, became obsessed with the idea. He not only had himself built a terracotta army of eight thousand men to protect him in the afterlife—which was rediscovered in 1974—he also visited the supposedly magic island of Zhifu three times to obtain alchemical drugs that were said to ensure his immortality. He sent a major maritime expedition of some hundred young men and women to find the mythical abode of the Eight Immortals, the island featuring the magic Mount Penglai. None of these ships ever returned, some perhaps discovering Japan instead but fearing to return without an immortal.

The traditional Chinese obsession and belief that immortality could be found and obtained is given full play in the early episodes of the adventures of Monkey as told in *The Journey to the West*. One of his monkeys tells the morose Monkey King that "the Buddhas, the immortals, and the holy sages . . . can avoid the Wheel of Transmigration . . . to live as long as Heaven and Earth" (Yu 1: 73). Excited by this information, Monkey King immediately plans to meet someone of this category and learn from them their secret.

Monkey King's first quest to obtain immortality serves a double narrative function: to humanize him further and to provide him with some astonishing supernatural powers, developing his trickster character. Leaving his mountain, Monkey King traverses an ocean to mingle with humans. He is quite ruthless in stripping a man of his garments to clothe himself and turns into a keen observer and commentator on humanity's ceaseless strive to seek more and more material goods. Finally, Monkey King crosses the Western Ocean for a second new continent. There, he finds a big mountain, which may be an allegorical allusion to Mount Penglai sought so desperately by the historical emperor Qin Shi Huangi. On this mountain, Monkey King finally finds an immortal, the Daoist sage Subodhi. In this, the trickster hero's persistence in his quest has been rewarded.

As a disciple newly named Sun Wukong, Monkey uses all his wits to learn as much as he can. He acquires immortality as well as significant new powers, yet he is taught a lesson in humility. Sun Wukong basically designs his own curriculum and will learn from Subodhi only what leads him toward immortality. His attitude borders on the insolent and foreshadows his rebellion against the gods of heaven. However, when Subodhi catches Monkey showing off his powers to other disciples, Subodhi dismisses him. Humbled only briefly, soon "rejoicing secretly," Monkey King uses his new power of cloud-skipping to arrive back home in no time at all (Yu 1: 93).

On Flower-Fruit Mountain, a situation develops in which Monkey King has to put his new powers to best use. This delights readers with an episode illustrating the capability of the trickster hero and functions well to showcase the character. Fighting Monstrous King of Havoc demands all the wit and skills of Monkey King to emerge victorious. Later, like a genuine king, Monkey arms his people and instructs them into defending themselves. In this, the plot joins the archetypal characteristics of trickster hero and charismatic ruler.

With a mix of trickery, bragging, and genuine accomplishment, Monkey King gains a mythical weapon worthy of his character from the dragon king of the sea. As befitting a mythical archetypal character, this magic staff becomes Monkey's attribute. Monkey is depicted

w th this staff in illustrated editions of *The Journey to the West* and prints featuring him and episodes from this popular novel.

Monkey's insolence, betraying the young trickster's lack of concern for others, makes him an increasing number of enemies. By threat of force, he acquires a splendid outfit of red phoenix feathers adorning a "gold cap, the gold cuirass, and cloud-treading shoes" from the brothers of the dragon king (Yu 1:107). As he leaves, he adds insult to injury by giving a mock apology to those whom he assembled by threat of his magic rod. This shows how the trickster hero increasingly gets out of bounds and self-assuredly transgresses against the order of society. With every fresh success, Monkey becomes emboldened to risk more.

In heaven, the Jade Emperor agrees on a strategy of inclusion to tame the rebellious Monkey. This reveals a standard political maneuver to eliminate a threat to social order. Listening to the advice of the "Spirit of the Planet Venus," who is male in Chinese tradition, the Jade Emperor offers Monkey a job in the celestial administration (Yu 1:114).

At first, it looks like this ruse to trick the trickster by co-opting him has worked. Monkey accepts the heavenly offer with delight. Yet when he discovers that his apparently ministerial rank of Bimawen, keeper of the horse stables, is one of the most menial in heaven, he rebels. He resigns his position in fury and returns to his own kingdom.

In his full-fledged rebellion against imperial authority, scholars, particularly from Communist China since 1949, have seen much to praise in the character of Monkey. As the archetypal trickster hero, Monkey refuses to be confined in his vital energy by a minor and subordinate post in imperial celestial bureaucracy. His violent rejection of this measly position appears to give literary voice to the frustration of quite a few members of the readership of the novel. They are invited by the text to see Monkey enacting a response they do not dare to enact themselves.

Expanding on the archetypal trickster hero's spirit of defiance, Monkey King bestows a new grandiloquent title upon himself, "Great Sage, Equal to Heaven" (Yu 1: 124). When an armed delegation of the Jade Emperor comes to try to arrest Monkey, he tells them that unless he is officially given this title by the emperor, he will carry his rebellion to the emperor's throne. Amazed at this reckless challenge, the imperial soldiers begin to battle Monkey. However, Monkey defeats them all:

HISTORICAL CONTEXT

The Chinese Buddhist monk Xuanzang (Hsüan-tsang), born Chen Yi or Chen Hui, left China for a journey to India in 627 CE. This was the second year of the reign of Emperor Taizong (T'ai-tsung) of the young Tang dynasty. This dynasty was established by Taizong's father in 618 and lasted until 907. Xuanzang went to India to obtain authentic Buddhist texts from the founding land of Buddhism.

Xuanzang left India in 643, carrying with him 657 Buddhist scriptures. He arrived back in China and met Emperor Taizong in 645. Until his death in 664, Xuanzang translated seventy-four of the Buddhist texts he brought to China. He also dictated a book about his journey to his disciple Bianji, entitled *Datang xiyu ji* (646; *The Great Tang Dynasty Record of the Western Regions*, 1996).

The story of Xuanzang's journey to India entered the Chinese popular imagination. During the Song dynasty, in the thirteenth century, two tales of Xuanzang's journey appeared. These tales introduce a monkey novice monk as guardian and escort of Xuanzang. Monkey saves Xuanzang in many encounters with their supernatural enemies. This represents evidence of the joining of the historical monk's journey with the adventures of Monkey in Chinese popular fiction in the Song dynasty.

After the rise of the Yuan dynasty in 1271, which exterminated the last vestiges of the Southern Song dynasty in 1279, the tale of the monk Xuanzang and his monkey protector appears to have remained popular in China, especially among storytellers. Ethnic Chinese wrested political control from the Mongols of the Yuan dynasty and established the Ming dynasty in 1368. Over a thousand fragments of a version of the tale of Xuanzang and Monkey exist in an encyclopedic collection assembled from 1403 to 1408.

In the later Ming dynasty, the definitive version of the tale, the one-hundred-chapter novel *Xiyou ji* (*Hsi-yu chi*; *The Journey to the West*) was printed in 1592. The printed book states that its author is anonymous. There has been considerable scholarly debate about the authorship of this novel, though many scholars agree that it was likely written by the minor official Wu Cheng'en (Wu Ch'eng-en). Regardless of its authorship, the novel has remained very popular in China, even despite its denunciation as a feudal text during Mao Zedong's Cultural Revolution (1966–76).

"Look at that Monkey King returning to his mountain in triumph!" (1: 130).

In some quiet despair, the Jade Emperor agrees to try co-opting Monkey once again into service in heaven. However, this second appointment ends up in disaster as well. Instead of guarding the orchard of the peaches of immortality, Monkey liberally helps himself to their fruits and wreaks further havoc. He is the archetypal trickster hero out of bounds. Yet he is ultimately shown the limits of his powers.

Ultimately, it is the Buddha himself who subdues Monkey, signaling the triumph of true religion over a rambunctious rebel. Monkey has been able to run wild against the secular celestial authorities, but he proves no match to the wisdom and compassion of the Buddha. He is allowed one final gesture of defiance in the narrative. Monkey unwittingly urinates against what turns out to be the fold of two fingers in the palm of the Buddha. After this transgression, however, Monkey is imprisoned under a mountain for the next five hundred years as punishment.

In the second cycle of Monkey episodes as told in *The Journey to the West*, Monkey is truly remorseful for his previous escapades. He promises to become a loyal guardian of the Buddhist pilgrim Xuanzang. Some critics have been uncomfortable with this seeming utter submission to authority. However, in the context of *The Journey to the West* as a popular and picaresque novel about the path toward enlightenment, Monkey's new function as a guardian of Xuanzang represents admirable spiritual progress.

Even as Xuanzang's protector, Monkey retains much of his energy as archetypal trickster hero. It is only because of Monkey's almost unbridled energy that Xuanzang is saved from danger in many of the eighty-one ordeals he has to face before bringing the Buddhist scriptures from India to China. As most critics have observed, Monkey is Xuanzang's most valuable and loyal guardian. Without Monkey, Xuanzang's pilgrimage would have ended in failure. This plot privileges the trickster hero over the figure of the earnest monk. In addition, Xuanzang is portrayed as peevish, small-minded, and perpetually frightened. He is helpless in the face of a multitude of dangerous episodes.

Archetypal analysis illustrates the allegorical nature of the numerous episodes featuring Monkey fighting demons and monsters to protect Xuanzang. Here, Monkey has to fight demons that represent lust, desire for power, and violence, or a mindless indulgence in earthly cravings. Many demons are shape-shifters, appearing first in human form before revealing their real demonic selves. Preoccupation with shape-shifting—fox spirits assuming human form to tempt men, for example—has long traditional cultural and mythological roots in China. The adventures of Monkey as told in *The Journey to the West* take up many of these traditional mythologies and meld them into a fascinating popular quest narrative.

Ultimately, Monkey, as a reformed trickster hero who puts his considerable skill and fighting prowess into the service of a higher religious cause, is rewarded with Buddhahood himself. Some critics have seen in this a narrative co-option and coercion of the rebellious, autonomous spirit into conventional social order. However, from the point of view of an archetypal character's development, Monkey's achievement of Buddhahood can be interpreted as spiritual triumph and accomplishment as well, as seen by other critics. In the end, the Buddha himself rewards Monkey: "Sun Wu-k'ung, when you caused great disturbance at the Celestial Palace, I had to exercise enormous dharma power to have you pressed beneath the Mountain of Five Phases. Fortunately your Heaven-sent calamity came to an end, and you embraced the teaching of Buddhism" (Yu 4: 425). For his repentance and conversion, Monkey is given the ultimate spiritual reward. This moves him out of his long incarnation as trickster hero. Logically, this transformation ends the narrative, as there is no more Monkey to perform any tricky and valiant deed. Structurally, Monkey's elevation to Buddhahood represents ultimate closure to all adventures of Monkey as told in the long popular novel *The Journey to the West*.

An analysis grounded in new historicism and cultural criticism reveals that it was the particular material fabric of the Ming dynasty that gave rise to a large readership for a novel like *The Journey to the West*. During the Ming dynasty (1368–1644), China's population rose from about 60 million to as much as 160 to 200 million.

There developed an urban, educated society that cherished popular novels written in the Chinese vernacular, like *The Journey to the West*. By incorporating traditional mythological stories about the adventures of Monkey and putting them in a coherent narrative form, *The Journey to the West* quickly gained a strong popular audience. The novel was reprinted over and over again after its authoritative version was established with the 1592 print version, to which only one chapter was later added. The relatively mild social satire presented through its archetypal trickster hero of Monkey helped ensure the success of the novel up to contemporary times. Ironically, though, popular novels were officially held in very low esteem by China's intellectuals of the time. This caused publication of quite a few anonymous works, as their authors did not want to see their literary reputations tarnished.

From a feminist point of view, *The Journey to the West* is interesting from two particular perspectives. First, the novel's nominal male hero, the Buddhist pilgrim Xuanzang, almost occupies the position of the damsel in distress. He is perpetually in need of rescue by strong, masculine Monkey. This idea is elaborated on by the plot device that many female demons and shape-shifters seek to seduce Xuanzang to profit from his flesh or semen as an elixir of immortality. Monkey is in the vanguard of protecting Xuanzang from sexual abuse at the hands of predatory female demons. These prey on Xuanzang much like male demons would upon the body of a princess. This curious gendering of Xuanzang as a victim of sexual desire traditionally ascribed to a female character creates an interesting narrative inversion of traditional gender roles in the novel. At its core stands Monkey, protecting the virginity and sexual innocence of his charge, the Buddhist pilgrim Xuanzang.

Second, at key moments in Monkey's battles with various demons, fiends, monsters, and shape-shifters, he has to rely ultimately on the help of Guanyin, the goddess of mercy. It is Guanyin who volunteers to find the Buddha a worthy pilgrim to travel to India and bring precious Buddhist scriptures to China. Guanyin selects both Xuanzang and his four guardians, including Monkey. Guanyin offers Monkey a chance at redemption and obtains his promise of repentance and religious sincerity. She is a female character instrumental for the plot of the novel and acts with great autonomy and power.

Guanyin provides Xuanzang with the only known means to discipline Monkey, the headband inside a cap that she instructs Xuanzang to trick the trickster into wearing: "When he returns, give him the shirt and the cap to wear; and if he again refuses to obey you, recite the spell silently. He will not dare do violence or leave you again" (Yu 1: 310). Guanyin's device of a headband, made from a hair of the Buddha, allows Xuanzang to control him by inflicting unbearable and unavoidable pain on Monkey's head, revealing her dominance over Monkey. While providing the means for his control, Guanyin also serves as Monkey's ultimate recourse when challenges prove almost too much for him.

By placing Guanyin in power over Monkey, *The Journey to the West* balances male power. Monkey is the most adept and valuable of Xuanzang's guardians. Yet even he has to rely on the help of the female Guanyin to ultimately ensure the success of the common quest.

CROSS-CULTURAL INFLUENCE

Cross-cultural influences on and of the adventures of Monkey as told in the Ming dynasty novel *The Journey to the West* fall into two patterns. First, international scholars have generally accepted the idea that Monkey has cross-cultural antecedents in the form of the Hindu monkey deity, Hanumān. Second, the popularity of Monkey has spread far beyond China and has inspired foreign adaptations of the adventures of Monkey in almost every medium, ranging from paintings to musicals and manga comics. Thus, with him being the product of cross-cultural influence and an inspiration himself, the popular character of Monkey in *The Journey to the West* has inspired in turn an international creation of art based on his mythical legends.

As scholars like Glen Dudbridge, Hera Walker, and Ramnath Subbaraman have all pointed out, the Chinese character of Monkey featured in *The Journey to the West* has been cross-culturally influenced by the legends of the Hindu monkey deity, Hanumān, as told in the Indian epic Rāmāyana. By the consensus of most scholars, the text of the Rāmāyana was created as early as the fourth century BCE or as late as the second century BCE.

The Rāmāyana is older by over one thousand years than the first appearance of the monkey character familiar from the adventures of Monkey, who is featured in two Song dynasty texts of the thirteenth century CE. These two tales, which present Monkey in connection with the pilgrimage of Xuanzang, have become considered the earliest direct Chinese ancestors of adventures of Monkey as told in *The Journey to the West*. Ironically, the only texts of these two Chinese tales that are known to have survived come from the library of Kōzanji

Monastery, located near the ancient Japanese city of Kyoto. Cross-cultural literary exchange thus saved these texts, which were rediscovered in the twentieth century.

The obvious and many similarities of the older Hanumān and the younger Monkey have been noticed by many scholars, whose findings are nicely summed up by Hera Walker. Their similarities begin at birth. Hanumān's father is the Wind God, and "exposed to the wind," the stone egg is "transformed into a stone monkey" in *The Journey to the West* (Yu 1: 67). Further prominent similarities are that both monkey characters begin life unruly, rambunctious, and disrespectful of authority. Then, they aid a nominally superior character in their quest. Hanumān serves Lord Rāma to find his wife, Sītā, who has been abducted by the evil demon Rāvana. Monkey helps Xuanzang find and bring Buddhist scriptures to China. Both monkeys have supernatural powers. Among them, shape-shifting is a striking similarity, as is their ability to cover vast distances by jumping up to travel through the air. Hanumān is strong enough to lift up a mountain in a famous episode, and Monkey's attribute is his heavy, golden-ringed iron staff weighing over seventeen thousand pounds. In addition, Subbaraman has pointed out that there are many similarities in the narrative structures of the episodes of Hanumān in the Rāmāyana and of Monkey in *The Journey to the West*.

Walker shows convincingly how the story of Hanumān reached China through Indian traders "along the maritime route of the Silk Road" beginning in the first century CE (16). Indian traders brought along their own myths and legends, which they shared with Chinese audiences and business and trading partners. This was true especially as the monsoon patterns of the region forced Indian traders to stay for extended periods in Chinese ports before they could sail back to India. Walker convincingly argues that this provided a natural setting for the exchange of Indian and Chinese popular tales, legends, myths, and folk stories. Indian trade settlements of the period show wall decorations "with iconographic images, including Monkey-headed figures of Hanuman" (Walker 80).

However, Monkey is not a mere derivative of Hanumān, but contains elements from indigenous Chinese monkey legends as well. Walker states with conviction that "Sun Wukong's development was in fact an amalgamation of indigenous and imported elements" (53). As Walker shows, Chinese sources of Monkey's eventual character as presented in *The Journey to the*

West include in particular the tale of the white monkey. This legend is recorded in a Chinese text from the third century BCE. In it, a white gibbon wreaks havoc at the Chu state's capital city. Later, a monkey cult developed in the Chinese state of Chu. Monkey legends were popular also in Sichuan (Szechuan) province. The Tang dynasty, during which the historical Buddhist monk Xuanzang lived and traveled to India in the seventh century, saw a few monkey cults in some locations of China. Thus, Monkey of *The Journey to the West* has both Chinese and Indian literary and cultural ancestors.

The Japanese were among the first non-Chinese people who took an interest in the adventures of Monkey and adapted him into their art and literature. In 1865, Japanese artist Tsukioka Yoshitoshi (pen name of Owariya Yonejiro) created a series of popular woodblock prints entitled *Tsūzoku Saiyūki* (*A Modern Journey to the West*). Here, Monkey is a central character. He is depicted with his trademark gold-bound iron staff and wearing his cloud slippers familiar from *The Journey to the West.*

Monkey has also become a popular character in Japanese films, television series, manga, and anime. The character of the mischievous trickster hero who supports a serious quest has clearly captured the Japanese popular imagination. In 2007, for example, the movie *Saiyūki* (Journey to the West) was the eighth highest-earning film in Japan. It is based on the popular television series *Saiyūki*, which ran from 1978 to 1980 and was revived for one season in 2006.

Japanese manga very often feature a character modeled on the Monkey King. These cross-culturally inspired characters include the light-hearted, loosely adapted Four-Tails (or Son Gokū, the Japanese name for Sun Wukong) in *Naruto* (1999–), a manga that also spawned an anime series. In *Naruto*, Son Gokū calls himself the Handsome Monkey King, King of the Sage Monkeys, and Great Sage Equaling Heaven. More serious treatment of the character is found in Katsuya Terada's manga *Saiyukiden Daienō* (2002–; *The Monkey King*, 2005–), which adds some sexual content to the many fighting episodes. In it, Monkey King is a serious, well-developed character. Buddhist themes and concepts are also incorporated in this manga with a generally darker, adult tone than in *Naruto*.

In America, Britain, and the English-speaking world, Arthur Waley's 1943 rendition of *Monkey: Folk Novel of China* is still a favorite version of the original novel and has been reprinted. Originally intended as a translation, Waley's substantial editing of the Chinese text has led scholars to consider his work a cross-cultural adaptation rather than a translation in the academic sense of the word. Encouraged by the Chinese writer and diplomat Hu Shih, who wanted to modernize the tale himself, Waley cut out all the poems from the original and downplayed allegory and religious motifs in favor of a humorous, satirical trickster story. Waley's rendition shortens the novel substantially and focuses primarily on Monkey. Sidekick characters are given anglicized names. Still, for an English reader interested primarily in a very readable and accessible rendition of Monkey's many capers, Waley's book is very appealing. His Monkey is a most vivid and mischievous character.

Internationally, the adventures of Monkey have been turned into plays and musicals. With its trickster hero and many episodes of supernatural encounters and fights, the novel *The Journey to the West* has lent itself especially well to international adaptations as a musical. Here, *Monkey: Journey to the West* stands out. Coproduced by Chinese opera director Chen Shi-zeng, British musician Damon Albarn, and British artist Jamie Hewlett, the stage musical premiered at the Manchester International Festival on June 28, 2007. It has been performed globally since, including shows in Paris, London, and Charleston, South Carolina.

The musical *Monkey: Journey to the West* features the adventures of Monkey in nine scenes from the highlights of the novel. The first two scenes show Monkey's birth and his acquisition of power. Scene 3 features Monkey creating mischief in heaven because he is not invited to the queen mother of heaven's birthday party. The cross-cultural transformation of the Jade Emperor's realm into a kingdom with recognizable British characters, such as the Queen Mother, adds a touch of bicultural humor to the musical. In scene 4, Monkey is captured in the Buddha's palm in a stage performance of magnificent virtuosity. Scenes 5 to 9 feature the pilgrimage of Tripitaka, chosen by the goddess of mercy, Guanyin, who is not turned into a more British character. Tripitaka is aided by Monkey, Pigsy, Sandy, and the Dragon Prince transformed into Tripitaka's horse. Here, the musical uses English names for the companions of Monkey, based on a creative translation of their names from the original Chinese.

The musical culminates in the pilgrims' arrival in paradise. There, they are given scriptures directly from the Buddha, and all get their appropriate awards as described in the original novel. For the 2007 premiere, Fei Yang performed the part of the Monkey King, including singing his songs. As a musical, *Monkey: Journey to the West* brings the adventures of Monkey to live in a splendid stage setting. Its musical compositions both draw on the original Chinese source and transform the story into songs for a spellbound global audience in the twenty-first century.

R. C. Lutz, PhD

BIBLIOGRAPHY

Dudbridge, Glen. *The Hsi-yu chi: A Study of Antecedents to the 16th-Century Chinese Novel*. London: Cambridge UP, 1970. Print.

Fu, James S. *Mythic and Comic Aspects of the Quest: Hsi-yu chi as Seen through Don Quixote and Huckleberry Finn*. Singapore: Singapore UP, 1977. Print.

Hayhurst, Darrell E., III. "Sun Wu-Kung." *Pantheon.org*. Encyclopedia Mythica, 6 Sept. 2006. Web. 25 Mar. 2013.

Hsia, Chih-tsing. "Journey to the West." *The Classic Chinese Novel: A Critical Introduction*. New York: Columbia UP, 1968. 115–64. Print.

Plaks, Andrew H. "*Hsi-yu chi*: Transcendence of Emptiness." *Four Masterworks of the Ming Novel*. Princeton: Princeton UP, 1987. 183–276. Print.

---. "The Journey to the West." *Masterworks of Asian Literature in Comparative Perspective*. Ed. Barbara Stoler Miller. Armonk: Sharpe, 1994. 272–84. Print.

Subbaraman, Ramnath. "Beyond the Question of the Monkey Imposter: Indian Influence on the Chinese Novel *The Journey to the West*." *Sino-Platonic Papers* 114 (2002): 1–35. Print.

Waley, Arthur, trans. *Monkey: Folk Novel of China*. New York: Day, 1943. Print.

Walker, Hera S. "Indigenous or Foreign? A Look at the Origins of the Monkey Hero Sun Wukong." *Sino-Platonic Papers* 81 (1998): 1–110. Print.

Yu, Anthony, trans. *The Journey to the West*. 4 vols. Chicago: U of Chicago P, 1977–83. Print.

Anansi

Author: Traditional
Time Period: 1001 CE–1500 CE
Country or Culture: Caribbean
Genre: Folktale

OVERVIEW

West African tales of a trickster spider came to the New World along with slavery. This spider was a liminal figure whose dwelling in the rafters of homes symbolized his suspension between earth and heaven. He was also a shape-shifter, appearing sometimes as a man or a woman and sometimes as a god. Even the spelling of his name changes throughout the tales: Ananse, Anansi, Aunt Nancy, Anancy, Hanansi, and Annancy.

This character became a means of subversive storytelling: slaves could relate Anansi's adventures, correlating them to their own lives and the ways in which they subverted the plantation order and triumphed over dull-witted masters. Ironically, many slave owners asked to hear these stories told, not realizing their import. Anansi's primary goal is the fulfilling of his own desires—for food, power, stories, or sex. To do so, he tricks other animals or eats his own children.

Like their protagonist, the tales shift in shape and emphasis, bearing more or less resemblance to other trickster tales found in African cultures, particularly among the Akan people. Folklorist Martha Warren Beckwith gathered *Jamaica Anansi Stories*, the collection of tales being examined here, during the 1920s in Jamaica. She had studied with the eminent ethnographer Franz Boas, who had encouraged Zora Neale Hurston's groundbreaking work among Afro-Caribbean people and who edited Beckwith's collection. Beckwith also included musical notation, riddles, and cross-references to tales from other cultures.

Beckwith took the unusual step of recording the stories in the Jamaican dialect, regarding the language worth saving as a testimony to the spirit of those who survived the Middle Passage and slavery in the Caribbean. She also gave the names of more than sixty storytellers and the locations where the stories were recorded. The tales were gathered during two trips to Jamaica in 1919 and 1921.

Anansi and his wife and children are major characters in the tales. (Tacoomah is sometimes the name of his wife, and in other tales, Tacoomah is Anansi's son or neighbor.) Other animals appear as well: Tiger is Anansi's natural enemy, and sheep are stolen and consumed. Various human characters, generally to be outwitted, also feature in the stories.

To study these tales, postcolonial theory is most appropriate. Postcolonial theory looks at the effects of Western colonialism and its aftermath, culturally and ideologically. Considered by most scholars to have begun with the 1952 publication of Martinique-born Frantz Fanon's *Black Skin, White Masks*, the theory studies the effect of colonialism on native peoples. Fanon, who was both a psychiatrist and a revolutionary, was interested in the language of Western colonizers and how it caused native peoples to internalize a sense of inferiority and a tendency to suppress their original culture.

According to Fanon, three distinct phases exist in colonialism. First, the colonized people assimilate the cultural model. Next, there is an internal examining of the response and a search for more authentic national roots. Finally, there is a choice for liberation, through violence if need be. Fanon himself worked for the Algerian National Liberation Front from 1957 to 1961. Although Fanon was focusing on the struggles for independence in Algeria, India, and the Middle East, his ideas have been applied to other areas, including the Caribbean.

SUMMARY

The majority of tales collected by Beckwith feature the cunning trickster Anansi, his family, and his enemies. Some of the tales are variants of others within the collection. A few include morals or explanations of natural phenomenon, such as why Anansi lives in the rafters of

"He [Anansi] saw a man giving a woman some money and telling her to put it up for 'rainy day.' After the man had left, Anansi went up to the woman and told her he was 'Mr. Rainy Day.' She said, 'Well, it's you, sah? My husband been putting up money for you for ten years now. He has quite a bag of it, and I'm so afraid of robbers I'm glad you come!' So Anansi took the money and returned home and lived contentedly for the rest of his days."

"Anansi Seeks His Fortune"

a house. Anansi is a shape-shifter as well as a trickster. Defining Anansi's form is therefore a seemingly impossible task. he is sometimes a woman (Aunt Nancy), sometimes a man, and sometimes a spider. He is noted for his cleverness, although he does not always succeed in his aims. In a few of the stories, he dies.

Anansi's overriding concern is to have his own needs met and does not make an effort to provide for his family's needs. Sometimes he eats all of the food or hides it, leaving his wife (named Tacoomah or Aso) and children (of varying numbers and names) hungry. Several tales highlight his use of cunning to obtain food. For example, in two versions of tale 11, "Throwing Away Knives," Anansi tells Tiger to toss away his knife, claiming to do the same. When they arrive at a pineapple field, however, Anansi still has his knife but refuses to share it with Tiger, and thus he alone can eat the pineapples. In the second tale, the other character is a sheep with a spoon. Anansi tricks the sheep into leaving his spoon behind. Anansi then eats all the food before the sheep returns from retrieving the spoon.

Some of the tales also explain why animals act a certain way, similar to the *Just So Stories* of Rudyard Kipling. Tale 18, "Goat on the Hill-side," for example, offers an explanation as to why goats remain on hilly ground: during a time of hunger, Anansi and Tacoomah

use the ruse of Tacoomah being ill to lure other animals to the house, one by one. Then they kill each animal and put it in a barrel to be preserved. Goat notices that many animals go into the small house but do not emerge. When Goat goes near the house to investigate, Tacoomah invites him in, but he runs back up the hillside, his now-preferred place.

Other Anansi tales offer explanations as to why crows are bald (tale 47, "Why John-crow Has a Bald Head"), why dogs watch people while they eat (tale 48, "Why Dog is Always Looking"), and why river rocks have moss (tale 49, "Why Rocks at the River are Covered with Moss"). Other tales in Beckwith's collection that explain habits and characteristics of other animals do not feature Anansi at all. For example, Anansi does not appear in tale 51, "Why Hog is Always Grunting," or in tale 52, "Why Toad Croaks."

Some of the tales have also been told in other slave-holding regions. The story of Anansi and the Tar-baby (tales 21 and 59), for example, may be familiar to American readers who remember the Uncle Remus stories, which were collected by Joel Chandler Harris in the late nineteenth century and were popularized by Walt Disney in the 1946 film *Song of the South*. In Beckwith's collection, tale 21 includes three variants, one of which claims to explain that Anansi lives under the rafters due to his shame at being caught by the Tar-baby.

Although Anansi is known as a trickster, he does not always prove to be clever. In "The Yam-hills," tale 31, Monkey tricks Anansi, which results in Anansi's death. It is forbidden to speak the word "nine" (which is the number of yam hills Anansi has planted), and whoever says the number aloud dies. Anansi tricks both Hog and Goat into counting all the hills. Each counts to nine and dies, and Anansi takes each animal home to eat. Monkey observes this from a tree and when asked to count the yam hills, he angers Anansi by counting one through eight and concluding with "an' the one Br'er [Brother] Anansi sit down upon." After he repeats this, Anansi grows impatient, tries to correct him, says the word "nine," and instantly dies.

The final sections of Beckwith's collections deal less directly with Anansi. Tales 50 through 62 do not directly concern Anansi, although they are stories of animals. In the section "Old Stories, Chiefly of Sorcery" (tales 63–99), a few of the tales feature Anansi. Tale 100, "Ali Baba and Kissem" begins the modern European stories, some of which do include Anansi tales. For example, in tale 130, "Clever Molly May," someone else outwits

Anansi; his servant eats the turkey she has roasted and blames the guest, after warning him that Anansi is sharpening his knives to cut off the guest's hands. Some of the songs recorded in "Song and Dance" (which are sometimes given with musical notation) include Anansi as well.

ANALYSIS

The folktales featuring Anansi as a character have sometimes been read as illustrative of psychoanalyst Carl Jung's trickster archetype. However, the use of postcolonial theory will provide a more useful analysis, as consideration is given to the effect of British colonization on the tales. Although postcolonialism became a major theory only in the 1990s, it has influenced subsequent critics and readers of colonial literature.

Postcolonial theory rejects the notion of a universal standard for judging literature, as though national, regional, social, or cultural differences do not affect narrative. Invariably, the supposed "universal" standard is found to be rooted in Eurocentric values. The first task of postcolonial criticism, therefore, is to become aware of depictions of non-Europeans as Other.

Frantz Fanon, originally from the French colony of Martinique, published *The Wretched of the Earth* (1961), a critique of France's empire in Africa. In that work, often considered the beginning of postcolonial criticism, he posited that colonized people first had to reclaim their past to find their own identity and voice. European colonizers generally devalued the native past, refusing to recognize cultural or historical events of significance before the arrival of Europeans. Often, they refused to attribute remarkable achievements (such as the ruins of Great Zimbabwe) to native peoples, believing them incapable of such endeavors.

According to Fanon, the second step in reclaiming identity called for the colonized peoples to reject this devaluation of their past and embrace the gifts of their past. Uncovering the truth of who they were before the colonial powers arrived is sometimes done by rejecting contemporary or modern society, which is seen as complicit in their colonization.

An additional concern of postcolonial criticism involves the use of language. This is particularly evident in Jamaica, where the British attempted to replace the Creole patois with Standard English, forbidding the teaching of Creole and its use in schools. Postcolonial writers may go so far as to refuse to write in the language of the colonizer, which is deemed to be tainted and implies acquiescence to the colonial powers. The Anansi stories, written and told in the Creole of Jamaica, offer an example of this refusal to adopt Standard English. Although English is Jamaica's official language today, many people continue to communicate only in patois.

Anansi stories may include words from Twi, the African language spoken by slaves from the Asante (Ashanti) tribes of West Africa. This use of language provides a further linkage to an African past; not only do many of the stories originate from West Africa, but some of the words do as well. In tale 23, "Cunnie-More-Than-Father," Anansi receives a rapidly growing yam:

So one day a man give him a yam-plant; that yam name 'yam foofoo.' The same day plant the yam, it been bear a very big one same day. So nobody in the yard know the name of that yam save him, Anansi, alone. So when he go home, he cook the yam an' call the wife an' chil'ren aroun' to eat, an' say, "Who know name, nyam; who no know name, don' nyam!" So as no one know the name, they didn't get none of it; Anansi alone eat off that yam that night. (28)

His son, here given the same name as the story itself, discovers the name of that special yam through trickery. He rubs a rock near the plant with okra, making it slippery, so that Anansi falls on the yam. He then cries out, "Lawd! All me yam foofoo mash up!" Unlike his selfish father, Cunnie-More-Than-Father races home to share the name of the yam with the rest of the family. "Yam foo-foo" is a term that comes from the Twi word *e-fufu*, which means "a white thing." Anansi, with his characteristic self-concern, says no one can eat of the plant unless he or she knows its name, but by gaining or retaining knowledge of the African language, the other members of his family can survive.

In tale 14, "New Names," Anansi assigns new names to Parrot, Tiger, Tacoomah, and himself. This renaming reflects the custom of slaveholders who gave new, anglicized names to African slaves, denying their African heritage. In this story, however, if the four come to their respective mother's home and she does not use the new name, she will be killed and eaten. Anansi warns his mother and teaches her his new name; she alone of the mothers is not eaten. This violence may be a reflection of the sort of brutal punishments that awaited slaves who were not compliant under the plantation system.

Names—and, by extension, languages—have power. Even in contemporary Jamaica, it is common for people to have a nickname or a "street name" that they use, rather than revealing their given name. The real name is shared only when an acquaintance becomes a friend and can be trusted to use the power of the name wisely.

Postcolonial theory maintains that the very identity of those formerly colonized is doubled or hybridized. This is certainly true in the Americas, where masters had sex with enslaved persons, creating a mixed race. Today, in Jamaica, there are many biracial descendents, creating a hierarchy built on skin color, with light-skinned persons considered most beautiful or desirable. For example, *Anancy and the Yella Snake* (1979), a more modern tale told by Louise Bennett, a Jamaican woman wants to marry a "yella skin man." She chooses a yellow snake, which plans to kill her and eat her, but Anansi rescues her by appealing to the snake's pride in his stature. Anansi captures the snake, taking it to the home of the girl's family, where her brother shoots it. The tale claims to explain why people shoot snakes, but it also demonstrates the preference for light-skinned partners and the presence of guns, a colonial import.

This doubled identity was perpetuated in Jamaica through the school system during colonization. Children were taught to write and speak in the language of the colonizers; Creole was not valued. At school, children were taught to belong to the colonizing culture; at home, they lived in the colonized oral tradition and local culture.

For contemporary writer Joyce Jonas (*Anansi in the Great House*, 1990), the "big house" of the plantation era represents the dualism of the colonial era: black versus white, slave versus free, First World versus Third World. Anansi, the symbol of folk culture, is despised by the colonial landowners but nevertheless makes his way into their homes through the enslaved women who tell the Anansi stories to the children under their care.

A second major work in postcolonial criticism is Edward Said's 1978 work, *Orientalism*. Said noted the European tendency to attribute to the East and its inhabitants all of the unwanted aspects of Westerners, such as sensuality and laziness. At the same time, though, the East was viewed as magical and mystical. The people are regarded not as individuals but as members of a nonwhite race; their actions are thought to be motivated by their race rather than by their relationships or circumstances.

Thus, in Jamaica, Anansi is noted for his limp, sometimes walking with a cane, and for his high-pitched falsetto voice and his lisp. Jamaicans refer to a lisp such as Anansi's, in which the *r* and *l* sounds are difficult to pronounce, as "Bungo talk." The term alludes to the Twi

language, which does not include an *r* sound. "Bungo" refers to the stereotype of an uneducated African or to a peasant of Jamaica, further evidence of the colonial pattern of undervaluing the native language.

Anansi tales were nevertheless popular with colonizers during the plantation era; in their journals, several plantation owners noted having listened to performances of the tales. Although some of the tales remained essentially the same, new stories were added. Some of the African conventions were also retained. The stories were told after dark by elders to children and young people and were bracketed by the assurance that they were not true.

Postcolonial critics also draw attention to the silence of literature on the subject of colonization and imperialism. The Anansi stories do not avoid this issue, although the language is coded. For example, in Beckwith's retelling of tale 30, "Dry-Head and Anansi," the spider tries to avoid sharing the hog he has tricked his wife into giving him to eat, telling Dry-Head that the meat belongs to buckra and that he is cooking it for him. "Buckra" was one of the names for an overseer, sometimes called "Massa." Dry-Head, also called Brar Go-long-go, is an obeah man, one with magical powers that would enable him to kill Anansi. Threatened, Anansi gives the cooked meat to Dry-Head, who eats it all. At the conclusion of the tale, though, the spider sets fire to Dry-Head, who has eaten all the meat and has not shared it. This tale exemplifies the violence in Jamaican plantation life. It also, along with many of the Anansi stories, highlights the continuing problem of hunger. The African versions of some of the Anansi stories often begin by stating that there was a drought or a famine; for Jamaican slaves, the problem of hunger was rooted in the unwillingness of the colonizers to share food fairly. Instead, many slaves were given a small plot of land on which to grow their own food. This ploy backfired, however, as slaves wanted more land and began to plan ways to escape and claim some of the island's land for their own use.

Serious collecting of the folktales began in the late nineteenth century, primarily by white women of the middle class living on the island. In 1899, a local Jamaican paper publicly praised Pamela Milne-Holme and Ada Wilson Trowbridge for publishing collections that attempted to approximate Creole. By 1900, about forty Anansi stories of Jamaican origin were in print in pamphlets, journals, and books. Walter Jekyll, who spent more than three decades in Jamaica, published the first major collection of tales in 1904, *Jamaican Song and*

Story. So popular was the work that it was reprinted in 1907 and 1966.

Anthropologists of the 1920s began collecting Anansi tales. Martha Beckwith's major collection of stories was published in 1924. Beckwith offered the tales as oral performances and transcribed from Creole storytellers to whom she gave full credit.

In *Annancy Stories* (1936), Philip M. Sherlock and A. J. Newman collected six Jamaican stories of Anansi for elementary-age British children. It was, of course, written in Standard English, and in the preface, the authors explained that the children would not be able to understand the original Creole. The illustrations, done by Rhoda Jackson, portray Anansi as a fat black man with eight thin legs, who wears a straw hat and is shoeless. This stereotype of a backward Jamaican peasant suited British thinking of the time.

No further collections were published until the 1950s and 1960s when Sherlock published two works written in Standard English. The tendency to rewrite the stories continued during the 1970s, when the stories that featured violence were further toned down for children.

Language thus became a matter of conflict in colonial Jamaica; the everyday Creole patois in which the traditional Anansi stories were told was held in low esteem. According to Fanon, colonized people may take on the judgments of the colonizers, and some older Jamaicans refused to tell Anansi stories.

When Jamaica won independence in 1962, a new appreciation of folk culture began. Folktales for children were collected and hailed as the start of a West Indian children's literature. Anansi tales have become accepted around the world; the spider has even been featured in *Gargoyles*, a Disney animated series. The resulting problem, however, is a dilution of the tales and a blandness to the stories that denies their subversive nature.

Encouraging native culture, a movement began to once again tell the Anansi stories as performance

HISTORICAL CONTEXT

The Spanish began to colonize Jamaica during the sixteenth century after Christopher Columbus discovered the island in 1494. The Taino, who were indigenous to the island, were wiped out and replaced by slaves, primarily from West Africa. Control of the island went to England in 1655. Coffee, cocoa, tobacco, and sugar plantations flourished and were dependent on slavery.

The European trade in human slaves centered in West Africa. "Slave castles" were built along the coast; captured slaves were housed there until the slave ships arrived. Human cargo was stored in the hold of ships, and overcrowding led to the spread of disease and death. Some believe that the cramped space was the site of the origin of the dance known as the limbo, as people tried to move about while shackled hand and foot. Presumably, the people of West Africa, many of whom shared a Twi dialect, also shared stories of the trickster spider known as Ananse.

An estimated fifteen to twenty million Africans were enslaved and taken to the New World. Of that number, some 840,000 Africans were taken to Jamaica between 1702 and 1808, when Britain outlawed the slave trade. In the mid-eighteenth century, sugar production reached its peak, and sugar exports had doubled from their rate fifty years earlier. This achievement was in part due to cruel overseers and violence; beating, branding, burning, and sexual exploitation were not uncommon occurrences. The British abolished slavery in 1834.

Not until 1958 did Jamaica, along with other British Caribbean countries, gain freedom as part of the Federation of the West Indies. Jamaica left the federation four years later.

Recent census data indicates that more than 90 percent of the population of nearly three million is black. As the Anansi tales demonstrate, the language of Jamaica may officially be English, but an English patois is also widely used and accepted.

literature. Anansi became a figure for resistance against Britain's cultural colonialism. Jamaica has experienced a rebirth of interest in pantomime, and Anansi stories were featured in ten productions in Kingston, Jamaica's capital city, between 1949 and 2004. Audiences laughed at every instance of Anansi speaking in a Creole patois. One researcher attributed this laughter to embarrassment at his use of the "uneducated" manner of speaking that the British had tried to eradicate. At the same time, people were pleased that the language was being used, leading to ambiguity in their response.

The only difficulty with these professional shows and with additional stage productions is the price of admission. By moving the stories from private homes to public spaces and charging for performances, Anansi is commodified rather than being available to all. Additionally, pantomime and theater are viewing media rather than participatory storytelling. As Emily Zobel Marshall puts it, "Through enabling a reflection on one's moral, philosophical, and political outlook and providing scope for a critique of one's sociopolitical situation, Anansi tales can encourage the use of intelligent means to survive disempowerment" (167).

Jamaicans themselves are ambivalent about the role of Anansi and other aspects of their African heritage, however. Following independence, Jamaican leaders during the 1960s celebrated that heritage while at the same time attempting to modernize the nation by relying on foreign capital and moving away from agrarian society. These early postcolonial policies destroyed the rural way of life connected to the folkways of traditional stories. In the face of this official activity, other people focused on Creole folk practices that were thought to be a solid place to stand in the face of rapid postindependence changes.

Jamaicans have made fruitful use of the Anansi tradition, extending even into the twentieth century, when seven- to fourteen-year olds were asked to reinterpret or to create new Anansi stories. From 1930 to 1931, Reverend Joseph Williams collected some five thousand written Anansi tales. Most of these were written in Creole, rather than in Standard English, despite the attempts of the British to wipe out Creole.

Edward Kamau Brathwaite highlights the similarities between jazz riffs and the language of Anansi stories. He regards the tales as improvisation, with repeated beats and language. In tale 27, "Anansi and Brother Dead," for example, the phrase that appears multiple times is "Man no 'peak." Brathwaite asserts that the phrase becomes a thematic element in the story, creating a rhythm not unlike a drumbeat.

Extreme poverty and violence in Jamaica led to a call to ban Anansi, whose exploits do not reflect the values of civil engagement. Some Jamaicans fear that Anansi's laziness and self-centeredness have become a Jamaican stereotype. They argue that while Anansi was valuable in a plantation economy, he no longer has validity and is merely a sentimental relic. In contrast, Anansi's defenders regard him as representative of the human condition. They also suggest that he is valuable for his potential as a satiric force. Marshall concludes, "In the postcolonial world, disadvantaged Jamaicans

continue to live in a climate of conflict, fear, and unpredictability and in these circumstances Anansi is still highly relevant" (179).

It is clear that Anansi is a cultural figure that has not yet been superseded by any other Jamaican literary character. Beloved for his quick wit and use of language, as well as for his ability to get his own needs met, he remains an important part of island culture. Anansi is as important in the postcolonial era as he was during the plantation economy, with new stories of his adventures coming to light.

CROSS-CULTURAL INFLUENCE

For centuries before Anansi tales were told in the Caribbean and southern United States, they were part of West African culture. The Akan tribes told of Ananse, a liminal trickster figure with access to the high god Nyame, who bequeathed him all the stories in exchange for a series of tasks completed. Thus, all stories in West Africa are known as *anansesem*, regardless whether the character Ananse appears.

A major difference in the tales from West Africa, particularly present-day Ghana, and those told in the New World is the absence of a religious dimension in the latter. In the West African tales, Ananse is involved with gods as well as men. He has dealings with Nyame and uses the (supposed) voice of Asase Yaa, the queen mother deity who rules with Nyame, to avoid being put to death. By the time Ananse had navigated the Middle Passage, however, the gods had disappeared from the stories. It may be that the concept of tribal, localized deities made it impossible for enslaved West Africans to include their names in the tales told in the Caribbean.

Perhaps Ananse survived at all because in the West African stories, he is the master of death. He returns from the land of the dead, a feat deemed impossible; he not only tricks Death out of rare gifts—a gold broom and gold sandals—but escapes with them. He fakes his own death in order to be buried near the ripening crops, of which he eats his fill. In another tale, he uses dead bodies, both animal and human, to gain increasingly more valuable gifts for Nyame.

According to scholar Christopher Vecsey, Ananse did not have the role of a cultural hero in West Africa. Although he is credited with bringing wisdom, the hoe, and weaving to the people, he is also the source of death, debt, and disharmony. Furthermore, he violates one of the major social mores in that he does not practice hospitality by sharing food. Instead, he makes sure that his own needs are met—in some cases even hiding the source of his meals from his own wife and children during famine.

The tales functioned as safety valves for the community, Vecsey posits. When Ananse fails in some venture, the tale concludes with a moral. Even within the tales, villagers sometimes disbelieve Ananse's reports because he is known to be untruthful. By beginning each tale with the repeated assertion that it was not true, the storyteller permitted his audience to mock the authority of both gods and local leaders, as well as to break the rules of the Akans. For, as the stories show, the rest of the events and characters in them all are acting in accordance with accepted behavior. The storyteller and the hearers are not being encouraged to be like Ananse but to enjoy a rest from the rigid society around them.

For Roman Catholic priest Robert Pelton, Ananse's most important function is that of trickster god: "The trickster speaks—and embodies—a vivid and subtle religious language, through which he links animality and ritual transformation, shapes culture by means of sex and laughter, ties cosmic process to personal history, empowers divination to change boundaries into horizons, and reveals the passages to the sacred embedded in daily life" (*Trickster* 3). The trickster represents the liminal state of those engaged in such events as coming-of-age rituals, which typically have a tripartite structure: leaving the known, enduring the ritual, and returning to the community. Without a clearly defined identity, living between cultural structures, the limen is dangerous. By living among the rafters, with access to both the god Nyame and humans, Ananse symbolizes the human on a quest. "He is a living connection between the wild and the social, between the potentially and the actually human," as Pelton puts it (*Trickster* 57). As a liminal figure, Ananse lives in the rafters, but within the house. He, too, is dangerous, with his often antisocial actions and his hungers.

Despite the importance of Ananse's stories to West African peoples, none of his stories relate to actual religious practices of the clans. Thus, Pelton would seem to agree with Vecsey: these tales are significant because they permit acting out and hearing of acts outside the parameters of acceptable society, not because they have shaped belief. Tales were told only after dark, prefaced by and concluded with the assertion that they were not true. Animal characters allowed mockery of humans without fear of reprisals.

In 1672, the Royal Africa Company was established after the English took Jamaica and other islands from the Spanish in 1655. The ratio of blacks to whites on the island increased rapidly thereafter; by 1740, there were ten times more blacks than whites. By the end of the eighteenth century, 60 percent of blacks worked on approximately four hundred sugar plantations on the islands. Life was harsh; many slaves did not live more than three or four years after arriving in the Caribbean.

The stories of Ananse migrated with the enslaved Africans during the heyday of plantation economy in the Caribbean. Slaves from the Asante tribes were particularly prized for their strength and height; they were also dangerous because they were well-trained warriors. Many of the Asantes, particularly those among the Akan tribe, were among those who resisted enslavement. Some scholars credit the Akans with being instigators of every slave rebellion in Jamaica. Indeed, most of the slave rebellions in the Caribbean occurred in Jamaica. According to Marshall, "Anansi tales were mechanisms of survival and sources of wisdom or knowledge, which could, in certain contexts, translate into resources for resistance and play a part in fueling slave revolt" (92). Caribbean slaves who managed to escape into the mountains were known as Maroons. Unsurprisingly, Jamaica had the largest Maroon population, with descendants into the present day. Although accurate historical data is scant, it may be that the first Maroons were enslaved by the Spanish; British slaves later joined that group. Maroons were said to have a "secret language," which some believe was the Akan dialect, Twi. This is a credible claim, given that many words in the Twi language have become loan words in Jamaican Creole. The Maroons, who, by 1739, had two established communities of about five hundred members each, signed a treaty with the British that year. They agreed to hunt and return runaway slaves in exchange for semi-autonomy. Taking their duties seriously, they ironically became a force that runaways feared. Borrowing from the Anansi stories, they attacked the vulnerable to maintain their own lifestyle. Anansi never minded subjecting others to a painful or difficult experience after his own brush with it.

Recognizing that the British treaty was not going to be upheld, the Maroons used guerrilla techniques and psychological warfare to frighten British soldiers during two major wars before the treaty was signed. Unused to an enemy that did not follow the protocols of

European warfare, the British forces were easily intimidated. Seven of these resistance fighters, including one woman, are still regarded as national heroes in Jamaica. As Marshall argues, the Anansi folktales offered practical guidance in the Maroon fight against oppression: Anansi stories could provide a form of mental training, illustrating tactics that could be implemented in the field—the arts of cunning and disguise, spying and surveillance, hiding and subterfuge.

Among all the Caribbean islands to which enslaved Africans were taken, Jamaica has proven a fertile soil for new and old tales of Anansi. Some Maroon communities take credit for the new stories, including more modern versions. During the late 1960s, Jamaican Michael Auld created a comic strip called *Anansesem*. It related the adventures of the Maroons during their resistance and imagined a role for Anansi. Various stories can be interpreted as including techniques valuable to the resistance and to rebellious enslaved persons.

Significant differences occur, however, in the stories of the Asantes and the Jamaicans. Names were given to the animal characters in African versions; in Jamaica, the characters are known by their species alone. Those species reflect the Jamaican, not the African, fauna. No elephants appear in Jamaican stories; Monkey and Tiger (who replaces Nyame as the keeper of the stories) are the only African animals. In addition, new Jamaican characters, such as Parrot and Cockroach, appear in the Jamaican stories. The animals engage in battles of wits with new characters such as Massa, Buckra or Backra the white boss, and Preacher. Jamaican food also replaces African food in the tales.

Although the African spider stories might mock authority, they upheld the social fabric and reinforced community values. This is not the case in the Jamaican stories, which play out against violence and conflict. The stories attempt to subvert the plantation order rather than to approve it. Another contrast is that in African tales, Ananse withholds food from his own family, caring only for himself. In the Jamaica tales, Anansi is still a trickster, but his wiles are practiced against the master, not against his own kind.

The folktales from Jamaica often include music, which Helen Roberts transcribed and Beckwith added to her collection of tales. By singing and by playing the fiddle (rather than African drums), Anansi courts women, hypnotizes other characters, and even kills some of them.

Due to the violence and lewdness of most Anansi tales, some Christians, particularly evangelicals, reject Anansi. Another factor in disregarding the stories is their association with the nine-night ceremony, an African import still popular in several Caribbean islands, including Jamaica. These events are part of an extended wake. The ninth night is the final watch; during this night, there is music and dancing, along with the telling of Anansi stories, so that none of the mourners become overly saddened by the death of a family member or friend. Many suggestions have been offered as to why Anansi stories are included, but one popular idea is that they amuse the "duppy" (ghost) of the newly deceased. Another interpretation is that they assist the duppy in making the transition to the other side.

Several twentieth-century writers and authors made use of Anansi in new ways. Jamaican poet and novelist Andrew Salkey, for example, used the spider in two collections, *Anancy's Score* (1973) and *Anancy, Traveller* (1992). The hero in the stories is placed in contemporary situations, as in "Vietnam Anancy and the Black Tulip" and "Anancy and the Atomic Horse." As Salkey writes him, Anansi is still not a knight in shining armor, but rather a guide and problem solver through difficult times.

For Jamaicans, a new pride in Anansi and a willingness to write and reinterpret the old tales signifies a coming to terms with their heritage, which is apart from the Spanish and British overlay. Through various media, including comic strips and theatrical productions, Anansi continues to shape Jamaican culture.

Judy A. Johnson, MLS, MTS

BIBLIOGRAPHY

Barry, Peter. *Beginning Theory*. 3rd ed. Manchester: Manchester UP, 2009. Print.

Beckwith, Martha Warren. *Jamaica Anansi Stories*. 1924. Charleston: BiblioBazaar, 2007. Print.

Brooker, Peter. *A Glossary of Cultural Theory*. 2nd ed. London: Arnold, 2002. Print.

Marshall, Emily Zobel. *Anansi's Journey: A Story of Jamaican Cultural Resistance*. Kingston: U of West Indies P, 2012. Print.

Pelton, Robert D. *The Trickster in West Africa: A Study of Mythic Irony and Sacred Delight*. Berkeley: U of California P, 1980. Print.

---. "West African Tricksters: Web of Purpose, Dance of Delight." *Mythical Trickster Figures: Contours, Con-*

texts, and Criticisms. Ed. William J. Hynes and William G. Doty. Tuscaloosa: U of Alabama P, 1993, 122–40. Print.

Van Duin, Lieke. "Anansi as Classical Hero." *Journal of Caribbean Literatures* 5.1 (2007): 33–42. Print.

Vecsey, Christopher. "The Exception Who Proves the Rules." *Mythical Trickster Figures: Contours, Contexts, and Criticisms*. Ed. William J. Hynes and William G. Doty. Tuscaloosa: U of Alabama P, 1993. 106–21. Print.

Gesar of Ling

Author: Traditional
Time Period: 1001 CE–1500 CE
Country or Culture: Tibet
Genre: Legend

OVERVIEW

Gesar of Ling is an old and popular Tibetan epic. Its powerful hero, Gesar, performs many great and legendary feats. Gesar may have been based on a historical person, but throughout the epic *Gesar of Ling*, the protagonist uses various forms of magic and primarily battles supernatural, demonic forces.

Gesar enters the world relatively lowborn, yet many magic portents hint at his truly exceptional nature, great powers, and extraordinary destiny. As a teenager, Gesar uses trickery, magic, intellect, and supernatural forces to win a beautiful bride, Sechan Dugmo, and become the king of Ling. Gesar is aided in his exploits by his magical steed, Kyang Go Karkar. After securing his rule and the power of his kingdom by magical means, Gesar receives his divine task from his sister, the goddess Manene. Gesar must defeat the four demon lords who rule the four countries surrounding Ling at the four cardinal directions of the compass.

There is no known author and no single, authoritative written text of the epic *Gesar of Ling*. Instead, most scholars believe that it developed as an oral epic in eastern Tibet around the twelfth century CE. By the time the Mongols received the surrender of Tibet in the 1240s, *Gesar of Ling* was widely popular in Tibet. The Mongols liked the epic so much that they translated, developed, and included it in their own literary tradition. It is in a Mongolian version that the epic was first printed in Beijing in 1716. However, with hundreds of individual storytellers handing down *Gesar of Ling* through many generations in a wide Central Asian geographical area including Tibet, Mongolia, and western China, many unique versions of the epic developed.

The first Western translations of the epic of *Gesar of Ling* were published in the nineteenth and early twentieth century in Germany and England. In 1996, American writer and Buddhist teacher Douglas Penick published *The Warrior Song of King Gesar*. This English version of the epic appears the most accessible for contemporary readers. Penick acknowledges a variety of Western translations and Tibetan sources. He combines his sources much as a contemporary Tibetan storyteller would. *The Warrior Song of King Gesar* includes all the key elements of the epic and is used as source text for this presentation and analysis.

An archetypal and structural analysis of *The Warrior Song of King Gesar* shows how the epic lays the groundwork for Gesar's appearance on earth. This is followed by the rites of passage for the young hero. The ultimate quest of Gesar is to rid the world of four demon kingdoms endangering his patrimonial realm of Ling. Its epic narration shows literary variation and imagination in dealing with key mythological themes. These include combating evil and displaying the valor, resourcefulness, and character of the hero. At the same time, the hero is challenged in an archetypical way and is required to use his considerable talents to fulfill his divine mission. Cultural criticism illustrates how Buddhist ideas coexist in the narrative with older, pre-Buddhist Tibetan traditional elements. These are highlighted in Penick's version. The analysis also addresses the question of the epic's historic development. Feminist criticism shows that there is multidimensionality in the epic's portrayal of female characters. This applies both to those women on the side of Gesar, such as his bride, and to those arrayed against him, such as various female demons and enchantresses.

SUMMARY

The Warrior Song of King Gesar begins with a portrayal of Gesar. The hero is depicted in full adult splendor as he and his warriors look down from heaven to earth.

Below, the world is in severe disarray. It is to save humanity that Gesar decides to be born. His mission will be "to establish the kingdom of freedom, confidence and joy" (Penick 6).

Gesar's mother, Dzeden, is a dragon princess who has assumed human form. As such, she serves the old king of Ling, Singlen. One night, Dzeden has the first in a series of mystical dreams that prepare her for giving birth to Gesar. Singlen's wife becomes suspicious that Dzeden is carrying her husband's child and mistreats her. On a special day when all of Dzeden's animals give birth to their young, including the foal that will become Gesar's warrior horse, Kyang Go Karkar, Gesar is born in an unusual way: "A white egg marked with three black spots pushes out of the top of Dzeden's head. She wraps it in a cloth and . . . the shell breaks open and a strong ruddy boy steps out" (Penick 8).

King Singlen's brother Todong fears that this boy will become the next king instead of him. Todong tries to kill Gesar, who survives all his physical assaults. In a duel of magic, Gesar defeats a magician employed by Todong to kill him.

Gesar grows up alone with Dzeden in the wilderness. When he is about fifteen, the bodhisattva Padma Sambhava appears to him in the morning sky. Padma Sambhava tells Gesar he must begin to fulfill his destiny. As Singlen has left Ling to meditate, his successor must be chosen. Gesar changes into a raven and persuades Todong to organize a horse race, open to all men of Ling. The winner shall receive the hand of the merchant's daughter Sechan Dugmo and be crowned new king. The raven disingenuously assures Todong that he will win.

Todong organizes the horse race. Gesar and Kyang Go Karkar join but look rather ragged. Through magic, Gesar wins. He and his horse assume their splendid selves. Gesar claims the beautiful Sechan Dugmo in marriage and ascends the throne of Ling.

Gesar establishes his pattern of going into a solitary retreat after each of his successes. One morning, Gesar is visited by his sister, "the goddess Manene, coming to him on an opaline rainbow" (Penick 25). Manene outlines Gesar's next task. He must gather his warriors and enter a secret cave on Mount Magyel Pomra, where he will find weapons and treasures for his upcoming battles. Gesar does as he is advised.

Next, Manene tells Gesar he must "destroy the Tirthika stronghold" (Penick 31). There, renegade priests have horded medicine and Buddhist scriptures,

"Your life here, Great Fearless Friend of Man, / Is without comfort or ease. It is ceaseless warfare. / Again and again, you must rouse yourself and raise yourself up. / Again and again, you must rely only on your discipline. / Again and again, you must confirm your dignity. / You must raise the Tiger, Lion, Garuda, Dragon victory banner. / Conquest over demonic degradation must be re-enacted again and again."

The Warrior Song of King Gesar

withholding them from the people. Gesar approaches the stronghold of the Tirthika alone. From Gesar's body, four warriors emerge. They are a tiger, a lion, a garuda (magic Buddhist bird), and a dragon. The warriors defeat the Tirthika priests, and Gesar brings bales of medicine and volumes of holy books back to Ling.

With his kingdom in order, Gesar receives a new set of divine tasks from Manene. She visits him one night "across a bridge of faint moonlight" and tells him that he must defeat the four demons ruling over lands surrounding Ling in the four directions of the compass (Penick 47). The next day, Gesar tells his wife and his people that he must leave them to begin his mission. Alone, he must kill the twelve-headed demon, Lutzen, ruling the north. As Gesar enters Lutzen's realm atop Kyang Go Karkar, a fierce bull attacks him. Kyang Go Karkar speaks to Gesar, exhorting him not to give up in this first crisis of his power. Gesar succeeds in killing the bull.

As Gesar approaches demon Lutzen's stronghold, he uses persuasion, battle skills, and trickery to overcome its three rings of guards. Gesar wins over Lutzen's warriors, who are descended from gods and from humans, by promising them their freedom if they kill the demon guards, which they accomplish. When Lutzen leaves his castle, Gesar enters. He persuades the demon's "elegant and beautiful" Chinese wife to betray

Lutzen (Penick 57). From the wife, Gesar learns how to defeat the demon by killing his two demon sisters and cutting off all of Lutzen's heads while he is asleep.

After Gesar kills Lutzen, the Chinese woman gives Gesar a potion. This makes him forget himself and his mission. He lives with her for six years while Kyang Go Karkar languishes in a cavernous stable. Gesar is visited finally by a headless falcon. The bird reveals itself as Gesar's half brother Gyaza, son of Singlen. It tells Gesar that Ling has been conquered by the white demon Kurkar, who rules the realm of Hor to the east of Ling. Kurkar has taken Sechan Dugmo as his wife and installed Todong as his deputy in Ling. Aroused by the bad news, Gesar shakes of the Chinese woman's spell. He confines her to a cave and rides Kyang Go Karkar back to Ling.

Gesar overthrows and imprisons Todong and prepares for war against the kingdom of Hor. With trickery, Gesar defeats Kurkar and his brothers by playing on their greed and superstitions. Assuming his true form, Gesar beheads Kurkar, takes Sechan Dugmo home, and reluctantly kills Sechan Dugmo and Kurkar's child, who is Gesar's mortal enemy. At home, Gesar forgives both Todong and Sechan Dugmo. Peace is restored to Ling.

Following his divine destiny, Gesar slays Jang, the demon king of the west. Jang prepares to attack Ling to please his new wife. Gesar anticipates this and defeats Jang and his armies through his combination of trickery, impersonation, and great physical strength.

After Jang is defeated, Gesar vows to meditate for thirteen years. After ten years, Manene appears to him. She tells Gesar he must break his personal vows for the benefit of his people and attack the last demon, Shingti of the south. Gesar assembles his army to advance on Shingti's realm. At the border, Gesar has messengers tell Shingti that the demon must give his daughter Metok Lhadze in marriage to the son of Todong. Otherwise, Shingti faces war and destruction. Shingti refuses. Gesar defeats and kills him and skins his body. Metok Lhadze chooses to marry Todong's son.

With his destiny fulfilled, Gesar moves atop a mountain platform in the east to meditate for three years, accompanied by Sechan Dugmo and a royal retinue. Afterward, Gesar bids farewell to his people. He, Sechan Dugmo, and select elite warriors stay behind. Gesar prepares them for their journey to the heavens: "Now that our work is done, There is no need for these bodies to perpetuate themselves" (Penick 135).

As morning comes, Gesar and his party depart for the sky. They leave behind their empty clothes, but their people know that Gesar will be with them always in spirit.

ANALYSIS

Archetypal and structural criticism shows that *Gesar of Ling* follows a familiar epic structure that accompanies the hero through his rites of passage to the episodes of his heroic feats. The epic's structure leads to perfect narrative closure when all tasks of Gesar's divine mandate are accomplished. Cultural criticism reveals some special plot devices resulting from the epic's particular unification of Buddhist teachings with older forms of Tibetan belief. A unique feature resulting from the Buddhist influence on *Gesar of Ling* is, for example, the idea that Gesar enters the world as reincarnation of an earlier self. As such, he possesses and uses strong magical powers immediately after his miraculous birth. As shown in *The Warrior Song of King Gesar*, the epic tries to unite core Buddhist beliefs regarding compassion and kindness with the plot of a fierce and determined warrior. This is accomplished in part by having Gesar confront and combat mostly demonic opponents. Those are defeated in graphic battles, while Gesar bestows characteristic mildness on his human adversaries, such as his "uncle" Todong. Feminist criticism illustrates that the epic develops multidimensional female characters. For instance, Gesar bases his reconciliation with his wife, Sechan Dugmo, on his realization, remarkable for a character in a traditional epic, that both he and she have violated their marriage. Sechan Dugmo accompanies Gesar to heaven, which is highly unlikely for a woman to do in many Buddhist traditions.

Structurally, even before presenting the birth of the hero, *The Warrior Song of King Gesar* establishes a strong Buddhist setting and privileges Buddhism as the philosophical frame of the narrative. Accordingly, the epic opens with its famous image of a smoke offering toward the sky, where the divine beings dwell: "The white smoke of the juniper rises Fragrant and dense from the burning coals" (3).

The epic emphasizes that Gesar enters the world of human suffering out of his own free will and out of compassion, a key Buddhist precept. Penick's version is less explicit in illustrating that this means Gesar is a bodhisattva, a person reincarnated to lead people toward their spiritual enlightenment. In some versions of *Gesar of Ling*, Gesar is seen as a reincarnation or representative of the historical Guru Rinpoche. This guru appears to Gesar in *The Warrior Song of King Gesar* as Padma Sambhava and exhorts him to begin fulfilling his destiny. To launch Gesar on his quest, Padma Sambhava tells Gesar, "You and I are one" (Penick 16). Historically, Guru Rinpoche/Padma Sambhava is considered to have led the second wave of introducing Buddhism to Tibet in the eighth century. The epic echoes this history as Padma Sambhava tells Gesar, "I have brought the Buddha's teachings to the land of snow" (16).

Padma Sambhava's strong association with Gesar in the epic indicates its narrative amalgamation of Buddhism with an older Tibetan folk tradition of the warrior hero. Most scholars believe that as the epic *Gesar of Ling* was developed by different Tibetan storytellers, they incorporated older themes, motifs, and subplots from Tibetan folktales into the epic. At the same time, since the twelfth century CE, the epic has had a strong Buddhist setting, which, through some special plot twists, the narrative aligns with a warrior's tale.

Gesar's miraculous birth follows traditional elements of the epic and sets him up as an archetypical protagonist. He has strong supernatural powers that he has to use unusually early to survive the first days of his life. In *The Warrior Song of King Gesar*, the relationship of Gesar to the royal house of Ling is established initially rather tenuously by the fact that Gesar's mother, dragon princess Dzeden, becomes a servant to King Singlen in her human form. Contrary to the jealous suspicion of Singlen's wife, Gesar is no biological son of the king. Instead, the epic uses the motif of the virgin birth to bring Gesar into the world of humanity.

Gesar acts as engine of his own birth. He has no biological father, and his mother neither conceives nor gives birth to him in a physically possible fashion. The fact that Gesar appears magically in an egg emerging from Dzeden's head signifies his singularity and his status as a legendary character with supernatural abilities. Structurally speaking, Gesar becomes the author of the narrative of his birth and sets up the parameters of his subsequent actions in the world of humanity.

Very early on, the epic introduces Todong, King Singlen's "cowardly malicious brother" (Penick 8). As such, within the structure of the epic, Todong is the archetypical opposite to Gesar. Todong functions to mirror the protagonist in the negative. Todong will also come to represent fallible, ordinary humanity as opposed to superhumanly brave, magnanimous, and compassionate Gesar. As such, the narrative does shows him some

sympathy. For all his evil, Todong remains part of the aristocracy of Ling to the end of the narrative, signifying the text's implied compassion for fallible humanity.

From a feminist and cultural criticism perspective, Todong's actions following Gesar's birth illustrate a struggle over lineage and legitimacy against the backdrop of patriarchal feudal society. Todong allies himself with King Singlen's wife, who worries that Dzeden may carry her husband's child. This could lead to her possibly losing her status in the feudal system, as she does not have a son of her own. When Gesar is born, Todong acts with chilling, if historically accurate, brutality. He puts on his armor and rides to Dzeden's tent. There, he picks up the baby and smashes his head against the tent post. Normally, this would kill the baby in a politically motivated infanticide. In the epic, the boy laughs at Todong, unhurt, as Gesar is protected by his magic powers. Even when Todong buries the child Gesar alive "in a deep pit, which he covers over with thorns and a large flat rock," Gesar miraculously reappears on the surface of the earth the next morning (Penick 9). When Todong tries to combat Gesar's magic with magic of a hired wizard, Gesar emerges victorious in the ensuing duel of magic forces.

From the point of view of cultural criticism, the fact that Gesar survives infanticide planned for reasons of feudal succession indicates that the epic is addressing an issue of concern in its original society. Structurally, the relevancy of this problem is repeated in a near parallel action by Gesar himself. When the demon Kurkar of Hor kidnaps Gesar's wife, Sechan Dugmo, she eventually yields to his advances, and the two have a son together. After Gesar kills Kurkar, he confronts the issue of this boy. The narrative eases Gesar's decision, which is in fact the same as that of Todong. This is done through the plot device of giving the boy "a mortal hatred of Gesar" and an incorrigible determination to exterminate Gesar once he reaches adulthood (Penick 96). Supplied with this comfortable moral excuse, Gesar appears justified in his actions. He reluctantly "arranges for a boulder to fall from a mountain pass where the boy is hiding, and he is crushed to death" (96). Thus, infanticide is excused by the plot in the case of Gesar himself. This solves the vexing issue of an illegitimate offspring threatening the structure of the patriarchal and feudal society mirrored by *Gesar of Ling*.

The plot prepares for Gesar's archetypal rites of passage once he reaches midadolescence. It is then that Padma Sambhava appears and exhorts Gesar to fulfill his destiny: "Wake Gesar, Lion King of Ling. You are

HISTORICAL CONTEXT

Most historians trace the origin of the Tibetan empire to the Tibetan king gNam-ri Srong-brtsan (Namri Songtsen), who was born around 570 CE and assassinated around 618 or 620 CE. His son Srong-brtsan sgam-po (Songtsen Gampo) is considered the first historically confirmed, nonmythical king of Tibet and ruled until his death around 649 CE. He is credited with introducing Buddhism to Tibet. However, the traditional Tibetan shamanistic Bön religion still prevailed. This religious conflict is echoed in *The Warrior Song of King Gesar*, in which Gesar destroys the stronghold of a Buddhist sect. This happens despite the epic taking place within a Buddhist framework and hints at the lingering of this religious struggle in Tibet well into the twelfth century and beyond.

Srong-brtsan sgam-po and his successors greatly enlarged the Tibetan Empire by military conquest of central Tibet and neighboring lands toward the west and south in the seventh and early eighth century CE. They were successful warrior kings who may have served as a model for the epic hero Gesar.

Around 747 CE, Tibetan king Khri srong Ide-btsan (Tri Songdetsen) invited Buddhist missionary Guru Rinpoche to Tibet. Also known as Padma 'byung gnas in Tibetan and Padma Sambhava in Sanskrit, this Buddhist scholar led the second wave of Buddhism in Tibet. There, he helped establish the first Buddhist monastery, Samye, in the 770s. According to Tibetan tradition, the king gave one of his young wives, Ye shes mtsho rgyal (Yeshe Tsogyal), as consort to Padma Sambhava, with whom she studied Buddhism. She is believed to have entered heaven as a female Buddha. This echoes the ending of *Gesar of Ling*, in which Sechan Dugmo accompanies her husband, Gesar, into the sky.

The Tibetan Empire fragmented over the issue of royal succession around 842 CE. No central authority was in place at the time of the Mongol conquest in the 1240s. Tibetan tradition often places Gesar's reign in the eleventh century. Contemporary historians, however, have expressed some doubt as to whether Gesar was a historical person.

---

now a man and your dream-like life of peace here is at an end" (Penick 16). Padma's speech to Gesar summarizes the subsequent actions that the epic will present, which is a typical oral narrative strategy. Gesar's tasks include mastering his rites of passage and performing all the epic feats he must accomplish on earth.

Padma Sambhava gives spiritual reasons for Gesar's quest that are aligned with Buddhist philosophy and teachings. In doing so, Padma Sambhava fulfills the same narrative function that the goddess Manene will serve later on in the epic. Like Padma Sambhava, Manene will motivate the hero, foretell the actions he must undertake, and put his tasks into a larger Buddhist framework. Padma Sambhava tells Gesar that his martial feats will serve humanity at large: "Join the ways of Heaven, Earth and Man, and bring into this world the kingdom of enlightenment, the deathless realm of true goodness and genuine dignity" (Penick 16).

The epic elegantly uses Padma Sambhava's speech to reconcile the apparent discrepancy between Buddhist teachings and the content of a warrior's epic. It is because people are deluded by demons that they cannot yet see the true nature and reason of Gesar's martial actions.

People, including perhaps at first any listener to the epic, will not be able to see easily that Gesar's warlike feats are grounded in compassion and empathy with human suffering. As Gesar's opponents are demons misguiding humanity, they must be overcome. Against demons, the use of physical force, reinforced by magic and the supernatural, is justified. It is applied by Gesar to cut through the delusions with which the demons influence the minds of humans. Through this double plot device of human delusions and demonic opponents, the narrative reconciles Gesar's warlike feats with Buddhist philosophy. Buddhist precepts govern interactions among humans and gentle divine forces but not interactions with evil demons. Therefore, the epic can tell its archetypal tale of a hero's martial triumph while adhering to the larger philosophical framework of Buddhism.

Trickery is a favorite means of Gesar to achieve success, yet he is no archetypal trickster hero. This is because unlike the trickster, who generally remains unaffected from episode to episode, Gesar relies also on his strength to follow up on his tricks. His character advances in status and position because of his achievements, unlike the typical unchanging trickster hero.

Right away with Gesar's first right of passage, *The Warrior Song of King Gesar* establishes the pattern that Gesar often begins his missions with a trick. His first challenge involves winning a bride and the kingship of Ling. All of this is done when he is about fifteen years old. Gesar sets up the framework for his ultimate success with his wily use of superstition. As his "uncle," Todong, likes to construct divine messages from the cries of ravens flying around his abode, Gesar changes into one of them. As a raven, Gesar tells Todong to set up a horserace to settle the issue of royal succession and provide the winner with a young, beautiful bride with a rich dowry. Insidiously, Gesar as raven assures Todong that he will be victorious.

The motif of an evil person's plans backfiring is employed in Gesar's first rite of passage. In addition, Todong's wife is given the wisdom to see through this ploy and to scold her husband accordingly. She says, "You are being led astray by greed and lust. You are drunk and a bird is a bird. If you go ahead with this, you'll regret it" (Penick 18). From a feminist critical perspective, the warning of Todong's wife could be traced to her self-interest in not being superseded by a young second wife. Polygamy was accepted in traditional Tibetan society, and Todong's wife has a vested interest in objecting to his plan. On the other hand, given that she is proven right in her apprehension, *The Warrior Song of King Gesar* shows some sympathy for a woman's position in the society the epic reflects, illustrates, and dramatizes.

On the appointed day of the horse race, Gesar successfully completes his first rite of passage. Again, as with his birth, Gesar appears as engine and author of his own success. As a raven, Gesar has deflected Todong's desire upon himself and made Todong the executor of his own downfall. When Gesar appears on Kyang Go Karkar, he and his magic horse have assumed a ragged look. Nevertheless, according to the rules set up by Todong, they are permitted to join the race against the kingdom's best riders, including Todong.

Structurally, the epic introduces the delay of an apparent crisis of confidence in the emerging hero. At the beginning of the race, Gesar momentarily stays behind on Kyang Go Karkar. In a pattern of encouragement repeated later when Gesar enters the land of the first demon he must slay, the horse appeals to Gesar's self-confidence to motivate and encourage him. The horse snorts at Gesar, "Are you having second thoughts?" (Penick 20). This Gesar emphatically rejects, and he responds with a thought in alignment with some Buddhist

beliefs, "What I will accomplish already is" (20). Gesar then spurs on Kyang Go Karkar. The horse employs its supernatural powers to fly through the air, landing in the field of riders ahead of them.

Within the narrative context of the epic's emphasis on the importance and inherent goodness of Gesar's destiny, *The Warrior Song of King Gesar* even allows Gesar to display a surprising streak of meanness. Riding up alongside Todong, Gesar asks Kyang Go Karkar to kick Todong's horse so that it and its rider fall to the ground. When Todong complains, Gesar responds cheekily that he only wanted to guard his treasure, or birthright. Obviously, the epic of *Gesar of Ling* does not share the Western concept of fair play in sportsmanship. Instead, it allows its hero to get away with this rather mean and unnecessary act of punishing those he is about to defeat through his magic anyway.

True to the epic's structure of spurring on its hero protagonist until he has accomplished all his divine tasks, winning his bride and his kingdom gives Gesar only a temporary respite. Yet *The Warrior Song of King Gesar* does like to pause at these instances of success and celebrate Gesar's triumph for a moment. This is often done through a description of Gesar feasting with his wife and his people. In these scenes, Gesar addresses his compatriots in heroic, dramatic speeches that illustrate his status, repeat his feats, and underline his importance for humanity under his leadership and protection. Warrior traditions are again aligned with Buddhist philosophy, as the goal of all martial struggle becomes popular enlightenment. This is not quite orthodox Buddhism but works generally well in embedding *The Warrior Song of King Gesar* in an overall Buddhist context.

The epic follows a clear structure to portray Gesar's heroic progress, which appears almost as an illustration of a young king successfully consolidating his rule. Spiritually exhorted and encouraged by his sister, the goddess Manene, Gesar obtains weapons for his warriors and treasure to support them from a cave in Mount Magyel Pomra that he enters by magical means. Next, he engages in a kind of religious war and destroys the sect of Tirthika, which has hoarded traditional medicine and Buddhist scriptures. Scholars have likened this action to the historical conflict in Tibetan society between clerical and shamanistic traditions. Gesar destroying a community of learned clerics, who are of course in the thrall of a demon, in favor of his own shamanistic use of their belongings places him on one side of this traditional struggle in Tibetan society.

The narrative plot of the epic takes the edge from a too-realistic depiction of a young king and his well-armed and well-supported warrior force readying themselves to attack and defeat neighboring kingdoms. In consequence, *The Warrior Song of King Gesar* presents Gesar alone, supported just by his horse, as he begins his quest. He must defeat the first of the four demon lords ruling and deluding humanity in kingdoms situated in the four directions of the compass. As with Todong, Gesar relies on trickery and dissimulation to prepare the way for his victories. He will continue to employ this strategy throughout his future battles.

One of the greatest crises of the archetypal hero comes when the Chinese widow of the demon king Lutzen, whom Gesar has slain with her help, nearly overcomes Gesar's will. Following the narrative strategy of explaining and, to some extent, excusing actions with the supernatural and with magic, it is her potion that makes Gesar forget his wife and his kingdom. For six years, Gesar stays at the side of the demon's widow. This major crisis in Gesar's life is overcome only with the help of Gesar's half brother. He reawakens Gesar's spirit when he talks to him in the unlikely incarnation of a headless falcon. This clearly surrealistic event highlights the spirit of the supernatural that permeates the epic *Gesar of Ling*.

From a feminist critical perspective, Gesar's resolution and resumption of his relationship with his wife, Sechan Dugmo, shows a remarkable divergence from expected patriarchal behavior patterns. For while Gesar is in the thrall of the demon's widow, the demon Kurkar of Hor conquers Ling with the help of the treacherous Todong. Todong helps Kurkar to win over Sechan Dugmo, whose resistance crumbles after two years. Kurkar and Sechan Dugmo then marry and have a child together. Once Gesar slays Kurkar and reluctantly kills the child, he sends Sechan Dugmo back to Ling.

The reconciliation of Gesar and Sechan Dugmo presents an emotionally moving climax of *The Warrior Song of King Gesar*. In song, Gesar confronts both his and her shortcomings:

> Sechan Dugmo, queen and wife,
> Remorse at what each of us has done
> . . . .
> Seem to separate us so, and yet,
> We share them utterly. (Penick 97)

Gesar's song shows how, out of a mutual acknowledgment of their sorrow at each other's behavior, there is hope that their love is strong enough to be renewed. As Sechan Dugmo goes out of her own free will from her tent to Gesar's palace the next morning, this reconciliation occurs.

Although many Buddhist traditions—including the Pure Land tradition, which has flourished in Tibet since the ninth century CE—hold that only a soul incarnated in a male body can enter heaven, Sechan Dugmo accompanies Gesar and his closest warrior companions to heaven at the end of *The Warrior Song of King Gesar*. Sechan Dugmo joining Gesar in heaven structurally closes the epic as it returns the hero to his status at the very beginning of the narrative. Sechan Dugmo's ascent to heaven represents a feminine achievement that mediates much of the more patriarchal sentiment in *The Warrior Song of King Gesar*, especially concerning infanticide and feudal struggle over succession.

CROSS-CULTURAL INFLUENCE

The epic *Gesar of Ling* is clearly a traditional Tibetan creation. Yet scholars have identified possible cross-cultural, non-Tibetan influences on the development of the epic. This concerns especially the origin of its archetypal hero, Gesar.

Scholarly inquiry into the possible origin of Gesar begins with his very name. In Tibetan and Sanskrit, *gesar* means either the anther or the pistil of a flower, the parts where either pollen is located or where pollen from another flower gathers to be led to a blossom's ova. However, either by phonetic accident or for a historical reason, Gesar is very similar to the Latin word *caesar*. Caesar came to be used as term for Roman and Byzantine emperors from the first century CE onward. It was known and recorded as such by the Turkish people of southwest Asia. This fact has led some Western scholars to propose that Gesar was originally modeled after an eighth-century Turkish prince from the region of Bactria, in contemporary Afghanistan and Uzbekistan. This historical prince is known from his coins as Phrom-kesar. If this theory is historically accurate, it would indicate that the Tibetan storytellers developing the epic *Gesar of Ling* took inspiration for their hero from a foreign prince. Tibetan and other Asian scholars dispute this origin, calling it a mere phonetic coincidence.

Refuting claims of a cross-cultural origin of the epic hero, Tibetan scholars have generally insisted that Gesar is modeled after a historical Tibetan ruler. According to their theory, the historical Gesar was born in the tenth or eleventh century CE and lived into his eighties. To reinforce their belief in a historic Gesar, some of these scholars have placed Gesar's birthplace in the Mgo log (Golok) region (now the autonomous district of Guoluo in China). In this theory, the magic mountain of Magyel Pomra is identified as the actual mountain Amnye Machen (Animaqing Shan in Chinese) in that district. In this area, there was also a kingdom called gLing-tshang (Lingtsang) that was established in the fourteenth century and survived into the early twentieth century.

However, during the time of the putative historical Gesar, there was no central royal rule among the various clans of Tibet. The Tibetan Empire previously expanded by its warrior kings had collapsed by the middle of the ninth century. For this reason, some scholars believe that the epic's hero of Gesar is a nostalgic construction modeled after an earlier king, either Tibetan or perhaps indeed foreign, and created during a time in the eleventh century when Tibetan audiences longed for the lost splendor and strength of their past.

This view can be reinforced by the opening of *The Warrior Song of King Gesar*. There, the world is in disorder. From the heavens, Gesar descends to earth via reincarnation to lead his people to a period of enlightenment, rescuing them from their present suffering. This yearning for a messianic hero has its counterparts in other cultures and societies as well. It appears to be a convincing explanation for the origin of the epic of *Gesar of Ling* during a troubled and fragmented period in Tibetan history.

Gesar of Ling proved extraordinarily appealing to non-Tibetan Central Asians whose societies came in contact with it. As a consequence, many non-Tibetan variants of the epic have developed over the course of many centuries. One of the first adaptations into another culture and oral literary tradition was developed by the Mongol conquerors of Tibet. The Mongolian version of *Gesar of Ling* became the first version of the epic to be recorded in written form in 1716. However, it is derived from the Tibetan original, which flourished as an oral tale long before this initial transcription.

The Mongolian text follows the Tibetan sources quite closely with regard to the origin of Gesar (Geser in Mongolian). It begins in the heavens with Geser deciding to enter the world of humanity to save them, which occurs through a miraculous birth. Geser wins his wife (here called Rogmo Goa) and the throne of Ling in a manner rather close to the Tibetan original. A new episode, in which Geser triumphs over a black striped tiger, has no equivalent in the Tibetan epic. Indicative of Mongolia's

close ties with China, the Mongolian Geser travels to China to marry his second wife, who is Chinese. Returning to Ling, he defeats a demon. Just as the Tibetan Gesar uses the help of demon Lutzen's Chinese wife to kill the twelve-headed demon of the north, so the Mongolian Geser kills his first demon opponent with the help of that evil character's wife. Yet the powerful dramatic interlude of Tibetan Gesar and Sechan Dugmo losing themselves to other romantic partners is left out of the Mongolian version. Similarly, the tight plot organization of the Tibetan version recounted in *The Warrior Song of King Gesar*, in which Gesar must kill four demons ruling four kingdoms in the four cardinal directions, is not followed in the Mongolian version. Instead, the Mongolian Geser kills the three kings of Sharaigol as well as a demon impersonating a lama (Buddhist holy man).

The Mongolian epic ends, as do some versions of the Tibetan *Gesar of Ling*, with Geser's travels to the underworld to meet and bring back his mother. In a 2009 sequel to his acclaimed *Warrior Song of King Gesar*, Penick published his version of this part of the Tibetan original. In *Crossings on a Bridge of Light*, Penick moves beyond the core episodes of the epic of *Gesar of Ling*. He assembles and translates the lesser known but still authentically Tibetan episodes around Gesar's descent into the Buddhist underworld to free his mother. Thanks to Penick's compilation and translation, these episodes have also become accessible to English speakers.

Another source text available to Western audiences was collected by Belgian French adventurer, explorer, and Buddhist Alexandra David-Néel, who visited Lhasa together with her adopted Sikkim son, Aphur Yongden, in 1924. She and Yongden transcribed and translated into French the version of the epic they heard during their two-month sojourn there. It was published as *La vie surhumaine de Guésar de Ling le héros thibétain* in 1931. In 1933, the English version, translated with the help of Violet Sydney, appeared as *The Superhuman Life of Gesar of Ling*. Scholars agree that this text captures well an authentic storyteller's version of the epic.

In 1991, American Buddhist composer Peter Lieberson approached Penick to write the libretto for Lieberson's opera *King Gesar*. This one-hour opera was designed as Lieberson's entry for the May 1992 Munich Biennial, an opera festival that features and celebrates new musical compositions. Lieberson and Penick collaborated to create a monodrama, an opera with one narrator accompanied by an orchestra.

On August 26, 1993, *King Gesar* enjoyed its United States premiere at the Tanglewood New Music Festival in Lenox, Massachusetts. Just as in Munich, the musicians included Yo-Yo Ma as cellist and Emanuel Ax and Peter Serkin on the piano. The narrator was Omar Ebrahim. *King Gesar* was designed by composer Lieberson as a modern version of a traditional campfire opera, to be told on a starry night to an enraptured audience. The narrator tells the story of Gesar, his miraculous birth, his rites of passage, and his subsequent heroic feats. The accompanying music is played on classical Western instruments but incorporates allusions to Tibetan chants and indigenous melodies.

Critical reception of *King Gesar*, which transposed the epic into a Western musical form, was generally favorable. Edward Rothstein for the *New York Times* lauded the performance for its musical experience and its sincere portrayal. Occasionally, however, he felt a sharp distance from what was for him the emotionally alien world of the epic. For the American critic, the traditional Tibetan alignment of a classic, violent warrior tale with Buddhist philosophy of compassion for human suffering was not completely accessible and meaningful for non-Buddhists.

Penick used his libretto for *King Gesar* as the basis for his version of the epic published as *The Warrior Song of King Gesar*. Through this accessible text, the epic has reached a larger American and English-speaking audience. Occasionally, when Penick uses contemporary terms such as "robots and zombies" (5), a critical reader may wish for less anachronistic and more literal closeness to the Tibetan source. However, as he sought to bring traditional Tibetan ideas to a contemporary American audience, Penick's choice of terms for his telling of the epic can be justified.

In 2005, American Buddhist literary scholar Robin Kornman revealed that his spiritual teacher, the controversial Tibetan exile Chos rgyam Drung pa (best known as Chökyi Gyamtso "Chögyam" Trungpa Rinpoche), had widely used the epic *Gesar of Ling* as a basis for his brand of Buddhist teaching in the United States. Trungpa (1939–87) fled from Chinese-occupied Tibet to India in 1959, relocated to England in 1963, and arrived in the United States via Canada in 1970. In the United States, Trungpa continued his contribution to the development of the Eclectic school of Buddhism and sought to familiarize his American disciples with its concepts. Yet Trungpa's use of alcohol, tobacco, and illicit drugs and his sexual promiscuity have made him controversial.

According to Kornman, Trungpa used *Gesar of Ling* to define his idea of the enlightened society. For Trungpa, the warrior aspects of Gesar were important in justifying a vigorous Buddhist lifestyle modeled after the tough indigenous populations of eastern Tibet even in the twentieth century. In 1978, Trungpa elucidated his ideas based on the Gesar epic in "a series of weekend public programs that he called Shambala Training" (Kornman 375). Trungpa's American disciples were fascinated by this uncommon combination of Buddhist philosophy and extolment of warrior spirit. Trungpa's explicit and implicit use of *Gesar of Ling* gave him a unique standing among Buddhist teachers and scholars in the United States.

The fascination that *Gesar of Ling* exerted among its American listeners at Trungpa's seminars appears to show the lasting global popular appeal of this traditional Tibetan legend. Just as Mongol storytellers adopted the epic into their own literary tradition, American Buddhist teachers such as Penick sought to make it widely available to a new English-speaking readership. The power of the epic *Gesar of Ling* seems to reach unbroken from the twelfth to the twenty-first century. It stretches in a wide arc from Central Asia to North America. Just as even in Tibet there is no single, authoritative text of the epic, each new version continues to add creativity and imagination of its own to an old, traditional core.

R. C. Lutz, PhD

BIBLIOGRAPHY

David-Néel, Alexandra. *The Superhuman Life of Gesar of Ling*. Trans. Violet Sydney. New York: Kendall, 1933. Print.

Kornman, Robin. "The Influence of the Epic of King Gesar of Ling on Chögyam Trungpa." *Recalling Chögyam Trungpa*. Ed. Fabrice Midal. Boston: Shambala, 2005. 347–79. Print.

Lieberson, Peter, comp. *King Gesar*. By Douglas Penick. Narr. Omar Ebrahim. Perf. Yo-Yo Ma, Peter Serkin, and Emanuel Ax. Cond. Lieberson. Sony, 1991. CD.

Li Lianrong. "History and the Tibetan Epic *Gesar*." *Oral Tradition* 16.2 (2001): 317–42. PDF file.

Penick, Douglas. *The Warrior Song of King Gesar*. Boston: Wisdom, 1997. Print.

Rothstein, Edward. "A Modern Voicing of Myth and Buddhist Belief." *New York Times*. New York Times, 28 Aug. 1993. Web. 22 Apr. 2013.

Gest of Robyn Hode

Author: Traditional
Time Period: 1001 CE–1500 CE
Country or Culture: England
Genre: Folktale

OVERVIEW

Of all antique heroes, Robin Hood is arguably the most popular today. Since its inception in the late Middle Ages, the story of the good outlaw who robs the wealthy to benefit the poor has been retold extensively in ballads, short stories, plays, and dozens of films and television shows. The oldest surviving long version of the story, *A Gest of Robyn Hode*, offers an intriguing snapshot of the early tradition and the hero's cultural significance. Dating back to about the mid-fifteenth century, the *Gest* (which means "adventure") was first printed in the early sixteenth century and was later collected by the nineteenth-century American scholar and folklorist Francis James Child in his five-volume *English and Scottish Popular Ballads* (1882–98).

The *Gest* is divided into eight fits, or sections, but the plot consists of three main parts with interlaced events: Robin Hood's adventures with the knight, with the Sheriff of Nottingham, and with the king. When Robin first sends his men to find a victim to rob, they produce a humble knight who, after borrowing money to save his son's life, is indebted to a loan-sharking abbot. Robin lends him money and other goods, enabling the knight to save his lands. Robin's companion Little John then assumes an alias and enters the service of the corrupt Sheriff of Nottingham. After fighting the sheriff's butler and cook, Little John steals the sheriff's silver and money and return to Robin. They then proceed to capture the sheriff and exact a promise of peace from him. Next, Robin robs two wealthy monks and considers the money repayment from the faithful knight, whom Robin eventually releases from his debt and even rewards with more money.

Meanwhile, Robin wins a shooting contest arranged by the sheriff, who then attacks the outlaw band, but they escape to the humble knight's castle. The sheriff appeals to the king and imprisons the knight in Nottingham after Robin and company return to the woods. The king arrives, disguises himself as an abbot, and is captured by Robin in the forest. After the king wins an archery contest, the band recognizes him, and Robin agrees to serve him at court. Yet Robin eventually returns to the forest, where he lives happily with his outlaw band for twenty-two more years before he is killed treacherously by his kinswomen and a knight named Sir Roger.

The figure of Robin Hood in the *Gest* is quite different from modern portrayals of the hero, and the meaning of his identity as an outlaw and his antiauthoritarianism are particularly intriguing in this medieval version. Often linked to the aristocracy in later renditions, Robin Hood in the *Gest* is of much lower station as a yeoman, or farmer, but the story is ambiguous about the meaning of his hostility toward authority figures. Some readers have insisted that the *Gest*, with its remarkable kindness toward the knight, is in fact relatively conservative, while others have aligned it with the radical sentiments underlying the English Peasants' Revolt of 1381. A thematic interpretation of antiauthoritarianism explores the meaning and extent of the hero's rebellion in the story and in the broad context of the medieval culture that produced the poem. Such an interpretation helps to identify the story's likely audience and its important differences from more recent creations in the Robin Hood tradition.

SUMMARY

The poem sets up the first adventure by introducing the good yeoman Robin and his companions Little John, William Scarlock, and Much the miller's son, who dwell in a forest in Barnesdale. When Little John suggests that Robin should dine, Robin replies that they have not yet found a suitable "guest" to rob to pay for the dinner, so

*" 'Therof no force,' than sayde Robyn; /
'We shall do wel! inowe; / But loke ye
do no husbonde harme, / That tilleth with
his ploughe. // 'No more ye shall no gode
yeman / That walketh by grenë-wode
shawe / Ne no knyght ne no squyer / That
wol be a gode felawe. // 'These bisshop-
pes and these archebisshoppes, / Ye shall
them bete and bynde; The hyë sheriff
of Notyingham, / Hym holde ye in your
mynde.' "*

A Gest of Robyn Hode

Little John asks Robin to advise him on the matter. Robin sends his men out to find a suitable victim, instructing
them not to harm ploughmen, good yeomen, or knights
or squires "that wol be a gode felawe" ("that would be a
good fellow"; 57, st. 14), but they should target these
types if necessary and should seek other members of the
gentry, such as earls and barons, higher clergymen such
as bishops and archbishops, and the Sheriff of Nottingham. The three men head off and return to Robin with a
sorry-looking knight who dines with them readily but
turns out to possess only ten shillings. The knight reports that after his son murdered a knight and squire, he
mortgaged his property to save his son's life and now
owes four hundred pounds to Saint Mary's Abbey, effectively the knight's loan shark. Robin lends the money
to the knight on the security of a pledge to the Virgin
Mary, to whom Robin himself is especially devoted. He
outfits the knight with new clothes and a horse and sends
him back to settle the debt with the abbey, with Little
John as his attendant.

The abbot of Saint Mary's and the high justice are eager to seize the knight's lands, but the prior of the abbey
argues against this corruption and urges them to wait
for the knight. When the knight arrives, he first asks for
more time to pay, but the abbot and justice instead offer money for his land. The knight then produces the
four hundred pounds and happily returns to his wife,
planning to recover the money to repay Robin. He sets

out to return to Robin with one hundred men, for whom
he has bought bows and arrows, but he is delayed by a
wrestling match, where he defends a yeoman who has
won but is being denied his victory. Then, Little John's
shooting prowess attracts the attention of the Sheriff of
Nottingham. With the knight's permission, Little John
enters the sheriff's service and assumes the alias Rey-
nald Greenleaf. Little Jon and the sheriff's cook fight
after the cook refuses to give Little John food and drink,
but the two soon reconcile, steal the sheriff's silver and
three hundred pounds, and return to Robin Hood. Little
John next lures the sheriff to the forest with promises
of plentiful deer to hunt. The outlaws then capture the
sheriff and dine with him using his silver. Robin tells the
sheriff he must stay for a year to learn to be an outlaw
but finally agrees to release him on an oath that he will
not harm Robin or his men.

Wondering why the knight has not returned, Robin is
reassured by Little John of the man's upstanding character. Robin sends his three comrades out for another
victim, and they find two wealthy monks from Saint
Mary's accompanied by fifty-two men, who flee after
the outlaws insist they join them for dinner with Robin
himself. Upon questioning, one of the monks swears
that he has only twenty marks, but Little John discovers
that he actually has over eight hundred pounds. Robin
praises Saint Mary for effectively repaying the knight's
loan, but then the knight finally returns. Robin informs
him that Mary has already repaid the loan, so the knight
gives him his bows and arrows, and Robin gives him
another four hundred pounds that remained from the
robbery of the monks.

Intent on revenge, the sheriff holds an archery contest, which Robin and his entire band attend. When Robin wins the gold and silver arrows, the sheriff tries to
capture him, prompting a battle between the outlaws and
the sheriff's men. When Little John is wounded, he begs
Robin to kill him so that the sheriff will not take him
prisoner. Instead, Robin and company carry Little John
on their horses, and they all fight and eventually escape
to the castle of the knight, now identified as Sir Richard at the Lee. The sheriff and his men attack the castle,
declare the knight a traitor, and finally seek the assistance of the king, who promises to come and capture
both Robin Hood and the knight. Robin Hood and his
men eventually return to the forest, and the sheriff captures the knight and imprisons him at Nottingham. The
knight's wife informs Robin of the trap, so the outlaws
go to Nottingham, and Robin himself kills the sheriff.

Robin frees the knight, and they all return to the forest to await the king's arrival.

When the king arrives in Nottingham, he seizes the knight's lands and promises them to whoever beheads the knight. An old knight advises the king that as long as Robin Hood prevails, no one will capture Sir Richard. After six months of dwelling in Nottingham, Robin hunts all of the king's deer, and the king disguises himself as an abbot and five of his men as monks. A forester leads them into the woods, where Robin promptly captures the men. The king swears truthfully that he has only forty pounds. Robin gives half to his men and returns the rest to the king, who urges Robin and his men to come to Nottingham. Robin declares allegiance to the king, who is struck by the extraordinarily loyalty of Robin's men to their leader. They have an archery contest, which Robin narrowly loses. He receives the customary buffet, or blow, from the king, whose true identity the men finally perceive. Robin and his men all agree to serve the king at court, but Robin stipulates that he will leave if he dislikes court life. The king assumes a green livery and returns the knight's lands at Nottingham, where a feast is held. Robin serves the king for one year and three months but finds court life expensive and dull, so he obtains the king's permission to visit the chapel of Mary Magdalene in Barnesdale for seven days. The story concludes as Robin returns to the forest to hunt deer and rule with his loyal band of outlaws. He never returns to court but lives happily for twenty-two years in the forest until he is murdered by the prioress of Kyrkesly, his kinswoman, and a knight named Sir Roger. The poem concludes by praising Robin as "a good outlawe" who "dyde pore men moch god" ("did poor men much good"; 78, st. 456).

ANALYSIS

Robin Hood tales fundamentally celebrate rebellion against authority, most commonly organized around the theme of class conflict: Robin Hood is above all a popular and social hero who robs the rich to benefit the poor. Perhaps surprisingly, however, the nature of the rebellion, conflicts, and the status of the hero himself vary quite a bit within the Robin Hood tradition. The Robin Hood familiar to most modern people from popular films, shows, and stories bears scant resemblance to the heroic outlaw of the late medieval English ballads. As the longest and most literary ballad of the medieval tradition, the Gest of Robin Hood offers a valuable glimpse into how Robin Hood was originally conceived, but its

portrayal of the outlaw and his famous antiauthoritarianism is far from straightforward. In this story, Robin does indeed steal from wealthy and corrupt clergymen and the Sheriff of Nottingham, but he also assists a knight, officially a member of the gentry, or upper class, and he swears loyalty to the king. Robin is also extraordinarily devoted to Saint Mary, suggesting his support of his society's official religion. On the other hand, Robin and his band are extremely violent, and Robin's departure from the king suggests a clear preference for the life of an outlaw rather than that of a courtier. These contradictions have prompted disagreement among scholars over the meaning of Robin's rebellion and whether the story is ultimately sympathetic to the aristocracy or to the masses increasingly oppressed by an irredeemably corrupt system. A thematic analysis of antiauthoritarianism in the story and its late medieval context explores these questions, revealing the Gest to be an especially intriguing and subtle representation within the early Robin Hood tradition.

A Gest of Robyn Hode clearly reflects the earlier ballads from which it was compiled, but it is also quite distinct from them. As is true of much medieval literature, including the early ballads, the author of the Gest is unknown, and its date is uncertain, though most scholars now date it to approximately the 1450s or 1460s (Rennison 14). The story is presented in the form of a poem written in quatrains, or stanzas of four lines each, with a rhyme scheme of abcb and a ballad meter of four stresses on lines 1 and 3 of each stanza and three stresses on line 2. The adventures of Robin and his band largely derive from shorter ballads that were created earlier, but the form of the Gest is undeniably distinct. With 456 four-line stanzas, the poem runs to just over 1,800 lines and is divided into eight fits. Though the poem's opening stanza implies orality by inviting the audience to "listin" (listen), the poem's length and division into fits indicate a literary form. In addition, the poem is not simply longer than the earlier ballads but reflects an attempt to create a structure of interlaced events. For example, the knight who appears in the first fit reappears in the second, fourth, and sixth fits; Little John's conflict and eventual alliance with the sheriff's cook in fit 3 derives from the outlaw's service to the knight and prompts the sheriff to arrange an archery contest in fit 5 and appeal to the king in fit 6. This interlaced structure might seem awkward to modern readers who are accustomed to the modern novel's emphasis on character and events driven by cause and effect, but it is typical of medieval narrative and indicates an ambitious attempt to create a sophisticated story that goes beyond the achievements of the earlier ballads (Knight, *Complete Study* 74–75).

Just as the *Gest* differs from its early sources, the character of Robin differs from what many modern readers who know the hero primarily from modern stories and films may expect. Over the centuries, the character of Robin became increasingly gentrified, or linked to the upper classes, eventually becoming a lord. He serves King Richard the Lionheart in many stories and is often said to have participated in the Crusades. The king named in the *Gest* in stanzas 353, 384, and 450 is in fact Edward, not Richard, and although later tradition sometimes imagines Robin's adventures in the context of ethnic struggles or a war between the Saxons and the Normans, there is no such struggle in the early stories (Rennison 19). Later renditions also supply a love interest for Robin in the form of Maid Marian, who likewise does not appear in the early medieval stories. In fact, these early narratives rarely include any women at all. In the *Gest*, the only female characters are the knight's wife, who informs Robin of her husband's capture, and the wicked prioress, who conspires to murder Robin at the story's end. These differences add up to a very different Robin in the *Gest* compared with later sources, but if the medieval outlaw is not a dispossessed lord, a loyal follower of the king, or a romantic leading man, who is he, and how should one interpret this version of his story?

This question can best be addressed by sketching a portrait of the medieval culture that produced the story. Although the date of the poem is not absolutely certain, the text reflects the linguistic forms of Middle English, which was active roughly between the late twelfth and fifteenth centuries. As noted, the story also names the king as Edward, which is not necessarily a reliable indicator of date, but kings named Edward in fact reigned in England continuously from 1272 to 1377. The language, sources, historical details, and place names (such as Nottingham and Barnesdale) firmly place the text in a medieval English setting in the late thirteenth to early fifteenth centuries. Of course, vast changes occurred in English society during this time, but the fundamental structure of society remained organized around the three estates, or classes: the nobles, who fought wars; the clergy, who prayed for all; and the peasants, who labored in the fields. Society was controlled by the nobles and the clergy in a rigid hierarchy dominated ultimately by the king. Beneath the king were barons and earls and

senior clergymen. Then came the lesser nobles, including knights and squires, and middle-ranking clergymen. The ranks of middle-class attorneys and merchants increased throughout the later Middle Ages as the money economy developed. Most people belonged to the lowest class of peasants. The society was thus monarchical but also feudal, which meant that anyone who held land did so in service of someone else of higher status. Ultimately all land belonged to the king, whose power was absolute and was believed to derive from God. Peasants had few, if any, rights and were forced to work on their lords' lands several days each week, historian David Baldwin explains. Poverty and scarce employment meant there was no chance of escape. Baldwin notes that in this society, "if there was a basic assumption, it was that everyone ought to look after him or herself. The medieval state did not concern itself with the well-being of its citizens, and those who became ill or who fell on hard times could only hope that their lord, or perhaps the local abbey, would show them some compassion" (18).

Nonetheless, English society was not as stagnant as these words imply. The development of an economy based on capital fueled the explosive growth of merchant activity in the fourteenth century, which led to the development of a growing new middle class that challenged the three-estate structure. This growth was enabled partly by better living standards and increased population from the eleventh to the thirteenth centuries, as Baldwin states. The swelling population created greater demand for peasants to produce more food. At the same time, widespread institutional corruption grew as churches obtained extraordinary wealth and used it to influence secular affairs, even forcing peasants to work on their land. Local governments were likewise regarded as corrupt, and after the bubonic plague ravaged England's population between 1348 and 1350, a labor shortage allowed some peasants to demand better conditions and higher wages. When lords in Parliament subsequently attempted to suppress these improvements, they angered the peasants. Another source of popular discontent was the introduction of poll taxes, designed to finance wars, which effectively turned the peasants against the upper echelons of society. These and other events partly inspired the Peasants' Revolt of 1381, which began when inhabitants of the Essex village of Fobbing drove out a tax collector and subsequently attacked the chief justice who came to restore order. The revolt grew, and a group of rebels eventually stormed the Tower of London, destroyed government buildings, released prisoners, and executed several high government officials. King Richard II agreed to negotiate with the rebels but subsequently broke his promise and defeated them, ending the rebellion in the summer of 1381. Despite this defeat, the poll tax was later revoked, and some peasants continued to leverage their valuable labor power.

The Peasants' Revolt reveals deep and widespread dissatisfaction among the lower classes in fourteenth-century English society, particularly regarding economic injustice, and this context helps to explain the emergence of Robin Hood as a popular hero. But was there a historical Robin Hood who fueled the character's celebration in the early ballads? Scholars have debated whether Robin Hood is based on an actual outlaw. Although numerous possibilities have been suggested, historians have not reached consensus, and Nick Rennison and other writers believe that definitive evidence is unlikely ever to emerge. Yet even without historical evidence of a real Robin Hood, his popularity in stories and ballads invites explanation. Did the medieval Robin Hood emerge from popular social discontent among the lower classes? This question can be addressed here only in terms of the *Gest*, rather than the whole Robin Hood tradition. The salient question involves the ambiguous presentation of the outlaw in the *Gest*. How does the story actually portray Robin Hood and his loyalties, and what do his actions imply about the tale's motivations and audience?

A Gest of Robyn Hode reveals significant evidence that its hero is neither as radically rebellious nor as dedicated to the poor as one might think. In the beginning of the poem, Robin explicitly instructs his fellow outlaws not to harm farmers or good knights and squires. Instead, they should target bishops, archbishops, the Sheriff of Nottingham, barons, and earls, and in stanza 19, he also mentions abbots and knights as potential victims. However, the story most prominently shows Robin and his men robbing not the upper aristocracy, such as earls and barons, but lower clergymen and the sheriff. When Robin takes the king's forty pounds toward the story's end, the king is disguised as an abbot, and the episode ends with Robin agreeing to serve him at court. In stanza 386, Robin even declares that he loves the king best of all: "I loue no man in all the worlde / So well as I do my kynge" (75). Furthermore, the story concludes by praising Robin as a good outlaw who did poor men much good, but the key recipient of Robin's generosity is not a peasant but the knight, a member of the lower gentry. This knight becomes a prominent character in the poem,

and J. C. Holt argues that Robin's generosity to him conforms to the medieval knightly code of conduct. Robin's actions—lending the knight money on the security of Saint Mary, outfitting him in new clothes, and providing a horse—are indeed reminiscent of those of a medieval lord. In turn, Robin and his fellows eventually agree to serve the king and thus acknowledge him as their rightful sovereign. These details undermine Robin's role as defender and benefactor of the poor.

Robin's devotion to Saint Mary is another conservative element that the story repeatedly underscores. Robin lends money to the knight on the security of Saint Mary and nothing more, a trust that he takes seriously when he later fears she is angry with him because she has not brought the knight back to repay his debt: "I drede Our Lady be wroth with me, / For she sent me nat my pay" (66; st. 206). He repeats this sentiment in stanza 235, and Little John also emphasizes his devotion to God when he defies the sheriff, telling him, "I make myn auowe to God" (64; st. 165). Yet Robin and his band are even clearer about their lack of respect for religious authorities. The story dwells on the abbot's corrupt behavior regarding the knight and his debt; the abbot and the justice clearly want nothing more than to dispossess the knight of his lands, and the whole point of the knight asking for more time to pay (when he actually has the money) is apparently to highlight the abbot's utter mercilessness. Later, when the outlaw band encounters the two monks and their retinue of fifty-two men, Little John remarks that they appear more regal than any bishop: "There rydeth no bysshop in this londe / So ryally" (67; st. 216). Finally, encountering the king disguised as an abbot, Robin explains in no uncertain terms why he robs him, distinguishing himself and his men as yeomen of the forest who live by the king's deer, while the abbot should donate some of his extreme wealth for the sake of holy charity:

> 'And ye haue chyrches and rentës bothe,
> And gold full grete plentë;
> Gyue vs some of your spendynge,
> For sayntë charytë.' (74; st. 378)

The story thus carefully preserves Robin's religious devotion while attacking the institutional representatives of religion as hopelessly corrupt.

From these details, Robin emerges not as a radical rebel but as a representative of a "higher form of law, a thief who only steals from those who should not possess

HISTORICAL CONTEXT

The figure of Robin Hood has captivated not only audiences through-out the ages but also historians, who have searched in earnest for a real Robin Hood who might have inspired the character. Such historians have been encouraged by historical findings about the social and political climate during the late medieval period in which Robin Hood may have lived, a time of growing class tensions and rampant corruption in both religious and secular institutions. These institutions were regarded by some as increasingly oppressive and partly led to the Peasants' Revolt of 1381, when bands of peasants stormed the Tower of London and murdered several prominent officials but were ultimately suppressed.

There were certainly real outlaws in England, and bands such as the Folville brothers are described as having gained the sympathy of the common people, much like Robin Hood. Some have claimed a man named Robert (or Robin) of Locksley, born in the time of Richard I, as a possible historical counterpart, but his biography is of dubious origin. The names Robert Hood and Little John turn up in Scottish chronicles of the fifteenth century, but these contain biographical and other details inconsistent with the tradition.

Encouraged by the historical scholarship of sixteenth-century Scottish writer John Major, later chroniclers and fiction writers began to link a "real" Robin Hood to the twelfth-century English king Richard I, known as Richard the Lionheart. In the mid-eighteenth century, the antiquarian William Stukeley invented a family tree for Robin Hood. Still inconclusive but less dubious is the work of scholars such as Joseph Hunter, who found records indicating an early fourteenth-century relationship between an outlaw named Robert (or Robyn) Hood and King Edward II. However, numerous other possible candidates of the same name and outlaw status have also been identified, without conclusive results.

with the king: adherence to traditional morality matters more than social or class status.

Conservative elements notwithstanding, it would be a mistake to conclude that the *Gest* is a gentrified text catering to an aristocratic audience. Peter Coss points out that even if knights and squires ally with Robin in the ballad, such members of the gentry would not have appreciated a humiliating story about being saved from ruin by a social inferior such as Robin. Coss also finds a bit of mockery and parody in Robin's and Little John's treatment of the knight. Furthermore, Robin and his band are aggressive and violent; Little John fights with the sheriff's butler and cook, and Robin readily not only kills but also decapitates the sheriff and shows no remorse whatsoever for the deed. Finally, though Robin serves the king at court, he agrees to do so only by reserving his right to leave and ultimately makes his escape by claiming that he wishes to visit the chapel of Mary Magdalene. For these reasons, Coss argues that the poem's ideal world is not so far after all from what English peasants envisioned in the revolt of 1381. Like Robin and his band, who serve him by popular consensus, the peasants swore loyalty to the king but chose their own leaders in an attempt to free themselves of corrupt secular and religious authorities

so much," but his robberies result less in charity than in protecting "those who are his own affiliates" (Knight, *Complete Study* 1, 79). For this reason, scholars such as Roy Pearcy conclude that even though Robin and his band reflect characteristics of outlaws, they are really "a kind of government in exile" (68), a government not so different from that of feudal culture. According to Pearcy, Robin and company only "wage guerilla warfare against the current regime" (68) because its legal and religious institutions have been hopelessly corrupted by an increasingly commercial society, not because they believe the conventional hierarchy to be inherently flawed. This interpretation would account for Robin's support of the knight and his willingness to make peace

who compromised their livelihoods. Whether the *Gest* and other early Robin Hood stories were in fact inspired by historical class struggles and meant for rebellious sympathizers will likely continue to be a matter of debate. It is worth remembering, however, that in Knight's words the *Gest* "advocates massive theft from the church, civic insurrection against and murder of a properly appointed sheriff, [and] breach of legitimate agreement with a king" (*Complete Study* 81), and for these deeds, Robin is rewarded with twenty-two years of happy life in the forest before he is murdered. If this rebellion is simply a better brand of lordship, it also presents the possibility of serious resistance to oppressive authorities, a type of resistance that clearly interested medieval peasants and continues to enthrall modern audiences.

CROSS-CULTURAL INFLUENCE

Robin Hood's connection to economic justice has made him especially appealing to the postindustrial world, in which labor and class issues have become prominent. For US audiences, the hero is further linked to the outlaw tradition of the Wild West, the idea of the noble outlaw cowboy who embodies a higher form of justice independent from the lawless society he confronts. Robin Hood's modern appeal has prompted the creation of scores of new adaptations and interpretations, particularly in film. Since 1990, there have been more than a dozen films and programs based on this hero who has fascinated audiences for at least six centuries. Some of the most prominent modern films have included the animated *Young Robin Hood* (1991); *Robin Hood: Prince of Thieves* (1991), starring Kevin Costner; *Robin Hood* (1991), starring Patrick Bergin and Uma Thurman; and director and screenwriter Mel Brooks's 1993 spoof, *Robin Hood: Men in Tights*, starring Cary Elwes. Brooks's comic treatment is particularly interesting because it was not as successful as some of his other popular comedies, most notably *Blazing Saddles* (1974). Some critics perceived Brooks's treatment of Robin Hood as not funny enough but also as straying too far from a tradition largely dedicated to the outlaw hero as a noble figure. In fact, Brooks's highly American treatment is far more traditional than it might initially appear, as he incorporates techniques such as borrowing with change, localization, and comic transgression, which have been integral to the Robin Hood tradition throughout the centuries. *Robin Hood: Men in Tights* is thus an unexpected example of a version that is both highly Americanized and deeply traditional.

The film begins with Robin Hood, called Robin of Loxley, captured and imprisoned in Jerusalem, where he is fighting in the Crusades. In prison, he meets Asneeze, who has been convicted of jaywalking, and the two successfully break out of prison and free all the inmates. Before Robin departs for England, Asneeze gives him a picture of his son Ahchoo and asks him to look after the young man. Robin agrees and then swims back to England, elaborately kissing the sand when he finally lands on the beach. Unfortunately, however, he discovers from his blind servant, Blinkin, that Prince John has usurped the throne from his brother, King Richard the Lionheart, who is fighting in Jerusalem. John has dispossessed

Robin of his family property, even killing his pets, and as Robin arrives at his castle, John's men are pulling it away on giant wheels. To recover his family's possessions, Robin plans to stop John, who has levied oppressive taxes against the people. To do so, Robin gathers a band of followers, first among them Ahchoo, the unusually large Little John, and Will Scarlett O'Hara, who claims to be from Georgia. Along the way, he meets Maid Marian, a princess at John's castle who wears a metal chastity belt with the Everlast athletic-wear logo stamped on it. Seeking her true love, who has the key to her chastity belt, Marian becomes Robin's love interest. The outlaw band also meets Rabbi Tuckman, who sells discount circumcisions and sacramental wine.

While Robin is training his buffoonish band of Merry Men, the Sheriff of Rottingham, who is in league with Prince John, hires a mafioso named Don Giovanni to kill Robin during an archery contest at an upcoming fair. Overhearing these plans, Marian informs Robin of the plot against his life and begs him not to go to the fair, but Robin cannot resist and goes disguised as an old man. During the competition, he reveals his identity only to lose in the final round. Stunned at his loss, he suddenly pulls out a copy of the film script and discovers that he is supposed to have one more shot, and John and the sheriff confirm this with their own copies. Robin wins the final shot by using an arrow labeled "Patriot Arrow," which parodies a smart bomb by making elaborate turns before it hits its target.

When the assassination plot fails, the Sheriff of Rottingham orders Robin be seized and killed. Marian intervenes and promises to marry the sheriff, who has pursued her throughout the story, if he will spare Robin's life. The sheriff agrees but has Robin brought to the hangman's scaffold, in view of the wedding altar, in case Marian should change her mind. During the wedding ceremony, which is conducted in pig Latin, Marian is about to pronounce her vow when the Merry Men ambush the executioner and rescue Robin. A battle ensues, during which the sheriff carries Marian off to rape her in the tower. Robin extricates himself from the battle and finds the sheriff attempting to remove Marian's belt with a drill. A sword fight ensues, which Robin finally wins accidentally by running the sheriff through while trying to sheathe his sword. As the sheriff is dying, the witch Latrine appears and saves his life with a magic pill on the condition that he agrees to marry her. Saved by the pill, the sheriff is dragged off by Latrine as he cries in despair that he has changed his mind. Just as Marian and Robin attempt to remove her belt with the key that he alone holds, Marian's German maid, Broomhilde, bursts in to stop them, insisting they marry first. Rabbi Tuckman presides over the wedding ceremony, which is interrupted by the return of King Richard, who insists on following the custom of kissing the bride before the wedding. Richard then has his brother John imprisoned and names all the toilets in the kingdom after him. After the wedding, Ahchoo is made the new sheriff. The film concludes with the credits rolling and Robin's and Marian's voices describing their wedding night, during which they must call for a blacksmith after the key will not unlock Marian's chastity belt.

The film is farcical from start to finish, and the relentless silliness suggests an overall product concerned with little more than pure parody of the Robin Hood tradition. The film's particular brand of lowbrow parody and the many corny and sometimes offensive jokes prompted poor reviews. In Stephen Knight's words, the film's "travesty of outlaw nobility" was "so crass it made [the critics] cross" ("*Robin Hood*" 461). To be sure, the story incorporates certain features basic to the later tradition, including the notion of Robin fighting with Richard in the Crusades, a noble hero dispossessed of his lands, and Maid Marian. The characters of Little John and Will are also preserved. Yet the story does not address in any way certain issues fundamental to the tradition: though Prince John levies oppressive taxes, there is no development of social or class conflict or of corrupt authorities who possess too much wealth. Likewise, the film does not explore issues of heritage, individualism, or nationalism. The romance found in the later tradition is mainly reduced to the joke of Marian's chastity belt.

In addition, the film's humor is constant but with uneven results, sometimes entertaining and sometimes falling flat. Characters and jokes that work well include the oversized Little John, who in one scene flails about, terrified of drowning in a few inches of water, and Rabbi Tuckman, played brilliantly by Mel Brooks, who offers discount circumcisions with the advertisement "half off." Certain of the silly jokes also work, including the ridiculous beach scene in which Robin chokes and sputters after kissing the sand and his accidental slaying of the sheriff after a long battle filled with impressive swordsmanship. However, some of the humor is tedious and conveys a sense of being overdone. Details such as the Rent a Wreck sign on the backside of Robin's horse, the men who literally throw their ears

when Robin commands, "Lend me your ears," and the attempt to send a message quickly by "foxing" (that is, strapping a message onto a fox), rather than faxing, pile up and rapidly become tiresome. Some of the film's humor is potentially offensive as well, such as the use of Blinkin's blindness to create bumbling slapstick scenes, the sheriff's attempted rape of Marian, and the stereotypical aspects of the characters Ahchoo and Broomhilde. For all of these reasons, critics were underwhelmed by the film.

However, as Knight argues, a closer look reveals that the film in fact uses conventional techniques in a way that establishes Brooks's treatment firmly within the long revisionist tradition of Robin Hood tales. Specifically, Knight argues that Brooks borrows elements while altering them slightly, uses local references, and employs comic transgression, which have all been common strategies throughout centuries of Robin Hood stories. The character of Marian is an example of borrowing with change, as Brooks makes her a noble lady as in earlier sources but hints at the saucy, unladylike Marian who appears early in the tradition as a friar's mistress. Perhaps the most significant use of borrowing with change occurs in the film's countless references to and parodies of the many films that preceded Brooks's version. According to Knight, the film's opening sequence of flaming arrows is a burlesque of an episode of the 1984 television series *Robin of Sherwood* and of *Robin Hood: Prince of Thieves*. In another opening scene, the villagers complain that their village is burned every time a film is made, a self-referential joke that also refers to *Robin of Sherwood*. With his accent, costume, and habit of stroking his beard, Cary Elwes, who plays Robin in Brooks's film, parodies Errol Flynn in the starring role of the 1938 film *The Adventures of Robin Hood*. In one of many references to Kevin Costner, the star of *Robin Hood: Prince of Thieves*, Brooks's Robin claims to be the true hero because, unlike Costner, he can speak with an English accent. These references to earlier films are therefore part of an aesthetic response that makes the film more sophisticated but is also a thoroughly traditional technique.

Localization is a very common feature in Robin Hood tales and began early in the tradition, as the *Gest of Robyn Hode* shows in its specific references to Barnesdale and Nottingham. Here, Brooks localizes the film firmly within the American Hollywood milieu, referring not only to previous Robin Hood films but also to many other classics. When Robin arrives on English shores, he sees a giant sign reading "ENGLAND" in the style of the famous Hollywood sign gracing the hills of Los Angeles. Will Scarlett O'Hara is an obvious reference to *Gone with the Wind* (1939), and the Don Giovanni character parodies Marlon Brando's performance as Don Vito Corleone in *The Godfather* (1972). The film is self-referential in general ways as well: when Robin initially loses the archery contest, he reacts in disbelief by pulling out the script to check what is supposed to happen. Knight claims that such "self-conscious burlesque is the essence of comic transgressiveness" ("*Robin Hood*" 466), which appears even in the earliest ballads. This self-consciousness is also prominent in the presence of an Arab maître d' named Felafel in the beginning dungeon scene, the repossession of Loxley castle on mobile home–type rollers, and Robin's promise to the people to protect forests and provide health care, among other scenes (466). These details emphasize the film's twentieth-century American cultural context, which is celebrated through highly traditional techniques. Ultimately, even if the film does not meet the artistic standards of greatness that audiences have come to expect of Robin Hood stories, Brooks nonetheless proves remarkably conservative in his comic lowbrow version of a tale that will no doubt continue to flourish.

Ashleigh Imus, PhD

BIBLIOGRAPHY

Baldwin, David. "Prologue: Robin Hood's World." *Robin Hood: The English Outlaw Unmasked*. Gloucestershire: Amberley, 2011. Print.

Child, Francis James, ed. *A Gest of Robyn Hode. The English and Scottish Popular Ballads*. Vol. 3. New York: Copper Square, 1965. 39–88. Print.

Coss, Peter R. "Aspects of Cultural Diffusion in Medieval England: Robin Hood." Knight, *Anthology* 329–44.

Hahn, Thomas. *Robin Hood in Popular Culture: Violence, Transgression, and Justice*. Cambridge: Brewer, 2000. Print.

Holt, J. C. "The Origins and Audience of the Ballads of Robin Hood." Knight, *Anthology* 211–32.

Knight, Stephen, ed. *Robin Hood: An Anthology of Scholarship and Criticism*. Cambridge: Brewer, 1999. Print.

---. *Robin Hood: A Complete Study of the English Outlaw*. Oxford: Blackwell, 1994. Print.

---. "*Robin Hood: Men in Tights*: Fitting the Tradition Snugly." Knight, *Anthology* 461–69.

Pearcy, Roy. "The Literary Robin Hood: Character and Function in Fitts 1, 2 and 4 of the *Gest of Robyn Hode*." *Robin Hood: Medieval and Post-Medieval*. Ed. Helen Phillips. Dublin: Four Courts, 2005. 60–69. Print.

Rennison, Nick. *Robin Hood: Myth, History & Culture*. Harpenden: Pocket Essentials, 2012. Print.

Maya Hero Twins: Hunahpu and Xbalanque

Author: Traditional Maya
Time Period: 999 BCE–1 BCE; 1501 CE–1700 CE
Country or Culture: Central America
Genre: Myth

OVERVIEW

The culture of the ancient Maya people has taken on something like a legendary status in modern times. Established around 2000 BCE near what today is the border of Mexico and Guatemala, Maya civilization would grow over thousands of years to include millions of people, diverse ethnic groups, thriving city-states, and some of the most advanced understandings of science and written languages in pre-Columbian Mesoamerica. Despite the many accomplishments of the Maya civilization, however, much of its history has been lost to time. This is largely due to two major periods of decline, one in the second century CE and one in the eighth to ninth, as well as to invasion and violent oppression by Europeans in the sixteenth century. While Maya culture thrived beyond the periods of decline and colonization, the destruction that came along with those periods has made it difficult for modern historians and archaeologists to re-create a detailed understanding of ancient Maya life. This lack of information, combined with evidence of extraordinary advancements by the Maya people, has made ancient Maya culture fascinating to many contemporary scholars as well as to the public.

What has remained despite the expanse of time is a rich and varied mythology, preserved through some extant literary traditions as well as through the ornate pottery, architecture, and artwork of the Maya people. One of the most popular myths from the ancient Maya world is that of Hunahpu (sometimes spelled Junajpu) and Xbalanque, the Hero Twins. Master players of the Maya ball game, the brothers go on many adventures through Maya mythology, conquering monsters with their legendary wits and exploring the Mesoamerican world. It is their origin story, however, for which they are most often celebrated. Born from their deceased father, Hun Hunahpu (One Hunahpu), the brothers are summoned to the underworld of Xibalba by the Lords of Death. There, they go through many trials that test their wits, only to survive and defeat the Lords of Death in a ball game. Sacrificing themselves so that they can be reborn, the brothers are ultimately clever enough to outwit the lords, killing the two most powerful among them and finally ascending to the sky as the sun and the moon.

The story of Hunahpu and Xbalanque extant today came down through a sixteenth-century text recorded by the K'iche' (Quiché) people of Guatemala but based on centuries of oral storytelling. Because of this, the myth of the Hero Twins provides a unique insight into Maya mythology. The sixteenth-century narrative, called the *Popol Vuh* (or *Popol Wuj*), shows how the K'iche' people during the end of the postclassic period understood the Hero Twins as well as some of the rituals and traditions associated with death. By looking also at ancient Maya architecture across North and South America, however, it becomes clear that the specifics of the myth were as varied over time as the diverse ethnic and cultural groups that told the stories. Ultimately, the myth of the Hero Twins offers a rare opportunity to understand ancient Maya culture as a dynamic, thriving civilization, its sophisticated understanding of death in a state of continual evolution.

SUMMARY

Before the birth of humanity live Hun Hunahpu (One Hunahpu) and Vucub Hunahpu (Seven Hunahpu), twin brothers who are excellent ballplayers. They spend all their time playing the game, causing a ruckus on the court, which is located on the road to the underworld, Xibalba. Eventually, the noise from their game bothers the twelve lords of Xibalba enough that they send for the brothers, instructing them to bring their equipment along. While the brothers answer the summons, they hide their ball-playing equipment in their mother's house.

The brothers travel across rivers of spikes, blood, and pus and follow Black Road at the crossroads, eventually coming to the courtroom of the Lords of Death. They see the lords standing there and greet them by name, only to realize that the figures before them are actually wooden statues. The brothers know they have been tricked when the actual lords step forward, telling them not to worry about their mistake and offering them a seat. The bench, however, is scalding hot, and when the brothers sit down, they are immediately burned. They then fail to keep their torch and cigar burning through the night they spend in Dark House. Having outwitted the twins three times, the Lords of Death sacrifice them, burying their bodies under the ball court.

The head of Hun Hunahpu, removed before the burial, is placed in a tree. One day, Xquic (Blood Woman), the daughter of one of the Xibalban lords, comes upon the tree, and when she investigates the head, it spits saliva into her hand. This saliva impregnates Xquic, greatly angering her father, who attempts to have her sacrificed. She convinces the would-be executioners to substitute the fragrant, gelatinous croton sap for her heart as the sacrifice and then makes her way to the upper world, where she eventually gives birth to the Hero Twins, Hunahpu and Xbalanque. As they grow older, the twins one day try to make a garden, but as soon as they clear any land, the animals of the forest drag brush back over it. Frustrated, the brothers catch a rat in the act of moving branches. They begin to burn it alive, but the rat tells them he knows something they are more suited for than making gardens. He then leads them to their grandmother's house, where he runs loose in the walls while the brothers convince their grandmother to make them chili sauce and to fetch them water. When she is gone, the rat releases the hidden ball equipment for the twins, the same equipment that their father and uncle had used.

The twins are likewise great ballplayers, and it is not long before their shouts attract the attention of the Lords of Death, who are upset that they have not learned to be more humble. The lords fetch the Hero Twins, and their grandmother is certain they will die. However, they have more wit than the previous twins. Arriving in Xibalba, one brother unleashes a mosquito on the lords. As

"'Get up!' he said, and Hunahpu came back to life. The two of them were overjoyed at this—and likewise the lords rejoiced, as if they were doing it themselves. One and Seven Death were as glad at heart as if they themselves were actually doing the dance.

And then the hearts of the lords were filled with longing, with yearning for the dance of Hunahpu and Xbalanque, so then came these words from One and Seven Death:

'Do it to us! Sacrifice us!' they said. 'Sacrifice both of us!'"

Popol Vuh

the mosquito bites every lord, the wooden statues stay perfectly still, while the real lords cry out in alarm. As the lords call each other by name, the Hero Twins are able to greet only the real rulers. Likewise, they recognize the bench to be a cooking griddle and decline the seat that is offered to them.

The Hero Twins, after having played two matches against the Lords of Death, are then set to new tasks. The lords put them in a number of test houses, including Jaguar House, Razor House, Fire House, and Cold House. Every house has its own challenges, and the brothers outwit every scenario. The only exception comes in the last house, where Hunahpu peeks outside their hiding spot and has his head cut off by a snatch-bat. As the head rolls onto the ball court, the brothers place a squash on top of Hunahpu's neck and tell a rabbit to hide in the goal. The Lords of Death then challenge them to a game on the field, using Hunahpu's head for a ball. During the game, however, the brothers deflect the ball at the same moment the rabbit goes running away from the field. With the lords distracted, they switch the squash for Hunahpu's head, and playing with the squash, they manage to defeat the lords on the court.

The Hero Twins know that the lords will not stop until they are dead, so when given the chance, they jump into a hot stove and are burned alive. The brothers know that through this form of death they can be resurrected, coming back first as fish and then in their original forms. Reborn, they are magical tricksters, traveling the realm and performing wonders for all people. The Lords of Death, hearing of their magic, summon them for a performance. Back in Xibalba, Xbalanque performs a trick in which he dismembers Hunahpu before the lords and then puts Hunahpu back together, resurrecting him. The lords are pleased and demand to be dismembered and resurrected by the brothers. The brothers agree, but after they have sacrificed the two most powerful lords, Hun Came (One Death) and Vucub Came (Seven Death), they instead leave them dead. In this way, the brothers outsmart death and rob Xibalba of its great glory. Knowing their success, they reassemble Vucub Hunahpu's body, leaving him beside the ball court and consecrating his calendar day for veneration of the dead. The brothers then ascend to the heavens, becoming the sun and the moon.

ANALYSIS
The ancient Maya myth of the Hero Twins comes to the modern day through a document known as the *Popol Vuh*. Recorded during the middle of the sixteenth century—around the time that the Spanish invaded and conquered the Maya lands—the document is a compilation of much older mythological stories, many of which seem to have existed in oral traditions for many centuries. In this way, while the *Popol Vuh* relays some of the myths and stories particular to the K'iche' people, one of the dominant ethnic groups within Maya culture during the time of Spanish invasion, it also provides one of the most detailed accounts of an older Maya mythology that was likely transmitted by multiple ethnicities for well over a millennium. However, because Maya civilization went into a heavy decline for unknown reasons at the end of what is known as the classic period, around the ninth century, little to no primary documentation of earlier mythologies and traditions remains today.

Because of this history, the story of the Hero Twins plays a significant role in modern understanding of ancient Maya culture and mythology. The Hero Twins are prominent in the *Popol Vuh*, with their origin story and subsequent adventures taking up a majority of the text. By connecting that narrative to surviving artwork and monuments as well as the scant other pieces of extant

literature, scholars have been able to piece together a far more detailed picture of ancient Maya belief than would otherwise be possible. While the implications of the story of the Hero Twins are far ranging, the story of their origin has a fairly clear meaning and focus. As in many Mesoamerican cultural traditions, myths in Maya culture primarily served to clarify the role between humanity and the cosmos. At times, this meant that myths would explore the relationship between humanity and various aspects of nature, between individual humans and the gods, or between human civilization and astrology. In the case of the origin of the Hero Twins, the myth is firmly rooted in the relationship between human culture and death itself. Instead of providing a firm moral or lesson about death, however, the myth develops the traditions that surround death, helping to infuse with meaning the games, rituals, and artwork that Maya culture associated with the underworld. Recorded during the sixteenth century, it also provides a unique look into the K'iche' culture at the time and its own relationship to Maya mythological history.

The myth begins not with the Hero Twins, Hunahpu and Xbalanque, but with their father and uncle, Hun Hunahpu and Vucub Hunahpu. This focus on the previous generation is important in that it establishes the myth as a story of transformation and growth. While some mythological and religious traditions develop a cosmology of the world that is fixed, viewing the relationship between humans and nature or humans and gods as permanent and unchanging, the Maya mythology is instead a mythology of change. Hun Hunahpu and Vucub Hunahpu, being the twins that precede the Hero Twins, represent an even earlier form of Maya culture in which the relationship between humans and the underworld is more limited, with humans having even less power and freedom than the Hero Twins will eventually demonstrate. Importantly, Hunahpu and Xbalanque themselves also precede humanity, their stories taking place in a time of deities and supernatural beings before the creation of humans. The myth of the Hero Twins, then, goes back beyond K'iche' culture and beyond the classic period, showing the roots of Maya civilization struggling with the reality of death. As one generation fails and another succeeds, that struggle is not a narrative of simple triumph but rather a narrative continually developing that relationship alongside civilization itself.

While Hun Hunahpu and Vucub Hunahpu are different in several ways from Hunahpu and Xbalanque, they share a commonality in their love for the ball game,

HISTORICAL CONTEXT

In addition to being one of the richest sources of Maya mythology, the *Popol Vuh* is also unique as a historical document, tracking the genealogy of rulers and other important political information from ancient K'iche' culture and the broader Maya world that surrounded it.

As early as the third century BCE, Maya civilization was the home of sprawling urban centers with populations numbering as high as 100,000. Most of these city-states, such as El Mirador, were located in what is today Guatemala, although the civilization itself stretched much farther than that. While these cities thrived for centuries, by the time that the *Popol Vuh* begins to detail the political history of the Maya civilization, those major city-states had been all but abandoned. The new city-states that arose helped usher in the classic period, a period in which political rulers organized millions of citizens, building giant pyramids and ornate temples to the gods, all funded by expansive trade routes.

Throughout the centuries, city-states rose and fell, the centers of power shifting through the Maya land. It was in this context that the K'iche' kingdom came to establish power toward the very end of the classic period. By the eighth or ninth century CE, the major centers of power in the lowlands of Guatemala were in serious decline, and the K'iche' kingdom in the highlands was able to establish some power. The K'iche' people would come to dominate the postclassic period, relying on a strict social class structure in order to support a military that expanded their borders and drew on the natural resources of the land. While the K'iche' kingdom might well have held power for much longer, it was conquered in 1524 by the Spanish invader Pedro de Alvarado, the K'iche' army having already been weakened by war with the Aztec people and diseases brought from Europe.

sometimes called *pitz*. Ball games were an important cultural event in ancient Maya civilization, just as they were in many other Mesoamerican cultures. The game often featured the use of a large rubber ball (rubber trees being common in many parts of Mesoamerica) and two teams of two or three players. While the particular rules varied greatly over time and location, generally players used their hips or shoulders to keep the ball moving, with a team losing points if the ball bounced more than twice, went out of bounds, or crossed a goal line. Players may have earned points by hitting markers or passing the ball through stone hoops set high around the court. There are no historical records detailing the specifics of how the ancient Mayas might have played this game or what its exact cultural meaning might have been. However, the large and ornate stone courts in almost all the major Maya cities have provided some clues. Likewise, equipment for cruder versions of the game has been found throughout the regions occupied by Maya and Aztec civilizations. Based on these artifacts, archaeologists have concluded that the game was played in casual settings among friends but also as an aspect of elaborate cultural and political rituals. The courts in major cities are all adorned with drawings of human sacrifice, war, and defeat, suggesting that the ritualized games might have been a way to dramatize major conflicts as well as mythological traditions, with the losing teams often becoming sacrifices to the gods in the preclassic and classic periods. Importantly, alongside these drawings there are almost always additional drawings of Hunahpu and Xbalanque, showing the link that connects the Hero Twins, the ball game, and death to be an ancient one.

When Hun Hunahpu and Vucub Hunahpu are summoned by the Lords of Death, this long tradition of ritualized games has not yet begun. Instead, they are simply two brothers excited by the recreation of the game and their own mastery over its challenges. They cannot raucously enjoy their sport, however, without incurring the ire of the Lords of Death, who are irritated both by the disruption the twins cause and by their audacious display of talent. One of the important ways that Maya mythology explains the relationship between humans and death is by explaining the roots of the rituals associated with the underworld. In this context, Hun Hunahpu and Vucub Hunahpu are representative of the risk that comes along with combat, competition, and displays of strength. They are at first simply playing their game as two brothers, but when they become too rowdy and too strong, that game is interrupted and they are dragged from the joyful realm of the ball court into the deadly and terrifying realm of Xibalba, punished for acting in a manner unfit for humans.

In contrast to the strength and physical prowess the brothers show on the ball court, in the realm of Xibalba, they are tested on their wit and intellect. There, they somewhat foolishly mistake wooden statues for the Lords of Death and agree to sit on a hot bench. While the mistakes themselves might seem relatively minor in the grand scope of the myth, the very fact that the Lords of Death trick the brothers is enough to secure the failure of the twins, resulting in their sacrifice. This scene is important as a moment of evolution in the Maya culture. While K'iche' people in the sixteenth century already had firmly established meanings attached to the ball game and to death rituals, they were also aware of competing traditions and of a long Maya history in which the ceremonies surrounding death had changed. Likewise, sacrificial death seems to have fallen out of favor within sixteenth-century K'iche' culture, and myths such as this helped to establish a distance between the sacrificial Maya traditions and the rituals that gained favor in the centuries before Spanish invasion. Hun Hunahpu and Vucub Hunahpu, then, are figures who fail because they do not understand the complicated and subtle rules of the "game" of death, both becoming too rowdy on the court of life and demonstrating a lack of awareness in Xibalba. While the Hero Twins themselves will go on to become champions of K'iche' culture, Hun Hunahpu and Vucub Hunahpu are a reminder that that the relationship between humanity and the underworld has not always been properly respected, often to the detriment of civilization.

While Hun Hunahpu and Vucub Hunahpu meet their death, they do, however, contribute to the eventual success of the Hero Twins. Before they learn to play the ball game, Hunahpu and Xbalanque first are led to the equipment that their father and uncle had hidden away. In using their wit to uncover the equipment, the Hero Twins both pick up the tradition started by the previous generation and use their own intelligence to move that tradition forward. This again makes clear that there is not a firm divide between the failure of the previous generation and the success of the K'iche' culture heroes; rather, every generation is obligated to sustain what has already been established while using its own wits to advance the meaning behind those traditions. Because of this, once the Hero Twins have acquired the equipment, they fall into the same pattern that Hun Hunahpu and

Vucub Hunahpu began, being as boisterous and shameless as their forebears. However, they have more knowledge to work from and so a better chance to succeed.

Once the Hero Twins enter Xibalba, however, they cease to follow the path of the previous generation. Instead, they begin a long process of gaining self-knowledge through death, eventually using that knowledge to overcome the Lords of Death themselves. While Hunahpu and Xbalanque appear to be alive throughout this myth, even transcending death and "living" forever as the sun and moon at its conclusion, they essentially die in order to enter the realm of the underworld. It is important to remember that they are continually in this liminal space between life and death, as it is only by dying that the Hero Twins can learn the lessons necessary to transcend the limitations of the underworld. This philosophy is reflected in the archaeology and artwork of the ball game as well as the role of sacrifice in ancient Maya culture. The end of life, while associated with the fearsome Lords of Death and certainly cause for lament, is also a fundamental aspect of the culture itself. The violent ball game and the ritual sacrifice of the losers that often followed ceremonial matches were not simply examples of lurid entertainment but rather rituals that emphasized death as an integral part of life, an inevitable experience in order to attain complete self-knowledge. While K'iche' culture came to separate itself from most ritual sacrifice, the value of death itself was still honored. The time the Hero Twins spend in Xibalba is a time during which they essentially sacrifice themselves, briefly becoming the objects of death in order that they might ultimately emerge and champion the Maya culture.

Within Xibalba, the triumph of the Hero Twins is again established not through physical strength but through their reliance on wit and intelligence. Hunahpu and Xbalanque are trickster figures, which distinguishes them from the Lords of Death, who are gods holding power over humanity. In Mesoamerican mythology, trickster figures, while often supernatural, rarely possess any power that allows them to control the world or other people. Instead, they represent individuals using their intelligence to overcome systems in which they have limited actual power. In the case of Hunahpu and Xbalanque, they face a firm reality (the inevitability of death) made real through the powerful Lords of Death. Just as humanity can never truly overcome physical death, the Hero Twins also must go through the process of dying, entering Xibalba and subjecting themselves to the challenges of the Lords of Death. However, they somewhat whimsically survive through these challenges, convincing the razors of Razor House to chop something else and feeding bones to the animals of Jaguar House to distract them. This creates a direct parallel with human life: individuals can use their intelligence and the tools of their culture to survive freezing temperatures, fires, animal attacks, and all the other challenges presented in Xibalba, even if they will inevitably still meet a physical death.

After the Hero Twins survive the mortal threats of the houses in Xibalba, their struggle with the Lords of Death moves again to the ball game. The ball game is the first instance in which the brothers begin to transcend death rather than simply endure their experience. When Hunahpu is decapitated, he does not die as he should but rather is kept alive with the assistance of numerous animals, a squash temporarily placed on his neck as a replacement head. This nod to the powerful gods of Maya mythology again establishes the inability of the trickster figures to overcome death on their own. What they are able to do, however, is succeed through the forum of the ball game, a symbol of Maya culture. In playing against the Lords of Death on the field, they perform an elaborate trick, winning back Hunahpu's head and ultimately winning the game as well. Based on the ancient drawings ornamenting the ball courts in major cities, this myth appears to be at the root of the ritualized games popular in ancient times. When teams played one another in spiritual ceremonies, then, they were acting out the triumph of Maya culture over the forces of death. That one team still had to admit defeat (and often face sacrifice) following these games acknowledges the inevitability of individual death while still celebrating the culture and traditions that survive.

For Hunahpu and Xbalanque to succeed, however, they cannot simply win the ball game. Instead, they must inhabit both roles, becoming victors as well as sacrificial objects. Because of this, while the Lords of Death continue scheming to find ways to kill the brothers, the Hero Twins instead jump into a burning furnace, knowing that through this form of death they can be resurrected. This self-sacrifice allows them access to magical knowledge, not only enabling them to resurrect one another but also giving them the ability to control fires and bring animals back to life. When they return, they also have different physical appearances, their forms altered but their essences remaining the same, further indicating the complex relationship between change and

tradition that is always at the heart of the myth. It is by completing the cycle of life, by literally and figuratively enduring sacrificial death, that the Hero Twins are able to gain this power. This again recognizes the history of human sacrifices while moving the culture forward to something more peaceful: because death is a natural and inescapable aspect of life, it should be treated with respect, honored as another aspect of the ongoing cycle.

Having acquired their new power, Hunahpu and Xbalanque trick the Lords of Death one last time, killing the two most powerful of them. While the remaining lords flee and are left to live, affirming the ongoing reality of death, the honor given to death and to Xibalba is greatly diminished: "Such was the beginning of their disappearance and the denial of their worship. . . . Such was the loss of their greatness and brilliance. Their domain did not return to greatness" (Tedlock 158). This conclusion firmly marks the critique by the K'iche' culture of earlier forms of Maya worship. The Lords of Death themselves are sacrificed, reversing the dynamic in which humans must be made subservient to the underworld and demonstrating that there is no longer a strong need for human sacrifice, even as the myth confirms that such a need once existed. In fact, the twins themselves announce, "There will be no cleanly blotted blood for you, just griddles, just gourds, just brittle things broken to pieces. Further, you will only feed on creatures of the meadows and clearings. None of those who are born in the light, begotten in the light will be yours" (157–58). This understanding of the myth is also tied firmly to the long history of the Hero Twins among diverse Maya ethnic groups. Rather than being a fixed story that celebrated the accomplishments of one group, the story of the Hero Twins is a set of oral narratives with details dependent on the cultures that told those narratives. In its conclusion, the story of Hunahpu and Xbalanque shows not only triumph over the underworld but also the continuation of K'iche' culture after the more violent cultural traditions that preceded it, Hunahpu and Xbalanque having secured a world in which constant subservience to the Lords of Death is no longer necessary.

The conclusion of the myth returns once more to the cultures of the past. Hunahpu and Xbalanque recover the body of their forefather Vucub Hunahpu, partially resurrecting him. They then rise into the sky as the sun and the moon. These two gestures affirm the continual, cyclical nature of Maya culture as a whole. Hun Hunahpu and Vucub Hunahpu can never be fully resurrected, their moment having passed. However, the twins are "respectful of their father's heart," and Vucub Hunahpu is left in a state of honor by the Place of Ball Game Sacrifice (159), signifying both the integration of the Maya world with the underworld and the respect the Hero Twins hold for the past. As the sun and the moon, they also then represent the cycles of life, with both figures traversing daily between the realm of day and the realm of night. These final affirmations confirm the Hero Twins as culture heroes. They explain the meaning of ancient rituals, secure the value of death within Maya culture, and elevate their own society. While so much of Mesoamerican cultural history is tragically lost to time, the enduring story of Hunahpu and Xbalanque remains a testament to the sophisticated Maya understanding of death and humanity not as oppositional forces, but rather as interdependent aspects of the universe, each honored through the continuation of ritual and myth.

CROSS-CULTURAL INFLUENCE

As Spanish invaders violently overtook the people of Mesoamerica in the sixteenth century, they brought with them their religious beliefs. While economic and material interests were certainly at the heart of the colonization of the Americas, many colonizers also justified their activities through religion, believing that they were justly spreading the word of Catholicism to a people they saw as primitive and unenlightened. For the people of Mesoamerica, there was hardly much of a choice between taking on the Christian religious practices brought by Spanish invaders (and later by colonizers from other European nations) and continuing their own traditions. Instead, amid the genocide and war of invasion, first Catholicism and then other forms of Christianity were forced upon the Maya people, as they were upon almost every indigenous group.

While the violence of colonization took a heavy toll on the indigenous spiritual traditions of Mesoamerica, the mythology and sacred beliefs did not die out. Instead, stories such as those from the *Popol Vuh* and the worship of indigenous gods continued through a practice called syncretism. Present in almost every cultural and spiritual tradition throughout the world, syncretism is the combination of different beliefs or practices into a new tradition. This practice occurs most often when two cultural groups with divergent spiritual traditions interact, whether through war, colonization, or trade. Groups then often find similarities between the two sets of beliefs, developing a symbolism and a tradition that

incorporates both in subtle and complex ways. In the case of K'iche' Maya culture, it is through syncretism that the Hero Twins most often survived into the modern day, the parallels between their own story and the story of Jesus Christ highlighted through a newly syncretic spirituality.

Before the syncretism necessitated by colonization began, however, Maya culture was involved in a constant exchange of traditions, both within its far-reaching borders and with other native people. This form of syncretism is more difficult for modern academics to track, both because of the destruction wrought by European colonizers and because most indigenous mythologies were spread through oral traditions, leaving no permanent record. This resulted in a type of continual syncretism, with different ethnicities repeatedly adapting new ideas and narratives into their own mythologies. The myth of the Hero Twins, for instance, ends with Hunahpu and Xbalanque ascending into the sky as the sun and the moon. Because of this, the brothers play an important role in the Maya calendar and in Maya astrology, especially among the K'iche' people. The same basic idea can be seen in the neighboring Aztec tradition, in which the gods Nanahuatzin and Tecuiçiztecatl sacrifice themselves by jumping into a hot fire so that they might be reborn as the sun and the moon. While the scene of the two figures jumping into the fire is a direct parallel with the myth of the Hero Twins, there are also several indirect parallels in the Aztec myth, primary among them the fact that the other Aztec gods, seeing how hot the sun burns, then sacrifice themselves in order to lessen its heat and ensure that humanity might live. While the death of the gods is presented differently in the Aztec narrative than in the K'iche' myth, the similarities in theme and story are enough to indicate the clear influence of one upon the other. However, because of the lack of historical information as well as the reality of constant syncretism, it remains unclear whether the Aztecs could be said to have influenced the Maya or vice versa.

Considering that the Aztec and Maya civilizations were in constant contact because of their geographical proximity, parallels such as those between the story of Hunahpu and Xbalanque and that of Nanahuatzin and Tecuiçiztecatl are hardly surprising. However, stories of twin brothers who serve as culture heroes are also relatively popular across North and South America. Certainly, human cultures around the globe have repeatedly featured heroic twins, including the Gemini twins

Castor and Pollux in Greek mythology and the twin horsemen of Hindu mythology, the Aśvins (Ashvins). However, the stories of heroic twins found in cultures across the Americas demonstrate far more similarities than any of the stories between continents.

One such example comes from the Winnebago and Ioway peoples of the Great Plains of North America. In the story, the hero Red Horn is killed by giants in a wrestling match. At the time of his death, however, two of his wives are pregnant, and they give birth to two young boys of legendary strength and skill in battle. While the boys are technically not twins, the drawings and depictions of them in the Winnebago and Ioway cultures almost always present them as identical to one another. As in the myth of the Maya Hero Twins, the two boys recover the decapitated head of their father, although in the Plains traditions that head is in the possession of the giants rather than hidden away in the underworld and protected by the Lords of Death. The sons of Red Horn engage in an astounding battle with the giants, slaughtering almost all of the monsters and exiling the surviving few to other parts of the world. Once they return with the head of their father, they use their powers to resurrect him, first scattering the powdered bones of the giants. While the parallels between the two myths are enough to suggest a strong link between the Maya story and the Plains story, there is no actual record of contact between the Maya and Plains peoples, and a large number of tribes and ethnic groups lived between the Great Plains of North America and the Mesoamerican region that was home to the Maya culture. Instead of suggesting a direct link, with the Plains peoples learning the story from the Mayas, the similarities between these mythological stories of heroic brothers suggest an influence and a syncretism that subtly spread over centuries. Considering the size of Maya culture and particularly of Maya trade routes, it is not surprising that popular stories—primary among them the mythology of the Hero Twins—might slowly have made their way to distant tribes and there been integrated into the mythologies that already existed.

In contrast to the mystery surrounding pre-Columbian mythology, it is much easier for scholars to track the syncretism of Mesoamerican mythology with Catholic spiritual beliefs following the Spanish invasion. There is still, of course, a great deal of information that remains lost from the classic period of Maya history, but the combination of written records and the presence of European mythology following the sixteenth century allows for a more detailed study of the myths' influences. One example studied by historian Margarita Vargas-Bettancourt comes through the mythology surrounding Tepozteco, a hero derived from Tepoztecatl, the Aztec god of drunkenness and the wind. Tepozteco was most popular in the southern Aztec region, near the K'iche' Kingdom. As it is recorded, however, his story seems to be a combination of Aztec mythology, the myth of the Maya Hero Twins, and Catholic symbolism. In the myth, Tepozteco is immaculately born, with many versions citing the wind as his father. Upon his birth, his parents abandon him, placing him in a box in a river and hoping he will be carried away. However, Tepozteco is saved and adopted, growing to become a skilled hunter. One day, Xochicalcatl, a horrible monster (or king, depending on the version) demands that Tepozteco's adoptive parents be given over to him as sacrifices. Tepozteco refuses to let this happen and instead travels to where Xochicalcatl lives, promising his family that he will kill the beast. Once there, Tepozteco transforms himself into a series of different animals until finally Xochicalcatl eats him. Inside Xochicalcatl, Tepozteco pulls out a flint he had grabbed from the ground and uses it to cut the monster's stomach open, killing him.

The story of Tepozteco is firmly rooted in the tradition of the Maya Hero Twins. Like the brothers, Tepozteco is created through an immaculate birth, goes on a great journey in which he overcomes a monster with his wit, champions and defends his ancestors, and ultimately becomes a mythical figure. Likewise, the moment in which Tepozteco jumps into the mouth of the monster parallels the moment when the brothers leap into the fiery oven, with the heroes miraculously living in both instances. Even more striking, some versions of the myth of the Hero Twins feature the grandmother and half brothers trying to kill the infant twins, while many others stress that the brothers become legendary hunters as well as legendary players of the ball game. Just as many links exist between the Maya and Aztec mythologies, so too do many exist between the Aztec and Catholic. The abandonment of Tepozteco in the river is a parallel story to the placing of baby Moses in a basket in a river, while his immaculate birth provides a clear link to the story of Jesus. The battle between Xochicalcatl and Tepozteco is a battle to free Tepozteco's people, just as Moses frees his own people from Pharaoh. Many other minor notes also reflect Catholic imagery, including Tepozteco's ascension as a star once he succeeds in his quest and the long journey to Xochicalcatl's lair. In a final note, later versions of the myth conclude by stressing that Tepozteco will return some day to earth, just as Catholicism promises an eventual return of Jesus.

The connections between the myth of Tepozteco and the Maya and Catholic narratives are diverse and often do not fit neatly onto one another. The story of divine birth and heavenly ascension becomes a complicated melding of different mythologies and spiritual ideas, rather than one neat, easily understood Aztec story. This, however, is typical of the influence the Hero Twins continue to have. The culture that created their legend was never a culture of fixed and permanent ideas, but rather one that freely exchanged myths, comfortable with their traditions evolving rather than staying the same over time. With the violent introduction of European spirituality, those stories only continued to transform, the ancient customs and narratives sustained through their integration into the beliefs of others. At the heart of all of this change, the myth of the Hero Twins continues to be one of the most powerful stories. The mythological brothers are present all across North and South America, appearing both as the recognizable warrior twins and as shadows of themselves, their narrative reflected subtlety in diverse mythologies. This ultimately speaks to the power of the myth and of syncretism in the face of colonialism. While entire nations suppressed Maya mythology, those narratives did not fade away but rather found new life, woven together with new spiritualities and adopted traditions. Resilient and powerful, the Hero Twins live on not in one story but through countless myths, rituals, and beliefs, every one adding greater depth to their already complex and ancient meanings.

T. Fleischmann, MFA

BIBLIOGRAPHY

Carrasco, David. *Religions of Mesoamerica: Cosmovision and Ceremonial Centers*. San Francisco: Harper, 1990. Print.

Foster, Lynn V. *Handbook to Life in the Ancient Maya World*. Oxford: Oxford UP, 2002. Print.

Hall, Robert L. "The Cultural Background of Mississippian Symbolism." *The Southeastern Ceremonial Complex: Artifacts and Analysis*. Ed. Patricia Kay Galloway and James B. Griffin. Lincoln: U of Nebraska P, 1989. 239–78. Print.

Markman, Peter T., and Roberta H. Markman. *Masks of the Spirit: Images and Metaphor in Mesoamerica*. Berkeley: U of California P, 1990. Print.

Milbrath, Susan. *Star Gods of the Maya: Astronomy in Art, Folklore, and Calendars*. Austin: U of Texas P, 1999. Print.

Radin, Paul. *Winnebago Hero Cycles: A Study in Aboriginal Literature*. Vol. 1. Baltimore: Waverly, 1948. Print.

Read, Kay Almere, and Jason J. Gonzalez. *Mesoamerican Mythology: A Guide to the Gods, Heroes, Rituals, and Beliefs of Mexico and Central America*. Oxford: Oxford UP, 2000. Print.

Taube, Karl. *Aztec and Maya Myths*. Austin: U of Texas P, 2003. Print.

Tedlock, Dennis, trans. *Popol Vuh: The Definitive Edition of the Mayan Book of the Dawn of Life and the Glories of Gods and Kings*. Rev. ed. New York: Simon, 1996. Print.

Vargas-Betancourt, Margarita. "Legend of Tepozteco: *Popol Vuh* and Catholic Mythology." *Human Mosaic* 35.1 (2004): 41–49. PDF file.

Myth of Māui

Author: Traditional
Time Period: 999 BCE–1 BCE
Country or Culture: Polynesia
Genre: Myth

OVERVIEW

The myth of Māui originated among the Polynesian peoples who settled the islands of Tonga and Samoa at the beginning of the first millennium BCE. The myth of Māui combines a land creation myth with the stories of its trickster hero, Māui. Generally, Māui is a young man with a great command of magic; he is sometimes even a demigod. His main feats are raising up parts of the ocean with his fishing hook to form islands and snaring the sun so that it moves more slowly in the course of a longer day. Māui is mischievous and can be quite violent.

In the first millennium CE and thereafter, the myth of Māui traveled with the Polynesians as they settled the islands of the eastern Pacific, including Hawaii and New Zealand. Due to this migration, the myth of Māui can be found in different variants in many Polynesian societies.

Interestingly, the oldest written version of the myth, "The Legend of Maui," comes from the Māori, the youngest Polynesian culture. Most scholars believe that the Māori began to settle in New Zealand, which they call Aotearoa ("long white cloud"), around 1280 CE. The first Europeans discovered the land in 1642 CE. The British established sovereignty over New Zealand with the Treaty of Waitangi on February 6, 1840. During Sir George Grey's term as the third British governor of New Zealand (1845–54), he learned the Māori language and began to collect Māori myths told to him by priests and chieftains. One particularly important source was the chief Wiremu Maihi Te Rangikāheke, son of an influential Māori priest. In 1855, Sir George Grey published "The Legend of Maui" in his influential anthology *Polynesian Mythology and Ancient Traditional History of the New Zealand Race, as Furnished by Their Priests and Chiefs.*

In his preface to this collection, Grey explains that he compiled his text not from a single oral Māori source, but from the myths and legends as told to him by a variety of storytellers from many different Māori tribes and over the course of many years. Contemporary critics have blamed Grey for not acknowledging his major source, Te Rangikāheke. "The Legend of Maui," for example, is closely based on Te Rangikāheke's Māori text that has survived as manuscript in Grey's collection. Grey assembled his English text of "The Legend of Maui" from Te Rangikāheke's source. For an English person of his time in the nineteenth century, Grey was remarkably free of prejudice, and he showed considerable sympathies for the Māori. This sympathy extended to his editing and translation of Māori texts into English. Grey's translation bowed only reluctantly to Victorian sensibilities, particularly concerning sexual matters. His editing settled on the absolute minimum required for a publication in his age. As a result of Te Rangikāheke and Grey's collaboration, "The Legend of Maui" is the first transcription and subsequent translation into English of the Polynesian myth of Māui.

A morphological analysis of "The Legend of Maui" shows that the Māori myth contains many elements familiar from similar myths around the world and locates them in the specific context of Māori and Polynesian culture. Cultural criticism indicates that "The Legend of Maui" addresses many issues of particular concern to traditional tribal Māori culture. Among them, for example, is the importance of lineage, illustrated by Māui's elaborate quest for his parents. Feminist criticism analyzes Māui's relationship with different women in the myth. Finally, a look at cross-cultural variants of the myth of Māui among different Polynesian societies reveals how the myth has both retained archaic core elements and developed a different focus in different cultures.

SUMMARY

"The Legend of Maui" begins with young Māui asking his older brothers where their parents live. To his surprise, none of the four brothers knows the answer. Startled, Māui asserts that he will find out on his own.

Māui's quest to find his parents is made especially important because of the circumstances of his birth. As a child, Māui suddenly appears at the communal hall where his mother and brother are dancing. When their mother counts her four sons, Māui appears as a surprise fifth child. At first, his mother rejects him. She tries to chase him away, saying, "You are no child of mine" (Grey 18).

In return, Māui reveals how he came into the world. He was born prematurely. When his brothers call him "this little abortion" (Grey 20), this refers to the older, nineteenth-century term for a miscarriage; it does not mean a voluntary termination of pregnancy.

When Māui is apparently born too early to survive, his mother, Taranga, cuts off part of her topknot, wraps the baby into it, and throws it into the surf. However, Māui survives this ordeal. Seaweed enfolds and protects him, and the waves carry him ashore again. There, jellyfish enfold him for protection. This is needed as "myriads of flies alighted on me to buzz about me and lay their eggs, that maggots may eat me, and flocks of birds collected round me to peck me to pieces" (Grey 18–19). Māui is rescued by his kindly great ancestor Tama-nui-ki-te-Rangi. In his house, Māui grows up.

Once Māui's mother, Taranga, hears from her son this story of miraculous rescue, she accepts him. She gives him the full name of Māui-tiki-tiki-a-Taranga, or "Māui formed in the topknot (*tiki-tiki*) of Taranga." For many nights, Māui's mother sleeps close to him. This causes the jealousy of the other brothers. Yet the two oldest ones insist on keeping the peace.

Every morning, Taranga disappears, only to return at night. Curious, one night Māui steals her clothes after she falls asleep. He blacks out their hut so that she will miss the morning light, the signal for her usual departure. Taranga finally wakes up in the middle of the day, rushes outside, covers herself with a rough cloak, and disappears down into a hole hidden by some rushes she pulls up and replaces over the hole.

Māui observes his mother and plans to follow her. To do so, he transforms himself into a pigeon with the help of the garments he stole from his mother. This impresses his brothers. Chasing after his mother down the hole, Māui flies into a cave. From there, he alights on

"Then forth rushed that bold hero, Maui-tiki-tiki-o-Taranga, with his enchanted weapon. Alas! the sun screams aloud; he roars; Maui strikes him fiercely with many blows; they hold him for a long time, at last they let him go, and then weak from wounds the sun crept along its course."

"The Legend of Maui"

a tree. He observes his father and mother sitting among other people below the tree. Changing back into a young man, Māui is acknowledged by his parents. His father, Makea-tu-tara, performs a ceremony akin to baptism for Māui. Yet he slips up in his prayers, which means that Māui will have to die eventually.

After returning to his brothers, Māui embarks on a series of mischievous adventures. In a rather casual act of violence, he kills a girl and destroys her father's crops. Next, Māui he obtains the magical jawbone of his ancestress Muri-ranga-whenua. The old woman gives it to Māui without feeling harm.

Māui decides to slow down the pace of the sun so that people will have more daylight to procure food. Together with his four brothers, Māui sets up an elaborate trap for the sun. Once they catch the sun in their ropes, Māui beats him until he becomes crippled and has to move at a slower pace from then on.

Later on, when married with "wives and children" (Grey 38), Māui tricks his brothers into letting him join their fishing expedition. He compels his brothers to paddle out even farther into the open sea, where he casts his special hook made from the jawbone of his ancestress. When his brothers deny him bait, Māui strikes his own nose and uses his blood as bait. Māui's hook catches the sill of the doorway of the submerged house of old Tonga-nui. With his fearful brothers listening, Māui chants incantations to force Tonga-nui to release his line, which comes up bearing a massive fish.

Back on shore, Māui instructs his brothers to wait before cutting up the fish until he has made an offering to the gods. Yet his brothers ignore him once he has gone. As they slaughter the fish, it thrashes and transforms the flat land into a hilly region. Thus, the fish becomes the North Island of New Zealand, "fished up" by Māui (Grey 45).

After this feat, Māui decides to extinguish the fires of his grandmother Mahu-ika. With this mischief on his mind, Māui puts out all the cooking fires in his village. Next, he commands his servants to bring him fire. When nobody volunteers, Māui asks his mother to show him the way to Mahu-ika.

When Māui meets Mahu-ika, the old woman treats him well. She offers him the fire he requests, tearing off one of her fingernails to give him the fire that comes out of it. Yet Māui moves out of her sight, extinguishes the fire, and returns to ask for more. He does this until Mahu-ika tears off all her fingernails and toenails save for a last one. Finally angry at Māui, Mahu-ika tears off her last toenail, which also becomes fire, and "as she dash[es] it down on the ground the whole place [catches] fire" (Grey 48). Māui is nearly burnt to death, even as he transforms himself into an eagle and jumps into water. He is saved by rains sent down by other ancestors. Mahu-ika saves a little bit of fire for humanity in some firewood trees.

Māui turns his mischief onto his sister Hinauri and her husband, Irawaru. He tricks Irawaru into joining him on a fishing expedition. There, Māui becomes angered at Irawaru for coming up with fish due to his barbed hook, while Māui catches none with his plain one. Back on shore, Māui beats Irawaru so that his brother-in-law becomes a dog. This saddens Hinauri, who commits suicide by drowning herself in the ocean.

Finally, Māui decides to overcome his ancestress Hine-nui-te-pō, goddess of thunder. Full of confidence, Māui gathers a flock of island birds as companions. Together, they come to the place where Hine-nui-te-pō is sleeping. Māui plans to enter Hine-nui-te-pō, crawl through her body, and pass out through her mouth. This will kill her and ensure Māui's immortality. However, Māui's plan will succeed only if none of the birds laughs at him in the process. Unfortunately for Māui, one of the birds cannot help but laugh once Māui is inside Hine-nui-te-pō. In consequence, the old woman awakes, and "she open[s] her eyes, start[s] up, and kill[s] Maui" (Grey 57).

Māui's surprise death means that all humans have become mortal. Humans will bear children, but all will have to die eventually.

ANALYSIS

An analysis that combines the approaches of morphological and cultural criticism reveals that the Māori myth told in "The Legend of Maui" addresses core concerns of traditional Māori culture and society. As an origin myth told from the perspective of its trickster hero, Māui, "The Legend of Maui" deals with the major questions of Māori society. These include parentage and lineage, shape shifting, the course of the day, human sustenance and the origin of the land, interaction with domestic animals, fire, and death. Through its human protagonist, Māui, the myth proposes answers and explanations to these questions that give its traditional society a collective identity based on shared beliefs. Feminist and cultural criticism illustrate that many of the actions of Māui—especially in his interactions with female characters, but not limited to them—appear rather antisocial from a contemporary international perspective. Here, the critical challenge is to look at the narrative of the myth in its original context to analyze its function in traditional Māori society.

Highlighting the absolute importance that traditional Māori culture places on lineage and genealogy, "The Legend of Maui" opens with Māui's quest to find the dwelling place of his parents. This is symbolic of the young protagonist's need, like that of all young people in traditional Māori society, to define his parentage in order to establish his own heritage. The quest of Māui is made complicated by the plot device of the absent parents. They no longer dwell with their five sons and have departed to an unknown location.

The common morphological motif of the unusual birth of the protagonist provides an edge and special urgency to Māui's quest to find his parents. Similar to other legendary characters in other cultural traditions, like the Greek Oedipus, or religious persons, like the biblical Moses, Māui is separated at birth from his mother, Taranga. As Māui is born prematurely, his mother does not deem the baby viable. As the editor of "The Legend of Maui," Sir George Grey informs the reader that Māui's mother did not follow the traditional course prescribed for such an event. This required a careful ceremonial burial to appease the spirit of the infant who died before having a chance to enjoy life. Otherwise, the dead infant would turn into a malicious spirit. On a level of collective psychology, such a ceremonial burial sought to heal through ritual the apparent breach in the desired, natural order of life, in which children are born to live.

Māui's mother designs a ritual of her own for her premature baby. Reunited with his mother later on, Māui repeats what her mother did to him at his birth: "I was born at the side of the sea, and was thrown by you into the foam of the serf [surf], after you had wrapped me up in a tuft of your hair, which you cut off for the purpose" (Grey 18). This private ritual indicates that Māui's mother is not totally indifferent to the fate of her premature baby. In turn, Māui's life becomes special following his mother's unique ritual. The exceptionality of the hero's birth is, of course, a well-known mythological motif.

Signifying the harmonious accord of nature and humanity at the beginning of his life, Māui is saved by a combination of natural and human interventions. In the ocean, seaweed enfolds the baby who is then shaped by the waves of the sea and washed ashore in a protective mantel of jellyfish. Just as realistic natural forces such as flies and birds threaten the baby, Māui's human ancestor Tama-nui-ki-te-Rangi arrives on the scene and rescues the infant. In the traditional fashion of Māori infant care, he hangs Māui up by the roof inside of his house to dry and warm him from the central cooking fire. Corresponding to a common trend in myths to disregard some aspects of reality, "The Legend of Maui" does not tell how baby Māui is raised by his old male relative without a mother's milk.

Incorporating the motif of the precocious infant, as soon as he can walk, Māui makes his way to the community hall where his mother and brothers engage in a communal dance. Even in contemporary Māori culture, many social activities are centered on these halls, called *wharenui*. It is here, in a common social setting, that Māui confronts his mother. Through Māui's vivid recollection of the circumstances of his birth and rescue, he convinces his mother to accept him publicly.

Māui's naming by his mother establishes his genealogy and legitimacy. Taranga gives him the full formal name of Māui-tiki-tiki-a-Taranga. This name alludes to his unique birth, folded in the topknot hair, or tiki-tiki, of his mother. It also puts him on par with his oldest brothers, all of whom share the first name of Māui. This emphasis on the need for personal genealogy, encoded under the Māori concept of *whakapapa*, has been a mainstay of Māori culture since archaic times.

Using the mythological motif of limiting access to moments of happiness, every morning Māui's mother departs from him and his brothers for the day. She returns only at night and will leave again at daybreak. This separation from his mother is unacceptable to Māui. He devises a scheme to entrap his mother and cause her to extend her stay. After she falls asleep at night, Māui steals her clothes and blacks out their hut. With no rays of sunshine entering the hut through its cracks as before to signal the coming of day, Māui tricks his mother into sleeping well into the morning. When she finally rushes out of the hut, just taking an old cloth to cover herself, Māui spies on her. He sees her lifting some grass from the ground and disappearing down a deep hole. Thus, Māui proves his growing power as a trickster and investigator of things important to him.

Māui's trickery and spying enable the success of his quest to find the dwelling place of his parents. Throughout "The Legend of Maui," Māui relies on trickery, imagination, magic, and physical strength to perform a series of remarkable feats. This makes him a model young warrior for his culture.

Even though Māui is only a human in "The Legend of Maui," he possesses some supernatural abilities tied to shamanism. From boyhood, Māui can transform himself into various birds. The myth leaves open the extent of this transformation, whether it is a resemblance or actual shape shifting. When Māui steals the garments of his mother to take on "the semblance of a pigeon" (Grey 26), the myth alludes to a shaman or priest impersonating a sacred animal through some choice objects. With the belt of his mother, Māui creates the distinct white breast plumage of the New Zealand pigeon that Māori call *kereru*, kukupa, or kuku. The black throat feathers of this indigenous pigeon are indicated by the mother's apron made of the hair of a dog's tail. All in all, Māui's impersonation of a bird impresses his brothers and indicates Māui's special talents for shamanistic practice.

Employing the motif of a human changing into an animal, Māui fully transforms into a pigeon in his quest to find his parents. As a pigeon, he flies to the spot where his mother descended into the ground. He opens the entrance, flies in, and replaces the disguise of the entrance. Next, Māui flies into the cave until he comes out upon a grove of trees called *manapau*. As Grey informs the reader, these legendary trees hail back to the mythical country from which, in Māori traditional beliefs, the Māori originate. Thus, the manapau trees tie Māui's quest for his parents to an allegory of the origin and travel of the Māori people to New Zealand.

Māui forces his parents to acknowledge him through his own initiative, indicating the resourcefulness, determination, and autonomy of the protagonist. Sitting in his tree, Māui spots his parents below. He mischievously makes himself known by throwing berries from the tree at his parents. They and their friends begin to pelt the pigeon with stones, none of which hit Māui. By design, Māui lets his father hit him "exactly upon his left leg" (30). This is significant and explains his name. In Māori and other Polynesian languages, Māui means the "left side," including the left hand or the left leg. Falling to the ground, Māui changes from pigeon to human.

The son lets his father inflict a symbolic wound on the part of his body that corresponds to the son's name given to him by his mother. This act strengthens the son's genealogical bond with his ancestors.

Māui's superhuman talents even persuade some bystanders to consider him a god—even though he is human, albeit one invested with strong magical powers. Māui is deemed a god by some because his eyes are red from his disguise as a pigeon, as the New Zealand pigeon has red eyes. Yet his mother, Taranga, remembers his features as that of her son. In a series of questions typical of a mythical discourse scene, Taranga establishes and proclaims Māui's identity as her son: "This indeed is my child" (Grey 32). As traditional Māori society was matrilineal, the acknowledgement from Taranga carries great significance. In turn, Māui's father, Makea-tu-tara, agrees to perform an acknowledgement ceremony that Grey translates as baptism. The reader should understand that this is an approximation only. The ceremony represents Māui's acceptance into the lineage, called *whakapapa*, of his ancestors. It is not related to Christian baptism.

Cultural critics have remarked that elaborate religious rituals combined with the threat of grave consequences for even minor infractions have tended to elevate the position, prestige, and power of religious authorities. The more elaborate religious ceremonies are, the more the general population will have to rely on the expertise of priests and other religious persons to perform them correctly. An example of this can be seen in "The Legend of Maui." Including the plot device of foreshadowing the end of the myth, it is revealed that Māui's father "hurriedly skipped over part of the prayers . . . of the services to purify Maui; he knew that the gods would be certain to punish this fault, by causing Maui to die" (Grey 32). From a feminist critical perspective, it is interesting that the error that will cause Māui to die is committed by his father. Māui's mother, before his father botches Māui's baptism, had predicted that Māui would be immune from death. Taranga believes that Māui will overcome

his fearsome ancestress Hine-nui-te-pō. Yet Hine-nui-te-pō will indeed cause his death at the end of the myth. Thus, the mother's predictions are invalidated by the father's fatal error.

The plot technique of foreshadowing Māui's death casts a brief pall on the ensuing narrative of "The Legend of Maui." Nevertheless, Māui emerges from his parents' dwelling place a youthful and invigorated hero.

In an act of casual violence that contemporary readers may find appalling, Māui proves his maturity by slaying his first victim. "The Legend of Maui" gives no concrete reason for Māui's behavior. In the traditionally warlike Māori society in which the myth was originally told, this action did not warrant further comment. Instead, Māui's deed stands on its own—though it portrays a protagonist who is rather alien to contemporary global society. According to the legend, Māui's first casualty is "the daughter of Maru-te-whare-aitu," and following this, "by enchantments, he destroyed the crops of Maru-te-whare-aitu, so that they all withered" (Grey 33).

After taking this step along his maturation into a warrior, the myth shows Māui cleverly enhancing his powers through more trickery. Māui persuades one of his grandmothers, Muri-ranga-whenua, to give him her jawbone for his magical purposes. Here, the myth employs a surreal logic of its own. This gift of Māui's grandmother does not physically harm the old woman. From a morphological point of view, the story follows the motif of the hero gathering magical objects to perform further feats.

One of the most archaic components of "The Legend of Maui" is Māui's taming of the sun. Here, Māui is motivated by his strong desire to help his community. He wishes to find a way to lengthen daylight for useful human activities. Cajoling his brothers to join him, Māui reveals that his purpose to battle the sun is "so we may compel him to move more slowly, in order that mankind may have long days to labour in to procure subsistence for themselves" (Grey 35). Combining the description of realistic hunting practices with a mythological quest, the legend tells how Māui and his brothers use the techniques of a traditional snare hunt to lay a trap for the sun. The hunters are successful, and the sun is caught in the snare devised by Māui and executed by his brothers. Privileged to perform the key action of the episode, Māui beats the sun to cripple it. Henceforth, it will move more slowly across the sky.

There is a brief transition from the slowing of the sun to the next episode, which shows that Māui has reached

HISTORICAL CONTEXT

Many historians and anthropologists have concluded that the ancestors of the Polynesians came primarily from the island of Taiwan, leaving there around 2500 BCE. The settlement of Polynesia proper, which encompasses the islands of the South Pacific Sea, began around 980 BCE at the island chain of Tonga. From there, Polynesians spread out as far northeast as Hawaii and as far southeast as the Easter Islands/Rapa Nui. These islands were most likely discovered and settled around 900 CE. Most historians agree that the two islands of New Zealand began to be settled by the Polynesian people known as the Māori by 1280 CE. New Zealand represented the last and outer reach of settlement of the South Pacific Sea by Polynesians.

The Māori brought with them common Polynesian myths and adapted them to their own culture. "The Legend of Maui" is part creation myth and part story of a trickster hero, Māui. At the end of the myth, there is a reference to the mythical ancestral land of the Māori, Hawaiki. This mythical land is not to be mistaken for the real Hawaii. According to the Māori myth, some of Māui's children came from Hawaiki to settle in Aotearoa, the Māori name for New Zealand.

Europeans first made contact with the Māori, who developed a fierce warrior culture, in 1642, when Dutch explorer Abel Tasman sailed to New Zealand's South Island. Captain James Cook visited New Zealand first in 1769. Contact with Europeans and Americans provided Māori tribes with muskets after 1805. Unfortunately, opposing Māori tribes used their newly gained firepower in a series of lethal internecine wars that greatly decimated the overall population.

In 1840, Great Britain signed the Treaty of Waitangi with a majority of Māori tribes. From the British point of view, this treaty established British sovereignty over New Zealand.

As the third governor of New Zealand, from 1845 to 1854, Sir George Grey collaborated with a bilingual Māori chief and son of a priest, Wiremu Maihi Te Rangikāheke. Te Rangikāheke transcribed many Māori myths, legends, and chants. He helped Grey translate his and other collected materials into English. In 1855, Grey published an English-language anthology of Māori myths, which includes "The Legend of Maui." Scholars have established that Te Rangikāheke's account of this myth, which was the basis of Grey's account, authentically renders the original myth of Māui as told by the Māori in the North Island of New Zealand.

the next step toward maturity and adult life. At his home, he has gained wives and children who berate him for "his laziness in not catching fish for them" (38). In the face of this criticism, Māui brags that he will prove an excellent provider and catch a fish so large that they cannot eat it in one setting. His brothers are reluctant to let Māui join them in their fishing canoe, as they are weary of his magic tricks. To join them, Māui uses trickery. He hides in their boat the next day and only appears when they are out at sea.

This opening incident of Māui's fishing episode points at the inherent dangers of social exclusion and even ostracism for anyone who stands out too much in a traditional society. Māui's reputation as trickster appears to endanger the success of ordinary collective action. Fishing from their many-crewed canoes enabled the Māori to join their paddling strength to travel farther into the sea than possible in a single-crewed boat.

A person excluded from this activity would face serious dietary consequences.

As shown throughout the myth, Māui has an ambiguous relationship with his brothers. They represent the ordinary people facing the trickster hero in their midst. Māui's brothers alternately obey, disrespect, belittle, or oppose him. Yet they cannot help but be impressed by his amazing feats. Accordingly, out at sea, Māui emerges from hiding and assumes a leadership role. He compels his brothers to venture out much farther beyond their usual fishing grounds. Yet his brothers do not share their bait with Māui and urge him to finish his fishing as quickly as possible. Showing his individualism and self-reliance as leader, Māui baits his magic hook with his own blood.

Māui's capture of a giant fish that becomes the land represents the second core, archaic element of the myth. At first, Māui's hook snares the roof of the submerged house of sea-dwelling "old fellow Tonga-nui" (Grey 42). Māui uses magic chants to persuade Tonga-nui to let go while he raises the house, which emerges from the sea like a new volcanic island. While his brothers are afraid, Māui finally lands his fish. The fish contains "a portion of the earth, of Papa-tu-a-Nuku" (43), who is the mother earth goddess in Māori religion. Māui's fish becomes a strong symbol of the maritime culture of the Māori, as well as other Polynesian cultures. The people depend on dry land, the islands, to live on, and fish is a major source of their nutrition. In "The Legend of Maui," these two elements are united in one item, Māui's fish.

For Māori culture, "The Legend of Maui" functions as an origin myth for key geographical elements of the North Island of New Zealand, where the original Māori source of Grey's tale, Te Rangikāheke, lived. Leading up to the climax, the narrative contrasts Māui's singularity with the folly of his ordinary brothers once the fishing party is magically propelled to the shore. Māui warns his brothers not to slaughter the fish until he has found a priest to perform the required rituals for such a big catch. Of course, his brothers cannot wait. They begin cutting the fish, which makes it toss and turn. This forcefully shapes the land, giving it distinct geographical features. Instead of lying there flat and plain, the island becomes rough terrain. Now, it sports mountains, valleys, and cliffs. Māui's fishhook becomes the semicircular strip of land forming the real bay called Heretaunga in Māori, or Hawke's Bay in English, on the North Island.

Continuing to use Māui to probe questions of major importance to traditional Māori culture, "The Legend of Maui" has Māui interact, somewhat maliciously, with the forces of fire and death. With typical self-confidence and a certain dose of spite, Māui sets himself the new task to "extinguish and destroy the fires of his ancestress of Mahu-ika" (45). The myth does not give any further information as to what motivates Māui to do so. An analysis informed by cultural criticism may look at this episode as an illustration of humanity's attempt to control fire and master its use. At the same time, Māui's action appears unprovoked, as Mahu-ika's fires do not threaten Māui or his community. To the contrary, the old woman quite willingly offers to help Māui when he asks her for her fire. It is only when she realizes she has been tricked that she tries to burn him in anger. Māui escapes nearly singed but alive. Mahu-ika saves some of her fire for humanity's subsequent continuous use. The episode

highlights how Māui's mischief increasingly leads him into danger, foreshadowing the myth's resolution.

In a final interlude before the climax of the myth, Māui shows again a rather malicious side of himself. On a joint fishing expedition with his brother-in-law Irawaru, Māui becomes jealous of Irawaru's better luck and better equipment, a barbed hook that surpasses his own plain one. They quarrel over a fish entangled in both lines. This incident hints at underlying conflicts in Māori society pitting fishermen against each other. Māui's resolution of the conflict, however, appears hardly appropriate for a hero to a Western reader. Māui tricks Irawaru into a helpless position below his canoe and nearly tramples him to death. Using his magic, Māui "transform[s] Irawaru into a dog, and [feeds] him with cung" (Grey 52). When Māui's younger sister Hinauri learns of her husband's transformation, she is so stricken with grief that she commits suicide. It is no real solace that Irawaru becomes the mythical ancestor of all Māori dogs. Here, Māui acts as an amoral trickster who uses his powers nearly at will. He is not restrained by kinship relations, nor does he show any feelings of empathy for his victims. The episode reveals the darker side of Māui.

Ultimately, Māui fails in his last quest to kill the goddess of thunder, Hine-nui-te-pō. From a feminist critical point of view, Māui tries to maintain his immortality through a form of reversing the birth process. He plans to enter Hine-nui-te-pō's body, crawl through her, and reemerge from her mouth. This would kill Hine-nui-te-pō and ensure Māui's immortality despite the faulty ceremony performed by his father. Even though Grey's text is silent on the details of Māui's proposed entry into Hine's body, the context makes it clear that it should be through the birth canal. Here, Māui attempts to triumph over the female body. He came into the world too soon as a premature baby, yet was saved, and he now hopes to live forever by reversing parts of his birth passage.

As structuralist critic Michael Jackson has pointed out, Māui's death corresponds well to the circumstances of his birth and life. Māui takes along a group of wild birds on his voyage to Hine. He instructs the birds not to laugh at the sight until he has emerged from Hine's mouth. As Jackson has noticed, this establishes a structural parallel to Māui's whole story. Māui relies on birds very often. Just as birds, and bird shape, aided Māui before, birds become his undoing. As one bird, "the little Tiwakawaka," cannot help but laugh while Māui is still inside Hine-nui-te-pō, the woman wakes up and kills Māui (57).

The life of the protagonist of "The Legend of Maui" comes full circle at the end of the myth. Born prematurely but saved by the help of nature and humanity, living a life of trickery and performing astounding feats, Māui fails to reverse part of the process of his birth to achieve immortality. With this end, "The Legend of Maui" turns into an allegory of the limited power of every human, including a hero and demigod like Māui. He comes to share in death, the ultimate fate of all humanity. Yet his myth illustrates how much humans can make of their lives despite their foreordained end.

CROSS-CULTURAL INFLUENCE

The myth of Māui originated among the Polynesian people of Tonga in the South Pacific Sea. Polynesians settled in Tonga around 980 BCE according to most historians. From Tonga, the myth of Māui traveled with the Polynesian people as they populated further South Sea Islands. For this reason, variants of the myth developed in nearly all Polynesian societies. There was a strong cross-cultural influence extending from the source in Tonga to each new culture emerging on a newly settled chain of islands. As shown, the myth of Māui was transcribed first in New Zealand, where it arrived around 1280 CE with the Māori people. A comparison of the Māori myth, "The Legend of Maui," with other, older Polynesian variants shows how each Polynesian culture gave the basic myth a shape of its own.

The most archaic version of the myth of Māui comes from Tonga. The central event is Māui dragging up the islands of Tonga from the sea with his magic fishhook. This narrative core is retained in "The Legend of Maui," when Māui catches a fish that is both part of the land of the North Island of New Zealand and forms its varied geographical shape through its violent thrashings on the shore.

As a creation myth, the Tongan version of Māui includes the variant in which Māui the land puller is the youngest of three brothers. He is known as the trickster, or Māui-kisikisi. It is from the old fisherman Tonga Fusifonua that Māui obtains the magic fishhook with which he raises the Tongan islands from the sea. First, he is only allowed to take the fishhook if he can find it in Tonga Fusifonua's collection of hooks. Māui achieves this with the help of the old man's wife, who betrays to young Māui the secret of which hook is the right one. After achieving his feat, Māui receives the honorific name of Māui-fusi-fonua, or "Māui the land puller," which is part of the old man's name as well.

From this Tongan variant, the idea of Māui's brothers traveled with the myth all the way to its later version as told in New Zealand. Similarly, the archaic Tongan root of the Māori fish-catching episode appears through the name of the old man living at the bottom of the sea. In "The Legend of Maui," his name is Tonga-nui. Māori Māui's incantations force the old man to release the magic fish that will give shape to the North Island of New Zealand.

In the Tongan versions of the myth of Māui, it is either Māui himself or his son, both called Māui-kisikisi, who discover how to make fire from kindling wood. Māui-kisikisi relates his discovery to the people so that they can use fire to cook food. Unlike "The Legend of Maui," in the Tongan version, Māui serves his people, rather than mischievously testing his powers with his grandmother, the keeper of fire. Yet the Tongan story element that fire is obtained from various kindling woods is found at the end of the fire episode of "The Legend of Maui." There, Mahu-ika saves "a few sparks" of her fire that she had thrown "to protect them, into the Kaiko-mako, and a few other trees" to allow humans to "use portions of the wood of these trees for fire when they require a light" (Grey 49). While the archaic Tongan myth focuses on the discovery of fire, the Māori myth focuses on its control.

When the myth of Māui traveled with Polynesian settlers to the islands of Samoa, around 800 BCE, the myth underwent some changes. In the Samoan version, the hero's name is changed to Ti'iti'i. His key accomplishment, like that of the Tongan Māui-kisikisi, is to bring fire to humanity. This may remind a reader of the independent Greek myth of Prometheus. The Samoan version indicates alike that such a key human discovery as the use of fire was often traced back to mythological origins in traditional societies.

To obtain fire, Ti'iti'i has to go to the underworld. There, he meets the god of earthquakes, Mafui'e, from whom he receives some fire. Back in the world above, Ti'iti'i uses this fire to cook his food. He is discovered by Mafui'e, who destroys Ti'iti'i's kitchen. As in the myth of Prometheus, the gods appear wrathful toward the human who uses the secret of fire. Ti'iti'i challenges the god Mafui'e to a wrestling match. Unlike American professional wrestling, the outcome of this competition is not predetermined. Ti'iti'i wins the contested match. As reward, he learns that fire can be found in kindling wood. This outcome relates to both the Tongan source of the Samoan myth and the later Māori version, in which fire is always obtained from kindling wood. Here, the myth in all its variants furnishes a legendary explanation for the common Polynesian technique of creating fire from kindling wood.

Just as some Tongan variants divide the feats of Māui among a father (the land puller) and a son (the fire catcher), the Samoan version ascribes the feat of Māui snaring the sun to another mythical figure. In the Samoan tradition, it is the child of the woman Mangamangai. This boy is conceived when his mother looks at the rising sun. When the boy grows up, he snares the sun and makes it promise to run a slower course.

Once Polynesian seafarers reached Tahiti around 700 CE and settled its island chain, the myth of Māui saw another local adaptation. In the Tahitian tradition, Māui became a priest and a sage. Only after his death does he become a god. The Tahitian Māui's prime achievement is stopping the sun so that he can finish his priestly work during daylight. He is credited with discovering that fire can be created from kindling wood. The Tahitian Māui appears more remote and less personal than the trickster encountered in most other Polynesian versions of the myth.

The myth of Māui reached the island of Mangareva as Polynesians settled there around the ninth century CE. The Mangarevan variant of the myth focuses on the two core episodes of Māui fishing the dry land from the sea and his capture of the sun. Rather than being born prematurely, the Mangarevan Māui is born from the belly button of his mother. This detail corresponds to a common Chinese nursery explanation as to where children come from. As such, it may relate to the possible origin of the Polynesian people as migrants from the island of Taiwan around 2500 BCE, or it may be an independent narrative invention by the Mangarevan community.

The myth of Māui flourished in Hawaii when the island chain began to be settled around 900 CE (the majority opinion of historians and archeologists). The key event of the Hawaiian myth is Māui raising the islands from the bottom of the ocean floor with his magic fishhook. Indeed, the second largest island of Hawaii, Maui, is named after the mythological hero.

In the Hawaiian tradition, Māui is a trickster hero. He is considered one of the *kupua*, or mischievous demigods. As such, he is a shape-shifter, similar to the Māori tradition. His story is closely entwined with that of his beloved mother, Hina. This parallels the relationship of Māui with Taranga in the Māori tradition. Hawaiian

Māui's key accomplishments are raising the islands of Hawaii, lifting the sky, snaring the sun, and bringing fire to his people. These feats closely mirror other Polynesian variants of the myth of Māui and add a strong mother-son bond to the myth.

In one Hawaiian version of the island-lifting episode, Hina helps Māui on his fishing expeditions with his brothers. She rises from the waters in the form of a gourd with which Māui bails water out of the communal canoe. Māui casts his line from the canoe, snatching the islands, while his brothers paddle along. Instructed not to look behind them, the brothers do so when a beautiful woman appears over the water. Māui's fishing line tears, and Hina disappears from the canoe. Instead of forming one continuous landmass, individual islands are lifted from the ground. The brothers' disregard for Māui's instructions is echoed in the Māori version of "The Legend of Maui," when their premature cutting of the fish roughs up the raised land.

In the Hawaiian tradition, Māui decides to snare the sun because his mother, Hina, complains that the daylight is too short to dry her traditional tree fiber clothes. His quest is motivated by filial affection, and he sets himself to the task vigorously. Māui's endeavor is aided by the help, indirectly or directly, of a female relative. In one version, he uses a rope made from his sister's hair to tie up the rays of the sun, immobilizing it. In exchange for its freedom, the sun agrees to longer days during the summer season. Another version has Māui enlist the help of his grandmother, echoing the Māori version in which he receives the magic jawbone of his grandmother Muri-ranga-whenua. Both versions tell tales in which Māui succeeds in altering the speed of the sun's movement across the sky, a major achievement for the protagonist.

The prevalence of the myth of Māui across almost all Polynesian cultures has led scholars such as William Westervelt to surmise a very ancient origin of this myth unique to Polynesia. For Westervelt, the myth of Māui may have originated even before people settled the Tonga islands, where the oldest forms of the myth are found. Westervelt surmises the origin of the myth to have taken place in India. However, if the myth traveled to Tonga from other regions, no traces of it have been found elsewhere outside Polynesia. The trickster hero Māui makes his first surviving appearance in Tonga. From there, his story traveled to the outer ends of Polynesia. The journey of the myth and the settlement of Polynesia terminate on New Zealand. There, "The

Legend of Maui" was first transcribed and recorded in writing for posterity.

R. C. Lutz, PhD

BIBLIOGRAPHY

Beckwith, Martha Warren. "Maui the Trickster." *Hawaiian Mythology*. 1940. Honolulu: U of Hawaii P, 1976. 226–37. Print.

Dixon, Roland B. "The Maui Cycle." *Oceanic Mythology*. 1916. New York: Cooper Square, 1964. 41–56. Print.

Grey, George. "The Legend of Maui." *Polynesian Mythology and Ancient Traditional History of the New Zealand Race, as Furnished by Their Priests and Chiefs*. 1855. Whitefish: Kessinger, 2004. 16–58. Print.

Jackson, Michael. "Some Structural Considerations of Māori Myth." *Journal of the Polynesian Society* 77.2 (1968): 147–162. Print.

Smith, Philippa Mein. *A Concise History of New Zealand*. 2nd ed. New York: Cambridge UP, 2012. Print.

Stafford, Don. *Introducing Māori Culture*. Auckland: Reed, 1997. Print.

Starzecka, Dorota, ed. *Maori: Art and Culture*. London: British Museum P, 1998. Print.

Westervelt, William Drake. *Legends of Ma-Ui: A Demi God of Polynesia, and of His Mother Hina*. 1910. London: Abela, 2011. Print.

Stagolee

Author: Julius Lester
Time Period: 1851 CE–1900 CE
Country or Culture: African American; North America
Genre: Folktale

OVERVIEW

Over the past century, Stagolee has become an astonishingly popular "badman" folk hero in African American oral traditions. A gambler, womanizer, and gunslinger who often displays supernatural powers, Stagolee becomes known for his chief exploit: his murder of a man named Billy Lyons for knocking off Stagolee's Stetson hat. The many versions of the tale present different consequences for this crime, and the Stagolee hero has evolved from early ballads, toasts, folktales, and rhythm and blues songs to rap versions in more recent years.

Julius Lester's 1969 folktale version introduces Stagolee as an outlaw from the age of five when he leaves home with nothing but a guitar, a deck of cards, and a .44 revolver. An infamous gambler and murderer feared even by white people, Stagolee plays cards with Billy Lyons, who becomes angry over his loss, so he knocks off Stagolee's Stetson hat and spits in it. Stagolee promptly shoots Billy and moves in with his wife. Then, he comically evades two white sheriffs who attempt to bring him to justice, killing the first and using his superhuman strength to survive the second sheriff's lynching rope. Because he escapes death for so long, Stagolee finally draws the attention of St. Peter and the Lord, who send Death, a disgruntled employee, to take Stagolee's life. Yet when the hero fends off even Death, the Lord must take matters into his own hands and strikes him with his thunderbolt. Honored with a lavish funeral, Stagolee flouts his final judgment and visits heaven, where he discovers that even the afterlife is segregated. With most blacks barred from heaven because of their propensity to sing the blues, Stagolee happily proceeds to hell, whose gate boasts a Black Power sign. He reunites with friends in a festive, air-conditioned hell and even

challenges a forlorn Devil to a duel. When the Devil declines, Stagolee crowns himself the new chief of hell.

The tale of Stagolee enjoyed a long history prior to Lester's entertaining account. In fact, the story began as a legend based on the nineteenth-century murder of a man named William Lyons by a pimp named Lee Shelton, which may partly account for the story's subsequent popularity. Yet Stagolee is the most popular example of a character type; numerous other "badman" heroes developed in nineteenth-century African American folklore have been celebrated for their total disregard for society's morals and laws, many of which guaranteed the oppression of African Americans. Indeed, Stagolee and his counterparts are the prototypes for the modern outlaw figure of the gangster rapper, and many extremely violent and disturbing Stagolee narratives emerged during the twentieth century. Stagolee's role as a culture hero who nonetheless fuels negative stereotypes about black men has thus created ambivalence about his meaning and value. How might the heroism of this outlaw be understood in the context of American culture and history? A cultural analysis examines how Julius Lester's Stagolee narrative incorporates features of the early legends and alters the story's problematic details to offer an entertaining portrait of Stagolee's "badness" that was current in 1969 and continues to resonate with audiences.

SUMMARY

Julius Lester's version of Stagolee introduces the protagonist as "undoubtedly and without question, the baddest nigger that ever lived" (172), so bad that flies avoid his head in the summer and snow refuses to fall on his house in winter. Born on a Georgia plantation, Stagolee decides at the age of two that he will not waste his life picking cotton and working for white people, and so at age five, he runs away carrying only a guitar, a deck of cards, and a .44 revolver. He plans to play cards for money, play the blues on his guitar to win any woman he

"Stack said, 'Well, that's all right. The Lawd'll take care of your children. I'll take care of your wife.' And with that, Stagolee blowed Billy Lyons away. Stagolee looked at the body for a minute and then went off to Billy Lyons's house and told Mrs. Billy that her husband was dead and he was moving in. And that's just what he did, too. Moved in."

— "Stagolee"

wants, and use his gun "whenever somebody tri[es] to mess with him" (172). As he grows up, Stack, as Stagolee is often referred to, wins fame by killing men over card games and using their bodies as tables or chairs. He is so bad that "even white folks [don't] mess with Stagolee" (173).

Stagolee plays cards with a man named Billy Lyons, who thinks he is better than others because he has "a little education, and that stuff can really mess your mind up" (Lester 173). Billy gets angry when Stagolee keeps winning, so he knocks Stagolee's Stetson hat off his head and spits into it. Naturally, Stagolee pulls his gun, and Billy immediately restores the hat and begs for his life, invoking pity for his wife and two children. Stagolee replies, "The Lawd'll take care of your children. I'll take care of your wife" (173), promptly shoots Billy, and moves in with Billy's wife. A new white sheriff in town hears of the murder and informs his deputies that they will arrest Stagolee, but the deputies fear Stagolee so much that they actually defend him, telling the sheriff that killing an occasional man is good for one's health. The sheriff agrees to this for a white man but not for Stagolee because "this is a nigger" (173). The deputies then reprimand the sheriff for his racial slur because they say that Stagolee is a community leader and "one of our better citizens" (174). When the sheriff accuses them of cowardice, the deputies explain that they have reached an understanding with Stagolee that guarantees all their safety. The sheriff persists, so the deputies lay down their guns, tell him to do the job alone, and

proceed to the undertaker to make arrangements for the sheriff's funeral.

Stagolee hears that the sheriff is looking for him, and "being a gentleman," he goes out to meet him in a bar (Lester 174). The sheriff confronts Stagolee, firing shots in the air, but when Stagolee ignores him, the sheriff tells him, "I'm the sheriff, and I'm white. Ain't you afraid?" (174). Stagolee replies with "you ain't Stagolee. Now deal with that" (174). When the sheriff tries to arrest him, Stagolee promptly kills him. The next day, he attends both the funerals of Billy and the sheriff before returning to Mrs. Billy. At this point, Stagolee is described as good looking and "always respectful to women" (175). His one fault is his tendency to drink himself into oblivion. The new sheriff waits until Stagolee gets too drunk to walk and then, accompanied by the "Ku Klux Klan Alumni Association" (175), breaks into his house with a lynching rope. But when the rope touches Stagolee's neck, he suddenly becomes sober and wide awake, prompting the white people to run in terror. Calmly stretching, Stagolee asks to get the lynching over with so he can "get on back to bed" (175). Stagolee magically causes the rope to fail and mocks his would-be murderers, who eventually give up and release him.

With his superhuman strength, Stagolee lives longer than he is supposed to, attracting the attention of St. Peter in heaven, who notes that Stagolee should "have died thirty years before" (Lester 176). St. Peter consults the Lord, who calls on Death to pay a visit to Stagolee. Overworked from "so many trips to Vietnam," Death is unhappy about receiving another assignment and cannot understand "why dying couldn't be systematized" with an organized structure that would utilize assistants (176). But the Lord will have none of it, so Death gets on his horse and meets the Lord, who upbraids his servant for neglecting to bring Stagolee on time. Death starts to complain about his working conditions, but the Lord cuts him off. So Death proceeds to find Stagolee but is completely flummoxed when Stagolee flatly refuses to die, threatening instead to shoot him. Death then consults his *Death Manual* but finds no solution. When Stagolee fires a shot that narrowly misses him, Death returns to heaven and tells the Lord that he must get Stagolee himself. The Lord then has St. Peter "tell the work crew" of angels to bring him his "giant death thunderbolt" (178). St. Peter helps him to spell correctly as he writes Stagolee's name on the thunderbolt, and the Lord then casts his eye on the world, marveling at the killing in Vietnam and sinful deeds elsewhere. St. Peter helps the Lord to locate Stagolee and strike him dead with the thunderbolt.

The final part of the story recounts Stagolee's funeral and journey to the afterlife. His lavish funeral goes on for days and is attended by people "from all over the country" (Lester 179), some of whom place messages in his pocket for their relatives in hell. Musicians honor him, while women of all ages worship and weep. Stagolee is buried in his own private cemetery, but naturally, he rises three days after death and decides to visit heaven on his own, unable to stomach the idea of being judged by a white man. Hearing hymns and harp music, Stagolee concludes that he must go to another side of heaven to find "the black part" (180), but instead he discovers St. Peter playing bridge. St. Peter tells Stagolee that because all the black people sang the blues, most were sent to hell. Stagolee then informs St. Peter that he "messed up" (180) because he is actually in hell, not heaven. Approaching hell, Stagolee smells barbecue cooking, hears jukeboxes, and sees a Black Power sign on the gate. Entering, he meets his friends and finds that hell has been renovated and is air-conditioned. Stagolee then asks if there are any "white folks down here" and is told, "Just the hip ones, and ain't too many of them" (181). He then notices an old man sitting alone and covering his ears. His friends tell him that this is the Devil, who cannot "get himself together" because he does not yet know "how to deal with niggers" (181). Stagolee invites the Devil to take up his pitchfork and "go one round" (181) with him. When the Devil simply looks sadly at Stagolee, the hero dismisses him and declares, "'I'm gon' rule Hell by myself!' And that's just what he did, too" (181).

ANALYSIS

If Stagolee is the most popular badman folk hero, his image as a lawless rebel has also provoked much ambivalence. The many variants of his name attest his popularity: in addition to Stagolee, he is known as Staggerlee, Stackerlee, Stackalee, and Stack (Prahlad 1245). The African American badman hero type that Stagolee exemplifies descends partly from African trickster characters and developed in the late nineteenth century as blacks struggled after the Civil War against laws and customs designed to oppress them. In a society whose laws were indifferent at best and more often harmful, the figure of the invincible black badman came to be celebrated for taking the law into his own hands or simply flouting it. Yet scholars have found that the figure

of Stagolee is also based in history, specifically in a conflict in which a St. Louis pimp murdered a man for knocking off his Stetson hat. This reality might account for Stagolee's amazing popularity, with hundreds of songs and narratives emerging in different forms, but it also raises the question of the extent to which he merits celebration. Moreover, many of the Stagolee toasts or folk poems are violent and sadistic, fueling negative stereotypes about black men and present-day gangster rappers. A cultural analysis considers how Julius Lester's 1969 story negotiates the popularity and ambivalence surrounding Stagolee to produce a version palatable to a general audience. Specifically, Lester incorporates traditional traits of the Stagolee character, such as his supernatural trickster qualities, while eliminating his cruelty and brilliantly incorporating humor. These elements effectively make Stagolee both less realistic and more sympathetic. On the other hand, Lester emphasizes politics and race relations to make the story provocative and relevant to a 1969 audience. In this way, a cultural analysis contextualizes and evaluates the relative success of Lester's engaging treatment.

Cecil Brown has argued that Stagolee is based on a real-life incident in 1895, in which a flamboyant pimp named Lee Shelton, or Stack Lee, murdered a man named William Lyons in a bar in the red-light district of St. Louis following a dispute about politics. When Lyons took Shelton's hat, the latter demanded that he return it and pulled a .44 revolver, killing Lyons when he refused to submit. Shelton then retrieved his hat from the dying Lyons and went home to bed. He was arrested and sentenced to prison. He served thirteen years and was released on parole but then later returned to jail for other reasons and died there in 1912. Even before Shelton's death, his story had become a legend in the bars and brothels of St. Louis, and there is evidence that blacks sang ballads about him in 1911 as far away as Georgia and North Carolina (Brown 99).

The legend of Stagolee is, of course, distinct from Shelton's actual life, which did not end in fanfare as it does in some renditions of the legend (Brown 115–16). The forces underlying the development of Stagolee as a celebrated "bad" hero are rooted in several cultural phenomena. The outlaw figure has long been celebrated in mainstream American culture in the form of white characters such as Billy the Kid and Jesse James, and these types are surely related to the development of the black "badman." Some scholars describe the badman as emerging from the figure of the town bully, a common character type in southern small towns whose behavior is rooted in tribalism, or leadership by prowess (Abrahams 123–4). However, the black outlaw type also developed in the context and legacy of slavery. By virtue of their status, slaves were already defined as inferior to whites, but slave owners labeled disobedient or rebellious slaves as "bad niggers." Obviously, this "badness" represented a righteous desire for freedom, which helps to explain how what whites viewed as bad came to signify what was good for black people (Bryant 2). This positive and subversive meaning of "bad" as fearless, rebellious, and cool applies to the folk figure of the heroic badman.

Yet John W. Roberts rightly argues that this nineteenth-century type did not arise simply from the image of the hostile slave or the angry, oppressed black man. Instead, the heroic badman emerged partly from the trickster character who populates African folktales that were narrated by slaves and partly from the historical realities of blacks after the Civil War ended in 1865 (Roberts 184–215). During this period, slavery did not simply disappear because many slave owners refused to break with custom, and states passed new laws designed to prevent freed slaves from exercising their rights. For many blacks, de facto slavery continued through various forms of white resistance. Blacks thus faced a situation in which they were technically free but were either afforded no protection by the law or were actively harmed by it. In this context, the black outlaw character emerges in folklore as a fearless hero with supernatural trickster-like traits, flouting the laws that would oppress him and showcasing his invincible manhood. According to Roberts, the badman's two worst enemies are in fact the law and the "bad nigger" who commits crimes, sometimes to exploit the law's "apparent indifference to the well-being of black people" (215); in this way, the black badman's behavior becomes heroic as he challenges whites and certain blacks threatening the values and material opportunities of the black communities.

Yet the figure of Stagolee specifically is complex precisely because he is based in history and because of the popularity and development of his legend, which has shown some disturbing trends. While the early ballads emphasize that real-life criminal Shelton is caught and punished, suggesting recognition that his behavior is not acceptable, they also sometimes celebrate his deeds by showing him outwitting the devil in hell, thereby confirming his mythic, heroic badness (Abrahams 126; Roberts 212). In the later twentieth century, the Stagolee

legend evolved into toasts, or oral folk poems in rhyming couplets, which emerged most prominently as part of black urban criminal subcultures, with many versions collected from prisoners (Wepman, Newman, and Binderman 2–7). In these toasts, performers boast of Stagolee's exploits, improvising new details and adopting his voice, but the vignettes are full of foul language as the protagonist sadistically murders people and brags of dominating his women through violent sex (135). This Stagolee is in fact the prototype of the gangster rapper who celebrates a life of crime. For this reason, critics such as Tonya Bolden reject Stagolee as a hero because, she argues, most narratives state that he resists white oppression but show him preying mostly on his own people. In addition, he contributes much to negative stereotypes about black men but nothing to real social change, instead encouraging some young people to emulate his behavior; she specifically cites Lester's version of the story as an exception written for a general audience (131). Therefore, to appreciate the meaning and value of Stagolee, one must follow Anand Prahlad's advice and distinguish carefully between the historical Lee Shelton and "the legendary motif" (1247), but also be aware of the profound differences among the many versions of the legend.

Julius Lester's story impressively negotiates these distinctions. To be sure, Lester introduces Stagolee as "the baddest nigger that ever lived" (172) but establishes his heroism by making him both more likable and less realistic than the historical Stagolee. Lester incorporates the supernatural trickster qualities that appear in some of the early ballads in which Stagolee outwits the Devil himself. The author conveys Stagolee's superhuman status early on in the second paragraph when he describes him as leaving home at the age of five with nothing more than a guitar, a deck of cards, and a gun. With this detail, the reader immediately understands that Stagolee is a mythical character. Similarly, when the second sheriff and his band of white racists attempt to hang Stagolee, he swings "ten feet in the air, laughing as loud as you ever heard anybody laugh" (175). After a half-hour, he is still laughing, so they give up and Stagolee simply goes home to bed. When Death himself flees Stagolee's gunshots, it becomes clear that the hero is totally invincible in human terms. Only the Lord's thunderbolt can take him from this world, but he never really dies because he gets "on up out of the grave" (180) after three days (an allusion to the resurrection of Christ) to continue his antics in the afterlife. Eventually, he unseats the forlorn Devil, who turns

HISTORICAL CONTEXT

The Stagolee legend flourished as a popular song in the early twentieth century long before award-winning author Julius Lester penned his version of the tale in 1969. Yet Lester's account of Stagolee is historically significant because it was written on the heels of the American civil rights movement and early in the black power movement, both of which significantly inform his version of the tale.

A central element of Lester's story is its emphasis on race relations between blacks and whites, specifically the racism that Stagolee fearlessly resists. This treatment reflects social movements against racial discrimination in the United States that inspired various forms of activism from approximately 1955 to the late 1960s. These acts of resistance included boycotts (most famously the Montgomery bus boycott that began in 1955 when a black woman named Rosa Parks refused to give up her seat to a white passenger), marches, sit-ins, and freedom rides, among other actions. This activism eventually led to a series of federal laws, including the Civil Rights Act of 1964, which outlawed major forms of discrimination based on race, color, religion, and nationality in employment and public accommodations. The Voting Rights Act followed in 1965 and was designed to restore and guarantee voting rights that had been repeatedly denied to African Americans in the years following the abolishment of slavery. These and other fundamental legal and social changes are reflected in Lester's direct and provocative treatment of race relations in his Stagolee tale. Another key influence was the black power movement, which began in the late 1960s and sought to advance the civil rights movement by fostering racial pride, freedom from racial injustice of all kinds, and political and economic independence. Lester directly refers to the black power movement at the end of his story when Stagolee in the afterlife arrives at the gates of hell, which are graced with a sign that reads Black Power.

out to be no match for the truly eternal Stagolee. These fantastic elements render Stagolee as not a literal badman but a mythical one who symbolizes superhuman strength and endurance. This supernatural quality makes Stagolee's lawlessness more acceptable to readers who might frown upon his lawlessness.

Also contributing to Stagolee's palatable image is his likability. He is certainly merciless as he kills Lyons while mocking him as he begs for his life, and he is happy to fight when he willingly goes to the bar after he learns that the sheriff is looking for him. Yet he is nothing like the sadistic murderer of the toast tradition in which Stagolee revels in killing out of sheer cruelty. In Lester's story, Stagolee kills Lyons and the first sheriff but then attends their funerals, suggesting that he harbors a measure of human decency. He displays no other violent behavior in the rest of the story except to defend himself against Death. Instead, he uses his superpowers and cool attitude to survive the second sheriff's lynching attempt, leaving his would-be murderers unharmed. Lester also departs from the toast tradition by making Stagolee kind to women: "He was always respectful to women, always had plenty of money, and, generally, he made a good husband, as husbands go" (175). This description makes Stagolee appear more sympathetic, but it is more than a little hard to believe that this badman is always respectful to women, especially given that they have no voice or choice in the story other than to praise or submit to him. He simply announces to Billy Lyons's wife that he is moving in with her, and women of every age fall over themselves in grief at Stagolee's funeral. Of course, these details are meant to be funny and are effective within that limited framework.

Lester's brilliant use of humor is arguably the strongest technique in support of Stagolee's likability and the story's overall success. Much of the tale is hilarious with witty dialogue and character sketches. Highlights include the first sheriff's interactions with his deputies, who are obviously terrified of Stagolee and defend him, telling their boss, "Ain't nothing wrong with killing a man every now and then" and "It's good for a man's health" (173). When the sheriff describes Stagolee with a racial slur, the deputies scold him: "Now, sheriff, you got to watch how you talk about Stagolee" (173). When the sheriff persists, the deputies go straight to the undertaker to start his funeral preparations, and people of the town urge him to stop "disturbing the peace" (174). Here, a comic inversion makes the sheriff the troublemaker while the deputies and townspeople defend Stagolee as a community leader. Another comic high point is the scene with St. Peter, the Lord, and Death, who is an overworked and dissatisfied employee and is exhausted from having to "make so many trips to Vietnam . . . not to mention everywhere else in the world" (176). Death has lobbied for a more systematized approach to dying, such as limiting deaths to certain countries on certain days of the week: "That way, he wouldn't have to be running all over the world twenty-four hours a day" (176). But the Lord "had vetoed the idea. Said it sounded to him like Death just wanted an excuse to eventually computerize the whole operation" (176). Lester's dialogue sparkles as Death and the Lord argue and again when Death confronts Stagolee, telling him, "Come on, man. I ain't got all day" (178). Death becomes increasingly feckless as Stagolee flat-out refuses to die, forcing Death to consult his useless *Death Manual*. He returns to the Lord empty-handed and is allowed to go back to bed.

At this point, the Lord turns to St. Peter and asks if anyone has recently applied for Death's job, to which St. Peter replies, "You must be joking" (178). The Lord then orders over three thousand angels to bring his thunderbolt, which he is able to pick up "like it was a toothpick" (178), but then he immediately asks St. Peter how to spell Stagolee's name. When St. Peter tries to point out that the Lord knows everything, the Lord interrupts with, "You better shut up and tell me how to spell Stagolee" (178). The Lord then casts his eye to the earth and is astonished at "all that killing down there" (179), which St. Peter informs him is not Georgia but Vietnam. The Lord then gets distracted by "all that sin down there," declaring, "Women wearing hardly no clothes at all. Check that one out with the black hair, St. Peter. Look at her! Disgraceful! Them legs!" (179). Impatient, St. Peter cries out, "Lord!" (179), and directs his boss to Fatback, Georgia, to find Stagolee. This hilarious treatment continues throughout to render Stagolee charismatic and appealing, but it also shows him as part of a larger comic cosmos that justifies his wit and irreverence.

Whereas Lester's use of humor transforms Stagolee into an irresistible hero, his emphasis on race relations makes the story current and especially significant for a 1969 audience. The reality of conflict between whites and blacks is prevalent throughout the story, structuring the events and driving the humor. Stagolee decides at age two that he will not work for "white folks" (172), and Lester is careful to point out that Stagolee is so bad that "even white folks didn't mess with [him]" (173). When the deputies tell the first sheriff that an occasional homicide is good for one's health, the sheriff counters them with his statement about white privilege and a racial slur against Stagolee. When he confronts Stagolee, his words reveal his crass presumptions: "Stagolee, I'm the sheriff, and I'm white. Ain't you afraid?" (174). Attempting to defeat Stagolee, the second sheriff enlists the help of the "Ku Klux Klan Alumni Association, which was every white man in four counties" (175). The Lord mentions in passing to St. Peter, "Speaking of folks living past their time. St. Peter, have the librarian bring me all the files on white folks. Seems to me that white folks sho' done outlived their time" (177). When Stagolee reaches heaven, he discovers that even the afterlife is segregated when he looks for "the black part of Heaven" (180) and fails to find it because, St. Peter informs him, "we had to get rid of" the black people because they kept singing the blues (180). Stagolee reacts to this by telling St. Peter, "Hey, man. You messed up . . . This ain't Heaven. This is Hell. Bye" (180–81). Stagolee then proceeds to hell, where he reunites with his friends in what appears to be an eternal party. When he asks whether hell includes any "white folks," he is informed, "Just the hip ones, and ain't too many of them. But they all right. They know where it's at" (181). Stagolee then notices the Devil, forlorn and sitting alone in a corner, and when he asks about him, someone explains, "He ain't learned how to deal with niggers yet" (181). The story then concludes with Stagolee challenging the Devil to "have some fun" and "go one round" with him (181). When the Devil refuses, Stagolee appoints himself as hell's new ruler.

Lester's relentless focus on race works well with his other narrative strategies to make the tale socially and political relevant. Because the story constantly reminds the reader that Stagolee lives in a world and even a cosmos defined by the unjust realities of racism, which is also a historical fact of American culture, the story becomes much more than simply an entertaining portrait of a folk hero who inspires but could never exist in the real world. Stagolee's fantastic superpowers, his over-the-top rebelliousness, and the story's farcical humor might all give the impression that true resistance to injustice is impossible or beside the point. But the story's focus on racial tensions, as well as its references to the Vietnam War, remind readers that Stagolee is partly a product of and a response to real racial injustice—injustice that was meeting profound challenges in the civil rights movement of the 1960s and 1970s when Lester wrote the story. Lester's Stagolee does not prey on his own people; rather, he has the power to defend himself against his white oppressors, and he changes the rules of their game in the physical world and in the afterlife. In this way, Lester transforms Stagolee from a somewhat dubious folk hero into a mythical social and political revolutionary, albeit a fanciful one. Granted, the story's obsession with polarized race relations is somewhat dated and is occasionally inconsistent within the tale itself: the Lord suggests that white people have outlived their time, but later St. Peter explains that they banished most black people from heaven. Overall, however, Lester navigates the cultural complexities of Stagolee to make this American legend both great and accessible.

CROSS-CULTURAL INFLUENCE

The badman folk hero is prominent in American culture but is not unique to it. In fact, this hero is an old type found in narrative traditions throughout the world. One of the most notable examples comes from late medieval Italy in Giovanni Boccaccio's *Decameron*, a fourteenth-century collection of one hundred novellas that is considered a literary masterpiece and the most important example of early Italian prose. Boccaccio offers his stories as advice to ladies in love, and he creates a frame structure in which the tales are narrated by ten young ladies and gentlemen leaving Florence to escape the bubonic plague, a historical pandemic that may have killed as many as 100 million Europeans by 1400. By making the real and devastating plague the context of his fictional *Decameron*, Boccaccio links his stories to historical events to suggest the power of his tales to reveal truth and to help one survive in a world that is not always propitious. His first story, however, provides no easy comfort. It tells of Ser Cepparello, a man so enmeshed in sin that he is proud of it and is described as the worst man ever. Near the end of his life, Ser Cepparello decides to help a Frenchman collect loans from the notoriously corrupt Burgundians, but when Cepparello falls ill, he endangers the reputation of his hosts. As his capstone achievement, Cepparello delivers an utterly false confession to a gullible friar in a performance so brilliant and convincing that it earns him sainthood. Long debated by scholars, Ser Cepparello's heroism makes sense in the context of late medieval Italian culture in which church corruption and the devastation of the bubonic plague (among other forces) had created a sense of chaos and lawlessness.

The narrator, Panfilo, introduces the story of Ser Cepparello by praising God and his grace, which allows human beings to approach divine benevolence through the intercession of saints. However, because human judgment is imperfect, sometimes society nominates to sainthood those who are in fact worthy of eternal damnation in hell. Nonetheless, God does not blame humans for such mistakes but hears their prayers in any case. Panfilo then declares that he will tell a story about such a flawed judgment concerning a man named Ser Cepparello. A wealthy French merchant and knight named Musciatto Franzesi is asked to accompany the French king's brother to Tuscany, so in preparation, he wishes to resolve his extensive and complicated financial business. He finds people to help him resolve all of his issues except one: he must recover several loans from the Burgundians, who are notoriously bad, "a quarrelsome lot, of evil disposition, and disloyal" (Boccaccio 26). Struggling to find a solution, he finally remembers a man named Ser Cepparello, who had often been his guest in Paris and was called Ciappelletto by the French.

Ser Cepparello revels in all things bad. A notary, he feels shame if his documents are found to be valid and offers fraudulent ones free of charge. He delights in bearing false witness, causing him to win many lawsuits. He also loves to stir up scandal and create enmity between anyone who falls for it. He happily witnesses murders when invited to do so and even kills men himself without a second thought. He openly mocks God, the saints, and the sacraments, never attending church but frequenting bars and "dens of iniquity with great pleasure" (Boccaccio 27). He also prefers men to women, is sexually deviant, thieves, and is a glutton and a cheating gambler. In short, he is "probably the worst man that ever lived!" (27). Because he regularly puts his evil in service of Musciatto, he is shielded from the people and the law.

Musciatto therefore enlists Cepparello to recover his loans from the Burgundians, promising further protection and a healthy portion of the profits. Cepparello agrees and departs for Burgundy, where he is virtually unknown. He lodges in the home of two Florentine moneylenders and begins to collect the loans. Not long after, however, he becomes ill and is told that he will soon die, which prompts the Florentines to worry about how to handle the situation: if they throw him out without any clear reason, they will find themselves condemned by the people, but Cepparello is so wicked that he will refuse to confess, which means that he will not receive a proper church burial and instead "be thrown into a ditch just like a dead dog" (Boccaccio 29). Even if he does confess, his sins are so terrible that he will end up the same way, and the people, who already disapprove of the money-lending brothers, will condemn them for their iniquity and rob and possibly kill them.

Overhearing the brothers as they vent their worries, Ser Cepparello calls them to his sick bed and confirms their assessment of the situation. He promises to help by committing one last sin against God, which "will make no difference," given the enormity of his lifelong transgressions (Boccaccio 29). Asking them to bring the holiest priest they can find, he promises to "set both your affairs and mine in order in a way that will satisfy you" (29). Not convinced, the brothers nonetheless find such a friar and bring him to Cepparello's bedside. Cepparello then offers a totally false confession. The friar first asks how long it has been since Cepparello's last confession. Having never confessed at all, Cepparello claims that although he usually confesses "at least once a week" (30), he has often confessed much more often but has been hindered by his illness from doing so for eight days. Pleased with this answer, the friar praises Cepparello and remarks that there will be little for him to hear. Cepparello objects to this response, saying that he always confesses by recounting every sin he has ever committed, and he requests that the friar question him in this manner.

The friar again praises Cepparello and begins to question him about the capital vices, beginning with whether he has "ever sinned in lust with any woman" (Boccaccio 30). With a deep sigh, Cepparello responds that he is "ashamed to tell the truth for fear of sinning from pride" (30). When the friar reassures him, he declares that he is "as virgin today as when I came from my mother's womb" (31). Jubilant, the friar commends Cepparello for doing so well, especially given his freedom to marry, unlike priests and other religious people. The friar then asks about gluttony, to which Cepparello admits that even though he fasts weekly for "at least three days on bread and water" (31), he had relished the water and had often greatly desired wild herb salads, enjoying food more than someone of his devotion should. When the friar reassures Cepparello that it is natural to want to eat and drink after fasting or hard work, Cepparello tells him, "Don't say this just to console me" (31), because unless man offers good deeds to God absolutely, he sins. Moving on to avarice, the friar asks if Cepparello has ever wrongfully coveted or kept anything. To this,

Cepparello urges the friar not to judge him because of his association with the money lenders. He declares that he came to their house to try to convince them to change their ways. Moreover, he claims to have given a large inheritance to charity and to have always given half of his profits to the poor.

When the friar praises him and asks if Cepparello has submitted to anger, Cepparello reports that he has often been angry watching so many sinners disobey and ignore God and his commandments. The friar commends his righteous anger but wishes to know if Cepparello has ever committed murder or similar abuse. At this point, Cepparello objects, saying, "How could you say such things and be a man of God?" (Boccaccio 32), for if he had committed such crimes, how could God have done so much for him? Cepparello continues his confession in this way, portraying the most minor sins as if they were deep offenses and even scolding the friar at several points. When the friar is ready to grant absolution, Cepparello stops him in order to confess several more sins, such as when he once unthinkingly spat in church, which the friar dismisses: "My son, that is nothing to worry about; we priests, who are religious men, spit there all day long" (33). To this, Cepparello replies, "Then you do great harm, for no place should be kept as clean as a holy temple in which we give sacrifice to God" (34). Finally, Cepparello weeps at length, keeping the friar in suspense as he insists that he can never be forgiven for the most terrible sin of all: cursing his mother when he was a small boy. The friar promises that God will forgive him and then absolves and blesses Cepparello, offering him burial in the monastery.

Eavesdropping on Cepparello's false confession, the Florentine brothers struggle not to laugh and marvel at the wickedness of their guest, unwavering even on his deathbed. Cepparello dies soon after, and when the brothers learn that he will receive burial, they use his own money to arrange an honorable funeral. Meanwhile, the friar describes Cepparello's exceedingly holy life to the brothers of his order and convinces them to treat the body with great honor in hopes that God will perform miracles through him. The brothers agree and arrange a great public funeral in which they honor Cepparello as a rare example of piety. The country folk believe everything and rush forward after the service to kiss Cepparello's body, and they tear off his clothes, believing it will bless them. He is buried in the chapel in a marble tomb, and people immediately begin to visit his tomb to pray and worship him, calling him Saint Ciappelletto and claiming miracles in his name. Panfilo concludes his story by stating that although it is possible that Cepparello is in heaven, since he might have truly repented at the last moment, he is more likely in hell, where he belongs. Nonetheless, he says, God is truly merciful because he cares more about the intentions than the accuracy of those who pray to someone like Cepparello. Thus, he encourages his audience to keep faith in God's mercy and grace.

Panfilo's condemnation of Cepparello is clearly ironic as his story delightfully showcases the hero's genius for comedy and rhetoric and the gullibility of the friar and the other Christians. Like Stagolee, Cepparello is described as the worst man who ever lived, and his badness is so brilliantly outrageous that it earns the respect of his audiences. In addition, Stagolee's badness is partially a response to the injustice of racism, a fact that serves to sanction his disregard for the law. Similarly, readers champion Cepparello not only for his humor and rhetorical brilliance but because his false confession exposes the deep fallibility of the friar and, by extension, the church as a whole. His nomination to sainthood underscores the power of language to construct belief and implies that the arbiters of God's truth are at best imperfect, at worst totally incompetent. This type of church satire was increasingly common in late medieval Italy, when the church's wealth, corruption, and interference in politics had spiraled out of control, leading many Christians to lose faith in an institution that dictated and constrained much of their lives. Indeed, it was partly the church's decadence that later fueled the Protestant Reformation in the sixteenth century. The scourge of the bubonic plague, the same disaster afflicting the storytellers of *The Decameron*, only intensified the spiritual crisis that had already arisen for other reasons. These crises thus help to explain the celebration of Cepparello's badness and the privileging of his story as the first in *The Decameron*. As different as they are in time, circumstance, and character, Stagolee and Ser Cepparello are surely badmen of the same ilk, both repelling and delighting audiences as they prove that no evil is too great for heroes like them.

Ashleigh Imus, PhD

BIBLIOGRAPHY

Abrahams, Roger D. *Deep Down in the Jungle: Black American Folklore from the Streets of Philadelphia.* New Brunswick: Aldine Transaction, 2006. Print.

Boccaccio, Giovanni. *The Decameron.* Trans. Mark Musa and Peter Bondanella. New York: New American Lib., 2002. Print.

Bolden, Tonya. *Strong Men Keep Coming: The Book of African American Men.* New York: Wiley, 1999. Print.

Brown, Cecil. *Stagolee Shot Billy.* Cambridge: Harvard UP, 2003. Print.

Bryant, Jerry H. *Born in a Mighty Bad Land: The Violent Man in African American Folklore and Fiction.* Bloomington: Indiana UP, 2003. Print.

Lester, Julius. "Stagolee." *Myths, Legends, and Folktales of America: An Anthology.* Comp. David Leeming and Jake Page. New York: Oxford UP, 1999. 172–80. Print.

Prahlad, Anand. "Stagolee." *The Greenwood Encyclopedia of African American Folklore.* Ed. Prahlad. Westport: Greenwood, 2006. Print.

Roberts, John W. *From Trickster to Badman: The Black Folk Hero in Slavery and Freedom.* Philadelphia: U of Pennsylvania P, 1989. Print.

Wepman, Dennis, Ronald Newman, and Murray Binderman. *The Life: The Lore and Folk Poetry of the Black Hustler.* Philadelphia: U of Pennsylvania P, 1976. Print.

SURVEY OF MYTH AND FOLKLORE

American Indian Trickster Tales: The Coyote Hero

Author: Traditional Shasta
Time Period: 1001 CE–1500 CE; 1901 CE–1950 CE;
   1951 CE–2000 CE
Country or Culture: North America
Genre: Folktale

OVERVIEW

Coyote is among the most popular figures in American Indian folklore and mythology, particularly in a story type known as trickster tales. These tales showcase protagonists who often use deception to carry out transformations, gain an advantage over others, or simply embark on adventures. The American Indian trickster often appears as an animal, such as a raven, spider, blue jay, mink, rabbit, or coyote, the latter the most popular trickster incarnation. Among the Shastas of the Pacific Northwest, Coyote appears in numerous tales and is especially intriguing in "The Death of the Grizzly Bears."

In this story, Coyote lives with his wife, Louse, and ten grizzly bears, one of whom mocks a neighboring orphan boy. As an act of revenge, the boy cuts off the chief bear's foot while the animal sleeps, leading the bears to suspect the boy as the culprit. Coyote wishes to befriend and protect the boy, so he insists on the boy's innocence, even though in reality he witnessed the crime. He repeatedly tells the bears that the chief's foot fell into the fire and offers to visit the boy to discover the truth. Coyote instructs the boy that when the chief bear questions him, he should consent to being swallowed by the bear. The boy does so, and once inside the bear's body, he cuts out the animal's heart, causing its death. Coyote then tells the other bears not to bury the animal in the ground, thus allowing the boy to escape from inside its body. Coyote pretends to visit the boy's grandmother but actually goes to help the boy transport the bear meat. The youngest surviving bear dreams of Coyote's betrayal, and one of the bears sets out to discover

the truth. He chases Coyote and the boy, who escape to the boy's house, the door of which the boy magically transforms into stone. As the bear tries to enter, the boy heats rocks and then allows the bear to enter, hind feet first. Trapping the bear in the door, he kills it with the hot rocks. In this way, all the bears are destroyed except for the youngest, who survives to become the ancestor of all future bears.

As complex as he is popular, Coyote is known to play many and often contradictory roles in American Indian stories. This Shasta tale is no exception, as Coyote deceives his friends to help the boy and possesses supernatural powers yet is clearly neither omniscient nor omnipotent. A symbolic analysis of this and several other Shasta tales addresses the mystery of Coyote's significance, which is notoriously difficult in folklore studies. Is he a semidivine rebel hero, living on the margins of society and challenging its norms, a comic and cosmic supernatural force of creativity, or a warning of the dangers of social chaos? Although there is no universal meaning of Coyote, a symbolic interpretation unearths several common features across a sample of Shasta tales and reveals Coyote's profound significance as a reflection of human nature, culture, and survival.

SUMMARY

"The Death of the Grizzly Bears" begins by introducing Coyote's household, which includes his wife, Louse, and ten grizzly bears. An orphan boy lives nearby with his grandmother and often visits the animals. One day, the boy arrives, and one of the bears greets him, declaring that he had known the boy's parents, who were good hunters and gatherers. The bear adds, "But now you are alone and poor" (Farrand 214). This comment brings the boy to tears, and when he returns home, his grandmother scolds him for visiting the bears: "The Grizzlies are mean, and always scoff at you. It was they who killed

"After a while one of the Grizzly Brothers recollected that on the previous day they had mocked the orphan boy, and expressed his belief that it was the boy who cut off the chief's foot. Thereupon Coyote said, 'I'll go to the boy and ask him.' The others agreed, and Coyote started out. He found the boy eating bear-meat. He warned him to keep quiet, and not to say anything when questioned about the happenings of last night."

"The Death of the Grizzly Bears"

your people" (214). That evening, the boy sharpens his knife and returns to the house of Coyote and the bears, hiding in the shrubbery until all are asleep, at which point he cuts off the chief bear's foot and dashes home. The bear later awakens in pain, lamenting that someone has cut off his foot. Coyote then shouts harshly at the other grizzlies to wake up because their chief has been injured.

In fact, Coyote witnessed the boy cutting off the foot and has thrown the bear's discarded foot bones and moccasin into the fire because he wants to befriend and protect the boy. Coyote tells the chief bear that his foot was burned in the fire after it slipped off of a footrest. The chief believes this, but his brothers are dubious, and Louse states, "I thought I saw someone go out last night" (215). Coyote claims that he was awake the whole night and that no one went out, repeatedly refuting his wife's words. Recalling the mockery of the orphan boy, one of the grizzly bears suggests that the boy cut off the chief's foot, so Coyote offers to visit the boy to get to the bottom of things. Coyote finds the boy eating bear meat and instructs him to "keep quiet" about the previous night's events. Coyote returns to the bears and declares, "The poor boy is crying. He is not feeling well. I am sure he did not cut off your leg" (215). When the bear insists that the boy is the culprit, Coyote is sent to bring the boy to be questioned by the chief. This time, Coyote tells the boy that if the chief asks if he should crush the boy with

his hands, the boy should say no, but if he asks, "Shall I swallow you," the boy should consent to this.

Confronted by the grizzly chief, the boy confesses to the deed, and when the bear asks if the boy cut off his foot because the bear had mocked him, the boy concedes this as well. When the bear asks if he should "pulverize" the boy, the child refuses but agrees to be swallowed by the bear. Inside the bear's body, the boy uses his knife to cut out the animal's heart, killing him. The other grizzlies plan to bury the chief in the ground, but Coyote tells them not to do this to prevent others from stealing the carcass for food. Instead, he tells them to build a fence to surround the bear and to cover the body with brush. The grizzlies follow these instructions, which allow the boy to come out of the chief's body when the other bears have gone.

Next, Coyote once again deceives the bears, telling them that he wishes to visit the grandmother to see "how she is getting on" (216). Finding the boy at home, Coyote explains everything he has done and then returns home to tell the bears that he plans to stay with the grandmother for a while. In fact, he wishes to help the boy transport the bear meat. That night, however, the youngest grizzly dreams that Coyote is "help[ing] the boy to carry the meat of his dead brother" and asks another bear the next morning to go out to verify the dream. One of the bears sees Coyote transporting the last piece of meat, so he chases the boy and Coyote, who arrive safely at the boy's home. The boy changes the door into stone simply by wishing that it happen. The grizzly then circles the house, demanding, "Boy, how can I get inside?" Meanwhile, the boy heats rocks and tells the grizzly that he must enter the house with his hind feet first. He opens the door to allow half of the bear's body in and then "wishe[s]" the door to close tight" (216). When the door traps the bear, the boy kills him with the hot rocks. He kills the other bears in the same way except for the youngest, who becomes the ancestor of all grizzlies.

ANALYSIS

Tricksters are fundamental rule breakers who appear in literary traditions throughout the world, often stealing, playing pranks, and generally delighting audiences with their antics. Yet the American Indian Coyote trickster is as distinct as he is perplexing. Unlike their counterparts in European and other traditions, Coyote and other American Indian tricksters are central figures that are both highly developed and maddeningly inconsistent.

Coyote reveals marked differences in his behavior across American Indian tales as well as within the traditions of individual tribes. For this reason, just as Coyote deceives his rivals in the tales, the many Coyote characters have bedeviled scholars trying to make sense of them. What is clear is that because no generalized Coyote figure exists across American Indian folklore, there is no universal symbolism for this trickster. Intelligent readings must therefore approach Coyote within the context of the tribe and, if possible, the narrator producing the stories. A symbolic analysis delineates Coyote's compelling roles in "The Death of the Grizzly Bears" and other tales of the Shasta people, an American Indian tribe in the Pacific Northwest region of North America. The analysis situates these roles in the context of debates that attempt to define Coyote as an individual in the societies in which he appears. Some readers highlight Coyote's heroic rebelliousness, whereas others underscore his semidivine creative powers or social functions. Although part of Coyote's effect is to subvert stable meanings, this sample of Shasta narratives emphasizes the trickster as a highly fallible, semidivine, creative force dedicated to both benevolence and deceit. Neither omniscient nor omnipotent, the version of Coyote presented in these tales displays more cunning than stupidity and warns of the complex human potential for deception that is both crucial for survival and potentially destructive.

As Richard Erdoes and Alfonso Ortiz note in the introduction to their anthology *American Indian Trickster Tales*, in much European folklore, tricksters appear as comic makers of mischief, but they are usually minor characters and are fairly one-dimensional compared with their American Indian counterparts. In addition, European tricksters are often male humans, whereas American Indian tricksters usually appear as animals. Franchot Ballinger notes that American Indians consider animals to be equal to humans in the sense of having "consciousness, intelligence, and spirits" and, citing scholar William Bright, states that American Indians describe animals, including trickster characters, as originally being "First People," or prototype creatures that existed prior to the arrival of humans (45). When humans arrived, these First People, who were similar to gods, became animals. Thus, tricksters are mythic figures who often play key roles in creation but also have comic or less admirable traits. Coyote is the most popular trickster for reasons not entirely clear, but Ballinger suggests that real-life coyotes are difficult to define and

are remarkably skilled survivors because of their high adaptability, two characteristics that also apply to Coyote in American Indian mythology.

The behavior of Coyote and other trickster animals is indeed complex, with many playing the roles of ambiguous culture heroes, according to Erdoes and Ortiz. Clever and foolish, a godlike savior and an impish destroyer, Coyote frequently displays supernatural and even sacred powers, but at times he is a comic, sniveling thief and glutton. Coyote not infrequently displays these opposing traits in the same culture and even in the same story, and Ballinger confirms that American Indian authors also find tricksters to be enigmatic. For readers grappling with Coyote's fascinating and deeply unsettling presence, this ambiguity is both horrifying and magnetic (Wiget 87). The interpretive difficulties have led many scholars to "take differences in characterization as part of a common essence and to define the trickster as a protean amalgamation of them all" (Hymes 109). A common solution to Coyote's contradictions has thus been to cast him as a heroic rebel, an individualistic spirit living on the margins and both challenging and affirming society's strict conventions (Ballinger 23). In fact, however, Coyote and other tricksters reflect significant differences across stories and cultures, and Dell Hymes and other scholars underscore the importance of interpreting Coyote within the context of specific American Indian cultures rather than as an expression of one universal culture or nature. Thus, it is best to limit the description of Coyote to how he appears within this particular group of Shasta tales.

In "The Death of the Grizzly Bears," Coyote appears to be a benevolent deceiver. He is benevolent because he wishes to help the orphan boy after the bears mock him, but to do so, he deceives the characters with whom he lives, which makes his deception hard to dismiss: he does not simply trick other animals to help an ostensibly worthier human but actually betrays those who are related to him. He even lies to his wife, Louse, by repeatedly denying that the orphan boy or anyone else has cut off the bear's foot. These details emphasize Coyote's deceitfulness. Yet Coyote also goes to great lengths to help the orphan boy, telling him how to survive the chief bear's interrogation and ensuring that the bear is not buried so that the boy can escape from his body. Later, Coyote helps the boy transport the bear meat. That Coyote chooses to protect a human from mockery and fierce animals further underscores his helpful and generous nature. The story thus establishes Coyote as a protector of humans, but his benevolence relies on treachery that is both deep and personal.

Coyote displays a similar type of benevolence in the Shasta tale "The Theft of Fire," but this time he deceives humans and is aided by his animal friends. In this story, Coyote grows tired of needing to pile rocks to obtain heat, so he declares that the animals must "change this rock so that [they] can have regular fire" (Farrand 209). When he reveals his intention to obtain "regular fire" from a shaman, the people try to dissuade him from such a perilous undertaking, but Coyote insists. Arriving at his destination, Coyote finds only children, because the "fire-keepers" have gone hunting. Coyote approaches the fire with a stick as the children question him about his identity, noting that they have been told to beware of Coyote, the only likely intruder. Coyote responds simply with "Nonsense" and plants himself next to the fire (209). He slyly moves his stick and blanket toward the coveted fire as he tells the children not to fear him because he is their cousin. As his stick burns, he attempts to distract the children by telling them to look away. They initially resist, but when he tells them to "look . . . at Coyote's house" (210), the children do so, and Coyote dashes away with his burning stick.

Just as Coyote is scuttling off, the shaman returns and chases him, but Coyote passes the firebrand to his accomplices stationed at various points. First, he passes the stick to Eagle, who gives it over to Buzzard, and Turtle receives it last. When the slow Turtle is nearly caught by the shaman, he hides the fire in his armpit and jumps into a river. Coyote is angry at the other animals for giving the stick to Turtle, but when Turtle emerges from the river, he throws the stick on the ground, starting a massive fire in the mountains. From this, "all people came to obtain fire, and there has been fire ever since" (210). Coyote then makes fire sticks, instructs his people, and establishes rules regarding their use. In this story, Coyote's theft is beneficial to others because it provides a fundamental benefit, but once again, his deed relies on trickery, which may hint at the skill required to create and maintain fire. Furthermore, Coyote's animal accomplices and deception of humans in this story reveal that he does not favor any one species or character. He is an equal-opportunity trickster.

One of Coyote's most interesting traits in "The Theft of Fire" and other Shasta tales is his marked fallibility. In "The Theft of Fire," Coyote upbraids the other animals because he mistakenly believes that they have erred in giving the firebrand to Turtle, and he even abuses Turtle

when the slow animal first emerges from the water. Only when Turtle proves Coyote wrong by throwing the firebrand on the ground is Coyote convinced of the truth. Not prominent in "The Death of the Grizzly Bears," this type of fallibility is quite notable in other Shasta tales, particularly "The Origin of Death." This story begins by stating that Coyote is "considered the wisest being to whom all people were wont to go for advice and help in times of distress" (Farrand 209). Spider and Coyote live together, and each has a son. When Spider's child dies, he tells Coyote, "I should like to have my child come back to life. What do you think of it?" Coyote responds that this would not be right because if all dead people were revived, the world would be overcrowded with spirits, leaving little room for the living souls already on earth. Spider silently accepts this verdict. However, when Coyote's child dies, he returns to Spider and attempts to revoke his former judgment, stating that he is willing to bring both their sons back to life. Yet Spider rejects this idea, saying, "My child is all spoiled now. It is too late" (209). Here, it is fascinating that Coyote displays wisdom but fails to apply it when he faces precisely the same situation that he had previously judged for another. In this way, the story might be intended to teach wisdom not by Coyote's words but by his deeds, demonstrating that profound wisdom is attained not merely through intelligence but through experience. Here, Coyote appears to represent indirectly the process of finding true wisdom.

On the other hand, several Shasta tales show Coyote failing entirely or with his power severely limited. At several points in "The Death of the Grizzly Bears," Coyote is shown to be neither omniscient nor omnipotent. He is unaware that the youngest bear accurately dreams of what Coyote is doing as he helps the boy transport the bear meat, and he and the boy are caught by surprise when the bear finds them. After the bear chases them to the boy's house, the boy effectively replaces Coyote as the principal actor, changing his door to stone, heating the rocks, trapping the bear in the half-open door, and killing the bear with the hot rocks. The boy then proceeds to kill nearly all of the other bears in the same way. By the end of the story, it is as if Coyote's agency has been transferred to the boy, who emerges as the real hero.

In "Coyote and Pitch" and "Coyote Tries to Kill the Moon," the "hero" utterly fails. The first story tells of how Coyote hears "that Pitch, the bad man, [is] coming," so he goes out and challenges him to a fight,

HISTORICAL CONTEXT

Storyteller Mary Carpelan reports that the Shastas traditionally inhabited an area in the Pacific Northwest extending from north-central California to southern Oregon. This area encompassed an extraordinarily large land base that the Shasta people inhabited for thousands of years prior to the nineteenth century. Their name derives from Mount Shasta, the region's most notable landmark, and the terrain was consequently rugged, with high elevations and extreme weather. Villages were inhabited year-round, and the Shastas survived by hunting deer, fishing for salmon, and gathering various berries, nuts, and bulb plants. In the early nineteenth century, the development of trade routes between California and Oregon began to deprive the Shastas of their rights to the land they had long inhabited.

The mid-nineteenth-century discovery of gold in northern California forever altered the Shastas' destiny when several hundred thousand people traveled there in the hope of striking it rich. For the Shastas and other American Indians, the massive influx of gold miners and settlers brought violence, enslavement, diseases, starvation, conflicts over natural resources, and environmental damage from mining. Despite the tragic loss and damage to the Shastas and other indigenous peoples, many tribes have survived and continue to work to preserve their culture and enjoy their full rights to land and resources.

The Shasta tales explored here are part of a collection that was gathered in 1900 by physician and anthropologist Livingston Farrand during a visit to the Siletz Reservation in northwestern Oregon. On that reservation, Farrand found individuals who narrated numerous Shasta tales of Coyote.

(222). He then realizes that he cannot kill the moon. These two stories reveal Coyote's ignorance of natural phenomena and even his foolishness, as he fails to understand the effect of the pitch until his entire body is immobilized. In these cases, he seems to represent the human propensity for stubbornness and stupidity.

Yet if Coyote is dimwitted in certain Shasta tales, his powers of protection and regeneration are far more prominent in the group of stories overall. In "The Death of the Grizzly Bears," he is quite skilled at inventing stories to protect the orphan boy, such as when he tells the bears that the boy is upset and instructs them not to bury the dead bear's body. Moreover, Coyote displays special knowledge when he instructs the boy to allow the bear to swallow but not crush him: somehow Coyote knows that the boy will be able to cut out the bear's heart and later escape from the animal's body. This special knowledge appears as a full-blown supernatural power in "The Flood," a story in which Coyote declares that the entire world will be flooded and that everyone will die. All of the people dismiss this warning because they believe that Coyote is joking, but he persists, warning everyone to prepare for a flood that will occur "in about ten years" (Farrand 210). When the flood indeed occurs, Coyote and two people retreat to a high mountain and are the only survivors. However, the rising water threatens to overtake them even on the mountain, so the desperate Coyote asks, "Am I going to die now?" (211). As the water rises, Coyote poses the same question to his tail, which replies "No!" He then asks his phallus, which responds to him that the last stage of the flood has arrived. When the floodwaters recede, "the people c[o]me to life again," and Coyote gathers them together and assigns them names: "Deer, Grizzly Bear, Black Bear, Panther, Spider, Rattlesnake," and so forth. The story concludes by explaining, "The people thereupon dispersed all over the country" (211).

In "The Flood," Coyote has prophetic and regenerative powers that appear to be rooted in his own flesh,

boasting, "I can whip you, no matter who you are" (Farrand 218). Pitch then tells Coyote that he cannot fight with his hands, so Coyote punches him, only to find that his fist sticks to Pitch. He then repeats the mistake with all of his limbs, his tail, his ear, and finally his head. He escapes only when his friend Spider arrives and scrapes him off of Pitch's body.

In the second vignette, Coyote observes "the Moon (man)" and declares, "I am going to see how he comes out" (222). Coyote sits on a mountain until the moon appears, at which point he shoots an arrow at it. But the moon keeps moving, so Coyote continues shooting until he has used all his arrows. The next day, Coyote looks over the mountain's edge and sees all of his arrows "sticking in the place whence the Moon had come up" as he predicts the flood and then addresses his tail and phallus with questions that coincide with the flood's end and the revival of the people. Coyote then names the people and allows them to disperse, suggesting his central role in the world's repopulation. Similarly, several other Shasta tales include etiological details, or explanations of the cause or origin of something. In "The Death of the Grizzly Bears," Coyote's support of the orphan boy leads to the death of all the grizzlies living with Coyote except the youngest, who is said to be the "progenitor of all Grizzly Bears that are alive now" (216). In "The Theft of Fire," his robbery results in the benefit of an essential element for all people. In these stories, then, Coyote is more than simply a benevolent deceiver; his powers of deception are linked to essential life forces.

However, as Ballinger points out, these etiological details do not appear to be the stories' main points; rather, they function as evidence of the stories' authenticity. Thus, "The Death of the Grizzly Bears" does not serve primarily to explain how the bears survived. Instead, the survival of the bears evidences the story's truth. This understanding allows the audience to focus on Coyote's behavior as the main point of the stories. "The Origin of Death" is not about how death first emerged but about Coyote's ambivalence toward this reality. Likewise, "The Theft of Fire" is about not fire itself but how Coyote obtains it. "The Flood" is important not for its depiction of the natural disaster but for Coyote's relationship to the event and to the people. Specifically, the story warns of the consequences of dismissing Coyote's wisdom, which seems to be a reasonable thing to do given his frequent deception and fallibility, such as in "The Origin of Death," when he sanctions and then rejects death when it does not serve his personal interest. His silly boasting in "Coyote and Pitch" and his ignorance in "Coyote Tries to Kill the Moon" lend further support to his marginalization.

Yet ultimately, Coyote in these Shasta tales is anything but a marginal hero, notwithstanding his rebelliousness, deception, and foolishness. Ballinger argues that to romanticize Coyote as a rebellious and individualistic culture hero living on the margins and challenging society's conventions is to prize individuality in a way that is sharply at odds with American Indian cultures, which do not exalt individuality for its own sake but rather value the crucial links among all individual destinies. These Shasta stories in fact exemplify Coyote's flaws as part of his centrality in society. It is Coyote's deception that leads the orphan boy to both defeat his enemies and ensure the grizzlies' survival. Coyote's robbery makes fire available to all. His ambivalence toward death dramatizes humans' philosophical acceptance of and yet personal resistance to the reality of death. His encounter with Pitch and his attempt to kill the moon illustrate the limits of human knowledge in the face of unfamiliar elements and natural phenomena. Like Coyote's supernatural powers, these flaws are fundamental to his meaning in these tales, which suggest powerful lessons in human survival. Scholar Patrick Hubbard suggests that Coyote perhaps represents "man as he tries to second-guess his environment" and understand his remarkable power to transform reality; he is "a comic echo of man's everyday struggle to maintain his niche in a world which is constantly becoming something else" (114). To be sure, Coyote challenges social limits in these tales, but as Ballinger notes, he does so to warn of the dangers inherent in human nature and the fragility of both culture and survival. Coyote thus becomes a culture hero who resembles the complexity of humans far more than he does an exceptional supernatural figure. At the same time, he is not a predictable Everyman, and his stories never fall into obvious moralizing but offer an intriguing, indirect sort of didactic experience. In this way, Coyote in these Shasta tales emerges paradoxically as a human culture hero as sophisticated as he is ambiguous.

CROSS-CULTURAL INFLUENCE

Coyote's popularity has earned him a place in children's literature, where he retains many of his key traits but becomes notably less contradictory in his behavior. Two American children's books reflect this tendency in very different ways. The first, titled *Coyote Fights the Sun*, was published in 2002 and written by Mary J. Carpelan, who is of Shasta heritage and learned the story from her grandfather. An intriguing variant of "Coyote Tries to Kill the Moon," the story reveals the flexibility with which Shasta narrators approach Coyote tales. Carpelan's story is more complex than "Coyote Tries to Kill the Moon," but her Coyote displays a poignant consistency in his behavior as he grieves the loss of his children. In contrast, Marty Kreipe de Montaño adapts her 1998 book *Coyote in Love with a Star* from a traditional tale of the Klamath people, another tribe of the Pacific Northwest. Here, Coyote's character is somewhat simplified as a hungry wanderer in search of work and love, but de Montaño, a member of the Potawatomis, crafts a humorous, current tale by setting Coyote's adventures in Manhattan. In this way, the author effectively reaches children by combining Coyote's traditional traits with modern touches. If both stories diminish Coyote's mysterious powers, they also shine in their ability to make Coyote appealing and meaningful to young readers.

In *Coyote Fights the Sun: A Shasta Indian Tale*, Coyote lives in Quartz Valley with his family, which includes two daughters. They store dried meat, fish, nuts, and berries and live on this food for the winter until one sunny day in March when Coyote sees the sun and believes that spring has arrived. He shouts to his daughters to go out and find some "icknish" (5), or wild celery, and to throw out all the old food because spring has brought them new, fresh food. The daughters throw the old food down the hill and then proceed to Quartz Hill to find the celery plants. As soon as they climb the hill, a dark cloud emerges, and snow begins to fall, reaching two feet deep. The girls freeze to death in the storm, so Coyote searches for them the next morning. When he discovers his dead children, he becomes angry at the sun for fooling him by making him believe that spring had arrived and decides to "shoot the sun" (13).

The next morning, Coyote sees the sun rise over "Oro Fino Hill," so he goes to sit on the hill to wait for the sun, but then he sees the sun rise "behind Duzel Rock, Moffett Creek" (14). Coyote concludes that the sun has purposely evaded him: "'Ohhh,' Coyote said, 'he must have seen me waiting here for him, so he comes up over there'" (14). Coyote then goes to Duzel Rock in the evening and hides behind rocks all night until the sun rises in the morning. This time, he sees the sun rise "way over behind Gazelle Mountain, towards Mount Shasta" (15). Coyote concludes that once again, the sun has purposely fled, so he decides to travel even farther to await his enemy. He climbs high onto the rocky mountain to wait for the sun "so he could shoot him" (18). The next morning, the sun rises far away behind Mount Shasta. Still believing that the sun has seen him and run away, Coyote descends the hill and sees what he thinks is a large lake, but in fact, it is a "valley of fog" (19). Coyote decides to jump into the lake to swim across to Mount Shasta, but he falls through the fog and rolls down the mountain. He then gets up and climbs onto a rock pile near Gazelle Mountain. The story then concludes somewhat unexpectedly: "And he is still sitting there, waiting for the sun to come up so he can shoot" (23).

This story is clearly a version of the Shasta tale "Coyote Tries to Kill the Moon." In that story, however, Coyote comes to realize that he cannot in fact kill the moon, whereas Carpelan's version concludes with Coyote still

waiting for the sun to rise so that he can shoot it. This difference is significant and verifies the claims of Hymes and other scholars about the remarkable variation and flexibility of American Indian treatments of Coyote. In this case, there are two versions of essentially the same story, both attributed to the Shasta people, that convey not only different but arguably contradictory messages. In "Coyote Tries to Kill the Moon," the protagonist is ignorant of natural phenomena but eventually learns something. Carpelan's Coyote evidently learns nothing, as the narrator leaves him frozen in his ignorance.

Yet Carpelan's story is actually more complex than the moon tale, as Coyote's behavior is implicitly driven by his reaction to the death of his daughters, for which he is partly responsible. Coyote's reaction to his loss, and implicitly to his own guilt, is anger and a desire for revenge against the sun, which he believes has tricked him. That the story leaves Coyote's wish for revenge unresolved might suggest his stupidity but more profoundly conveys the effect of grief. With this recognition, Coyote in Carpelan's story stands in for human beings and their relationships with larger phenomena beyond human control, such as death, weather, and the elements that appear to control these events. Coyote's reaction to the sun is natural as he grapples with the death of his children, and the fact that he never comes to terms with the sun's true nature reminds the reader that grief is a recurring process that all must face. Carpelan supports this interpretation in her author's notes, which state that members of her family told the story repeatedly throughout their lives, and her mother was careful to watch for dark clouds as she climbed Quartz Hill in the spring to gather wild celery. For Carpelan and her family, and ostensibly for many American Indians, mountain snowstorms in early spring were a real threat. Coyote's experience thus represents a moving negotiation of humans' limited power in the face of nature.

Coyote in Love with a Star offers a quite different portrait of this peripatetic hero. The story introduces "Ol' Man Coyote" as he wanders along a dry pasture in Kansas, hungry and looking for work. But "unemployment [is] high on the Potawatomi reservation," and so on the advice of a friend, he sets out for New York City, where people are paid "to open doors and run elevators" (6). Coyote is also lonely and hopes "maybe he could find someone special in the big city." He prepares some fry bread, packs up his van, and heads "toward the place where the sun comes up" (6). Coyote drives for a long time and camps along the way, living on fry bread. He finally crosses the George Washington Bridge and discovers skyscrapers, music blaring from street corners, people "all in a big hurry," and "many neighborhoods, each one like a different country, with its own food, smells, language, and music" (10).

Once Coyote gets settled, he hits the pavement to look for work. Coming upon a subway entrance, he looks down into the "deep hole" and hears a rumbling underground that sounds "like a whole herd of buffalo" (12). Coyote descends and finds iron bars and a turnstile blocking the entrance. He sees some flower sellers pushing through "a gate in the fence" toward the subway train (16). Wanting to ride the train but not knowing how to gain access, Coyote transforms himself into a sunflower, prompting a flower seller to pick him up and place him in his basket. In this way, Coyote boards the train. He rides it to the last stop, where he changes himself back to his normal shape and emerges to find the Twin Towers, "two huge towers that stretched to the sky" (18). He sees crowds of people entering the buildings to go to work and believes that he can get hired as well. Fortune serves him well: "He found a job, and it was in his field too. He became the Rodent Control Officer in the World Trade Center" (20).

Despite his success, Coyote feels homesick. At night, he stargazes from the World Trade Center's observation deck. One evening when the stars appear especially bright, Coyote falls in love with "one star that [is] more beautiful than all the rest" (20). Coyote spends every night waiting for his star to appear, at which point he howls and begs for her to "take him up into the sky" so he can "dance with her" (22). The star ignores him for some time but finally accepts Coyote: "As they danced across the sky, he was so happy he thought his heart would burst" (22). Soon, however, Coyote realizes that the star does not speak to him, and none of the stars speak to each other: "they just danced, cold and beautiful, across the night sky" (24). He becomes chilled and feels dizzy when he looks down, so he asks the star to return him to earth. She dances with him and then drops him over the edge of the sky. He falls for four days and nights, eventually landing in Central Park. When he hits the ground, his body makes a huge cavity, which "became known as the Reservoir" (26). The story concludes, "So now, whenever you hear coyotes howling at the night sky, you know they're scolding the star that dropped their grandfather. That's what the people say" (26).

In her notes to the story, de Montaño states that she offers a "somewhat autobiographical" adaptation of a more traditional version of the story, which originates among the Klamaths of southern Oregon. In that version, the Klamaths explain the creation of Crater Lake, a detail that de Montaño incorporates with the formation of the reservoir in Central Park. In this story, Coyote obviously stands in for human beings as he leaves Kansas to find work and ends up employed at the World Trade Center. Yet he retains some of his supernatural trickster aspects, such as when he changes himself into a flower and when he magically dances in the sky with his beloved star. The story also echoes traditional Coyote tales with the etiological details of the reservoir and the explanation for why coyotes howl at the night sky. In this way, the story combines traditional traits with new and comic elements, such as Coyote's adventures in New York, to make the Coyote figure current. Yet in this story, Coyote lacks his more problematic traits, notably his love of theft and deception. Instead, he emerges as less perplexing and more likable, a toned-down version of the troubling figure in much American Indian folklore.

In this sense, *Coyote in Love with a Star* is similar to *Coyote Fights the Sun*, as both tales, which are intended for juvenile audiences, present Coyote as consistent, presumably to avoid confusing young readers. To some degree, these presentations diminish Coyote's fascinating powers of benevolence and corruption and his complex depiction as a semidivine creator and silly fool who leave readers intrigued and wanting to know more. The strength of these stories, however, is the way in which each animates Coyote with a touching humanity: Coyote fights grief even as he believes he fights the sun and falls in love with a cold, lifeless star, only to realize his silly mistake and wish for home. These plots communicate experiences of sadness and love in ways that young readers can begin to understand, effectively preserving elements of Coyote's human symbolism and preparing readers for the bedeviling trickster who waits a bit farther down the road.

Ashleigh Imus, PhD

BIBLIOGRAPHY

Ballinger, Franchot. *Living Sideways: Tricksters in American Indian Oral Traditions*. Norman: U of Oklahoma P, 2004. Print.

Bright, William. *A Coyote Reader*. Berkeley: U of California P, 1993. Print.

Carpelan, Mary J. *Coyote Fights the Sun: A Shasta Indian Tale*. Berkeley: Heyday, 2002. Print.

de Montaño, Marty. *Coyote in Love with a Star*. Washington: Natl. Museum of the American Indian, Smithsonian Inst., 1998. Print.

Erdoes, Richard, and Alfonso Ortiz, eds. *American Indian Trickster Tales*. New York: Viking, 1998. Print.

Farrand, Livingston, comp. "Shasta and Athapascan Myths from Oregon." Ed. Leo J. Frachtenberg. *Journal of American Folklore* 28.109 (1915): 207–42. Print.

Hubbard, Patrick. "Trickster, Renewal and Survival." *American Indian Culture and Research Journal* 4.4 (1980): 113–24. Print.

Hymes, Dell H. "Coyote, the Thinking (Wo)man's Trickster." *Monsters, Tricksters, and Sacred Cows: Animal Tales and American Identities*. Ed. A. James Arnold. Charlottesville: UP of Virginia, 1996. 108–37. Print.

Wiget, Andrew. "His Life in His Tail: The Native American Trickster and the Literature of Possibility." *Redefining American Literary History*. Ed. A. Lavonne Brown Ruoff and Jerry Washington Ward. New York: MLA, 1990. Print.

The Hero's Journey in *Harry Potter and the Philosopher's Stone*

Author: J. K. Rowling
Time Period: 1951 CE–2000 CE
Country or Culture: England; Scotland
Genre: Myth and Fantasy

OVERVIEW

J. K. Rowling's debut novel, *Harry Potter and the Philosopher's Stone*, was published in Great Britain by Bloomsbury in 1997. A year later, Scholastic published an American edition, retitled *Harry Potter and the Sorcerer's Stone*. Though the initial print run was small, the book soon soared into the ranks of best sellers and stayed on top of those lists for the next several years. Rowling's successive novels in the series also reached the top spots in sales and popularity, and the Warner Bros. films based on the novels were similarly successful.

The Harry Potter series comprises seven titles. *Harry Potter and the Philosopher's Stone* introduces readers to eleven-year-old Harry Potter, his friends, his teachers, the wizarding world, and the ultimate enemy, Lord Voldemort; his adventure in the first novel revolves around a stone that provides the elixir of life. In *Harry Potter and the Chamber of Secrets* (1998), Harry must save his best friend Ron's little sister, Ginny, from a serpentine monster that has been released from a hidden chamber in the school. *Harry Potter and the Prisoner of Azkaban* (1999) introduces Sirius Black, Harry's godfather. *Harry Potter and the Goblet of Fire* (2000) provides a training ground for Harry as he competes in the Triwizard Tournament and announces Voldemort's return to power. In *Harry Potter and the Order of the Phoenix* (2003), the war against Voldemort has begun, and one society of those who will fight against him is reunited while another is born. It is in this novel that Harry hears the prophecy that doomed his parents and forced him into the role of Voldemort's most dangerous foe. The sixth book, *Harry Potter and the Half-Blood Prince*

(2005), provides a glimpse into Voldemort's past as the war escalates. *Harry Potter and the Deathly Hallows* (2007), the final novel in the series, showcases the final battles that Harry must fight not only within himself but also with his greatest enemy.

Harry Potter is undoubtedly a hero, and it seems clear that Rowling developed his story with the hero's journey pattern in mind. This pattern, also known as the monomyth and defined by comparative mythologist Joseph Campbell in *The Hero with a Thousand Faces* (1949), is evident not only in each individual book but also over the course of the series. Campbell's journey consists of three major stages (departure, initiation, and return), introduces the hero to a variety of helpers (supernatural and otherwise), and follows the hero through a series of tests and trials. *Harry Potter and the Philosopher's Stone* not only provides the call to adventure for the series-long journey but also depicts a self-contained journey that revolves around Harry's entry into the wizarding world and Lord Voldemort's first attempt at a return to power.

SUMMARY

Harry Potter and the Philosopher's Stone begins with a celebration among wizards throughout the United Kingdom. Lord Voldemort, the most evil wizard of all time, has been defeated. Unfortunately, Lord Voldemort's defeat has come at a price; wizards James and Lily Potter are dead, leaving their one-year-old son, Harry, orphaned. Harry is left in the questionable care of his mother's sister, Petunia Dursley, and her husband, Vernon.

Life with the Dursleys is not easy. Vernon is a businessman who hates anything out of the ordinary, while Petunia is a busybody who was jealous of her sister's magical abilities. Their only child, Dudley, is a spoiled bully who makes Harry's life miserable. Harry is made to sleep in a closet under the stairs and to wear Dudley's old clothes. Though the Dursleys are awful to

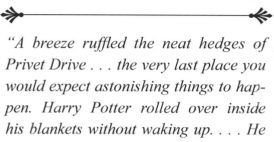

"A breeze ruffled the neat hedges of Privet Drive . . . the very last place you would expect astonishing things to happen. Harry Potter rolled over inside his blankets without waking up. . . . He couldn't know that at this very moment, people meeting in secret all over the country were holding up their glasses and saying in hushed voices: 'To Harry Potter—the boy who lived!'"

Harry Potter and the Philosopher's Stone

Harry throughout his time with them, perhaps the worst thing they do is hide his true nature from him. He grows up doing unexpected things, such as growing his hair back after a particularly horrible haircut and turning his teacher's hair blue, but he does not know how he is doing these things or even that he is, in fact, doing them.

Right before Harry's eleventh birthday, a letter arrives for him, but Vernon quickly confiscates it. He and Petunia are horrified by the contents, an invitation for Harry to attend Hogwarts School of Witchcraft and Wizardry. The Dursleys are unable to ignore the invitation, as hundreds of letters follow the first, so Vernon instead takes his family on a cross-country trek in an effort to escape the taint of magic. Just when he thinks he has found the perfect hiding spot, a shack on a rock off the coast, magic makes an undeniable appearance. At midnight on Harry's birthday, the imposing Rubeus Hagrid knocks down the door of the shack and introduces Harry to his birthright.

Hagrid, the gamekeeper for Hogwarts, has been sent to hand-deliver Harry's school invitation. Harry is thrilled to learn that something is finally going right in his life: he is a wizard. Since Harry's aunt and uncle have avoided telling him about his heritage, Hagrid must relate Harry's background. He explains that Harry's parents were murdered by Lord Voldemort but that Harry survived and is credited with destroying Voldemort, as the evil wizard disappeared after the attack. Ignoring the Dursleys' protests, Hagrid takes Harry on a wondrous

journey to purchase his school supplies in Diagon Alley, the hidden magical district of London, where he visits wizard bank Gringotts, bookstore Flourish and Blotts, and wand shop Ollivanders. The only blot on the day, the best birthday of Harry's life, is his brief encounter with Draco Malfoy, who will become Harry's biggest rival at school.

A month later, Harry goes to King's Cross Station to meet the Hogwarts Express. Struggling to find his train, he quickly realizes that he does not know how to cross the magical barrier that conceals Platform Nine and Three-Quarters. Harry asks the help of a friendly-looking woman accompanied by five red-haired children, thus meeting the Weasley family and the boy who will become his best friend, Ron Weasley, for the first time.

The journey on the Hogwarts Express begins Harry's true immersion into the wizarding world. He realizes that he is a celebrity; nearly all of the other children have grown up knowing who Harry is—the Boy Who Lived. Harry becomes friends with Ron, and other major characters are introduced, including Hermione Granger and Neville Longbottom. Upon arrival at Hogwarts, the new students are sorted into the four school houses: Gryffindor, Hufflepuff, Ravenclaw, and Slytherin. Harry and his new friends all join Gryffindor, a house known for its students' bravery.

Harry's year at school progresses as one might expect, with highs and lows depending on his schoolwork and extracurricular activities. He enjoys classes with Charms teacher Professor Flitwick and Transfiguration teacher Professor McGonagall. He hopes to be fascinated by Professor Quirrell's Defense against the Dark Arts class, and he dreads History of Magic with boring Professor Binns, a teacher who is a ghost, and Potions with Professor Snape, who seems evil and hates Harry. He learns to fly a broom and is appointed to the position of seeker on the Gryffindor Quidditch team. Adventures include a fight with a mountain troll, an encounter with a dragon, and a trip into the Forbidden Forest. Then, Harry and his friends learn of a break-in at Gringotts that occurred on the day he was there with Hagrid. He realizes that the vault that was broken into was the very same vault Hagrid had cleared.

The specific adventure of the first novel ensues as Harry, Ron, and Hermione seek information about the item that Hagrid removed from the vault for safekeeping: the Philosopher's Stone, a magical object capable of creating an elixir of life. Harry and his friends realize that the stone is now hidden in Hogwarts, protected by enchantments created by the teachers. Harry believes Professor Snape is going to steal the stone to help Lord Voldemort return and terrorize the wizarding world once again, so at the end of the school year, the trio tackles the obstacles protecting the treasure. As they overcome these tests, Ron and Hermione are forced to remain behind, and Harry must continue on alone.

After arriving in the room where the Philosopher's Stone is being kept, Harry learns that it is not Professor Snape but Professor Quirrell who has been aiding Voldemort in his attempted return to power. Harry outsmarts both Quirrell and Voldemort in his desire to save the stone. As a result, he triumphantly prevents Lord Voldemort from returning to physical form and ultimately helps the Gryffindors win the coveted House Cup. Harry returns to the Dursleys for the summer with a lighter heart and the knowledge that his cruel relatives do not know he is not allowed to do magic outside of school.

ANALYSIS

Campbell's hero's journey cycle can be found in mythology, fairy tales, literature, and film. In works that follow this pattern, the hero is called to adventure and crosses a threshold that leads to a new and different world. Along the way, the hero undergoes a variety of tests and trials, encounters supernatural aid, battles dark forces, and experiences a return to his or her world with a boon that will benefit the larger group. The journey can be either a psychological journey in which the hero moves from innocence to maturity or a physical journey that culminates in a point of psychological growth. Each novel in Rowling's series presents an adventure that leads Harry to some new understanding about himself, and the series overall presents a journey in which Harry develops into a hero for the rest of his society. *Harry Potter and the Philosopher's Stone* follows Harry's first individual journey as a hero, and it serves as the call to adventure for the hero's journey that takes place over the course of the series. As a piece of children's literature, however, *Philosopher's Stone* modifies some aspects of the journey to allow for an eleven-year-old child to complete the cycle.

Campbell's description of the human hero begins with comments specifically on the hero's childhood. He argues that "the tendency has always been to endow the hero with extraordinary powers from the moment of birth, or even the moment of conception" and that "herohood is predestined, rather than simply achieved"

(319). The hero is described as "the despised one, or the handicapped: the abused youngest son or daughter, the orphan, stepchild, ugly duckling, or the squire of low degree" (326). As a result, the childhood of the hero is often difficult, including persecution as well as banishment and homecoming.

Harry spends most of his formative years living with the Dursleys, despite Professor Minerva McGonagall's early warning to Hogwarts headmaster Albus Dumbledore that the Dursleys will be unsuitable caretakers. Within hours of Harry's parents' murder, Dumbledore places him with the Dursleys in order to keep him safe from Voldemort's followers and untarnished by the fame that will inevitably follow the Boy Who Lived. In surviving Voldemort's attack, which was initiated by the evil wizard's knowledge of the prophecy identifying the person who would be his downfall, Harry is "predestined" as a hero and gains "extraordinary powers" at the point he becomes an orphan. Having been placed with the Dursleys, he further becomes "despised" and "abused." As the unwanted nephew and cousin, Harry is both literally the orphan and symbolically the "stepchild," and since he is forced to wear Dudley's huge hand-me-downs, he becomes the "ugly duckling."

Once the hero's identity is established, he is called to an adventure that will change his life. Harry's early introduction suggests a cowering, unintelligent child, but he has, surprisingly, turned out to be an engaging and likable boy. His ability to interact well with others proves helpful on his journey. Campbell's adventure is introduced by a herald, includes a transition into a new dimension of life via a threshold crossing, and presents a variety of helpers. For Harry, the adventure begins just before his eleventh birthday. One morning while he is helping prepare breakfast for the Dursleys, an invitation to attend Hogwarts School of Witchcraft and Wizardry arrives in the mail, but Vernon Dursley intercepts it and attempts to keep it from Harry. Despite Vernon's continued endeavors to keep magic out of his family's lives, the call of magic will not be put off, and when hundreds of invitations are ignored, a herald is sent. The herald, who is "often dark, loathly or terrifying," according to Campbell (53), arrives at the moment Harry turns eleven. Hagrid is a half-giant whose "face [is] almost completely hidden by a long, shaggy mane of hair and a wild, tangled beard," with eyes "glinting like black beetles under all the hair" (46). As herald, Hagrid will neither be ignored nor allow Vernon to stop Harry from accepting his call back into the world where he belongs. In taking Harry to Diagon Alley, Hagrid leads him through both the figurative threshold that separates the everyday Muggle (nonmagical) world from the magical world and a literal threshold in the form of a hidden gateway that invites Harry into a world unlike anything he could have imagined. Though he must make a brief return to the Muggle world, Harry crosses another threshold when he enters Platform Nine and Three-Quarters at King's Cross Station and catches the Hogwarts Express train to school. It is at the platform that he meets the Weasley family and accepts supernatural aid from Molly Weasley, who shows him how to go through the barrier around the platform. More supernatural aid follows as Harry befriends Ron Weasley, who provides him with basic information needed to survive in the wizarding world. At Hogwarts, Harry meets a variety of teachers who will also be influential supernatural helpers throughout his journey.

The monomyth cycle continues with a series of tests and trials that the hero must overcome as he crosses the threshold of psychological maturation. Though these events help the hero move from childhood to adulthood, they can be physical and mental challenges as well as emotional ones. Harry experiences brief versions of Campbell's wonder journey and night-sea journey, more complex confrontations with the dragon battle and the brother battle, symbolic variations of the belly of the whale, and adapted versions of the crucifixion, dismemberment, and nadir. In the process, he also undergoes an experience that represents a sacred marriage (Campbell 245).

The wonder journey is a voyage in which the hero experiences wonders that he has never known. He may be drawn into these wonders in such a way that he does not want to return to his normal existence. For Harry, the trip to Diagon Alley inducts him into the miracles of the wizarding world, thus fulfilling the wonder journey. The novel clearly shows his awe at his new surroundings: "Harry wished he had about eight more eyes. He turned his head in every direction as they walked up the street, trying to look at everything at once: the shops, the things outside them, the people doing their shopping" (71). Once introduced to the wizarding world, Harry dreads returning to the Dursleys' home, even for the rest of the summer, but he does go back, only to be rewarded at the end of his brief return with a second wonder journey on Hogwarts Express. Platform Nine and Three-Quarters serves as both a threshold guardian and a threshold crossing into the bulk of Harry's adventure.

In its role as a guardian, the magical platform prevents those who are not worthy of the journey from accessing the train. When Harry watches the Weasley boys go through the barrier and asks Molly Weasley how to get across himself, his worth becomes clear, and he is able to conquer the guardian, cross the barrier, and enter into the journey. At the end of the journey on the Hogwarts Express, the first-year students are ferried to Hogwarts, a large castle, in a "fleet of little boats":

> the first boats reached the cliff; they all bent their heads and the little boats carried them through a curtain of ivy that hid a wide opening in the cliff face. They were carried along a dark tunnel, which seemed to be taking them right underneath the castle, until they reached a kind of underground harbor, where they clambered out onto rocks and pebbles. (112)

Though this trip is brief, it allows Rowling's hero to experience yet another threshold crossing as he begins school.

Campbell defines the dragon battle as one in which the hero fights against a terrifying beast as he struggles to move forward in his quest. In Harry's first journey, Rowling combines the dragon battle with the brother battle. This combined battle begins when Harry first meets Draco Malfoy (whose name literally means "dragon") in Diagon Alley. Upon encountering Draco, Harry knows this boy is a bully; the narrator points out that "Harry [is] strongly reminded of Dudley" during this first meeting (77). Draco's physical contrast to Harry—Draco is blond, while Harry is dark haired—and the differences in their personalities suggest that he is Harry's foil and will be the character with whom Harry will engage in a brother battle. The two boys' clashes throughout the book clearly position Draco as a series-long opponent. Other dragon battles occur when Harry and Ron defeat a troll in the girls' bathroom, when Hagrid adopts the dragon Norbert, and when Harry and his friends encounter Fluffy, a three-headed dog.

In order for a sacred marriage to take place, Campbell's hero must undergo a "meeting with the goddess," a female character who "represents the totality of what can be known" (116). Hermione is the symbolic goddess of the novel. The smartest student in her year, she is effectively an encyclopedia of knowledge. However, Hermione's bossy, know-it-all demeanor at the beginning of the school year alienates her from many of the other children. Thus, a crisis becomes necessary for

HISTORICAL CONTEXT

The publication of *Harry Potter and the Philosopher's Stone* was not an easy process. J. K. Rowling has often stated that the idea for the Harry Potter books came to her while she was riding on a train in 1990. After developing the basic premise of the first novel, she began to write a draft in her spare time. Rowling spent several years teaching English in Portugal, where she completed the first chapters of the book. After her divorce and return to Great Britain with her young daughter, she continued to work on the novel that would bring her fame and also pursued additional education as she struggled to support herself and her child. A strong supporter of government assistance programs, Rowling has credited such programs with helping her survive during this difficult period.

In 1995, literary agent Christopher Little agreed to represent Rowling, but he had difficulty finding a publisher for *Philosopher's Stone*, which was considered too long by many children's publishers and focused on life at a boarding school, a seemingly old-fashioned topic associated with elitism. The book was rejected by numerous publishers before it was accepted by Bloomsbury, which published the book in the summer of 1997. Although the initial print run of the book was small, reviews and enthusiastic reader recommendations generated significant publicity, and Scholastic soon bought the rights to publish the novel in the United States.

the mirror, he sees his family and becomes so enamored of this connection to people who love him that he almost loses himself to the obsessive desire to be with them. Dumbledore clarifies the dangers of the mirror by telling Harry, "This mirror will give us neither knowledge or truth. Men have wasted away before it, entranced by what they have seen, or been driven mad, not knowing if what it shows is real or even possible. . . . It does not do to dwell on dreams and forget to live" (213–14). In sharing this information, Dumbledore helps Harry to move on from this potential obsession.

Another symbolic variation on this low point for Rowling's hero is when he is given detention after helping Hagrid send Norbert to Ron's brother Charlie. Harry, with Hermione's help, actually succeeds in getting Norbert safely away from the castle, but Hogwarts caretaker Filch catches the two of them attempting to get back to Gryffindor Tower. The detention and loss of house points that result from their capture throw Harry into the role of outcast: "From being one of the most popular and admired people at the school, Harry was suddenly the most hated. Even Ravenclaws and Hufflepuffs turned on him" (244). Harry becomes further discouraged as he sees Hermione and Neville deal with this rejection.

A third, more literal immersion into an enclosed space that suggests the hero's death occurs when Harry, Ron, and Hermione plunge into the pit under the trapdoor that leads to the Philosopher's Stone. The three have cemented their union as a three-part hero at this point of the story, so Ron and Hermione's involvement in the attempt to find the stone is not surprising. Once in the bowels of Hogwarts, where the Philosopher's Stone has been hidden, the heroes are confronted by a variety of obstacles. First, a plant known as the devil's snare attempts to strangle them, but working together, they escape and move on to the next challenge. Harry uses his Quidditch skills to conquer the obstacle of the flying keys, Ron uses his knowledge of wizard's chess to get them past McGonagall's strategic challenge, and Hermione uses her brain to figure out Snape's logical task.

the hero to unite with the goddess. Harry—along with Ron, who serves as a connected limb of the hero—is able to create a link with Hermione after rescuing her from a troll that the boys had accidentally locked in the bathroom with her. Hermione's insistence to Professor McGonagall that she is at fault and the boys are blameless creates a union that will hold throughout the series: "from that moment on, Hermione Granger became their friend" (179).

For Campbell's hero, the belly of the whale is the point in which the hero, "instead of conquering or conciliating the power of the threshold, is swallowed into the unknown, and would appear to have died" (90). The hero "goes inward, to be born again" (91). There are several points in *Philosopher's Stone* in which Harry must tackle his own immaturity before he can move on in his journey. One such challenge occurs when he discovers the Mirror of Erised, which shows the person looking into it what he or she desires most. Harry encounters the Mirror of Erised over Christmas break, while he is testing out his invisibility cloak. When he looks into

The chess challenge offers both a crucifixion as Ron sacrifices himself to gain the win needed to leave the room and a dismemberment as the friendship unit loses one of its parts. Ron seems to have died as a result of his actions, but he will be resurrected before the end of the journey. The heroic group is further dismembered when Harry loses Hermione, the third piece of this trinity, as she solves Snape's challenge and realizes that only one person can move forward.

The nadir, or lowest point of the hero's journey, awaits Harry on the other side of this last threshold. Harry enters the last chamber and finds the Mirror of Erised, in which the Philosopher's Stone has been hidden, and Professor Quirrell, the person he had least expected to be the villain. When Quirrell reveals that Voldemort has taken residence within his body, Harry is horrified: "Harry would have screamed, but he couldn't make a sound. Where there should have been a back to Quirrell's head, there was a face, the most terrible face Harry had ever seen. It was chalk white with glaring red eyes and slits for nostrils, like a snake" (293). Voldemort reveals his plan, explaining, "Once I have the Elixir of Life, I will be able to create a body of my own" (293–94). Rowling's language here is deliberate. She points out that Voldemort's elixir will return him to power, but she allows the shortsighted Voldemort to ignore the opposite nature of Harry's elixir. Harry is able to remove the stone from the mirror because of his purity, but his defeat of Voldemort is even more important. Voldemort's temporary defeat becomes a boon that Harry can take back to the larger wizarding community.

This last chapter of the novel covers the final portion of Campbell's cycle. Harry and Voldemort engage in a threshold struggle, fighting while Harry attempts to flee with the stone. Harry sacrifices himself to keep the stone safe from Voldemort, creating a second moment of crucifixion. In order to survive this battle, Harry receives rescue from without in the form of a protective charm that his mother cast over him as she died. Further, even as Harry seems to have died, he is resurrected. After his encounter with Voldemort, Harry is taken to the school's hospital wing, where he remains for three days before rejoining his fellow students at the feast celebrating the end of the school year. It is his return to the school body that brings him the greatest recognition, for his bravery, along with that of his friends, earns Gryffindor enough house points to win the House Cup, defeating rival house Slytherin and its most prominent representative, Draco Malfoy.

Harry comes full circle as he departs from King's Cross to return to the Dursleys' home for the summer. He has lived through the original threshold crossing into the magical world to which he has always belonged. He has conquered various tests and trials during his initiation into the life of a wizard. He has made friends who will become lifelong helpers, and he has learned that supernatural aid will be there to protect and guide him as he grows. In the wake of these changes in his life, he has grown in maturity while maintaining the purity needed to save the Philosopher's Stone from Voldemort's grasp, and he has not only defeated Voldemort yet again but also shared a reward with his fellow Gryffindors. He even knows that he now has power over the Dursleys and is able to leave his friends with a smile when Hermione wishes him a happy break: "'Oh, I will,' said Harry, and they were surprised at the grin that was spreading over his face. 'They don't know we're not allowed to use magic at home. I'm going to have a lot of fun with Dudley this summer'" (309). He truly has become the "master of two worlds" (Campbell 229).

CROSS-CULTURAL INFLUENCE

In addition to inspiring a successful film franchise, the Harry Potter series prompted a surge in publication of children's and young-adult books that share many of the basic themes and archetypes found in Rowling's novels. British writer Jenny Nimmo's eight-book Children of the Red King series, following the adventures of protagonist Charlie Bone, begins with *Midnight for Charlie Bone*, published in 2002. On the eve of his best friend's tenth birthday, Charlie opens a package that he believes contains a photograph that he had taken for his friend's birthday card. However, the photo in the package is not the correct print. As he looks at the picture, Charlie begins to hear voices, and he quickly realizes that the voices belong to the subjects of the photo and the photographer who took the photo. Though his paternal grandmother, who comes from a family of "endowed" people, is thrilled, this new power marks a confusing change in his life: "Charlie was very bewildered. In the morning he had been an ordinary boy. He hadn't been touched by a magic wand or banged his head. He hadn't an electric shock or fallen off a bus, or, as far as he knew, eaten a poisoned apple. Any yet, here he was, hearing voices from a piece of photographic paper" (10). With this discovery, Charlie sets off on a journey that will alter his understanding of who he is, what happened to the father he thought was dead, who his friends are, and what his father's family is really like.

Similarities to the Harry Potter series run through the Charlie Bone books, though Nimmo does twist the details by creating a few contrasts. At the beginning of the series, Charlie is around the same age as Harry in *Philosopher's Stone*. Though Charlie's mother is alive and cares for him, Charlie has been told his father died when he was two years old. In addition, Charlie has an evil set of relatives similar to the Dursleys in Rowling's books. In contrast to the Dursleys, who hate magic of any form, Charlie's paternal grandmother and great-aunts attempt to control his life and his endowment. They are not afraid to use Charlie as a tool to gain power and wealth, and Charlie learns that his relatives are so evil that they cooperated in the disappearance of Charlie's father years before. After Charlie's endowment is discovered, he, like Harry, is sent to a special school. Though Harry is excited to attend Hogwarts, Charlie is a bit nervous about going to Bloor's Academy. He tells his mother, "I don't want to go. It's a boring old place for geniuses. I won't fit. It's halfway across the city and I don't know anyone there" (32). Despite his reluctance, Charlie is sent to the school, where the children are separated into groups depending on their talents.

At Bloor's Academy, Charlie meets a number of other children with powers. He befriends Fidelio Gunn, a character similar to Ron Weasley who introduces Charlie to the rules and conditions of this new world, and Olivia Vertigo, a Hermione-like character who knows more than the other students about the school. Charlie also meets characters who will make his life difficult. Mr. Carp, the English teacher, gives Charlie detention, and Manfred Bloor, the son of the school's director and a prefect, makes his life as miserable as possible. Like each of the Harry Potter novels, each book in Nimmo's series contains its own adventure and leads to an understanding of an overall journey. The basic premise in which a student gradually matures over the course of his quest to understand himself and to overcome the evil force that threatens his world is clearly modeled on the hero's journey pattern that Rowling's series follows.

Another series that shares significant similarities with the Harry Potter series is American writer Rick Riordan's Percy Jackson and the Olympians. The Percy Jackson books include *The Lightning Thief* (2005), *The Sea of Monsters* (2006), *The Titan's Curse* (2007), *The Battle of the Labyrinth* (2008), and *The Last Olympian* (2009). The major differences between Riordan's books and Rowling's books are the setting and magical premise. Whereas Rowling's books are set in England and feature witches and wizards, Riordan's series is set in the United States and follows the adventures of characters who are descended from the gods of Greek mythology. Despite these differences, there are many similarities between the Harry Potter and Percy Jackson series.

Like the Harry Potter and Charlie Bone series, the Percy Jackson series focuses on magical training, the development of friendships, and the hero's journey. At the beginning of *The Lightning Thief*, Percy is a twelve-year-old who struggles in school because strange things keep happening to him. Field trips are especially bad, as he tells readers:

> At my fifth-grade school, when we went to the Saratoga battlefield, I had this accident with a Revolutionary War cannon. I wasn't aiming for the school bus, but of course I got expelled anyway. And before that, at my fourth-grade school, when we took a behind-the-scenes tour of the Marine World shark pool, I sort of hit the wrong lever on the catwalk and our class took an unplanned swim. (2)

Percy's blunders before he is formally called to adventure are reminiscent of Harry's accidents early in *Philosopher's Stone*, such as when he talks to a snake at the zoo and accidentally sets it free. Unfortunately, Percy's bad luck continues when his sixth-grade class takes a field trip to the Metropolitan Museum of Art. During this trip, he discovers that teacher Mrs. Dodds is truly evil when she turns into a monstrous creature and attacks him. He defeats her with a pen that turns into a sword, but afterward, his classmates claim that she never existed.

Like Harry, Percy is sent away from home to train once he learns that he possesses magical powers. At Camp Half-Blood, Percy deals with teachers, meets friends and enemies, and learns to control his powers. In a humorous contrast to Hogwarts headmaster Dumbledore, Riordan's camp director is Dionysus, the Greek god of wine, who has been appointed to the position as punishment for past misdeeds. The centaur Chiron becomes the teacher who provides Percy with the most guidance, serving as a kind of combination of Rowling's Professor McGonagall and Remus Lupin (a Defense against the Dark Arts professor who first appears in *Harry Potter and the Prisoner of Azkaban*). The humor continues as Grover, Percy's best friend and protector, is revealed to be a satyr, a part-human, part-goat creature from Greek mythology. Their friendship with fellow Camp Half-Blood resident Annabeth Chase, like that of Harry and Ron with Hermione, develops gradually over the course of the book.

After Percy is accused of stealing the god Zeus's lightning bolt, he embarks on a journey with the goal of identifying the true thief. Percy travels the United States with Grover and Annabeth, confronting tests and trials along the way. One of the major Campbellian trials that Percy faces is atonement with the father, which occurs as Percy learns that Poseidon is his father and that he had not been completely abandoned by his father during his developmental years. After successfully retrieving the lightning bolt, Percy believes he has conquered both the mythological world and the human one, but he overlooks a prophecy that told him he would be betrayed by someone he thought was a friend. Luke, an older camper who helped Percy throughout his quest, reveals himself to have been the thief and sends a scorpion to sting Percy. Thus, *The Lightning Thief*, like *Philosopher's Stone*, draws toward the end with the hero injured. When Percy recovers enough to leave the camp's hospital ward, he is told that he can and should stay at Camp Half-Blood all year round. However, Percy needs a break from magic, and he decides to return to his mother's care until the next summer.

As illustrated, *Midnight for Charlie Bone* and *The Lightning Thief* share a number of themes, character archetypes, and broad categories of events with *Harry Potter and the Philosopher's Stone*. To some extent, these similarities can be attributed to the overwhelming popularity of the Harry Potter series and the desire of writers and publishers to tap into the widespread reader interest in books about young heroes who overcome great evil with the help of their friends. Perhaps more importantly, however, all three books follow the overarching hero's journey pattern defined by Campbell in *The Hero with a Thousand Faces*; each features a call to adventure, numerous challenges to be overcome, and significant personal growth on the part of the protagonist. In chronicling the journeys of such heroes, Rowling, Nimmo, and Riordan have firmly placed their works within a tradition that is thousands of years old.

Theresa L. Stowell, PhD

BIBLIOGRAPHY

Anelli, Melissa. *Harry, a History*. New York: Pocket, 2008. Print.

Campbell, Joseph. *The Hero with a Thousand Faces*. Princeton: Princeton UP, 1949. Print.

Heilman, Elizabeth E. *Critical Perspectives on Harry Potter*. 2nd ed. New York: Routledge, 2009. Print.

Kronzek, Allan Zola. *The Sorcerer's Companion: A Guide to the Magical World of Harry Potter*. New York: Broadway, 2010. Print.

Nimmo, Jenny. *Midnight for Charlie Bone*. New York: Scholastic, 2003. Print.

Prinzi, Travis. *Harry Potter and Imagination: The Way between Two Worlds*. Allentown: Zossima, 2009. Print.

---, ed. *Hog's Head Conversations: Essays on Harry Potter*. Allentown: Zossima, 2009. Print.

Riordan, Rick. *The Lighting Thief*. New York: Miramax, 2005. Print.

Rowling, J. K. *Harry Potter and the Philosopher's Stone*. London: Bloomsbury, 1997. Print.

Whited, Lana A., ed. *The Ivory Tower and Harry Potter: Perspectives on a Literary Phenomenon*. Columbia: U of Missouri P, 2002. Print.

"Warlike Women": Amazons in the Americas

Author: Christopher Columbus; Walter Raleigh
Time Period: 1001 CE–1500 CE; 1501 CE–1700 CE
Country or Culture: Greek; Caribbean
Genre: Legend

OVERVIEW

Stories of warlike women might be the most persistent and mystifying legends in Western civilization. From ancient Greek civilization to the discovery of the New World, stories of such women, often called Amazons, have done far more than thrill readers: throughout history, prominent writers and explorers have used these Amazon myths to shape Western cultures.

Amazon legends relevant to the Americas include the accounts of European explorers who set out to discover and conquer the New World. Of particular interest are descriptions by the late fifteenth-century Italian explorer Christopher Columbus and Sir Walter Raleigh (or Ralegh), an English courtier and favorite of Queen Elizabeth I. Inheriting a long history of Amazon narratives, both men offer fairly stock descriptions of warlike women. In his letter of March 4, 1493, to Spanish sovereigns Isabella and Ferdinand, Columbus announces his discovery of what he believed were the Indies. This letter, only recently proclaimed to be the most authoritative version, reveals the challenges and goals of Columbus's journey, including financial information, the beauty and richness of the islands, and the friendliness and innocence of the native people. His description of warrior women and the cannibalistic men who mate with them appear at the letter's conclusion as part of a catalog of exotic people encountered. After the women mate with the wild men, Columbus claims, they retain female children and send the males to another island once the boys are old enough to feed themselves.

Sir Walter Raleigh echoes Columbus in his narrative *The Discovery of Guiana* (1596), which recounts his

voyage to a land corresponding to modern-day Venezuela, where a native tells him of the Amazon women who dwell there. Like Columbus's account, Raleigh's description is brief and focuses on the women's mating habits, but he is more flamboyant in his account of the women's lasciviousness, cruelty, and stores of gold.

Originating in ancient Greece and evolving over the centuries, the stock descriptions employed by Columbus and Raleigh are best understood not as historically true but for what they symbolize to the individuals and the cultures perpetuating them. In both ancient Greece and Renaissance Europe, the mythical warrior women represent aspects of the men who encounter or hear of them. At the same time, the Amazons act as foils to the personal and cultural identities the men wish to construct. However, the stories fulfill these functions differently for the Greeks, for Columbus, and for Raleigh. In ancient Greece, the Amazons appear both as a group and as specific characters who play key roles in defining Greek cultural and military dominance. For Columbus and Raleigh, the Amazons are no longer individual characters but function as strategies for the writers to cast themselves as legendary explorers and conquerors. Particularly for Raleigh, who wrote his narrative as part of an effort to regain the favor of Queen Elizabeth I, the Amazon legend bears rich and complex meanings. A symbolic analysis that contextualizes Amazon legends within key narrative histories reveals the stories' crucial roles in the self-fashioning and cultural conquest enacted by two celebrated New World explorers.

SUMMARY

Columbus's description of "warlike women" appears at the end of his letter of March 4, 1493, addressed to the Spanish sovereigns Isabella and Ferdinand. The letter begins with Columbus victoriously announcing his discovery of "the Indies" (Zamora 3), a series of islands that he claims to have possessed without opposition; he specifically states that he has given the islands Spanish names and marked each harbor discovered with a large cross. He describes his initial exploration of the islands, his attempts to communicate with the natives he had captured, and some problems he encountered with supplies and his crew. Columbus then proceeds to praise the temperate climate, exotic vegetation, abundant rivers and harbors, and the mostly naked, friendly natives, who have stone tools and only sharp sticks for weapons. The indigenous people appear to share a common language but have no private property or religion, although they seem to understand "that all powers reside in heaven" (5). Believing that Columbus and his crew are divine, the natives venerate the European men.

Columbus then particularly praises the island he has named La Spañola for its fruit, trees, and gold. He thanks God, who enabled him, difficulties notwithstanding, to discover "gold and mines and spicery and innumerable peoples" (6). Columbus reports that he has left on the island of Española some of his crew, with enough weapons and provisions for one year so that they may "subjugate the entire island without danger" (6). He states that the island is rich in gold, pepper, mastic, lignum aloe, cotton, slaves, and possibly rhubarb and cinnamon, and he stresses that he considers the islands to belong to the crown. Moving on to financial matters, Columbus promises to pay Isabella and Ferdinand a sufficient sum to finance the conquest of Jerusalem, "for which purpose this enterprise was undertaken" (7). He encourages all Christians to celebrate the discovery as a divine blessing and emphasizes the ease with which the pagans will be converted to Christianity. Columbus then voices several complaints, declaring that despite his loyalty and sacrifices, he has received no favor, and "nothing of what was promised [him] has been fulfilled" (7). He requests that his sponsors ask the church to endow a cardinalate on his son and that they appoint one of his crew paymaster of the expedition.

At this point, Columbus describes the marvelous women he encountered on the island that lies closest to Spain. This island, he states, is called Matenino and is "populated entirely by women, without a single man, and their comportment is not feminine, but rather they use weapons and other masculine practices" (8). These weapons include bows and arrows, and they use the abundant copper available to them for their "adornments" (8). Columbus then claims that a second island called Caribo is inhabited by a warlike, cannibalistic

"They which are not far from Guiana do accompany with men but once in a year, and for the time of one month, which I gather by their relation to be in April; at that time all the kings of the borders assemble, and the queens of the Amazones, and after the queens have chosen, the rest cast lots for their valentines. This one month they feast, dance, and drink of their wines in abundance."

The Discovery of Guiana

people feared by all surrounding groups of natives. He confesses that he hopes to capture these cannibals as slaves and declares that they mate with the women of Matenino, who keep the resulting female children but send the males to another island once the boys can feed themselves. Columbus moves on to describe the island known as Cuba, where he has heard that everyone is born with a tail, and Jamaica, where everyone is bald and where there is "gold in immeasurable quantities" (8). He concludes by wishing his royal sponsors the protection of the "Holy Trinity" (8).

Raleigh's account of warrior women appears early in *The Discovery of Guiana* in the context of reviewing the explorations of his Spanish predecessors. After briefly recounting the journey from England, Raleigh describes his arrival in Trinidad, the island itself, the Spaniards he encounters, and the pertinent information they provide. He then touches on previous English-Spanish conflicts in the region and reveals his desire to capture a particular Spaniard named Berreo, whom he does eventually apprehend. He introduces his description of "warlike women" as a digression in the context of discussing the gold and other commodities that lie between the Orinoco and Amazon Rivers. Raleigh then states that he inquired of some of the oldest and "best travelled of the Orenoqueponi" indigenous people to learn about the "warlike" women, whose existence is a matter of debate (61). He states that a leader, called a "cacique," reported to him that the women dwell on the southern parts of the river near provinces called Topago. Raleigh then refers to similar women in ancient Africa (with Medusa as their queen) and Asia, specifically Scythia. He names Lampedo and Marthesia as queens of the ancient "Amazones," declaring that "in many histories they are verified to have been, and in divers ages and provinces" (61).

Next, he describes the Amazon women said to exist in Guiana chiefly by focusing on their mating habits. The women, he says, "do accompany with men but once in a year, and for the time of one month, which I gather by their relation to be in April" (61). The Amazon queens first choose their mates, and then the other women "cast lots for their valentines" (61). After a month of feasting and mating, the men depart. The women keep the daughters, even sending a gift of thanks to the fathers, who also receive any sons conceived. Raleigh then states that his source refutes the popular notion that the women cut off their right breast. He concludes by stating that the women are reportedly "very cruel and bloodthirsty" (61), both coupling with and murdering prisoners of war. The women are especially cruel to those who attempt to invade their land, and they have "great store of these plates of gold" (61), which they obtain by trading a highly prized green stone. At this point, Raleigh resumes his discussion of Spanish explorations.

ANALYSIS

Stories of warlike "Amazon" women are a special type of legend. Although the existence of such women has never been proven, scholars have attempted for millennia to verify them, partly because some ancient Greek historians insisted that the women existed and because the legends were so important to Greek culture. As Abby Wettan Kleinbaum notes, the Athenians' supposed victory over Amazon women was represented widely in paintings, sculptures, and temple facades. Lacking other evidence for the Amazons' existence, twentieth-century historians such as Guy Cadogan Rothery argued that these culturally relevant women represent something else that actually did exist, possibly barbarians, the Persians, warrior priestesses, or beardless men. This dominant approach means that critics have only recently addressed the issue of what warlike women symbolize for the various cultures and peoples who have mythologized them in a long narrative history stretching from the ancient world to the twentieth century. A symbolic analysis addresses how these persistent stories developed in key periods and eventually fuelled the narratives

of New World adventurers such as Columbus and Raleigh. For both the Greeks and the Renaissance men, warlike women embodied traits both enviable and repulsive, traits that heroes share: military valor and wildness. Whereas specific Amazon characters symbolized general cultural dominance for the Greeks, Columbus and Raleigh employ stock descriptions to construct narratives of conquest both cultural and personal. In these personal narratives, the New World explorers fashion themselves as legendary, upstanding men worthy of fame, honor, and riches.

The plentiful Amazon legends of ancient Greece are essential to understand because they laid the foundation for all subsequent narratives of conquest in the West. The first-century BCE Greek historian Diodorus of Sicily tells of a group of warrior women who rule over men and live on Hespera, a large island in western Libya. According to legend, the women are called Amazons because in Greek, *a-mazos* signifies "without breasts," and the women are said to cut off their breast to facilitate fighting (in fact, the word's etymology is uncertain). These Amazon women dominate nearly all cities on the island and then defeat many tribes and territories, including Egypt, Arabia, Syria, Cilicia, Tauris, Greater Phrygia, coastal cities in Asia Minor, and an Aegean island the women call Samothrace. The Amazon queen Myrina is eventually defeated, and the women are driven back to Libya. The Amazons then assist Dionysius, the god of wine, in defeating the Titans, but when the women become angry because the god claims all the credit for his victory, he nearly destroys the entire race. The Greek hero Heracles then subdues the women as one of his twelve labors, and an earthquake subsequently destroys the Amazon city of Cherronesus (Sobol 19–31).

In a region northeast of the Caucasus Mountains, another group of Amazon women were said to have arisen among the Scythians. When the Scythian men were defeated, the women retreated to the mountains near the Sea of Azov to form an all-female society. The women trained themselves in warfare and mated with men in nearby communities, keeping the female babies and returning the males to their fathers. Under the guidance of their military leader, Lysippe, they eventually migrated to the south bank of the Black Sea and founded their capital, Themiscrya. These Amazons of Asia Minor spread west into Thrace and east into Syria, later crossing Asia Minor and establishing cities. It is these Amazons who encounter several Greek heroes in mythology, such as the monster-slayer Bellerophon. Accused by a queen of attempted rape, Bellerophon is commanded by the queen's father, Iobates, to conquer the Amazons. Flying on a winged horse named Pegasus, Bellerophon defeats the women with arrows and crushes their town with boulders. After the death of Bellerophon, the Amazons return to the Greek world when the hero Heracles is commanded to steal the sword belt of Queen Hippolyte as one of his twelve labors. Heracles wins the belt not with his prodigious army but with romance: when Hippolyte meets Heracles, she is so smitten that she offers the belt as a love gift. It is a gift too late, however, because as she ungirds it, the sounds of battle between Greeks and Amazons are heard. After a savage battle, the Greeks defeat the women, and Heracles presents the belt to Eurystheus, who had commanded the deed (Sobol 33, 37–46).

The Greek defeat of Amazons through forces both military and romantic becomes a pattern essential to the most important Greek legend of these women, which is the Amazons' attack on Athens. The hero of this episode is Theseus, who becomes king of Athens after he conquers the Minotaur, a half-man, half-bull monster, and his father dies of grief when he believes that Theseus has been defeated. Seeking gold and desiring to emulate Heracles, Theseus travels with a friend to the Amazonian coast. The women greet him with gifts rather than swords, and their queen, Antiope, takes Theseus as her lover, while his men mate with the other Amazon women (in some versions, Theseus seduces Hippolyte, not Antiope). When another Greek named Soloon commits suicide out of love for Antiope, Theseus decides to bring her back to Athens. Antiope goes willingly, but her sisters Hippolyte and Oreithyia are outraged and plan to attack the city. With their troops, the sisters travel to Athens and battle the Athenians for many months, with heavy casualties on both sides. When the Amazons are finally outnumbered, a truce is called. Theseus buries the Amazon dead honorably, treats the wounded, and establishes sacrificial offerings to the women on the eve of the Festival of Theseus. After this defeat, the Amazon states never recover their numbers, and the women eventually die off or are assimilated into other cultures (Sobol 50–60).

The Athenians' victory is not the final Amazon legend (the Greeks defeat the Amazon warrior Penthesilea in Homer's *Iliad*), but it is the most significant in terms of what the Amazons meant in Greek culture. Respected scholars such as the first-century CE historian Plutarch discredited many Amazon legends but accepted as incontrovertible fact the Athenians' victory, which came to represent a fundamental event shaping Greek culture and "national spirit" (Sobol 84). Why did the Greeks insist on their defeat of the Amazons? Kleinbaum reports that after defeating the Persians, the Athenians rebuilt their temple and decorated it with battle scenes between Greeks and centaurs, giants, and Amazons, which suggests that the Greeks viewed the women's powers as supernatural: "Any plucky mortal could kill a Persian, but it takes a hero to triumph over an Amazon" (11–12). These female warriors represented the ultimate in military force, the transcendent battle prowess that every Greek male desired.

Yet as women, the Amazons were considered barbaric and unnatural, the antithesis of the ideal Greek woman, who was to be utterly submissive and chaste and whose sole purpose was to produce male heirs and preserve the family; the Amazon women, in contrast, repelled and murdered men, ruled themselves, and had no families (Powell 403). To Greek patriarchal culture, these qualities were intolerable and had to be subdued but also transformed, which explains the use of romance in the tales of conquest. Greek heroes not only were physically stronger than Amazon warriors but also were able to turn the women into submissive Greek wives. The Greeks thus combined gender and military prowess to create an irresistible image of an Other: an enviable warrior and a savage woman to be seduced and conquered. A true hero could melt the heart of even the most dire warrior woman, confirming that the traditional system of male domination would always prevail, Kleinbaum asserts. Theseus's seduction and the Amazon invasion of Athens encapsulate this symbolism, allowing Greek men to identify with, conquer, and assimilate Amazon women simultaneously.

The Greek legends' power to invite both emulation and revulsion proved seductive for medieval and Renaissance explorers. By the time Columbus penned his letter to Isabella and Ferdinand in 1493, Amazon women had evolved to become religious symbols and fantastic, erotic, and wealthy creatures. Medieval Christians transformed the women into beastly pagans in need of conversion, and poets retold the stories of Penthesilea aiding the Trojans and of other exotic Amazons who lived far off in the East. When the famous explorer Marco Polo actually traveled to the East in the thirteenth century, he did not claim to meet Amazons but did describe a community of peaceful Christian women who lived alone on an island, admitting their husbands from a neighboring island for three months of the year for mating purposes. Sir John Mandeville, a famous fourteenth-century traveler, claimed to have discovered Amazonia, an island of one-breasted warrior women who repelled men except for brief periods of mating, rejected or killed their male children, and imprisoned the lost tribes of Israel (Kleinbaum 72–73).

Both Marco Polo and Mandeville also told of visiting the realm of Prester John, a legendary Christian ruler who was said to have mysteriously vanished somewhere in the East. The myth of John originated in a twelfth-century letter in which John claims to be the king of India and invites the emperor of Rome and king of France to liberate the Holy Land from infidels. He promises great riches and claims to rule over realms of fantastic animals and humans, such as multicolored lions and unicorns, half-human creatures that are half-dog or half-horse, cannibals, one-eyed and four-eyed men, and a land he calls "Great Feminie" that matches previous accounts of Amazons. Significantly, John describes the sexual appeal of these women, who allow men to mate with them for several days. He also mentions the women's proximity to a river flowing from the earthly paradise that Christians believed the first man and woman had inhabited. John claims that another nearby river contains precious gems and a fountain of youth. This account, verified by Mandeville, eroticizes the Amazons and links them to fantastic creatures, wealth, and prosperity. In an age of limited geographical knowledge and narratives populated by brave knights, damsels in distress, dragons, infidels, sorcerers, and magic potions, late medieval and early Renaissance readers were thrilled and convinced by stories of fantastic journeys that promised a better, ideal life somewhere far away (Kleinbaum 74–76). This fantasy life allowed late medieval and early Renaissance readers to imagine themselves as exotic and transcendent heroes who were just as great as the Greek men of ancient tradition.

Columbus's letter both draws heavily on and justifies these fantasies. Discovered in the late 1980s and translated in 1993, this letter is now believed to be more authoritative than a previous version dated February 15, 1493 (Zamora 1–2). In the March 4 letter, Columbus's portrait of warlike women includes stock Amazon characteristics: women who live without men, practice warfare, mate for brief periods, retain female children, and send the boys elsewhere. The women are not presented as individuals; the specific Amazon characters and detailed encounters of Greek legends are nowhere to be found. In comparison, Columbus's description seems mundane, but he incorporates fantastic elements from medieval travel narratives that suggest the women as part of a suite of exotic creatures. First, he states that the warlike women of Matenino mate with a group of cannibal men who live on a nearby island and that these men "wear their hair very full, like women" (8). Next, he goes on to describe the island of Borinque and the western part of Cuba, specifically a province called Faba, which he did not witness directly but where "everyone is born with a tail" (8). Finally, he mentions Jamaica, "where all the people are bald" (8) and which he has been assured contains abundant gold.

This exotic conclusion seems somewhat unexpected, even an afterthought, but the context of the letter clarifies how Columbus uses the Amazon description to support his cultural and highly personal objectives. When Columbus links the women to cannibal men and humans with tails and no hair but also to copper and gold, he clearly invokes previous stories of lands with fantastic, sexually deviant (and available) creatures and great riches. He thus implicitly elevates himself to level of Marco Polo and Mandeville; like these famous men, he finds a promised land and is therefore worthy of their status. Moreover, prior to his portraits of exotic people, Columbus vacillates between bland and benevolent descriptions, complaints, and demands. He recounts that the islands are fertile, temperate, and well populated with "the best people under the sun; they have neither ill-will nor treachery" (4), stressing the peoples' trusting nature and the rich potential for agriculture, gold, and spices. He further assures that these people will be "with very little effort . . . converted to our Holy Faith" (7). Yet Columbus also complains of "a thousand indignities and disgrace" he has endured for seven years, pointedly reminding Ferdinand and Isabella of promises they have not kept (7). He then demands favors for his son and his crew member.

In this context, the final description recuperates the letter and the journey, not to mention Columbus himself. First, the exotic features make the letter more interesting; the new lands are full not only of riches and friendly natives but also of the same astonishing things found by previous heroes. Second, the warlike women and others make Columbus's complaints and demands seem less offensive; an explorer who discovers such creatures surely deserves to be well rewarded for his exploits. Finally, the closing description justifies Columbus's journey of conquest, which is about constructing his reputation but also dominating new lands as part of Spain's colonial empire. For Columbus and his Christian patrons, it is easier to justify their invasion of foreign lands for precious metals, spices, and slaves if those lands contain not just pagans in need of conversion but wild cannibals, unnatural warrior women, and humans with tails—in short, dangerous creatures that must be subdued. In this sense, Columbus casts himself, his crew, and his Spanish patrons as civilized Christians who wish to tame wild pagans, an image that became literal in drawings of European explorers encountering naked, savage women (Montrose 179). Yet as a courageous, worldly explorer who seeks to dominate indigenous people and their lands, Columbus also embodies the lawlessness of the people he describes. He uses the warlike women and other deviants to justify and project the wild enterprise of colonial conquest that he represents.

Amazons for Columbus symbolize not just adventure, wealth, and reputation, but also danger both personal and cultural—danger that Raleigh understood quite well. Born to a modest English family around 1552 or 1554, Raleigh worked his way into Queen Elizabeth I's court through his manifold talents, writing poetry, engaging in military campaigns, and captaining a ship in an attempted voyage to Asia in 1578–79. Attractive, fashionable, and witty, he embodied the Renaissance ideal of the self-fashioning, bold, and dynamic courtier. By the 1580s, he was the queen's favorite, her constant companion and recipient of many honors. During this time, he obtained patents to initiate voyages to discover the New World, which led to the Roanoke voyages and the naming of Virginia after the Virgin Queen.

Raleigh thus "inaugurated England's imperial project in America," as Benjamin Schmidt puts it in his introduction to Raleigh's text, but England was far behind Spain in attempts to colonize the New World, partly because the English were busy fighting the Spanish at home. Raleigh himself was partially credited with the English victory over the Spanish Armada, a naval battle initiated in 1588 by Spanish forces wishing to overthrow

HISTORICAL CONTEXT

Amazon stories originated in ancient Greece and flourished throughout the Middle Ages and early Renaissance, evolving to shape the subsequent legends of New World explorers such as Christopher Columbus and Sir Walter Raleigh. The New World accounts, however, appear in the context of European colonialism. The European colonization of the Americas was initiated by Spain just before 1500 and lasted until approximately 1900. The Spanish were interested in discovering new lands, trade routes, and resources, particularly gold, spices, and slaves, and they claimed interest in converting pagans to Christianity.

In his journey to the New World, Columbus intended to reach Asia by attempting a new route, sailing westward rather than east as previous explorers had done. After several attempts, Columbus finally received permission and financing from the Spanish monarchs Ferdinand and Isabella in 1491. He undertook his first journey in August 1492 and arrived in the islands of the Bahamas several months later, believing that he had reached Asia. Columbus made several more journeys to the New World, claiming many territories and resources for his Spanish patrons.

Over the next four centuries, Spain established an empire in the New World that included present-day Central and South America, western and southwestern regions of North America, and the Caribbean islands. The Spanish were later joined by their English competitors, who began exploring and colonizing the Americas in the second half of the sixteenth century.

Elizabeth. The two countries competed for dominance in the New World, which partly motivated Raleigh's voyage to Guiana in 1595.

An even more important motivation for the journey, however, was Raleigh's falling out with Elizabeth in 1592, when she discovered that he had secretly married one of her ladies in waiting, prompting the queen to imprison the couple in the Tower of London. Partly because he wished to regain the queen's favor and partly because his previous journeys had not succeeded, Raleigh sailed to Guiana in search of land, riches, and glory. Although this journey was also unfruitful, *The Discovery of Guiana* was a narrative success that helped Raleigh to mend his reputation to some degree.

His description of warlike women is notable for its appeal to earlier authorities and its use of stock elements to build a flamboyant portrait of lustful, violent women. Raleigh first reports the location of the women and then states, "The memories of the like women are very ancient as well in *Africa* as in *Asia*" (61). He goes on to name the Amazon queens Medusa, Lampedo, and Marthesia and the Scythian tribes. These "verified" histories bolster his own account and explicitly link him to Greek and other heroes who encountered ancient Amazons. His own description of the women is more titillating than fantastic. He livens up the stock elements by dwelling on the women's mating party: after the queen chooses her lover, "the rest cast lots for their valentines" (61). Then follows a month-long orgy of "feast, dance, and drink," after which the women who bear daughters are civil enough to send "unto the begetters a present" (61). There are no cannibals or humans with tails, but the women have gold, and they are lascivious and bloodthirsty, both copulating with and murdering their male prisoners.

These sexual overtones recall earlier accounts but take on special significance given that Raleigh both assimilates and contrasts the Amazon women to Queen Elizabeth. In the final pages of his narrative, he makes his case for why Guiana is worth the investment of conquest, stating, "Guiana is a country that hath yet her maidenhead, never sacked, turned, nor wrought" (109). Several pages later, he assures Elizabeth that whichever sovereign possesses Guiana "shall be greatest" and claims that "where the south border of Guiana reacheth to the dominion and empire of the Amazones, those women shall hereby hear the name of a virgin, which is not only able to defend her own territories and her neighbours, but also to invade and conquer so great empires and so far removed" (112). By describing Guiana as a country that is still virginal, Raleigh personifies the land as a feminine body that will inevitably and "naturally" be deflowered by masculine dominance, a metaphor that Louis Montrose connects with Raleigh's aggressive attempts to regain the goodwill of the virgin queen herself. Moreover, when Raleigh tries to persuade Elizabeth to conquer Guiana, he contrasts her virginity with the violently sexual Amazons. Yet the contrast dangerously blurs the lines in that he encourages her to be both like the conquering women and unlike them in her virginity, a precarious argument from a male courtier who had lost the queen's favor because of his own sexual incontinence. As Montrose reveals, Raleigh is careful throughout the narrative to portray his continent behavior in contrast to that of his Spanish competitors, on whom he nonetheless relies for information and guidance.

Like the Greeks, both Columbus and Raleigh use Amazon narratives to define themselves and their cultures.

The Greeks use highly specific narratives to create larger cultural meanings, whereas the New World explorers use stock descriptions to authorize colonialist claims and to negotiate their personal desires and risks. Stock descriptions of Amazons had proliferated by Raleigh's time and served to authorize public proclamations of dominance, which, as Schmidt points out, were far more important than actual discoveries. These descriptions are especially fascinating for how they become personal symbols. For Raleigh in particular, the Amazons represent heroic conquest that explicitly invokes the great Greek heroes and the unimaginable wealth described in medieval and other accounts. Yet the women also symbolize sexual adventure and transgression in an especially complex way, given Raleigh's own fall from grace and subjection to a female monarch who was prized for her virginity. Ironically, however, the symbolism of warlike women, so essential for New World explorers and their colonialist patrons, did not do much for Raleigh personally. Ultimately, *The Discovery of Guiana* was an innovative, entertaining narrative that helped restore Raleigh to Elizabeth's court but never to her inner circle, as Schmidt notes. Upon the queen's death in 1603, Raleigh was again imprisoned in the Tower of London by James I, and he was beheaded in 1618 on charges of treason

CROSS-CULTURAL INFLUENCE

Many Americans know of Wonder Woman, the popular superhero of twentieth-century comics and cartoons. Less well known is that a man named William Moulton Marston introduced Wonder Woman in 1941 as an Amazon who leaves her island of women to help the Americans defeat the Nazis in World War II. In his creation, Marston incorporates key elements of Amazon legends throughout history, tapping Greek, medieval, and Renaissance features. Yet he also changes previous legends by making all of the Amazons and Wonder Woman herself heroes, not defeated victims or fantastic, dangerous creatures. Furthermore, given that the character was introduced a few months after the United States entered the war, Marston created Wonder Woman as a specifically American mythical figure in support of the strong roles that women played in the war effort. Ultimately, however, Wonder Woman's Amazon origins and female identity have faded even though her character has endured, leaving unclear the extent of her power as an Amazon symbol.

The first Wonder Woman episode introduces its heroine as a mysterious woman of unknown identity "to whom the problems and feats of men are mere child's play," a woman "as lovely as Aphrodite—as wise as Athena—with the speed of Mercury and the strength of Hercules" (8). The story begins when Wonder Woman and one of her companions discover a wrecked plane on "Paradise Island," their home (8). The women are shocked to discover a man in the wreckage and immediately transport him to the hospital as alarmed bystanders run to inform their queen. Queen Hippolyte arrives at the hospital, where a nurse delivers papers found at the scene. The papers identify the man as Captain Steven Trevor, a US army intelligence officer. Hippolyte decides, based on this information, that the man cannot be allowed to die, but she orders the nurse to keep his eyes covered "so that, if he should awake, he will see nothing!" (9). She also commands that his plane be repaired immediately so that he may leave the moment as he recovers. The queen departs, and her daughter, Wonder Woman, remains with the man constantly, refusing to leave his side. The nurse then visits Hippolyte to report her suspicions that Wonder Woman has fallen in love with Trevor. The queen promises to "take steps immediately" (9) and summons her daughter, who admits that she does indeed love the man.

Hippolyte responds by stating, "I was afraid, daughter, that the time would some day arrive that I would have to satisfy your curiosity" (10). She then reveals their amazing shared history that begins "in the days of Ancient Greece, many centuries ago," when the all-female Amazonia was the most powerful nation (10). Wishing to prove his manly valor, the renowned hero Hercules arrives and accepts Hippolyte's challenge to single combat. The queen defeats him with her magic girdle, a gift from Aphrodite, but then Hercules takes the girdle "by deceit and trickery" and makes the Amazons slaves (10). An angry Aphrodite first refuses to help but then assists the women after Hippolyte's second entreaty. The queen regains the magic girdle and, at Aphrodite's command, leads her women to steal a fleet of ships to depart and establish a new world free of men. The goddess also commands the women to wear the special bracelets imposed by their masters "as a reminder that [they] must always keep aloof from men" (10). The women sail the seas until founding a new society on Paradise Island, where there is not only "no want, no illness, no hatreds, no wars" but also eternal life as long as the queen retains the magic girdle and no men "beguile" them (11). For this reason, Hippolyte explains, Trevor must be expelled right away.

Hippolyte then shows her daughter the magic sphere given to her by the goddess Athena. By looking into the sphere, Hippolyte gains access to all knowledge of the outside world and can even know the future. She has used the sphere to learn all the world's technology so that Amazons exceed the "so-called manmade civilization" (11). Mother and daughter then gaze into the sphere, which provides a flashback of how Trevor ended up on their island. Having gained special information about German spies, Trevor is shown requesting permission to capture them personally. His commander grants the permission, and Trevor lies in wait for the spies to pass in their car. When they do, Trevor confronts them at gunpoint, but the Germans crash the car, knocking Trevor unconscious. They place him inside an American robot plane and then fly the plane remotely over American forces, dropping bombs but making it seem as if the American plane is responsible. When Trevor regains consciousness, he begins to pursue the German bomber plane, which diverts him far out to sea. Trevor pursues the German plane until he runs out of gas, finally crashing on Paradise Island.

Having learned Trevor's history, Wonder Woman insists that he must be taken back to the United States. Hippolyte asks for time alone to seek the advice of Aphrodite and Athena, while her daughter silently wishes, without much hope, that she could be the one to escort Trevor. The goddesses Aphrodite and Athena appear to Hippolyte to declare that the "gods have decreed" Trevor's appearance on Paradise Island. He must be returned to the United States to "help fight the forces of hate and oppression" because "American liberty and freedom must be preserved!" (15). The goddesses command Hippolyte to send her "strongest and wisest Amazon—the finest of [her] wonder women" to the United States, for "the last citadel of democracy, and of equal rights for women, needs [her] help!" (15).

Hippolyte agrees to send her best woman to defend both liberty and "all womankind" (15). She organizes a tournament to identify her most capable Amazon but prohibits her daughter from participating, protesting that the winner must leave the island permanently, and she cannot bear to lose her daughter. Donning a mask, Wonder Woman enters and wins the tournament, defeating her final competitor in a shooting contest in which only Wonder Woman can deflect bullets with her metal bracelets. When Wonder Woman unmasks herself, Hippolyte claims that she had suspected her daughter's disguise and declares, "It's too late now!

You've won and I'm proud of you!" (16). She renames her daughter Diana after her godmother, the goddess of the moon, and presents a red, white, and blue costume she has sewn for her to wear in the United States. Wonder Woman exclaims, "Why Mother, it's lovely!" (16), and the first episode concludes with a caption celebrating Diana for "giving up her heritage, and her right to eternal life . . . to take the man she loves back to America—the land she learns to love and protect, and adopts as her own!" (16).

This remarkable story attests to the amazing persistence of Amazon legends and reflects Marston's use of key elements from earlier narratives. He includes Hercules's encounter with the Amazons from the Greek legends but omits their romantic features and makes the women ultimately victorious, with the Greek goddesses as protectors who serve to legitimate the women by making them a central part of Greek myth. Interestingly, Marston also taps some of the medieval and Renaissance features of Amazon legends in his portrayal of Paradise Island, where sickness and war are unknown and the women enjoy eternal life, features that recall the mythical Prester John's descriptions of the earthly paradise and fountain of youth. Moreover, Marston's description of Paradise Island as a "new world" recalls the Renaissance explorers who claimed to have seen or heard of Amazons in their New World journeys.

This "new world" might also refer to the cultural context in which Marston actually created Wonder Woman as a character: the United States as the exceptional "new world" defending freedom against fascism during World War II. In this context, Wonder Woman serves a clear cultural purpose, both reflecting and encouraging the strong American women who were needed to support the war effort. In this sense, she represented an Amazon legend supporting the image of Rosie the Riveter, an icon for the strong American women who took the place of men by working in factories to support the liberation of Europe (Collins 6).

Wonder Woman was also intended to provide a more general, positive model of a strong, independent woman capable of defending herself and making her own choices, and there is no question that Marston achieved this model to some degree. Wonder Woman is a true warrior who is squarely in charge of her destiny, and Marston repeatedly makes her female identity central to her heroism. On the other hand, Marston makes Wonder Woman's love for a man the defining event that leads her away from Paradise Island and motivates her to fight for the United States. In this sense, he repeats the well-worn formula of Amazons ultimately controlled by the power of romance, but it is significant that romance in this case does not subdue Wonder Woman. As Kleinbaum notes, she remains the hero, defeating male villains and saving her man with her intelligence and physical strength, not to mention her invisible plane, bulletproof wristbands, and magic lasso.

Yet as Kleinbaum documents, after Marston died in 1947, Wonder Woman's Amazon origins gradually faded away, as did her strong female identity, until finally she was merely an "incidentally female" superhero, a female version of Superman. Kleinbaum argues that this loss of Amazon identity reflects a pattern in which some male authors consistently eradicate Amazon characters either by domesticating them as wives or having them die, whereas some modern female authors preserve the identity. Yet if individual Amazon characters come and go, it is clear enough after more than two millennia that Amazon legends are too compelling to ever truly die.

Ashleigh Imus, PhD

BIBLIOGRAPHY

Collins, Judy. Foreword. *Wonder Woman Archives*. Vol. 1. By William Moulton Marston and H. G. Peter. New York: DC Comics, 1998. Print.

Greenblatt, Stephen, ed. *New World Encounters*. Berkeley: U of California P, 1993. Print.

Kleinbaum, Abby Wettan. *The War against the Amazons*. New York: McGraw-Hill, 1983. Print.

Marston, William Moulton, and H. G. Peter. *Wonder Woman Archives*. Vol. 1. New York: DC Comics, 1998. Print.

Montrose, Louis. "The Work of Gender in the Discourse of Discovery." Greenblatt 177–218.

Powell, Barry P. *Classical Myth*. 3rd ed. Upper Saddle River: Prentice Hall, 2001. Print.

Ralegh, Walter. *The Discovery of Guiana*. Ed. Benjamin Schmidt. Boston: Bedford/St. Martin's, 2008. Print.

Rothery, Guy Cadogan. *The Amazons*. London: Griffiths, 1910. Print.

Sobol, Donald J. *The Amazons of Greek Mythology*. South Brunswick: Barnes, 1972. Print.

Zamora, Margarita. "Christopher Columbus's 'Letter to the Sovereigns': Announcing the Discovery." Greenblatt 1–12.

Warrior Legend in Akira Kurosawa's
Seven Samurai

Author: Akira Kurosawa
Time Period: 1951 CE–2000 CE
Country or Culture: Japan
Genre: Legend

OVERVIEW

When Japanese filmmaker Akira Kurosawa decided to direct his movie *Shichinin no Samurai* (*Seven Samurai*, 1954), he performed painstaking historical research and included well-known samurai legends in his film. *Seven Samurai* tells the story of a group of masterless samurai led by the expert swordsman Kambei Shimada. In the year of 1587, the samurai are hired by the inhabitants of a village threatened by plunder from bandits once their harvest has come in. As the villagers can offer them only rice for their services, the seven samurai primarily fight for the villagers out of a sense of honor, self-respect, and disgust with the bandits preying on the weakest members of Japan's feudal society.

Once the villagers, led by their elder, Gisaku, and the rash young Rikichi, have managed to persuade the samurai, the film focuses on the distinct personalities of the seven valiant warriors. Kambei Shimada has leadership qualities and outstanding sword-fighting abilities. His self-appointed young disciple Katsushirō Okamoto strives to become a battle-hardened samurai. Shichirōji, who once served under Kambei as a junior officer, rejoins his former commander. Gorōbei Katayama is an archer whose good-humored nature stands in contrast to his lethal skills with his bow and arrows. He recruits charming and witty Heihachi Hayashida for the group, even though Heihachi's skills are not fully developed yet. Finally, there is taciturn Kyūzō and the clownish Kikuchiyo, who attaches himself to the group and shows the most sympathy toward the peasants. Kikuchiyo was added to provide some comic relief and to prevent the movie from becoming too solemn and thus less likely to interest its audience. He is the most dynamic character of all seven samurai.

In contrast to the villagers, who are individualized, the bandits remain a literally nameless force of evil. They are distinguished only by their different functions as leader, scouts, and fighters.

Akira Kurosawa went into retreat with his two favorite screenwriters, Shinobu Hashimoto and Hideo Oguni, in December 1952 to craft the script for *Seven Samurai*. Secluded at a traditional Japanese inn, the three men worked for almost seven weeks on the screenplay. During this time, Kurosawa began to immerse himself in samurai legends. He continued to look at these legends as he studied the period of the film, Japan's Sengoku (or Warring States) period, for the subsequent three months of preproduction of the movie. *Seven Samurai* was filmed during 148 shooting days spread out over one year. It was released on April 26, 1954. The film quickly gathered national and international acclaim for the director and his cast.

A filmic analysis of how Kurosawa incorporated, developed, and adapted popular samurai warrior legends in *Seven Samurai* is particularly intellectually rewarding, as Kurosawa spent considerable thought and artistic talent on this issue. Cinematic analysis shows how Kurosawa worked with his source material from Japan's diverse samurai legends to adopt them into a filmic masterpiece that is both about the past and about Japan's post–World War II present of 1954. A close critical look analyzes the portrayal of Kurosawa's individual samurai as archetypical characters. Their interplay and function in the dramatic plot to save a village from the forces of evil is analyzed in light of Kurosawa's success in bringing into film, the medium of the twentieth century, the legends of Japan's feudal past.

SUMMARY

The movie *Seven Samurai* opens with bandits gazing at a village in the near distance. Because they plundered it the preceding fall, they decide to wait for the next harvest before raiding it again. Unbeknown to the bandits, they have been overheard by a peasant. He rushes to inform the villagers of the event. In great despair, a peasant woman cries out, "There are no gods here anymore" (Kurosawa 2). One young villager, Rikichi (played by Yoshio Tsuchiya), proposes to fight the bandits: "Let's kill them—kill them all" (3). Yet the other villagers know they stand no realistic chance. The revenge of the bandits for peasant resistance would be brutal and lethal.

The village elder, Gisaku (played by Kokuten Kodo), proposes that the village hire samurai for their protection. As the peasants can only offer food, namely rice, as payment, Gisaku tells the recruiting party led by Rikichi, "You must find hungry samurai" (Kurosawa 7). This is possible, since the Sengoku period in Japan, during which the movie takes place, has left many samurai without a lord to provide for them.

Initially, Rikichi's party cannot find samurai willing to serve for food. In one village, they witness how a samurai uses the self-effacing guise of a priest to overcome and kill a thief who has taken a boy hostage. This samurai, who identifies himself as Kambei Shimada (played by Takashi Shimura), attracts two samurai followers impressed by his feat to save the boy. One is Katsushirō Okamoto (Isao Kimura). Katsushirō comes from a wealthy landowning family and aspires to become a valiant samurai through Kambei's teaching. The other is the comical young man Kikuchiyo (Toshiro Mifune), who appears to have a rather shady background. Impressed by the determination of the villagers who approach him, Kambei agrees to their proposal. He tells them, "I accept your sacrifice," meaning the giving of their best food, rice, to the samurai (Kurosawa 29). Both Katsushirō and Kikuchiyo join Kambei, the latter initially against Kambei's will.

In due course, four more samurai agree to protect the villagers. Like Kambei, they have lost their lords and been reduced to the status of *rōnin* (masterless samurai). They include master archer Gorōbei Katayama (played by Yoshio Inaba); Kambei's former lieutenant, Shichirōji (Daisuke Katō); Heihachi Hayashida (Minoru Chiaki), who has been reduced to cutting wood for a townsman in exchange for food; and the silent, mysterious Kyūzō (Seiji Miyaguchi).

"Years ago, when all of you were still babies, our village was burned out by bandits. When I was running away I saw something. There was one village left unburned. It has hired samurai."

Seven Samurai

As the samurai enter the village, the peasants hide out of fear. One of them, Manzo (Kamatari Fujiwara), orders his beautiful daughter Shino (Keiko Tsushima) to cut her hair "so [she] can look like a boy," as he fears sexual predation by the samurai (Kurosawa 51). The samurai are alienated by the peasants' shyness. To break the tension, clownish Kikuchiyo raises a false alarm about the bandits returning. Suddenly the villagers implore the samurai to save them. This breaks the ice as Kikuchiyo berates the villagers: "Look, you idiots. We come all this way and then look at the welcome you give us!" (62).

There is another crisis when Kikuchiyo discovers samurai armor in the village. The other samurai realize that the peasants have killed samurai defeated in battle and have taken their armor. Kikuchiyo resolves the situation. On the one hand, he denounces the peasants as devious and "most cunning . . . animals" (Kurosawa 75). Then he turns around and blames the samurai of making them thus with their endless battles and predations on the villagers. This reveals that Kikuchiyo is of peasant stock and explains his prior comic antics; Kikuchiyo's intervention also results in the samurai and peasants joining forces.

The seven samurai fortify the village and instruct the peasants in self-defense, primarily with bamboo spears. Katsushirō begins a relationship with Shino.

Eventually, as harvest time nears, three bandit scouts appear, and Kikuchiyo involuntarily betrays the presence of the samurai in the village. The samurai decide to intercept the scouts. Two are killed by Kyūzō, and the third reveals the location of the bandit camp before the enraged villagers put him to death.

Three samurai go on a raiding party against the bandits' stronghold, guided by Rikichi. They succeed in surprising and killing some bandits. As they torch the bandits' huts, a woman emerges from one of them. She looks at Rikichi and then turns back into the inferno. She was Rikichi's wife, kidnapped by the bandits. Rikichi tries to go after her but is stopped by Heihachi. Suddenly, a bandit's musket shot fells Heihachi. The samurai retreat after this first loss of one of their own. Heihachi is buried in the village in a solemn ceremony.

Next, the bandits assault the village. Several are killed, but their three muskets pose a grave danger. Kyūzō slyly captures one musket from a bandit. This earns him the undying admiration of young Katsushirō, who tells Kyūzō, "You are . . . really great" (Kurosawa 146).

Kambei's strategy is to let one or two bandits through a gap in the village's fortification and then kill them there while the peasants close the gap. This works well during the next bandits' assault.

Katsushirō continues to praise Kyūzō, saying, "He has the real samurai spirit" (Kurosawa 155). This riles Kikuchiyo, who tries to get a musket himself. Lacking discipline, he abandons his post to do so. He succeeds but is scolded by Kambei on his return: "Your going off like that merits no praise at all" (160). To save the situation at the post abandoned by Kikuchiyo, Kambei sends reinforcements there. In the melee, Gorōbei is shot and falls in battle. Wearily, the samurai prepare themselves for the final assault of the surviving bandits. Katsushirō has sex with Shino. In a scene cut from the original American release of *Seven Samurai*, there is a disturbance at night when Shino's father, Manzo, discovers his daughter with Katsushirō. As Katsushirō looks on in shame, Manzo beats Shino.

The next morning, the surviving thirteen bandits attack. They are allowed into the village by Kambei according to his plan to finish them off there. This nearly succeeds in a fierce battle as one mounted bandit after another is felled and killed. However, the bandit chief (Shinpei Tagaki) escapes into a hut full of village women. He emerges to battle the samurai only to retreat again. From the hut, he shoots Kyūzō fatally in the back with his musket. Kikuchiyo attacks the hut and is mortally shot, but he manages to pursue the bandit chief by sheer force of will. With his last strength, Kikuchiyo kills the bandit chief with his sword before collapsing in his own death.

As the peasants bring in their harvest, they play musical instruments. As one of the three surviving samurai, Katsushirō spots Shino. However, she retreats from him, ending their relationship. A sad Kambei sums up the outcome of the battle, after which the film ends with a fade to black: "We've lost again. No, the farmers are the winners. Not us" (Kurosawa 186).

ANALYSIS

Close filmic and literary analysis of *Seven Samurai* illustrates how creatively film director Akira Kurosawa incorporated traditional Japanese warrior legends of the samurai into his cinematic masterpiece. To introduce Kambei, the leader of the samurai, Kurosawa uses a famous legend concerning a samurai who saves a boy held hostage by a robber, which has antecedents in the tenth century CE. Similarly, a legendary duel of the historical samurai Yagyū Jūbei Mitsuyoshi is incorporated to present and characterize another of Kurosawa's samurai, the taciturn Kyūzō.

A look at the warrior legends of Japan reveals that in addition to the direct incorporation of specific legends, Kurosawa developed his film based on general themes and motifs taken from warrior legends. Examples discussed in the analysis are a samurai's need for constant alertness and presence of mind, the requirement of individual discipline for a common mission, and perhaps surprisingly, the permitted escape from a fight and certain death. Comedy exists as well in some samurai legends. Accordingly, Kurosawa used this comic element for the characterization of Kikuchiyo. A feminist literary and filmic analysis looks at how legends about the relationship of samurai with women provide the backdrop for Kurosawa's development of the relationship between junior samurai Katsushirō and peasant girl Shino. Cultural criticism indicates how Kurosawa selected and developed warrior legends for *Seven Samurai* within the context of post–World War II Japanese society.

For the introduction of Kambei, the first samurai who will agree to protect the villagers, Kurosawa utilizes the warrior legend of historical samurai Kamiizumi Hidetsuna. This legend itself has an older antecedent. Kamiizumi Hidetsuna was born into a minor noble family in Kōzuke Province in eastern Japan around 1508. This places Kamiizumi right within Japan's Sengoku period, ranging from about 1467 to 1600; *Seven Samurai* takes place in 1587. Kamiizumi became an active participant in quite a few battles of this period.

After a turbulent military career, either in 1563 or 1566, the historical Kamiizumi became a minor official of his former enemy, the warlord Takeda Shingen. Impressed by Kamiizumi's valor, Takeda allowed Kamiizumi to use a character from his own personal name for his own, so Kamiizumi changed his first name to

Nobutsuna. Soon after, Kamiizumi's legendary fame developed as a teacher of a new school of sword fighting that he called Shinkage-ryū. Attracting many disciples, Kamiizumi also traveled across central Japan.

It is during one of Kamiizumi's travels as a renowned *kengō* (major swordsman) that the legend used in *Seven Samurai* takes place. This legend was first written down as a historical story in the Japanese anthology *Honchō bugei shōden*, published about two hundred years after the event in the eighteenth century. In English, it is retold by Hiroaki Sato in his *The Sword and the Mind* (1984) and by Stephen R. Turnbull in *The Samurai Swordsman* (2008).

According to this warrior legend, Kamiizumi is traveling the countryside toward his destination of Myōkōji Temple in Owari Prefecture. In a village on the way, he is informed that a robber has taken a boy hostage at knifepoint and has barricaded himself in a barn. The robber threatens to kill the boy if anybody tries to apprehend him. With calm deliberation, Kamiizumi cuts off his topknot, the visual symbol of his status as samurai, and shaves his head. Next, he borrows a robe from a priest. Unarmed, with two rice balls as food offerings in his hands, Kamiizumi approaches the robber in the barn, looking like a priest. When the robber is distracted by the food, Kamiizumi seizes, disarms, and overcomes him, and the boy is freed.

Japanese scholar Sato notes in his *Legends of the Samurai* (1995) that this legend of Kamiizumi may be based on an older warrior legend from the tenth century CE. The older legend concerns a feat by Minamoto no Yorinobu, who lived from 968 to 1048 CE. The legend takes place when Minamoto no Yorinobu was governor of Kōzuke. This is the province where Kamiizumi was later born, which points to a local connection between the two legends.

As governor, Minamoto no Yorinobu is informed that a shackled burglar brought into the house of his lieutenant, Chikataka, managed to free himself. Unable to escape from Chikataka's home, the burglar takes Chikataka's boy hostage. With extreme calmness of mind and emanating the authority of his office, Minamoto enters the house and approaches the burglar at the threshold to the inner storage quarter. Sternly, Minamoto questions the motive of the burglar: "Did you take that boy hostage because you wanted to keep yourself alive, or because you wanted to kill the boy?" (Sato, *Legends* 73). When the burglar admits to the first alternative, Minamoto orders the burglar to give himself up. Surprisingly,

the burglar is convinced by Minamoto's reasoning and the unflinching assertion of his authority, and he surrenders, saying, "Thank you, sir. I don't think I can refuse to do what you tell me to. I will throw the sword away" (73–74).

After the boy is saved, the legend takes another surprising turn. Rather than executing the burglar as demanded by Chikataka, Minamoto sets him free. Minamoto explains that the burglar is to be rewarded for giving up his hostage and shows his compassion for the destitution that drove the man to steal. Minamoto no Yorinobu even provides a horse, bow and arrows, and provisions for the burglar as he sends him away. This greatly contributed to "Yorinobu's reputation as a warrior" (74).

The two related warrior legends of Minamoto and Kamiizumi share the same basic plot conundrum but solve the situation differently. In the older legend, Minamoto's authority is sufficient to convince the burglar he has to release his hostage. This indicates a more stable social situation during Japan's Heian period, when the older legend takes place. The newer, related legend takes place during the much more turbulent, almost anarchic Sengoku period. Here, the feat of Kamiizumi is to disarm the robber by stealth. The robber totters on the brink of insanity and is not open to reason like his older counterpart. This is another sign of the more troubled political and social times expressed in this more modern version of the legend.

Akira Kurosawa builds and develops this legend further in *Seven Samurai* and tells it in a cinematographically brilliant way. He places the episode at the beginning of the movie, before the peasants have found a single samurai willing to help them. Kurosawa's plot restricts audience knowledge by putting the audience on the same level as the traveling peasants who stumble upon an intriguing scene at a large country house. From their point of view, the camera shows a samurai, a priest, and a rich commoner emerging with a large throng of people from the gates of a mansion. The samurai, later revealed as Kambei, takes a knife out of his belt as onlookers, including the film audience, watch tensely. A medium close up shows the samurai cutting off his topknot with his knife. On the soundtrack, there is a gasp from the onlookers, signifying their surprise that a samurai would cut off this symbol of his rank.

Tension builds with the next action shown. After the samurai washes his hair in the stream nearby, the priest carefully shaves his head. Kurosawa's camera shoots the scene alternating with close-ups of the samurai's impassive face and medium shots of the onlooking multitude observing the action. Eventually, one of the peasants, Mosuke, asks a woman from the compound what is happening. She reveals to him, and to the audience, that a thief has been discovered and has run into the barn. Among the onlookers, a young samurai appears, later known as Katsushirō. As the people return to the mansion's compound and the camera focuses on the barn, another man tells the peasants that the thief has taken a boy hostage and threatens to kill him if anybody should enter the barn. To sonically reinforce the drama, the soundtrack reveals the crying of boy. Throughout the scene, Kurosawa limits his visuals to the point of view of the people outside, never cutting to an interior shot of the barn. This highlights the tension and mystery of the scene.

The people tell the peasants that they have asked the samurai to save the boy. The samurai agreed, asked for two rice balls, and then asked to be shaved and given the robes of a priest. With this story information conveyed, Kurosawa's camera cuts to the samurai, dressed as a priest by now. The camera reveals another samurai onlooker, later known to be the clownish Kikuchiyo. Tension builds as Kambei, watched by Katsushirō, Kikuchiyo, the peasants, and the people of the manor, slowly approaches the barn. The thief yells out to him and warns him to back off. Undeterred, Kambei continues, kneels, and places the two rice balls on a stone by the entrance to the barn. He informs the thief of his assumed status: "I'm a priest" (Kurosawa 16).

As the frantic thief continues his threats to kill the boy if anybody approaches, Kambei explains that the food is for both the boy and the thief. Kambei slides open the barn door, but the audience, like the onlookers, cannot see inside. He offers the food to the thief: "Here, take it. It's alright" (Kurosawa 16). The thief orders Kambei to throw in the two rice balls, and Kambei complies. Raising himself, Kambei waits for a moment and then rushes into the barn. Dramatic tension is created by a momentary pause during which the child's scream is heard, and wind blows dust through the barn door. Next, the thief emerges running, which is shot in slow motion. The child's mother rushes to Kambei holding her child, then the camera cuts to Kambei's bloodied sword before showing the dying thief collapsing in slow motion. Kambei appears ready to walk away from the scene.

Analytical comparison of Kurosawa's development of the legend and its antecedent shows his use of the

techniques of the medium of film to highlight the inherent drama of the episode. The actual climax takes place inside the barn and is not visible to the audience. At the same time, Kurosawa makes the outcome more lethal than the original legends. In *Seven Samurai*, the thief is killed, very effectively and offscreen. Only the symbol of the blood on Kambei's sword indicates that it has been used to deliver a mortal blow. As Kambei is a masterless samurai, or rōnin, like his six eventual companions, sheer reliance on authority, as in the oldest version of the legend, would not have worked within the narrative logic of the film. At the same time, given the overall theme of violence of the movie, well grounded in the historical period in which it is set, killing the thief rather than disarming him would have been anticlimactic.

The legend serves Kurosawa in introducing Kambei and the next two samurai to the story of his film. Structurally, the legend is alluded to again at the very end of the film, creating a strong narrative parallel. This is done as the bandit chief runs into a hut where many women of the village have been hiding. From this vantage point, he manages to shoot and kill Kyūzō, triggering Kikuchiyo's charge at the bandit. Kikuchiyo is shot, but by sheer power of will, he survives long enough to confront the bandit chief inside the hut. Now, Kurosawa shows the interior and their ensuing duel. This ends as Kikuchiyo runs the bandit chief out of the house and stabs him to death before dying himself. Structurally, this inversion of the earlier legendary episode perfectly closes the drama of the movie's battle scenes.

A second warrior legend directly incorporated into *Seven Samurai* concerns a duel of legendary renown, fought by historical samurai Yagyū Jūbei Mitsuyoshi. Yagyū was born in 1607, just after the Sengoku period had ended with the establishment of the Tokugawa shogunate in 1603. As a teenager, Yagyū served as sparring partner for the future Shogun Iemitsu, who assumed power in 1623. In his twenties, Yagyū became considered a master swordsman. Suddenly, for reasons no longer known, the shogun dismissed Yagyū from court. For twelve years, Yagyū embarked on a *musha shigyō*, or warrior's pilgrimage, before regaining the shogun's favor.

It was during Yagyū's warrior pilgrimage that the legend of his encounter with a presumptuous rōnin takes place. As Hiroaki Sato retells the legend, based on the Japanese version by Kaionji Chōgorō, Yagyū is visiting the mansion of a daimyo during his warrior pilgrimage. There, a showy rōnin challenges Yagyū to a duel. Yagyū declines. Upon the insistence of the curious daimyo, Yagyū agrees "to fight with wooden swords" (Sato, *Legends* xiii). The match is over in an instant, "with their wooden swords hitting each other's body, apparently simultaneously" (xiii). The boisterous rōnin declares it a draw, to which Yagyū calmly objects that he won. Outraged, the rōnin asks for a rematch. The rematch takes place with the same results; the rōnin claims another draw and Yagyū insists again that he has won.

Outraged, the rōnin demands a match with real swords. Yagyū declines, but the daimyo insists on the real fight, which is described as quick and lethal: "As soon as the two men face each other, the fight is over—with the rōnin keeling over, his head split in two" (xiv). Yagyū shows the daimyo where the rōnin's sword has touched his body. There, "part of his outer jacket is slightly cut, but not the clothes underneath, let alone his flesh" (xiv).

The original warrior legend of Yagyū stresses both the expert swordsman's incredible skill and his becoming modesty in letting a foolish challenger come to harm. The setting in front of a daimyo provides an interesting frame. Historically, masterless samurai, the rōnin, sought generally to regain employment from a new daimyo. They often found it quickly during the Sengoku periodbut much less so thereafter. In the legend, Yagyū's challenger is motivated to prove his martial skills to recommend himself to the daimyo. At the same time, Yagyū, enjoying the hospitality of the daimyo, feels pressured to oblige his host. The legend ends by solving the puzzle of the apparently simultaneous hits. While Yagyū's strike was mortal, the rōnin's merely grazed his jacket. This greatly appeals to the audience's taste for samurai legends.

Kurosawa brilliantly translates the legend into a very dramatic cinematic episode. Again, Kurosawa limits the audience's knowledge of what is happening to the point of view of the onlookers. These include the peasants and the group of five samurai they have convinced to help them at this point. The group comes upon two samurai combatants on a temple ground. This setting removes the third party of the daimyo, which would not fit so well into the plot of the film. *Seven Samurai* shows both a tall samurai and the samurai later revealed to be Kyūzō as they cut themselves staffs from bamboo growing at the temple. Watching the two opponents prepare their staffs heightens the tension.

The first match unfolds with minor but telling variations from the legend. The tall samurai shouts for the

match to begin, and Kurosawa's camera shows the two samurai assuming their positions. With a great yell, the tall samurai rushes at Kyūzō. This is intercut with shots of the audience. When the tall samurai strikes at Kyūzō, Kyūzō parries that blow. The combatants remain with locked staffs for a moment before disengaging. Then the tall samurai claims:

TALL SAMURAI: Too bad—a tie.

Medium shot of KYŪZŌ standing impassively.

KYŪZŌ: No.

Close-up of the TALL SAMURAI: he grins and then stares in amazement.

Close-up of KYŪZŌ.

KYŪZŌ: I won. (Kurosawa 39)

Cutting out the legend's rematch with nonlethal weapons, the tall samurai insists on a real sword fight right away. Kyūzō refuses initially to engage in a lethal duel and tells his brash opponent about the futility of such a match.

KYŪZŌ: There is no need.

TALL SAMURAI: What?

KYŪZŌ: If I use a sword, I'll kill you. It's stupid. (40)

Since the tall samurai insists on the duel, it takes place. Kurosawa uses editing and cinematography effectively to dramatize the climax of the warrior legend at the root of his episode. Kurosawa crosscuts from the two samurai to the people watching to create tension with this editing. Then, the camera shows the tall samurai attacking Kyūzō with a loud yell. Kyūzō quickly strikes the neck of his adversary, who comes to a sudden stop. Keeping up the suspense, the camera shows the tall samurai standing and then sinking to the ground in slow motion, mortally struck.

This use of the warrior legend of Yagyū serves well to characterize Kyūzō in *Seven Samurai* and places him in the tradition of a Japanese sword-fighting legend. The fact that the legend takes place in the historical period after that of the movie does not matter much. The warrior legend is used fruitfully to illustrate the enduring theme of an ideal samurai's prowess and his self-restraint in using his lethal skills until absolutely challenged to do so.

HISTORICAL CONTEXT

The first historical reference to Japanese samurai dates from a poetry anthology of the tenth century CE. Samurai were named after the verb *saburau*, meaning "to serve, or to wait upon a member of aristocratic and imperial society." By the twelfth century CE, samurai were understood to be members of the warrior class who nominally served the aristocracy. Samurai followed a strict code of conduct that became known as *Bushidō*. The earliest warrior legends of the samurai date from the tenth to the twelfth centuries.

Samurai rose continuously to power and began to form military governments, relegating the emperor to a ceremonial figurehead in the twelfth century CE when they gained power as rulers of Japan. This began with the rule of the Kamakura shogunate; founded by the Minamoto samurai clan, it lasted from 1185 to 1333.

After a period of relative internal stability, Japan descended into the chaos of the Sengoku period, also called the Warring States period. Historians commonly see this period as beginning with the Ōnin War of 1467 to 1477. By the time *Seven Samurai* takes place in 1587, the Warring States period neared its end. This trend began in the 1560s, when Oda Nobunaga emerged as a warlord with the possible strength to unify Japan by force. However, there were still many battles ahead. This conflict led to a general arming of the populace and much chaos and destruction, thus creating many near-lawless regions such as the one shown in *Seven Samurai*.

Tokugawa Ieyasu's victory at the Battle of Sekigahara in 1600 consolidated the power of the Tokugawa clan. When Ieyasu became shogun in 1603, he established a period of astonishing inner peace. This became known as the Edo period, named after the shogun's capital of Edo (contemporary Tokyo). The Edo period lasted until the Meiji Restoration of 1868 returned the emperor to real power. Many warrior legends of the Edo period glamorize the samurai.

In addition to his direct use of warrior legends for *Seven Samurai*, Kurosawa's film also incorporates more indirectly some key themes and motifs of the samurai legends. A prominent example is a samurai's need for constant alertness and self-discipline. This quality is outlined in the legends about Minamoto no Raikō, known also as Yorimitsu, who lived from 948 to 1021 CE, for example. In his *Legends of the Samurai*, Sato offers a translation of the story "Minamoto no Raikō: Alert and Penetrating." Here, the protagonist escapes the assault of a mischievous demon boy by remaining alert during a light sleep even after having drunk some sake. "He sensed" what the boy was up to, and the boy, in turn, gives up his plan of assault when he notices the samurai is aware of him (Sato, *Legends* 63). Another legend given by Sato involves the legendary robber Hakamadare of the tenth and eleventh century CE. In "Muraoko no Gorō and Hakamadare," the samurai is not fooled into giving up his alertness even when he comes upon Hakamadare lying "completely naked . . . by the roadside," pretending to be dead (35). A less circumspect samurai is killed by Hakamadare when he lets down his guard at this sight.

Kurosawa uses the theme of a samurai's need for alertness as illustrated by these warrior legends in Kambei's ploy to test potential partners. In a village, Kambei sets himself up in an inn, visible from the outside. He instructs Katsushirō to hide behind the doorframe and to hit any samurai who enters with a stick. Two samurai either fend off Katsushirō's stroke or see right through the ruse; Gorōbei has the same reaction. It is only Kikuchiyo, who has drunk too much, who gets hit. As he is the comic character, he gets to join the group nevertheless.

It is also Kikuchiyo who violates the samurai principle of group discipline, especially in battle. A warrior legend, "The Unwelcome Combat," presented by Turnbull, concerns the ensuing disciplining of a samurai for his selfish—even if successful—action. During the siege of Ueda Castle in 1600, two enemy samurai appear in front of the besiegers, challenging samurai for a duel. From among them, Ono Taadaki and another warrior "responded to the shout by heading over the line towards the challenger" (Turnbull 70). Even though Taadaki and his comrade successfully kill an enemy, Taadaki is placed on one year's probation for having "broken ranks without permission for a private battle" (71). In *Seven Samurai*, Kambei censors Kikuchiyo for abandoning his post to get a bandit's gun by himself:

"Listen carefully – in war, you never fight individually" (Kurosawa 160).

Yet as Kikuchiyo is a comic character, this transgression, while noticed, does not detract from his overall sympathetic portrayal. Indeed, there are a few comic warrior legends, such as "Guardian Kings and the Oxcart: A Comic Interlude," presented by Sato in English translation. Here, three samurai with a rustic background hire an oxcart to bring them to a viewing spot to observe the festive procession of the Kamo Festival. However, unaccustomed to the rough ride of the oxcart, the three samurai get sick, vomit, and "in their sickness all three fell asleep" during the procession (Sato, *Legends* 67).

Even a samurai's flight from danger is a theme in some warrior legends. While a samurai was not generally expected to flee from danger, there were certain traditionally recognized mitigating circumstances. In the legend "Taira no Koremochi, aka General Yogo," presented by Sato, the protagonist escapes the onslaught of his home by superior forces. He lives to fight another day and wins that battle by valor, presence of mind, and surprise. Similarly, the legend "Taira no Sadatsuna: When Not to Risk Your Life," translated by Sato, explicitly praises the protagonist for his decision to flee robbers. Sadatsuna's explanation, "I don't want to risk my life with robbers" (*Legends* 91), is fully validated by the legend. In *Seven Samurai*, Kambei's former lieutenant, Shichirōji, describes how he survived a battle: "Well, I lay right down in the ditch there, in the water. But when the castle finally burned down and then almost fell on me, I thought I was gone" (Kurosawa 35). Nevertheless, he is welcomed to join a fresh fight.

From a feminist critical perspective, the peasant woman Shino's termination of her romantic relationship with young samurai Katsushirō, once the bandits are defeated, is strongly justified. Given the deep historical class structure of traditional Japanese society, any relationship between a samurai and a peasant woman could not have existed in the realm of an official marriage. Even as a consort, a young village woman would not have been accepted. In addition, samurai warrior legends show women often at peril when attracting the romantic interest of a samurai. In the legend "Kō no Moronao: When a Warrior Falls in Love," rendered by Sato, the powerful samurai Moronao's love for a married woman is fatal—it ultimately leads to the death of the woman, her children, and the ritual suicide of her husband. Little does it help that "Moronao thereafter piled up evil acts and was in time destroyed" (Sato, *Legends* 203).

Shino is a wise character to end her relationship with Katsushirō.

From the point of view of cultural criticism, Kurosawa places *Seven Samurai* in the cultural context of post–World War II Japanese society as well as in its historical period. The most telling detail is perhaps that all four samurai who do not survive are killed by bandit guns. Historically, guns entered Japan first from China in a very basic version in the thirteenth century, making no impact. However, the introduction of Western muskets by the Portuguese in 1543 dramatically altered Japanese warfare. Guns quickly became manufactured in Japan and were widely used during the later part of the Sengoku period. However, the Tokugawa shogunate, established in 1603, severely limited gun possession to selected forces of its own only, even though guns continued to be mass-produced in Japan. Similarly, warrior legends rarely focus on guns as weapons of a warrior. As historian Noel Perrin states, the gun is seen as an alien, especially Western, weapon at odds with the traditional warrior spirit. In *Seven Samurai*, it is the bandits who introduce guns on the battlefield. Only by necessity do the samurai obtain some guns from the bandits. In a general cultural context, guns may be likened to the atomic bomb. This was a weapon against which the traditional samurai spirit proved as mismatched as the sword against the gun.

CROSS-CULTURAL INFLUENCE

The international success of *Seven Samurai* led to a cross-cultural influence on a variety of films that incorporate the central theme of a group of diverse heroes banding together to fight for an often highly idealistic cause. The most direct movie adaptation of *Seven Samurai* is *The Magnificent Seven* (1960), by director John Sturges. Sturges turned the story into a Western and otherwise remained relatively close to Kurosawa's original. The period commonly known as the Wild West seemed to lend itself well to the plot. This era of the American West gave rise to outlaws and bandits in the absence of a strong and lawful central authority in the second half of the nineteenth century. It could be compared to Japan's Sengoku period.

Sturges places the besieged village in northern Mexico. The seven gunfighters are recruited across the border in the United States. Like *Seven Samurai*, the film opens with a group of bandits. They are led by Calvera, played by Eli Wallach, who promises to return to raid a beleaguered village for food and supplies. Initially, the villagers only want to buy guns and ammunition in America. However, they meet the experienced gunslinger Chris Larabee Adams (played by Yul Brynner), who persuades them to hire gunmen for protection instead.

Similar to Kurosawa's use of warrior legends to characterize his individual samurai, Sturges uses common character traits from the Western movie tradition for his own group of hired gunmen. There is young, wild but inexperienced Chico (Horst Buchholz) performing the role of the apprentice samurai Katsushirō. Then there is Chris's old friend Harry Luck (Brad Dexter), similar to Kambei's former lieutenant Shichirōji. The others are gambler and drifter Vin Tanner (Steve McQueen), similar to down-on-his-luck Heihachi; the Irish Mexican Bernardo O'Reilly (Charles Bronson); cowboy Britt (James Coburn); and a genuine gunman, Lee (Robert Vaughn). Lee, unlike his samurai counterpart Kyūzō, is given a crisis of self-confidence. All in all, Sturges's movie thoroughly Americanizes his cast of seven. The film does not attempt to mold the characters into samurai but gives them very similar plot functions within the narrative.

The cultural difference between the highly stratified feudal Japanese society depicted in *Seven Samurai* and the much more open Mexican and American society of the Wild West period is apparent when Chris and his men arrive at the village. They begin training the villagers and bond with them. There is much less of a fearful gap between the two groups, even though it is clear they are different. The romance of Chico, who is Mexican, and the village girl Petra (Rosenda Monteros), while following the subplot of Katsushirō and Shino, is much less doomed by an unbridgeable class division.

The battle with the bandits differs quite significantly from that in *Seven Samurai*. Yet structurally, it follows the overall pattern of a successful, if costly, defense of the village. In *The Magnificent Seven*, the bandits' first attack is repulsed without the loss of any of the seven gunmen but with plenty of bandit casualties. Chico pretends to be a fellow bandit and follows the retreating bandits to their camp, only to learn the bandits plan to come back because they are out of food. This echoes the scene of Kikuchiyo infiltrating the bandit's siege by pretending to be one of their own and by interacting with a bandit before killing him for his gun. Even though Kurosawa's episode appears much later in his film, this parallel indicates how closely Sturges wanted to follow his original, down to individual plot episodes even when using a different chronological order for them.

In *The Magnificent Seven*, the preemptive raid on the bandit camp modeled after that of the group of samurai fails. The bandits have left for the village already, and the villagers have accepted their rule over them. This is a major divergence from *Seven Samurai*. It serves to highlight, in a different cultural setting, the large division between the gunmen and the villagers, just like the gap between the samurai and the peasants. Again, Sturges aligns both his theme and content with that of the Japanese film.

In an act of apparent magnanimity, Calvera lets the outnumbered gunmen live and has them escorted ignobly from the village. Calvera voices his belief that the gunmen will no longer fight for such a pointless goal as protecting villagers. He also worries about an intervention by the US Army should he kill American citizens. This is a unique plot element, as the Japanese bandits never worry about feudal authorities intervening with their raids on villages that are nominally under the protection of the provincial governor. It is one of the few moments when the world of *The Magnificent Seven* differs significantly from that of its Japanese model.

Another minor issue of divergence, here in the degree of realism portrayed, is that Mexican authorities insisted on clean costumes for the actors playing the villagers. This violated the kind of historical authenticity Kurosawa's costumes and set—a village built to life-size scale—sought to portray for his time period. When Mexican authorities demanded fresh clothes to avoid the stereotype of dirtily dressed Mexican villagers, Sturges and his crew complied because they were shooting on location in Mexico. This indicates that, to some degree, contemporary international political issues affected the production of *The Magnificent Seven*.

Of their own free will, all but one of the gunmen, Chris's old friend Harry, decide to return to liberate the village from Calvera. As they engage the bandits in a gunfight in the streets of the village, the villagers gain courage and join the fight. However, Bernardo, Britt, and Lee are killed, all after taking out a substantial number of bandits. Just as Chris is in danger of falling, Harry reappears to rescue him. Harry is killed in the process, but the bandits are overcome. Finally, it is Chris who shoots Calvera. Dying, Calvera utters his astonishment at the gunmen's return.

While the number of killed and surviving samurai and gunmen is the same, at three survivors each, there is a difference in the characters still alive at the end. The leaders, Chris and Kambei, survive, as do the youngest,

Chico and Katsushirō. However, while Kambei's trusted former lieutenant, Shichirōji, survives, Chris's friend Harry dies. Instead, Vin the luckless gambler survives. While Kurosawa's survivors are those with the strongest bond among them—captain, lieutenant, and disciple—Sturges's are a more mixed group. This may indicate Sturges's greater sense of individualism despite modeling his movie so closely after the Japanese original.

Another divergence is emphasized at the end when Chico decides to stay in the village together with Petra. Sturges's Wild West is less class stratified as a society than Kurosawa's feudal Japan. A romance between outlaw and village woman can flourish, unlike that of samurai and peasant woman. However, as a final homage honoring Kurosawa, Sturges's ending lines very closely echo Kambei's sentiment at the end of *Seven Samurai* that it was the villagers, not their protectors, who truly won the battle.

Apart from this direct, acknowledged adaption of *Seven Samurai* by John Sturges, film critics have identified numerous American and international movies that incorporate core plot ideas from Kurosawa's masterpiece. A common idea taken is to have a group of relatively unrelated, diverse characters unite for the purpose of a common cause. Each member of the new group is characterized individually. This strategy allows for some heroes to be killed, heightening audience tension. In this vein, movies such as Lewis Milestone's *Ocean's Eleven* (1960) and Steven Soderbergh's 2001 remake, J. Lee Thompson's *The Guns of Navarone* (1961), Robert Aldrich's *The Dirty Dozen* (1967), Ramesh Sippy's *Sholay* (1975), Stephen Spielberg's *Saving Private Ryan* (1998), and Quentin Tarantino's *Inglorious Basterds* (2009) all bear plot influences from Kurosawa's *Seven Samurai*.

Steward Lee's "Bounty Hunters," a 2010 episode of *Star Wars: The Clone Wars* (2008–), a 3-D animated television series produced by George Lucas, is a direct homage to Kurosawa's movie. "Bounty Hunters" transcribes the samurai film's plot into the world of science fiction. This indicates the genre-transcending, wide cross-cultural artistic influence of *Seven Samurai*.

In "Bounty Hunters," the team of Anakin, Ahsoka, and Obi-Wan Kenobi crash-land on the agrarian planet Felucia. There, they decide join a group of bounty hunters led by Sugi to come to the aid of local farmers whom pirates threaten with the repeated theft of their crop. The leader of the pirates is a recurring villain of the series, Hondo Ohnaka. Written by Drew Z. Greenberg, the episode acknowledges its clear inspiration from and modeling after *Seven Samurai*.

In early 2013, there were industry rumors that Zack Snyder may plan a *Star Wars* film based on *Seven Samurai*. This rumor was denied by Snyder's associates. However, Kurosawa's movie has already made it into space through animation. *Seven Samurai*'s vast cross-cultural influence appears to be strong and sustained across many genres and many filmmakers.

R. C. Lutz, PhD

BIBLIOGRAPHY

"Bounty Hunters." *Star Wars: The Clone Wars—The Complete Season Two*. By Drew Z. Greenberg and George Lucas. Dir. Steward Lee. Cartoon Network, 2010. DVD.

Kurosawa, Akira, Shinobu Hashimoto, and Hideo Oguni. *Seven Samurai*. Trans. Donald Richie. Santa Barbara City College School of Media Arts, 24 June 2010. PDF file.

The Magnificent Seven. Dir. John Sturges. Perf. Yul Brynner, Eli Wallach, and Steve McQueen. MGM, 1960. DVD.

Perrin, Noel. *Giving up the Gun, Japan's Reversion to the Sword, 1543–1879*. Boston: Godine, 1979. Print.

Sato, Hiroaki. *Legends of the Samurai*. Woodstock: Overlook, 1995. Print.

---, trans. *The Sword and the Mind*. Woodstock: Overlook, 1984. Print.

Seven Samurai. Dir. Akira Kurosawa. Perf. Toshiro Mifune, Takashi Shimura, and Keiko Tsushima. Toho, 1954. DVD.

Stafford, Roy. *Seven Samurai*. Harlow: Longman, 2001. Print.

Turnbull, Stephen R. *The Samurai Swordsman: Master of War*. North Clarendon: Tuttle, 2008. Print.

Yoshimoto, Mitsuhiro. *Kurosawa: Film Studies and Japanese Cinema*. Durham: Duke UP, 2000. Print..

APPENDIXES

MYTHOLOGY IN THE CLASSROOM

With the great interest in mythology—both classical and comparative—a plethora of books have emerged appealing not only to the general reader but also to teachers and students. The books in this series are part of this profusion. How then are teachers and students to make the best use of the reference works in this series?

In order to evaluate the role that volumes in this series would play in a classroom course, it may be useful to briefly outline the goals and challenges in teaching a mythology course. There are basically two major approaches. At a minimal level students should become competent in recognizing the stories, characteristics, and attributes (many instructors would include visual representations here) of mythological characters. Such competency should also allow students to recognize allusions from later literature and art to contemporary political slogans and commercials. Here, textbooks with summaries of the stories would serve the purpose. Through this basic recognition of the stories and allusions it is argued that students will improve their reading and understanding of texts. The second approach is to read translations of the primary texts of mythology. This approach teaches a different type of reading in which students encounter multiple levels of meaning, nonlinear presentation, archaic thought patterns, and so forth. Such an approach is challenging both for students and teachers.

Other challenges confront instructors of mythology courses. These courses call upon instructors to be knowledgeable in more areas of expertise than any other course that they teach: language and literature, myth theory, archeology and art, history, anthropology, and psychology, to name a few. In comparative or world myth courses, instructors often teach stories that are outside their field of expertise. How then do the volumes of this series address these goals and challenges?

A brief overview of the format of each volume gives a starting point in answering this question. Each volume consists of articles summarizing and analyzing myths, fairy tales, legends, sagas, and folktales on a certain theme (e.g., love, heroes) from various cultures around the world. Each article, where possible, highlights an interpretative or theoretical approach. Part of the article focuses on cross-cultural comparisons and closely analyzes at least one retelling of the tale in art, film, music, and so forth.

COMPARATIVE MYTHOLOGY

Given the diversity of the texts and genres, these volumes would appeal more to a comparative mythology course rather than to a classical mythology class, although instructors in the latter course could still refer their students to relevant articles on Greco-Roman myths. In comparing myths from different cultures, scholars have focused on accounting for the similarities between them. In this respect, many myth courses outline two basic approaches: diffusion and similar thought patterns. The diffusionist approach received its greatest impetus from the discovery of the Indo-European languages in the late 1700s and the subsequent development of I-E linguistics in the following century. Just as linguists could compare words and grammatical and syntactical forms and attempt to reconstruct a protolanguage, those analyzing mythology also hoped to work out relations between mythologies. The method often involves locating common elements that are unique to the two myths being compared. An example would be the birds sent out in the Mesopotamian and biblical flood stories. If enough of these unique common elements can be found, then a genetic relationship can be posited about the two myths. The other approach postulates that the similarities between myths arise from similar thought patterns. Thus Carl Jung posited the universal unconscious and its archetypes, and Joseph Campbell regarded myths as following his monomythic pattern. Yet interpreters of mythology must also take context into account (and the best interpreters of either stripe do). Sources need to be evaluated; learning as much as one can about the dating, storytellers, and audience is a necessity. Differences between the stories should also be explored in detail (discussed below under Interpretative Approaches).

For a comparative mythology course, the articles in these volumes could serve as a basis for the exploration of a theme. Whether the student has been reading primary sources or a summary of the tale, the article furnishes a starting point for obtaining a deeper understanding of the story under consideration. The articles are written by scholars knowledgeable in their respective fields. This aspect of expertise is one of the major challenges in the teaching of comparative mythology, as noted above. Apart from calling in colleagues who are experts in their fields, such articles as are found here fulfill this pressing need. They show how a scholar who studies the culture from which the story arises interprets the tale. Clearly understanding the ways in which the culture understood the story is the first step in any comparison. The articles also give references for further reading so that students can explore the tale from different perspectives.

Once the myth has been explored in detail from the culture's viewpoint, the volumes offer various comparisons. The summary versions allow students to look for other similar stories without having to read the often longer primary sources. The subdivisions of the themes (e.g., lover's quest, tales of transformation, animal lovers) allow the student to focus on a more detailed comparison. From the articles, the students then could go to the primary sources, again gaining from the article a preliminary understanding of how the myths are or were understood within their cultures.

Summary versions of the myth, fairy tale, legend, or folktale also allow the students to encounter the tale in multiple versions. Primary sources often do not present a complete version of the tale but rather focus on a part. Summaries can provide an overall presentation with variations. Students then would be able to choose the most interesting source or version for comparison. As each version may have different emphases, it is crucial for students to understand not only how the story is interpreted within the culture, but also how the culture's understanding of the tale has developed and evolved over time. The later versions of the story also show how later generations have adapted the tale or another culture has assimilated the tale into their culture.

INTERPRETATIVE APPROACHES

As noted earlier, the authors of the articles, where possible, have highlighted their interpretive or theoretical approach. These include the following theories: nature, etiological, ritual, charter, Freudian, Jungian, and structuralist theories. Folktales as well as many myths and other tales are also analyzable in terms of Vladimir Propp's "wonder tale" pattern, and hero stories can be fit into Campbell's or other hero patterns. Folklorists have cataloged the different types of folktales. Feminist analyses also abound. These theories are universalist, i.e., *all* myths are explained by the theory. However, most instructors employ an eclectic approach in which several theories are used in interpreting a myth. Since myths are multivalent, theories are applicable at different levels in the story. Thus, for example, the Demeter-Persephone story can be examined in connection with nature theory (goddess as explanation for the growth of vegetation),

etiological theory (origin of seasons), ritual theory (origin of the Eleusinian Mysteries and in relation to marriage), and psychological theories (e.g., Jung's great mother archetype).

However, many universalist approaches often focus on similarities and force disparate material into a "one-mould-fits-all" pattern. Thus, some recent scholarship has reacted against these universalist theories, arguing that context and culture-specific aspects of a tale are undermined by such approaches. In these reactions, differences play just as important a role as similarities. In fact, differences may be of great interest in revealing aspects of a culture not found in the other culture being compared.[1]

In the end, however, a middle ground between similarities and differences would offer a productive way of comparing myths. After all, there must be some basic similarity to compare. Differences would then provide a more nuanced comparison. The articles deal with both universalist and culture-specific approaches. Students will thus be able to choose the most interesting method to follow in comparing the tales.

FAIRY TALES IN THE COLLEGE CLASSROOM

The inclusion of fairy and other tales, in contrast to myth, will also offer the student interesting comparisons. Much of the study of the fairy tale and folklore has focused on identifying types and motifs within the tales. Developing from the work of Antti Aarne and Stith Thompson, folklorists have been cataloging the stories of the world into type and motif. Unfortunately, this scholarly revolution has for the most part bypassed studies in classical mythology.[2] In this respect, the inclusion of fairy tales in this volume in part provides an opportunity to assimilate the findings of folklorists.

While distinctions between these genres are made, folktale story patterns often appear in other genres. Thus, a definition of a fairy tale or folktale might include that it takes place in the timeless past ("once upon a time"), has protagonists with common names (e.g., Jack), and contains helpers (e.g., fairies, magical objects) and hinderers (e.g., ogres). A myth, however, might be defined as a story about the gods and heroes from a definite locale, and so on. Nevertheless, similar story patterns turn up in both genres. For example, the Oedipus myth is type 931 (hereafter AT 931) in Aarne and Thompson's 1961 publication *The Types of the Folktale*. Although it is often difficult to determine whether there are any tendencies in stories moving from one genre to another, William Hansen in *Ariadne's Thread* (2002) has argued that "genre variance" usually moves from folktales (indefinite place and time) to legend or myth in a definite place (e.g., Oedipus in Thebes).[3] As folklorists have cataloged various traditional genres from around the world, the analysis of stories into types and motifs offers a thorough method to find comparisons.

One example may be given here. The story of Cupid and Psyche in Lucius Apuleius's *Metamorphoses* has often been regarded as "the most fairy tale–like of all ancient stories." Even with its mythological coloring (e.g., the god Cupid as the male protagonist and the goddess Venus filling the role of the witch or evil stepmother), the story can be clearly classified as AT 425B (*The Disenchanted Husband*), a subtype of AT 425 (*The Search for the Lost Husband*). In AT 425B, a marriage is arranged for the heroine to an enchanted husband; a taboo is imposed by the husband, but the bride violates this and thus loses her husband. In her search for her husband, the heroine meets a witch-goddess who imposes seemingly impossible tasks upon her. With the help of her husband or others, she accomplishes these tasks and wins him back. An examination of AT 425B will lead the student to numerous parallels from around the world. Then the student will be able to explore themes found in these parallels, e.g., the theme of anxiety over arranged marriages—it is not surprising that another subtype of AT 425 is AT 425A (*The Monster [Animal] as Bridegroom*), the Beauty and the Beast theme (which has its own subtype, AT 425C). Again, the differences must be explored as well. Another interesting theme to explore is that these stories focus on women and were told by women. An old woman relates the tale of Cupid and Psyche in Apuleius, describing it as one of her "old women's tales," the precursor of "old wives' tales." Much feminist criticism has focused on female storytellers and the themes connected with women (e.g., arranged marriages, incest). While we

must be careful not to project more recent ideas into the past, the examination of similar stories in a variety of genres offers students a mutually illuminating way to approach these stories.[4]

These then are some ways in which these volumes may be incorporated into a mythology course.

NOTES

1. See Bruce Lincoln's essay, "Theses on Comparison," in his *Gods and Demons, Priests and Scholars: Critical Explorations in the History of Religions* (2012), pages 121 to 130. See also Daya Krishna's essay, "Comparative Philosophy: What It Is and What It Ought to Be," in *Interpreting across Boundaries: New Essays in Comparative Philosophy*, edited by Gerald J. Larson and Eliot Deutsch (1988), pages seventy-one to eighty-three. While the latter is strictly about philosophy, much of Krishna's arguments are relevant for comparative studies in general.
2. See William F. Hansen's essay, "Mythology and Folktale Typology: Chronicle of a Failed Scholarly Revolution," in the *Journal of Folklore Research*, volume thirty-four (1997), pages 275 to 280.
3. William F. Hansen, *Ariadne's Thread: A Guide to International Tales Found in Classical Literature* (2002). See pages eight to nine on genre variance and pages fifteen to sixteen on the movement of story patterns from folktale to legend or myth.
4. The material in this paragraph is indebted to Hansen's (supra note three) analysis of AT 425 and the Cupid and Psyche story on pages one hundred to 114. He summarizes four parallel stories and cites the literature that will lead students to further sources. Marina Warner's *From the Beast to the Blonde: On Fairy Tales and their Tellers* (1994), among others, explores the Cupid and Psyche story in light of the Beauty and Beast theme, focusing on the role of the heroine as well as female storytellers. See in particular chapters two and seventeen.

LESSON PLAN

UNWINDING GENDER IN HOMER'S PENELOPE AND THE SUITORS

Students will analyze the story of Penelope and the suitors in Homer's *Odyssey* in order to understand the significance of gender and social prescription; in addition, students will examine the representation of gender across cultures through a common theme of weaving.

Materials: Homer's *Odyssey*; Wilhelm and Jacob Grimm's "Spindle, Shuttle, and Needle."

Overview Questions

One of the most studied female heroines in Greek mythology, Penelope is often characterized at once as a faithful spouse and a cunning protagonist. To what extent does Penelope endorse the patriarchal society she inhabits? In what ways does Penelope negotiate her gender and social position to challenge these structures?

Discussion Questions (select passages as evidence)

1. In Penelope's interactions with the suitors, what is suggested about the expectations of women in her society? What are the social constraints surrounding Penelope's position?

2. Without knowledge of Odysseus's fate, Penelope makes a choice to remain in her home. How is Penelope's choice a moral decision?

3. Study closely the language of marriage. What is Penelope's perspective on marriage? How do her actions endorse marriage as society prescribes it for women?

4. In books 16–24, in what ways does Odysseus have greater liberty than Penelope to act? Select one instance of this authority.

5. In her speech to the suitors, Penelope relents in her refusal to marry (bk. 18). How does this scene complicate Penelope's character in the story?

6. Examine the depiction of the marriage bed. How does the bed reinforce the patriarchal system Penelope inhabits?

7. Apart from her ploy of weaving and unwinding the shroud, how does Penelope challenge the social constraints upon her? In what ways is Penelope heroic in terms attributed to Odysseus?

Comparative Study

Weaving serves as an important activity in many myths and folktales, holding social and cultural meaning across cultures. Compare the story of Penelope with that of Wilhelm and Jacob Grimm's "Spindle, Shuttle, and Needle," writing on the following prompts.

1. Examine the scene of Penelope weaving (bk. 24). In what ways does the activity of weaving and unwinding her work embody Penelope's thoughts and feelings? In what ways does weaving represent the negotiation of gender roles?

2. In "Spindle, Shuttle, and Needle," weaving serves as a domestic activity and source of financial support. In what ways does the young woman's weaving depart from the meaning of weaving in Homer's tale?

3. What are common themes or metaphors for weaving in both tales?

Response Paper

Word length and additional requirements set by Instructor. Students answer the research question in the Overview Questions. Students state a thesis and use as evidence passages from the primary source document as well as support from supplemental materials assigned in the lesson.

TIMELINE

BCE	
4000–2270	Sumerian civilization begins
3000–1500	Minoan period in Greece
2649–2181	Old Kingdom in Egypt
2600–2470	Reign of Gilgameš (Gilgamesh), first dynasty of Uruk
2055–1650	Middle Kingdom in Egypt
1792–1750	Hammurabi's reign, height of Babylonian Empire
1600–1100	Bronze Age in Greece
1540–1070	Olmec civilization in Central America
1500	Aryans invade India; Vedic period begins
1360	The Assyrians conquer the lands of Mesopotamia
1250	Moses leads Israelite slaves from Egypt, establishes monotheistic worship at Mt. Sinai (formerly sacred to the Mesopotamian moon god Sîn)
1200–1000	Earliest Hindu literature, the *Rig-Veda*
1200–900	Early Vedic period
1100	Trojan War
900–600	Late Vedic period
800–700	Birth and life of Homer, the Greek epic poet
600–400	Athens is the center of Greece
599–500	Laozi (Lao-Tzu), founder of Daoism (Taoism), active in China
590–527	Birth and life of Mahāvīra, founder of Jainism
563–483	Birth and life of Siddhartha Gautama, the Buddha, founder of Buddhism
551–479	Konguzi (Confucius)
509–31	The Roman Republic
500	Purāṇas, Hindu religious texts, begin to be compiled
356–323	Birth and life of Alexander the Great
31	Roman Empire is established
CE	
30–33	Jesus of Nazareth preaches in Galilee
200–300	Hindu tales of the *Pañcatantra* (*Panchatantra*) composed
250–900	Maya civilization in Central America
400–499	King Arthur, legendary Briton ruler, active in British Isles
476	The Roman Empire falls
500–600	Teotihuacán, Mesoamerican city, grows to 200,000 and influences rest of Mesoamerica

528	Buddhism is officially recognized as the state religion in Silla on the Korean Peninsula
570–682	Birth and life of the prophet Muhammad, founder of Islam
593–622	Prince Shōtoku writes his commentaries on the Buddhist sutras in Japan
629–645	Xuanzang (Hsüan-tsang) travels to India and Southeast Asia, advancing the spread of Buddhism
632–750	Islam spreads to the Near East, North Africa, Spain, and France
700–800	Swahili culture emerges on the East African coast
700–1000	The Viking Age of expansion in Europe, North Atlantic islands, and Asia Minor
762–1055	Founded by the Abbasid caliphate, Baghdad is cultural center of the Islamic world
796–804	Single volumes of the Bible that include the Old and New Testaments begin to be published in France
800	*The Book of Kells* is created in Ireland
850	Ife, in contemporary Nigeria, flourishes as a center of Yoruba culture
850–860	The first version of "Cinderella" composed in China
900–1050	*Beowulf* is recorded by Anglo-Saxon scribes in the British Isles
900-1100	Topiltzin-Quetzalcóatl, legendary Toltec ruler, active in Central America
1000	The Puranic age of Hindu literature ends
1090–1150	The Iroquois Confederacy in North America forges the Great Law of Peace
1325–1521	Aztec empire in Central America
1350–1400	*Sir Gawain and the Green Knight* composed by unknown author in England
1438–1532	Inca Empire in South America
1492	Christopher Columbus explores Hispaniola
1518–1521	Hernán Cortés conquers the Aztec Empire
1623	William Shakespeare's collection of plays are published in the First Folio
1634–1636	Giambattista Basile publishes *Lo cunto de li cunti* (The tale of tales) in Italy
1697	Marie-Catherine d'Aulnoy introduces the term *conte de fées* ("fairy tales") in France
1697	Charles Perrault publishes "Le petit chaperon rouge" ("Little Red Riding Hood") in France
1740	Gabrielle-Suzanne de Villeneuve publishes "La belle et la bête" ("Beauty and the Beast") in France
1812	Jacob and Wilhelm Grimm publish *Kinder- und Hausmärchen* (Children's and household tales) in Germany
1835	Hans Christina Anderson publishes *Eventyr fortalte for børn* (Fairy tales told for children) in Denmark
1889	Andrew Lang publishes *The Blue Fairy Book*, the first of his *Fairy Book* series in England

GUIDE TO ONLINE RESOURCES

Akhet: The Horizon to Ancient Egypt

http://www.akhet.co.uk/mainpage.php

Offers a diverse set of selected texts, including mythology, and photos of masks, sculpture, tombs, and temples. Highly illustrative, the site offers an excellent survey of Egyptian objects.

American Folklore

http://www.americanfolklore.net

Presents a large collection of full-text entries covering all major areas of traditional North American literature. Includes African American, Asian American, and Native American literature, as well as traditional works from Mexico, Latin America, and Canada.

Encyclopedia Mythica

http://www.pantheon.org

Provides A-to-Z reference information on the major mythology and folklore subjects and regions, organized by continent and by major subjects in the literature. The site also offers special sections on bestiary literature, an image gallery, and genealogical tables from various pantheons and prominent houses.

International World History Project

http://history-world.org

Offers introductory articles on all major geographical and cultural areas of interest for background research on ancient civilizations, including Mesopotamia, western and eastern Asia, early Europe, and the Americas.

Internet Sacred Text Archive

http://www.sacred-texts.com

Includes the full text of publications in all major areas of mythology, folklore, and religion, including many esoteric and occult topics across cultures.

Luminarium: Anthology of English Literature

http://www.luminarium.org

Offers full-text selections encompassing the medieval era through the Restoration. Many of the major legends and myths are covered, with an introduction, a list of online texts, and links to study resources.

Perseus Digital Library

http://www.perseus.tufts.edu/hopper/collections

Full-text literature concentrated in the areas of Greek and Roman, German, and Renaissance subjects. Literature varies across the arts, historical periods, and religions.

SurLaLune

http://www.surlalunefairytales.com

An introduction to the major fairy tales and folklore literature. Offering selected full-text entries of many major tales, each title is annotated with its history, a list of similar tales across cultures, and a bibliography. Many articles include a gallery of illustrations and book covers. A forum is available for discussion.

Theoi Greek Mythology

http://www.theoi.com

Contains over 1500 pages on Greek literature, family trees, and illustrations. An excellent resource for primary source literature with introductory material and annotations. The illustration library includes Greek and Roman art from the classical period as well as European paintings and sculpture.

BIBLIOGRAPHY

Abrahams, Roger D. *Deep Down in the Jungle: Black American Folklore from the Streets of Philadelphia.* New Brunswick: Aldine Transaction, 2006. Print.

Abusch, Tzvi. "The Development and Meaning of the Epic of Gilgamesh: An Interpretive Essay." *Journal of the American Oriental Society* 121.4 (2001): 614. Print.

Aeschylus. *Eumenides.* Ed. Alan H. Sommerstein. Cambridge: Cambridge UP, 1989. Print.

Ahl, Frederick, and Hanna M. Roisman. *The Odyssey Re-Formed.* Ithaca: Cornell UP, 1996. Print.

Al-Dīn, Rashīd. *The Successors of Genghis Khan.* Trans. John Andrew Boyle. New York: Columbia UP, 1971. Print.

Alter, Robert. *The David Story: A Translation with Commentary of 1 and 2 Samuel.* New York: Norton, 1999. Print.

Anderson, Sherwood. *Winesburg, Ohio.* 1919. New York: Penguin, 1960. Print.

Anelli, Melissa. *Harry, a History.* New York: Pocket, 2008. Print.

Apollodorus. *The Library of Greek Mythology.* Trans. Keith Aldrich. Lawrence: Coronado, 1975. Print.

Apollonius Rhodius. *Apollonius Rhodius, the Argonautica.* Trans. R. C. Seaton. Cambridge: Harvard UP, 1961. Print.

Aristophanes. *The Birds.* Trans. William Arrowsmith. Ann Arbor: U of Michigan P, 1961. Print.

Arnold, Bill T., and Bryan E. Beyer. *Encountering the Old Testament: A Christian Survey.* 2nd ed. Grand Rapids: Baker, 2008. Print.

Aron, Melanie Sylvia. "Hero in Drag: Victorian Gender Identity and the Fairy Tales of Andrew Lang." MA thesis. California State U, Fresno, 2008. Print.

Atwood, Margaret. *The Penelopiad.* New York: Canongate, 2005. Print.

Baldwin, David. "Prologue: Robin Hood's World." *Robin Hood: The English Outlaw Unmasked.* Gloucestershire: Amberley, 2011. Print.

Ballinger, Franchot. *Living Sideways: Tricksters in American Indian Oral Traditions.* Norman: U of Oklahoma P, 2004. Print.

Barber, Elizabeth Wayland. *Women's Work: The First 20,000 Years.* New York: Norton, 1994. Print.

Barber, Richard. *King Arthur: Hero and Legend.* New York: St. Martin's, 1986. Print.

Baring, Anne, and Jules Cashford. *The Myth of the Goddess: Evolution of an Image.* London: Viking, 1991. Print.

Barnard, Alan. *History and Theory in Anthropology.* Cambridge: Cambridge UP, 2000. Print.

Barolini, Teodolinda. *The Undivine Comedy: Detheologizing Dante.* Princeton: Princeton UP, 1992. Print.

Barry, Peter. *Beginning Theory: An Introduction to Literary and Cultural Theory.* 3rd ed. Manchester: Manchester UP, 2009. Print.

Bassett, Samuel E. "The Suitors of Penelope." *Transactions and Proceedings of the American Philological Association* 49 (1918): 41–52. Print.

Beckwith, Martha Warren. *Jamaica Anansi Stories.* 1924. Charleston: BiblioBazaar, 2007. Print.

Beckwith, Martha Warren. "Maui the Trickster." *Hawaiian Mythology.* 1940. Honolulu: U of Hawaii P, 1976. 226–37. Print.

Bernardo, Susan M. "Abandoned or Murdered Children: Motifs S300–S399." Garry and El-Shamy 404–8.

The Bible. 3rd ed. Oxford: Oxford UP, 2001. Print. New Revised Standard Vers. with the Apocrypha.

The Bible. New York: American Bible Soc., 1999. Print. King James Vers.

Bieman, Elizabeth. *William Shakespeare: The Romances.* New York: Hall, 1990. 66–89. Print.

Biran, Michal. *Qaidu and the Rise of the Independent Mongol State in Central Asia.* Richmond: Curzon, 1997. Print.

Boccaccio, Giovanni. *The Decameron.* Trans. Mark Musa and Peter Bondanella. New York: New American Lib., 2002. Print.

Bolaki, Stella. "'It Translated Well': The Promise and the Perils of Translation in Maxine Hong Kingston's *The Woman Warrior.*" *Melus* 34.4 (2009): 39–60. Print.

Bolden, Tonya. *Strong Men Keep Coming: The Book of African American Men.* New York: Wiley, 1999. Print.

Bonnefoy, Yves. *Asian Mythologies.* Chicago: U of Chicago P, 1991. Print.

Borroff, Marie, trans. *Sir Gawain and the Green Knight.* New York: Norton, 1967. Print.

"Bounty Hunters." *Star Wars: The Clone Wars—The Complete Season Two.* By Drew Z. Greenberg and George Lucas. Dir. Steward Lee. Cartoon Network, 2010. DVD.

Boyer, Régis. "Archetypes." Brunel 110–17.

Bremmer, J. N., and N. M. Horsfall. *Roman Myth and Mythography*. London: Inst. of Classical Studies, 1987. Print.

Bright, William. *A Coyote Reader*. Berkeley: U of California P, 1993. Print.

Brodsky, Joseph. *A Part of Speech*. New York: Farrar, 1980. Print.

Brooker, Peter. *A Glossary of Cultural Theory*. 2nd ed. London: Arnold, 2002. Print.

Brown, Cecil. *Stagolee Shot Billy*. Cambridge: Harvard UP, 2003. Print.

Brown, Jonathan. "Minerva, Arachne and Marcel." *Tout-Fait: The Marcel Duchamp Studies Online Journal* 2.5 (2003): n. pag. Web. 1 May 2013.

---. *Painting in Spain: 1500–1700*. New Haven: Yale UP, 1998. Print.

Brunel, Pierre, ed. *Companion to Literary Myths, Heroes and Archetypes*. London: Routledge, 1996. Print.

Bryant, Jerry H. *Born in a Mighty Bad Land: The Violent Man in African American Folklore and Fiction*. Bloomington: Indiana UP, 2003. Print.

Bryant, Nigel. *The Legend of the Grail*. Rochester: Brewer, 2004. Print.

Buckley, Jerome. Foreword. *Idylls of the King*. By Alfred, Lord Tennyson. New York: Houghton, 1963. Print.

Budge, E. A. Wallis, trans. *The Kebra Nagast*. 1922. New York: Cosimo, 2004. Print.

Bulfinch, Thomas. *Bulfinch's Mythology*. New York: Modern Lib., 2004. Print.

Burkert, Walter. *Greek Religion*. Cambridge: Harvard UP, 1985. Print.

Campbell, Joseph. *The Hero with a Thousand Faces*. Princeton: Princeton UP, 1949. Print.

Campbell, Joseph. "The Ritual Love-Death." *Masks of God: Primitive Mythology*. Vol. 1. London: Secker, 1960. Print.

---. *Masks of God: Occidental Mythology*. New York: Viking, 1964. Print.

---. *Mythology: The Voyage of the Hero*. Oxford: Oxford UP, 1998. Print.

---. *Myths of Light: Eastern Metaphors of the Eternal*. Novato: New World, 2003. Print.

Carandini, Andrea. *Rome: Day One*. Trans. Stephen Sartarelli. Princeton: Princeton UP, 2011. Print.

Carpelan, Mary J. *Coyote Fights the Sun: A Shasta Indian Tale*. Berkeley: Heyday, 2002. Print.

Carrasco, David. *Quetzalcoatl and the Irony of Empire*. Chicago: U of Chicago P, 1982. Print.

Carrasco, David. *Religions of Mesoamerica: Cosmovision and Ceremonial Centers*. San Francisco: Harper, 1990. Print.

Carson, Anne. *Autobiography of Red*. New York: Vintage, 1999. Print.

Carter, Susan. "Athena and the Mirror." *She Is Everywhere! An Anthology of Writing in Womanist/Feminist Spirituality*. Ed. Lucia Chiavola Birnbaum. New York: iUniverse, 2005. 209–25. Print.

Cellini, Benvenuto. *Perseus with the Head of Medusa*. 1890. *Image Collection*. Web. 24 Sept. 2012.

Chambert-Loir, Henri, and Anthony Reid. *The Potent Dead: Ancestors, Saints, and Heroes in Contemporary Indonesia*. Honolulu: U of Hawaii P, 2002. Print.

Child, Francis James, ed. *A Gest of Robyn Hode. The English and Scottish Popular Ballads*. Vol. 3. New York: Copper Square, 1965. 39–88. Print.

"Chi Li Slays the Serpent." *egog-industries.deviantart.com*. deviantART, 29 Apr. 2010. Web. 1 Feb. 2013.

Cicora, Mary A. *Modern Myths and Wagnerian Deconstructions: Hermeneutic Approaches to Wagner's Music-Dramas*. Westport: Greenwood, 2000. Print.

Clapp, Nicholas. *Sheba: Through the Desert in Search of the Legendary Queen*. New York: Houghton, 2001. Print.

Clark, Elizabeth. *Women in the Early Church*. Collegeville: Liturgical, 1983.

Clauss, James Joseph. *The Best of the Argonauts: The Redefinition of the Epic Hero in Book One of Apollonius's Argonautica*. Berkeley: U of California P, 1993. Print.

Collins, Judy. Foreword. *Wonder Woman Archives*. Vol. 1. By William Moulton Marston and H. G. Peter. New York: DC Comics, 1998. Print.

Colum, Padraic. "Quetzalcoatl." *Myths of the World*. New York: Grosset, 1930. 298–300. Print.

Cornell, T. J. "Aeneas and the Twins: The Development of the Roman Foundation Legend." *Proceedings of the Cambridge Philological Society* 21 (1975): 1–32. Print.

Coss, Peter R. "Aspects of Cultural Diffusion in Medieval England: Robin Hood." Knight, *Anthology* 329–44.

Croker, T. F. Dillon. *Romulus and Remus; or, Rome Was Not Built in a Day*. London, 1859. Print.

Curtis, Paul. *Stesichoros's Geryoneis*. Leiden: Brill, 2011. Print.

Dante. *The Inferno*. Trans. Robert Hollander and Jean Hollander. New York: Anchor, 2002. Print.

David-Néel, Alexandra. *The Superhuman Life of Gesar of Ling*. Trans. Violet Sydney. New York: Kendall, 1933. Print.

David and Goliath. Dir. Ferdinando Baldi. Perf. Orson Welles. Echo Bridge, 1960. Film.

Day, David. *The Search for King Arthur*. New York: Facts on File, 1998. Print.

Deacy, Susan. *Athena*. London: Routledge, 2008. Print.

Deane, William J. *David: His Life and Times*. New York: Revell, 1889. Print.

DeForest, Mary Margolies. *Apollonius' Argonautica: A Callimachean Epic*. New York: Brill, 1994. Print.

De Jonge, Nico, and Toos Van Dijk. *Forgotten Islands of Indonesia*. Hong Kong: Periplus, 1995. Print.

de Montaño, Marty. *Coyote in Love with a Star*. Washington: Natl. Museum of the American Indian, Smithsonian Inst., 1998. Print.

Denuccio, Jerome D. "Fact, Fiction, Fatality: Poe's 'The Thousand-and-Second.'" *Studies in Short Fiction* 27.3 (1990): 365. Print.

Dewald, Carolyn. "Women and Culture in Herodotus' Histories." *Women's Studies* 8.1–2 (1981): 93–128. Print.

Dexter, Miriam Robbins. "The Ferocious and the Erotic: 'Beautiful' Medusa and the Neolithic Bird and Snake." *JFSR* 26.1 (2010): 25–41. Print.

DiGaetani, John Louis. *Wagner outside the Ring: Essays on the Operas, Their Performances, and Their Connections with Other Arts*. Jefferson: McFarland, 2009. Print.

Diodorus Siculus. "Theseus and the Minotaur." *Library of History*. Vol. 3. Trans. C. H. Oldfather. London: Heinemann, 1993. 11–13. Print. Loeb Classical Lib. 340.

Dixon, E., ed. "The Third Voyage of Sinbad the Sailor." *Fairy Tales from* The Arabian Nights. London: Dent, 1910. 85–91. Print.

Dixon, Roland B. "The Maui Cycle." *Oceanic Mythology*. 1916. New York: Cooper Square, 1964. 41–56. Print.

Dong, Lan, ed. *Transnationalism and the Asian American Heroine: Essays on Literature, Film, Myth and Media*. Jefferson: McFarland, 2010. Print.

Doré, Gustave. *The Doré Bible Illustrations*. London: Dover, 1974. Print.

Dudbridge, Glen. *The Hsi-yu chi: A Study of Antecedents to the 16th-Century Chinese Novel*. London: Cambridge UP, 1970. Print.

Dundas, Judith. *Pencils Rhetorique: Renaissance Poets and the Art of Painting*. Newark: U of Delaware, 1993. Print.

Edwards, Louise. "Transformations of the Woman Warrior Hua Mulan: From Defender of the Family to Servant of the State." *Nan Nü: Men, Women, & Gender in Early & Imperial China* 12.2 (2010): 175–214. Print.

Eliot, T. S. *The Waste Land and Other Poems*. New York: Penguin, 1998. Print.

Eliot, T. S. "A Commentary." *Criterion* 3.9 (1924): 1–5. Print.

Erdoes, Richard, and Alfonso Ortiz, eds. *American Indian Trickster Tales*. New York: Viking, 1998. Print.

Euripides. *Medea and Other Plays*. Trans. James Morwood. New York: Oxford UP, 1997. Print.

Farmer, Philip José. *To Your Scattered Bodies Go*. New York: Putnam, 1971. Print.

Farrand, Livingston, comp. "Shasta and Athapascan Myths from Oregon." Ed. Leo J. Frachtenberg. *Journal of American Folklore* 28.109 (1915): 207–42. Print.

Faure, Bernard. *The Power of Denial: Buddhism, Purity, and Gender*. Princeton: Princeton UP, 2003. Print.

Feiler, Bruce. *America's Prophet: Moses and the American Story*. New York: Harper, 2009. Print.

Feng, Lan. "The Female Individual and the Empire: A Historicist Approach to Mulan and Kingston's *Woman Warrior*." *Comparative Literature* 55.3 (2003): 229–45. Print.

Feng Menglong, comp. "Madam White Is Kept Forever under the Thunder Peak Tower." *Stories to Caution the World: A Ming Dynasty Collection*. Vol. 2. Trans. Shuhui Yang and Yunqin Yang. Seattle: U of Washington P, 2005. 474–505. Print.

Fiorenza, Giancarlo. "Penelope's Web: Francesco Primaticcio's Epic Revision at Fountainebleau." *Renaissance Quarterly* 59 (2006): 795–827. Print.

Flanagan, Victoria. *Into the Closet: Cross-Dressing and the Gendered Body in Children's Literature and Film*. New York: Routledge, 2008. Print.

Florescano, Enrique. *The Myth of Quetzalcoatl*. Trans. Lysa Hochroth. Baltimore: Johns Hopkins UP, 1999. Print.

Foley, Helene P. "Penelope as Moral Agent." *The Distaff Side: Representing the Female in Homer's Odyssey*. Ed. Beth Cohen. New York: Oxford UP, 1995. 93–116. Print.

Foster, Lynn V. *Handbook to Life in the Ancient Maya World*. Oxford: Oxford UP, 2002. Print.

Frazer, James George. "Moses in the Ark of Bulrushes." *Folk-Lore in the Old Testament: Studies in*

Comparative Religion, Legend, and Law. Vol. 2. London: Macmillan, 1919. 437–55. Print.

Freeman, Philip. "Lessons from a Demigod." *Humanities* 33.4 (2012): 34. Print.

Freitas, Lima de. "Labyrinth." *Encyclopedia of Religion*. Ed. Mircea Eliade. Vol. 8. New York: Macmillan, 1987. 411–19. Print.

Freud, Sigmund. *Moses and Monotheism*. Trans. Katherine Jones. 1939. New York: Random, 1967. Print.

Freund, Richard A. "Searching for King David and King Solomon." *Digging through the Bible: Understanding Biblical People, Places and Controversies through Archaeology*. New York: Rowman, 2009. 107–46. Print.

Frontain, Raymond-Jean, and Jan Wojcik. "Introduction: Transformations of the Myth of David." *The David Myth in Western Literature*. Ed. Frontain and Wojcik. West Lafayette: Purdue UP, 1980. 1–11. Print.

Fu, James S. *Mythic and Comic Aspects of the Quest: Hsi-yu chi as Seen through Don Quixote and Huckleberry Finn*. Singapore: Singapore UP, 1977. Print.

Gan Bao. "Li Chi Slays the Great Serpent." *In Search of the Supernatural: The Written Record*. Trans. Kenneth J. DeWoskin and James Irving Crump. Stanford: Stanford UP, 1996. 230–31. Print.

Ganjavī, Nizāmī. "Bahrām Sits on Tuesday in the Red Dome." *The Haft Paikar (The Seven Beauties)*. Trans. C. E. Wilson. London: Probsthain, 1924. 171–87. Print.

Garber, Marjorie, and Nancy Vickers, eds. *The Medusa Reader*. New York: Routledge, 2003. Print.

Garber, Marjorie. *Vested Interests: Cross-Dressing and Cultural Anxiety*. New York: Harper, 1993. Print.

Garry, Jane, and Hasan El-Shamy, eds. *Archetypes and Motifs in Folklore and Literature: A Handbook*. Armonk: Sharpe, 2005. Print.

Geertz, Clifford. *Interpretation of Cultures*. New York: Basic, 1973. Print.

Genovese, E. N. "Hercules and His Twelve Labors." *Masterplots*. 4th ed. Ed. Laurence W. Mazzeno. Pasadena: Salem, 2010. Print.

Georgievska-Shine, Aneta E. "Velazquez and the Unfinished Story of Arachne." *Subject as Aporia in Early Modern Art*. Ed. Alexander Nagel and Lorenzo Pericolo. Burlington: Ashgate, 2010. 175–93. Print.

Gerber, John C. *Mark Twain*. Boston: Twayne, 1988. Print.

"Gilgameš and Huwawa (Version A)." *Electronic Text Corpus of Sumerian Literature*. Faculty of Oriental Studies, University of Oxford, 19 Dec. 2006. Web. 1 Apr. 2013.

Gillard, Stuart, dir. *Riverworld*. Perf. Jeananne Goossen and Peter Shinkoda. SyFy Channel, 2010. Film.

Gimbutas, Marija. *The Goddesses and Gods of Old Europe, 6500–3500 BC: Myths and Cult Images*. Berkeley: U of California P, 1982. Print.

Gimbutas, Marija. *The Goddesses and Gods of Old Europe*. Berkeley: U of California P, 1974. Print.

---. *The Language of the Goddess: Unearthing the Hidden Symbols of Western Civilization*. San Francisco: Harper, 1989. Print.

---. *The Living Goddesses*. Ed. Miriam Robbins Dexter. Berkeley: U of California P, 1999. Print.

Ginzberg, Louis. *The Legends of the Jews*. Vol. 4. 1913. Philadelphia: Jewish Publication Soc. of Amer., 1987. Print.

Goldberg, Christine. *Turandot's Sisters: A Folktale Study*. New York: Garland, 1993. Print.

Greenblatt, Stephen, ed. *New World Encounters*. Berkeley: U of California P, 1993. Print.

Grey, George. "The Legend of Maui." *Polynesian Mythology and Ancient Traditional History of the New Zealand Race, as Furnished by Their Priests and Chiefs*. 1855. Whitefish: Kessinger, 2004. 16–58. Print.

Grierson, Roderick, ed. *African Zion: The Sacred Art of Ethiopia*. New Haven: Yale UP, 1993. Print.

Gurewitsch, Matthew. "Her Brother's Keeper." *Opera News* 62.13 (1998): 24. Print.

Hahn, Thomas. *Robin Hood in Popular Culture: Violence, Transgression, and Justice*. Cambridge: Brewer, 2000. Print.

Hainsworth, J. B. *The Idea of Epic*. Berkeley: U of California P, 1991. Print.

Hall, Edith. Introduction. *Medea and Other Plays*. By Euripides. Trans. James Morwood. New York: Oxford UP, 1997. Print.

Hall, Robert L. "The Cultural Background of Mississippian Symbolism." *The Southeastern Ceremonial Complex: Artifacts and Analysis*. Ed. Patricia Kay Galloway and James B. Griffin. Lincoln: U of Nebraska P, 1989. 239–78. Print.

Hamerton-Kelley, Robert, ed. *Violent Origins*. Stanford: Stanford UP, 1987. Print.

Harris, Wilson. "Quetzalcoatl and the Smoking Mirror (Reflections on Originality and Tradition)." *Review of Contemporary Fiction* 17.2 (1997): 12. Print.

Hayhurst, Darrell E., III. "Sun Wu-Kung." *Pantheon.org*. Encyclopedia Mythica, 6 Sept. 2006. Web. 25 Mar. 2013.

Hayslip, Ly Le. *When Heaven and Earth Changed Places*. New York: Plume, 1993. Print.

Heilman, Elizabeth E. *Critical Perspectives on Harry Potter*. 2nd ed. New York: Routledge, 2009. Print.

Heitman, Richard. *Taking Her Seriously: Penelope and the Plot of Homer's* Odyssey. Ann Arbor: U of Michigan P, 2005. Print.

Hesiod. The Works and Days, *Theogony, and* The Shield of Herakles. Trans. Hugh G. Evelyn-White. Mineola: Dover, 2006. Print.

Hesiod. "From *The Shield of Herakles* and *Theogony* (c. 700 B.C.E.), translated by Richmond Lattimore: Medusa and Perseus." Garber and Vickers 11–13.

Hirst, Michael. *Michelangelo and His Drawings*. New Haven: Yale UP, 1988. Print.

Holroyd, Michael. *Bernard Shaw: The One-Volume Definitive Edition*. New York: Norton, 2006. Print.

Holt, J. C. "The Origins and Audience of the Ballads of Robin Hood." Knight, *Anthology* 211–32.

Homer. *The Odyssey*. Trans. A. T. Murray and George E. Dimock. Cambridge: Harvard UP, 1995. Print.

Homer. "From *The Iliad* (c. 750–725 B.C. E.), translated by Richmond Lattimore: Medusa as Shield and Sign." Garber and Vickers 9–10.

Hood, Steven J. *Dragons Entailed: Indochina and the China-Vietnam War*. New York: East Gate, 1992. Print.

Hsia, Chih-tsing. "Journey to the West." *The Classic Chinese Novel: A Critical Introduction*. New York: Columbia UP, 1968. 115–64. Print.

Hubbard, Patrick. "Trickster, Renewal and Survival." *American Indian Culture and Research Journal* 4.4 (1980): 113–24. Print.

Hunter, Matthew L. *Jason and Medea: A Whirlwind of Ruin*. New York: IUniverse, 2005. Print.

Hurwit, Jeffrey M. *The Athenian Acropolis: History, Mythology, and Archaeology from the Neolithic Era to the Present*. Cambridge: Cambridge UP, 1999. Print.

Hyginus. *The Myths of Hyginus*. Trans. Mary Grant. Ed. Grant. Lawrence: U of Kansas, 1960. Print.

Hymes, Dell H. "Coyote, the Thinking (Wo)man's Trickster." *Monsters, Tricksters, and Sacred Cows: Animal Tales and American Identities*. Ed. A. James Arnold. Charlottesville: UP of Virginia, 1996. 108–37. Print.

Irwin, Robert. The Arabian Nights*: A Companion*. New York: Tauris, 2005. Print.

Jackson, Michael. "Some Structural Considerations of Māori Myth." *Journal of the Polynesian Society* 77.2 (1968): 147–162. Print.

Jacobus de Voragine. "St. George." *The Golden Legend: St. George*. American Buddha, n.d. Web. 12 Mar. 2013.

James, Sharon L., and Sheila Dillon. *A Companion to Women in the Ancient World*. Malden: Wiley-Blackwell, 2012. Print.

Jarman, Mark. "When the Light Came On: The Epic 'Gilgamesh.'" *Hudson Review* 58.2 (2005): 329–34. Print.

Jensen, Adolf E. *Myth and Cult among Primitive Peoples*. Chicago: U of Chicago P, 1951. Print.

Jones, Ann Rosalind, and Peter Stallybrass. *Renaissance Clothing and the Materials of Memory*. Cambridge: Cambridge UP, 2000. Print.

Jones, David E. *Women Warriors. A History*. Washington: Brassey's, 2000. Print.

Joyce, James. *Ulysses*. New York: Vintage, 1990. Print.

Kendall, Carol, and Yao-wen Li. "The Serpent-Slayer." *Sweet and Sour: Tales from China*. New York: Clarion, 1978. 33–38. Print.

Kingston, Maxine Hong. *The Woman Warrior: Memoirs of a Girlhood among Ghosts*. New York: Vintage, 1989. Print.

Kirsch, Jonathan. *King David: The Real Life of the Man Who Ruled Israel*. New York: Ballantine, 2000. Print.

Kirsch, Jonathan. *Moses, A Life*. New York: Ballantine, 1998. Print.

Kleinbaum, Abby Wettan. *The War against the Amazons*. New York: McGraw-Hill, 1983. Print.

Kleiner, Fred S. *Gardner's Art through the Ages: A Global History*. Boston: Wadsworth, 2011. Print.

Knight, Stephen, ed. *Robin Hood: An Anthology of Scholarship and Criticism*. Cambridge: Brewer, 1999. Print.

---. *Robin Hood: A Complete Study of the English Outlaw*. Oxford: Blackwell, 1994. Print.

---. "*Robin Hood: Men in Tights*: Fitting the Tradition Snugly." Knight, *Anthology* 461–69.

Kornman, Robin. "The Influence of the Epic of King Gesar of Ling on Chögyam Trungpa." *Recalling Chögyam Trungpa*. Ed. Fabrice Midal. Boston: Shambala, 2005. 347–79. Print.

Kronzek, Allan Zola. *The Sorcerer's Companion: A Guide to the Magical World of Harry Potter*. New York: Broadway, 2010. Print.

Kurosawa, Akira, Shinobu Hashimoto, and Hideo Oguni. *Seven Samurai*. Trans. Donald Richie. Santa Barbara City College School of Media Arts, 24 June 2010. PDF file.

Lacy, Norris et al., eds. *The Arthurian Encyclopedia*. New York: Bedrick, 1986. Print.

Lafaye, Jacques. *Quetzalcóatl and Guadalupe: The Formation of Mexican National Consciousness*. Chicago: U of Chicago P, 1976. Print.

Lang, Andrew, ed. *The Violet Fairy Book*. New York: Dover, 1966. Print.

Lanham, Richard A. *The Motives of Eloquence: Literary Rhetoric in the Renaissance*. New Haven: Yale UP, 1976. Print.

Lawrence, D. H. "Quetzalcoatl Looks Down on Mexico." *Selected Poems*. Ed. Kenneth Rexroth. New York: Viking, 1959. 122–25. Print.

Leal, Paloma Esteban. "Picasso/Minotaur." *Picasso: Minotauro*. Madrid: Museo Nacional Centro de Arte Reina Sofía, 2001. 223–38. Print.

Leeming, David Adams. *Mythology: The Voyage of the Hero*. 3rd ed. New York: Oxford UP, 1998. Print.

Leeming, David. *Myth: A Biography of Belief*. Oxford: Oxford UP, 2003. Print.

The Legend of the White Serpent. Dir. Shirō Toyoda. Frank Lee International, 1956. Film.

Leitao, David D. *The Pregnant Male as Myth and Metaphor in Classical Greek Literature*. New York: Cambridge UP, 2012. Print.

Leslie, Richard. *Pablo Picasso: A Modern Master*. New York: SMITHMARK, 1996. Print.

Lester, Julius. "Stagolee." *Myths, Legends, and Folktales of America: An Anthology*. Comp. David Leeming and Jake Page. New York: Oxford UP, 1999. 172–80. Print.

Lévi-Strauss, Claude. *The Savage Mind*. Paris: Librairie Plon, 1962. Print.

Lieberson, Peter, comp. *King Gesar*. By Douglas Penick. Narr. Omar Ebrahim. Perf. Yo-Yo Ma, Peter Serkin, and Emanuel Ax. Cond. Lieberson. Sony, 1991. CD.

Li Lianrong. "History and the Tibetan Epic *Gesar*." *Oral Tradition* 16.2 (2001): 317–42. PDF file.

Li Qingxin. *Maritime Silk Road*. Beijing: China International, 2009. Print.

Lockard, Craig. *Southeast Asia in World History*. New York: Oxford UP, 2009. Print.

"Lohengrin." *Opera News* 70.10 (2006): 54. Print.

Long, Christopher P. "The Daughters of Metis: Patriarchal Dominion and the Daughters of Between." *Graduate Faculty Philosophy Journal* 28.2 (2007): 67–86. Print.

The Magnificent Seven. Dir. John Sturges. Perf. Yul Brynner, Eli Wallach, and Steve McQueen. MGM, 1960. DVD.

Maier, Paul L., ed. and trans. *Josephus, The Essential Works*. Grand Rapids: Kregel, 1994. Print.

Mair, Victor H., and Mark Bender, eds. *The Columbia Anthology of Chinese Folk and Popular Literature*. New York: Columbia UP, 2011. Print.

Makdisi, Saree, and Felicity Nussbaum, eds. The Arabian Nights *in Historical Context: Between East and West*. New York: Oxford UP, 2008. Print.

Malkin, Irad. *The Returns of Odysseus: Colonization and Ethnicity*. Berkeley: U of California P, 1998. Print.

Malory, Thomas. *Le Morte d'Arthur*. Ed. Keith Baines. Introd. Robert Graves. New York: Mentor, 1962. Print.

Markman, Peter T., and Roberta H. Markman. *Masks of the Spirit: Images and Metaphor in Mesoamerica*. Berkeley: U of California P, 1990. Print.

Marr, David G. "The Question of Women." *Vietnamese Traditions on Trial, 1920–1945*. Berkeley: U of California P, 1981. 190–251. Print.

Marshall, Emily Zobel. *Anansi's Journey: A Story of Jamaican Cultural Resistance*. Kingston: U of West Indies P, 2012. Print.

Marston, William Moulton, and H. G. Peter. *Wonder Woman Archives*. Vol. 1. New York: DC Comics, 1998. Print.

Martínez Alfaro, María Jesús. "A Tapestry of Riddling Links: Universal Contiguity in A. A. Byatt's 'Arachne.'"*Journal of the Short Story in English* 45 (2005): 145–61. Web. 1 May 2013.

Marzolph, Ulrich, ed. The Arabian Nights *in Transnational Perspective*. Detroit: Wayne State UP, 2007. Print.

Matthews, John. *Sir Gawain: Knight of the Goddess*. Rochester: Inner Traditions, 2003. Print.

McCullough, Helen Craig. *The Tale of the Heike*. Stanford: Stanford UP, 1988. Print.

Milbrath, Susan. *Star Gods of the Maya: Astronomy in Art, Folklore, and Calendars*. Austin: U of Texas P, 1999. Print.

Miller, Geordie. "Shifting Ground." *Canadian Literature* 210–211 (2011): 152–67. Print.

Montrose, Louis. "The Work of Gender in the Discourse of Discovery." Greenblatt 177–218.

Monty Python and the Holy Grail. Dir. Terry Gilliam and Terry Jones. Perf. Gilliam et al. Python Pictures, 1974. Film.

Moon, Beverly. "Archetypes." *Encyclopedia of Religion*. Ed. Mircea Eliade. Vol. 1. New York: Macmillan, 1987. 379–82. Print.

Morford, Mark P. O., and Robert J. Lenardon. *Classical Mythology*. 8th ed. New York: Oxford UP, 2007. Print.

Morgan, Giles. *St. George*. Edison: Chartwell, 2006. Print.

Morgan, J. R., ed. *Longus: Daphnis and Chloe*. Oxford: Aris, 2004. Print.

Morgan, Pauline. "Hercules and His Twelve Labors." *Cyclopedia of Literary Places*. Ed. R. Kent Rasmussen. Pasadena: Salem, 2003. Print.

Morris, Linda A. *Gender Play in Mark Twain: Cross-Dressing and Transgression*. Columbia: U of Missouri P, 2007. Print.

"Moses: The Birth of a Leader." *Chabad.org*. Chabad-Lubavitch Media Center, 2013. Web. 6 Mar. 2013.

Mueller, Melissa. "Helen's Hands: Weaving for *Kleos* in the *Odyssey*." *Helios* 37.1 (2010): 1–21. Print.

Murgatroyd, Paul. *Mythical Monsters in Classical Literature*. London: Duckworth, 2007. Print.

Murray, Stuart J. "The Autobiographical Self: Phenomenology and the Limits of Narrative Self-Possession in Anne Carson's *Autobiography of Red*." *English Studies in Canada* 31.4 (2005): 101–22. Print.

New Oxford Annotated Bible. 3rd ed. New York: Oxford UP, 2007. Print. New Revised Standard Version with the Apocrypha.

Nimmo, Jenny. *Midnight for Charlie Bone*. New York: Scholastic, 2003. Print.

Oakley-Brown, Liz. *Ovid and the Cultural Politics of Translation in Early Modern England*. Aldershot: Ashgate, 2006. Print.

"Ode of Mulan." *The Flowering Plum and the Palace Lady: Interpretations of Chinese Poetry*. Trans. Hans H. Frankel. New Haven: Yale UP, 1976. 68–72. Print.

Olson, Charles. *The Collected Poems of Charles Olson*. Berkeley: U of California P, 1987. Print.

---. *Collected Prose*. Ed. Donald Allen and Benjamin Friedlander. Berkeley: U of California P, 1997. Print.

Ovid. *Metamorphoses*. Trans. A. D. Melville. Oxford: Oxford UP, 1998. Print.

Ovid. "Minos and the Minotaur." *Metamorphoses*. Vol. 2. Trans. Brookes More. Francestown: Jones, 1941. 342–44. Print.

Oxford Classical Dictionary. 3rd ed. Ed. Simon Hornblower and Anthony Spawforth. Oxford: Oxford UP, 2009. Print.

Oyler, Elizabeth. *Swords, Oaths, and Prophetic Visions: Authoring Warrior Rule in Medieval Japan*. Honolulu: U of Hawaii P, 2006. Print.

Paine, Albert Bigelow. *Mark Twain: A Biography; The Personal and Literary Life of Samuel Langhorne Clemens*. New York: Harper, 1912. Print.

Pearcy, Roy. "The Literary Robin Hood: Character and Function in Fitts 1, 2 and 4 of the *Gest of Robyn Hode*." *Robin Hood: Medieval and Post-Medieval*. Ed. Helen Phillips. Dublin: Four Courts, 2005. 60–69. Print.

Felliot, Paul. *Notes on Marco Polo*. Vol. 2. Paris: Adrien-Maisonneuve, 1963. Print.

Pelton, Robert D. *The Trickster in West Africa: A Study of Mythic Irony and Sacred Delight*. Berkeley: U of California P, 1980. Print.

---. "West African Tricksters: Web of Purpose, Dance of Delight." *Mythical Trickster Figures: Contours, Contexts, and Criticisms*. Ed. William J. Hynes and William G. Doty. Tuscaloosa: U of Alabama P, 1993, 122–40. Print.

Penick, Douglas. *The Warrior Song of King Gesar*. Boston: Wisdom, 1997. Print.

Perrin, Noel. *Giving up the Gun, Japan's Reversion to the Sword, 1543–1879*. Boston: Godine, 1979. Print.

Peyronie, André. "The Minotaur." Brunel 814–21.

---. "Theseus." Brunel 1110–23.

Pindar. The Odes *and Selected Fragments*. Trans. G. S. Conway and Richard Stoneman. London: Dent, 1997. Print.

Pinsky, Robert. *The Life of David*. New York: Nextbook, 2005. Print.

Plaks, Andrew H. "*Hsi-yu chi*: Transcendence of Emptiness." *Four Masterworks of the Ming Novel*. Princeton: Princeton UP, 1987. 183–276. Print.

---. "The Journey to the West." *Masterworks of Asian Literature in Comparative Perspective*. Ed. Barbara Stoler Miller. Armonk: Sharpe, 1994. 272–84. Print.

Plath, Sylvia. "Medusa." Garber and Vickers 102–3.

Plutarch. *The Lives of the Noble Grecians and Romans*. Trans. John Dryden. Chicago: Encyclopedia Britannica, 1952. Print.

Poe, Edgar Allan. "The Thousand-and-Second Tale of Scheherazade." *The Complete Stories and Poems of Edgar Allan Poe*. New York: Doubleday, 1984. Print.

Polo, Marco. "Of the Exploits of King Caidu's Valiant Daughter." *The Book of Ser Marco Polo*. Vol. 2. 3rd ed. Trans. Henry Yule. Ed. Yule. London: Murray, 1903. 463–65. Print.

Pomeroy, Sarah B., et al. "The Late Dark Age (Homeric) Society." *Ancient Greece: A Political, Social, and Cultural History*. New York: Oxford UP, 1999. 53–66. Print.

Poole, Josephine. *Joan of Arc*. New York: Knopf, 1998. Print.

Powell, Barry B. *Classical Myth*. 3rd ed. Upper Saddle River: Prentice Hall, 2001. Print.

Prahlad, Anand. "Stagolee." *The Greenwood Encyclopedia of African American Folklore*. Ed. Prahlad. Westport: Greenwood, 2006. Print.

Prinzi, Travis. *Harry Potter and Imagination: The Way between Two Worlds*. Allentown: Zossima, 2009. Print.

---, ed. *Hog's Head Conversations: Essays on Harry Potter*. Allentown: Zossima, 2009. Print.

Pritchard, James B., ed. *Solomon and Sheba*. London: Phaidon, 1974. Print.

Pseudo-Apollodorus. *The Library of Greek Mythology*. Trans. Keith Aldrich. Lawrence: Coronado, 1975. Print.

Pseudo-Apollodorus. *The Library*. Trans. J. G. Frazer. 1921. Cambridge: Harvard UP, 1996. Print.

Puccini, Giacomo. *Turandot. Seven Puccini Librettos*. Trans. William Weaver. New York: Norton, 1971. Print.

Pétis de la Croix, François. "The History of Prince Calaf and the Princess of China." *Persian Tales; or, The Thousand and One Days*. Vol. 1. Trans. Ambrose Philips. London: Lane, 1800. Print.

The Qur'an. Trans. M. A. S. Abdel Haleem. Oxford: Oxford UP, 2005. Print.

Radin, Paul. *Winnebago Hero Cycles: A Study in Aboriginal Literature*. Vol. 1. Baltimore: Waverly, 1948. Print.

Ralegh, Walter. *The Discovery of Guiana*. Ed. Benjamin Schmidt. Boston: Bedford/St. Martin's, 2008. Print.

Rank, Otto. "Cyrus." *The Myth of the Birth of the Hero: A Psychological Exploration of Myth*. Trans. F. Robbins and Smith Ely Jelliffe. New York: Journal of Nervous and Mental Disease, 1914. 24–38. Print.

Rank, Otto. "Lohengrin." *The Myth of the Birth of the Hero and Other Writings*. New York: Vintage, 1959. 59–64. Print.

Rayor, Diane J., trans. *The Homeric Hymns*. Berkeley: U of California P, 2004. Print.

Read, Kay Almere, and Jason J. Gonzalez. *Mesoamerican Mythology: A Guide to the Gods, Heroes, Rituals, and Beliefs of Mexico and Central America*. Oxford: Oxford UP, 2000. Print.

Reece, Steve. *The Stranger's Welcome: Oral Theory and the Aesthetics of the Homeric Hospitality Scene*. Ann Arbor: U of Michigan P, 1993. Print.

Rennison, Nick. *Robin Hood: Myth, History & Culture*. Harpenden: Pocket Essentials, 2012. Print.

Riches, Samantha. *St. George: Hero, Martyr and Myth*. Phoenix Mill: Sutton, 2000. Print.

---. "Saint George as Male Virgin Martyr." *Gender and Holiness: Men, Women and Saints in Late Medieval Europe*. Ed. Samantha Riches and Sarah Salih. New York: Routledge, 2002. 65–85. Print.

---. "Virtue and Violence: Saints, Monsters and Sexuality in Medieval Culture." *Medieval Sexuality: A Casebook*. Ed. April Harper and Caroline Proctor. New York: Routledge, 2008. 59–78. Print.

Riordan, Rick. *The Lighting Thief*. New York: Miramax, 2005. Print.

Roberts, John W. *From Trickster to Badman: The Black Folk Hero in Slavery and Freedom*. Philadelphia: U of Pennsylvania P, 1989. Print.

Roberts, Moss. "Li Chi Slays the Serpent." *Chinese Fairy Tales and Fantasies*. New York: Pantheon, 1979. 129–31. Print.

Rossabi, Morris. "Khubilai Khan and the Women in His Family." *Studia Sino-Mongolica: Festschrift für Herbert Franke*. Ed. Wolfgang Bauer. Wiesbaden, Germany: Steiner, 1979. 153–80. Print.

Rothery, Guy Cadogan. *The Amazons*. London: Griffiths, 1910. Print.

Rothstein, Edward. "A Modern Voicing of Myth and Buddhist Belief." *New York Times*. New York Times, 28 Aug. 1993. Web. 22 Apr. 2013.

Rowling, J. K. *Harry Potter and the Philosopher's Stone*. London: Bloomsbury, 1997. Print.

Sacks, Jonathan. 2012. "Freud's Great Freudian Slip." *Chabad.org*. Chabad-Lubavitch Media Center, 2013. Web. 6 Mar. 2013.

Salmonson, Jessica Amanda. *The Disfavored Hero*. Boulder Creek, CA: Pacific Warriors, 1999. Print. Rpt. of *Tomoe Gozen*. 1981.

---. *The Golden Naginata*. New York: Ace, 1982. Print.

---. *Thousand Shrine Warrior*. New York: Ace, 1984. Print.

Sandys, George. *Ovid's Metamorphosis Englished, Mythologized, and Represented in Figures by George Sandys*. 1632. Whitefish: Kessinger, 2003. Print.

Sarton, May. "The Muse as Medusa." Garber and Vickers 107–8.

Sato, Hiroaki. *Legends of the Samurai*. Woodstock: Overlook, 1995. Print.

---, trans. *The Sword and the Mind*. Woodstock: Overlook, 1984. Print.

Seven Samurai. Dir. Akira Kurosawa. Perf. Toshiro Mifune, Takashi Shimura, and Keiko Tsushima. Toho, 1954. DVD.

Shakespeare, William. "A Winter's Tale." *The Riverside Shakespeare.* Vol. 2. Boston: Houghton, 1974. Print.

Shaw, George Bernard. *Saint Joan.* 1924. New York: Penguin, 2003. Print.

Showalter, Elaine. "The Feminist Critical Revolution." *The New Feminist Criticism.* Ed. Showalter. New York: Pantheon, 1985. 3–17. Print.

Silver, Arnold Jacques. *Saint Joan: Playing with Fire.* New York: Twayne, 1993. Print.

Slone, Thomas. *One Thousand Papua New Guinean Nights.* Oakland: Masalai, 2001. Print.

Smith, John Z. *Map is Not Territory: Studies in the History of Religions.* Chicago: U of Chicago P, 1978. Print.

Smith, Philippa Mein. *A Concise History of New Zealand.* 2nd ed. New York: Cambridge UP, 2012. Print.

Sobol, Donald J. *The Amazons of Greek Mythology.* South Brunswick: Barnes, 1972. Print.

Spatt, Hartley S. "The Gilgamesh Epic." *Masterplots.* 4th ed. Ipswich: Salem, 2011. Print.

Ssu-ma Ch'ien. *The Grand Scribe's Records.* Vol. 2. Trans. Tsai-fa Cheng et al. Ed. William H. Nienhauser Jr. Bloomington: U of Indiana P, 2002. Print.

Stafford, Don. *Introducing Māori Culture.* Auckland: Reed, 1997. Print.

Stafford, Roy. *Seven Samurai.* Harlow: Longman, 2001. Print.

Stanley, Sandra K. "The Woman Warrior." *Masterplots II: Women's Literature Series* (1995): 1–3. Print.

Starzecka, Dorota, ed. *Maori: Art and Culture.* London: British Museum P, 1998. Print.

Subbaraman, Ramnath. "Beyond the Question of the Monkey Imposter: Indian Influence on the Chinese Novel *The Journey to the West.*" *Sino-Platonic Papers* 114 (2002): 1–35. Print.

Taube, Karl. *Aztec and Maya Myths.* Austin: U of Texas P, 2003. Print.

Taylor, Keith Weller. *The Birth of Vietnam.* Berkeley: U of California P, 1983. Print.

Tchana, Katrin. "The Serpent Slayer." *The Serpent Slayer and Other Stories of Strong Women.* New York: Little, 2000. 1–5. Print.

Tedlock, Dennis, trans. *Popol Vuh: The Definitive Edition of the Mayan Book of the Dawn of Life and the Glories of Gods and Kings.* Rev. ed. New York: Simon, 1996. Print.

Tennyson, Alfred. *Idylls of the King.* New Haven: Yale UP, 1983. Print.

Turnbull, Stephen R. *The Samurai Swordsman: Master of War.* North Clarendon: Tuttle, 2008. Print.

Turnbull, Stephen R. *The Samurai: A Military History.* New York: Macmillan, 1977. Print.

"Turandot." *Operapaedia.* San Diego Opera, 2013. Web. 8 Apr. 2013.

Turzynski, Linda J., and Walter E. Meyers. "Parzival." *Masterplots.* Ed. Laurence W. Mazzeno. 4th ed. Vol. 8. Pasadena: Salem, 2011. 4315–18. Print.

Twain, Mark. *The Complete Essays of Mark Twain.* Ed. Charles Neider. 1963. Cambridge: Da Capo, 2000. Print.

---. *Personal Recollections of Joan of Arc.* New York: Oxford UP, 1996. Print.

---. *Sieur Louis de Conte: Personal Recollections of Joan of Arc. Internet Medieval Sourcebook.* Fordham University, n.d. Web. 1 Apr. 2013.

---. *What Is Man? and Other Essays.* New York: Harper, 1917. Print.

Tyler, Royall. "Tomoe, the Woman Warrior." *Heroic with Grace: Legendary Women of Japan.* Ed. Chieko Irie Mulhern. New York: Sharpe, 1991. 129–61. Print.

Underberg, Natalie. "The Hero Cycle, Various Motifs in A." Garry and El-Shamy 10–23.

Vandiver, Elizabeth. "'Strangers Are from Zeus': Homeric Xenia at the Courts of Proteus and Croesus." *Myth, Truth, and Narrative in Herodotus.* Ed. Emily Baragwanath and Mathieu Bakker. New York: Oxford UP, 2012. 143–66. Print.

Van Duin, Lieke. "Anansi as Classical Hero." *Journal of Caribbean Literatures* 5.1 (2007): 33–42. Print.

Vargas-Betancourt, Margarita. "Legend of Tepozteco: *Popol Vuh* and Catholic Mythology." *Human Mosaic* 35.1 (2004): 41–49. PDF file.

Vautier, Sylvie. "Picasso's Minotaur: A Myth Too Human." *Picasso: Minotauro.* Madrid: Museo Nacional Centro de Arte Reina Sofia, 2001. 238–46. Print.

Vecsey, Christopher. "The Exception Who Proves the Rules." *Mythical Trickster Figures: Contours, Contexts, and Criticisms.* Ed. William J. Hynes and William G. Doty. Tuscaloosa: U of Alabama P, 1993. 106–21. Print.

Virgil. *The Aeneid.* Trans. Robert Fitzgerald. New York: Vintage, 1984. Print.

Voragine, Jacobus de. *The Golden Legend; or, Lives of the Saints.* Vol. 3. Ed. F. S. Ellis. London: Dent, 1900. Print.

Waley, Arthur, trans. *Monkey: Folk Novel of China*. New York: Day, 1943. Print.

Walker, Hera S. "Indigenous or Foreign? A Look at the Origins of the Monkey Hero Sun Wukong." *Sino-Platonic Papers* 81 (1998): 1–110. Print.

Wall, Kathleen. *The Callisto Myth from Ovid to Atwood: Initiation and Rape in Literature*. Kingston, ON: McGill-Queen's UP, 1988. Print.

Warner, Marina. *Joan of Arc: The Image of Female Heroism*. New York: Knopf, 1981. Print.

Weatherford, Jack. *The Secret History of the Mongol Queens*. New York: Crown, 2010. Print.

---. "The Wrestler Princess." *Roundtable*. Lapham's Quarterly, 3 Sept. 2010. Web. 10 Apr. 2013.

Wepman, Dennis, Ronald Newman, and Murray Binderman. *The Life: The Lore and Folk Poetry of the Black Hustler*. Philadelphia: U of Pennsylvania P, 1976. Print.

Westervelt, William Drake. *Legends of Ma-Ui: A Demi God of Polynesia, and of His Mother Hina*. 1910. London: Abela, 2011. Print.

Weston, Jessie L. *From Ritual to Romance*. 1920. Garden City: Doubleday, 1957. Print.

---, trans. *Sir Gawain at the Grail Castle*. Vol. 6 of *Arthurian Romances, Unrepresented in Malory's* Morte d'Arthur. London: Nutt, 1903. Print.

Wharton, Edith. *Artemis to Actaeon and Other Verse*. New York: Scribner, 1909. Print.

White, T. H. *The Once and Future King*. New York: Ace, 1987. Print.

Whited, Lana A., ed. *The Ivory Tower and Harry Potter: Perspectives on a Literary Phenomenon*. Columbia: U of Missouri P, 2002. Print.

Whiting, B. J. "Gawain: His Reputation, His Courtesy, and His Appearance in Chaucer's Squire's Tale." *Gawain: A Casebook*. Ed. Raymond H. Thompson and Keith Busby. New York: Routledge, 2006. 45–95. Print.

Wiget, Andrew. "His Life in His Tail: The Native American Trickster and the Literature of Possibility." *Redefining American Literary History*. Ed. A. Lavonne Brown Ruoff and Jerry Washington Ward. New York: MLA, 1990. Print.

Wilk, Stephen R. *Medusa: Solving the Mystery of the Gorgon*. Oxford: Oxford UP, 2000. Print.

Williamson, George S. *The Longing for Myth in Germany: Religion and Aesthetic Culture from Romanticism to Nietzsche*. Chicago: U of Chicago P, 2004. Print.

Wiseman, T. P. *Remus: A Roman Myth*. Cambridge: Cambridge UP, 1995. Print.

Wright, Melanie. *Moses in America*. New York: Oxford UP, 2003. Print.

Yoshimoto, Mitsuhiro. *Kurosawa: Film Studies and Japanese Cinema*. Durham: Duke UP, 2000. Print..

Yu, Anthony, trans. *The Journey to the West*. 4 vols. Chicago: U of Chicago P, 1977–83. Print.

Yuan, Shu. "Cultural Politics and Chinese-American Female Subjectivity: Rethinking Kingston's *Woman Warrior*." *Melus* 26.2 (2001): 199–223. Print.

Zamora, Margarita. "Christopher Columbus's 'Letter to the Sovereigns': Announcing the Discovery." Greenblatt 1–12.

Ziolkowski, Theodore. *Gilgamesh among Us: Modern Encounters with the Ancient Epic*. Ithaca: Cornell UP, 2011. Print.

Ziolkowski, Theodore. "The Minotaur: The Beast Within and the Threat Outside." *Minos and the Moderns: Cretan Myth in Twentieth-Century Literature and Art*. New York: Oxford UP, 2008. 67–116. Print.

Zipes, Jack. *Fairy Tales and the Art of Subversion*. New York: Routledge, 2006. Print.

Zukofsky, Louis. *"A."* New York: New Directions, 2011. Print.

INDEXES

COUNTRY AND CULTURE INDEX

CHRONOLOGICAL INDEX

INDEX